The Routledge Companion to Nonprofit Marketing

This timely collection of cutting-edge articles offers a complete overview of marketing in the nonprofit sector. Written by a leading team of international experts, the book examines the issues faced by public and nonprofit organizations in marketing and raising funds, and provides a comprehensive review of the latest research.

An introductory section reviews the history of ideas in nonprofit marketing and examines those fundamental marketing principles of special relevance to nonprofit organizations. The book then explores in depth the latest thinking in each of the most important nonprofit arenas, including:

- voluntary sector marketing
- fundraising
- arts marketing
- education marketing
- political marketing
- social marketing
- volunteer recruitment, management and retention
- public sector marketing and e-government

Containing real-world examples and case study material throughout, *The Routledge Companion to Nonprofit Marketing* makes an important contribution to our understanding of marketing theory and practice in the nonprofit sector. It is an essential reference for all students, researchers and practitioners working in nonprofit marketing, fundraising or philanthropy.

Adrian Sargeant is the Robert F. Hartsook Professor of Fundraising at Indiana University, USA. He is Editor of the *International Journal of Nonprofit and Voluntary Sector Marketing*.

Walter Wymer is Associate Professor of Marketing at the University of Lethbridge, Canada. He is Editor of the *Journal of Nonprofit and Public Sector Marketing*.

The Routledge Companion to Nonprofit Marketing

Edited by
Adrian Sargeant and
Walter Wymer

Routledge
Taylor & Francis Group

LONDON AND NEW YORK

First published 2008
by Routledge
2 Park Square, Milton Park, Abingdon, Oxon OX14 4RN

Simultaneously published in the USA and Canada
by Routedge
270 Madison Avenue, New York NY 10016

Routledge is an imprint of the Taylor & Francis Group, an informa business

© 2008 Adrian Sargeant and Walter Wymer for editorial matter and selection; individual chapters, the contributors

Typeset in Bembo by RefineCatch Ltd
Printed and bound in Great Britain by
TJ International Ltd, Padstow, Cornwall

British Library Cataloguing in Publication Data
A catalogue record for this book is available from the British Library

Library of Congress Cataloging in Publication Data
A catalog record has been requested for this book

ISBN10: 0–415–41727–9 (hbk)
ISBN10: 0–203–93602–7 (ebk)

ISBN13: 978–0–415–41727–3 (hbk)
ISBN13: 978–0–203–93602–3 (ebk)

Contents

List of figures and tables

Figures

Tables

List of contributors

Michael Basil, Ph.D. is a Professor of Marketing at the University of Lethbridge, USA. His background in social marketing came from work with Porter Novelli and the US Centers for Disease Control and Prevention. His research has been published in communication, marketing, psychology and public health journals.

Steve Downing, Ph.D. is an Associate Professor in the School of Reputation and Relationships at Henley Management College. He is a founding member of the John Madejski Centre for Reputation. His research focuses on strategy and change management, acquisitions, entrepreneurship, leadership, organizational learning, reputation and sustainability.

John B. Ford, Ph.D. is a Professor of Marketing and International Business at the College of Business and Public Administration, Old Dominion University, USA. His research interests include international advertising strategy, cross-cultural issues in marketing research, nonprofit marketing issues and gender issues in marketing. Among others his publications have appeared in the *Journal of Advertising*, the *Journal of Advertising Research* and the *Journal of the Academy of Marketing Science*.

Dave Gelders, Ph.D. is an Assistant Professor at the Leuven School of Mass Communication Research and the Public Management Institute, K.U. Leuven, Belgium. He is involved in several government-communication-related projects, and has published in several international scientific and professional journals.

Ross Gordon, BA, M.Sc. is a Research Officer at the Institute for Social Marketing at the University of Stirling, UK. He researches social and commercial marketing theory and practice, with a particular focus on critical marketing and upstream social marketing. He has published in the *Journal of Public Health Policy, Health Education, Public Health* and authored various book chapters.

Michelle Govekar, Ph.D. is an Associate Professor of Management at Ohio Northern University, USA, where she teaches undergraduate courses in management and business policy and strategy. Her publications focus on the management of international operations, determinants of using sweatshops, management of nonprofit organizations and strategic change in northwest central Ohio organizations.

Paul Govekar, DBA is an Assistant Professor of Management at Ohio Northern University where he teaches undergraduate courses in business ethics, organizational behaviour, nonprofit management and management decision-making. His publications focus on the management of nonprofit organizations, ethics in businesses and nonprofit organizations and management history.

Ted Hart is President of the consulting firm Hart Philanthropic Services (http://tedhart.com) and is Founder and President of the international ePhilanthropy Foundation (www.ephilanthropy.org), headquartered in Washington, DC, the global leader in providing training to charities for the ethical and efficient use of the Internet for philanthropic purposes through education and advocacy.

Gerard Hastings, Ph.D. is Director of the Institute for Social Marketing (www.ism.stir.ac.uk), a collaboration between Stirling and the Open Universities, UK. He has been researching and teaching in social and critical marketing for twenty-five years, and consults widely for government and non-government bodies, including the World Health Organization, the European Commission and Cancer Research UK. He is the author of *Social Marketing: Why should the Devil have all the best tunes?* (Butterworth Heinemann, 2007).

Carola Hillenbrand is an Academic Fellow in the School for Reputation and Relationships at Henley Management College, UK. She leads a variety of research projects on Corporate Reputation and Corporate Responsibility and teaches Statistics and Quantitative Research Methodology on Henley's different MBA programmes and on the doctoral programme.

Jane Hudson, Ph.D. is Senior Lecturer in Marketing at Bristol Business School, University of the West of England, UK. Her research interests are in nonprofit marketing, fundraising and branding. Her work has appeared in journals, including the *Service Industries Journal* and the *International Journal of Nonprofit and Voluntary Sector Marketing*.

Theresa A. Kirchner is an Assistant Professor of Marketing in the Marketing Department of the School of Business at Hampton University, USA. Her background includes work with nonprofit arts boards for more than twenty years. Her research interests include strategic management, marketing of nonprofit organizations and organizational business continuity and disaster-recovery planning.

Kersti Krug, Ph.D. is Assistant Principal in the College for Interdisciplinary Studies at the University of British Columbia, Canada. Her research and teaching interests include nonprofit and social marketing, interdisciplinarity, organizational culture, leadership, and change, and arts administration. She has significant professional and senior management experience in universities, government and museums.

Diana Leat, Ph.D. is Research and Development Director at Carnegie UK Trust, a Visiting Professor at the Centre for Charity Effectiveness, Cass Business School, London and a Visiting Research Fellow at UCLA, USA. Diana has held research and teaching posts in a number of universities and research centres in the UK, the USA and Australia. She is the author of over 100 articles and books on the nonprofit sector and social policy.

Jennifer Lees-Marshment, Ph.D. specializes in political marketing and party behaviour, having published the books *Political Marketing and British Political Parties* (Manchester University

Press, 2001), *The Political Marketing Revolution* (Manchester University Press, 2004) and *Political Marketing in Comparative Perspective* (co-edited, Manchester University Press, 2005). Currently at the University of Auckland, she is working on the differences between political marketing practice and theory.

Mei-Na Liao, Ph.D. is Lecturer in Marketing at the Bradford University School of Management, UK. Her research interests are in the field of nonprofit marketing. In 2000, she won an Emerging Scholar Award at the Association for Research on Nonprofit Organizations and Voluntary Actions annual conference, New Orleans, USA. Dr Liao has published in various international research journals.

Jenny Lloyd, Ph.D. is Lecturer in Marketing at Bristol Business School, University of the West of England, UK. Her research interests are in the domain of political marketing, where she has published a number of scholarly articles and book chapters. She is also the author of numerous conference presentations in this field.

Laura McDermott is a Research Officer at the Institute for Social Marketing at the University of Stirling and the Open University in the UK, where she specializes in social marketing research in relation to food and nutrition. Her research includes work undertaken for clients such as the World Health Organization and the UK Food Standards Agency.

Charles S. Madden, Ph.D. is the Ben H. Williams Professor of Marketing at Baylor University, USA. He has published numerous articles and given numerous presentations over his productive career. More recently Dr Madden has been researching marketing activities in higher education.

Kym Madden, Ph.D. is Senior Research Fellow at the Centre of Philanthropy and Nonprofit Studies in the Faculty of Business at the Queensland University of Technology, Australia. She researches in various areas of philanthropy, fundraising and volunteerism. Her philanthropy research has investigated the giving behaviour of wealthy individuals and small to medium-sized businesses.

Arthur Money, Ph.D. is Emeritus Professor in the School of Projects, Processes and Systems at Henley Management College, UK. Prior to joining Henley Management College, he was Professor of Business Administration in the Graduate School of Business, Deputy Dean of the Faculty of Commerce and served as Director of the Graduate School of Business of the University of Cape Town, South Africa. He is the author of over 100 journal articles, working papers, book chapters, co-author of nine books and co-editor of two books.

Kevin Money, Ph.D. is Director of the School of Reputation and Relationships and the John Madejski Centre for Reputation at Henley Management College in the UK. He teaches on the MBA programme and he is a mentor and tutor on Henley's Executive Development Programme. His research interests include the building of strong relationships with stakeholders, CSR and the reputation and commitment of corporate funders to charities.

Yvonne Moogan, Ph.D. is a Principal Lecturer at Liverpool John Moores University, UK. Her position is MBA Director responsible for UK and overseas students (approximately 300), she also teaches Research Methods, Statistics and Marketing.

Gillian Mort, Ph.D. is an Associate Professor in the Department of Marketing, Griffith Business School, Australia. She is a member of the editorial board for the *International Journal of Nonprofit and Voluntary Sector Marketing* and the author of numerous scholarly works in the domain of nonprofit marketing. Her research interests include social entrepreneurship, nonprofit marketing, arts marketing and the marketing of services.

Sandra Mottner, Ph.D. joined the faculty of Western Washington University, USA, in 2001, where she is now an Associate Professor. Prior to her academic career, Dr Mottner had twenty-five years of business experience in retail, general business management and marketing. Her research interests include nonprofit marketing, church marketing, retailing of thrift stores (charity shops) and nonprofit marketing education.

Paulette Padanyi, Ph.D. is Associate Professor and Chair of the Department of Marketing and Consumer Studies in the College of Management and Economics at the University of Guelph in Ontario, Canada. Her research is concentrated in the areas of market orientation and performance evaluation in nonprofit organizations and student volunteerism.

Dayananda Palihawadana, Ph.D. is Senior Lecturer in Marketing at Leeds University Business School, UK. He has published extensively in the areas of service quality and international marketing. As programme director for the M.Sc. in International Marketing at the University of Leeds, he is responsible for developing a globally competitive research base in advancing international services theory.

Jennifer Radbourne, Ph.D. is Head of School of Communications and Creative Arts, Deakin University, Australia. Jennifer's recent Australian Research Council-funded research has focused on audience reception analysis and audience connectivity in the performing arts. She has provided research and consultancy services to governments and arts organizations in Australia, Hong Kong and Vietnam in strategic planning, marketing and governance.

Ruth Rentschler, Ph.D. is Executive Director of the Centre for Leisure Management Research in the Bowater School of Management and Marketing, Deakin University, Australia. She has published many books, articles and reports on arts management and marketing. Her most recent research is on authenticity, indigenous art and cultural tourism. She has conducted funded research projects on arts governance and audience segmentation.

Adrian Sargeant, Ph.D. is the Robert F. Hartsook Professor of Fundraising at the School of Public and Environmental Affairs, Indiana University, USA. He is Professor of Nonprofit Marketing at Bristol Business School at the University of the West of England, UK and a Visiting Professor of Philanthropy at the Centre of Philanthropy and Nonprofit Studies, at Queensland University of Technology, Australia.

Mark N. K. Saunders, Ph.D. is Assistant Dean (Director of Research and Doctoral Programmes) and Professor of Business Research Methods at Oxford Brookes University Business School, UK. His main areas of research interest include research methods, organizational justice and trust.

Wendy Scaife, Ph.D. is Senior Research Fellow, Centre of Philanthropy and Nonprofit Studies, at Queensland University of Technology, Australia. Previously a health charity CEO, she researches medical research marketing/funding, corporate community involvement, best-practice fundraising/fundraising education, nonprofit marketing and public relations, and promoting a philanthropic culture.

Paul G. Schervish, Ph.D. is Professor of Sociology and Director of the Center on Wealth and Philanthropy at Boston College, USA. He is also Senior Adviser to the John Templeton Foundation and National Research Fellow at the Indiana University Center on Philanthropy.

Haseeb A. Shabbir, Ph.D. is Lecturer in Marketing at Leeds University Business School, UK. His interests are in nonprofit and social marketing and in the application of psychology in developing marketing theory. He is particularly interested in the Dimensional Qualitative Research (DQR) approach and has published in *Psychology and Marketing* and the *Journal of Advertising*, exploring the versatility of this technique.

Des Thwaites, Ph.D. is Senior Lecturer in Marketing at Leeds University Business School, UK. He has published over seventy journal articles, textbook chapters and case studies in the marketing area. His sport-specific work has been presented at the North American Society for Sport Management and the Sport Management Association of Australia and New Zealand conferences.

Jay Weerawardena, Ph.D. is Lecturer in Marketing at the University of Queensland Business School, Australia. He has published in many scholarly journals and has presented papers at reputed conferences in marketing, management and entrepreneurship/small business, including conferences conducted by the American Marketing Association and the Academy of Management.

Charles B. Weinberg, Ph.D. is President of SME Vancouver Professor of Marketing, Sauder School of Business, University of British Columbia, Canada. His research and teaching interests include analytical marketing and public and nonprofit (social) marketing. In the latter area, his work has included arts management, marketing healthy and safe behaviours, portfolio management, pricing and competition.

Christine S. Williams, MBA is Head of the Department of Marketing and Strategy and a member of the Centre for Research in Service, the Business School, University of Gloucestershire, UK. Her main areas of research interest include service quality, customer satisfaction and service management.

Lucy Woodliffe, Ph.D. is Senior Lecturer in Marketing at Bristol Business School, University of the West of England, UK. She has published on the subjects of consumer disadvantage and charity fundraising and her current research and teaching interests include nonprofit and social marketing.

Walter Wymer is an Associate Professor of Marketing at the University of Lethbridge in Alberta, Canada. His research interests are focused upon the marketing needs of nonprofit/ nongovernmental organizations. This includes marketing to volunteers, cause marketing, Internet marketing, and fundraising. Dr Wymer has published articles and books on nonprofit marketing topics and given presentations at numerous academic conferences. He is editor of the *Journal of Nonprofit and Public Sector Marketing*, North American editor of the *International Journal of Nonprofit and Voluntary Sector Marketing*, and former president of the Atlantic Marketing Association. He is co-author of *Nonprofit Marketing: Marketing Management for Charitable and Nongovernmental Organizations* (2006). Most recently, he was keynote speaker for the 2007 Australasian Nonprofit and Social Marketing Conference in Brisbane, Australia.

Introduction: the growth of a discipline

Adrian Sargeant and Walter Wymer

Welcome to *The Routledge Companion to Nonprofit Marketing*. After forty years of academic debate and research, it seems timely to conduct a review of the current state of research in this field and to highlight the challenges and opportunities those of us working and writing in this field will face in the future. In commissioning our 25 chapters, we have sought to provide a broad coverage, with contributions from leading nonprofit scholars in a variety of different countries. It is our hope that the *Companion* will become an invaluable reference tool for graduate students and researchers and develop with subsequent editions into a chronicle of the development of the body of knowledge. In this brief introduction, we begin this process by charting the development of nonprofit marketing, thereby setting the current work in its historical context.

Just as the origins of marketing can be traced back to the earliest forms of trade, non-profit marketing, too, is far from a new idea, particularly in the realm of philanthropy, where Mullin (1995) charts the significance of organized fundraising activity to early Jewish charity. In this tradition, individual volunteers were clearly assigned within each community to take responsibility for specific fundraising tasks, taking into account the needs and situation of each prospective group. The use of the mail for the purposes of fundraising also has a surprisingly long history. Indeed, there is evidence that professional coaching in the development of fundraising letters has existed since the Middle Ages. A fourteenth-century 'fundraising' hand-book developed by monks at a Cistercian monastery in Austria, for example, advocated that an applicant's letter must consist of:

- a honeyed salutation;
- a tactful exordium (an introduction to the purpose of the application);
- a narration (to set the scene with a description of the present situation or problem);
- a petition (the detailed presentation of the application); and
- a conclusion (a graceful peroration).

The monks even went so far as to supply twenty-two model letters to illustrate the application of this approach, each of which, on the basis of their experience, was framed to offer a different justification for the merit of philanthropy. These included 'generosity to avoid ridicule'; 'the wealthy's obligation to give'; 'do as you would be done by'; 'to be kind is better than being an animal', and so on (Sargeant and Jay 2004).

As many readers will already be aware, Kotler and Levy (1969) are credited with opening the academic debate on the relevance of marketing to nonprofit organizations. They argued that marketing had for too long been regarded as a narrow business function and rebuked both academics and practitioners for ignoring the broader relevance of marketing ideas, or considering only specialized applications, such as public relations. At the time, their ideas met with some discussion in the literature, particularly in the early 1970s (see, for example, Luck 1969; Ferber 1970; Lavidge 1970; Ardnt 1978). Lovelock and Weinberg (1990) argue that the debate 'fizzled-out' in the latter part of that decade, as marketers became more concerned with other variants of their discipline and in particular turned their attention to the issue of whether service marketing might be any different from the marketing of products. Kotler and Levy's revised definition of marketing as 'serving human needs and wants sensitively' (Kotler and Levy 1969: 15) was no longer controversial.

In 1971 the *Journal of Marketing* provided an entire issue devoted to marketing's social/ environmental role and number of empirical articles then followed (see, for example, Meade 1974; Miller 1974; Smith and Beik 1982; Schlegelmilch 1979). It was not until the early 1980s, however, that the first generic nonprofit marketing textbooks were to appear, with work by Rados (1981), Kotler and Andreasen (1982) and Lovelock and Weinberg (1989) being particularly noteworthy. Textbooks also began to appear in the fields of healthcare (Kotler and Clarke 1986; Cooper 1979; Frederiksen *et al.* 1984) education (Kotler and Fox 1985), the arts (Mokwa *et al.* 1980), the marketing of ideas (Fine 1981) and social marketing (Manoff 1985; Kotler and Roberto 1989). It is interesting to note that the only major facet of nonprofit marketing that lacked a formal textbook was the topic of fundraising. It was not until 2004 that this gap was to be filled (Sargeant and Jay 2004).

The 1980s and early 1990s saw the introduction of a number of scholarly journals, including the generic *Journal of Nonprofit and Public Sector Marketing* and *International Journal of Nonprofit and Voluntary Sector Marketing*. Sector-specific journals also emerged including *New Directions in Philanthropic Fundraising*, *Journal of Educational Advancement*, *Health Marketing Quarterly*, *Journal of Health Care Marketing*, *Journal of Marketing for Higher Education* and *Social Marketing Quarterly*. It was also not unusual to find journals from other disciplines printing studies from the field of marketing. Andreasen and Kotler (2003) note studies in fields as diverse as library science, art history and hospital management.

The 1990s also saw an explosion of conference interest in the topic with nonprofit tracks being introduced to many American Marketing Association, Academy of Marketing Science and Atlantic Marketing Association events and in Europe the Academy of Marketing and European Marketing Academy (EMAC) conferences. Marketing papers were also becoming commonplace at the Association of Researchers in Nonprofit and Voluntary Action (ARNOVA) events in the USA and at the ISTR (International Society for Third Sector Research) biannual conferences. The following decade saw the introduction of a series of sector-specific conferences, including the American Marketing Association's annual nonprofit event and in Europe the Annual Colloquium on Nonprofit, Social and Arts Marketing hosted by Henley Management College and London Guildhall (now Metropolitan) University. A nonprofit conference was also introduced in Australia where the Australian Non-profit and Social Marketing Conference (ANSMAC) is now a well-attended annual event.

Concomitant with the level of academic interest in the topic has been a rise in the number of universities offering courses in nonprofit management. Indeed, the ten years to 2006 have seen a tripling in the number of universities in the USA offering courses in this field (Young 1999; Mirabella 2006). Mirabella (2006) notes:

> The current universe of programs that focus on the management of nonprofit organizations found over two-hundred and fifty-five colleges and universities with courses in nonprofit management. Seventy-two programs offer noncredit courses such as Fundraising, Managing Your Nonprofit Organization, and Governance. Many of the fifty-seven programs with courses through continuing education, have similar courses designed for the nonprofit manager, including Strategic Planning, Human Resource Management and Financial Management. An additional one-hundred and twenty-nine schools offer at least one course for undergraduate credit . . . (and) one hundred and fifty-seven colleges and universities have at least one course within a graduate department.

The picture elsewhere is less rosy. In the UK, for example, fewer than 2 per cent of further and higher education institutions were found to be offering accredited courses in nonprofit marketing and/or fundraising in 2006 (Sargeant *et al.* 2006). A similar analysis remains to be conducted of programmes in other countries, but a brief web search conducted for this volume suggests that considerable opportunities to expand provision still exist. Indeed, although our foregoing discussion makes it clear that there has been a growth in nonprofit scholarly output, there is less evidence that this is being effectively communicated to those who would benefit.

Of course one could argue that marketing need or societal issues requires identical skills and thought processes to the marketing of cars, perfume and other consumer products. The requirement to consider nonprofit marketing as a distinct discipline in its own right is thereby greatly diminished. But is it? Is it really possible to adopt commercial marketing practice to making a potential donor aware of a starving baby or encouraging a committed smoker to quit? Does it make sense to regard nonprofit marketing as a distinctive discipline?

As long ago as 1977, the eminent marketer scholar Shelby Hunt provided some insight into this issue, arguing that the profit–nonprofit dichotomy would be valuable until:

1 The broadening of the marketing concept was no longer regarded as controversial.
2 The nonprofit sector and the issues that must be addressed therein was completely integrated into all marketing courses and not treated as a separate subject.
3 Nonprofit managers perceived their organizations as having marketing problems.
4 Nonprofits established marketing departments (where appropriate) and employed marketing personnel.

The past thirty years have seen a good deal of progress. The adoption of marketing ideas in the nonprofit arena is certainly no longer controversial and many nonprofits now employ marketing personnel to address marketing issues. The second of Hunt's tests seems the only area of difficulty. Nonprofit marketing has yet to be properly integrated into 'mainstream' marketing courses, quite possibly because it is seen as being of less interest to the majority of marketing students and/or employers. While this may be intuitive, it fails to reflect the pattern of the majority of modern careers, where the majority of individuals will now work for a variety of employers and quite possibly in a variety of different contexts. The need for a broader perspective on the subject has therefore never been greater. Indeed, it is also the case that with an increasing number of nonprofits creating professional marketing and/or fundraising positions, it may be in the career interests of many graduates/undergraduates to develop expertise/ knowledge that would allow them to compete for jobs in this sector.

That is not to say, however, that we necessarily agree with Shelby Hunt that it is desirable that nonprofit and for-profit marketing be merged. While we would certainly applaud greater coverage of the subject in generic marketing courses and modules, we believe that the body of knowledge that comprises nonprofit marketing is beginning to develop to a point where it would be difficult to do more than merely scratch the surface of the topic in any such course. The bodies of knowledge, in particular, for fundraising/volunteering and social marketing are now well developed, as is the evidence that simply applying for-profit ideas to these contexts would be sub-optimal in the extreme. There is thus a need to teach perspectives and tools/ techniques that are more applicable to the nonprofit sector and for these to be grounded in and substantiated by an ongoing stream of high-quality research.

High-quality research ought to be directed in areas which provide the greatest need for nonprofit managers (Smith 1999). These areas still include individual fundraising, marketing to corporate supporters, volunteer recruitment and retention, using Internet technologies for effective marketing, social and advocacy marketing, public relations, and nonprofit branding and positioning (Wymer et al. 2006).

As discussed previously, the field of fundraising has only recently been credited with a formal textbook (Sargeant and Jay 2004). Fundraising is, however, a crucial marketing activity in many, if not most, nonprofit, non-governmental and charitable organizations. Marketing practitioners in these organizations could benefit by more research on how to better attract new donors (Gainer and Moyer 2004). For example, to whom should fundraising appeals be directed? Can donor markets be segmented in a manner similar to consumer markets? And, if so, how should donor markets be segmented? What variables and factors should be used to segment effectively donor markets? Can appeals be developed and delivered to donor targets with such segment differences in mind? Adrian Sargeant and Lucy Woodliffe have authored a reading on individual donor behaviour for this book to enhance our understanding in this area.

Perhaps one of the most critical areas in fundraising at the time of writing is retention. With many organizations routinely losing 50 per cent of their donors between the first and second donation there is an urgent need to understand more about the relationship dynamic in this context. Papers by Kevin Money (et al.) and Haseeb Shabbir illuminate this issue.

Planned giving, a subtopic of fundraising, is also of increasing importance to nonprofit managers. From the perspective of the nonprofit marketer, planned giving is:

> A systematic effort to identify and cultivate a person for the purpose of generating a major gift that is structured and that integrates sound personal, financial, and estate-planning concepts with the prospect's plans for lifetime or testamentary giving. A planned gift has tax implications and is often transmitted through a legal document, such as a Will or a trust.
>
> (NSFRE Fund-Raising Dictionary 1996: 58)

Marketers need to better understand how to identify potential planned givers. They need to better understand the process that potential planned givers use in deciding whether or not to give and which worthy causes to support (Brown 1996). Paul Schervish has contributed a reading for this book on the motivations for giving by wealthy individuals, a frequent target for planned giving appeals.

Many nonprofit organizations organize special events for fundraising purposes. Marketers could benefit from research that adds to our knowledge on how to more effectively plan and organize special events. For example, what is the best type of event to develop? When to have the event? Whom to invite? Under what circumstances should nonprofits solicit corporate event sponsors (O'Mahony and Polonsky 2006)?

In addition to fundraising from individual contributors, managing corporate support is emerging as an important marketing function. Corporate support of charities has changed considerably during the last fifty years, evolving from straightforward financial contributions thirty years ago to complex cause-marketing arrangements in which corporations derive marketing benefits from their associations with nonprofits (Himmelstein 1997; Wymer and Samu 2003). Kym Madden and Wendy Scaife have contributed a review of corporate philanthropy for this book.

Although there have been numerous works on cause marketing and other dimensions of business–nonprofit sector collaborations, much of this prior work has the corporate perspective in mind. More research is needed to enhance our knowledge of how to manage more effectively this marketing function for the nonprofit. For example, how does a nonprofit decide which business to target? How can smaller, local nonprofits attract business support? How can nonprofit managers manage more effectively their relationships with business supporters? How do nonprofit managers manage communications publicizing their business supporters? What are the audience effects from these communications?

Fundraising and attracting corporate support are two important marketing activities for nonprofit organizations which focus upon obtaining needed resources. Recruiting and retaining volunteers represents another important marketing activity (Wymer and Self 1999). Many challenges lie ahead for managers responsible for this form of marketing. The proportion of women in the employee workforce is at an all-time high and women typically comprise about two-thirds of the volunteer workforce. Modern culture is such that many people feel a constant state of time-poverty and economic pressure. Baby boomers are entering retirement. A new generation is coming of age, a generation feeling less responsibility for civic participation. How can younger individuals be recruited? What are their motivations for volunteering? What do they expect from the volunteer experience? Walter Wymer, Paul Govekar and Michele Govekar have contributed two readings on volunteer issues to this book.

To communicate with the coming-of-age generation, nonprofit managers will rely more heavily upon newer technologies. Interesting works on virtual volunteering (www.serviceleader.org) and e-philanthropy (www.ephilanthropy.org) have been harbingers in this area. However, the academic community needs to participate more fully in adding to our knowledge in using the Internet and related technologies as vehicles to achieving marketing goals. How can nonprofit managers more effectively use their Internet capabilities for fundraising planned giving, e-philanthropy? More needs to be known about how potential volunteers, contributors and other supporters use the nonprofit's website. What information are they seeking? How can appeals be directed more effectively on the nonprofit's website? With regard to volunteer marketing, how can the website be used to recruit and retain volunteers? Can the organization's Internet tools be used for volunteer/donor community building? Finally, how can the website be used more effectively as a public relations tool? The reading by Ted Hart addresses many of these issues.

Another area of great interest to the nonprofit sector is social marketing, the application of marketing concepts to influence positive social changes. Marketing campaigns directed to reduce smoking, pollution, obesity and unsafe sex are examples of social marketing. Changing human behaviour is challenging and complex. More research will always be needed to better understand how to influence behaviour. More research is also needed to deal with challenges faced by social marketers. Modern industrialized societies, populations that have been exposed to corporate marketing messages, often from a very young age, are often oppositional to the objective of social marketers. Corporate advertising encourages people to over-consume, smoke, drink, gamble, eat convenience foods, and so forth. Social marketers must compete with corporate-marketing messages in this environment (Wymer *et al.* 2006). In this book, two critical readings on social marketing topics have been contributed by Gerard Hastings, Michael Basil, Ross Gordon and Laura McDermott.

In addition to the areas discussed previously, practitioners in different parts of the nonprofit sector have special challenges. There are too many to list in this brief introduction, but as an example, faith-based institutions represent the largest nonprofit subsector, yet have been the focus of surprisingly little research. Sandra Mottner reviews this literature and offers numerous suggestions for expanding the field. Equally, in the 1980s and 1990s, political marketing struggled to assert itself as a serious subject for academic study. Thanks to an explosion of interest in recent years, the appearance of textbooks and a number of journal special issues, the application of marketing to this field is no longer controversial. Jenny Lloyd and Jennifer Lees-Marshment, two of the leading thinkers in this area, have contributed chapters to this book, reviewing the current state of our knowledge and challenging the way that we view political parties and brands.

Throughout, this companion book presents readings by leading scholars in the field to present a body of work that deals with nonprofit marketing at both the conceptual and practical levels. Conceptual topics, such as developing a marketing orientation or customer–relationship management, are presented in a context specific to the nonprofit sector. Topics of practical importance, such as e-philanthropy or volunteerism marketing, complement the more conceptual subjects.

This companion book also balances the breadth and depth of nonprofit marketing. A broad variety of topics are addressed and, within specific subject areas, reviews are provided to give the reader a sense of the scope of our knowledge on that topic. However, in certain instances, readings with narrowly focused topics add depth to our coverage of nonprofit marketing. These more narrowly focused readings provide the reader with greater insights into special topics of interest to both researchers and practitioners. We commend them to you.

References

Andreasen, A. and Kotler, P. (2003) *Strategic Marketing for Nonprofit Organizations*, 6th edition, Upper Saddle River, NJ: Prentice Hall.

Ardnt, J. (1978) 'How broad should the marketing concept be?', *Journal of Marketing*, 42 (January):101–3.

Brown, W. (2006) 'What research tells us about planned giving', *International Journal of Nonprofit and Voluntary Sector Marketing*, 9(1):86–95.

Cooper, P.D. (1979) *Healthcare Marketing: Issues and Trends*, Germantown, MD: Aspen Systems Corporation.

Ferber, R. (1970) 'The expanding role of marketing in the 1970s', *Journal of Marketing*, 34(1):29–30.

Fine, S. F. (1981) *The Marketing of Ideas and Social Issues*, New York, NY: Praeger.

Frederiksen, L. W., Solomon, L.J. and Brehony, K.A. (1984), *Marketing Health Behavior*, New York, NY: Plenum.

Gainer, B. and Moyer, M. S. (2004), 'Marketing for nonprofit managers', in Robert D. D. Herman (ed.) *The Jossey-Bass Handbook of Nonprofit Leadership and Management*, San Francisco, CA: Jossey-Bass Publishers, pp. 277–309.

Himmelstein, J. (1997). *Looking Good and Doing Good: Corporate Philanthropy and Corporate Power*, Indianapolis, IN: Indiana University Press.

Humboldt Area Foundation (2001), glossary, including definition of planned giving, available online at: http://hafoundation.org/about/glossary (accessed 17 January).

Hunt, S. D. (1977) 'The three dichotomies model of marketing: An elaboration of issues', in C. C. Slater (ed.) *Macro-Marketing: Distributive Processes from a Societal Perspective*, Boulder, CO: University of Colorado, pp. 52–6.

Kotler, P. and Andreasen, A. (1982) *Strategic Marketing for Nonprofit Organizations*, Englewood Cliffs, NJ: Prentice Hall.

—— and Clarke, R. N. (1986) *Marketing for Health Care Organizations*, Englewood Cliffs, NJ: Prentice Hall.

—— and Fox, K. F. A. (1985) *Strategic Marketing for Educational Institutions*, Englewood Cliffs, NJ: Prentice Hall.

—— and Levy, S. J. (1969) 'Broadening the concept of marketing', *Journal of Marketing*, 33(2):10–15.

—— and Roberto, E. L. (1989) *Social Marketing: Strategies for Changing Public Behavior*, New York, NY: Free Press.

Lavidge, R. J. (1970) 'The growing responsibilities of marketing', *Journal of Marketing*, 34(1):27.

Lovelock, C.H. and Weinberg, C.B. (1989) *Marketing for Public and Nonprofit Managers*, 2nd edition, Redwood City, CA: Scientific Press.

—— (1990) *Public and Nonprofit Marketing: Readings and Cases*, San Francisco, CA: Scientific Press.

Luck, D. J. (1969) 'Broadening the concept of marketing too far', *Journal of Marketing*, 33(2):53–5.

Manoff, R. K. (1985) *Social Marketing*, New York, NY: Prager.

Meade, J. (1974) 'A mathematical model for deriving hospital service areas', *International Journal of Health Services*, 4:353–7.

Miller, S. J. (1974) 'Market segmentation and forecasting for a charitable health organization', Proceedings: Southern Marketing Association Conference, Atlanta, Georgia.

Mirabella, R.M. (2006) 'Nonprofit management education: Current offerings in university-based programs', available online at: http://tltc.shu.edu/npo/ (accessed 22 August).

Mokwa, M.P., Dawson, W. D. and Priere, E. A. (eds) (1981) *Marketing the Arts*, New York, NY: Praeger.

Mullin, R. (1995) *Foundations for Fundraising*, London: ICSA.

NSFRE Fund-Raising Dictionary (1996) AFP/Wiley Fund Development Series, New York, NY: John Wiley & Sons.

O'Mahony, B. and Polonsky, M. (2006) 'Special events', in W. Wymer, P. Knowles and R. Gomes, *Nonprofit Marketing: Marketing Management for Charitable and Nongovernmental Organizations*, Thousand Oaks, CA: Sage Publications, pp. 246–78.

Rados, D. L. (1981) *Marketing for Non-Profit Organizations*, Dover, MA: Auburn House.

Sargeant, A., Hudson, J. and Jay, E. (2006) *Fundraising Training in the UK: An Assessment of Current Provision*, London: Institute of Fundraising.

—— and Jay, E. (2004) *Fundraising Management: Analysis, Planning and Practice*, London: Routledge.

Schlegelmilch, B. B. (1979) 'Targeting of fundraising appeals', *European Journal of Marketing*, 22:31–40.

Smith, J. P. (1999) 'Nonprofit management education in the United States', speech delivered to the Building Bridges Initiative Conference in Buenos Aires, Argentina, 7 October.

Smith, S. M. and Beik, L. L. (1982) 'Market segmentation for fundraisers', *Journal of the Academy of Marketing Science*, 10(3):208–16.

Wymer, W., Knowles, P. and Gomes, R. (2006) *Nonprofit Marketing: Marketing Management for Charitable and Nongovernmental Organizations*, Thousand Oaks, CA: Sage Publications.

—— and Samu, S. (2003). *Nonprofit and Business Sector Collaboration: Social Enterprises, Cause-Related Marketing, Sponsorships and Other Corporate-Nonprofit Dealings*, Binghamton, NY: Best Business Books.

—— and Self, D. (1999) 'Major research studies: An annotated bibliography of marketing to volunteers', *Journal of Nonprofit and Public Sector Marketing*, 6(2/3):107–64.

Young, D. R. (1999) 'Nonprofit management studies in the United States: Current developments and future prospects', *Journal of Public Affairs Education*, 5:13–23.

Part 1

Voluntary sector marketing

1

Operationalizing the marketing concept

Achieving market orientation in the nonprofit context

Paulette Padanyi

Introduction: the relationship between marketing, the marketing concept and market orientation

Marketing is generally acknowledged to be an essential strategic management function. In particular, marketing expertise is critical when an organization has to appeal to outside groups to generate revenue and/or to compete with other organizations for its sources of revenue.

Within the for-profit sector, it is also generally accepted that no organization can claim to have fully adopted marketing as a strategic component of its operations if it is not guided by 'the marketing concept'. The marketing concept, a business philosophy which maintains that the customer should be at the centre of the firm's thinking about strategy and operations, was first articulated by Drucker in 1954 (Day 1994). It directs an organization to look outward and to be open to external trends and events that can provide market opportunities (Warnaby and Finney 2005). Outward-looking organizations understand their customers, their competitors and the environment in which they operate, and offer products and services that have a greater chance of being successful because they have been developed and promoted based on this knowledge. By comparison, inward-looking organizations offer products and services based on anecdotal assessments of what they think the market wants or what they want to offer given their existing human and financial resources. In other words, they produce and sell the products they want to, not what the market necessarily wants or needs (Gonzalez *et al.* 2002).

For-profit marketing practitioners and academics further maintain that, in order to implement the marketing concept, a firm must have a 'market orientation'. Since a firm with a high level of market orientation stays close to its customers and ahead of its competition, it is better equipped to respond to market requirements and anticipate changing conditions (Day 1994). A market orientation is therefore a prerequisite for organizational success and profitability (Raju *et al.* 1995).

Although the term 'market orientation' came into use shortly after Drucker articulated the marketing concept, it was not well defined. Indeed, as of this writing, there is still no accepted definition for 'market orientation'. The title of a classic *Harvard Business Review* article, 'What the hell is market-oriented?' (Shapiro 1988), expresses the continued frustration that practitioners and academics have experienced in trying to come to grips with the term.

Nevertheless, academic acknowledgement of market orientation as a construct worthy of investigation in the for-profit sector began in 1989 with a *Journal of Marketing* article tying it to the organizational culture literature from organizational behaviour (Deshpande and Webster 1989). Empirical research to prove that there is a direct, positive relationship between market orientation and organizational performance in the for-profit sector has been under way since 1990, when Narver and Slater developed the first valid, reliable scale to measure the market orientation construct. Results have been mixed but, for the most part, they indicate that market orientation should increase and improve organizational results (Lovelock and Weinberg 1989; Kotler and Andreasen 1996; Vasquez *et al.* 2002)

The idea of extending the marketing concept to the nonprofit sector was first advocated publicly by Kotler and Levy (1969), who posited that marketing is a pervasive societal activity performed by all organizations, whether they are profit-seeking or not. They maintained that all organizations are concerned with their 'products' in the eyes of certain 'consumers' and seek to find 'tools' for furthering their acceptance. Thus, Kotler and Levy basically initiated an idea that has since become an article of faith among marketing academics, that the marketing concept has no boundaries.

The discussion generated by Kotler and Levy's article regarding the applicability of marketing and the marketing concept to the nonprofit sector is reviewed in the next section. The remainder of this chapter focuses on what is currently known about market orientation and the conclusions that can be reached about operationalizing it for academic or managerial purposes.

The applicability of marketing and the marketing concept to the nonprofit sector

The 'yes' arguments

Following Kotler and Levy's 1969 article, Shapiro (1973) declared that 'marketing is as intrinsic to the nonprofit sector as it is to the business community'. He sought to justify the applicability of marketing and the marketing concept to the nonprofit sector by demonstrating that marketing principles, such as the marketing mix, readily apply to the nonprofit challenges of resource attraction, resource allocation and non-donor persuasion.

Typical of many academics since Shapiro, Lovelock and Weinberg (1989) supported the extension of the concept into the nonprofit arena by framing nonprofit management challenges and actions in marketing strategy terms. For example, they talked about nonprofits becoming more selective in the market segments that they target, as well as being market-oriented in terms of developing and maintaining products and services, determining price policies and building awareness of their offerings.

Other theorists have supported applying the marketing concept to the nonprofit sector by arguing that:

- nonprofits are just as profit-oriented as other businesses because they need an excess of revenues over expenses to survive; therefore, the difference with nonprofits is not that profits cannot be made, but that profits cannot be distributed (Hay 1990);
- nonprofits operate in the same environment and face similar demands with regard to effectiveness and efficiency as for-profits (Anthony and Young 1990); and
- competition is a reality for all organizations, thus nonprofits must deal on an ongoing basis with rivalry for capital, labour, customers and revenues, just like for-profits (Tuckman 1998).

The 'no' arguments

The first argument against Kotler and Levy's treatise appeared shortly after its publication. Luck (1969) felt that the authors were defining marketing in terms that were too broad, and that the marketing concept was developed for a different type of organization. He felt it was developed for businesses that are based on market transactions, i.e. 'buying and selling', and thus are focused on tapping customer markets to achieve a profit goal.

Another concern raised was the emphasis that the marketing concept places on competition. Bush (1992) suggested that cooperation among nonprofit organizations should be the basis for organizational and managerial orientation in the nonprofit sector, not competition. He maintained that a competitive mindset provokes an 'insular mentality' and a predisposition to see relationships with other organizations as potentially threatening. In his opinion, this insular attitude would make it difficult, if not impossible, for nonprofit agencies with similar goals to share information and resources, which is a desirable and necessary form of collaboration given the ongoing resource limitations faced by nonprofits.

Sheth (1993) also pointed out that application of the marketing concept entails offering users what they want, as opposed to what they need, which is inappropriate in need-driven nonprofit areas like health care and education. He also noted that a market orientation is incongruous with the nonprofit approach since it is openly discriminatory against non-targeted segments and thus unequal in its provision of services.

The 'compromise'

At this point in time, many nonprofit-sector academics and practitioners have taken the position that the marketing concept is applicable in the nonprofit sector, but that, when it is implemented as a 'market orientation', it requires modification due to the unique aspects of the sector (Liao *et al.* 2001). The unique aspect of the sector that receives most attention is its greater complexity, which is caused by the fact that nonprofit organizations typically:

(a) maintain a higher number of relationships that can be considered vitally important, in large part because the attraction and assignment of resources are two separate tasks (Vasquez *et al.* 2002); and

(b) have much more varied organizational objectives, which are mission-based and less tangible than the financially oriented objectives in the for-profit sector (Forbes 1998; Kotler and Andreasen 1996).

The greater number of relationships maintained by nonprofit organizations results in the need to view at least some of their stakeholders as separate target markets that warrant separate annual marketing plans. Having multiple target markets further complicates the application of the marketing concept because it requires spreading already strained marketing resources to understand the needs and expectations of the different stakeholder groups, and to plan and undertake multiple, possibly divergent activities.

With regard to performance assessment, the 'soft' and often subjective nature of nonprofit organizational objectives makes it difficult to establish whether and how strategies and tactics based on the marketing concept are impacting upon mission achievement (Lovelock and Weinberg 1989). Furthermore, the existence of multiple constituencies complicates matters because different stakeholders have different goals and therefore differ in the criteria they use to evaluate the effectiveness of an organization (Herman and Renz 1997).

13

Other characteristics of nonprofit organizations which claimed to influence the implementation of the marketing concept in the nonprofit sector include:

■ the potential conflict that exists between the organizational mission and consumer
satisfaction, because the behaviour of nonprofit organizations is often not determined by
the market but by other concerns (Vasquez *et al.* 2002);
■ the fact that competitors for resources may also be collaborators on various projects
(Kara *et al.* 2004); and
■ the lack of true markets for nonprofits in the economic sense of the term, and the
subsequent inappropriateness of the concept of exchange (Liao *et al.* 2001).

Given the many unique aspects of the nonprofit sector, operationalizing market orientation
in the nonprofit context for research or managerial purposes involves considering at least five
issues:

1   What is market orientation in the nonprofit context?
2   How should market orientation be measured in the nonprofit context?
3   Is market orientation a single construct or multiple, constituent-specific constructs?
4   Does market orientation impact upon nonprofit organizational performance?
5   Does market orientation impact upon organizational performance in all nonprofit
subsectors?

The following sections review the academic discourse in these areas.

Issue 1: what is market orientation in the nonprofit context?

Until very recently, thinking about market orientation in the nonprofit sector was entirely
based on for-profit conceptualizations. Therefore, a review of the key for-profit literature in this
area is a necessary starting point for understanding the nonprofit discourse about market
orientation.

As noted earlier, academic acknowledgement of market orientation as a construct worthy
of investigation in the for-profit sector began with a 1989 *Journal of Marketing* article by
Deshpande and Webster. They related market orientation to an organization's culture and
climate, with culture being the history, norms and values that members of the organization
believe underlie climate, and climate being how organizations operationalize the themes that
pervade everyday behaviour. Their landmark article spawned two very different interpretations
of market orientation: (a) market orientation as a form of organizational culture; and (b) market
orientation as a specific set of activities that implements the marketing concept.

Market orientation as organizational culture

Narver and Slater (1990) championed this interpretation of market orientation. They characterized market orientation as the organizational culture that produces the necessary behaviours
to create superior value for customers and attain a sustained competitive advantage. More
specifically, they envisioned market orientation as consisting of three behavioural components:
customer orientation (the sufficient understanding of one's target buyers to be able to create
superior value for them continuously), competitor orientation (understanding the short-term
strengths and weaknesses and the long-term capabilities and strategies of both current and

potential competitors) and interfunctional coordination (the coordinated utilization of company resources in creating superior value for target customers).

Slater and Narver (1994) rejected the notion that management should attempt to adjust market orientation according to market conditions. They said that adjustment would be complex, time-consuming and expensive. Furthermore, because all markets will encounter slow growth, hostility and changing buyer preferences over time, it is better for management to develop and maintain a high level of market orientation to deal with conditions as they arise.

Market orientation as organizational activities

Deshpande and Webster (1989) also said that culture could be viewed as a lever or tool to be used by managers to implement strategy and to direct the course of their organizations more effectively. Therefore, Kohli and Jaworski (1990) defined market orientation as 'specific activities that translate the (marketing concept) philosophy into practice', making deliberate engendering of a market orientation possible. According to their view, market orientation is composed of three sets of activities: organization-wide generation of market intelligence pertaining to current and future customer needs, dissemination of this intelligence across departments, and organization-wide responsiveness to this intelligence through developing and executing plans (Jaworski and Kohli 1993). They considered market orientation an elective business strategy, the adoption of which may or may not be desirable depending upon supply- and demand-side factors (Kohli and Jaworski 1990).

Tying market orientation to specific activities is defended by supporters as being directly related to the implementation of the marketing concept, whereas culture is broader, the way that things are done generally across the firm (Greenley 1995). These supporters also claim that tying market orientation to specific activities allows it to be measured at all levels of the firm (organizational, departmental, individual), whereas tying the construct to culture limits the measurement of market orientation to the firm level only (Siguaw *et al.* 1994).

Market orientation in the nonprofit sector

The two for-profit interpretations of market orientation have very distinct implications for the operationalization of the marketing concept in the nonprofit world. A market orientation that is purely cultural in nature requires that management actively develop and maintain market orientation norms throughout the organization (Day 1994; Greenley 1995; Slater and Narver 1994). Alternatively, a market orientation that is behavioural in nature requires that management plan and implement activities depending upon environmental circumstances (Kohli and Jaworski 1990). For pragmatic reasons, the latter interpretation is more attractive for the nonprofit sector, since acute resource limitations, both human and financial, make it prohibitive for most nonprofit organizations to expend the time and money needed to build a market orientation culture (Slater and Narver 1994).

Many nonprofit researchers have resolved the issue of which interpretation is more appropriate by taking the position that culture is an antecedent variable (Shoham *et al.* 2006), making market orientation a set of activities by default. Gonzalez *et al.* (2002) and Gainer and Padanyi (2005) challenged this approach, suggesting that market orientation is both market-oriented culture and market-oriented activities. As posited in Gonzalez *et al.* (2002: 64), 'a nonprofit organization's full market orientation requires that its adoption be made from the dual philosophical–cultural and behavioral perspective that defines it. These perspectives should be considered complementary, not exclusive.'

15

The theoretical model developed by Gonzalez *et al.* (2002) recognizes market orientation as a management philosophy that requires three conditions to transform it into a form of organizational culture: an external orientation (which results in orientation towards beneficiaries, donors, competitors and the environment), integration and internal coordination (with the aim of satisfying beneficiaries and donors, and achieving the organization's mission), and adoption of a long-term management perspective (leading to continuity and permanence of activities directed towards beneficiaries and sustained permanent relationships with donors). Their model further indicates that market orientation is a function of carrying out a series of activities: the generation of intelligence, the internal dissemination of this intelligence and the development and initiation of responsive actions.

Gainer and Padanyi's (2005) empirical study involved collecting data from nonprofit service organizations and analysing alternative models incorporating separate cultural and behavioural market orientation constructs. Their results indicate that a positive relationship exists between market-oriented behaviours and organizational performance which is mediated by market-oriented culture.

Other researchers have gone further, arguing for moving away from for-profit-based interpretations of market orientation and completely redefining market orientation for nonprofit purposes. Vasquez *et al.* (2002: 1027) suggest that, within the context of private foundations, market orientation is 'adopting a sensitive attitude toward the beneficiaries' and donors' real and latent needs and expectations'. Liao *et al.* (2001) advocate replacing the term 'market orientation' with an entirely new term, 'societal orientation'. They reject the term 'market orientation' because it implies an orientation towards markets in the true economic sense of the term (which they maintain the resource acquisition and resource allocation markets are not) and because it implies some form of exchange (which they do not consider to be a helpful concept in the nonprofit context). They also contend that the recognized components of market orientation are problematic because: (a) nonprofits often seek longer-term benefit to society rather than simply customer satisfaction; (b) the notion of competition is less relevant; and (c) market orientation implies focusing on one or two stakeholder groups rather than the large number that nonprofits must deal with. Therefore, they theorize that 'societal orientation' should comprise stakeholder orientation, competitive orientation, collaborative orientation and interfunctional coordination.

Bennett (2005) has further advanced discussion about the shortcomings of the for-profit interpretations of market orientation in a nonprofit context by recognizing that market orientation implies a short-term transactional marketing approach rather than the longer-term relationship marketing approach that charities and other caring organizations need to deal effectively with their beneficiaries and donors. His study of charitable service organizations in the UK indicates that market orientation must be operationalized by relationship marketing methods (such as advertising, direct marketing and the use of sales promotion devices) to achieve a nonprofit organization's goals.

Issue 2: how should market orientation be measured in the nonprofit context?

The recent progress made towards moving the conceptualization of market orientation in the nonprofit sector beyond the frameworks established by Narver and Slater and Kohli and Jaworski has not yet been translated into accepted measurement schemes. As a result, the scales they developed continue to be the most frequently used means of measuring the construct in nonprofit marketing research.

To measure culture-based market orientation, Narver and Slater (1990) developed a fifteen-item scale (MKTOR) with multiple-item measures of customer orientation (e.g. we express commitment to our customers; we create value for our customers; we understand the needs of our customers), competitor orientation (e.g. our personnel share information about our competitors; we respond rapidly to competitive actions; our managers discuss competitors' strategies) and interfunctional coordination (e.g. we coordinate customer contacts between our departments; we share information about customers among our departments; we integrate departmental strategies with regard to our customers).

With the MKTOR scale, a researcher derives an overall market orientation index for a respondent firm by averaging the item scores across all the items of the three components. Although Narver and Slater (1990; Slater and Narver 1994) claimed that their scale was unidimensional, a recent study by Ward *et al.* (2006) indicates that it is multidimensional. These authors recommended a nine-item unidimensional alternative to minimize the larger scale's potential for mixed results and to resolve some of the activities-oriented wording problems they saw with MKTOR.

Kohli *et al.* (1993) developed the twenty-item MARKOR scale to operationalize their activities-based definition of market orientation and to address the weaknesses they saw with the Narver and Slater scale. Personal interviews conducted with managers led to the identification of three basic components of market orientation (intelligence generation, dissemination and responsiveness). Multiple-item measures were then developed to reflect intelligence generation (e.g. we meet with customers at least once a year to discuss their needs; we conduct research studies on our customers; we poll customers at least once a year to assess the quality of our products or services), intelligence dissemination (e.g. we hold periodic department meetings to discuss trends and developments relating to our customers; marketing personnel spend time discussing future customer needs; data on customer satisfaction is disseminated at all levels of this organization on a regular basis) and responsiveness (e.g. customer complaints are attended to rapidly; we respond to competitive actions quickly; in planning and developing new activities, we focus on what is of value to our customers).

The advantage of the MARKOR scale is that it focuses on specific organizational activities which are more tangible than measures of culture and less vulnerable to the overgeneralization possible with using self-administered questionnaires. However, the authors never verified that it measures the three components of market orientation that they hypothesize. Attempts at factor analysis (e.g. Pelham 1993) have also been unsuccessful, consistently suggesting that the scale measures more than three dimensions.

For-profit researchers investigating the relationship between market orientation and business performance have typically elected to use either the culture-oriented MKTOR scale or to use the activities-oriented MARKOR scale, or to develop their own scale based on one approach to market orientation or the other. They have rarely provided a rationale for the route they have selected (Padanyi 2001).

The vast majority of nonprofit marketing academics have used adapted versions of the MARKOR scale (Shoham *et al.* 2006). In a study designed to determine whether MARKOR is appropriate to measure market orientation in nonprofit services, Kara *et al.* (2004) justified their preference for the MARKOR scale by noting that the three basic functions that it operationalizes (intelligence generation, intelligence dissemination and responsiveness) incorporate the activities referenced in some of the specific items used in the MKTOR scale. Based on reliability tests of the three dimensions and confirmatory factor analysis, they concluded that MARKOR is a valid and reliable measure of market orientation in nonprofit organizations, and further noted that 'when presented with the scale, executives had little difficulty relating to its items' (Kara *et al.* 2004: 68).

Notably, Vasquez *et al.* (2002) attempted to generate an entirely new scale based on their proposed redefinition of market orientation (cited earlier: 'adopting a sensitive attitude toward the beneficiaries' and donors' real and latent needs and expectations'). In developing this scale, they claimed that they disregarded any existing scales, but their new scale is clearly based on the Kohli and Jaworski framework, since it is a sixteen-item scale with three basic categories of measures: intelligence generation, intelligence dissemination and responsiveness. They claim that this scale is unidimensional, and that it is both valid and reliable for the nonprofit context of private foundations.

Issue 3: is market orientation a single construct or multiple, constituent-specific constructs?

The discussion thus far suggests that market orientation is a singular mindset that pervades all of an organization's external dealings. However, the fact that organizations have multiple constituencies is acknowledged throughout the marketing literature, and 'multiple constituency theory' suggests that an organization should deal with each of their constituencies as separate markets, using different strategic and targeted marketing appeals and techniques to achieve specific performance goals.

A multiple constituency approach is often not achieved in practice, because fielding different marketing efforts to appeal to different constituencies is costly and inevitably taxes organizational resources. As a result, organizations often focus their efforts on the one group they deem to be most important. In the case of the for-profit sector, the final users of the products or services sold have historically been viewed and treated as the most important constituency because of the financial dependence of commercial enterprises on the goodwill and satisfaction of their customers (Kimery and Rinehart 1998).

In borrowing the market orientation construct for nonprofit-sector use, nonprofit academics initially accepted it as a singular mindset focused on the client/customer market. This was consistent with early assertions that the nonprofit sector needed to adopt marketing principles and techniques because customer satisfaction is very important to 'mission-driven' organizations (Kanter and Summers 1987). It is not surprising, then, that the first studies dealing with market orientation in the nonprofit sector focused exclusively on clients and customers (e.g., Naidu and Narayana 1991; Raju *et al.* 1995; Kumar *et al.* 1997; Wood *et al.* 2000; Voss and Voss 2000).

However, since nonprofit marketing serves many other purposes (such as attracting human and financial resources, and setting up commercial ventures), and given the current economic, public relations and information challenges facing nonprofit managers (Sheth 1993), it is increasingly being recognized that market orientation in the nonprofit context must be treated by academics in more complex terms (Gonzalez *et al.* 2002).

According to Kotler and Andreasen (1996), there are at least sixteen constituencies that nonprofit organizations must deal with: three *input publics* (donors, suppliers and regulatory agencies), four *internal publics* (management, boards of directors, staff, volunteers), four *intermediary publics* (merchants, agents, facilitators, marketing firms) and five *consuming publics* (clients, local publics, activist groups, general publics and the media). A comparable list developed by

Liao *et al.* (2001) includes individual donors, corporates, trusts/foundations, trustees, employees, volunteers, recipients, government, umbrella bodies and society in general.

To date, empirical nonprofit marketing researchers have dealt with very few of these groups. Padanyi (2001) focused on three stakeholders: funders (governments and foundations), donors and clients/customers. Vasquez *et al.* (2002), Gonzalez *et al.* (2002), Kara *et al.* (2004), Bennett (2005) and Macedo and Pinho (2006) all focused on two key stakeholders, beneficiaries and donors. Most nonprofit researchers have studied only one (Liao *et al.* 2001).

The few studies conducted to date involving multiple constituencies have achieved mixed results. Based on data collected in Canada, Padanyi and Gainer (2004) found that organizations cluster into four groups in dealing with their government funders and clients/customers. These clusters are organizations with (a) low client orientation and high government funder orientation; (b) high client orientation and low government funder orientation; (c) high client orientation and high government funder orientation; and (d) low client orientation and low government funder orientation. Macedo and Pinho (2006) conducted a study of Portuguese nonprofit organizations (NPOs) investigating their market orientation towards users/ beneficiaries and donors. They found that these organizations favour a market orientation towards users/beneficiaries but are less proactive with regard to having a donor market orientation. On the other hand, Bennett's (2005) study of charitable service organizations in the UK found that charities that were market-oriented towards donors were also market-oriented towards their beneficiaries.

Issue 4: does market orientation impact upon nonprofit organizational performance?

Despite general agreement that market orientation should increase and improve a nonprofit organization's results, relatively few studies have been conducted to date on the relationship between market orientation and organizational performance in the nonprofit context (Kara *et al.* 2004). The primary difficulty associated with conducting studies of this nature is goal definition at the organizational level. Evaluation at the programme level has been a common practice in the nonprofit sector for years, but evaluation at the organizational level is a relatively recent pursuit, caused in part by growing demands for accountability by funders and donors (Padanyi 2001). Furthermore, at the organizational level, nonprofits do not define themselves based on financial returns, but rather based on the more amorphous goal of achieving their mission (Liao *et al.* 2001).

In 1987, Kanter and Summers stated that the key issues associated with performance measurement in nonprofit organizations are: (a) the number of stakeholders; (b) the need for input as well as output measures (because the effectiveness of a nonprofit organization is as dependent upon its ability to attract resources as it is on its ability to provide service); (c) the need to incorporate short-term, intermediate and long-term perspectives (because the ultimate criterion for the performance of a nonprofit may be long-term survival); and (d) the need to incorporate subjective as well as objective measures (because nonprofits typically provide intangible services). Several attempts have been made to model nonprofit performance in multidimensional terms (e.g. Herman 1990; Kushner and Poole 1996). In practice, however, empirical researchers have either used single measures, such as the effectiveness of the organization in carrying out its mission or changes in revenues and annual operating budgets (e.g. Bradshaw *et al.* 1992; Crittenden *et al.* 1988; Herman and Tulipana 1985) or a limited set of multidimensional performance indicators (e.g. Padanyi 2001; Kara *et al.* 2004; Gainer and

Padanyi 2005). At the time of writing, operationalization of nonprofit performance remains 'problematic' (Shoham *et al.* 2006).

For a recent meta-analysis of studies conducted to date on the relationship between market orientation and organizational performance in the nonprofit and voluntary sector, the authors found seventeen empirical studies, most of which identified a positive market orientation–performance link, albeit with 'high deviation' (Shoham *et al.* 2006). To explain this deviation, they identified three potential moderators of the market orientation–organizational performance link: location, market orientation operationalization and performance measure used. With regard to study location, they found that US samples exhibited a weaker market orientation–organizational performance relationship than samples from other countries. Based on this, they suggested that market orientation may have its greatest effect in nations where high standards of consumer service and expectations are still evolving. With regard to market orientation operationalization, they found that using the MARKOR scale resulted in a stronger relationship than using proprietary scales, which they maintain supports the importance of using previously validated scales with proven reliability. Finally, with regard to performance measures used, they found that the impact of market orientation on subject measures of performance is stronger than its impact on combinations of subjective and objective measures.

Issue 5: does market orientation impact upon performance in all nonprofit subsectors?

There are a large number of 'subsectors' or 'industries' in the nonprofit sector, as illustrated by the schemas used by the Canadian and American governments to categorize registered charities. The Canadian government uses six basic groupings: social welfare, health, education, religion, benefits to community and 'others' (primarily service clubs), which are divided into over fifty subgroups (Revenue Canada 1998). The US government recognizes twenty-four non-business categories, including: health, arts and culture, environmental quality and protection, consumer protection, crime and delinquency prevention, and youth development (Kotler and Andreasen 1996).

No matter how they are classified, the activities and purposes of different types of nonprofit organizations are highly diverse. Thus, nonprofit observers claim that a management process that works for one subsector will probably not work for another (Anthony and Young 1990). Furthermore, a tenet of nonprofit marketing education, based on anecdotal evidence, is that the subsectors tend to select different marketing strategies and tactics due to differences in sources of funding, extent of public scrutiny, reliance on volunteers, the types of objectives they set, the product/services they offer and the nature of the markets they serve (Hay 1990; Kotler and Andreasen 1996).

Given the differences known to exist between nonprofit subsectors, studies of the application of marketing principles should involve more than one subsector if results are to be truly generalizable across the entire nonprofit sector. Nevertheless, most studies of the market orientation–organizational performance relationship in the nonprofit sector have focused on one subsector, such as hospitals, or social service agencies, or arts and culture organizations (Shoham *et al.* 2006). This has allowed these researchers to incorporate performance measures actually used in practice by a given subsector into their studies. Therefore, they have used not only subjective measures of effectiveness but sector-specific objective data, such as hospital occupancy rates (Naidu and Narayana 1991) or subscriber attendance at cultural events (Voss and Voss 2000) or fundraising practices (Kara *et al.* 2004).

Padanyi and Gainer (2004) took the approach recommended by Herman and Heimovics (1994) and measured organizational performance using 'widely-shared' performance measures (client satisfaction, peer reputation and resource attraction). This allowed them to claim that their finding that client/customer orientation and government funder orientation both have significant, positive relationships with organizational performance was generalizable across three important subsectors of the nonprofit sector (social services, community support, and arts and culture).

Conclusions: operationalizing market orientation in the nonprofit sector

It should be apparent at this point that much work remains to be done to understand market orientation in the nonprofit context and to provide definitive answers to the questions raised in this chapter. Nevertheless, several conclusions can be drawn in relation to its operationalization for both managerial and scholarly purposes.

Managerial operationalization of market orientation

Although market orientation is still ill-defined, the information gathered to date indicates that nonprofit managers who ignore this strategic approach in their operations do so at their own peril. In an economic sector increasingly oriented towards competition for new resources and collaboration to extend existing resources, a nonprofit organization which is determined to survive must recognize that 'its beneficiaries and donors should feel that they are receiving a nonprofit offer that satisfies their needs and expectations to a greater degree than any other alternative to which they might resort' (Gonzalez et al. 2002: 65).

The current academic literature clearly indicates that market orientation involves both culture and activities, even if one or the other is not technically considered to be part of its definition. From a managerial perspective, initiating client-oriented activities prior to attempting to instil a client-oriented culture, as suggested by Gonzalez et al. (2002) and Gainer and Padanyi (2005), has practical advantages. Success with market-oriented activities may help to overcome employee resistance to change. It should also reduce the risk to human and financial resources associated with imposing cultural change in a deliberate, top-down manner (Harris 1999).

The starting point for developing market orientation is self-analysis to understand what the organization currently does. More specifically, the organization must determine who its key stakeholders are, what market-oriented behaviour it currently directs towards them, and whether or not it can already be characterized as having a market-oriented culture. In determining its key stakeholder groups, obvious considerations are beneficiaries, donors, competitors and collaborators. However, other groups which should be considered include volunteers (Shoham et al. 2006), suppliers who provide components of the organization's service or product offerings (and can thus impact upon the satisfaction of beneficiaries) or interest groups that have the potential to impact upon a nonprofit organization's capacity to fulfil its mission (Gonzalez et al. 2002). The organization must then inventory the activities it currently undertakes with each of its stakeholders and, based on this, assess its existing culture in terms of the attitude or 'sensitivity' of all of its personnel towards these various groups.

In addition, if it has not already done so, the organization must determine how to assess its own performance and set specific standards or goals which it can use to judge its success. These goals should be based on what is relevant to achieving the organization's mission, rather than on what is simply easy to measure, e.g. a library should measure user satisfaction rather than number of books borrowed (Harrison and Shaw 2004). Well-defined means to assess performance are needed to determine the contribution that each stakeholder group makes or could make to the organization's performance. This understanding provides the basis for judging the relative importance of each group, and for determining whether or not appropriate levels of effort and resources are being devoted to each one. Furthermore, since the purpose of market orientation is to improve organizational performance, it is not worthwhile developing it without also having the means to determine whether the effort has been worthwhile and should be continued.

Self-analysis and goal-setting provide the organization with the strategic foundation needed to build multiple market orientations. A variety of market-oriented activities has been identified that can be undertaken with different constituent groups. The activities selected may vary by stakeholder group and must be determined based on the priority that the organization places on a given constituency and its available human and financial resources. Using the Kohli and Jaworski (1990) framework, these activities can be grouped into intelligence generation, intelligence dissemination and responsiveness categories as follows:

Intelligence generation includes:

- meeting with or polling or conducting some other form of regular and systematic research on stakeholders to determine their needs, desires and expectations (Gonzalez et al. 2002);
- collecting and analysing information on organizations competing for the attention and loyalty of the same donors or beneficiaries (Bennett 2005);
- using the information gathered to profile the strengths and weaknesses of competition in order to identify one's own competitive advantage, or to identify opportunities for self-improvement or collaboration (Gonzalez et al. 2002); and
- understanding the specific and generic environmental forces that may impact upon the organization's capacity to deal with its various stakeholders (Gonzalez et al. 2002).

Intelligence dissemination includes:

- sharing, jointly considering and processing information across all the departments within an organization pertaining to stakeholders' requirements (Bennett 2005);
- using all of the formal and informal tools at hand (e.g. holding meetings, making use of information technology and creating taskforces) to analyse, interpret, discuss and forecast trends and events relating to both stakeholders and competitors (Gonzalez et al. 2002); and
- using learning systems such as 'communities of practice' and networks of collaborating organizations to interpret the environment (Murray and Carter 2005).

Responsiveness includes:

- developing a full response action plan for targeted groups (Vasquez et al. 2002); and
- putting the action plan into practice with a budget which adequately covers the costs associated with its generation, distribution and communication (Gonzalez et al. 2002).

It must be noted that, in a multiple-constituency situation, it is important that nonprofit managers continue to recognize and treat different stakeholder groups as distinct entities. Therefore, as activities are undertaken to generate and disseminate market intelligence, or to build relationships, each constituent group should be researched, consulted and communicated with separately. Attempts to collapse data on them to simplify distribution across the organization, or to combine communication efforts should be avoided.

Once the organization has fielded the various market-oriented activities that it has selected for each stakeholder group, it cannot automatically claim to have a market-oriented culture. Development of a market-oriented culture involves more than 'merely implementing tactically-oriented marketing practices more effectively' (Warnaby and Finney 2005: 193). To assess whether it has achieved a market-oriented culture, an organization must consider whether it:

- unconditionally assumes the ongoing need to generate exchanges of value with beneficiaries and other stakeholders (Gonzalez *et al.* 2002);
- has a learning orientation that results in improved intelligence generation and dissemination (Murray and Carter 2005);
- responds to stakeholder needs and wants, rather than placing emphasis on what the organization has considered most appropriate for the stakeholders (Harrison and Shaw 2004);
- allocates resources to support multiple market orientations based on a systematic evaluation and prioritization of its various stakeholders (Padanyi 2001);
- recognizes the existence of competition and is aware that competitive offerings and performance provide a basis for stakeholders to judge their own organization's performance, as well as providing ideas for upgrading their offerings (Harrison and Shaw 2004);
- provides superior value creation and delivery (Warnaby and Finney 2005);
- has a commitment from everyone in the organization to undertaking market-oriented behaviours, and maintaining and generating mutually beneficial relationships with the targeted markets (Gonzalez *et al.* 2002);
- has some degree of formalization of the communication and activity processes adopted by the organization (Vasquez *et al.* 2002);
- has fully integrated marketing into the organization, with all employees recognizing that they all 'market' their services and/or products and that effective marketing has long-term benefits for the organization (Harrison and Shaw 2004); and
- recognizes or rewards personnel (employees or collaborators) to the extent that their performance is adapted to market orientation principles (Vasquez *et al.* 2002).

Academic operationalization of market orientation

From an academic perspective, it is clear that market orientation is still fertile ground for exploration and investigation. It is also apparent that a researcher interested or involved in this area must make a conscious decision to either: (a) continue attempting to adapt the for-profit conceptualizations of market orientation to the nonprofit context; or (b) build on recent efforts to reconceptualize market orientation and specifically tailor it to the nonprofit context.

If the chosen path is to adapt for-profit conceptualizations of market orientation to the nonprofit context, the researcher must recognize that some for-profit dimensions (e.g. competitor orientation with regard to clients/customers) may only apply to nonprofit organizations operating in environments where organizations compete for customer/client patronage and loyalty, such as theatres or hospitals (Shoham *et al.* 2006), and that for-profit conceptualizations do not allow for relationships with certain key stakeholders (such as collaborators).

These weaknesses, combined with a body of research to date showing that the impact of market orientation on the performance of nonprofits is 'positive, but with high deviation' (Shoham *et al.* 2006), argue for taking the alternative path, i.e. reconceptualizing market orientation in a way that specifically tailors it to the nonprofit sector. One alternative conceptualization has been developed, societal orientation, which is worthy of consideration (Liao *et al.* 2001). It must be noted, though, that the similarity of its proposed components (stakeholder orientation, competitive orientation, collaborative orientation and interfunctional orientation) to the Narver and Slater components (customer orientation, competitor orientation and interfunctional coordination) might encourage merely adapting MKTOR, with its problematic blend of both cultural and behavioural items, to create a societal orientation scale. Thus, there is room for further reconceptualizations of market orientation in the nonprofit context that can potentially lead to totally new measurement scales and complex models which incorporate various antecedents and moderators specific to the nonprofit sector.

No matter which path is taken, multidimensional, 'widely-shared' organizational performance measures that can be applied to a variety of subsectors are needed to determine the applicability of the marketing concept across the nonprofit sector (Herman and Heimovics 1994). Liao *et al.* (2001) further recommend distinguishing between two critical dimensions of performance: efficiency and effectiveness. Effectiveness involves the analysis of the extent to which an organization fulfils its mission (plus other measures or constructs that relate to the achievement of this goal), while dealing efficiently with fundraising and administrative costs/ allocation of scarce resources.

Researchers following either path must also seek to overcome the many limitations associated with previous research on market orientation in the nonprofit context. Thus, consideration must be given to:

- gathering data in a variety of types of nonprofit organizations (Vasquez *et al.* 2002; Kara *et al.* 2004);
- encompassing other key nonprofit constituencies such as time donors (volunteers), current and potential collaborators and mass-media contacts (Padanyi 2001);
- going beyond self-described behaviour to consider the perceptions of targeted stakeholder groups regarding the organization and its market orientation (Vasquez *et al.* 2002);
- exploring interactions between multiple market orientations by identifying and surveying each individual organization's entire set of constituent groups (Rowley 1998);
- evaluating the moderating role that factors such as market dynamism and uncertainty or existing competitive intensity may exert on the market orientation–organizational performance relationship (Vasquez *et al.* 2002); and
- using longitudinal data collection methodologies, rather than continuing to rely on cross-sectional data, in order to understand long-term effects (Kara *et al.* 2004).

Overcoming the last limitation is particularly critical to proving the value of market orientation and its impact on organizational performance in the nonprofit context. It is difficult to infer causality between these variables with cross-sectional design because 'precedence' or temporal priority, a condition for establishing causality, is not present (Lehman *et al.* 1998).

References

Anthony, R. N. and Young, D. W. (1990) 'Characteristics of nonprofit organizations', in David L. Gies, J. Steven Ott and Jay M. Shafritz (eds) *The Nonprofit Organization: Essential Readings*, Pacific Grove, CA: Brooks/Cole Publishing Co.

Bennett, R. (2005) 'Competitive environment, market orientation and the use of relational approaches to the marketing of charity beneficiary services', *Journal of Services Marketing*, 19(6/7):53–469.

Bradshaw, P., Murray, V. and Wolpin, J. (1992) 'Do nonprofit boards make a difference? An exploration of the relationships among board structure, process, and effectiveness', *Nonprofit and Voluntary Sector Quarterly*, 21(autumn):227–49.

Bush, R. (1992) 'Survival of the nonprofit spirit in a for-profit world', *Nonprofit and Voluntary Sector Quarterly*, 21(winter):391–410.

Crittenden, W. E., Crittenden, V. L. and Hunt, T. G. (1988) 'Planning and stakeholder satisfaction in religious organizations', *Journal of Voluntary Action Research*, 17:60–73.

Day, G.S. (1994) 'The capabilities of market-driven organizations', *Journal of Marketing*, 58(October):37–52.

Deshpande, R. and Webster, Jr., F. E. (1989) 'Organizational culture and marketing: Defining the research agenda', *Journal of Marketing*, 53(January):3–15.

Forbes, D. P. (1998) 'Measuring the immeasurable: Empirical studies of nonprofit organization effectiveness from 1977–97', *Nonprofit and Voluntary Sector Quarterly*, 27(June):183–202.

Gainer, B. and Padanyi, P. (2005) 'The relationship between market-oriented activities and market-oriented culture: Implications for the development of market orientation in nonprofit service organizations', *Journal of Business Research*, 58(6):854–62.

Gonzalez, L. I. A., Vijande, M. L. S. and Caseilles, R. V. (2002) 'The market orientation concept in the private nonprofit organization domain', *International Journal of Nonprofit and Voluntary Sector Marketing*, 7(1):55–67.

Greenley, G. E. (1995) 'Forms of market orientation in UK companies', *Journal of Management Studies*, 32(January):47–66.

Harris, L. C. (1999) 'Barriers to developing market orientation', *Journal of Applied Management Studies*, 8(June):85–101.

Harrison, P. J. and Shaw, R. N. (2004) 'Intra-organizational marketing culture and market orientation: A case study of the implementation of the marketing concept in a public library', *Library Management*, 25(8/9):391–8.

Hay, R. D. (1990) *Strategic Management in Nonprofit Organizations: An Administrator's Handbook*, New York, NY: Quorum Books.

Herman, R. D. (1990) 'Methodological issues in studying the effectiveness of nongovernmental and nonprofit organizations', *Nonprofit and Voluntary Sector Quarterly*, 19(autumn):293–307.

—— and Heimovics, R. D. (1994) 'A cross-national study of a method for researching nonprofit organizational effectiveness', *Voluntas*, 5:86–100.

—— and Renz, D. O. (1997) 'Multiple constituents and social construction of nonprofit organization effectiveness', *Nonprofit and Voluntary Sector Quarterly*, 26(June):187–206.

—— and Tulipana, F. P. (1985) 'Board–staff relations and perceived effectiveness in nonprofit organizations', *Journal of Voluntary Action Research*, 14(4):48–59.

Jaworski, B. J. and Kohli, A. K. (1993) 'Marketing orientation: Antecedents and consequences', *Journal of Marketing*, 57(July):53–70.

Kanter, R. M. and Summers, D. V. (1987) 'Doing well while doing good: Dilemmas of performance measurement in nonprofit organizations and the need for a multiple constituency approach', in Walter W. Powell (ed.) *The Nonprofit Sector: A Research Handbook*, New Haven, CT: Yale University Press.

Kara, A., Spillan, J. E. and DeShields Jr., O. W. (2004) 'An empirical investigation of the link between market orientation and business performance in nonprofit service providers', *Journal of Marketing Theory and Practice*, 12(2):59–72.

Kimery, K. M. and Rinehart, S. M. (1998) 'Markets and constituencies: An alternative view of the marketing concept', *Journal of Business Research*, 32:117–24.

Kohli, A. K. and Jaworski, B. J. (1990) 'Market orientation: The construct, research propositions, and managerial implications', *Journal of Marketing*, 54(April):1–18.

—— and Kumar, A. (1993) 'MARKOR: A measure of market orientation', *Journal of Marketing Research*, 30(November):467–77.

Kotler, P. and Andreasen, A. R. (1996) *Strategic Marketing for Nonprofit Organizations*, 5th edition, Upper Saddle River, NJ: Prentice Hall.

—— and Levy, S. J. (1969) 'Broadening the concept of marketing', *Journal of Marketing*, 33(January):10–15.

Kumar, K., Subramanian, R. and Yauger, C. (1997) 'Performance-oriented: Toward a successful strategy,' *Marketing Health Services*, 17(summer):10–20.

Kushner, R. J. and Poole, P. P. (1994) 'Exploring structure–effectiveness relationships in nonprofit arts organizations', *Nonprofit Management and Leadership*, 7(winter):119–36.

Lehman, D. R., Gupta, S. and Steckel, J. H. (1998) *Marketing Research*, New York, NY: Addison Wesley.

Liao, M. N., Foreman, S. and Sargeant, A. (2001) 'Market versus societal orientation in the nonprofit context', *International Journal of Nonprofit and Voluntary Sector Marketing*, 6(3):254–68.

Lovelock, C. H. and Weinberg, C. B. (1989) *Marketing for Public and Nonprofit Managers*, 2nd edition, Redwood City, CA: Scientific Press.

Luck, D. J. (1969) 'Broadening the concept of marketing – too far', *Journal of Marketing*, 33(July):53–63.

Macedo, I. M. and Pinho, J. C. (2006) 'The relationship between resource dependence and market orientation: The specific case of nonprofit organizations', *European Journal of Marketing*, 40(5/6):533–53.

Murray, P. and Carter, L. (2005) 'Improving market intelligence through learning systems and knowledge communities in not-for-profit workplaces', *Journal of Workplace Learning*, 17(7/8):421–35.

Naidu, G. M. and Narayana, C. L. (1991) 'How marketing oriented are hospitals in a declining market?', *Journal of Health Care Marketing*, 11:23–30.

Narver, J. C. and Slater, S. F. (1990) 'The effect of a market orientation on business profitability', *Journal of Marketing*, 54(October):20–35.

Padanyi, P. (2001) 'Testing the boundaries of the marketing concept: Is market orientation a determinant of organizational performance in the nonprofit sector?', unpublished thesis, York University, UK.

—— and Gainer, B. (2004) 'Market orientation in the nonprofit sector: Taking multiple constituencies into consideration', *Journal of Marketing Theory and Practice*, 12(2):43–58.

Pelham, A. M. (1993) 'Mediating and moderating influences on the relationship between market orientation and performance', unpublished thesis, Pennsylvania State University.

Raju, P. S., Lonial, S. C. and Gupta, Y. P. (1995) 'Market orientation and performance in the hospital industry', *Journal of Health Care Marketing*, 15:34–41.

Revenue Canada (1998) *Database of Registered Charitable Organizations*, Government of Canada.

Rowley, T. J. (1998) 'Moving beyond diadic Ties: A network theory of stakeholder influences', *Academy of Management Review*, 22(October):887–910.

Shapiro, B. P. (1973) 'Marketing for nonprofit organizations', *Harvard Business Review*, 51(September–October):123–32.

—— (1988) 'What the hell is "market-oriented"?', *Harvard Business Review*, 66(November–December):119–25.

Sheth, J. N. (1993) 'User-oriented marketing for nonprofit organizations', in D. C. Hammach and D. R. Young (eds) *Nonprofit Organizations in a Market Economy*, San Francisco, CA: Jossey-Bass.

Shoham, A., Ruvio, A., Vigoda-Gadot, E. and Schwabsky, N. (2006) 'Market orientations in the nonprofit and voluntary sector: A meta-analysis of their relationships with organizational performance', *Nonprofit and Voluntary Sector Quarterly*, 35(3):453–76.

Siguaw, J. A., Brown, G. and Widing, II, R. E. (1994) 'The influence of the market orientation of the firm on sales force behavior and attitudes', *Journal of Marketing Research*, 31:106–16.

Slater, S. F. and Narver, J. C. (1994) 'Does competitive environment moderate the market orientation–performance relationship?', *Journal of Marketing*, 58(January):46–55.

Tuckman, H. P. (1998) 'Competition, commercialization, and the evolution of nonprofit organizational structures', *Journal of Policy Analysis and Management*, 17(2):175–94.

Vasquez, R., Alvarez, L. I. and Santos, M. L. (2002) 'Market orientation and social services in private nonprofit organizations', *European Journal of Marketing*, 36(9/10):1022–46.

Voss, G. B. and Voss, Z. G. (2000) 'Strategic orientation and firm performance in an artistic environment', *Journal of Marketing*, 64(January):67–83.

Ward, S., Girandi, A. and Lewandowska, A. (2006) 'A cross-national validation of the Narver and Slater market orientation scale', *Journal of Marketing Theory and Practice*, 14(2):155–67.

Warnaby, G. and Finney, J. (2005) 'Creating customer value in the not-for-profit sector: A case study of the British Library', *International Journal of Nonprofit and Voluntary Sector Marketing*, 10(3):183–95.

Wood, V. R., Bhuian, S. and Kieker, P. (2000) 'Market orientation and organizational performance in not-for-profit hospitals', *Journal of Business Research*, 48(June):213–26.

Relationship marketing and the not-for-profit sector

An extension and application of the commitment–trust theory

Kevin Money, Arthur Money, Steve Downing and Carola Hillenbrand

Introduction

Relationship marketing has been one of the major paradigms in the marketing literature over the last ten years. In this time it has also had a major impact on marketing activities in the for-profit sector, being credited with increased customer cooperation, increased purchases and decreased customer defection (Morgan and Hunt 1994; Gummesson 1999). Traditional marketing has emphasized the importance of acquiring new customers (Gummesson 1997). Relationship marketing, however, has put a more overt emphasis on the importance of developing long-term supportive relationships with existing customers and posits that energy and resources are better spent on this group (Gronroos 1997) than on attempting to attract new customers. Several theorists have suggested that relationship-marketing activities would be particularly suited to the non-profit sector (Sargeant 2001a; Burnett 1998).

This seems particularly relevant as non-profit organizations (NPOs) operate in a highly competitive environment (Sargeant 2001a). Sargeant argues that competition from the increasing number of NPOs, combined with a decreasing funder pool (Pharoah and Tanner 1998) has led many NPOs to rely increasingly on a small number of key funders (NCVO 1999). To survive and thrive in this competitive environment, theorists such as Burnett (1998), Sagawa (2001) and Sabo (2002) propose that NPOs should concentrate on maintaining and developing relationships with existing funders.

Applying relationship marketing to funder relationships

While relationship-marketing concepts have been applied to many different stakeholders such as employees, suppliers and communities, most studies focus on relationship marketing in the context of the customer. This is because customers are the group that drive the cashflow and business success most directly (Zadrozny 2006; Gronroos 1997). In the not-for-profit context, funders are often seen as the group that drive cashflow most directly (Burligame 2001). It is for this reason that funder–organization relationships will be the key focus of this chapter. But what are the similarities and differences between funder and customer relationships and how can relationship-marketing concepts be applied to the not-for-profit sector?

Rothschild (1979) argues that funder relationships with NPOs are fundamentally different from orthodox customer–organization relationships. He believes that individuals in customer relationships are usually the direct consumers of the organization's services. Funders, however, are not the direct consumers of an NPO's services, nor do they normally have direct experience or involvement in service delivery. Consequently, this is why theorists have argued that funder trust in NPOs is critical (Sargeant and Lee 2001). Even when there is a direct customer transactional relationship with an NPO, Garbarino and Johnson (1999) found that trust is more important in generating long-term loyalty than the benefits received in the exchange itself.

Trust is central to relationships with organizations (Kramer and Tyler 1996). The development of trust is a key activity in relationship marketing generally (Gummesson 1997) and in the NPO sector (Thomas *et al.* 2002). Trust has been associated with many positive organizational outcomes, not specifically related to NPOs. These include, for example: buffering against poor economic conditions (e.g. Taylor 1996); long-term competitive advantage (e.g. Silinpaa and Wheeler 1998); long-term financial success and shareholder value (e.g. Collins and Porras 1998); innovative solutions to organizational challenges (e.g. Kay 1993) and organizational advantage from intellectual capital (e.g. Nahapiet and Goshal 1998).

The organizational outcomes are the consequence of the various supportive behaviours. These behaviours, in turn, are anteceded by trust. These include, for example, long-term commitment and loyalty (e.g. Bagozzi 2000); lower levels of coercion and opportunism by stakeholders towards their organizations (e.g. Cummings and Bromiley 1996); cooperation and positive functional conflict between stakeholders and their organizations (e.g. Morgan and Hunt 1994); flexibility (e.g. Young-Ybarra and Wiersma 1999) and creativity (e.g. Nahapiet and Goshal 1998). Commitment is perhaps the most important of these supportive behaviours as it drives many of the other behavioural outcomes (Morgan and Hunt 1994). Funder commitment is important to NPOs because this group often provides the NPO with its main source of income. But what type of relationship will generate this commitment? While trust is still likely to be a key driver of commitment, the key question is how NPOs cause funders to trust and be committed to them when there is no direct consumer transaction.

The drivers of trust and commitment

Figure 2.1 presents the Morgan and Hunt (1994) model of relationship marketing. According to Morgan and Hunt (1994), trust and commitment are at the heart of any successful relationship with customers. They believe that commitment depends on four variables: relationship benefits, relationship termination costs, shared values and trust. Trust itself is dependent upon three variables: shared values, communication and opportunistic behaviour.

The view that commitment is dependent on the above antecedents has a long history, based on a number of theories. The prediction that relationship benefits and termination costs drive commitment has its origins in exchange theory (e.g. Blau 1964; Chadwick-Jones 1976). The shared values–commitment link, on the other hand, can be seen to be derived from the social–psychological theory of attraction based on similarity (e.g. Berscheid 1985). The link between trust and commitment is based on theories of long-term exchange (Perlman and Duck 1987).

The view that trust is developed from the history of a relationship, through shared values, communication and opportunistic behaviour, can also be supported from other sources

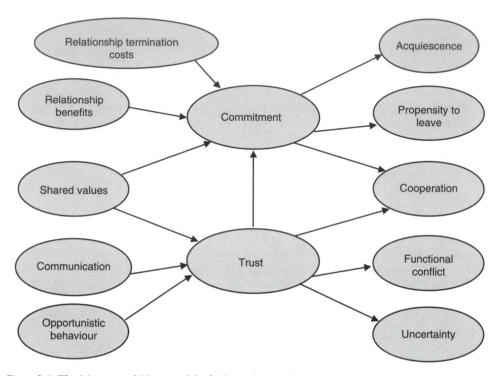

Figure 2.1 The Morgan and Hunt model of relationship marketing

deriving from the interpersonal relationship literature (for reviews of these theories, see Duck 1997; Duck and Ickes 2000; Hinde 1997; Seligman 1997). In essence, all these antecedents of trust have the same theoretical foundations and are based on socio-cognitive learning theories (e.g. Heider, 1958, 1980), which assume that individuals are rational and learn from the past. Individuals interact, experience and observe the actions of a relationship partner (e.g. how they have communicated, whether they have kept commitments or been honest, etc.) and use these perceptions to develop a view of how the partner will act in the future (i.e. their trust in the organization).

Material and non-material benefits

Morgan and Hunt (1994) see the benefits from customer relationships in terms of product profitability, customer satisfaction and product performance. Clearly, these dimensions are less directly applicable in NPO–funder relationships. A more in-depth look at exchange theory provides insights into the selection of more appropriate benefits in this context. Rempel *et al.* (1985), for example, categorized the benefits in relationships into three types: 'extrinsic', 'instrumental' and 'intrinsic'. Of these, they found that extrinsic and intrinsic were the most important and were thus chosen as sub-constructs of benefits in this study. Extrinsic benefits are the material benefits that are exchanged in a relationship. Intrinsic benefits, on the other hand, are the benefits inherent in the relationship. They are more intangible than extrinsic benefits and are usually tacit.

A series of exploratory qualitative interviews was carried out with organizational funders to investigate the nature of the benefits they received in their relationship with the NPO. The general nature of intrinsic and extrinsic benefits was explained to funders, who were asked to identify examples under each category to verify the dichotomy and to develop appropriate measures (Strauss and Corbin 1990). In the process, the terms were renamed 'material' and 'non-material' benefits. These material benefits included, for example, funders learning from the NPO and receiving positive publicity from their relationship with it (Polonsky and Macdonald 2000). Non-material benefits, on the other hand, included the belief that the NPO was making efficient use of its donated funds and that it was having a positive impact on the people for whom these funds were intended. This is similar to the concept of operational competence, identified by Mayer *et al.* (1995) and Sirdeshmukh *et al.* (2002).

Given that Rothschild (1979) emphasized the non-transactional nature of funder relationships with NPOs, supported by other theorists who have argued that funder trust in NPOs is critical in these relationships, it is likely that non-material benefits will be closely associated with trust. In fact, we advance this further, suggesting that trust is the key antecedent of non-material benefits. In the absence of direct consumption, we suggest that trust will be one of the major factors used to assess the non-material benefits provided by NPOs.

Communication

Communication, as operationalized by Morgan and Hunt (1994), has three sub-constructs. These are the frequency, relevance and timeliness of communication from the organization to the customer. However, a review of the literature on NPO fundraising suggested that this was a rather limited view of communication. Burnett (1992), for example, has recognized the importance of dealing with funders individually, recognizing their motivation for giving and their expectations of the NPO. Sargeant (2001b) found that when funders were asked about the communication process, their loyalty increased. Thus, we can infer from these sources that communication must be a two-way process involving listening to as well as informing funders. Listening would include seeking funders' opinions about the NPO and identifying their needs and motivations in the relationship.

In the interviews, funders often made judgements about the NPO on the basis of contacts they had experienced with the NPO's staff. Staff interactions can therefore be considered as an important element in NPO communication with funders. This statement is consistent with the points made by Brennan and Brady (1999) who suggest that NPO marketing relationships will be strengthened by the behaviour of employees in a variety of roles. Reichheld (1993) found that employee behaviour had a significant impact on customer loyalty. Building on this, Flood *et al.* (2000) found that good communication by employees had a positive impact on the financial performance of organizations.

Garbarino and Johnson (1999), in reviewing theories of relationship marketing, include both transactional and relational exchanges. Transactional exchanges refer to encounters in which customers relate to any number of interchangeable employees for strictly transactional ends. In relational exchanges, on the other hand, customers interact with key individuals for both transactional and relational reasons (Gronroos 1997). Peltier *et al.* (2002) endorse the importance of this distinction in the NPO sector. Moreover, Sirdeshmukh *et al.* (2002) identified front-line employee behaviour as a key driver of trust in relationship marketing. In designing the questionnaire, therefore, a number of questions were included that addressed funder perceptions of the NPO staff.

The following employee behaviours were mentioned in the interviews by funders as important in shaping their positive perceptions of the NPO: a knowledgeable and professional approach, friendly service and employees who appeared passionate about their work. This may serve as a proxy for the impact of the NPO on its clients. We may therefore hypothesize that communication is a key antecedent of non-material benefits, given the close association of both concepts with trust. In the absence of direct consumption, we suggest that funders will have to rely on both communication and trust when judging the non-material benefits provided by an NPO.

The outcomes of trust and commitment

The Morgan and Hunt model (see Figure 2.1) also included the outcomes of commitment of trust. They posit five outcomes. In the NPO context, these outcomes would be:

- *acquiescence*: the degree to which a funder accepts or adheres to the NPO's requests;
- *propensity to leave*: the likelihood that the funder will leave the NPO relationship in the (reasonably) near future;
- *cooperation*: the funder sharing information with the NPO and working with it to achieve mutual goals;
- *functional conflict*: the extent to which a funder seeks to resolve disputes amicably and in a way that can enhance understanding in the relationship, or negatively, i.e. dysfunctionally;
- *decision-making uncertainty*: the extent to which the funder perceives it has enough information to make key decisions, can predict the consequences of these decisions and has confidence in those decisions.

It is likely that some of these variables will be strongly linked to trust, such as the extent to which a funder is prepared to cooperate and treat conflict in a constructive way. MacMillan *et al.* (2004) provide other outcomes, that are suggested as generic themes that can be customized and adapted to different organizations and stakeholder groups. These are now contextualized to the funder–NPO context as a way of illustrating other outcomes in funder–NPO relationships:

- *retention*: the extent to which a funder intends to stay with an organization;
- *extension*: the extent to which funders are likely to extend their relationships with an NPO. For example, funding different and new projects outside those they already fund, or supporting the NPO in a different role (e.g. as a volunteer);
- *advocacy*: the extent to which a funder is likely to recommend and defend an NPO;
- *cooperation*: the extent to which a funder will both actively and reactively cooperate with the NPO, by sharing information, solving conflicts in a functional way and seeking mutual benefit in the relationship;
- *subversion*: the extent to which a funder will actively seek to harm the NPO, by, for example, using coercive power or seeking the support of others to harm the NPO.

Following more recent works such as MacMillan *et al.* (2004) and Money and Hillenbrand (2006) it seems reasonable that outcome variables can be tailored to specific circumstances. For example, advocacy – the extent to which a funder will recommend and defend the NPO to others – may be of particular importance in certain circumstances, and so on. Measurement of negative outcomes, such as subversion – the extent to which funders may seek to harm the NPO – may also be relevant. It is thus suggested that the exact nature of outcomes should be defined in a process which draws upon perceived organizational need and the current circumstances in a relationship. As the work of Money and Hillenbrand (2006) suggests, it is envisaged that the outcome variables should be customized on each occasion.

The model

The Morgan and Hunt model was amended to include both material and non-material benefits as shown in Figure 2.2, with trust being an antecedent of non-material benefits.

Case study: applying the model to organizational funders of an NPO in South Africa

Many NPOs rely on donations from both individuals and organizations (such as corporations, trusts and governments). While both sources of funding are important, the average value of each organizational funder is often suggested to be higher than that of each individual (see Burlingame 2001; Sargeant and Stephenson 1997). Therefore, NPOs would benefit from focusing on strengthening their relationships with organizational funders. It is for this reason that organizational funders were chosen as the focus of the case study.

A crime-prevention NPO based in South Africa was chosen as the setting for the research. The majority of the NPO's funders are organizations, including many leading trusts and companies in South Africa. Of these organizational funders, approximately 50 per cent also funded other NPOs while 50 per cent only funded the NPO in question. The entire sample was drawn from one sector in one country. The benefit of this was that the whole sample was subject to the same business environment and public policy context, thus minimizing extraneous sources of variation. Furthermore, the study set out to test the applicability of relationship-marketing approaches to the NPO sector while not seeking to develop a general model of NPO funding. A study based on one NPO and its funders was therefore appropriate. For reasons of simplicity and focus, the case study excludes consideration of the outcome variables, which are left as suggestions for further research later in the chapter. At this stage, we concentrate only on the drivers of trust and commitment.

Exploratory fieldwork was done in two ways. First, a focus group was held with the board of the NPO to identify their perceptions of the relationship dimensions with organizational funders. The Morgan and Hunt factors were used as prompts in this discussion. Second, a series of in-depth, onsite interviews was conducted with fifteen senior managers of the funding companies. In addition to exploring the specific benefits of the relationships as noted above, the study also aimed to gain a holistic understanding of the relationship and assess the validity of the main concepts used in the Morgan and Hunt model. Respondents were encouraged to suggest any changes that were necessary to fit the NPO context. From these discussions, it became clear that some of the Morgan and Hunt concepts were appropriate while others required modification. A draft questionnaire was designed using the measures explained below and sent to a different sample of senior managers in funding organizations. After receiving their feedback and making the relevant changes, a final draft of the questionnaire was developed.

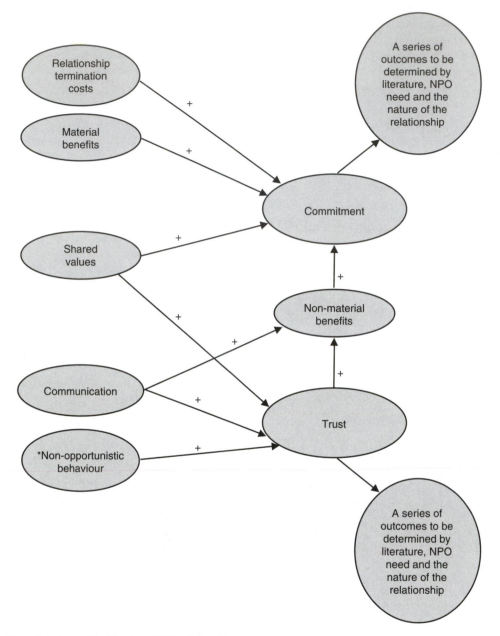

Figure 2.2 A model of funder–NPO relationships

* Morgan and Hunt (1994) use a construct labelled opportunistic behaviour. We use a construct labelled non–opportunistic behaviour. This is done to simplify the model for the reader, because with this labelling, all the links in the model can be hypothesized to be positive.

Data collection

The questionnaire was administered by post to senior managers (responsible for funding decisions) of all 120 funding organizations, i.e. the total population of organizational funders for this particular NPO. A total of 41 responded, representing a response rate of just over 33 per cent. This response rate is in line with typical response rates where respondents are top managers or organizational representatives (Baruch 1999).

Of the 41 respondents, 21 (51 per cent) were commercial organizations, 6 (15 per cent) were government departments, 8 (20 per cent) were either trusts, foundations or development organizations and 6 (15 per cent) organizations did not indicate what sector they were from. Participants were asked to indicate the extent to which they agreed or disagreed with a set of statements concerned with their commitment to the NPO and this was done with reference to a 7-point Likert-type scale. Point 1 on this scale indicated strong agreement with a statement, point 7 strong disagreement and point 4 neither agreement nor disagreement.

Measures

The constructs in the Morgan and Hunt model (see Figure 2.1), were used as the basis for finding appropriate measures for our initial model shown in Figure 2.2. The multi-item scales used by Morgan and Hunt to measure their constructs were adapted by adding or removing items/questions so as to make the domains of the constructs relevant to this study. New questions were developed through expert focus groups and by drawing upon the literature. The measures that are shown in Figure 2.2 are described in more detail in Table 2.1.

Preliminary testing of the measures

Some preliminary analysis was carried out to test the reliability and validity of the multi-item scales. The methods used were those recommended by Churchill (1979).

First, each scale was subjected to a Cronbach Alpha reliability test. The Cronbach Alphas ranged from 0.74 to 0.89, and thus were all in excess of the generally accepted required level of 0.70 (Foreman et al. 1998).

Second, a principal component factor analysis was performed on each of the multi-item scales. The scales factored as expected with loadings for items being in excess of 0.5. This demonstrated convergent validity.

Finally, composite equally weighted scales were created to obtain measures of the constructs in the model. The correlations between these scales were calculated and are shown in Table 2.2.

NB: Some of the N figures are less than the sample size of 41, revealing that there are a small number of missing values. While all the measures exceeded the minimum of 30 observations needed for partial least squares (PLS) analysis (Wixom and Watson 2001), the missing values were replaced with the mean, as suggested by Chin and Newstead (1999) when using PLS to perform the structural modelling exercise.

All but one of the correlations is significant at the 1 per cent level. The exception is the correlation between termination costs and commitment. This link is therefore removed from the initial model, leaving shared values, non-material and material benefits as the only antecedents of commitment. It should be noted that both the qualitative and quantitative research suggested the level of termination costs to be very low in this relationship. This is likely to have contributed to the lack of a significant link between termination costs and commitment.

Table 2.1 Measures used in the case study

Commitment	Communication	Benefits	Shared values	Trust	Non-opportunistic behaviour	Termination costs
The conceptualization of commitment is that of Morgan and Hunt. It is described in terms of statements relating to the participant's intention to stay in the relationship with the NPO, and willingness to put in an effort to maintain the relationship with the NPO.	The conceptualization of communication is based on a subset of the informing measures provided by Morgan and Hunt. To these were added the listening aspects suggested by Burnett (1992) and the NPO staff behaviour aspects suggested in the interview stage of the research. It is thus described in terms of statements relating to providing information to (i.e. informing) funders (characterized by the frequency, relevance and timeliness of communication), listening to funders (i.e. seeking information about funders' needs and motivations), staff interactions (i.e. with staff who are responsive, knowledgeable and passionate about the NPO).	As no appropriate instrument for the measurement of these benefits is available in the literature, an instrument was specifically developed for this study. This was derived from Rempel et al. (1985). A distinction is made between material – the tangible benefits explicit in the relationship (e.g. receiving positive publicity from their relationship with the NPO, learning skills from the NPO) and non-material benefits: the benefits inherent to the relationship (e.g. believing that funds were making a positive impact on the targeted clients and that funds were used efficiently). These sub-scales are intended to function as independent measures.	Following Morgan and Hunt (1994), shared values are described in terms of statements relating to the participants' perceptions that an NPO has similar values to themselves. An instrument developed by Swasy (1979) embraces the conceptualization as described above in a context-free set of statements. It was, therefore, adapted for use in this study. The adaptation involved changing the wording of individual statements in the Swasy (1979) instrument to capture individuals' perceptions of the extent to which they share the same values as the NPO.	The Morgan and Hunt conceptualization of trust, having been developed for a commercial customer–company relationship, was seen to be too transactional and thus not adopted. Instead, the measure of trust was based on a conceptualization of Rempel et al. (1985), in terms of the following sub-constructs: *reliability*, the extent to which a funder expects the NPO to be consistent and predictable in keeping its commitments; *dependability*, the extent to which funders expect the NPO will tell them the truth, act in their interests, and not take advantage of them in the future, and *faith*, the extent to which funders expect the NPO to act in their interests in an unpredictable and uncertain world.	Morgan and Hunt (1994) use a construct labelled opportunistic behaviour. We use a construct labelled non-opportunistic behaviour. This is done to simplify the model for the reader, because with this labelling all the links in the model can be hypothesized to be positive. The items used to measure non-opportunistic behaviour are therefore represented by statements relating to the participants' perceptions that an NPO has not taken advantage of them in the past. An instrument developed by Cummings and Bromiley (1996) embraces such a conceptualization and has, therefore, been adapted and adopted for use in this study. This, however, involved changing the wording of the individual Cummings and Bromiley statements to capture funders' perceptions of the extent to which they perceived they have, or have not been, treated opportunistically.	The conceptualization of termination costs is an extension of that used by Morgan and Hunt to incorporate their suggestions for further research and is described in terms of statements relating to the financial costs of ending a relationship (i.e. switching and opportunity costs, dissolution expenses) and the non-financial costs of ending a relationship (e.g. loss of reputation, aggravation). Questions were added to obtain a measure incorporating both dimensions.

Table 2.2 Correlation matrix of the construct measures

		Termination costs	Material benefits	Non-material benefits	Shared values	Communication	Non-opportunistic behaviour	Trust	Commitment
Termination costs	Pearson	1.00	.211	.021	.085	.353*	-.059	-.003	.159
	Sig. (1–tailed)	.	.098	.450	.305	.016	.367	.494	.171
	N	39	39	39	38	37	35	36	38
Material benefits	Pearson	.211	1.00	.695**	.419**	.528**	.374*	.411**	.440**
	Sig. (1–tailed)	.098	.	.000	.004	.000	.011	.005	.002
	N	39	41	41	40	39	37	38	40
Non-material benefits	Pearson	.021	.695**	1.00	.507**	.539**	.470**	.598**	.549**
	Sig. (1–tailed)	.450	.000	.	.000	.000	.002	.000	.000
	N	39	41	41	40	39	37	38	40
Shared values	Pearson	.085	.419**	.507**	1.00	.361*	.260	.630**	.465**
	Sig. (1–tailed)	.305	.004	.000	.	.012	.060	.000	.001
	N	38	40	40	40	39	37	38	39
Communication	Pearson	.353*	.528**	.539**	.361*	1.00	.363*	.582**	.395**
	Sig. (1–tailed)	.016	.000	.000	.012	.	.014	.000	.007
	N	37	39	39	39	39	37	38	38
Non-opportunistic behaviour	Pearson	-.059	.374*	.470**	.260	.363*	1.00	.648**	.378*
	Sig. (1–tailed)	.367	.011	.002	.060	.014	.	.000	.012
	N	35	37	37	37	37	38	38	36
Trust	Pearson	-.003	.411**	.598**	.630**	.582**	.648**	1.00	.436**
	Sig. (1–tailed)	.494	.005	.000	.000	.000	.000	.	.003
	N	36	38	38	38	38	36	38	37
Commitment	Pearson	.159	.440**	.549**	.465**	.395**	.378*	.436**	1.00
	Sig. (1–tailed)	.171	.002	.000	.001	.007	.012	.003	.
	N	38	40	40	39	38	36	37	40

* Correlation is significant at the 0.05 level
** Correlation is significant at the 0.01 level

The amended NPO–funder research model is shown in Figure 2.3 below. This model is now formally tested through the application of structural equation modelling.

Data analysis

The data were analysed in two separate, but sequentially related, stages of analysis by means of structural equation modelling, using PLS. These stages were:

Stage 1: Testing the measurement model by performing a validity and reliability analysis on each of the measures of the research model.

Stage 2: Testing the structural model by estimating the paths (links) between the variables in the model, determining their significance as well as the predictive ability of the model.

Structural equation modelling: partial least squares

Partial least squares (PLS), a structural equation modelling technique, was used in this study to perform the analysis for the NPO–funder model depicted in Figure 2.3. PLS is the preferred approach when one or more of the following is present: the model includes formative constructs; the sample size is relatively small; assumptions of normality are not satisfied (Chin and Newstead 1999). The software used was PLS-Graph Version 3.0.

A PLS application requires a minimum sample size which is ten times the greater of: (a) the number of items comprising the most formative construct; or (b) the number of independent constructs directly influencing a dependent construct (see Wixom and Watson 2001: 28). In

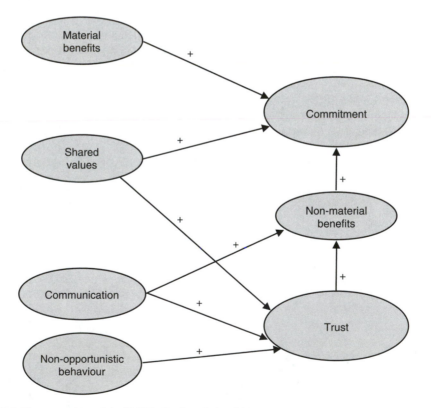

Figure 2.3 The research model of NPO–funder relationships

this study, none of the constructs are formative – all are reflective. A discussion on reflective and formative indicators can be found in Chin (1998: ix).

Trust is the dependent construct, with the three most independent antecedents influencing it being shared values, communication and opportunistic behaviour. This application of PLS therefore requires a minimum sample size of 30 which is exceeded by our sample size of 41. The outputs from the PLS software are used first to test the measurement model and then to test the fit and performance of the structural model. The results for the two stages of analysis now follow.

Stage 1: The measurement model: reliability and validity of the measures

The measures used for the constructs are assessed in terms of:

1   Reliability by means of the Fornell and Larker internal consistency index (Fornell and Larker, 1981). These are not part of the PLS output and have to be computed from the loadings and average residuals reported in the PLS output. Consult Hair *et al.* (1998: 612) for the formula. A measure is considered reliable if the reliability index is at least 0.70 (Nunally 1978). The reliability of the measures is reported in Table 2.3.

Table 2.3   Reliability and convergent validity (AVE) report

	Mean	Standard deviation	Loading
Shared values (Fornell and Larcker reliability = 0.84; AVE = 0.64)			
1 In general, their opinions and values are a lot like ours.	4.83	1.43	0.73
2 We like and respect their values.	5.71	0.89	0.82
3 We share a very similar set of values (e.g. in terms of their beliefs about the way staff be treated . . .).	5.29	1.10	0.84
Trust (Fornell and Larcker reliability = 0.87; AVE = 0.53)			
1 The NPO are very unpredictable. I never know how they are going to act from one day to the next.	5.63	1.13	0.55
2 I can never be sure what the NPO are going to surprise us with next.	5.74	0.99	0.80
3 I am confident that the NPO will be thoroughly dependable, especially when it comes to things that are important to my organization.	5.55	1.03	0.89
4 In my opinion, the NPO will be reliable in the future.	5.69	0.92	0.75
5 Though times may change and the future is uncertain, I know that the NPO will always be willing to offer my organization the support it may need (e.g. even if we had not funded them recently).	5.26	0.85	0.62
6 The NPO would not let us down, even if they found themselves in an unforeseen situation (e.g. competition from other funders, changes in government policy).	5.10	0.94	0.69
Non-material benefits (Fornell and Larcker reliability = 0.86; AVE = 0.54)			
1 The chance to support programmes that will have a good long-term impact on society.	6.05	0.80	0.80
2 Innovative and cutting-edge solutions to the problems it faces (e.g. crime-related issues and opportunities in South Africa).	5.51	1.12	0.81
3 The knowledge that our support is used in an ethical way (e.g. good accounting systems, staff who do not waste money).	5.59	1.26	0.74
4 The opportunity to target our support to issues that we care about.	5.56	1.03	0.58
5 Being able to see that our support has an impact on the people for whom it is really intended.	5.41	1.26	0.73

Table 2.3—continued

	Mean	Standard deviation	Loading
Commitment (Fornell and Lacrker reliability = 0.94; AVE = 0.85)			
1 The relationship my organization has with . . . is something we intend to maintain in the long term (e.g. over the next two years, possibly beyond).	5.59	1.43	0.90
2 The relationship my organization has with . . . is something that we will put a lot of effort into maintaining in the future.	5.30	1.40	0.96
3 The relationship my organization has with . . . is something we are very committed to.	5.62	1.08	0.89
4 The relationship my organization has with . . . is very important to us.	5.34	1.46	0.93
Non-opportunistic behaviour (Fornell and Larcker reliability = 0.88; AVE = 0.71)			
1 In the past the NPO have succeeded partly because they have taken advantage of my organization.	5.51	1.43	0.80
2 I feel that the NPO generally try to get the upper hand when they deal with us.	5.67	1.11	0.87
3 The NPO have taken advantage of my organization when it was in weak position.	6.23	0.83	0.86
Communication (Fornell and Larcker reliability = 0.88; AVE = 0.56)			
1 Staff who talk with passion and experience about the work of . . .	5.63	0.89	0.78
2 The opportunity to work with knowledgeable, professional and approachable staff.	5.0	1.22	0.79
3 The NPO keep me informed about new developments that are relevant to us.	5.08	1.47	0.61
4 The NPO provide frequent communication about issues that are important to us.	4.83	1.52	0.74
5 Even when things don't go quite according to plan, the NPO do their best to listen to us (e.g. my own and my organization's ideas, concerns and suggestions).	5.28	1.24	0.72
6 Whatever the circumstances, the NPO usually take notice of the suggestions I make about my organization's work with them.	4.97	0.95	0.80
Material benefits (Fornell and Larcker reliability = 0.87; AVE = 0.70)			
1 Opportunities to be involved with projects that tie in with our company's vision (funding something that in some way matches our strengths, builds our reputation).	5.57	0.99	0.89
2 An efficient use of our support (whatever form this takes).	5.66	1.39	0.79
3 Being able to support programmes that will ultimately also benefit my organization and its staff (e.g. creating a society that is good for our business and our people and their families).	5.39	1.18	0.83

2 Convergent validity by assessing the average variance extracted (AVE). This is standard output from PLS. Measures with AVE 0.50 or higher are said to exhibit convergent validity (Chin 1998). The AVEs reported in Table 2.3 all exceed 0.50, confirming that all measures demonstrate satisfactory convergent validity.

3 Discriminant validity is established from the latent variable correlation matrix. This matrix has the square root of AVE for the measures on the diagonal and the correlations among the measures as the off-diagonal elements. The matrix has to be constructed from

Table 2.4   The latent variable correlation matrix: discriminant validity

	Shared values	Trust	Non-material benefits	Commit-ment	Non-opportunistic behaviour	Communi-cation	Material benefits
Shared values	0.797						
Trust	0.623	0.726					
Non-material benefits	0.519	0.680	0.737				
Commitment	0.535	0.469	0.684	0.921			
Non-opportunistic behaviour	0.335	0.668	0.474	0.359	0.844		
Communication	0.437	0.614	0.603	0.524	0.438	0.741	
Material benefits	0.413	0.403	0.652	0.507	0.431	0.605	0.836

Square root of AVE is on the diagonal

the PLS output. Discriminant validity is determined by looking down the columns and across the rows. Should the diagonal elements be larger than off-diagonal elements, discriminant validity is deemed satisfactory. Discriminant validity is demonstrated as these conditions are satisfied (see Table 2.4).

The structural model is now tested.

Stage 2: Testing the structural model: path coefficients and predictive ability

The key PLS outputs for this analysis are:

1   R^2 values, reported in Figure 2.4, which provide an indication of the predictive ability of the independent variables. Trust, non-material benefits and commitment with R^2 values of 0.68, 0.52 and 0.52 respectively are considered to provide adequate evidence of the predictive ability of the model.
2   Path coefficients and their statistical significance, reported in Figure 2.4. PLS, being a distribution-free technique, uses the bootstrapping resampling technique to determine the significance of the paths. Two hundred resamples were taken in performing the bootstrap. The results reveal that all the links in the model, except material benefits to commitment, are significant at the 5 per cent level.

The findings, reported in (1) and (2) above, indicate that a relationship-marketing approach can be applied to a funder relationship with an NPO. This provides much needed empirical support to previous theoretical arguments and endorses the assertions of Burnett (1998) and Brennan and Brady (1998) that relationship marketing can be applied to the NPO sector.

Non-material benefits is the main driver of funder commitment, since it has the highest path coefficient of 0.51. Material benefits, however, is not identified as being a significant link and is eliminated from the model. It should be noted that there is a high correlation between material and non-material benefits (see Table 2.1). Thus, if non-material benefits are removed from the analysis, the impact of material benefits on commitment approaches significance. Receiving a certain level of material benefits is, therefore, important in influencing funders' commitment to an NPO. Nevertheless, in this case, differences in non-material benefits are the main predictor of continued giving.

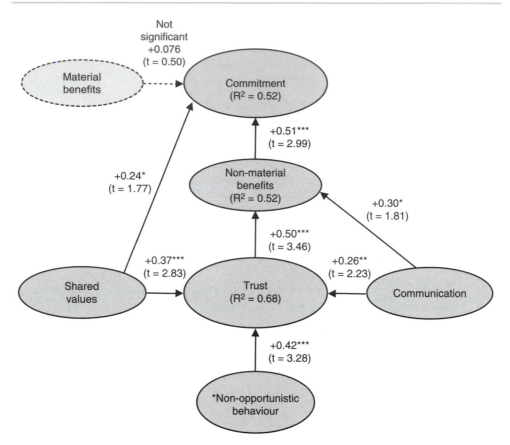

Figure 2.4 The fitted model of NPO–funder relationships based on the results

* indicates significance at the p < 0.05 level.
** indicates significance at the p < 0.01 level.
*** indicates significance at the p < 0.001 level.

It is noted that trust is developed directly by the behaviours of the NPO towards its funders. This is through communication and non-opportunistic behaviour. To develop commitment, it is essential to provide non-material benefits. Trust, in turn, is the key driver of non-material benefits. Clearly, therefore, NPOs must engage in behaviours that will develop the trust of their organizational funders.

The drivers of trust and commitment

The results relating to the drivers of commitment are now discussed. We subsequently examine the drivers of trust.

Termination costs

The results suggest that NPO–funder relationships may be differentiated from customer relationships in the commercial profit-orientated sector in at least one key respect. This appears to be the lack of impact of termination costs on funder commitment to the NPO. In so far as funders are not usually dependent on the NPO, this result is not surprising. In the South African interviews it was clear that funders had taken much effort in selecting the NPO to avoid negative consequences in other respects, for example, the effect on their reputation if they ceased funding. Even though termination costs were measured, they did not seem to have an impact on the commitment of funders to the NPO. Moreover, the low level of such costs was not attributable to a poor relationship that funders were eager to leave. The general tenor of the relationship between the NPO and the funders seemed to be positive.

Shared values

In the Morgan and Hunt model, shared values impact upon both commitment and trust. This is also the case with our results. These impacts imply that funders need to believe in the cause of the NPO to trust it and to maintain and put further effort into the relationship. In fact, shared values have a direct and indirect impact on commitment via trust and non-material benefits.

Material and non-material benefits

It was hypothesized that material and non-material benefits would be distinct. It was also hypothesized that both of these benefits would have a positive impact on the commitment of funders to the NPO. The findings revealed, however, that non-material benefits were more important in predicting commitment than material benefits. In fact, the material benefits–commitment link was not found to be significant. This is particularly surprising given that more than 50 per cent of the organizations in the sample were profit-making corporations, who, it was assumed, would be interested in material benefits, such as marketing and branding associations. This finding suggests that NPOs would be advised to focus on the non-material benefits they provide to their funders.

This raises the question whether non-material benefits are particularly important more broadly in the NPO sector and why this should be the case. We noted above the view of Rothschild (1979) who emphasized the importance of trust in funder relationships, given that funders do not directly consume the outputs of an NPO. In the absence of direct consumption, funders must trust NPOs at one stage removed, to serve the interests of the NPO's clients. Non-material benefits are beliefs or assumptions about the NPO, for example, that it is making a positive impact and using its funds efficiently. These beliefs will inevitably rely on trust in the absence of sufficiently hard evidence about the NPO's behaviour.

Our results indicate that there is a highly significant link between non-material benefits and trust.

Non-opportunistic behaviour

This is the most important determinant of trust. Of all the antecedents, it explains the highest proportion of the variance. It implies that the way the NPO has treated funders in the past affects whether funders believe the NPO will keep its commitments and not take advantage of them in the future. If the NPO has exploited its relationship with the funder – to promote itself, for example – the funder may well feel that the NPO will behave in a similarly negative way in the future. Thus the funder's trust in the NPO will be undermined. Conversely, good experiences are likely to enhance funder trust in the positive behaviours of the NPO towards its client group.

Communication

Communication is the most complex antecedent of trust but it is a factor that NPOs can change, by their own behaviour. Improving communication offers NPOs a lever to improve trust. NPOs cannot easily change their values, but they can employ strategies to improve their communication with funders. These might include:

- informing funders about their client group;
- keeping funders informed about forthcoming events, the use of their funds and by undertaking networking activities and initiating events to allow funders to have experience of NPO client activities;
- seeking information about funder needs and motivations; and
- using staff that are responsive, knowledgeable and also passionate about the NPO.

From the interview stage of the research, it was clear that funders relied on their interaction with NPO staff in developing their trust in the NPO. In particular, it was important for these staff to have direct experience of the NPO's client activities. This was seen as important in enabling staff to talk passionately and with conviction about the NPO. The results also suggest that listening and staff interaction have a significant impact on the non-material benefits received by funders. In the absence of direct consumption, the experience of NPO staff in client interaction is likely to act as a proxy for this consumption.

Applying relationship marketing in a wider context

As previously discussed, a focus on relationships is one of the major paradigms in marketing literature and practice. As outlined in this chapter, relationship marketing has its roots in research with customers, as exemplified in the work by Morgan and Hunt (1994). In an extension to this focus, the case study in this contribution suggests that a relationship-marketing model can be applied to the NPO sector in the particular context of the relationship between funders and an NPO. Importantly, the results suggest that the composition and interplay of factors varies compared to the commercial sector, but confirm the importance of trust and commitment as central elements in relationships.

As we noted earlier, much is left to be achieved by future researchers. Such questions are, for example: how can relationship marketing concepts be applied to other stakeholder groups? What will the key differences be with relationships in the commercial sector? And can a holistic picture of relationship marketing be developed for the NPO sector?

Answers to these questions can only be found by conducting more research. Methods for conducting this research may usefully begin with research conducted in the commercial sector. Much can be learned from studies that have applied relationship-marketing approaches to different stakeholder groups in the commercial sector. A study of note is that of MacMillan et al. (2004), in which the authors propose a generic model of business relationships. This model is customized through a research process (which includes a literature review, focus groups, questionnaire development and data analysis) to provide insights into the drivers and out-comes in relationships with various stakeholders, such as employees, customers, communities (Hillenbrand and Money in press) and investors (Zaman 2004). The results of the studies presented suggest that relationship-marketing concepts can be applied successfully to a number of different organizations, stakeholder groups and cultures. The results suggest that each relationship is dependent upon a range of dynamic issues, with different outcome variables being judged as critical. A common denominator seems to be the importance of trust and commitment in each of these different relationships in underpinning relationship success. When conducting future research within the NPO sector, it would be useful for researchers to adapt and adopt the techniques provided by researchers such as these, to provide a more holistic picture of how relationship marketing could be applied to different stakeholders in the NPO sector.

Limitations

The quantitative study is based upon a sample of forty-one organizational funders of one NPO in South Africa. Although appropriate statistical methods have been applied to the data, the generalizabilty of the findings would be strengthened if it were to be replicated with a larger sample and extended to other NPOs. It would also be helpful to apply the research in a wider variety of countries to overcome potential cultural limitations. At present it is not possible to determine how specific these results are to the South African context. It is thus not possible to make confident generalizations from this study. It does seem, however, that if the Morgan and Hunt model can be adapted from a North American industrial context to the area of our own research without too much difficulty, it could also be applied to many other contexts. A further benefit of additional applications would be to incorporate cases of relationships which were less supportive. In the case of this NPO, it will be recalled, most relationships were positive and supportive.

Conclusions

There are few academic empirical studies which apply relationship-marketing models to the NPO sector. A contribution of this study is the extension of the relationship-marketing literature to NPO funders. Both the relationship-marketing area and the NPO sector can benefit from the validation of current understandings and the extension and development of new ideas. The fitted model presented in Figure 2.4 explains 52 per cent of the variance in the commitment of funders to continue funding a NPO through the key constructs of non-material benefits and shared values. NPOs would, therefore, be well advised to engage in strategies which develop non-material benefits, since it is this factor that is the major driver of commitment.

The introduction of the concept of non-material benefits offers the potential for application to a wide variety of service and non-profit organizations, particularly where there is a disconnect between users and funders. The research also provides valuable insights into how organizations can improve the non-material benefits that they offer to their funders. For example, organizations can develop non-material benefits by allowing funders greater involvement in their activities, demonstrating the achievements of the organization and offering greater transparency of their operations.

There appears to be a particularly close set of links between non-material benefits, trust and communication. Communication impacts directly on non-material benefits as well as indirectly via trust. Communication is therefore crucial and we have suggested three subdimensions, namely informing, listening and staff interaction. Both the qualitative and quantitative results provide evidence to support these subdimensions and fundraisers may make use of this finding in their professional role.

Fundraisers may provide information about the NPO, but funders are not likely to believe this unless they trust the organization in the first place. Our qualitative interviews suggest that it is particularly important for an NPO to listen to its funders to build trust. This, in turn, validates the information that is provided by the NPO. Fundraisers, therefore, need both to inform and to listen.

The qualitative results also suggest that the type of person used in fundraising is important. Funders want to be informed and listened to by a person who has direct experience of the NPO's client activities, rather than an expert in fundraising per se. NPOs should devise a fundraising strategy which reflects this.

To build trust, communication needs to be supported by two other factors: shared values and non-opportunistic behaviours. The former relates to funders' identification with the cause of the NPO and the latter to the NPO not taking unfair advantage of funders by, for example, exploiting its contacts without their consent.

More research is required to develop further our understanding of other contexts and cultures. There is also scope for applying this model to other stakeholder groups and expanding the model to include outcome variables consequent on commitment and trust.

Note

This chapter is based on original research first published in the *Journal of Business Research*, by Keith MacMillan, Kevin Money, Arthur Money and Steve Downing. Previously published material reproduced by kind permission of Elsevier Inc.

References

Bagozzi, R. P. (2000) 'On the concept of intentional social action in consumer behavior', *Journal of Consumer Research*, 27:388–96.
Baruch, Y. (1999) 'Response rate in academic studies – a comparative analysis', *Human Relations*, 52(4):421–38.
Berscheid, E. (1985), 'Interpersonal attraction', in G. Lindzey and E. Aronson (eds) *Handbook of Social Psychology*, 3rd edition, New York, NY: Random House.
Blau, P. M. (1964) *Exchange and Power in Social Life*, New York, NY: Wiley.
Brennan, L. and Brady, E. (1999) 'Relating to marketing? Why relationship marketing works for not-for-profit organizations', *International Journal of Nonprofit and Voluntary Sector Marketing*, 4(4):327–37.
Burlingame, D. (2001) 'Corporate giving', *International Journal of Nonprofit and Voluntary Sector Marketing*, 6(1):4–6.
Burnett, K. (1992) *Relationship Fundraising*, London: White Lion Press.
—— (1998) *Relationship Fundraising*, 2nd edition, London: White Lion Press.
Chadwick-Jones, J. K. (1976) *Social Exchange Theory: Its Structure and Influence in Social Psychology*, London: Academic Press.
Chin, W. W. (1998) 'Issues and opinions on structural equation modelling', *MIS Quarterly*, 22(1):7–16.
—— and Newstead, P. R. (1999) in R. H. Hoyle (ed.) *Statistical Strategies for Small Sample Research*, London: Sage Publications.
Churchill, G. A. (1979) 'A paradigm for developing better measures of marketing constructs', *Journal of Marketing Research*, 26:64–73.
Collins, J. C. and Porras, J. I. (1998) *Built to Last: Successful Habits of Visionary Companies*, London: Century Business.
Cummings, L. L. and Bromiley, P. (1996) in R. M. Kramer and T. R. Tyler (eds) *Trust in Organizations*, London: Sage Publications.

Duck, S. (ed.) (1997) *Handbook of Personal Relationships: Theory, Research and Interventions*, Chichester: John Wiley & Sons.

—— and Ickes, W. (eds) (2000) *The Social Psychology of Personal Relationships*, Chichester: John Wiley & Sons.

Flood, P. C., Hannan, E., Smith, K. G., Turner, T., West, M. A. and Dawson, J. (2000) 'Chief executive leadership style, consensus decision-making and top management team effectiveness', *European Journal of Work and Organizational Psychology*, 9(3):401–20.

Foran, N. J. and Theisen, B. A. (2000) 'The business of charity', *Journal of Accountancy*, 190(6):77–80.

Foreman, S., Money, A. H. and Page, M. J. (1998) 'How reliable is reliable? A note on the estimation of Cronbach Alpha', Proceedings of the International Management Conference, Cape Town, South Africa, 1–26.

Fornell, C. and Larcker, D. F. (1981) 'Evaluating structural equation models with unobservable variables and measurement error', *Journal of Marketing Research*, 18:39–50.

Garbarino, E. and Johnson, M. S. (1999) 'The different roles of satisfaction, trust and commitment in customer relationships', *Journal of Marketing*, 63(April):70–87.

Gronroos, C. (1997) 'Value-driven relational marketing: From products to resources and competencies', *Journal of Marketing Management*, 13:407–19.

Gummesson, E. (1997) 'Relationship marketing as paradigm shift: Some conclusions from the 30R approach', *Management Decision*, 35(4):267–72.

—— (1999) 'Total relationship marketing: Experimenting with a synthesis of research frontier', *Australasian Marketing Journal*, 1999(7).

Gutek, B. A. (1997) 'Dyadic interactions in organizations', in C. L. Cooper and S. E. Jackson *Creating Tomorrow's Organizations*, Chichester: John Wiley & Sons.

Hair, J. F., Anderson, R. E., Tatham, R. L. and Black, W. C. (1998) *Multivariate Data Analysis*, 5th edition, New Jersey, NJ: Prentice Hall.

Heider, F. (1958) *The Psychology of Interpersonal Relations*, Hillside, NJ: Lawrence Erlbaum Associates.

—— (1980) in D. Gorlitz (ed.) *Perspectives on Attribution Research and Theory*, Cambridge: Bellinger.

Hillenbrand, C. and Money, K. (2007) 'Corporate responsibility and corporate reputation: two separate concepts or two sides of the same coin?', submitted to the *Reputation Review* (in press).

Hinde, R. A. (1993) *Relationships: A Dialectical Perspective*, London: Psychology Press.

Kay, J. (1993) *Foundations of Corporate Success: How Business Strategies Add Value*, Oxford: Oxford University Press.

Kistner, W. G. (2000) 'Supporting organizations give donors more control', *Journal of the Healthcare Financial Management Association*, 54(8):82–85.

Kramer, R. M. and Tyler, T. R. (1996) *Trust in Organizations*, London: Sage Publications.

MacMillan, K., Money, K., Downing, S. and Hillenbrand, C. (2004) 'Giving your organization SPIRIT: An overview and call to action for directors on issues of corporate governance, corporate reputation and corporate responsibility', *Journal of General Management*, 30(2):15–42.

Mawr, B. and Allen Jr., J. R. (1999) 'The charitable remainder trust as an executive benefit tool', *Journal of Financial Service Professionals*, 53(4):34–9.

Mayer, R. C., Davis, J. H. and Schoorman, F. D. (1995) 'An integrated model of organizational trust', *Academy of Management Journal*, 20(3):709–34.

Money, K. and Hillenbrand, C. (2006) 'Using reputation measurement to create value: An analysis and integration of existing measures', *Journal of General Management*, 32(1):1–12.

Morgan, R. M. and Hunt, S. D. (1994) 'The commitment–trust theory of relationship marketing', *Journal of Marketing*, 58:20–38.

Nahapiet, J. and Goshal, S. (1998) 'Social capital, intellectual capital and organizational advantage', *Academy of Management Review*, 23(2):242–67.

NCVO (National Council for Voluntary Organizations) (1999) *Research Quarterly*, (6), London: NCVO.

Nunally, J. C. (1978) *Psychometric Theory*, New York, NY: McGraw Hill.

Payne, A. (1995) 'Keeping the faith', *Marketing*, February: 13–15.

Peltier, J. W., Schibrowsky, J. A. and Schultz, D. E. (2002) 'Leveraging customer information to develop sequential communication strategies: A case study of charitable-giving behaviour', *Journal of Advertising Research*, July–August:23–41.

Perlman, D. and Duck, S. (1987) *Intimate Relationships: Development, Dynamics and Deterioration*, London: Sage Publications.

Pharoah, C. and Tanner, S. (1998) 'Trends in charitable giving', *Fiscal Studies*, 18(4):427–43.

Polonsky, M. J. and Macdonald, E. K. (2000) 'Exploring the link between cause-related marketing and brand building', *International Journal of Nonprofit and Voluntary Sector Marketing*, 5(1):46–57.

Reichheld, F. F. (1993) 'Loyalty-based management', *Harvard Business Review*, 71(2):64–73.

Reinartz, W. J. and Kumar, V. (2000) 'On the profitability of long-life customers in a noncontractual settting: An empirical investigation and implications for marketing', *Journal of Marketing*, 64(4):17–35.

Rempel, J. K., Holmes, J. G. and Zanna, M. P. (1985) 'Trust in close relationships', *Journal of Personality and Social Psychology*, 49:95–112.

Rothschild, M. L. (1979) 'Marketing and communications in non-business situations or why it's so hard to sell brotherhood like soap', *Journal of Marketing*, 43:11–20.

Ryan, J. (2000) 'Keeping it real', *Target Marketing*, 23(5):24–5.

Sabo, S. R. (2002) 'Profitable pairings', *Association Management*, 54(3):52–5.

Sagawa, S. (2001) 'New value partnerships: The lessons of Denny's/Save the Children Partnership for building high yielding cross-sector alliances', *International Journal of Nonprofit and Voluntary Sector Marketing*, 6(3):199–215.

—— (2001a) 'Relationship fundraising: How to keep donors loyal', *Nonprofit Management and Leadership*, 12(2):177–93.

Sargeant, A. (1998) 'Donor lifetime value: An empirical analysis', *Journal of Nonprofit and Voluntary Sector Marketing*, 3(4):283–97.

—— and Asif, S. (2001b) 'Botton Village', *Case Research Journal*, 21(1):93–110.

—— and Lee, S. (2001) *Trust and Confidence in the Voluntary Sector*, Henley Working Papers, 01/08.

—— and Stephenson, H. (1997) 'Corporate giving – targeting the likely donor,' *Journal of Nonprofit and Voluntary Sector Marketing*, 2(1):64–79.

Scott, A. (2000) 'A golden opportunity to boost biotech's image?', *Chemical Week*, 162(38):37.

Seligman, A. B. (1997) *The Problem of Trust*, Chichester: Princetown University Press.

Sharma, A. and Lambert, D. M. (1994) 'Segmentation of markets based on customer service', *International Journal of Physical Distribution and Logistics Management*, 24(4):50–9.

Silinpaa, M. and Wheeler, D. (1998) *The Stakeholder Corporation*, London: Financial Times Prentice Hall Publishing.

Sirdeshmukh, D., Singh, J. and Sabol, B. (2002) 'Consumer trust, value and loyalty in relational exchanges', *Journal of Marketing*, 66:15–37.

Strauss, A. L. and Corbin, J. (1990) *Basics of Qualitative Research: Grounded Theory Procedures and Techniques*, Newbury Park, CA: Sage Publications.

Swasy, J. L. (1979) 'Measuring the bases of social power', *Advances in Consumer Research* 6: 340–6.

Taylor, A. (1996) 'The man who put Honda back on track', *Fortune*, 17(September):28–36.

Thomas, J. L., Cunningham, B. J. and Williams, J. K. (2002) 'The impact of involvement, perceived moral intensity and satisfaction upon trust in non-profit relational contexts: Processes and outcomes', *Journal of Nonprofit and Public Sector Marketing*, 10(1):93–115.

Werbel, J. D. and Carter, S. M. (2002) 'The CEO's influence on corporate foundation giving', *Journal of Business Ethics*, 40(1):47–60.

Wixom, B. H. and Watson, H. J. (2001) 'An empirical investigation of the factors affecting data warehousing success', *MIS Quarterly*, 25(1):17–41.

Young-Ybarra, C. and Wiersma, M. (1999) 'Strategic flexibility in information technology alliances: The influence of transaction cost economics and social exchange theory', *Organization Science*, 10(4):439–59.

Zadrozny, W. (2006) 'Leveraging the power of intangible assets', *MIT Sloan Management Review*, 48(1):84–91.

Zaman, A. (2004) 'Reputation and risk', London: FT Briefing.

3

The dynamics and implications of relationship quality in the charity–donor dyad

Haseeb A. Shabbir, Dayananda Palihawadana and Des Thwaites

Introduction

The notion that quality perceptions have driven the relationship-marketing paradigm is well documented (Gronroos 1990, 1994). Indeed, an understanding of the processes and the development of the 'relationship quality' between the buyer–seller dyad is considered central to implementing any relationship-marketing strategy (Storbacka *et al.* 1994; Bejou *et al.* 1996). Determining the quality of relationships has become a fundamental precursor to managing relationship marketing, for managerial and practical purposes but also from a conceptual and theoretical perspective (Sheth and Parvatiyar 1995). Furthermore, Gronroos (2002) considers a relationship quality orientation as a prerequisite to effective relationship marketing. Liljander and Strandvik (1996), for instance, propose that the relationship quality construct is critical in guiding relationship management and Storbacka *et al.* (1994) suggest that relationship quality and its understanding will guide the field of services management in general.

However, the absorption of the relationship quality metaphor has been characteristically much slower than the relationship marketing (Dwyer and Oh 1987) and the relationship fundraising metaphors (Shabbir *et al.* 2007). Nevertheless, relationship quality has emerged as an increasingly important construct central to implementing any relationship-marketing (Dwyer and Oh 1987; Gronroos 2002) or relationship-fundraising strategy (Bennett and Barkensjo 2005a; Bennett and Barkensjo 2005b; Shabbir *et al.* 2007).

In the context of charitable giving, Burnett (1992), Sargeant (2001), Bennett and Barkensjo (2005a) and Shabbir *et al.* (2007) equate the development of donor loyalty and the implementation of relationship fundraising with an emphasis on a relational approach to donor care. Therefore, this notion of relationship quality as central to developing quality–care programmes is not restricted to the commercial sector alone but considered instrumental to donor developmental activity. The aim of this research is to help to guide charities in today's increasingly competitive and sophisticated donor marketplace by focusing on sound and coherent theoretical approaches to understanding the quality of relationships that donors have with the charities they support. Highlighting the importance of determining the structural nature and processes inherent in donor-perceived relationship quality is the cornerstone of this review of relationship quality in the fundraising sector.

Relationship quality

Smith (1998: 78) defines relationship quality as 'an overall assessment of the strength of a relationship and the extent to which it meets the needs and expectations of the parties based on a history of successful or unsuccessful encounters or events'. Additionally, relationship quality refers to a 'customer's perceptions of how well the whole relationship fulfils the expectations, predictions, goals and desires the customer has concerning the whole relationship' (Jarvelin and Lehtinen 1996). Consequently, it forms the overall impression that a customer has concerning the whole relationship including different transactions (Gronroos 2002). Hennig–Thurau and Klee (1997: 751) define relationship quality as the 'degree of appropriateness of a relationship to fulfil the needs of the customer associated with the relationship'. This definition entails a relational perspective to perceived service quality since Gronroos (2002: 81) describes relation-ship quality as the 'dynamics of long-term quality formation in ongoing customer relation-ships' and furthermore 'is their (customers) continuously developing quality perception over time' (2002: 82). The premise behind the relationship quality conceptualization, therefore, is that customers' quality perceptions develop and change over time as the relationship continues.

Despite the general consensus that relationship quality is 'perceived quality in a relationship framework' (Gronroos 2002: 83), conceptual work to highlight this (Holmund 1997; Liljander-Strandvik 1995) and attempts, recently, to synthesize the literature on relationship quality (Roberts et al. 2003), there remains no consensus regarding the structural nature of relationship quality, i.e. the dimensionality of the relationship quality construct and its organization. It is evident that relationship quality is a complex multidimensional construct or one that is 'a higher-order construct consisting of several distinct, although related dimensions' (Dorsch et al. 1998: 130); yet, there appears to be no agreement as to the nature or content of these dimensions. Furthermore, research into the development or evaluation of relationship quality perceptions is also lacking in the extant literature. This is especially pertinent within the fundraising sector (Shabbir et al. 2007).

Although early studies within the commercial sector focused predominantly on constructs, such as satisfaction and service quality, the relationship quality construct 'is (now) emerging as a central construct in the relationship marketing literature' (Smith 1998: 4). Leuthesser (1997: 246) states that 'in the area of relationship marketing, the primary emphasis of studies to date has been on understanding the factors that influence relationship quality'. Here, Leuthesser (1997) is asserting the fact that most studies in relationship marketing deal with constructs and empirical validation of constructs that have been posited more recently as comprising the relationship quality construct; such factors or constructs include satisfaction, commitment and trust, for instance (Roberts et al. 2003).

Within the commercial sector, the majority of authors view satisfaction and trust as the key underlying dimensions of relationship quality (Bejou et al. 1996; Crosby et al. 1990; Lagace et al. 1991; Roberts et al. 2003; Wray et al. 1994). Commitment is also cited as a potential dimension (Kumar et al. 1995; Hennig-Thurau and Klee 1997; Dorsch et al. 1998; Moorman et al. 1992; Roberts et al. 2003). Other key dimensions of relationship quality proposed in the literature include opportunism (Dwyer et al. 1987; Dorsch et al. 1998), involvement (Moorman et al. 1992), cooperative norms (Baker et al. 1999), customer orientation and ethical profile (Dorsch et al. 1998), conflict, willingness to invest and expectation of continuity (Kumar et al. 1995) and, finally, perceived benevolence (Roberts et al. 2003; Bennett and Barkensjo 2005a, 2005b). Although there is a growing consensus that satisfaction, trust and commitment are the central dimensions of relationship quality within the commercial sector (Crosby et al. 1990; Dorsch et al. 1998; Garbarino and Johnson 1999; Wray et al. 1994; Roberts et al. 2003), the dimensionality of relationship quality within the fundraising context remains completely unexplored. Only Bennett and Barkensjo (2005a, 2005b), adapting the work of Roberts, Varki and Brodie (2003), have modelled beneficiary and donor-perceived relationship quality as comprising trust, commitment and perceived benevolence.

Research context of relationship quality evaluation

Modelling relationship quality in the interpersonal literature, predominantly within the parent–sibling, marriage and general family studies, has focused predominately within nonprofit contexts, which is in stark contrast to work carried out in the marketing literature. These nonprofit contexts are wide ranging but some examples include: exploring the association between relationship quality and alcohol consumption as predictors of condom use (Woodrome et al. 2006), parent–child relationship quality's effect on alcohol use (Jordan and Lewis 2003), relationship quality's effect on social understanding of children (Cutting and Dunn 2006), differential parental treatments' effects on parent–child relationship quality (Richmond et al. 2005), the effect of relationship quality on bipolar symptoms (Yan et al. 2004) and the association between relationship quality and well-being in adolescent mothers (Stevenson et al. 1999). Indeed, all of the studies investigating relationship quality in the interpersonal literature could be classified as 'nonprofit contexts' had they been published in the managerial or organizational research literature. Indeed, only Hennig-Thurau et al. (2001) and Bennett and Barkensjo (2005a, 2005b) have modelled relationship quality in nonprofit contexts within the marketing literature. Hennig-Thurau et al. (2001) model relationship quality in the education context, a classic nonprofit marketing context (Sargeant, 2001). Bennett and Barkensjo (2005a, 2005b) explore relationship quality of marketing activities and general relationship quality as perceived from the charity beneficiary and donor's perspective respectively. More recently, Shabbir et al. (2007) have explored relationship quality within the charity donor context. However, the majority of studies focusing on relationship quality in the management sciences clearly focus on commercial contexts.

Structure of relationship quality evaluation

A key finding which emerges from the extant literature is that both formative and indicative conceptualizations of relationship quality are used in the extant literature. These forms of measurement used for relationship quality have important implications for how it is conceptualized by managers in terms of its structure and consequently its management.

The entire debate about how relationship quality is evaluated, along a continuum of good- and bad-quality perceptions, or as a general judgement at global-level evaluation, or domain-specific evaluations based on several judgemental criteria, has at its roots the issue of how humans process information for decision-making purposes. The idea that several domain-specific constructs interact with each other to generate a state of cognitive satisfaction or equilibrium, which is reflective of relationship quality evaluations, is conducive to the connectionist approach (Smith 1996). The connectionist approach is derived from the field of exploring the philosophy of the mind with classical philosophers such as Bechtel and Abrahamsen (1991) advocating the potential role of connectionism in understanding decision-making. Each of the domain-specific judgemental criteria can therefore be considered to be simple units with their own unique inputs, but which converge to reflect an overall relationship quality evaluation. Connectionist or multidimensional conceptualizations of relationship quality have been proposed for commercial contexts (e.g. Hennig-Thurau *et al.* 2002; Hennig-Thurau and Klee 1999) and for the charity context (Shabbir *et al.* 2007). This approach infers that donors may evaluate relationship quality based on a number of underlying composite judgemental criteria but these are independently evaluated, although the degree and nature of one affects or could affect the other. Therefore, this would assume that a donor, for instance, might trust a charity but not be committed to it or may be committed to a charity but not trust it; however, both trust and commitment of the donor could affect each other. Classically, this has been proposed in the relationship marketing (Morgan and Hunt 1994) and relationship fundraising literatures (Sargeant and Lee 2004; Sargeant *et al.* 2006). The individual effects and their codependent effect on the conjoint variable or construct becomes part of the evaluation of overall relationship quality. Relationship quality evaluations in turn involve such combinations of independent and dependent evaluations of constructs.

The alternative approach to modelling relationship quality is based on the computational approach or the classic social cognitive approach. This type of evaluation would imply that donors have a fixed and stable judgement concerning the quality of their relationships. In this case trust and commitment, for instance, would therefore share an equal amount of relationship-formation importance, and even if overall judgement takes into consideration importance weightings of each construct, then the effect of change from external sources on each construct cannot be modelled due to the assumption of stability across each underlying dimension (Rossiter 2002). Therefore, different developmental stages of relationships, personality variables and the nature of the relationship may generate their own unique effects on each underlying construct, negating any form of stability in evaluation; that is, this form of structure is not affected by the array of intervening variables that may or may not shape the donation exchange process from decision-making models.

Indeed this connectionist-versus-computational debate parallels closely the reflective-versus-formative construct measurement debate recently reinvigorated in marketing science (Rossiter 2002; Diamantopolous and Winkfhofer 2001; Jarvis *et al.* 2003). It appears that the formative construct approach to modelling lies firmly in computational or classic social cognitive psychology. The computational approach advocates that mental activity is computational, that mental processing does not vary with different goals, beliefs, perceptions or cognitive states. This would imply that a formative structure for relationship quality would remain fixed, stable and consistant with time, space and situation. Formative conceptualizations of relationship quality have been proposed by Roberts *et al.* (2000) for commercial contexts and by Bennett and Barkensjo (2005a, 2005b) for the charity context.

This debate not only has implications for marketing and fundraising but has become increasingly important in the wider interpersonal relationship quality literature. The exploration of different composites of relationship quality, for example, commitment, trust, passion and love (Fletcher *et al.* 2000) to determine the nature of overall relationship quality evaluation and its development has been a burgeoning one in the marriage literature. It is not difficult to imagine relationships with varying degrees of these variables, such that an individual may be committed to the relationship but not trust the partner, or may trust the partner and not show any commitment. The same argument applies within the charity–donor dyad. Clearly, to summate the two variables as convergent would mean declaring null the myriad relationship patterns that may exist in real life. This is so indeed, yet for others commitment may be seen as an outcome of relationship development and trust as a determinant or vice versa. The literature supports the view that myriad constructs have been put forward as underlying dimensions of relationship quality. This vast array of possibilities and combinations concerning the relationships between these constructs raises an important issue: how are these dimensions, with varying divergent and convergent elements, organized to evaluate relationship quality development? Clearly, two options exist: the summated route or a global-level evaluation judgement, such that individuals store one overall judgement about their partners or relationship along a good-versus-bad continuum (i.e. formative route), which then dictates specific evaluation judgements or alternatively a multidimensional structure (reflective route). The summated approach negates the existence of separate underlying constructs such as trust and commitment and instead 'parcels' these constructs as underlying isomorphic indicators or antecedents of relationship quality. Many scales have followed this presumption and the development of indexes or scales has this *modus operandi* as its core presumption.

Shabbir *et al.* (2007) developed a framework of relationship quality which assumes a multidimensional structure for relationship quality evaluation. The model was derived from thirty-four in-depth interviews with regular donors to charity and is presented as a generic model of relationship quality evaluation for relational donors. The sample size – thirty-four regular donors – used represents the number of respondents that were necessary to achieve a position whereby each of the emergent categories and relationships was saturated (Strauss and Corbin 2002). This form of theoretical sampling ensures that the emergent theory is not unevenly developed or lacking in density or precision (Strauss and Corbin 2002). The respondents, when approached in a city high street, volunteered to be contacted at a later date and subsequently interviews were arranged at the respondents' convenience. This ensured that respondents felt more relaxed by being able to select their own times and venues (McCracken 1988). Subsequently all interviews took place in the respondent's business, recreation or home environment. All interviews were recorded with the participant's permission. The interviews took place over an eight-month period, allowing for the theoretical sampling process to develop, a characteristic of the grounded theory method.

Interviews were only conducted with respondents who had made donations to charity on at least four occasions during the past year. Study participants comprised 20 females and 14 males, with an age range from 21 to 76. The respondents contributed to a wide range of charities but support for children, medical, animal, international relief and social welfare proved most popular. The diversity of respondents used is reflective of theoretical sampling in that it assumes the sample characteristics are not developed a priori, but in conjunction with the coding and analysis of the data as it proceeds. The data from each interview transcript were entered into the qualitative analysis software package QSR*NUDIST. The model is presented in Figure 3.1.

The model shows that perceived relationship benefits, service quality, trust, commitment and satisfaction are the key antecedents of donors' perceptions of the quality of the relationship they have with the charity they support. The dimensions found in the model are consistent with those found in the extant relationship fundraising literature. Indeed, among the constructs discussed in the context of relationship fundraising those which have been found to be the important underlying dimensions of relationship fundraising outcomes include: donor perceived service quality (Sargeant 2001; Sargeant *et al.* 2002; Peltier *et al.* 2002), exchange benefits (Sargeant 2001; Peltier *et al.* 2002; Cermack *et al.* 1996) and trust and commitment (Peltier *et al.* 2002; Sargeant and Lee 2002; Sargeant and Lee 2004). More recently Bennett and Barkensjo (2005a) have also found service quality and satisfaction to have a positive impact on relationship fundraising outcomes. The model also depicts relationship benefits, service quality and trust as cognitive or knowledge based in nature, satisfaction and commitment as affective in nature and finally loyalty and word-of-mouth communications as behavioural in nature. The antecedent dimensions are now briefly discussed.

The antecedent and outcome properties of individual constructs and subsequent hypotheses development are discussed in detail in Shabbir *et al.* (2007). This study therefore does not seek

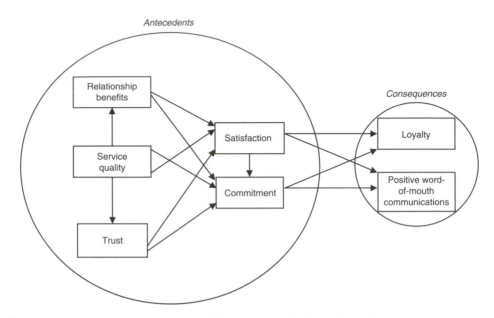

Figure 3.1 Antecedents and consequences of donor-perceived relationship quality

to focus on the development of the framework or on the nature of individual components but rather the implications of relationship quality research most pertinent for fundraising managers. This is not to say that the actual interrelationships are not important; indeed they form the central aspect of the model, but rather the implications for general relationship quality research that emanate for fundraisers are considered more of value for the purpose of this discussion.

The key implication for fundraisers arising from the model is that the aforementioned dimensions of donor-perceived relationship quality are closely interrelated, at the conceptual level, with each other and with relationship fundraising outcomes; loyalty and word-of-mouth communications. In the existing relationship fundraising literature, these dimensions have been, in the main, modelled as separate variables interacting in a wider relationship marketing or fundraising framework. This model depicts them as reflective of overall perceived relationship quality. This has important implications for fundraising managers. For instance, the interactions between service quality and satisfaction would previously have been considered as a relationship between two related but distinct variables. This study shows that the two, service quality and satisfaction, are part of one overarching construct: relationship quality. Therefore, the proposed model shows that in order to manage relationships with donors and implement the type of donor care programmes recommended by Burnett (1992), it is inappropriate to consider focusing on satisfaction or trust or improving service quality alone. Rather, it is paramount to consider all of the interacting relationships that constitute relationship quality evaluation and adopt an integrated approach to managing relationships. The implementation of programmes that integrate each of the interacting dimensions serves to facilitate the overall development of relationship quality.

Two further key implications arising from the model include the structural evaluation of relationship quality that has already been discussed and the decision-making perspective of donors' evaluation of relationship quality which are explained further. These implications have not been discussed in the existing literature (see e.g. Shabbir *et al.* 2007) and therefore form the remainder of this discussion.

Relationship quality evaluation

Although this model supports the notion that relationship quality evaluation for relational, or regular, donors follows the 'classic connectionist' approach which proposed that a state of 'stability or equilibrium is reached through the simultaneous interactions of all the elements in a cognitive system' (Smith 1996), that is, a multidimensional evaluation, this may not always be the case (Bennett and Barkenjso 2005a).

Figure 3.1 supports the position that relational donors may constantly, albeit unconsciously, be assessing the relationship's nature, or 'quality', by evaluating a number of interrelated but distinct constructs, without realizing their overall individual impact along the cognitive–affective–behavioural pathway or how these individual evaluations are reflective of the overall nature, degree or 'quality' of the relationship. Relational donors evaluate their relationships with the charity that they support using a combination of constructs and this evaluation does not take place along a negative–positive continuum but rather is 'multidimensional' and thus individual indicators may fluctuate in levels from other indicators. This results not in one global quality assessment but a more diffused and abstract generalization concerning the nature of the relationship.

The interactions between the individual composites often involve the satisfaction concept itself which is able to shape the degree and nature of the mental equilibrium or stable state reached. It is not surprising therefore to find that satisfaction acts as a potential mediator between the cognitive and behavioural states. Such an evaluation would not require the formulation of a second-order or higher-order 'global'-level relationship quality construct. Therefore, in such cases where the classic connectionist approach is adopted an index or summated scale would not accurately represent the underlying processes that are involved in the evaluation of relationship quality, simply because its development is far more complex than the presumption of a unitary higher-order node. Therefore, given that domain-specific or composite-level judgements may differ, this reflects the arbitrary nature of relational donors' relationship evaluation. Hypothetical cases of such relationship interactions have been discussed earlier, but such examples include where relationships exist with high degrees of commitment but low degrees of trust, or high trust and commitment but low satisfaction levels. It is not necessary for people to make consistent assessments of relationship quality composites. Often these composites do not exist in a tangible form and cannot be captured as exclusive domains of one order, such as that of relationship quality. Rather, they may operate at multiple levels and orders, such that commitment and trust may belong as outcomes and antecedents of unrelated concepts in human decision-making, which converge when assessing the quality or 'degree and nature' of relationships. Trust and commitment may therefore be used to assess a number of concepts, and not only relationship quality, and as such belong to much wider strata of interpersonal and impersonal situations faced by conscious and unconscious decision-making and processing. It would be unrealistic for charities, government or regulatory bodies to assume that one single indicator such as 'efficiency in terms of percentage donation given to cause' or 'administration costs' would suffice in indicating which charities are 'better or worse'. The situation is far more complex. Some charities require a greater degree of complexity and may well have greater administration costs; in such and indeed in general cases evaluation of the degree of relationship quality is based on 'all-important' variables and not only one or two selected through popular discontent from media scandals, for instance. Any quality mark, therefore, or register or directory of 'quality charities' would simply not work as it would not be in tune with how donors may potentially be evaluating their existing relationships.

Bennett and Barkensjo (2005a, 2005b) however have positioned relationship quality as a unitary order measurement for the charity beneficiary (2005a) and for the charity donor (2005b) and therefore support the standard social cognitive processing for evaluation; that is, the existence of a stored higher–order attitude exerting top-down pressure on individual evaluations; that is, a causal or formative structure. This approach would assume that donors constantly store a higher–order or global evaluation which can be tapped into and recalled when appropriate triggers act as cues. This 'global-level evaluation' generates a standard or consistent level of evaluation across underlying domains such that it generates the same or relatively consistent evaluations across trust, commitment, satisfaction and service quality per-ceptions, for instance. These domains then inversely or retroactively confirm the global-level evaluation and therefore form further stability in the stored higher-order function. Usually, such higher-order attitudes are manifested in situations where biological or high cognitive interaction or involvement characterize the interaction form, classically within the parent–infant relationship, where unlike the charity–donor relationship, it is more important to evalu-ate the immediate value of any interactions. Examples of giving behaviour whereby such a form may exist include volunteering behaviour or physical interaction with the charity or its work. Here, levels of credence are less and evaluation therefore can operate using a simple rule-of-thumb criteria or a heuristic unlike direct-debit situations where less active involve-ment with the charity or its work may lead to higher credence properties and therefore a more complex form of evaluation such as that proposed in Figure 3.1. Thus, face-to-face givers, for instance, should not be neglected on the basis that they have 'formed stable judge-ments' and therefore probably having displaying greater resistance to change. Such high inter-action or involvement levels, in volunteering, for instance, also automatically cue a cognitive system designed to minimize resources and time in evaluation and use instead pre-existing attitudes towards such behaviour that act as a form of heuristics and therefore bypass domain-specific evaluations. Bennett and Barkensjo (2005a) presume that such a system may operate for evaluating relationship quality by charity beneficiaries and this presumption would make sense, since the interactions by a beneficiary, whether conscious or unconscious, physical or non-physical, involve greater risk, interaction and involvement itself than interactions between charities and their direct-debit donors, for instance. Bennett and Barkensjo (2005b) also model this formative judgement for relationship quality of marketing activities by donors and again marketing activities are more visible, have thus less credence, high in experience properties and thus more susceptible to a preformed attitude rather than this constantly fluctuating multidimensional form of evaluation for direct-debit donors towards their supported charity, not the marketing activities of the supported charity. A paid fundraiser's level of relationship quality with a charity would, for instance, also be expected to involve a higher-order attitude motivated primarily by the wage whereas an unpaid fundraiser's attitude may not be developed as such and involve a more complex interaction of processes or domain-specific evaluations.

A second key implication arising from Figure 3.1, aside from the actual relationship between components, is the interplay at different decision-making levels. This is briefly discussed below before practical implications for fundraising managers are discussed.

The cognitive–affective interface

Another important implication of the model is the decision-making perspective that it adopts. It can be summarized that the underlying antecedent dimensions of evaluation can be classified as cognitive or affective and outcomes as behavioural. This supports the view that development of relationship quality follows the classic 'cognitive–affective–behavioural' pathway common to many decision-making contexts both within marketing and in general decision-making contexts (Tsal 1985).

Perceived service quality (or perceived impact) and trust are modelled as cognitive constructs preceding the effects of the affective constructs; satisfaction and commitment, that is, affective emotional pleasure from giving, mediates the knowledge that one is helping another. Inversely the knowledge that one is helping another strengthens the emotional bonds with relational behaviour. This mediating role of affect between cognition and behaviour has been documented extensively in the consumer behaviour literature (Shiv and Fedorikhin 1999). This positive cognitive appraisal will lead directly to positive affect which drives donor loyalty. The 'winning hearts and then minds' (Burnett 2006) strategy of relationship fundraising therefore holds through the mediating effects of the heart on the mind; both are intrinsically linked and cannot be separated in the loyalty path. Therefore, focusing on hearts, without providing evidence that can augment affective appraisal with a cognitive one, is like telling donors 'we need help' but not telling them how to and why this may be the case. Inversely, focusing on cognitive appraisal without appreciating that the natural evolution of this is positive emotional appraisal which drives giving and loyalty behaviour, is like telling donors 'we need help' but not providing mechanisms of channelling the positive emotional drive to give and support.

The implications of this conjoint cognitive and affective appraisal are that fundraising managers should focus on designing communication campaigns for relational-level givers, using a combination of both elaboration-cognitive and peripheral-affective elicitation cues. A combination of cognitive and affective elicitation allows both forms of evaluation to ensue simultaneously and therefore the cognitive–affective–behavioural path can take course on its own. If only affective cues are presented, this may 'win hearts but not minds'. Conversely, if presenting cognitive cues is the focus, then 'minds may be won at the expense of hearts'. However, the latter would assume that the natural progression of donors' cognitive appraisal would lead to emotive responses consequent to the cognitive appraisal but not strengthening this progression would be one shortcoming of such an approach. It appears that for relational donors, informational and emotional appeals should be conjoint and not separate since both complement each other. Presenting both simultaneously harnesses the complicity of decision-making and evaluation and offers the cognitive–affective and indeed the reversed affective–cognitive pathway to operate simultaneously and therefore 'pushing' and 'pulling' respectively the donor towards relationship development. It may be that initial support may be stimulated by emotional and affective triggers but it appears that as the donor becomes more relational, he or she requires more cognitive maintainers. If these cognitive factors are not provided the affective factors may not be maintained or strengthened. Even low levels of cognitive appraisal may be adequate to strengthen the affective modalities in the donor's decision to develop their relationship with the charity. Note that for new or prospective donors this would be a contrary approach since new or prospective donors need to know the degree of need, and informing them that the charity is already making headway in helping beneficiaries may preclude that charity as deserving of the new donors' commitment (Smith and Berger 1996). Relational donors, however, have already internalized their decision to support their charity and only seek maintaining factors to strengthen support and act as inertial barriers to competing charities.

Therefore, for relational donors, ideally a combination of cognitive and affective cues should exist as this would preclude the assumption that relationships should develop at the pace set by the charity rather than the key partner within the charity–donor dyad, the donor. How long it takes a donor to feel or become relational is unknown, but what is clear is that it may be spontaneous and be a matter of seconds before a donor is stimulated to feel they are within a relationship with the charity or inversely it may be considered and evaluated over time and may thus take longer (Hill 2003). This is further elaborated using the case of direct–debit donors.

Hill (2003) pointed to the lack of appreciation of understanding how the direct-mail recipient processes the creative content of the direct-mail content. Hill (2003) explains that although psychographics and demographics act as external signposts for targeting, the element of persuasion in direct marketing can only be thoroughly achieved through understanding that the end result or desired goal is an emotionally affiliated or triggered response to behaviour. His model of sense–feel–(think)–do is expanded here to sense–feel–think–(feel)–do. Passing through the initial sensory stages of dealing with the direct mail therefore needs to be a sensory–emotional attachment that takes the recipient a step further to engage with the content of the direct-mail shot. It is at this stage where the model of this investigation has its most implications. At this point the direct mail has three options based on the prospective recipient's decision-making route: either to make the content emotional or rational and informative or use a combination approach. This investigation proposes the dual use of emotive and informative content in synchrony so that the recipient can simultaneously shift between one decision-making phase to another, since given the myriad uncontrollable factors at the point of decision-making it is impossible to state at what stage of the decision-making process the donor actually is or headed towards or using which particular pathways. If the recipient is for instance cognitively inclined, then the informational cues are present to shift the decision-making from cognitive to affective phases. However, if the recipient is affectively orientated – and much of charity communications is based on appealing to prospective donors' emotional or inner drives – then cognitive cues can be presented to buffer or supplement the emotional content.

Focusing on either of emotional or cognitive elements on the assumption that one of either the peripheral or central routes will be elected by relational donors, does not take into consideration a myriad intervening and often uncontrollable variables such as mood. This set of intervening variables can affect the donors' mood, orientation, proneness and so on, towards the charity, the mail shot and recipients. A highly emotional appeal to one donor may appear like the charity is 'shouting signals' of 'junk mail' (Hill 2003) whereas an informational appeal may not reach the attention threshold of the donor and therefore be considered as 'trash' mail (Hill 2003). A combination of both, it is envisaged, would seek to criss-cross both peripheral and central paths when and where the inner psychology of the donor requires.

The results provide support for the strong affiliation that relational donors have with usually one charity by means of brand name recognition. The brand signals a degree of trust and perceived impact or benevolence which automatically shifts the donor towards the emotional attachment stage. For not-so-well-known charities to reach this group of relational donors, a more effective informational phase of content may be required to 'convince' the donor that they are a credible charity and worthy of emotional-level consideration. Such charities are not advised therefore to cold-target with emotionally laden appeals to relational donors, since for this group of donors cognitive processing serves to screen the mailshot on the basis of credibility inferred through an already established name or experience. Given the intense levels of competition and the high costs of attrition even more-established charities are advised to supplement emotional material with cognitive cues so that the elements of trust and perceived benevolence are affirmed and strengthened. For instance, if a new mailshot from a charity signals a cognitive cue that they are number one in helping the cause and not provide evidence purporting towards this, this could easily switch loyal donors or engender low cognitive appraisal. Sargeant (2001) found that 16 per cent of donors stop supporting a charity because they feel another deserves their support and almost 60 per cent based on some failing of perceived delivered service quality. Failing signals of trust and service quality also make switching to competition more likely and this is among the key issues facing fundraisers in attempting to reverse attrition today (Sargeant and Jay 2004; Burnett 2002). A strategic communications plan based on the cognitive–affective–behavioural pathway would go some way to alleviate attrition. It must be said however that charities should conduct context-based research and decide in terms of cost–benefit analysis the benefits for a segmented approach.

This research therefore demonstrates that emotional attachment should be the desired goal for charities but this emotional attachment can be strengthened through cognitive reassurance of trust and service quality. Furthermore, there exist clear pathways from cognitive to emotive phases and this should be developed into the creative content of mailings. The cognitive material should seek to reassure the donor that the charity is credible and provide evidence of this through perceived benevolence of the charity towards the cause and recipients of the support. This is despite established charities being in the heart of relational donors since the competitive environment of fundraising is increasingly turbulent and as Hill (2003) points out the psychology of direct-mail givers is more prone to switching behaviour than previously thought.

Implications for fundraising managers

In managing donor developmental programmes, fundraising managers are advised to determine how their segments process information, or evaluate the degree and nature of relationships, or quality, for instance. By knowing whether different donor groups use multidimensional or formative-processing structures, charities are better placed to design the delivery of their communication media for maximum efficiency. Providing a benchmark to beneficiaries of the successful outcome of the charity's work towards them, that is, a formative cue, may work better than a multidimensional approach in some contexts (Bennett and Barkensjo 2005b). However, this study shows that for relational donors, a combination of related but distinct constructs such as trust, service quality, satisfaction and commitment and the pathways between each of these constructs may need to be organized to move the donor along a decision-making path towards behavioural outcomes. Although the costs of such research would involve some form of complex statistical analysis, to map the structural paths (Bennett and Barkensjo 2005a; 2005b), these costs are no doubt offset by the increased efficiency and effectiveness of communication programmes designed to engender donor support.

Second, a greater understanding and refocus on the decision-making perspective adopted by donor or general supporter segments would also certainly assist charities to offset the costs of what are becoming increasingly more expensive donor recruitment and retention programmes. Indeed, where donors use a multidimensional evaluation structure to assess relationship quality, for instance, such an understanding becomes necessary in the design and development of communication media content. By emphasizing relationship benefits, service quality and trust prior to satisfaction and commitment is a reflection of fundraisers having to recognize that donor care is about what the donor wants, and not what fundraisers feel donors should receive. Fundraisers must implement a strategy to leverage donors based on the development of relationship quality needs. Central to this need for relationship evaluation is the processing of cognitive modalities prior to affective-based ones. This would imply that the first step to donor care is in fact an informational or rational stage, where the donor's knowledge base is developed, and the second is an emotional-based stage, designed at facilitating positive feelings to eventually positive behavioural relational outcomes. Ultimately, the behavioural outcomes are convergent as common goals for both charity and donor, with each seeking loyalty and preferably the empowerment of advocacy throughout positive word-of-mouth communications. If, for instance, fundraisers attempt to 'load' emotional appeals and communications on first-time donors, without first engendering a sense of understanding and purpose, then donors will not feel positive but rather negative given the lack of essential preceding informational cues. These informational cues may be suggestive of building trust, of recognizing donor efforts, or rewarding the donor, rather than seeking to achieve the aforementioned through emotional-based imagery or cues.

Therefore, it is important to have fundraisers who are knowledgeable about the development of relationship quality, its components and different levels expected by donors. While it has long been acknowledged in the literature that being trustworthy can improve donor confidence, it is also important to know that donors seek trust as part of an integral chain of relationship quality development. This suggests that training should focus on teaching fundraisers how to learn what standard of affective care they seek, in addition to supplying them with cognitive stimulation in the form of service quality, trust and relationship benefits. Clearly, fundraisers need to be apt in communicating benefits, service quality, trust, satisfaction and commitment-engendering messages. Fundraisers should, therefore, spend time developing their communication skills in relation to managing each of the components of relationship quality.

In summary, a donor-oriented integrated approach is therefore more suited to managing relationships. The benefit of formulating relationship fundraising communications based on service quality, relationship benefits and trust recognizes that these elements of relationship quality are more central to making even small donors feel like major donors; that is, moving donors up the loyalty ladder. A central aspect of this approach, however, is the longer time-frame required for implementation; therefore rather than a one-year time-frame and for achievement of goals, a three- or five-year time-frame and achievement of goals should be established. This would ensure sufficient time for donors to move up the loyalty ladder and appropriate transformation based on communications. The generation of 'affective stage' donors from 'cognitive-based' ones must not be seen as a 'quick-fix' solution but rather as an approach that needs relationship development itself within the time and resources of the charity.

Donor care is dependent on making the donor aware of certain 'relationship essentials' which should in themselves lead to the generation of positive feelings and attitude formation. Just as the adage 'relationships take time', similarly, donor relationships need nurturing. Tim Hunter, the head of the direct marketing department at the NSPCC (National Society for Prevention of Cruelty to Children), in the UK, recognizes explicitly the danger of overpowering a donor relationship: 'We don't want donors to feel they are part of some big marketing machine and that once they have responded they will be bombarded with mailings for the rest of their lives' (Burnett 2002: 17). Allowing the relationship to develop along time recognizes the need for donors to move along a path at their own choosing, and avoids upsetting them from the onset, when they are most vulnerable to leaving the charity.

Implications for future research

This chapter focused on the issues relating to relationships from the donor's perspective only. However, because relationships involve more than one party, it is also important to look at the issues studied here from the charities' or the fundraisers' perspective. What do fundraisers think makes a good relationship, or how do they determine when a relationship is of good quality? Looking at the fundraisers' side of the story might provide further insight into why relationships between charities and donors are not always good and may suggest additional ways to improve them. Many of the same variables might be relevant from a fundraising perspective, but other factors such as accountability and inter-team communication might also be important to consider.

To investigate other possible antecedents of relationship quality, future research should examine the impact of other independent variables that are potentially important. For example, variables such as value can also have an effect on overall relationship quality. In addition, due to the dynamic nature of relationships, it is unlikely that relationship quality follows a process of sequential development but rather of constant flux with each component multidirecting each other in a complex multicausal multidirectional manner not reflected in this chapter. Donors in their interactions may react differently depending on the different phases in the relationship formation and development process and are constantly open to myriad intervening variables, often unique for each individual.

It is important to consider the total relationship quality paradigm and its potential for advancing further the research proposed in this chapter. The intervening extrinsic, intrinsic and processing determinants should be incorporated with donor-perceived relationship quality, as reflecting the donor's potential judgemental criteria for processing giving behaviour, within a total relationship quality (TRQ) framework. This TRQ framework could incorporate certain organizational-level variables, such as staff motivation and relationship orientation. Important organizational-level variables, such as donor orientation (Bennett 1996) and relationship quality of marketing activities (Bennett and Barkensjo 2005), could shed important insights surrounding the optimal organization-wide effects.

Indeed, Burnett (2002: 15) identifies vertical and horizontal barriers as the 'Dependency on other departments, who won't cooperate . . . and lack of commitment, particularly from senior managers' as central barriers to relationship fundraising success. This chapter advocates that, given the role of relationship quality in developing donor loyalty and positive word-of-mouth communications, donor-perceived relationship quality is ideally suited to act as a foundation or basis for integrating relationship fundraising skills and knowledge.

References

Baker, T. L., Penny, M. S. and Siguaw, J. A. (1999) 'The impact of suppliers' perceptions of reseller market orientation on key relationship constructs', *Journal of the Academy of Marketing Science*, 27(winter):50–7.

Bechtel, W. and Abrahamson, A. (1991) *Connectionism and the Mind: An Introduction to Parallel Processing in Networks*, Cambridge, MA: Blackwell Publishers.

Bejou, D., Wray, B. and Ingram, T. N. (1996) 'Determinants of relationship quality: An artificial neural network analysis', *Journal of Business Research*, 36:137–43.

Bennett, R. and Barkensjo, A. (2005a) 'Causes and consequences of donor perceptions of the quality of the relationship marketing activities of charitable organizations', *Journal of Targeting, Measurement and Analysis for Marketing*, 13(2):122–39.

—— and Barkensjo, A. (2005b) 'Relationship quality, relationship marketing and client perceptions of levels of service quality of charitable organizations', *International Journal of Service Industry Management*, 16(1):81–97.

Bowlby, J. (1969) *Attachment and Loss*, New York, NY: Basic Books.

Burnett, K. (1992) *Relationship Fundraising*, London: White Lion Press.

—— (2002) 'Relationship fundraising ten years after: How do we turn the promise into reality?', International Fundraising Congress, Amsterdam, Holland.

Clarke, M. S. and Mills, J. (1979) 'Interpersonal attraction in exchange and communal relationships', *Journal of Personality and Social Psychology*, 37:12–24.

Crosby, L. A., Evans, K. R. and Cowles, D. (1990) 'Relationship quality in services selling: An interpersonal influence perspective', *Journal of Marketing*, 54:68–81.

Cutting, A. L. and Dunn, J. (2006) 'Conversations with siblings and with friends: Links between relationship quality and social understanding', *British Journal of Developmental Psychology*, 24(1):73–87.

Diamantopoulos, A. and Winklhofer, H. (2001) 'Index construction with formative indicators: An alternative to scale development', *Journal of Marketing Research*, 38(2):269–77.

Dorsch, M. J., Swanson, S. R. and Kelley, S. W. (1998) 'The role of relationship quality in the stratification of vendors as perceived by customers', *Journal of the Academy of Marketing Science*, 26(2):128–42.

Dwyer, R. F., Schurr, P. H. and Oh, S. (1987) 'Developing buyer–seller relationships', *Journal of Marketing*, 55(January):11–27.

Erikson, E. R. (1968) *Identity: Youth and Crisis*, New York, NY: Norton.

Fletcher, G. J. O., Simpson, J. A. and Thomas, G. (2000) 'The measurement of perceived relationship quality components: A confirmatory factor analytic approach', *Personality and Social Psychology Bulletin*, 26(3):340–54.

Garbarino, E. and Johnson, M. (1999) 'The different roles of satisfaction, trust and commitment in customer relationships', *Journal of Marketing*, 63(April):70–87.

Gronroos, C. (1990) 'Relationship approach to marketing in services contexts: The marketing and organizational behaviour interface', *Journal of Business Research*, 20(1):3–11.

—— (1994) 'From marketing mix to relationship marketing: Towards a paradigm shift in marketing', *Management Decision*, 32(2):4–20.

—— (2002) *Service Management and Marketing – A Customer Relationship Management Approach*, Chichester: John Wiley & Sons.

Hennig-Thurau, T. and Klee, A. (1997) 'The impact of customer satisfaction and relationship quality on customer retention: A critical reassessment and model development', *Psychology and Marketing*, 14(8):737–64.

—— Gwinner, K. P. and Gremler, D. D. (2002) 'Understanding marketing relationship marketing outcomes', *Journal of Services Research*, 4(3):230–47.

—— Hansen, M. F. and Langer, U. (2001) 'Modeling and managing student loyalty: An approach based on relationship quality', *Journal of Services Research*, 3(4):331–34.

Fornell, C. (1992) 'A national customer satisfaction barometer: The Swedish experience', *Journal of Marketing*, 56:6–21.

Jarvis, C. B., MacKenzie, S. B. and Podsakoff, (2003) 'A critical review of construct indicators and measurement model misspecification in marketing and consumer research', *Journal of Consumer Research*, 30:199–218.

Jarvelin, A. M. and Lehtinen, U. (1996) 'Relationship quality in a business-to-business context', in B. B. Edvardsson, S. W. Johnston and E. E. Scheuing (eds) *QUIS 5 Advancing Service Quality: A Global Perspective*, Lethbrige, Canada: Warwick Printing, pp. 243–54.

Jordan, L. C. and Lewis, M. L. (2003) 'Paternal relationship quality as a protective factor: Preventing alcohol use among African-American adolescents', *Journal of Black Psychology*, 31(2):152–71.

Hill, D. (2003) 'Tell me no lies: Using science to connect with consumers', *Journal of Interactive Marketing*, 17(4):61–73.

Kelley, H. H. and Thibaut, J. W. (1978) *Interpersonal Relations*, New York, NY: John Wiley & Sons.

Kumar, N., Scheer, L. K. and Steenkamp, J. E. M. (1995) 'The effects of supplier fairness on vulnerable resellers', *Journal of Marketing Research*, 32:54–65.

Lagace, R. R., Dahlstrom, R. and Gassenheimer, J. B. (1991) 'The relevance of ethical salesperson behaviour on relationship quality: The pharmaceutical industry', *Journal of Personal Selling and Sales Management*, 11(4):39–47.

Leuthesser, L. (1997) 'Supplier relational behaviour: An empirical assessment', *Industrial Marketing Management*, 26(3):245–55.

Liljander, V. and Strandvik, T. (1995) 'The nature of customer relationships in services', in T. A. Swartz, D. E. Bowen and S. W. Brown (eds) *Advances in Services Marketing and Management*, 4, Greenwich, CT: JAI Press, pp. 141–67.

Malim, T. (1994) *Cognitive Processes (Introductory Psychology)*, New York, NY: Palgrave MacMillan.

McCracken, G. (1988) *The Long Interview*, Newbury Park, CA: Sage Publications.

Moorman, C. R., Zaltman, G. and Deshpande, R. (1992) 'Relationships between providers and users of market research: The dynamics of trust within and between organizations', *Journal of Marketing Research*, 26:314–29.

Naude, P. and Buttle, F. (2000) 'Assessing relationship quality', *Industrial Marketing Management*, 29(4):351–61.

Polonsky, J. (2006) 'Who receives the most help? The most needy or those with the best marketers?', *International Journal of Nonprofit and Voluntary Sector Marketing*, 8(4):302–4.

Reichheld, F. F. (1993) 'Loyalty based management', *Harvard Business Review*, 71(2):64–73.

Richmond, M. K., Stocker, C. M. and Rienks, S. L. (2005) 'Longitudinal associations between sibling relationship quality, parental differential treatment and children's adjustment', *Journal of Family Psychology*, 19(4):550–9.

Roberts, K., Varki, S. and Brodie, R. (2003) 'Measuring the quality of relationships in consumer services: An empirical study', *European Journal of Marketing*, 37(1/2):169–96.

Rossiter, J. (2002) 'The C-OAR-SE procedure for scale development in marketing', *International Journal of Research in Marketing*, 19(4):305–35.

Rust, R. T. and Oliver, R. L. (1994) 'Service quality: Insights and managerial implications from the frontier', in Roland T. Rust and Richard L. Oliver (eds) *Service Quality: New Directions in Theory and Practice*, Thousand Oaks, CA: Sage Publications, pp. 1–19.

—— and Zahorik, A. J. (1993) 'Customer satisfaction, customer retention, and market share', *Journal of Retailing*, 69(2):193–215.

Sargeant, A. (1999) 'Charitable giving: Towards a model of giving behaviour', *Journal of Marketing Management*, 15:212–38.

—— (2001) 'Relationship fundraising: How to keep donors loyal', *Nonprofit Management and Leadership*, 12(2):177–92.

—— and Jay, E. (2004) *Fundraising Management*, London: Routledge.

Saxton, J. (1999) 'Getting Britain Giving campaign', *Guardian*, November.

Shabbir, H., Palihawadana, D. and Thwaites, D. (2007) 'Determining the antecedents and consequences of donor perceived relationship quality – A dimensional qualitative research approach', *Psychology and Marketing*, 24(3):271–93.

Sheth, J. N. and Parvatiyar, A. (1995) 'The evolution of relationship marketing', *International Business Review*, 4(4):397–418.

Shiv, B. and Fedorikhin, A. (1999) 'Heart and mind in conflict: Interplay of affect and cognition in consumer decision making', *Journal of Consumer Research*, 26:278–82.

Smith, E. R. (1996) 'What do connectionism and social psychology offer each other?', *Journal of Personality and Social Psychology*, 70:893–912.

Smith, G. E. and Berger, P. D. (1996) 'The impact of direct marketing appeals on charitable marketing effectiveness', *Journal of the Academy of Marketing Science*, 24(3):219–31.

Smith, J. B. (1998) 'Buyer–seller relationships: Similarity, relationship management and quality', *Psychology and Marketing*, 15(1):3–21.

Stevenson, W., Maton, K. I. and Teti, D. M. (1999) 'Social support, relationship quality and well-being among pregnant adolescents', *Journal of Adolescence*, 22(1):109–21.

Strauss, A. and Corbin, J. (1998) *Basics of Qualitative Research: Grounded Theory Procedures and Techniques*, 2nd edition, Thousand Oaks, CA: Sage Publications.

Storbacka, K., Strandvik, T. and Gronroos, C. (1994) 'Managing customer relations for profit: The dynamics of relationship quality', *International Journal of Service Industry Management*, 5(5):21–38.

Thibault, J. W. and Kelley, H. H. (1959) *The Social Psychology of Groups*, New York, NY: Wiley.

Tsal, Y. (1985) 'On the relationship between cognitive and affective processes: A critique of Zajonc and Markus', *Journal of Consumer Research*, 12(3):358–63.

Woodrome, S. E., Zimet, G. D., Orr, D. P. and Fortenberry, J. D. (2006) 'Dyadic alcohol use and relationship quality as predictors of condom non-use among adolescent females', *Journal of Adolescent Health*, 38(3):305–6.

Wray, B., Palmer, A. and Bejou, D. (1994) 'Using neural network analysis to evaluate buyer–seller relationships', *European Journal of Marketing*, 28(10):32–48.

Yan, L. J., Hammen, C., Cohen, A. N., Daley, S. E. and Henry, R. (2005) 'Expressed emotion versus relationship quality prediction of recurrence in bipolar patients', *Journal of Affective Disorders*, 86(2–3):337.

4

The branding of charities

Jane Hudson

Introduction

The twenty-first century has seen increasing numbers of companies recognizing the power of a strong brand. At a time when the global economy is subject to changing market dynamics and heightened competition, the role of brands in the commercial domain has never been greater (Brymer 2004). Brands and brand management have become focal areas for academics and practitioners alike and the ability of a strong brand to offer critical benefits such as the ability to differentiate an organization from competitors is no longer in question (Hankinson 2001).

Nonprofit branding too appears to have come of age. The Habitat for Humanity brand, for example, was recently valued at $1.8 billion (Quelch *et al.* 2004), reinforcing the significance of the practice of branding to nonprofit organizations. Such recognition, it is argued, is well overdue (Sargeant and Jay 2004). Historically nonprofits have been relatively slow to adopt branding practices because of difficulties in committing internal stakeholders to the process (Grounds and Harkness 1998) and a perception on the part of some nonprofit managers that branding is too 'commercial' or even immoral (Ritchie *et al.* 1998). This reluctance to use the term is something of an anomaly since nonprofit organizations have long been concerned with 'maintaining a consistent style and tone of voice and conducting periodic reviews of both policies and actions to ensure that a consistent personality is projected' (Tapp 1996: 335). As Tapp rightly notes, such practices are the very essence of brand management, regardless of whether an organization's management chooses to regard them as such.

In this chapter it is intended to review what we presently understand about branding in the nonprofit sector and how the application of brand management tools, techniques and concepts may differ in this context. Opportunities for further research will also be highlighted. We begin, however, by defining what we mean by the term 'brand' and why nonprofit brands have recently been in the ascendancy.

What is a brand?

In Europe the English word 'brand' was probably conceived in the Middle Ages as a degenerate of the old Norse word *brandr*, which refers to the branding of cattle to denote ownership. After the Middle Ages, the use of branding developed as trade increased and tradesmen wished to be recognized for their products. The demand for branded goods as modern society knows them notably increased with the advent of the Industrial Revolution (1830–1870) and many brands that originated then are still available today, such as Levi's and Heinz (Riezebos 2003). As brands have developed in the course of the last century they have evolved into a complex communications system between a manufacturer and consumer. This complexity has spawned a variety of different definitions of branding, each of which tends to emphasize rather different dimensions of brands or the way in which they may enhance or detract from consumer relationships.

Gardner and Levy (1955: 7), for example, define a brand as:

> a complex symbol that represents a variety of ideas and attributes. It tells the consumer many things, not only by the way it sounds (and its literal meaning if it has one) but, more important, via the body of associations it has built up and acquired as a public object over a period of time.

In the nonprofit context this is a particularly helpful definition as it highlights the need to consider the associations that are derived from a brand name and all the activities that the brand undertakes. Many of these associations can be critical to success in income generation and in many cases to success in achieving the organization's mission.

However, as the reader will appreciate this definition is now somewhat dated and it fails to highlight the outputs from a brand. Many writers now prefer to emphasize the ability of a brand to facilitate the building of relationships with consumers and even to form a focus for that relationship. The definition is also a little narrow in scope. The National Society for the Prevention of Cruelty to Children (NSPCC), in stark contrast, defines its brand as 'everything we are, everything we say, everything we do'. It is this more holistic conception of brand that will be adopted in this chapter.

Why brand?

Pragmatically, branding should be a critical issue for nonprofits because it has been shown to impact dramatically on income generation (Dixon 1996; Kennedy 1998; Denney 1998; Grounds and Harkness 1998). A strong brand can convey the values and beliefs of a nonprofit to potential donors and suggest very potent reasons why it might be worthy of support (Harvey and McCrohan 1988; Dixon 1996). This is highly significant, since as Bendapudi *et al.* (1996) state, where donors lack knowledge of the charities' image they may either ignore a communications message or 'distort' it to excuse themselves from making a gift.

So how does this process work? Why do brands improve fundraising performance? First, brands are considered an aid to learning and can be used as a tool to educate progressively members of the public about the work undertaken. If members of the public are already familiar with a charity's brand, their name and the values associated with that name, then fundraisers are not working from a 'zero base'. Indeed, some organizations feel that fundraising benefits to such a degree from branding activity that they actually charge a percentage of the communications budget to the fundraising function. In an age when nonprofits are highly concerned with their reported fundraising costs, this is a not insignificant development.

Second, it is argued that branding reduces risk for a donor. 'Agency theory' is key in this, as in making donations donors are in effect using nonprofits to act as their agents in disbursing funds. The brand image of a nonprofit will provide numerous clues as to how well an individual charity will perform in this capacity. This is particularly the case in impersonal forms of fundraising like direct mail, press or radio advertising where the donor may be entirely reliant on their perception of the organization in deciding whether or not to offer a donation. Tapp (1996) also argues that brands can serve to enhance trust between a nonprofit and its donors/ potential donors. They provide assurance that an organization is worthy of trust and that funds donated will be used in a manner consistent with the standards that have been established over time (Ritchie *et al.* 1998).

Brands are also significant since, as we noted earlier, they can provide the focus for a supporter relationship. If a brand can be personified, through the 'is, says, does' approach of the NSPCC, consumers may not just perceive them, but may also be able to have a relationship with them (Blackston 1992; Kapferer 1992). Indeed, there is now evidence that individuals do develop relationships or 'bonds' (Veloutsou 2001) with specific brands. When the bond is strong, customer sentiments towards the brand extend beyond simple repeat purchase or cognitive preference. The tie can become emotional and based on intense affective considerations which may defy logical understanding (Fournier 1994; Schlueter 1992; Schwadel 1987; Morris and Martin 2000). In the nonprofit context this is particularly critical as in addition to income generation many organizations will seek to leverage their brand to effect societal change (e.g. in the case of the NSPCC, to put an end to cruelty to children, full stop). Effecting behavioural change will be greatly facilitated if individuals can identify with a brand and develop an emotional attachment to its goals and aspirations.

Branding can also offer a form of reputation insurance to a nonprofit. Having built up a consistent image over time that becomes trusted and increasingly well understood, short-term crises can be survived. The Aramony scandal, for example, rocked the United Way in the USA when the chief executive was accused of wasting donated funds on unnecessary flights on Concord. This had a dramatic impact on donations in the short term, but the reputation of the organization was such that it quickly regained its share of gifts and its relative position in the market.

Components of a brand

To achieve these benefits, nonprofits need to develop their understanding of the various components of a brand and investigate how these might be managed actively over time. While there are many generic models of brand that have been developed by various authors in the commercial context, most may be reduced to a number of similar components. Indeed they can be satisfactorily analysed by considering the rational and emotional elements of brands (de Chernatony and Dall'Olmo 1998). The rational elements of brands include, for example, the physical benefits of the brand and its functional attributes. The emotional elements of brands include brand image, brand identity, brand personality, brand essence and the added value that it offers the consumers. The purpose of models that depict this dichotomy is to increase managers' understanding of both dimensions so that they may achieve sustainable differentiation in one or more areas and thus protect the long-term value of the brand among targeted consumers. However, such models are not without limitations in that they are largely generic as

67

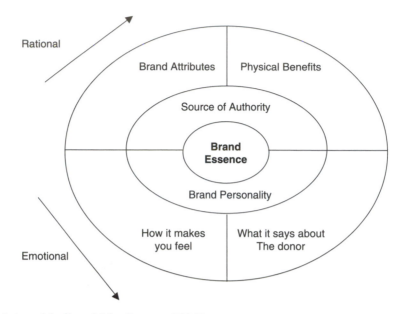

Figure 4.1 A model of brand (after Sargeant (2004))

opposed to context specific and as such are open to interpretation in each brand category situation. The model (presented in Figure 4.1.) developed by Sargeant (2004) is the only model specifically developed within the nonprofit context.

This model has much in common with those developed in the commercial sector by Kapferer (1992), de Chernatony (1993) and Aaker (1996). All seven elements of the model are areas where brands may be differentiated from those of other nonprofit organizations in order to gain competitive advantage and ultimately enhance donations or increase the take-up of service provision/campaigning.

At the centre of the model is what the author refers to as the brand's essence, which he considers to be the core of what the brand stands for and how it differentiates it from other brands. The Royal National Lifeboat Institution (RNLI) in the UK, for example, leverages the heroism of its lifeboat teams, placing them at the core of the institution's brand. The essence defines the core of the organization enabling those who come into contact with it to have a clear representation of what makes it unique. De Chernatony (1993) argues that it is the brand essence that enables a brand owner to summarize verbally the key functional benefits that allow the brand to make a rational claim for purchase/donation (and which may be linked with emotional rewards) in one short statement. Following through on the RNLI example, donors know that by supporting the organization they will save lives at sea and make it easier and safer for the crews to do their job. To facilitate this, the brand allows the individual to identify with the heroism of the crews.

The next layer in this model of the brand comprises two elements. On the rational side of the brand, the source of its authority and on the emotional side of the brand, its personality. The source of authority refers to the quality, credence or expertise of the charity brand in a particular cause. For example, Cancer Research UK has a powerful national brand associated with research into curing cancer. Through the brand, the consumer recognizes the charity's specialism and its claim to be the leading provider of high-quality research in this field. Brand personality on the other hand is a more complex construct and illustrates the manner or style in which the organization will fulfil its tasks. Greenpeace, for example, has an action-oriented brand that supporters know they can trust to take action, even in the most difficult of circumstances. The critical concept of personality is explored in detail in the next section of this chapter.

The outer layer of the model illustrates the final four elements of the brand. These are once again categorized as rational or emotional. Considering first the rational elements, both the 'attributes' and the 'physical benefits' refer to the functional elements of the brand. In the Cancer Research UK example, the brand may be used to convey information about the range of research undertaken and the very practical benefits (e.g. improving survival rates) that have resulted from work undertaken in the past.

Considering next the emotional elements of the brand, these are concerned with how the brand makes the donor feel and what the brand says about that donor. The Dogs Trust, in the UK, for example, has a brand that is designed to make donors feel good about their ongoing support. Its communications are designed to entertain the recipients, with donors receiving Valentine's Day cards from the animals they have adopted and letters purporting to come from the animals themselves. The organization is obviously very serious about its work, but the brand allows donors to buy into their mission without focusing on the more distressing aspects of dealing with unwanted pets. Brands can also be used by donors to express something of their self-identity. Witness how many people in public life will be seen sporting a Royal British Legion poppy in the days running up to Remembrance Sunday.

Brand personality

The idea of a brand personality is familiar and accepted by practitioners and academics alike in the commercial sector (see e.g. Plummer 1985; Crask and Laskey 1990; Aaker 1997). Furthermore it is becoming of increasing interest in the nonprofit sector. Research has argued that brand personality is important because it can help to differentiate brands (Crask and Laskey 1990), develop the emotional aspects of the brand (Landon 1974) and augment the personal meaning of a brand to the consumer (Levy 1959). Further to this, brand personality has been variously defined as:

> The set of human characteristics associated with the brand.
>
> (Aaker 1997: 393)

Allen and Olsen expand on the Aaker (1997) definition as follows:

> Creating brand personality literally involves the personification of a brand. Attributions of personality to a brand require that the brand performs intentional behaviours. To do so, the brand must be 'alive' – the brand must be an active figure that intentionally does things. Based on the observed behaviours, consumers can make attributions about the brand's personality – 'inner character', goals and values.
>
> (Aaker 1995: 392)

The management of brand personality is thus an attempt to consider how brands can be imbued with certain human and emotional characteristics. Authors, such as McEnally and de

Chernatony (1999), have argued that these 'emotional' elements have come to dominate the practice of modern consumer branding. The authors use a social interactionist perspective to develop the notion that consumers choose representative brand personalities that are symbolic of their lifestyle. They state that individuals form self-concepts based on their perception of the responses of others. As consumers share common symbolic values, through socialization, they ascribe attributes or status to others by their ability to purchase particular brands. The purchases they make themselves can therefore be used to reinforce their self-concept. Indeed, McEnally and de Chernatony (1999) argue that individuals purchase brands that are consistent and representative of their self-concept and display these brands to others as a means of communicating to others. When consumers choose between competing brands, they assess actively the fit between the personalities of competing brands and the personality that they wish to project (Zinkhan et al. 1996).

Turning to the methods by which the brand's personality is built and communicated to the consumer, advertising, packaging and other elements of the marketing mix are critical (Aaker 1996; Batra et al. 1993; Levy 1959; Plummer 1985). It is from these communications that consumers add new benefits and attributes to their knowledge of the brand (Keller 1993). Where consumers have accepted the brand's personality they develop an 'active awareness' of the brand. Consumers know what the brand stands for and have developed opinions about the brand. The intangible aspects of the brand are also added to their memory networks and the brand becomes more than just a 'product' (Aaker 1996).

In a strategic sense Aaker describes brand personality as a metaphor that:

> can help brand strategists by enriching their understanding of people's perceptions of and attitude toward the brand, contributing to a differentiating brand identity, guiding the communication effort and creating brand equity.
>
> (Aaker 1995: 8)

Turning to the nonprofit sector, despite widespread acceptance that branding can facilitate more efficient fundraising, there has been little empirical work conducted into the nature of charity brand personalities and the role that these can play in this process. As argued in the commercial sector, people buy things not only for what they do, but also for what they mean. In electing to purchase brands with particular personalities consumers can thus seek to convey representation of themselves (Fournier 1991; Ligas 2000) and/or to reinforce their self-image. As Wee et al. (2003: 216) note, 'symbolic values and meanings are desirable and useful to consumers for the construction of their self, whether that is self-enhancement or self-reinforcement'. This may be an equally important factor in the nonprofit context, as extant research has shown that the act of offering a donation can confer an identity on the donor (Schwartz 1967). While the nature of this identity will undoubtedly vary, work by Yavas et al. (1980) suggests that in general, possessing a generous, loving self-image is more important for donors than for non-donors.

Of particular interest in the UK, where charities have a distinct legal status (akin to 501[C]3 in the USA), is how such personalities might be structured. Sargeant et al. (forthcoming) consider whether there are, for example, brand personality traits (e.g. 'trustworthy' or 'caring') that are ostensibly 'charitable' in nature. They argue that the extent to which nonprofit brand personalities are unique or shared with others in the sector or same category of cause is important. It is of particular significance, since if certain traits accrue to an organization's brand by virtue of that organization being a charity, the need to focus on that trait in individual marketing practice is greatly reduced. Equally, if some traits apply at the level of the cause (e.g. animal welfare) the need to promote or manage that trait becomes one for the subsector as a whole to address, rather than a single organization per se.

Drawing on earlier work, Aaker (1997) attempted to clarify the underlying structure of brand personalities and identified five similar dimensions, namely sincerity, excitement, competence, sophistication, ruggedness (certainly, the first three of these are congruent with earlier work in human psychology). However, the extent to which Aaker's framework could legitimately be generalized to all commercial brand contexts (Austin *et al.* 2003) and in particular to the nonprofit sector remains unclear. Doubts have also been expressed over Aaker's original methodology. Writers such as Azoulay and Kapferer (2003) have noted that her operationalization of personality included a number of demographic variables, which are typically inferred from users rather than brand personality per se and that her personality scale is culture specific (Davies *et al.* 2001). The traits 'western' and 'small town' have very different meanings outside the USA, for example.

The Aaker model is difficult to apply in the nonprofit context because it appears that a number of personality traits may be shared across the sector as a whole. Malloy and Agarwal (2001), for example, posit that the dominant climate in nonprofits is based on an individual caring or 'feminine' model and that this is key to the stimulation of ongoing public support. We might therefore expect that traits such as being caring, considerate or sympathetic would be common to many charities. Writing from a sociological perspective Sternberg (1998) postulates that the charity sector needs to maintain an identity as a force for change and for promoting a fair society. This is a view echoed by Putnam *et al.* (2003) and Korten (1995) who view the distinctive identity of the voluntary sector as important for the wider health of society. There would thus appear to be something distinctive about the nature of nonprofit or charity values and in the light of the foregoing, some contribution at least to nonprofit personality that accrues by virtue of charitable or voluntary status. To complicate matters further, many practitioners have argued that distinct personality traits may derive from certain forms of voluntary activity, such as animal welfare, the prevention of child abuse, cancer research, and so on (Pidgeon 2002; Elischer 2001; Growman 2000).

Sargeant *et al.* (forthcoming) therefore revisited Aaker's work to explore brand personality in the nonprofit context. They sought to determine not only those traits that are capable of differentiating between charities, but also to determine whether any might typically be shared between causes or across the sector as a whole. The research highlighted that donors appear to 'imbue' an organization with particular characteristics, by virtue of its charitable status. Furthermore, the analysis suggested that these common or shared characteristics reflect the voluntary, benevolent nature of nonprofits and the role that they play in attempting to instigate change. Furthermore they recommended that when seeking to differentiate their brand, charity marketers consider the nature of the emotional stimulation engendered by the organization, the nature of the voice projected by the charity, the character of their service provision and the extent to which the organization might be viewed as traditional. In respect of causal differences, the authors conclude that few personality characteristics are shared, with the exception of the faith-based and human service sectors where some commonality was exhibited.

The work by Sargeant *et al.* indicates that charity brands may not be as distinctive as previously thought. The public has a strong sense of what it means to be a charity, but within this finds it difficult to distinguish between causes, much less specific charities. It also tells us that charities may be competing more on simple name recognition than on the basis of a strong individual identity. Further research is clearly warranted in this interesting domain.

Conclusion

This chapter has discussed the key elements of branding that may be pertinent to the nonprofit sector. In doing so I have painted a rather rosy picture of what branding can offer a nonprofit, but it is important to understand that despite the advantages, some constituencies, including donors, may be antagonistic towards the organization spending money on branding. Indeed a number of major charities have recently been criticized openly in the press for spending on this, rather than on service activities per se. While this may be just a matter of reassuring the public of the benefits, there are a number of legitimate criticisms of branding expenditure that can be raised.

First, Spruill (2001) argues that branding can create barriers that prevent nonprofits from building collaborative partnerships with each other for either service delivery or fundraising. Managers are understandably reticent about diluting their brand and thus unwilling to develop partnerships as a consequence. Spruill also argues that branding can develop a spirit of unhealthy competition for visibility, prompting others to undertake similar expenditure, none of which will directly benefit beneficiaries. There may also be a sense that the voice of smaller causes is buried under the noise created by high-profile names. Meyers (1995) notes that such concerns prompted Planned Parenthood to drop the idea of licensing condoms, which could have earned about $300,000 a year in royalties.

Of course, such objections assume that it is possible for a nonprofit not to brand. Regrettably, nonprofits have brands whether or not they choose to call them that. The issue is rather whether an organization should take steps to manage its brands and it would be puerile to suggest that this would in some sense be inappropriate. That is not to say that organizations should simply plough ever greater sums into brand-building communications without giving a second thought to the impact on others; merely that the development of effective brand management is a matter that deserves serious management attention and thought.

In this chapter I have reviewed why this might be and examined a model of brand to illustrate the components that an organization may seek actively to manage. The issue of brand personality is critical and, as has been illustrated in the previous section, the management of this facet of nonprofit brands is particularly complex. Some aspects of personality may be beyond the direct control of the specific organization. This is rarely the case in the for-profit sector and would therefore make an interesting topic for further research.

Indeed, more clarity is generally required in respect of the lessons that may legitimately be applied from the commercial sector in respect of how nonprofit brands should be managed. Nonprofit branding should be a subject of study in its own right. In particular the branding themes suggested in Sargeant's model could be further explored as could the antecedents and consequences of brand relationships. Further research might also examine the role of branding in other nonprofit contexts such as campaigning or lobbying and the consequence of donor relationships that span a number of these different activities. The issue of campaign integration in this context is also little understood.

References

Aaker, D. A. (1995) *Building Strong Brands*, New York: Free Press.
Aaker, J. L. (1997) 'Dimensions of brand personality', *Journal of Marketing Research*, 34(3): 347–56.
Allen, D. and Olson, J. (1995) 'Building bonds between the brand and the consumer by creating and

managing brand personality'. Presentation to Marketing Science Institute Conference on Brand Equity and the Marketing Mix, Tuscon, Arizona, March 2–3.

Austin, J. R., Siguaw, J. A. and Mattila, A. S. (2003) 'A re-examination of the generalizability of the Aaker brand personality measurement framework', *Journal of Strategic Marketing*, 11: 77–92.

Azoulay, A. and Kapferer, J. (2003) 'Do brand personality scales really measure brand personality?', *Brand Management*, 11(2): 143–55.

Batra, R., Lehmann, D. R. and Dipinder, S. (1993) 'The brand personality component of brand goodwill: Some antecedents and consequences', in: *Brand Equity and Advertising*, David A. Aaker and Alexander Biel (eds), Hillsdale, NJ: Lawrence Erlbaum Associates.

Bendapudi, N., Singh, S. N. and Bendapudi, V. (1996) 'Enhancing helping behavior: An integrative framework for promotion planning', *Journal of Marketing*, 60(3): 33–54.

Blackston, M. (1992) 'Observations: Building brand equity by managing the brand's relationships', *Journal of Advertising Research*, 32(2): 79ff.

Brymer, C. (2004) 'What makes brand great?', *Marketing*, 15 January: 20–4.

C A F (2002) *Dimensions of the Voluntary Sector*, West Malling, Kent: Charities Aid Foundation.

Charity Commission (2005) *The Register of Charities*, http://www.charity-commission.gov.uk/ (accessed 5 March 2007).

Crask, M. R. and Laskey, H. A. (1990) 'A positioning-based decision model for selecting advertising messages', *Journal of Advertising Research*, 30: 32–8.

Davies, G., Chun, R. and da Silva, R. V. (2001) 'The personification metaphor as a measurement approach for corporate reputation', *Corporate Reputation Review*, 4(2): 113–27.

de Chernatony, L. (1993) 'Categorizing brands: Evolutionary processes underpinned by two key dimensions', *Journal of Marketing Management*, 9(2): 173–88.

—— and Dall'Olmo, R. F. (1998) 'Defining a "brand": beyond the literature with experts' interpretations', *Journal of Marketing Management*, 14: 417–43.

—— and McWilliam, G. (1990) 'Appreciating brand as assets through using a two-dimensional approach', *International Journal of Advertising*, 9: 111–19.

Denney, F. (1998) 'Not-for-profit marketing in the real world: An evaluation of Barnardo's 1995 promotional campaign', *International Journal of Nonprofit and Voluntary Sector Marketing*, 4(2): 153–62.

Dixon, M. (1996) 'Small and medium sized charities need a strong brand too: Crisis' experience', *Journal of Nonprofit and Voluntary Sector Marketing*, 2(1): 52–7.

Elischer, T. (2001) 'Organizational identity and brand issues', Institute of Fundraising Annual Conference (July), Birmingham, UK.

Fournier, S. (1991) 'A meaning-based framework for the study of the consumer–object relations', in: Holman R. and Soloman M. (eds), *Advances in Consumer Research*, 18: 736–42.

—— (1994) 'A consumer–brand relationship framework for strategy brand management', unpublished doctoral dissertation, University of Florida.

Gardner, B. B. and Levy, S. J. (1955) 'The product and the brand', *Harvard Business Review*, 33(March–April): 33–9.

Grounds, J. and Harkness, J. (1998) 'Developing a brand from within: Involving employees and volunteers when developing a new brand position', *Journal of Nonprofit and Voluntary Sector Marketing*, 3(2): 179–84.

Growman, L. (2000) 'Leveraging the brand', Association of Fundraising Professionals Annual Conference (March), New Orleans.

Hankinson, P. (2001) 'Brand orientation in the top 500 fundraising charities in the UK', *Journal of Product and Brand Management*, 10(6): 346–60.

Harvey, J. W. and McCrohan, K. F. (1988) 'Fundraising costs: Societal implications for philanthropies and their supporters', *Business and Society*, 27(1): 15–22.

Kapferer, J. (1992) *Strategic Brand Management*, New York: Free Press.

Keller, K. L. (1993) 'Conceptualizing, measuring and managing customer-based brand equity', *Journal of Marketing*, 57 (January): 1–22.

Kennedy, S. (1998) 'The power of positioning: A case history from the Children's Society', *Journal of Nonprofit and Voluntary Sector Marketing*, 3(3): 224–30.

Korten, D. C. (1995) *When Corporations Rule the World*, San Francisco, CA: Berrett-Koehler, Inc.

Landon, Jr, E. L. (1974) 'Self concept, ideal self concept, and consumer purchase intentions', *Journal of Consumer Research*, 1 (September), 44–51.

Levy, S. J. (1959) 'Symbols for sales', *Harvard Business Review*, 37(4):117–24.

Ligas, M. (2000) 'People, products and pursuits: Exploring the relationship between consumer goals and product meanings', *Psychology and Marketing*, 17: 983–1003.

McEnally, M. R. and de Chernatony, L. (1999) 'The evolving nature of branding: consumer and managerial considerations', *Academy of Marketing Science Review*, (02), available online at: www.amsreview.org/.

Malloy, D. C. and Agarwal, J. (2001) 'Ethical climate in nonprofit organizations', *Nonprofit Management and Leadership*, 12(1): 39–55.

Meyers, W. (1995) 'The nonprofits drop the "Non" ', *New York Times*, 24 November.

Morris, R. and Martin, C. (2000) 'Beanie Babies: A case study in the engineering of a high-involvement/relationship-prone brand', *Journal of Product and Brand Management*, 9(2): 78–98.

Pidgeon, S. (2002) 'Developing donor lifetime value', Institute of Fundraising Annual Conference (July), Birmingham, UK.

Plummer, J. (1985) 'How personality makes a difference', *Journal of Advertising Research*, 24 (December/January): 27–31.

Putnam, R. D., Feldstein, L. and Cohen, D. (2003) *Better Together: Restoring The American Community*, New York: Simon & Schuster.

Quelch, J. A., Austin, J. E. and Laidler-Kylander, N. (2004) 'Mining gold in not-for-profit brands', *Harvard Business Review*, 82(4): 24.

Riezebos, R. (2003), *Brand Management: A Theoretical and Practical Approach*, Harlow: Pearson Education Limited.

Ritchie, R. J. B., Swami, S. and Weinberg, C. (1998) 'A brand new world', *International Journal of Nonprofit and Voluntary Sector Marketing*, 4: 26–42.

Sargeant, A. and Jay, E. (2004) *Fundraising Management*. London: Routledge.

—— West, D. C. and Ford, J. B. (2001) 'The role of perceptions in predicting donor value', *Journal of Marketing Management*, 17: 407–28.

—— West, D. C., and Ford, J. B. (2004) 'Does perception matter? An empirical analysis of donor behaviour', *Service Industries Journal*, 24(6): 19–36.

—— Hudson, J. and West, D. C. (forthcoming) 'Conceptualising brand values in the charity sector: The relationship between sector, cause and organisation', *Service Industries Journal*.

Schwartz, B. (1967) 'The social psychology of the gift', *American Journal of Sociology*, 73: 1–11.

Spruill, V. (2001) 'Build brand identity for causes, not groups', *Chronicle of Philanthropy*, 13 (June): 45ff.

Sternberg, P. (1998) 'The third way: The repositioning of the voluntary sector', *Journal of Nonprofit and Voluntary Sector Marketing*, 3(3): 209–17.

Tapp, A. (1996) 'Charity brands: A qualitative study of current practice', *Journal of Nonprofit and Voluntary Sector Marketing*, 1:327–36.

Veloutsou, C. (2001) 'Essential qualitative methods for business and management', Les Oakshott: Palgrave (2nd edn); *European Management Journal*, 20 (6): 711–12.

Wee, T., Ming, T. T. and Matthew, C. H. (2003) 'Leveraging on symbolic values and meanings in branding', *Journal of Brand Management*, 10(3): 208–18.

Yavas, U., Riecken, G. and Clabaugh, M. (1980) 'Perceived risk in store choice in the second order market', *Developments in Marketing Science*, 5: 1–4.

Zinkhan, G., Haytko, D. and Ward, A. (1996) 'Self-concept theory', *Journal of Marketing Communication*, 2(1): 1–19.

5

Marketing strategies and portfolio analyses

Kersti Krug and Charles B. Weinberg

Marketing strategies

The long-run growth and success of a not-for-profit organization depend on developing strategies which deliver the organization's mission and carry it to its goals. Although the formulation and implementation of such strategies can be viewed as the fundamental responsibility of management, managers typically find their days filled with short-run operating decisions and other time-consuming responsibilities. Strategic thought, planning, action and reviews tend to get put aside. As a result, too often organizations lose sight of their missions and fail to achieve their goals because they are overwhelmed by day-to-day operating problems. Consequently, strategic plans are not revised as market, competitive and environmental circumstances change, or possibly are never developed in the first place.

Strategic planning involves defining the organization's mission or purpose, setting objectives, formulating strategy, managing resources, and evaluating processes and results. The larger the nonprofit, the more layers of strategy are necessary. A group organized to teach blind youngsters to swim would have a much simpler strategy than a regional community college that serves a large and varied constituency; equally, the regional community college would have a simpler marketing strategy than an international, multipartnered non-governmental organization (NGO). The strategies for the college and the NGO would have many layers, each providing more detailed operational guidance, and coordinated with the levels above and below.

Strategy is concerned with both obtaining resources (through revenues and fundraising) and allocating these resources across the organization's products. In this context, we use the term 'product' broadly to refer to programmes, activities, services, social change initiatives and any other framework that the nonprofit uses to organize itself. Our view is that an organization should take a portfolio approach to the range of activities in which it engages, so that different programmes serve different goals. Overall, too few organizations achieve a balanced portfolio, As a result, they sometimes find themselves overextended financially, participating in markets where they have neither an inherent competency nor a competitive advantage, or are performing inadequately. Examples abound of organizations that have lost their way, with some eventually saved by governments in embarrassing public bail-outs. A Canadian example is the

Vancouver Museum which has struggled since its near demise in the 1990s to recapture its relevance with audiences, donors and city government.

The challenge for not-for-profits is to ensure that revenues can be sustained while focusing on essential purposes. Not only must the heads of these organizations understand how each programme within a complex portfolio of programmes advances mission, how it contributes to revenues and how well it is delivered, but so should staff, board members, volunteers and funding agents – if they are to share the strategic knowledge necessary to support effectively the organization's long-term well-being.

Our main goals in this chapter are threefold: first, to demonstrate that a portfolio approach, specifically designed for not-for-profits, is an effective way to manage an organization strategically; second, to develop a particular approach that suggests that portfolio performance can be evaluated (and resource decisions made) on three dimensions – mission contribution, performance quality and financial impact; and third, to present a graphical approach that allows senior managers to analyse visually their portfolio position and promote alternative views on the organization's current performance and future direction.

Managing the nonprofit portfolio

To help organizations manage their product portfolio, we developed and tested a dynamic, three-dimensional model. As shown in Figure 5.1, which uses the standard programmes in a museum to illustrate the model, the three dimensions involve measures of mission, performance quality and money (revenue/cost coverage). The first dimension measures whether the organization is 'doing the right things'; the second, whether it is 'doing things right' in terms of

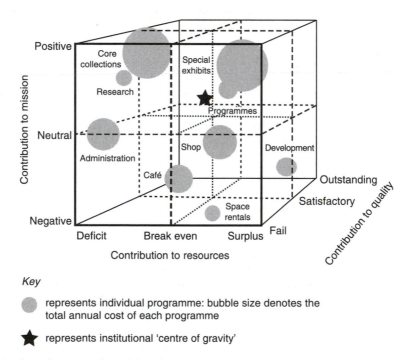

Key

    represents individual programme: bubble size denotes the total annual cost of each programme

    represents institutional 'centre of gravity'

Figure 5.1 Three-dimensional portfolio of ten programmes in a large museum

quality; and the third, whether it is 'doing things right' financially. It can be problematic to support a programme that covers its own costs but does not advance mission, just as it can be problematic to support one that advances mission and covers its own costs but delivers poor service.

The circles, or bubble sizes, represent the associated cost of each programme, allowing the organization to see quickly relative 'price tags' or the organization's annual investment in individual programs. Bubble locations allow management to see how well each programme stacks up against the advancement of mission, how well it is performed, and how well it covers its own costs with associated revenues. By visualizing the quadrant in which different pro-grammes are positioned, managers can more easily isolate which should be bolstered, cut or restructured. By weighting bubble dimensions and assigning locations on the graph, the non-profit can mark its 'centre of gravity' – a pointer that permits it to see where the organization as a whole stands relative to these dimensions. Over time, management can measure progress as it moves programmes in positive directions on mission, resources and performance axes – or changes the relative size of bubbles.

Our empirical testing was initially undertaken in museums – in large part because the political, economic and social environment for museums has changed significantly over the past twenty years. With decreasing government support, museums had entered a new world in which many forgot what their original missions were or actively abandoned them because 'old' mission activities were considered unhelpful in their search for new funding sources. For many, this became a world where increasing budget deficits created cycles of cuts, layoffs and some-times complete elimination of core programmes. It resulted in great turmoil but also significant rethinking of organizational purposes.

This complex environment provided an excellent testing ground for our portfolio approach. As we describe below, the benefits of using the portfolio analysis accrue both from the process of implementing the model and from the outputs of the portfolio analysis.

Mission, merit and money: the portfolio model

This conceptual model was developed and tested in Canadian and American museums, as well as an international charitable organization and a multinational professional accounting firm, and was presented for comment at three nonprofit conferences covering North America, Europe and Australia. The detailed research project was originally published in Krug and Weinberg (2004). Earlier development of the portfolio approach in a two-dimensional frame-work can be found in Lovelock and Weinberg (1989) and Krug (1992).

The tested model has four principal elements:

- the programme and its cost;
- mission;
- performance (or quality); and
- resources (or revenue/cost coverage).

The programme

This is the portfolio's fundamental building block. The definition of what constitutes a pro-gramme (i.e., what is included or excluded) is unique to each organization, and often reflects historic accounting, governing or structural breakdowns. It is important to recognize that management accounting and organizational structures can significantly affect how decision-makers perceive the contribution of a programme or an organizational unit, and how they then plan and make change. Although the portfolio model cannot solve problems inherent in historic structural and reporting relationships, it can help to focus attention on relationships between parts and the whole. It can thereby help to rationalize responsibilities, resources and priorities to better achieve agreed-upon goals. It can also illuminate how structures and cost accounting systems do, or do not, aid organizational decision-making.

Once each programme is defined, a critical input is its total annual cost, preferably including all direct and indirect costs, whether internally or externally directed. Programme cost is an estimate of the nonprofit organization's overall investment in any programme. In Figure 5.1, cost defines the size of each bubble to give management a quick overview of where its resources are deployed and where intervention might have greatest financial, strategic or operational impact.

Mission contribution

This is a subjective judgement based on each manager's appraisal regarding existing mission statements. Input can be sought from one person or many, then combined to form an average assessment. The average may reflect a genuine consensus, but may only be a trade-off among widely divergent opinions about mission contribution. Both can be made explicit by the portfolio model which illuminates hidden assumptions that guide managers' judgements. In the process of exploring how managers arrive at their assessments, the organization gets an opportunity to test its mission as well as expose differences in mission interpretations. It can thereby correct misdirected managerial opinions and actions.

Contribution to quality (or performance)

This indicates how well a programme is delivered. It combines qualitative and quantitative measures depending on what criteria are relevant, what standards are applied and what research instruments are used. For example, attendance or number of people served is a quantitative measure; assessment of what users or clients take from the experience is a qualitative one. Resistance to such output or performance measurement is not uncommon in not-for-profit organizations because evaluation may be seen to restrict professional freedom and challenge expert judgement – especially when the providers of services are so well intentioned. These attitudes do much to alienate programme evaluators, visitor researchers, and auditors whose studies and useful advice are often ignored. The portfolio model, and the process of using it, can bring these different professions together in a common cause to improve long-term organizational effectiveness.

Resource contribution

This requires both cost and revenue data. These are usually quantitative measures taken from financial tables, but are often not organized in a format that allows for strategic judgements. Moreover, cost accounting involves underlying qualitative judgements and accounting precedents for how common services, fundraising, administrative overheads or general revenues are allocated to specific programmes. Use of the portfolio model can both indicate the importance of accurate cost and revenue attribution and show differences in interpretation and understanding of the organization's economic situation. The resource dimension of the portfolio illustrates most clearly the unique situation of nonprofit organizations, which can be great in programme execution and mission advancement yet short of a balanced budget – a deficit they can sometimes make up with fundraising.

We believe that the last three elements are the most important dimensions for portfolio analysis. Other axes can be added as organizations identify what else is important to know for effective, strategic decision-making (see also Kaplan and Norton 1996). However, any model or management tool ceases to be useful if it merely mirrors the complex reality it is intended to simplify. Models should illuminate, not reproduce, reality.

Building a portfolio model

The model is built by converting all elements, both quantitative and qualitative dimensions, to numbers. This includes creating and positioning programme bubbles. Figure 5.2 assumes a large museum with three programmes – Special Exhibitions, Core Collections and Space Rentals. The first, Special Exhibitions, has high curatorial, research, design, construction, public security, publication, insurance, programming, advertising and other costs adding to $10,000,000. Its bubble would be big. The second, Core Collections, has collections registration, storage, loans, database management, conservation and restoration and twenty-four-hour building security costs, adding also to $10,000,000. Space Rentals would have marketing, coordination, event staffing, security, and set-up and cleaning costs, adding to $1,000,000. Its bubble area is one-tenth that of the other two.

As programme definitions often depend on institutional history, they should not include so much detail that people cannot get their minds around what each contains, nor so little that the organization is represented by so many different activities as to be visually meaningless. Six to ten programmes on one graph are ideal. To avoid problems inherent in comparing very large programmes with very small ones, programmes in a graph should vary in size by no more than a factor of ten. A balance must be struck between capturing detail that is meaningful to professional staff and middle managers, and providing a broad overview to senior managers and board members. This can be achieved by rolling activities up from small to large through branching layers that permit both the small to be tracked and the large to be seen.

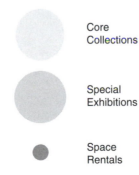

Core
Collections

Special
Exhibitions

Space
Rentals

Figure 5.2 Relative bubble sizes of three sample museum programmes

Providing inputs

Once programmes are defined, they can be positioned on the graph (Figure 5.3). To construct comparative analyses, position values also must be converted to numbers. Organizational participants input their assessments directly to a simple spreadsheet programme which translates individual and collective input to dynamic visuals. Numbers allocated to the three axes should have intuitive meaning. For example, the mission axis uses zero for a neutral contribution to mission (i.e. neither advancing nor detracting), +5 for a maximum positive contribution, and −5 for maximum negative contribution (i.e. anything with a minus sign is not neutral but actively detracts from mission). The goal is to have all programmes above or on the neutral line.

The performance axis uses the familiar grading structure of outstanding, satisfactory and fail, with the maximum score a ten, the mid-point score, five and the minimum, zero.

On the resource axis, programmes that cover 100 per cent of their own costs with revenues they attract are positioned at the break-even point. Other programmes are placed to the left or the right of the break-even point, depending upon whether they produce a deficit or surplus respectively. Surpluses subsidize other programmes. The goal of a not-for-profit organization is typically not to seek profits from every programme, but to achieve a balanced budget from the total mix of programmes. One use of the portfolio approach is both to evaluate fundraising programmes and to mobilize fundraising efforts to overcome identified weaknesses. Alternatively, organizations which face budget deficits may recognize that they need to consider the controversial option of charging for services, which historically were provided at no charge.

In some applications, managers provide their assessment of each programme on each dimension as a single number. In other settings, managers may prefer to provide a range that covers upper and lower limits to their judgements.

While some organizations may only wish to display an overall mean across all managers who participated in the process, it is often interesting to also show individual judgements. Introducing these may produce dynamic dances of programme bubbles which can elicit humour, rich discussions, critical reflection and organizational learning. For example, a programme bubble that flies dramatically from one extreme of the graph to the other suggests that there is significant diversity of opinion or knowledge among managers, or perhaps a lack of internal

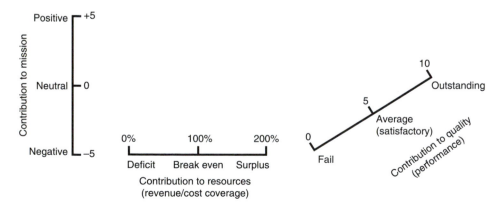

Figure 5.3 Navigation points for assessing contribution to mission, resources and performance

consistency in how the organization delivers that programme. When a programme bubble moves little or not at all, it may be a sign of wide organizational consensus, shared managerial understanding, or, perhaps, the troubling sign of uncritical group-think.

Interpreting the results of a portfolio analysis

Continuing our previous example, we assume that ten senior managers have individually participated in assessing how the three programmes contribute to mission, resource and quality dimensions. Although only a simple representation of an actual museum, it draws on the empirical work that was conducted in museums and on discussions held with museum managers and professionals in the USA, Canada, Australia and Europe.

Contribution to mission

Figure 5.4 shows that the average assessment of ten managers places Core Collections at +4 on the advancement of mission axis, Special Exhibitions at +3, with Space Rentals clearly detracting from mission at −4. Given the different cost weightings (or bubble sizes) of the three programmes, the average (or centre of gravity) for all managers is about +3. Each manager's qualitative judgement regarding mission would normally have drawn on an existing written mission statement

Effective mission statements are a critical part of both using the portfolio approach and building not-for-profit organizational health. Their development, however, is not as easy as it seems. Peter E. Drucker describes the importance of mission (and its lesson for the for-profit sector) to 'focus the organization on action' (1989: 89). He argues that:

> It defines the specific strategies needed to attain the crucial goals. It creates a disciplined organization. It alone can prevent the most common degenerative disease of organizations, especially large ones: splintering their always limited resources on things that are 'interesting' or look 'profitable' rather than concentrating them on a very small number of productive efforts. The temptation to content oneself with the 'goodness of

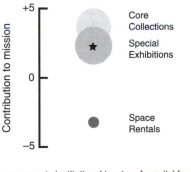

★ represents institutional 'centre of gravity' for three
programmes against mission dimension

Figure 5.4 Management-assessed contribution to mission of museum programmes

our cause' – and thus to substitute good intentions for results – always exists in nonprofit organizations.

Portfolio analysis can contribute not so much to the writing of a mission statement as to its refinement. By working through the model, the organization approaches its mission state-ment in a sense backwards, starting not from a blank piece of paper but from its ultimate impact – as assessed by those who produce the results. The portfolio model unveils the assumptions that colour interpretations of what is written in an existing mission statement, exposing what is ambiguous or open to incorrect interpretation or simply not working as intended.

Once all the input is collected and entered, the museum can see how various programmes contribute to its overall mission – thus answering the question: are we doing the right things? Although the weighted centre in Figure 5.4 is well above the neutral line, manage-ment might now focus on moving Space Rentals up the mission axis. For example, the museum could decide to stop renting space for real estate or investment seminars which only seek convenient locations and cover walls with their own posters and displays, and rent instead to sponsored community service or educational events that find value in this particular space.

To test the presence or lack of consensus, managerial judgement of the contribution of programmes to mission can be displayed. In group discussions, new insights about diverse underlying assumptions can emerge. As discovered during field tests (see below, Anecdote A), some managers may assume that the relevance of Special Exhibitions is tested through exhibit content, whereas others assume that the test has to do with its attractiveness to the museum's visiting public. The exposure of these different perceptions and the breaking down of defences enables the museum to arrive at better decisions and achieve a more genuine consensual support for difficult decisions as individuals begin to understand why decision-making in the past has evoked unexpected dissent, or, in reaction against such dissent, why the quality of decisions has settled for the lowest, least troublesome, common denominator. Revealing hidden assumptions helps to resolve broad institutional issues and improve quality of decision–making.

Anecdote A

The mission statement of a large regional museum spoke of service to the people of their region, including the founding peoples of the area. Despite the existence of their recently revised mission statement, senior managers differed significantly in their interpretation of how or whether the museum's special or temporary exhibitions advanced that mission. One manager concluded the following: 'Last year, when our main exhibition showed [the inventions of a European], mission was not advanced because this inventor has nothing to do with our region. But this summer, when we produced our exhibition jointly with [a nearby community of originating people], our mission was perfectly advanced.' A second manager concluded the opposite: 'This year mission was not well advanced because not many visitors came to see our local, community-based show – so apparently it was only marginally relevant to the public we claim to serve. But last year, when we got huge crowds of visitors from all across this region to see [the inventor's] show, mission was far better advanced because that exhibition obviously reached and was relevant to our public.'

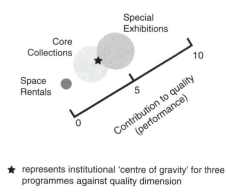

★ represents institutional 'centre of gravity' for three
programmes against quality dimension

Figure 5.5 Management-assessed contribution to quality of museum programmes

Contribution to quality

Quality considerations, or performance, can be analysed through the second axis of the model. In Figure 5.5, the average of managers' assessments shows a rather lacklustre organization. Here Space Rentals are an embarrassment (event organizers bring in their own velvet paintings to cover up the museum's collection of Impressionist art); and Core Collections are deteriorating (objects are dusty, thefts have occurred and conservators have left for jobs which entail higher professional standards). Both do little to bolster uneven productions of Special Exhibitions (websites fail to provide timely information on openings, closings and content, and are visually unattractive; good exhibitions are interspersed with bad, not only confusing visitor expectations, but also, over time, undermining word-of-mouth communication on which nonprofits rely). Poor performance of activities that may advance mission can do damage to that mission. But as we illustrate in Anecdote B, there are often systemic, professional or cultural barriers to evaluating performance rigorously. The degree to which programmes perform in advancing organizational mission without considering performance is, in itself, poor managerial performance. Mission is not enough.

After considering the performance dimension, the nonprofit can answer the question: are we doing things well? It can now better see where to put its efforts to improve programme performance, raise standards and, possibly, discontinue or replace programmes which it does poorly, knows it can never improve and are best left to others. The personal tastes and critical standards of managers are exposed, again launching conversations which strengthen partici-patory decision-making. The museum also discovers what it currently does not know, impel-ling it to conduct marketing research, programme evaluations, audits and other studies to understand better what works and what does not, and how programmes can be nudged in more positive directions.

Anecdote B

In one museum, some senior staff suggested that only peers could judge the quality of their work, but as there were so few experts who actually know which standards to apply, judgements about quality 'are best left to those insiders who are properly trained to assess it'. Some also suggested that if their organization's mission was to educate the visiting public, it made little sense to allow those mass publics to comment on what was delivered. 'It's like getting students to evaluate the professor's work. They don't know enough.' At a subsequent meeting with programme evaluators, auditors and visitor researchers from Australia, Europe and North America, it became clear that these attitudes are widespread. Resistance to evaluations of performance and outputs, these researchers argued, places museums at risk, especially at a time when not only governments but wider publics are demanding accountability and evidence of relevance to justify their financial support. 'The third side of this multidimensional model,' one concluded with visible pleasure, 'can make the studies we conduct more useful to and used by museum professionals and managers who might now see the connection between doing the right thing and doing it right.'

Contribution to revenues

Figure 5.6 shows the results of the ten managers' assessments about where each programme lies relative to the ratio of its revenues to total annual costs. If these three programmes were all that the museum delivered, the institution would be in deficit, perhaps rapidly going broke.

Although Special Exhibitions more than cover their own costs, and Space Rentals provide subsidies to other programmes, the large cost of Core Collections pushes the centre of gravity below the break-even point. Management can now concentrate on specific programmes when considering potential actions: for example, pushing Rentals to be more profitable, reducing the overall cost of Collections, tightening up project management of Exhibitions, or concentrating fundraising efforts in more innovative ways.

Often discussion of the resource dimension is followed by a presentation from the organization's financial/budget staff about accounting issues and estimates of costs and revenues. Both averages and extremes of opinion can be checked as well. In the process of checking, as we show in Anecdote C, the organization can expose underlying assumptions of managers some of whom may have been quite ignorant of the real costs and contributions of programmes. In field tests, managers acknowledged that they had not really appreciated the high cost of Collections or had expected that Space Rentals brought in much more revenue than it did. Many added that they should know these things or that their ignorance had unfairly judged the programmes of their colleagues. Ultimately, the organization can better answer the question: are we doing things right financially?

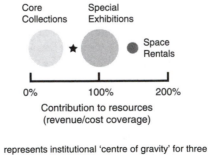

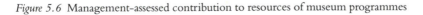

Figure 5.6 Management-assessed contribution to resources of museum programmes

Anecdote C

In a medium-sized museum, evidence of dissent among programme managers was attributed in part to how costs were apportioned to programmes – specifically because the significant costs of public programmes and development were not counted in those units but in other units such as collections and curatorial research that provided these services. For example, when public programmes needed a curator to make a presentation, or when a fundraising event needed collections staff to create the right museum ambience, those resource costs were not passed on to public programmes or development. As a result, these two programmes were considered 'lean' while collections and curatorial were 'fat' – albeit 'necessary burdens' to a museum. Myths about lean and fat programmes were doing much to damage organizational culture and management teamwork, and were risking the organization's capacity to make intelligent adjustments based as they were on misleading and historically skewed or emotionally loaded information.

Combining dimensions

The three model dimensions can be juxtaposed in a single graphical display as illustrated in Figure 5.1. In three dimensions, the organization can get a full overview of how its managers, on average, view its programmes. Although it is difficult in print to show how programmes are positioned dynamically in these three dimensions, we can describe some implications of their overall placements.

First, Special Exhibitions shows up in the top right quadrant in every case – though sometimes only squeaking in. It suggests that further improvements can be effected with minimum interventions in cost containment, revenue enhancement and quality stabilization. Second, Space Rentals provides surplus revenues to subsidize other programmes, but half a million in net revenue against a million-dollar cost may not be enough of a rationale for a large museum to keep it running when the programme is badly performed and seriously detracts from mission. Eventually, if not already, it may be doing more damage than its surplus justifies. Certainly, it needs change. Third, Core Collections may be at the heart of a museum's mission, but the programme has become enormously expensive and not one of whose performance the museum can be proud. It is possible that the poor performance is an outcome of inadequate financial support, but as easily, it could be that grants are not forthcoming because agencies do not see this museum's care of collections as worthy of support. Such a negative cycle is alarming.

Looking further at this hypothetical organization, we find the Shop hovering near the centre lines of all axes. This may suggest that small efforts could enable the programme to make more positive contributions. The types of goods sold could be changed or information provided about Shop goods could be enhanced such that this programme not only advances museum mission better but also attracts more revenue through better performance. The Café with its high prices, tasteless food, dirty tables and slow service falls into the most negative corner of the graph and needs dramatic management attention. Despite its usefulness to tired and hungry museum visitors, it could be replaced by a contracted service whose management knows something about running food services, or simply with comfortable chairs and vending machines.

Research, like Collections, is high on the mission axis, but not performimg well nor able to cover its own costs. Unlike Collections, its cost is small, so management is directed first to improving the quality of scholarship and publications, and later to improving grant applications, developing joint publishing ventures and charging for expert advice or consulting services. Development, which is doing much to keep the organization financially viable, uses overly aggressive methods to attract donors, makes promises to sponsoring corporations which run counter to museum values, and abuses the time of professional staff for ill-conceived, but often 'profitable,' ventures. It needs a deep review of both professional ethics and re-education in museum values.

Administration is generally a cost centre, but its poor performance could be a contributor to the poor performance of several other programmes, to the financial mismanagement of a few programmes, and to inadequate managerial knowledge among heads of programme units. Programmes, small in cost and high in quality, may need to be left alone for the time being to be subsidized by other programmes. Not everything needs to be worked on at the same time.

The centre of gravity shows that the organization as a whole may be positively contributing to mission, but its financial centre shows a current deficit which, if not quickly turned around, will force more draconian action in future. The apparently mediocre performance of several programmes requires equally rapid turnaround before they begin to erode not only mission contribution, but the organization's capacity to attract funding through grants and earned revenue. Management can use the model to play what-ifs, to visualize how much change is required in what programmes to bring the centre to a more positive place. In future, management can review their past actions to see how the centre of gravity has shifted in more positive directions in response to specific interventions. It can also learn whether positive or negative movements on one axis affect movements on other axes.

From institutional to individual input

The examples above have illustrated average ratings of all organizational participants. The variability among managers is not yet visible. Since inputs are entered one person at a time, each individual's estimates (including upper and lower limits, if included) are available. If the organizational culture is safe enough and managers mature enough (although identities need not be exposed), the unveiling of individual judgements can tell the organization and its managers even more. Using as an illustration two different managers' assessment of their museum's three sample programmes on all three axes of the model, we might see the results as represented by Figure 5.7.

The first manager is the one who in our first anecdote (Anecdote A) stated that this year the museum's main Special Exhibition contributed perfectly (a rating of +5) to the mission because it had been done jointly with one of the originating communities in the region. He also gives a high rating for Core Collections, but puts Space Rentals at the far extreme of negative contribution to mission. On the resource axis, he places the two large programmes close to the break-even line: Collections a little under, Exhibitions a little over. He believes that Space Rentals is bringing in twice its cost, so puts it far into surplus. On the performance axis, he assesses the quality of each programme to mirror his rating of its contribution to mission: perfect or very high for Collections and Exhibitions, and a failure for Space Rentals.

Four interpretations of this manager's assessments are possible: first, he may reflect the more 'traditional' museum professional view that values core or educational programmes and involvement with cultural communities over 'commercial' activities; second, he has incomplete knowledge of the actual costs and revenues of programmes; third, he does not bring

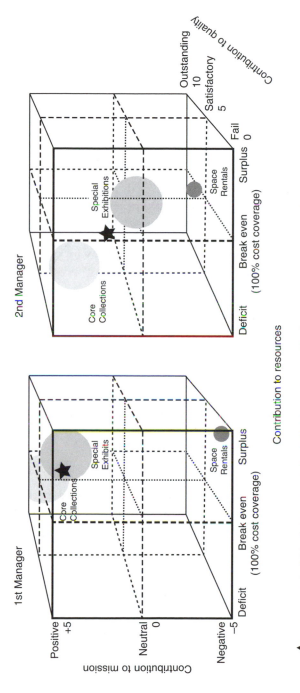

Figure 5.7 Management-assessed contribution to three dimensions of museum programmes

a discriminating eye to programme performance, perhaps assuming that if a programme contributes to mission, it must be well done, and if it does not, that it is poorly done; and fourth, given the very high placement of his centre of gravity, he may see what the museum does as inherently good.

This second manager is the one who said that because this year's main exhibition did not attract many visitors from the museum's region, it did not advance mission (although she acknowledges that it did not detract from mission). She puts Special Exhibitions at 0, or on the neutral mission line. She agrees that Collections Care is what a museum is about, so places that high on mission advancement, but does not relegate Space Rentals to the mission and performance basement. Her assessment of performance does not indicate an automatic relationship to a programme's contribution to mission.

Four interpretations also are possible here: first, this manager brings a less traditional, perhaps more 'business-like' view to what is meant by museum mission; second, she has better knowledge of what programmes actually cost and what they bring in; third, she does not link programme performance to mission; and fourth, given the less positive placement of her centre of gravity, she may be more critical about what the museum does.

Seeing how individuals deviate from the overall institutional average contributes further to individual learning through collective discussions about what the institution is actually doing. For example, it can encourage managers to be more aware of what programmes actually cost and what they bring in, and to disentangle the evaluation of programme quality from its contribution to mission.

This and similar questions are not easy for any management to answer, but the purpose of the portfolio model is not only to answer questions; it also poses and illuminates them. Good questions can be worth more than bad answers.

Conclusion

To repeat, the value of portfolio analysis lies in the process of both conducting and seeing the actual outputs from the process. In our field tests, we found that implementing portfolio analysis based on three critical dimensions of strategic success and in an easy-to-use spread sheet format greatly enhanced its value to managers. The lessons we took home are summarized in Table 5.1.

One of the most useful contributions of management tools such as portfolio analysis is that they can make the complex manageable, the hidden visible and the familiar strange. Computer-aided decision tools can hold and manipulate a huge amount of information in multiple dimensions, yet represent these data with simple graphics or visuals that make complexity understandable to the human mind.

In this chapter, we developed and presented a portfolio management approach to strategic decision-making which can enhance managerial processes and organizational outcomes for not-for-profit organizations.

Table 5.1 Summary of findings

Define programmes properly	Get acceptance	Fit the organization	Assure confidentiality	Separate opinion from fact	Keep it simple	Make it timely
Programmes need to be distinct in meaningful ways to justify separate treatment and evaluation. In the model, six to ten programmes of significance work best.	Not everyone uses models intuitively nor interprets data visually. Disappointment or rejection of the model is a natural response. Patient building up of its features helps.	The portfolio model works best in open organizational cultures and in nonprofits with adequate programme complexity, though breakdowns of single programmes are possible.	Ensuring participant confidentiality, especially at the beginning, is important and can be aided by selecting the right person for information management. As the process proceeds, managers begin to self-reveal.	Dependability of input needs more than majority opinion and acknowledgement that territorial biases exist. Accurate figures, rigorous analyses, systematic research, evidence and experience still have a place in management.	Although the model can accommodate other dimensions, the three here provide sufficient complexity. Familiar, off-the-shelf software eases the process.	Using the model is best in normal strategic planning and annual budgeting cycles – perhaps twice a year. As the portfolio approach can be used at different levels of the organization, the process can be sequenced to build up or pass down the organization.

Table 5.1—continued

Invite broader input	Test future what-ifs	Require performance evaluation	Consider summary measures	Learn safely and enjoyably	Expose systemic issues	Improve mission statements
Computer capacity enables input from individuals beyond the management cadre (e.g. volunteers, staff, board members) and offers a natural extension towards more robust decision-making.	Testing of proposed new directions and changed priorities provides a potential new tool to better-considered decisions as well as buy-in to change.	The merit (performance) axis invites input of often-resisted expertise. It supports the nonprofit's demonstration of accountability to boards, governments, and other publics.	The centre of gravity is an aggregate measure. Though optional, it provides a quick fix on where the nonprofit as a whole stands. Its comparative value comes over time.	Expressing opinions as numbers and showing them as dynamic graphics are more likely to evoke learning and enjoyment than defensive interpersonal reactions.	In the process of making underlying assumptions concrete and visible, portfolio analyses expose organizational and accounting issues (e.g. inclusions, exclusions, balances, impacts) which would otherwise be hidden.	By assessing programmes against mission, not only are programmes scrutinized, but so are the mission statements themselves and their varying interpretations by managers.

References

Andreasen, A. and Kotler, P. (2003) *Strategic Marketing for NonProfit Organizations*, Don Mills, ON: Pearson Professional.

Doyle, P. and Stern, P. (2006) *Marketing Management and Strategy* (4th edn), Harlow, UK: Prentice Hall Financial Times.

Drucker, P. F. (1989) 'What business can learn from nonprofits', *Harvard Business Review*, July–August: 2–7.

Kaplan, R. S. and Norton, D. P. (1996) *The Balanced Scorecard: Translating Strategy into Action*, Boston: Harvard Business School Press.

Krug, K. (1992) 'Profit or prostitution: Portfolio analysis for museum marketing', *MPR News* (International Council of Museums Bulletin), 2(2).

—— and Weinberg, C. B. (2004) 'Mission, money, and merit: Strategic decision-making by nonprofit managers', *Nonprofit Management and Leadership*, 14(3): 325–42.

Lovelock, C. (2004) *Services Marketing: People, Technology, Strategy* (5th edn), Upper Saddle River, NJ: Prentice Hall.

—— and Weinberg, C. B. (1989) *Public and Nonprofit Marketing* (2nd edn), Redwood City, CA: Scientific Press.

Lowy, A. and Hood, P. (2004) *The Power of the 2x2 Matrix*, San Francisco, CA: Jossey-Bass.

McLeish, B. J. (1995) *Marketing Strategies for Nonprofit Organizations*, New York, NY: John Wiley & Sons.

Winer, R. S. (2007) 'A strategic marketing framework', Ch. 2 in *Marketing Management*, 3rd edn, Upper Saddle River, NJ: Pearson Prentice Hall.

6

Marketing and religion

Sandra Mottner

Introduction

Marketing as a recognized practice and subject of study is a veritable infant when compared with the practice and study of religion. Since prehistoric times, humankind has been attempting to explain the world around it through religious beliefs and practices. Even with the advent of 'organized religion', the notion of marketing being used on behalf of a religion is a very modern concept (Moore 1994). Although many religious groups have been practising marketing, they have been calling the practices 'tithing' rather than fundraising, or 'evangelism' as opposed to recruitment. In fact, the very idea of marketing and religion used in the same phrase is considered sacrilegious to many individuals (Cutler 1991; Moncreif *et al.* 1986). However, leaving these judgements aside, there is ample evidence of marketing tactics and tools being strategically used to further the goals and objectives of religious organizations (Fielding 2006). In a world where many churches have experienced declining attendance, such as in the UK and the USA, the use of marketing tactics to reverse that trend is timely. In fact, as many US churches experience declining attendance, others have increasingly adopted marketing tactics and reversed the visitation trend (Wellner 2001). This chapter examines the use of marketing to further the goals and objectives of religious organizations in a nonprofit marketing framework and brings together the major literature extant in the field and identifies specific research needs. First, however, it is important to review the world of religion and put the concept of marketing activities of religious organizations into context.

Religious beliefs vary widely, but most often are used to explain things that people cannot understand or give an individual or group of people something in which to trust other than themselves (Harrison 2006). Religions also serve to define rules for behaviour (Harrison 2006). While some people have the freedom to choose their own beliefs and practices, other groups of people have no choice. Obviously, when a group of people have freedom of choice about their religious beliefs and/or practices there is an increased ability for marketing to play a role. One of the founding principles of the USA was the strong belief in freedom of religious choice. Consequently, the USA has a greater degree of religious freedom than many countries, and therefore many of the examples used in this chapter are US based. Interestingly, the largest segment of funds raised for US nonprofits is for religious organizations (Giving USA

Foundation 2006). Even though the USA has freedom of choice with respect to religion, it does have a strong Christian tradition in which all types of Christian religions and denominations are represented. Consequently, most examples in this chapter will also be based on the Christian religion and when an organized religious body is mentioned in this chapter the word used is often 'church', when in fact a mosque, synagogue or other religious organization could be substituted in many cases.

This chapter is primarily concerned with marketing being used to influence people to change their behaviour with respect to religion in some way. The behaviours that are being changed include: (a) joining an organized religious group, either from another religion (conversion) or from having no religion; (b) maintaining or increasing 'loyalty' to a certain type of religion; (c) increasing the level of 'religiosity' and conformity to a specific religion's norms; (d) increasing one's depth of belief or faith in a religion; and (e) financial support of religious organizations. These behavioural changes are both public and social as groups of people change their behaviour. However, the changes take place on an individual basis as well. Marketing tactics being used to change a public behaviour fit the description of social marketing. However, the behavioural change has at its core a fundamental change in an individual's beliefs. Consequently, the marketing of religion will tread on some very personal space and is a matter that needs to be dealt with in a highly sensitive and ethical manner.

Besides fitting the social marketing construct (Abreu 2006), marketing practices of religious organizations also fit with the idea that marketing can be used in the nonprofit arena and for social causes and not just for products and services (Kotler and Levy 1969). Religious organizations, churches and synagogues and their hierarchies are classified as nonprofit organizations in the USA as are most religious organizations worldwide. However, while the goals and objectives of individual religious organizations vary by religion the hallmarks of nonprofits, scarcity of resources, use of volunteers, multiple stakeholders and a perceived mission to do 'good works' (Sargeant 1999) fit churches well.

The nature of marketing and religion in the USA has changed with time. For example, the last few decades have seen the growth of a number of mega-churches in the USA. Some of these churches use tactics such as Internet marketing, television campaigns and sophisticated micro-targeted efforts. Some churches, such as the Church of Latter Day Saints (Mormon) have grown their number of believers through missionary efforts worldwide. These personal selling campaigns rely on personal testimony, 'sales' training, skilled openings and closing and other personal selling devices. Word-of-mouth campaigns also function effectively and represent organized marketing efforts in many cases. As can be seen, all of these examples can be examined in marketing terms. This chapter discusses how marketing can be related to furthering the goals and objectives of religious organizations. The topics covered in this chapter include:

- religion and the market orientation paradigm – a discussion of the orientation models of religious organizations and the implications for marketing;
- religion's customers and consumers – identification of the publics involved in marketing of belief systems;
- strategy – strategic planning in religious marketing;
- brand – how branding strategies are used by religious organizations;
- money – fundraising and revenue generation;
- the service – how the services marketing framework fits the marketing of religion and helps to define the marketing tools;
- performance measurement – using marketing metrics; and
- a research agenda – a brief recap of many of the things that we need to know.

Overall, this chapter is reviewing much of the existing literature. Further, the chapter discusses the application of marketing theories and practices to the aforementioned topics. Faith-based parachurch organizations such as the Salvation Army will only be nominally discussed. Parachurch organizations are faith-based organizations whose primary mission is to provide social services, raise consciousness and mobilize political action (Sargeant 2005). Finally, the chapter concludes with a research agenda for scholars, religious leaders and religious and marketing practitioners.

The chapter will not be discussing the major role that religious beliefs or affiliation or the strength of those beliefs (religiosity) play in consumer behaviour and markets (Mittelstaedt 2002). Additionally, this chapter does not seek to explore the use of religion, religious metaphors and religious symbols in for-profit marketing communications. Nor do the discussions seek to promote or in any way denigrate any religious beliefs or practices. It is hoped that this very interesting and fundamentally important area of research and discourse will not remain as underresearched and underdiscussed as it has in the past (Cutler 1991) and this chapter will provide some 'food for thought' and inspiration towards further reading, writing and research.

Religion and the market orientation paradigm

The paradigm in marketing today is the construct of marketing orientation, the concept that organizations are most successful when they are customer driven. However, as posited by Sargeant et al. (2002) this is not necessarily a good model for explaining marketing in the context of the nonprofit organization. They (Sargeant et al. 2002) offer a model of societal orientation in which mission, values and beliefs are antecedents of a societal orientation which produces societal benefits. Social orientation includes a focus on stakeholders, competition, collaboration, interfunctional coordination and responsiveness. This model fits religion fairly well.

Religious organizations are mission driven by definition. Their mission is determined by their beliefs. However, in order to reach the goals and objectives of a religion and thereby achieve their overall mission, they will assume different perspectives or orientations. Wymer et al. (2006) define four different orientations in which a nonprofit (or social) organization rationalizes what is important. Wymer et al. (2006) name these respectively as: (a) cause orientation; (b) offer orientation; (c) fundraising orientation; and (d) needs-centred orientation. Obviously, nonprofit organizations fit into one or more of these orientations. However, organizations that are needs centred are most likely to develop and implement successful mission-based marketing strategies. Hence, the work of Wymer et al. (2006) in developing indicators for the differing orientations has provided a method of evaluating the orientation of a nonprofit.

As noted in Table 6.1, the indicators developed by Wymer et al. (2006) have been reformulated for churches. While it is likely that churches that are primarily needs centred will be most successful in meeting their goals and objectives, all religious organizations would likely deem that their mission and beliefs must be central and paramount to all plans. When the public perceives that a church organization is moving away from its central mission, then public trust and perceptions will fall. For example, churches which are perceived as being primarily focused on fundraising might enjoy a short-term financial success, but have limited long-term success in achieving their mission and could even have their downfall celebrated by many, thus damaging the religion itself. A good example of this is the case of the televangelist Jim Bakker and his PTL

Table 6.1 Nonprofit orientations adapted for churches (based on Wymer *et al.* 2006: 64)

	Churches with a:			
	Cause orientation	*Offer orientation*	*Fundraising orientation*	*Needs-centred orientation*
Have an organizational focus on,	the mission and beliefs of the church	the church offerings★ (salvation, programmes, services, rituals, etc.)	raising funds	needs of the population
Hire employees or seek volunteers to do marketing who,	believe in the religion and its mission	are knowledgeable about what the church offers★	are knowledgeable about fundraising and financial management	have marketing knowledge
Believe that competition comes,	from other churches or lack of deep belief	only from similar churches such as denominations who have similar offerings★	from any other church or religiously based organization	from other religions, churches, charities and a large number of other choices
Answer questions by,	looking to church teachings and beliefs	looking to what the church or religion offers★	looking at past fundraising efforts or the fundraising efforts of other churches	relying on research
Believe that when it comes to market segmentation,	their religion is for everyone and no market segmentation is needed	that their religion should recognize the correctness of their religious practices and therefore no segmentation is needed	everyone is a target for fundraising and little segmentation if any is needed	their beliefs are for everyone but targeting segments is important
Believe that when it comes to market strategies,	their religion is the 'true way' so people will be naturally drawn to it	the focus should be on what the church offers but not on the other parts of the marketing mix	the focus should be on persuading anyone who may be a target for fundraising through promotion	a well-planned marketing strategy using all parts of the marketing mix for a variety of marketing segments is important
Believe that when marketing strategies fail,	the un-churched or believers in other religions or members of other churches just don't care, are influenced by Satan (or other dark forces!), are too lazy or have some other defect that does not allow them to see the truth	the people don't fully understand the meaning and importance of the offerings★	fundraisers aren't doing their jobs well	the marketing strategy is flawed and needs to be researched and redeveloped

★ Offering(s) in this context is used to describe such things as programmes, services and activities.

Club (Praise the Lord Club), which built a tremendous financial base and then had the ministry disintegrate with a sex scandal, bankruptcy, mail and wire fraud convictions, and income tax issues (Knight Ridder Tribune News Service 2002).

An example of being needs centred and mission driven is the case of unchurched parents who perceive a need for moral reinforcement and learning outside of the home for their children. A needs–centred church organization will recognize this unmet need in its community and develop offerings such as Sunday school classes, pre-schools, day care and promote these offerings to parents. Churches learn of the need through feedback from church members, market research or other means and realize that it applies to one primary segment of the population (the parents) and a secondary or derived market (the children). The result of this effort is that parents' need for moral training for their children is met. The mission-driven church, however, also has the opportunity to work with both the children and the parents to change possibly their beliefs and bring them into the church community. The more thorough the church is in determining the size, scope and attributes of the need, the more effective they can be at meeting the need.

Religion's customers and consumers

One of the hallmarks of a nonprofit organization is that there are numerous and varied stakeholders (Sargeant 1999) and often multiple customers and/or consumers. This is very true in the case of religious organizations. An excellent tool for defining the various stakeholders is the model used by Wymer et al. (2006) which identifies four major groups: (a) input publics; (b) internal publics; (c) partner or intermediary publics; and (d) consuming publics. Understanding and identifying the various stakeholders helps to understand better the multiple marketing strategies that could be employed by religious organizations.

Input publics

Input pulics are the people or organizations who provide resources and constraints to a nonprofit organization (Wymer et al. 2006). It could easily be argued that among all organizations, religious organizations have a most unique input public and that is a higher power, God, a supreme being, prophet(s) or a divine being. As in the Judaic Christian tradition, God has set forth laws and prophecies that have been received by prophets, apostles and others and have become written documents (Torah and Bible) that provide a guide for the beliefs of the religious organization as well as a source of regulation and constraint. The supreme power (or powers) also serves as a strong internal public as well, directing the believer/leaders of the religious organizations' actions. This unique role of a supreme being, a God or some type of higher power is unique among organizations and reinforces that the beliefs of the religion and the overriding mission perspective of religious organizations must be honoured in all actions.

The cross-public role also applies to donors of the religious organization who most often are the members of the religious organization and who carry out the mission of the organization as well. The donor-members not only donate their money, but their time and abilities and talents. Ecumenical efforts between Christian denominations also represent an input public type of role being exercised. Local, state and national governments can regulate the behaviour of religious organizations, particularly through tax regulations which constrain behaviour and also supply tax relief to churches thereby also modelling input public behaviour.

Internal publics

The internal publics (the staff and volunteers who carry out the organization's mission) of religious organizations vary depending upon the size and complexity of the church organization. The Roman Catholic Church, for example, has a long tradition of management of its church organization starting with the Pope and descending through cardinals, archbishops, bishops, priests, and so on. Volunteer parishioners often supply additional public support to gain converts, minister to the needy, and perform outreach and other good works to their communities. Any person working directly for the religious organization either paid or volunteer is an internal public.

Partner or intermediary publics

Partner publics include marketing agencies, consultants and other professionals who are hired or volunteer their firm's services in order to help the organization to realize its objectives. There are also examples of partner publics in outreach parachurch organizations such as St Vincent DePaul, for example. There are also limited examples of for-profit and religious cooperation in a form of cause-related marketing.

Consuming publics

The consuming public is the population of believers and populations that the believers serve. The believer, the consuming public, is analogous to a customer and a consumer in the for-profit world. Understanding the nature of the greater body of consuming publics, both believers and non-believers, is key to the ability of an organization to implement a marketing strategy.

'Consumer behaviour' with respect to choosing a church or religious belief system, behaviour within the religion and other aspects of the consuming public sector is a relatively understudied area from the marketing perspective in particular. While the study of religious beliefs, religiosity and related topics has been examined in terms of consumer behaviour outside of the religion and church organization, much needs to be addressed within religions itself. While some scholarly work has been done in the *Journal for the Scientific Study of Religion* and the *Journal of Religion and Society*, much is needed from a marketing perspective. One phenomenon which is of particular interest to marketing strategists is the 'church shopping' phenomenon, which is particularly of note in the last two centuries as Protestants shopped between denominations.

This also underscores the need for market research on the part of religious organizations. An interesting example of how this has been used effectively is in the mega-church phenomenon in the USA. Two mega-churches have keyed into the need on the part of many individuals and families for a feeling of community and belongingness (Fielding 2006). Both the message of the churches' advertising and the services provided for families and individuals give those who join these congregations a feeling of 'home' in the sense of a community of like-valued people.

Strategy

Among other things, a marketing strategy defines target market(s), the competitive advantage, competitive positioning and the marketing-mix tools. The strategic marketing process also includes decisions about branding and fundraising. A discussion follows of target markets, competitive strategies, branding and fundraising with respect to religious organizations followed by a discussion of the tools in the marketing mix discussed in a services marketing context.

Target markets

In beginning the planning process of a marketing strategy, the religious organization identifies all the 'publics' mentioned earlier, assesses the current external and internal situation and then keeping its mission foremost the target market is developed. These target markets could include market segments that are already being served, segments that are underserved, or segments that are not being served at all. In the USA today there is a sizeable group of 'unchurched' (Wellner 2001), a clear target market that forms part of an underserved population. Segmentation implies a thorough knowledge and understanding of the markets, including information from market research. The use of market research is inconsistent in religious organizations at the current time.

Competition and competitive strategies

It could be argued that there are several levels on which organized religions compete. On one level, there is competition for the hearts, minds and souls of any given population as opposed to other religious faiths or lack of religious faith. On another level, there is competition between differing religious denominations. Religious organizations also compete for their market's time and attention against entertainment options, time commitments, consumer distractions, peer pressure and lack of a perceived need for religion. Clearly defining the competition becomes as important as determining one's target market segments and is a key challenge for the strategic marketer. Offer-oriented organizations (see Table 6.1) can easily become disoriented here because they will tend to define the competition by their offerings rather than by what needs the competitors are serving.

There are a number of different competitive strategies and their use in the marketing of religion is particularly underresearched. Most of the competitive strategies of religious organizations are not 'head to head'. Rather, most competitive strategies are reflected in how an organization positions itself in the minds of its consuming public. Brand-positioning strategies, which are discussed in the following section of this chapter, are the primary strategies used to position differing organizations. Just as with for-profit marketing, some religious organizations will position themselves as mass marketers, while others have adopted or made small niche markets (Busenitz and McDaniel 1990).

Examples of a niche strategy being very successfully used is that of small, African-American MEA churches throughout small communities in southeastern USA. These often historic churches serve a vibrant and cohesive community with very similar needs and histories. Niche strategies on an even smaller scale are often used for newly arrived groups of people in the USA who form small churches which speak their native language and use native customs. Examples of mass-appeal strategies are those of the nondenominational mega-churches which meet the needs of very large and often very geographically extended communities (Fielding 2006). These mega-churches have successfully identified themselves as having a mass and wide appeal versus other religious choices partially through the use of very successful branding strategies.

Branding

The concept of branding is an increasingly accepted practice in the nonprofit venue (Hankinson 2001) and indications of branding being used in the religious sector are becoming more evident (Abreu 2006; Fielding 2006). The key concept to consider in branding is the image or identity of the organization. The identity of any religious organization is clearly tied to its beliefs and its mission. Merely renaming the 'brand' does not change the image or identity. Branding is as much an internal process as an external one and in the case of nonprofits affects and involves all of the various publics described earlier. New churches, especially the new nondenominational mega-churches in the USA, have the ability to develop easily a brand identity when compared with such venerable institutions as the Church of England. For non-profits in general, and churches in particular, the core beliefs, the mission, do not change; however, some of the tools of branding can be used to meet the churches' goals and objectives.

Branding language helps to identify some of the tools and strategies that may be used. These include: (a) brand name; (b) brand personality; (c) brand equity; (d) brand positioning; (e) brand image; (f) brand campaign; (g) brand identity; and (h) brand promise. The last phrase, 'brand promise', should be the first addressed as it goes to the core of not only the beliefs of a religion but also implies that religion does offer a 'promise' to its believers. The brand promise means different things to different market segments and individuals at different times. An example of a 'brand promise' is the feeling of community promoted in advertisements that appeal to a certain segment of society (Fielding 2006). However, in offering a community of like believers, the mega-church is staying true to its mission and its core beliefs which must be the overriding issue in religious marketing (Abreu 2006). The brand image, brand personality, brand identity and the brand name all serve to help to position the brand in people's minds. These are powerful and effective tools that can help a religious organization deliver its brand promise. Brand positioning is often used to not only appeal to certain market segments but as a powerful competitive tool as well (Hankinson 2001).

Money

Fundraising for religious organizations is a form of nonprofit fundraising. However, in some religious organizations, fundraising is not always seen in a positive light. For example, Christians have often heard the story of Jesus driving the money-changers and merchants out of the temple (Holy Bible, John 2:14–16). This story is often used as a metaphor for not mixing matters of money and matters of belief and faith. However, the reality is that churches and religious organizations need money with which to pay their expenses, including their ministers and priests, marketing expenses, providers of music and other services, maintenance of church buildings and property and all the other products and services needed to achieve their goals and objectives. Further, major capital expenditures are needed at times and specific fundraising is undertaken for these causes. Finally, there are a number of outreach programmes sponsored by churches that need funds with which to accomplish their goals. Hence, money is often a major issue and need on the part of church organizations. Not surprisingly, Christian church leaders will often quote Bible passages to support the idea that giving to the church is a good idea as in this passage:

> Each one must do as he has made up his mind, not reluctantly or under compulsion, for God loves a cheerful Giver. And God is able to provide you with every blessing in

abundance, so that you may always have enough of everything and may provide in abundance for every good work.

(Holy Bible, 2nd Corinthians 9: 7–8)

Similarities between church fundraising efforts and nonprofit fundraising abound. Major gifts in various forms from outright cash gifts to bequests and property transfers are often pursued using relationship-building similar to those used by sectarian nonprofit organizations. Understanding the motivations of the potential donor (input public) takes time and careful attention. Major capital campaigns to construct new buildings, establish other locations, send missionaries to new locations, buy organs, fund the establishment of a church school, and so on, are the types of campaigns with which nonprofits are very familiar. Numerous plans for raising funds for these projects abound and professional fundraising services provide assistance as do many religious headquarter organizations.

Annual fundraising commitments, pledge drives and similar 'membership' financial efforts are common in many churches. Often the 'pledge drive' is led by church members and/or the clergy and is intended not only as a fundraising tool but also as a means of planning a budget for the next year. Members are often encouraged to tithe during this process, although the manner of figuring the tithe can be ambiguous and open to self-serving bias (Dahl and Ransom 1999). Banks have also become involved in lending money to churches based on tithing, pledges and/ or capital-fundraising campaigns (Harris 2001).

The raising of funds for the church can result in 'positive effects for donors and nonprofits' (Thornton 2006: 204). Fundraising in the church, just as with nonprofit organizations in general, needs a good understanding of the motivations and needs of the donors. Donors will obviously donate funds to the organization that most matches their own ideology (Thornton 2006) and as such the membership base of the church is the first market segment looked to for fundraising.

Beyond fundraising efforts, whether through major gifts, campaigns for specific causes or regular membership giving, many churches also pursue revenue from other sources. These activities include church stores similar to those at museums (Ford and Mottner 2003). Fielding (2006) notes the example of churches having concession stands with some of their activity venues. The traditional rummage sales, bake sales and even silent auctions continue to raise revenues as well. Often the money brought in through revenue-raising activities is directly targeted at a specific mission or outreach project (Ford and Mottner 2003).

The service

Religious organizations fit neatly into the framework of services marketing primarily due to the intangibility of what they offer (Santos and Mathews 2001). Tangible products, if any, are minimal. Consequently, in discussing the marketing tools that are used by religious organizations it is helpful to use the framework of the 7 Ps of services marketing: (a) product or service offering; (b) price; (c) promotion; (d) place; (e) physical evidence; (f) process; and (g) people (Booms and Bitner 1981). Finally, the evaluation of service quality is discussed as an essential part of the marketing tools associated with a service.

Product

The primary offerings (services) of religious organizations are layered. The foundation layer is the offering of a belief system and includes such things as salvation, spirituality, and so on. The more immediate service offering includes worship services, educational programmes and recreational activities (Coleman 2002). Different parts of the offerings have more importance for different age cohorts than others. For example, while the worship service is very important to all ages, service music associated with the service is more important to older cohorts than to younger cohorts, while the reverse is true of sports and activities (Coleman 2002). The application of product/service strategies such as market segmentation, positioning and differentiation could all conceivably play a significant role in the strategic plan of a religious organization. Anecdotal evidence indicates that strategic planning of this sort is occurring in mega-churches in particular, but academic research is lacking. New product development, however, may differ in some respects for for-profit practices and bears investigation. While Bennett and Savani (2004) have found a strong indication of parallel product/service development patterns between nonprofit and for-profit practices in civic organizations, the unique and intensely personal nature of religion may indicate differing product development practices for religious organizations.

Price

Attending a worship service is ostensibly 'free'. However, looking at what religious organizations 'offer' in terms of a 'value proposition' could yield some interesting findings both in terms of the perceived benefits received as well as the 'costs' to potential and/or current attendees. Research in this area is underdeveloped.

Promotion

An array of promotional tools is being used by religious organizations in order to communicate with their target market segments. The tools include advertising, personal selling/personal communication and public relations. Personal communication whether through word of mouth or personal visit is widely used by churches and is a form of relationship building and personal selling. Personal communication takes the form of visits by clergy, acknowledgement of visitors during services, orientation class for prospects and similar personal contacts (McDaniel 1986b).

Indeed, personal communication in the form of word of mouth is one of the most effective means of promotion by churches (Coleman 2002). An example of a word-of-mouth promotion tool in action is the Alpha International non-denominational programme which started in the UK as a means of bringing non-Christians into the Christian church. The programme specifically targets people under 34 years of age and involves local discussion courses. While Alpha International also sponsors conferences and publications, its success is generally attributed to non-threatening, non-denominational friendly communication (Anon. 2003). Word of mouth is also used by evangelical Christian mega-churches which, unlike traditional churches, 'normally exist to serve people who want to enter the door and adhere to the ways of the Bible. Seeker churches would rather figure out ways to tailor their services and sermons to the needs of attendees' (Buss 2002: 42).

Advertising is increasingly being used by churches in the USA (McDaniel 1986a). Advertising is still a problematic choice for some church members, but clergy are generally more approving of advertising, handbills, radio, TV and newspaper use than the general public. Both generally approve of onsite signage and Yellow Pages listing (McDaniel 1986a). Advertising can be used to target specifically a particular market. For example, in an effort to reach the declining Generation X cohorts, advertising agencies were hired to produce professional advertising pieces including subway advertisements, websites and others while adjusting offerings to reflect the need for non-traditional meetings. Coffee shops, cafés, entertainment, music concerts or even a partnership with a Manhattan jazz club were part of a Generation X-targeted campaign (Wellner 2001). Moncrief *et al.* (1986) noted that advertising was used in a wide variety of denominations in a regional multidenominational sample of Christian churches. The perception was that some denominations (Baptists) advertised more than others. Advertising media choices were topped by Yellow Pages, then newspapers, direct mail, signs, radio, flyers, TV, billboards and finally magazines. In 2002 Coleman found that word of mouth led media choices followed by Yellow Pages, the Internet, TV, newspaper, and radio – although this differed somewhat by age group.

Just as evangelists found television in the later part of the twentieth century, many churches are currently using the Internet as a communication tool. Using a virtual church experience through the Church of Fools website (http://www.churchoffools.com), sponsored by the Methodist church, researchers found that the Internet communication tool first attracted people out of curiosity. Subsequently, the website served a significant religious need for a large number of website visitors. With the exception of the sacrament of communion which had some mixed reactions, the satisfaction with the website has been significantly positive (Ostrowski 2006).

Place

While place usually refers to the distribution of goods in the marketing world, in the case of religious organizations the place issue is one of location – not unlike the retail decision about store placement. Like retail stores, the location of the church, mosque, synagogue, temple or shrine represents a major and long-term commitment on the part of a religious organization, which is difficult and costly to change. In many locations, decaying inner-city neighbourhoods with large older church buildings (even cathedrals) restrict the organizations from drawing in new members. The marketing implications become many of those faced by retailers. Proximity to attendees (core customers), distance from competition among other variables play a part in retail location decisions (Karande and Lombard 2005) just as they may play a role in religious organizations' location decision.

Physical evidence

Because the offerings of religious organizations are intangible, physical cues make the offerings more 'real' to the population being served (Booms and Bitner 1981). Therefore, tangible attributes (or atmospherics) of a religious organization that are visible, audible, touchable, and even things that can be tasted and smelled are important. Religious organizations have a long and rich tradition of doing a very good job of this through such things as their structures, whether small or large. The building offers a very visible sign often of strength, tradition and identity. However, just as the traditional architecture of banks has changed from imposing stone structures (built to engender trust on the part of their customers) to ATM machines in the shopping mall to meet the changing needs of consumers, the religious organization is altering its physical image as well. Physical symbols used in and on churches are part of the organization's identity and bear a striking resemblance to the use of logos in marketing.

Mega-churches tend to be modern, spacious, often pristine and with soaring ceilings. While some people deride these buildings for their similarities to conference centres or shopping malls the case has been made that these new buildings leave behind the image and symbolism of 'older' religious institutions. The new mega-church buildings are more functional; in fact they are multifunctional, and systematic interviews with the leaders of these churches indicate that they see their modern new buildings as one of their key tools for achieving their mission not only because of its functionality but because of the freedom from traditional design (Loveland and Wheeler 2003). Hence, while the Gothic style of many traditional Christian churches are meaningful to some segments, the new churches are meaningful to other segments. Similarly, the use of light, stained glass and modern lighting systems is also important physical evidence of a strategy that helps to bring meaning to the consuming public.

Other physical cues beyond the buildings include both music and spoken word. Again, the religious organizations have a long and rich tradition in this area – as well as with writings in many religious traditions. Physical evidence is an area in which many religions have been using marketing strategies unwittingly to help to tangibilize their message and help it to become more 'real'. Many of these practices are part of ritual and even sacrament depending upon religion. However, as a religion develops a marketing strategy it is an area that demands attention and is underresearched from a marketing perspective.

People

People who provide the service offerings of a religious organization include clergy, priests, lay ministers, church elders, councils, professional musicians, cantors, volunteers of all sorts, and many more. The lesson offered by the service marketing field is that training, selection and scheduling of the right people at the right place and time is essential. Since much of the work of religion is also done by volunteers, the issues of managing often enormous volunteer staffs become critical in implementing a marketing strategy. This area is in need of research and development. While priests, clergy and other leaders have long and extensive training in theology and even the management of a church in some cases, the evidence is that their marketing training is patchy at best.

Process

Process in services marketing refers to a diversity of topics. However, an example of process in religion is the use of multiple Sunday services being offered at different times to not only handle large groups of people but also to serve best the needs of different groups with different services. Since religion is both an individual and a group practice, religious organizations need to address both the process of servicing individuals as well as groups. Application of marketing practices from theatre in terms of group process would bear researching. Further, implementation of systematic fundraising processes should maximize fundraising efforts (Bennett 2005).

Service quality

In considering the marketing of religion within a service framework, it is appropriate and important to evaluate the service offered using one of the service quality measurement tools available. Santos and Mathews (2001) developed a specific scale to measure service quality in religious organizatios. Responsiveness, credibility and commitment were found to be the most critical elements of service quality in the perception of a wide variety of church-goers. Gender was the only factor that was significantly different among a variety of demographic attributes tested (Santos and Mathews 2001). Extending this significant contribution to the literature to different religious populations and practical applications should further the effectiveness of fine-tuning service marketing strategies.

Performance measurement

Beyond measuring the service quality as mentioned above, the last part of developing a strategic marketing plan (after planning and implementation) is devising specific means for evaluating the outcomes and making adjustments to the plan as needed. As professional marketers know, the measurement of performance is critical in evaluating the use of certain marketing tools, the allocation of assets (money and people) and future marketing plans. Most marketing outcomes are best evaluated in terms of the objectives and goals of the organization and the strategies used to achieve them. Evaluation can include attendance at worship service and other events and activities as well as the number of converts, number of members, funds received from various sources and new members. Forms of 'market share' between religious organizations also help. Busenitz and McDaniel (1990) used the following performance measurement tools: attendance, number of visitors, rate of growth, baptisms, new members, financial contributions and personal growth (including personal discipline, outreach to non-members, helping one another with personal needs and participation in church leadership). Many of these types of statistics have been historically collected by most religious organizations. However, getting more information with respect to public perceptions of offerings and marketing tools, service quality perceptions, value perceptions and more sophisticated measures of efficiencies (marketing inputs versus results) would be helpful for future marketing decisions.

One particularly interesting performance measurement system is an adaptation of Kaplan and Norton's (1992) 'balanced scorecard' which Keyt (2001) adapted for religious organizations. While traditional measures are important, the adaptation of the four measures of the balanced scorecard help to emphasize the marketing processes and multiple outcomes that occur in a developed marketing environment (Keyt 2001). An adaptation developed by Keyt (2001) is shown along with examples of how it might be used in Table 6.2.

Table 6.2 Balanced scorecard adapted for churches (based on Keyt 2001)

Kaplan and Norton (1992)		Keyt (2001)	
Perspective	Indicator example	Perspective	Indicator example
customer	market share	members/attenders	% of regular attendees
internal business for new	level of customer service support	internal ministry	provide support programmes
financial	stock price	ministering	number of individuals served in outreach programme
innovation/learning	new product introductions	innovation/ learning	new programme introductions

A research agenda

It is obvious that there are many areas of the marketing of religion which lack academic research and that considerable discussion and thought is warranted in this intriguing and often controversial field. Throughout future discussions and research, however, one key principle is important to remember and that is that the mission of any given religion is the central cause and reason for being. Marketing, however much it aligns itself with religious practices or with for-profit practices, is merely a tool which can be used to reach more effectively and efficiently the goals and objectives of a religion. The following is a list and discussion of just some of the areas where research is warranted.

First, a better knowledge of the consuming publics and the other publics is needed. For example, do we know what the attributes of specific marketing tools are that are most important to differing market segments? One interesting book that demonstrates how a consumer culture moderates religious belief/practice and offers an interesting perspective is Miller (2003). Another research project by Coleman (2002) looks at which church practices, activities and programmes attract new visitors but this needs further development and extension.

The internal public of religious leaders, both professional and volunteer, needs examination as well. How do they view the marketing of religion? A cross-cultural analysis was made by Sherman and Devlin (2000) who looked at British and US clergy. Further, how do religious leaders get training in professional, mission-based marketing? Moncrief et al. (1986) found that journals and magazines were used most often to learn about marketing and that formal training in seminary or business classes was very low and that church members, other ministers and consultants provided most of the information. There are obvious signs that this has altered since that article but information is scant.

Which marketing tools are most effective in which situations? When and how should they be used? What is the state of marketing and religion in different cultures and different faiths? How do some of the specific tools of a services marketing framework work in the venue of organized religion? For example, complaint behaviour, part of the service quality literature, has been examined for one church (Hansen and Woolridge 2002) and that study could be extended. How do different marketing tools work in different cultures? A study of the use of religious advertising in Hong Kong (Au 2000) helps to illuminate the reaction from both Christians and non-Christians in a multiculturally based primarily ethnically Chinese society. There are so many other settings and cultures to review. Branding research is also limited as is the research on church fundraising and social outreach through 'parachurch' organizations such as the Salvation Army, Habitat for Humanity, Bread for the World, and so on. This area was well discussed in an editorial (Sargeant 2005) which reflected on how doing something tangible – rather than the more intangible of giving money to the church – is an important act and point of difference for many donors. Now, empirical support is needed. On a very broad scale, the use of the American Marketing Academy's newer definition of marketing which emphasizes relationships versus the older definition which emphasizes exchange could help to understand and discuss the role of marketing in religion.

The preceding is just a partial list of the research that is needed but it is hoped that this chapter gives the reader a sense that marketing can be used in religion, that there is much to learn and that discussion of the topic is appropriate and helpful.

References

Abreu, M. (2006) 'The brand positioning and image of a religious organization: An empirical analysis', *International Journal of Nonprofit and Voluntary Sector Marketing*, 11(2): 139–46.

Anonymous (2003) 'Case study – Religion: A is for alpha, C is for Christ', *Brand Strategy*, October: 3.

Au, A. K. M. (2000) 'Attitudes toward church advertising in Hong Kong', *Marketing Intelligence and Planning*, 18(1): 39–45.

Bennett, R. (2005) 'Implementation processes and performance levels of charity Internet fundraising systems', *Journal of Marketing Channels*, 12(3): 53–78.

—— and Savani, S. (2004) 'New product development practices of urban regeneration units: A comparative international study', *International Journal of Nonprofit and Voluntary Sector Marketing*, 9(4): 291–308.

Booms, B. H. and Bitner, M. J. (1981) 'Marketing strategies and organization structures for service firms', paper in the proceedings of the Marketing of Services Conference, Chicago.

Busenitz, L. and McDaniel, S. W. (1990) 'Focused versus general marketing strategies in a religious setting', *Journal of Professional Services Marketing*, 61(1): 167–82.

Buss, D. (2002) 'Peddling God', *Sales and Marketing Management*, 154(3): 42–8.

Church of Fools (2006) 'Sponsored by the Methodist Church of America', available at http://www.churchoffools.com (accessed 27 November 2006).

Coleman, B. C. (2002) 'Appealing to the unchurched: What attracts new members', *Journal of Nonprofit and Public Sector Marketing*, 10(1): 77–91.

Cutler, B. D. (1991) 'Religion in marketing: Important research area or a footnote in the literature?', *Journal of Professional Services Marketing*, 8(1): 153–64.

Dahl, G. B. and Ransom, M. R. (1999) 'Does where you stand depend on where you sit? Tithing donations and self-serving beliefs', *The American Economic Review*, 89(4): 703–28.

Fielding, M. (2006) 'Tend to the flock', *Marketing News*, 15 May: 14–17.

Ford, J. B. and Mottner, S. (2003) 'Retailing in the nonprofit sector: An exploratory analysis of church-connected retailing ventures', *International Journal of Nonprofit and Voluntary Sector Marketing*, 8(4): 337–48.

Giving USA Foundation (2006) *Giving USA 2006: Annual Report on Philanthropy*, Indianapolis, IN: Giving USA Foundation.

Hankinson, P. (2001) 'Brand orientation in the charity sector: A framework for discussion and research', *International Journal of Nonprofit and Voluntary Sector Marketing*, 6(3): 231–42.

Hansen, S. W. and Woolridge, B. R. (2002) 'An empirical investigation of complaint behaviour among church members', *Journal of Consumer Satisfaction, Dissatisfaction and Complaining Behavior*, 15: 33–51.

Harris, K. (2001) 'Banks take a look at faith-based lending', *American Bankers Association Banking Journal*, 93(9): 7–8.

Harrison, V. S. (2006) 'The pragmatics of defining religion in a multicultural world', *International Journal for Philosophy of Religion*, 59: 133–52.

Holy Bible, the, revised standard version, Cleveland: World Publishing Co.

Kaplan, R. S. and Norton, D. P. (1992) 'The balanced scorecard – Measures that drive performance', *Harvard Business Review*, 70(1): 71–80.

Karande, K. and Lombard, J. R. (2005) 'Location strategies of broad-line retailers: An empirical investigation', *Journal of Business Research*, 58(5): 687–95.

Keyt, J. C. (2001) 'Beyond strategic control: Applying the balanced scorecard to a religious organization', *Journal of Nonprofit and Public Sector Marketing*, 8(4): 91–102.

Knight Ridder Tribune News Service (2002) 'Bakkers went from PTL fame to IRS debtors', *Knight Ridder Tribune News Service*, 11 October:1.

Kotler, P. and Levy, S. J. (1969) 'Broadening the concept of marketing', *Journal of Marketing*, 12(2): 10–15.

Loveland, A. C. and Wheeler, O. B. (2003) *From Meetinghouse to Megachurch: A Material and Cultural History*, Columbia: University of Missouri Press.

McDaniel, S. W. (1986a) 'Church advertising: Views of the clergy and general public', *Journal of Advertising*, 15(1): 24–9.

McDaniel, S. W. (1986b) 'Marketing communication techniques in a church setting: Views of appropriateness', *Journal of Professional Services Marketing*, 1(4): 39–54.

Miller, V. J. (2003) *Consuming Religion: Christian Faith and Practice in a Consumer Culture*, New York, NY: Continuum.

Mittelstaedt, J. D. (2002) 'A framework for understanding the relationships between religions and markets', *Journal of Macromarketing*, 22(1): 6–19.

Moncrief, W. C., Lamb, C. W. Jr. and Hart, S. H. (1986) 'Marketing the church', *Journal of Professional Services Marketing*, 1(4): 55–63.

Moore, R. L. (1994) *Selling God: American Religion in the Marketplace of Culture*, New York, NY: Oxford University Press.

Ostrowski, A. (2006) 'Cyber communion: Finding God in the little box', *Journal of Religion and Society*, 8: 1–8.

Santos, J. and Mathews, B. P. (2001) 'Quality in religious services', *International Journal of Nonprofit and Voluntary Sector Marketing*, 6(3): 278–89.

Sargeant, A. (1999) *Marketing Management for Nonprofit Organizations*, Oxford: Oxford University Press.

—— (2005) 'Editorial-church and parachurch fundraising in the United States? What can we learn?', *International Journal of Nonprofit and Voluntary Sector Marketing*, 10(3): 133–6.

—— Foreman, S. and Liao, M. (2002) 'Operationalizing the marketing concept in the nonprofit sector', *Journal of Nonprofit and Public Sector Marketing*, 10(2): 41–65.

Sherman, A. and Devlin, J. F. (2000) 'American and British clergy attitudes towards marketing activities: A comparative study', *Services Industries Journal*, 20(4): 47–62.

Thornton, J. (2006) 'Nonprofit fundraising in competitive donor markets', *Journal of Nonprofit and Voluntary Sector Quarterly*, 35(2): 204–24.

Wellner, A. S. (2001) 'Oh come all ye faithful', *American Demographics*, 23(6): 50–6.

Wymer, W. Jr., Knowles, P. and Gomes, R. (2006) *Nonprofit Marketing*, Thousand Oaks, CA: Sage Publications.

Part 2

Fundraising

7

Individual giving behaviour

A multidisciplinary review

Adrian Sargeant and Lucy Woodliffe

Introduction

In the USA, total giving to the nonprofit sector in 2004 stood at $248.52 billion, representing a 2 per cent increase over the previous year (AAFRC Trust 2005). A staggering 90 per cent of Americans offer donations to nonprofits with people giving on average 2 per cent of their income and contributing 76 per cent of the total income accruing to the sector (the balance coming from corporations, foundations and bequests) (AAFRC Trust 2005).

Explaining this generosity is a topic that has long been of interest (Wispe 1978). Over the past three centuries, several schools of thought have emerged from the economics, clinical psychology, social psychology, anthropology and sociology literatures. More recently, marketing's contribution to the subject has been recognized and a succession of authors has now demonstrated its utility (Bendapudi *et al.* 1996). The intention of this chapter is to draw together the disparate strands of this literature, highlighting the implications of prior research, and developing a composite model of giving behaviour.

The model proposed is illustrated in Figure 7.1. In the review that follows, each dimension of the model is considered and justified in turn. A review of all pertinent work is presented and the key findings from empirical studies are summarized in a table accompanying the explanation of each stage of the model. For the sake of brevity, the more intuitive findings are omitted and those most likely to be of interest to fundraising practitioners focused on.

The literature presented was compiled in 2006/7 by reference to the Proquest, PsychINFO and Business Source Premier databases. In addition, since a number of the nonprofit journals are not abstracted on these services, a manual review was undertaken of all articles published in these sources. Finally, a review was undertaken of books stored in the Indiana University Philanthropic Studies Library. The keywords donor, donation, fundraising and fund-raising were employed for the purposes of each search. While it is impractical here to cite every work identified, the works listed in the review that follows are felt to be representative of the current state of research in this field.

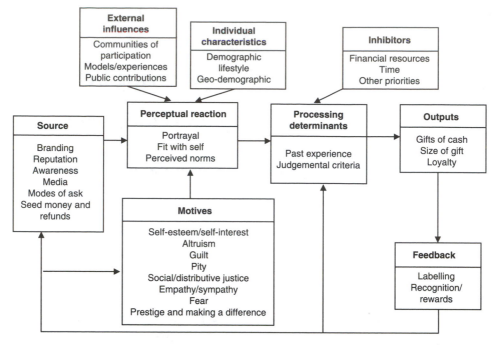

Figure 7.1 Giving-behaviour model

Source

Analysis begins by examining extant work on the 'source' of the fundraising solicitation. Emergent work on nonprofit branding, the impact of awareness, the use of specific media and the overall approach adopted have developed our understanding of the characteristics of successful fundraising solicitations.

Branding

As Tapp (1996: 335) notes, while 'charities do not describe much of what they do as "branding", organizations have long been concerned with maintaining a consistent style and tone of voice and conducting periodic reviews of both policies and actions to ensure that a consistent personality is projected'. In his view, the clarity with which this 'personality' is projected will have a direct impact on an organization's ability to fundraise (see also Grounds and Harkness 1998). Venable *et al.* (2005), following Aaker (1997), identify four dimensions to the nonprofit brand personality, namely integrity, nurturance, sophistication and ruggedness. Sargeant and Hudson (2005) argue that the picture is more complex, identifying three facets of charity personality shared by the sector as a whole. In a study of 9,000 individual donors the authors find that only values pertaining to the dimensions of 'emotional stimulation', 'service', 'voice' and 'tradition' are capable of distinguishing between organizations. Interestingly, it is only those facets of personality perceived to be distinctive that are linked to donor behaviour.

Reputation and awareness

Work by Kelman (1961) suggested that messages are more likely to be accepted by donors when the organization is already known to them and is perceived as reputable. McNair (2005) demonstrates empirically a link between awareness and donations, while Bendapudi et al. (1996) offer a potential explanation, suggesting that if understanding of the nonprofit's image is lacking, donors may either ignore communications or 'distort' them to preclude their support. Stark (1989) highlights the significance of agency theory in relation to this issue, since in making donations donors are in effect requiring nonprofits to act as their agents in disbursing funds. The reputation of a nonprofit will provide numerous clues as to how well a particular nonprofit will perform in this capacity.

Social impact theory (Latane 1981) also tells us that the role of reputation may vary by context. In less personal forms of fundraising, for example, direct mail, press or radio advertising, donors may be entirely reliant on their perception of the organization in deciding to offer a donation. In face-to-face forms of fundraising, the donor will have a number of more immediate cues that may trigger a donation, such as the number, gender and appearance of solicitors.

Media

Nonprofits currently engage in a variety of different fundraising techniques employing media such as direct mail, telemarketing, face to face (on the street), door to door, press advertising, radio advertising and DRTV (direct response television) (Sargeant and Kaehler 1998). An emergent body of literature on benchmarking the performance of specific media suggests that both initial returns and the lifetime value of supporters recruited will vary by media employed (Sargeant and McKenzie 1998; Sargeant et al. 2006). Extant work also reports that the profile of the donors recruited by each media may vary in terms of their demographic, lifestyle and behavioural characteristics (Jay 2002; Aldrich 2004).

Mode of ask

As Levis (1990) reminds us, to get a donation it is necessary to ask, since few gifts arrive unsolicited. The form of the solicitation, or mode of ask, has received considerable attention. Authors such as Fraser et al. (1988), Reeves et al. (1987) and Weyant (1984) identified that legitimizing low-value contributions (i.e. with a phrase such as 'every penny will help') can greatly improve compliance in face-to-face forms of solicitation. Brockner et al. (1984), Reeves et al. (1987) and Weyant and Smith (1987) conclude that this approach is less effective in other less personal forms of fundraising such as direct mail (see also Weyant 1996). The appeals scale (i.e. the discrete menu of amounts from which potential donors choose the level of their donation, for example, $2, $10, $25, $50, etc.) used by the fundraiser has also been shown to influence donor behaviour, notably the distribution of donations received (Desmet and Feinberg 2003). This suggests that fundraisers should use appeals scales as a way to optimize, rather than facilitate donations, by considering whether the scale is in line with donor expectations and reference systems.

Work by Wang et al. (1989: 181) notes the impact of 'reciprocal concession' on fundraising. Individuals, they note, 'are obliged to respond with a favor after other individuals have made a concession to them'. Thus in personal forms of solicitation, the authors argue it is better to begin by asking for a high sum and then if the donation is refused at that level to offer a concession (see also Cann *et al.* 1975; Cialdini and Ascani 1976; Mowen and Cialdini 1980). It is interesting to note, however, that other studies have found that multiple asks will also be effective where the initial request is *lower* than the target (Cann *et al.* 1975; Freedman and Fraser 1966), so we may only conclude that multiple asks are more effective in generating compliance than solus asks.

Freedman and Fraser (1966) argue that charities should solicit new donors by beginning with requests for small sums and then building these up over time. This is echoed in modern fundraising practice where many UK charities solicit gifts of as little as $5 per month (Pidgeon 2001). Zuckerman *et al.* (1979) suggest that this process works well since a low-value ask eliminates many potential barriers to giving. Where donors cannot post-rationalize their giving as a response to social or other pressures they are significantly more likely to attribute their first donation to caring about the cause and hence to continue to support the organization.

The utilization of techniques which engender a stronger sense of relationship has also been found to increase compliance (Roloff 1987; Roloff *et al.* 1988; Aune and Basil 1994), with a number of writers noting the 'foot-in-the-mouth' effect. In essence, there is strong evidence to suggest that on commencing a solicitation, asking people how they feel, acknowledging their response and then asking for a donation greatly enhances compliance. Howard (1990) argues that people will behave in a manner consistent with the state that they have described themselves as feeling. If prospects reply that they 'feel great' they will strive to maintain a consistency in what Osgood and Tannenbaum (1955) refer to as their 'general affective state'. It is therefore much less likely that a donation will be refused (see also Bem 1965; Howard 1990; Cialdini and Schroeder 1976). It is interesting to note that the gender of the asker would also appear to have an impact (Lindskold *et al.* 1977), as would the level of familiarity the prospect has with the individual making the request (Macaulay 1975).

Empirical studies pertaining to mode of ask are summarized in Table 7.1.

Table 7.1 Empirical studies pertaining to mode of ask

Author(s)	Method	N	Key findings
Aune and Basil (1994)	Field experiment; face-to-face solicitations	153 (students)	Foot-in-the-mouth (FITM) approaches generate positive relational perceptions, but relational obligations approaches produce more positive relational perceptions than the FITM approach.
Brockner *et al.* (1984)	Field experiment; telephone and face-to-face solicitations	90	Requests for smaller sums increase compliance without lowering the value of the mean contribution. Compliance greater in face-to-face contexts.
Cann *et al.* (1975)	Field experiment	60	In face-to-face contexts it is optimal to ask for a high sum and then offer a concession on refusal.
Cialdini and Ascani (1976)	Experiment	189	Rejection then retreat procedures are superior to techniques that do not involve the offering of a concession.
Cialdini and Schroeder (1976)	Two field experiments; door-to-door solicitations	84 + 169	Utilizing the phrase 'even a penny will help' enhances compliance without lowering the mean contribution – hence maximizing donated funds.

Table 7.1—continued

Author(s)	Method	N	Key findings
Desmet and Feinberg (2003)	Experiment	'large-scale'	Both the appeals scale used and the values on the scale influence the distribution of donations received. Three reference systems (points on the appeals scale, values of common denominations, intended or anticipated amount) should be taken into account when designing the appeals scale, to avoid donors 'resisting' the options on the scale and engaging in habitual behaviour.
Fraser *et al.* (1988)	Field experiment; house-to-house solicitation	640	Utilizing the phrase 'even a penny will help' enhances compliance without lowering the mean contribution – hence maximizing donated funds.
Freedman and Fraser (1966)	Two field experiments; telephone solicitation	156 + 127	Multiple asks effective where initial request is lower than the target. Finding holds even where second ask is unrelated and carried out by a different person.
Howard (1990)	Multiple field experiments; telephone solicitations	80, 120, 160	Asking someone how they feel, and then acknowledging that response facilitates compliance with a charitable request.
Lindskold *et al.* (1977)	Field experiment; face-to-face solicitations	3,000 (students)	Female solicitors generate more compliance in personal asks.
List and Lucking-Reiley (2002)	Field experiment	3,000	Increasing seed money from 10% to 67% of a campaign goal produces a nearly sixfold increase in contributions.
Macaulay (1975)	Experiment	131	Increase in familiarity leads to increased positive action irrespective of the attractiveness of the requester.
Mowen and Cialdini (1980)	Two field experiments; face-to-face solicitation	192 +216	By making a second request for a reduced proportion of the original the researcher can increase a target's perception of a concession which invokes the norm that concessions should be reciprocated.
Reeves *et al.* (1987)	Field experiment; house-to-house solicitation	240	Requests for smaller sums increase compliance without lowering the mean value of the contribution.
Reingen (1978)	Field experiment; face-to-face solicitation	224 (student sample)	Utilizing the phrase 'even a penny will help' enhances compliance without lowering the mean contribution – hence maximizing donated funds.
Roloff *et al.* (1988)	Questionnaire	60 (students)	Increasing intimacy with a potential helper increased obligations to grant requests for resources.
Staub and Baer (1974)	Field experiment	58	Individuals more likely to help when 'escape' is hindered, or subject is in their path. *continued*

115

Table 7.1—continued

Author(s)	Method	N	Key findings
Wang *et al.* (1989)	Field experiment; house-to-house solicitation	409	In face-to-face contexts it is optimal to ask for a high sum and then offer a concession on refusal.
Weyant (1984)	Field experiment; house-to-house solicitation	359	Requests for smaller sums increase compliance without lowering the value of the mean contribution.
Weyant and Smith (1987)	Field experiment; postal solicitation	6,000	Requests for smaller sums increase compliance without lowering the mean value of the contribution.
Zuckerman *et al.* (1979)	Experiment; telephone solicitation	127	Foot-in-the-door technique increased the likelihood of compliance with a relatively large demand.

Seed money and refunds

Some professional fundraisers believe that a substantial amount (40 to 50 per cent) of the total fundraising goal should be pledged as seed money before starting a public campaign (Fundraising School 1999). This is in keeping with Andreoni's (1998) positive theory of capital campaigns (for example, an initiative to build a new university building) for public goods. Later, Andreoni (2006) argues that 'leadership giving' – where a large donation is made by an individual, foundation or even government at the start of a fundraising project – can inspire others to donate, as it acts as a signal of the quality of the charitable good. List and Lucking-Reiley (2002) were the first to provide quantitative empirical support for this model of charitable giving, finding that increasing seed money from 10 per cent to 67 per cent of the campaign goal produced a nearly sixfold increase in contributions, both through more individuals contributing, and larger sizes of gifts.

Perceptual reaction

Whatever form the ask might eventually take, there are a number of variables which the literature suggests will tend to impact on a potential donor's perceptual reaction to the message being conveyed. In particular, donors receiving positively framed messages, designed to make them feel good, are statistically more likely to respond than those donors offered primarily negative messages, designed to make them feel bad (Benson and Catt 1978). The key variables impacting on perceptual reaction would appear, however, to be the portrayal of the individual(s) in need, the fit of the charity with a given donor's self-image and the existence of perceived norms of behaviour. Each of these variables will now be considered in turn.

Beneficiary portrayal

The portrayal of the charitable 'product' can have an impact on recall, attitudes towards support and actual giving behaviour. Donors will tend to support those charities that represent the needy in an acceptable way (Eayrs and Ellis 1990). Pictures of, for example, an overtly handicapped child have been shown to actually decrease the response to door-to-door giving solicitations. Similarly Isen and Noonberg (1979) report that a picture of a starving child in door-to-door solicitations reduced compliance. Brehm (1966) argues from reactance theory that people possess a number of behavioural and attitudinal freedoms. Distressing photographs act to reduce a prospective donor's perceived ability to be able to spend their monies elsewhere and hence, ironically, create barriers to the gift being made (see also Brehm and Brehm 1981). It has also been argued that donors perceive depictions of 'excessive' need as manipulative and, hence, compliance falls (Moore *et al.* 1985). The balance of evidence thus suggests that the strength of need depicted should be strong enough to indicate the worthiness of the case, but not so strong that it is seen as a 'hard sell'.

Appeals for charities concerned with disability often emphasize the dependence of those individuals with the respective disability. There is now considerable evidence that such appeals are successful in engendering feelings of sympathy (Brolley and Anderson 1986; Feldman and Feldman 1985; Lattin 1977; Jones 1985; Roehler 1961) and feelings of guilt and pity (Feldman and Feldman 1985; Krebs and Whitten 1972; Pieper 1975). The literature is less united, however, in respect of the degree to which dependency should be exhibited. Writers such as Berkowitz and Daniels (1962) and Midlarsky (1971) conclude that greater degrees of perceived dependency are related to greater degrees of help. Wagner and Wheeler (1969) meanwhile conclude that when the level of dependency is perceived as permanent, the level of dependency has no effect on the amount likely to be given. Using different terminology, Adler *et al.* (1991) identify that portraying recipients as succumbing to their condition (in contrast to coping) has no impact on the pattern of donations. They do however identify a strong impact on the subsequent attitudes of the donor towards the recipient group.

This latter point is of particular interest since many authors argue that portraying people with disabilities as dependent may well harm the long-term interests of the beneficiary group by reinforcing negative stereotypes and attitudes (Elliot and Byrd 1982; Harris and Harris 1977). Positive portrayals, on the other hand, seem to engender positive attitudes (Harris 1975; Shurka *et al.* 1982). On a related theme, there is evidence that attractive people are perceived as more worthy than unattractive people (Latane and Nida 1981) and that female subjects would appear to engender greater rates of compliance than male subjects (Feinman 1978; Gruder and Cook 1971). The portrayal of the responsibility of recipients for their own condition can also impact on compliance. Piliavin *et al.* (1975) identified that the extent to which an individual could be blamed for his/her needy condition would directly impact on both the degree of compliance and the levels of support proffered.

The discussion above has focused on portrayals made on behalf of the beneficiaries by the charity. In some cases, the appeal may be made and donation received directly by the beneficiary. While research on direct donations is limited, Hibbert *et al.* (2005) have studied beneficiary portrayal in the case of the *Big Issue*, a magazine produced by independent UK companies and sold by homeless, ex-homeless and vulnerably accommodated individuals on urban streets, as part of a social franchise. The vendors make a profit on each magazine, which provides them with an income. Hibbert *et al.* (2005) found that consumers preferred to buy the magazine from those who appeared more needy than those who were getting back on their feet. They conclude that the manner and behaviour of vendors is assessed by buyers and potential buyers, which influences whether they purchase or repeat purchase.

Empirical studies pertaining to portrayal are summarized in Table 7.2.

Table 7.2 Empirical studies pertaining to portrayal

Author(s)	Method	N	Key findings
Adler *et al.* (1991)	Experiment	148 (students)	Coping portrayals led to more positive attitudes towards people with disabilities than subjects in a succumbing condition. No differences were found between the two conditions in respect of the sums donated.
Berkowitz and Daniels (1962)	Experiment	32 (students)	Significantly greater levels of performance are associated with a high dependency condition.
Brolley and Anderson (1986)	Experiment and questionnaire	91 (students)	Positive advertisements do not foster more positive attitudes towards disabled persons than negative advertisements.
Eayrs and Ellis (1990)	Experiment	100	Commitment to give money is most closely associated with feelings such as guilt, sympathy and pity and was negatively associated with posters which illustrate people with a mental handicap as having the same rights, values and capability as non-handicapped persons.
Feinman (1978)	Experiment	156	Female subjects receive more help than male subjects.
Feldman and Feldman (1985)	Experiment	60 (students)	Telethons have a strong positive influence on the viewing public's perception of disabled persons. These attitudes do not impact significantly on donation behaviour.
Gruder and Cook (1971)	Experiment	113 (students)	Dependency made no difference to the help given to males, but females who were dependent received significantly more help than females who were not dependent. They also received marginally more help than males who were dependent.
Hibbert *et al.* (2005)	Focus groups and questionnaire (interviewer administered)	645	The appearance and manner of *Big Issue* vendors influences public reactions towards the initiative.
Midlarsky (1971)	Experiment	80 (students)	Greater degrees of perceived dependency are related to greater degrees of help.
Milgram (1970)	Experiment	160	Female subjects receive more help than male subjects.
Moore *et al.* (1985)	Panel	360 (198 of which present in all time periods)	A significant direct relationship was found between labelling conditions and attitudes towards giving and perceptions of the nonprofit organization.
Piliavin *et al.* (1975)	Field experiment	166 trials	The natural appearance of a victim impacts on the rendering of help. Attractive subjects generate more help than unattractive subjects. The extent to which a subject could be blamed for their own condition also impacts on helping behaviour.

Table 7.2—continued

Author(s)	Method	N	Key findings
Shurka *et al.* (1982)	Four experiments	Four groups of 24 (students)	The order of favourability for portrayals is 'coping not responsible', 'coping responsible', 'succumbing not responsible', 'succumbing responsible'.
Wagner and Wheeler (1969)	Experiment	144	Need as defined by the solicitor had no impact on helping, but adjunctive analyses suggested that models could influence need as perceived by the prospective donor, which in turn could affect helping.

Fit with self

In respect of the second variable, fit with desired self-image, Coliazzi *et al.* (1984) noted that individuals are more likely to help those who are perceived as being similar to themselves. They will thus tend to filter those messages from charities existing to support disparate segments of society. The extremely wealthy, for example, tend to avoid causes involving the overtly poor (such as homelessness) and are much more likely to patronize organizations from which they, or members of their social class, can draw benefit. As Ostrower (1997: 133) notes, they carve out a separate and exclusive arena for themselves quite distinct from the 'philanthropic arena of the economically disadvantaged', supporting causes such as the arts, education and healthcare. Similarly, Millett and Orosz (2001) identify that those from ethnic minorities are significantly more likely to filter out messages from nonprofits not serving members of their community. Similarity may also take the form of similarity of values, which as Heider (1958) notes, may be just as powerful as physical similarity. Interestingly, differences in response to perceived similarity have been reported between individuals of different personality types. Individuals with authoritarian personalities are much more likely to be motivated by perceived similarity than those with egalitarian personalities (Mitchell and Byrne 1973).

Perceived norms

A factor closely related to the above is the issue of perceived norms. Donors will be motivated to filter messages on the basis of normative concerns (Morgan *et al.* 1979). People appear to pay considerable attention to what others contribute within their respective societal group. According to Rege (2004), the social approval a person gets from adhering to the norm is positively correlated with the share of the population adhering to this norm. Thus not only will donors tend to support individuals perceived as similar to themselves, the pattern of that response (or lack thereof) will be made in terms of beliefs about what is normative for the group (Blake *et al.* 1955; Macaulay 1970).

Cialdini (1984), for example, notes that the knowledge that others are contributing legitimizes contribution, and Reingen (1978) identified that showing prospective donors a fictitious list of previous donors led to higher donations and increased compliance. It is interesting to note that the length of the list of previous contributors also appeared to be an issue with longer lists outperforming shorter ones. More recently, Jones and McKee (2004) demonstrate that feedback information on relative sizes of received contributions during a fundraising campaign impacted positively on individual and total contributions, although Andreoni and Petrie (2004)

found that revealing the identity of the donor, as well as the contribution amounts was necessary for giving to increase significantly. Experimental research by Gächter and Fehr (1999)
reveals that social approval incentives (revealing the identity and contributions of each subject,
and making subjects discuss the contributions) have a significant effect on giving behaviour, but
only on those who know each other. However, Rege and Telle (2001) found that this effect
extended to strangers too – the social approval incentive of writing contributions on a black-
board in front of subjects unknown to each other increased contributions by as much as 100 per
cent.

Empirical studies pertaining to 'fit with self' and 'perceived norms' are summarized in
Table 7.3.

Table 7.3 Empirical studies pertaining to fit with self and perceived norms

Author(s)	Method	N	Key findings
Andreoni and Petrie (2004)	Experiment	200 (students)	Revealing the identity of the donor, as well as the contribution amounts is necessary for giving to significantly increase.
Blake et al. (1955)	Experiment	50 (students)	Size of a donation is governed by the size of gift presumed to be 'standard' by the group as a whole.
Bryan and Test (1967)	Four field experiments	4000 + 730 + 140 + 3703	Presence of a helping model significantly increased helping behaviour. Interpersonal attraction is a relevant variable in affecting donations.
Callero et al. (1987)	Postal questionnaire	685	Role-person merger strongly associated with a history of helping. Role-person merger predicts helping behaviour.
Cialdini et al. (1990)	Multiple experiments	139 + 358 + 484 +127 +87	If other members of a particular group are contributing, then the pressure to comply to social norms mounts.
Coliazzi et al. (1984)	Experiment	128	Factors which facilitated altruism include amount of need, similarity to the person in need and cost to the helper.
Gächter and Fehr (1999)	Experiment		Social approval incentives have a significant effect on people who have some knowledge of each other, but no effect among subjects who are strangers.
Jones and McKee (2004)	Experiment	90 (students)	Feedback information on relative sizes of received contributions offered during a fundraising campaign impacted positively on individual and total contributions.
Keating et al. (1981)	Telephone interviews	1,000	Rates of giving are positively related to social pressure and income. More personal forms of solicitation are more effective.
List and Lucking-Reiley (2002)	Experiment	3000	Increasing seed money from 10% to 67% of a campaign total increased contributions by a factor of six.
Macaulay (1970)	Experiment	131	Increase in familiarity leads to increased positive action irrespective of the attractiveness of the requester.

Table 7.3—continued

Author(s)	Method	N	Key findings
Mitchell and Byrne (1973)	Experiment	139	Individuals with authoritarian personalities are much more likely to be motivated by perceived similarity than those with egalitarian personalities.
Radley and Kennedy (1995)	Semi-structured interview	49	Charitable giving reflects variations in the relationship of the individual to the community of which they are a part.
Rege and Telle (2001)	Experiment	80 (students)	Contributions to a public good enhanced by allowing stakeholders to monitor others' behaviour.
Yavas *et al.* (1980)	Self-administered questionnaire	100	Donors appear to be more sympathetic, generous, loving and helpful than non-donors.

Processing determinants

Two key categories of variable appear to impact on the manner in which the giving decision is processed, namely the donor's past experience with a given charity (and with charitable giving in general), and the criteria he/she might use to evaluate potential organizations for support. Each of these dimensions will now be considered in turn.

Judgemental criteria

Economists have long argued that donors make decisions in respect of their giving by reference to the degree of utility they will attain (Collard 1978). While historically it was argued that this would take material form, it has recently been accepted that utility may also derive from the emotions evoked from giving (Arrow 1972). Under this view donors will select charities to support on the basis of whether they have benefited in the past or believe that they will in the future (Krebs 1982; Frisch and Gerrard 1981; Amos 1982). Individuals could, for example, give to those organizations that will do them political good and/or serve to enhance their career, perhaps through the networking opportunities that will be accorded (Amos 1982; Frisch and Gerrard 1981). Donors may also evaluate potential recipient organizations against the extent to which their support will be visible, or noticeable by others within their social group, thereby enhancing the donor's standing therein (Stroebe and Frey 1982; Cnaan and Goldberg–Glen 1991).

Individuals will also evaluate potential recipient organizations on the basis of the extent to which their performance is viewed as acceptable (Cutlip 1990). Glaser (1994: 178) found that the variable 'an adequate amount spent per program' was the most important factor in the decision to contribute to charitable organizations. Donors appear to have a clear idea of what represents an acceptable percentage of income that may be applied to both administration and fundraising costs. Warwick (1994) identified that donors expect that the ratio between administration–fundraising costs and so-called charitable expenditure would be 20:80. It is interesting to note that despite this expectation most donors believe that the actual ratio is closer to 50:50. For example, Bennett and Savani's (2003) research shows that respondents perceived that only 46 per cent of the focal charities' expenditures reached beneficiaries, when in reality the average figure was 82 per cent. Harvey and McCrohan (1988) found that 60 per cent was a significant threshold, with charities spending at least 60 per cent of their donations on charitable programmes achieving significantly higher levels of donation. Steinberg (1986) suggests that this is something of an anomaly since fundraising costs in particular are sunk, and should therefore not enter into a donor's decision to support a given charity.

On a related theme, perceived effectiveness is also an issue. Sargeant *et al.* (2001) identify that the degree to which the organization is seen to achieve its stated goals impacts on compliance, the total amount donated and the lifetime value of individual donors. To help individuals rate charity performance more accurately, it has been shown that charitable organizations need to provide relevant information in the public domain such as the ratio of salary costs to total income, or the rate of change in charity income for each £1 spent on marketing (Bennett and Savani 2003).

The extent to which an organization is regarded as being professionally run has also received attention in the literature. In two separate studies, Sargeant *et al.* (2001) and Sargeant *et al.* (2004) conclude that the extent to which an organization's management may be regarded as professional impacts on the value of gifts, the lifetime value of donors and their loyalty to the organization. It is interesting to note that in the USA the relationship is positive, while in the UK the relationship is negative, implying that an increase in perceived professionalism would lower donations. It appears as though the British public regards amateurism as a virtue.

Past experience

A variety of authors have argued that once recruited to support a charity, a given donor will be significantly more likely to give again in the future (see e.g. Kaehler and Sargeant 1998). This may be because donors begin to build trust with the organization, which in turn fosters commitment and higher levels of support over time. Indeed, these relationships were tested empirically by Sargeant and Lee (2004) who were able to explain 20 per cent of the variation in giving by reference to their model. Further quantitative work by Sargeant *et al.* (2006) shows a significant positive causal link between trust and commitment, and commitment and giving behaviour (measured by average donation). In this study, the drivers of trust were identified as the performance of the organization (as discussed above), and the quality of the communications received from the organization after making a donation.

The issue of donor loyalty has received comparatively little attention, although empirical work by Sargeant (2001) identified that the perceived quality of service provided by the fundraising department to the donor, the perceived impact of previous donations and the extent to which the donor felt that he/she had been able to exert influence and control over his/her relationship with the nonprofit were all positively correlated with retention and lifetime value (see also Burnett 2002). Donors indicating they were 'very satisfied' with the quality of service provided were twice as likely to offer a second or subsequent gift than those who identified themselves as merely 'satisfied'. More empirical work (albeit based on a relatively small sample) by Bennett and Barkensjo (2005) also provides support that there is a significant and positive relationship between a donor's perception of the quality of marketing activity undertaken and his/her future intentions/behaviour, particularly their intended level of donation.

Empirical studies pertaining to 'judgemental criteria' and 'past experience' are summarized in Table 7.4.

Table 7.4 Summary of empirical studies pertaining to judgemental criteria and past experience

Author(s)	Method	N	Key findings
Amos (1982)	Analysis of secondary data including income tax returns	N/A	Both indirect and Kantian motives for support of voluntary organizations can be identified.
Bennett and Barkensjo (2005)	Face-to-face survey	141	Donors' perceptions of a charity's relationship-marketing activities are strongly associated with perceptions of the organization's advertising (presenting personally relevant messages, generating feelings of trust in and commitment to charity, convince donor of charity's desire to interact with them), and with two-way personal contact methods such as special events and PR. Direct marketing has the lowest, although still significant impact on perceptions of relationship-marketing activities.
Bennett and Savani (2003)	Survey	286	The provision of small amounts of relevant information about a charity improves the accuracy of a person's ratings of the charity across a range of disparate attributes, such as level of efficiency. An individual's general knowledge and familiarity with the charity sector is a significant determinant of how they feel about charities, and their ability to rate accurately their performance attributes.
Frisch and Gerrard (1981)	Postal survey	195	Younger individuals place greater emphasis on self-serving motives for volunteering.
Frumkin and Kim (2001)	Panel	2,359 Nonprofits	Nonprofits with low administrative to total expense ratios perform no better in fundraising from individuals, trusts and corporations than those with higher expense ratios.
Harvey and McCrohan (1988)	Self-administered questionnaire	5,000	Perceived organizational efficiency is positively correlated with level of giving.
Sargeant *et al.* (2003)	Postal survey	10,000	Factors including the demonstrable/familial utility deriving from the gift, organizational effectiveness, the perceived professionalism of an organization, together with the quality of service supplied, all have the capacity to influence gift levels, lifetime value and the longevity of the donor–nonprofit relationship (UK sample).
Sargeant *et al.* (2003)	Postal survey	10,000	Factors including the demonstrable utility deriving from the gift, organizational effectiveness, the perceived professionalism of an organization, together with the quality of service supplied, all have the

Continued

Table 7.4—continued

Author(s)	Method	N	Key findings
			capacity to influence gift levels and the value of particular donors (US sample).
Sargeant *et al.* (2006)	Postal survey	1,300	There is a significant positive causal link between trust and commitment, and commitment and giving behaviour.
Sargeant and Lee (2004)	Postal survey	1,000	Commitment mediates the impact of trust on giving behaviour.

External influences

Models/experiences

Schervish and Havens (1997) argue that models and experiences from one's youth will shape future adult giving behaviour. Thus those growing up in a family with a strong tradition of charitable support will be significantly more likely to exhibit such behaviours themselves. Sociologists have also argued that the provision of 'models' (e.g. a celebrity seen to be offering support) can influence contributory behaviour. This occurs through the creation of social norms, thereby legitimizing and encouraging the giving behaviour (Krebs 1982; Krebs and Miller 1985; Wilson and Petruska 1984). Role models are regarded as particularly effective in situations of social ambiguity, where the behaviour is rare or unusual (Festinger 1954). Sargeant *et al.* (2003) thus argue that it is particularly effective in bequest solicitations where an individual will often be considering such a gift for the first time and may be unaware of the behaviour of others.

Communities of participation

Communities of participation are networks of formal and informal relationships entered into either by choice or by circumstance (e.g. schools, soup kitchens, soccer groups) that bring an individual into contact with need. Authors such as Schervish (1993, 1997) argue that a basic connection to a cause (e.g. being a graduate of a school) is not enough in itself to prompt subsequent donations to that school and that some degree of socialization is required. This, the author argues, is experienced through communities of participation and thus donors will be predisposed to give to causes connected in some way with these communities. Schervish and Havens (1997) found empirical support for this proposition.

Similarly Conley (1999) in a study of the predictors of alumni giving found that involvement in school activities and involvement in alumni activities were both primary indicators of whether an individual would give. Lohmann (1992) also found that giving frequently related to personal membership of networks, societies, political groups, social movements or religious, artistic or scientific communities. This reflects many of the themes developed in the psychology and sociological literatures where the concept of 'we-ness' is seen as a spur to caring (e.g. Piliavin *et al.* 1981; Jenks 1990; Coleman 1990). Indeed Brady *et al.* (2002) in a study of university giving, focus on organizational identification or 'oneness' towards the organization. They find that the construct is a key determinant of 'intent to give'.

It is important however, for a nonprofit not to overemphasize the role of communities of participation. Self-perception theory (Bem 1972) tells us that external triggers for giving can cause a donor to discount any intrinsic motives they might have had (Scott 1977), making it difficult to sustain that giving in the longer term, particularly when contact with that community comes to an end.

Empirical studies pertaining to 'models/experiences' are summarized in Table 7.5.

Public policy contributions and crowding out

The majority of studies on this topic suggest that government contributions discourage or crowd out private contributions, but that the crowding out is incomplete. However, the extent of the crowding-out effect varies from under 30 per cent (Abrams and Schmitz 1978; Clotfelter 1985; Kingma 1989; Andreoni 1993; Ribar and Wilhelm 2002), to approximately 70 per cent (Andreoni 1993; Bolton and Katok 1998). Simmons and Emanuele (2004) found that crowding out takes place for both donations of money and time. The accepted explanation for crowding out has been that givers treat government contributions as imperfect substitutes for private giving. According to Andreoni and Payne (2003), it may also occur as a result of a charity's behavioural response to receiving a government grant, leading to a reduction in fundraising efforts. Research is not conclusive, however, and Nyborg and Rege (2003) acknowledge that whether public policy contributions crowd out or indeed crowd in (see e.g. Khanna and Sandler 2000) private contributions, and the extent of this effect depends largely on which model of moral-based motivation (altruism, norm, fairness, commitment and cognitive evaluation) is adopted. They also suggest that the policy implications of each model are likely to be quite different.

Table 7.5 Summary of empirical studies pertaining to models/experiences

Author(s)	Method	N	Key findings
Brady et al. (2002)	Postal survey	595 (students)	Organizational identification, philanthropic predisposition and perceived need influence intention to give.
Sargeant et al. (2003)	Postal survey	5,000	Factors determining bequest giving include role models, family connections to the cause, perceptions of efficiency and impact on cause.
Schervish and Havens (1997)	Secondary analysis of survey of giving and volunteering in the USA	2,671	Variables/constructs associated with giving behaviour include participation and commitment to religious institutions, household income, retirement status, invitation to participate and communities of participation.
Scott (1977)	Field experiment	315	Compliance with a small initial request under conditions of no incentive enhances the likelihood of positive behavioural intentions for subsequent moderate and large requests.
Wilson and Petruska (1984)	Experiment	112 (students)	Esteem-oriented individuals were more likely to initiate helping behaviour and were more strongly influenced by competence models.

Individual characteristics

Demographics

A variety of demographic factors can influence giving. Variables such as age (Halfpenny 1990; Nichols 1992; Pharoah and Tanner 1997), gender (Mesch *et al.* 2002; Hall 2004), social class (Jones and Posnett 1991; Bryant *et al.* 2003; McClelland *et al.* 2004), social norms (Morgan *et al.* 1979; Piliavin and Chang 1990; Radley and Kennedy 1995) and the degree of religious conviction (Halfpenny 1990; Pharoah and Tanner 1997; Jackson 2001) have all been shown to impact on giving behaviour.

The variable 'gender' warrants some elaboration. Marx (2000) identified that women are more likely to support human services organizations and to be committed to the organization. In the USA, the Council of Economic Advisors determined that women tended to give more frequently than men, although they donate very similar amounts in aggregate. Further attitudinal and behavioural differences have been identified. Braus (1994: 48), for example, identified that women tend to want more information about how the money is actually going to be used, prefer one-off donations as opposed to regular (or committed) giving and to give more 'from the heart than the head'.

How potential gender differences are resolved within a marriage may also impact on giving behaviour. Andreoni *et al.* (2003) found that when bargaining over charitable giving takes place within a marriage (rather than one spouse taking charge), household giving is reduced by at least 6 per cent. Joint decisions are more likely to reflect the husband's, rather than the wife's tastes, and the husband is more likely to become the chief decision-maker if he earns more, or is more highly educated than the wife. These findings suggest that there are complex interrelationships between the variables of gender, marital status, education and income in the context of charitable giving.

Not surprisingly, the variable social class/income has also received considerable attention. Writers such as Mears (1992) and Jones and Posnett (1991) see giving as income elastic, although it is important to note that not only the amounts given will vary as one moves up the social strata, but also the rationale for support. Radley and Kennedy (1992, 1995) identified that the lower socio-economic groups tend to see the needy as a group to be pitied because of their treatment at the hand of fate. Promotional messages stressing the ability of even a small gift to alleviate pain and suffering are therefore likely to be most effective. The higher socio-economic groups by contrast, particularly those from the professions, give not only for the amelioration of suffering but also for the longer-term change in their situation. Authors such as Amato (1985) add that professional people tend to become more involved in their charitable giving, while preliminary evidence provided by Kottasz (2004) suggests that the profession itself may be associated with giving behaviour. In her study of high-earning male professionals, lawyers tended to donate larger amounts of money to charity and on a more regular basis than respondents working in financial services, possibly because the former were significantly more empathetic than the latter, an empathetic disposition being positively associated with giving.

Interestingly, in the USA the poor and extremely wealthy give a much higher proportion of their income than the middle class (Silver 1980) and those living in small-town/rural settings are more willing to exhibit helping behaviours than city dwellers (Latane and Nida 1981).

Lifestyle/geo-demographic

Schlegelmilch (1988) shows that attitudinal and lifestyle variables improve the prediction of whether an individual will give versus chance by 32 per cent and Yankelovich (1985) reported that the most important characteristics of the generous giver are all related to the donor's perceptions and values. Perceptions of financial security, discretionary funds, attendance at religious services and whether an individual volunteers time for charity were all shown to be good indicators of a propensity to give. Hansler and Riggin (1989) also report success using the geo-demographic system VISION to segment potential support for the Arthritis Foundation.

In addition to this work, a small number of authors have explored the potential for such variables to be used in predicting *which* nonprofit organizations might be supported. Schlegelmilch and Tynan (1989), for example, identified that no significant differences could be found between the donors to a number of different charities in respect of lifestyle. However, the authors defined lifestyle somewhat narrowly as what people like to do in their spare time. Other authors such as Sargeant (1996) and Bennett (2003) have found lifestyle and values offer significant utility in distinguishing donors from one category of cause to another.

Personality

Studies in the field of psychology have shown that empathy and other prosocial tendencies emerge during childhood, and are then relatively stable across a person's lifetime (see e.g. Eisenberg *et al.* 2002). According to Penner *et al.* (1995), the 'prosocial personality' consists of two dimensions, which have significant associations with prosocial behaviours and actions. The first concerns 'other-orientated empathy', such as a sense of responsibility and ability to experience cognitive and affective empathy, and the second concerns 'helpfulness', the self-perception of being a helpful and competent individual (Penner *et al.* 2005). Other authors to find an association between empathetic tendencies and donating and volunteering behaviours include Davis *et al.* (1999). 'Agreeableness', a trait from the big five theory of personality (developed by Goldberg, 1981, 1993) has also been shown to influence an individual's propensity to act prosocially (Graziano and Eisenberg 1997; Ashton *et al.* 1998). Agreeableness is the tendency to be compassionate and cooperative, and is measured by 'likeability', 'friendly compliance' and 'need for affiliation.'

Personality inventories have been used by some authors (Piferi *et al.* 2006; Rytting *et al.* 1994) to assess an individual's prosocial disposition, including the multiple perspectives inventory (Gorenflo and Crano 1998), (empathy) and the empathy subscale from the impulsiveness, venturesomeness and empathy (IVE) inventory (Eysenck *et al.* 1985). The Myers–Briggs-type indicator has also been applied to philanthropic donors. It was found that the thinking–feeling factor helped to identify the motives for giving (for example, 'feelers' give for more personal and internal reasons), but it did not influence whether or not an individual donates to charity (Rytting *et al.* 1994).

Empirical studies pertaining to individual characteristics are summarized in Table 7.6.

Motives

There are a variety of intrinsic motives for charitable support. Motives can assist donors in filtering out those charity appeals that are likely to be of most relevance and can help in structuring the evaluation process that will subsequently be conducted to define ultimately the pattern of support exhibited. Each major category is now reviewed in turn.

Table 7.6 Summary of empirical studies pertaining to individual characteristics

Author(s)	Method	N	Key findings
Amato (1985)	Diary and self-administered questionnaire	97 (Students)	People in helping professions have higher levels of involvement in everyday planned helping than do people in non-helping professions. Attitudinal and demographic variables predict participation in formal helping situations.
Andreoni *et al.* (2003)	Secondary analysis of Gallup surveys	4,180 households	Women give to more charities than men, but offer lower amounts. In marriage, bargaining over giving preferences appears to reduce giving by at least 6%.
Ashton *et al.* (1998)	Self-administered questionnaire	118 (students)	Empathy positively related to 'agreeableness' and negatively related to 'emotional stability'.
Bennett (2003)	Interviews	250	Possession of certain personal values correlated significantly with specific organizational values that the respondents most admired.
Boris (1987)	Interviews	100	Giving among the wealthy motivated by civic responsibility, egoism, progressivism and scientific problem-solving.
Davis *et al.* (1999)	Three experiments	191 (students)	Empathy influences choice of situations where needy individuals may be found.
Graney and Graney (1974)	Panel study	60 + 46	Giving to charity may be viewed as a form of pseudo-social interaction among the wealthy.
Hansler and Riggin (1989)	Database analysis	N/A	Giving to the Arthritis Foundation is related to membership of VISION (geo-demographic) categories.
Jones and Posnett (1991)	Secondary analysis of family expenditure survey	7,000	Participation in giving is sensitive to income, the tax-price of income, demographic variables and the level of giving varies primarily with income.
Kottasz (2003)	Survey (email and face-to-face)	158	High-earning professional males represent a distinct market segment, attracted to giving to arts and cultural charities, well-established organizations with a good reputation and image and enjoying invitations to special events. Profession may have a bearing on giving behaviour which suggests that occupationally differentially marketing strategies and communications may be a useful approach for charitable organizations.
Mears (1992)	In-home interviews	239	Strong donors had higher educations, higher incomes and higher general awareness of charities.
Midlarsky and Hannah (1989)	Two experiments	2,715 + 2,735	Linear increase with age in numbers of people donating. When controlled for financial costs, elderly persons proved to be the most generous.

Table 7.6—continued

Author(s)	Method	N	Key findings
Piferi et al. (2006)	Survey	343 (students)	Of the six motives investigated, only the motive to relieve others' distress was associated with sustained giving.
Radley and Kennedy (1992)	Interviews	49	Motives for giving vary between socio-economic groups.
Radley and Kennedy (1995)	Interviews	49	Charitable giving reflects variations in the relationship of individuals to the community of which they are a part.
Sargeant (1996)	Postal survey	3,000	Donors to three distinct categories of cause differ significantly in psychographic/lifestyle characteristics.
Schlegelmilch (1979)	Postal survey	800	Attitude and lifestyle variables improve prediction of giving versus non-giving by 32% over chance.
Schlegelmilch and Tynan (1989)	Postal survey	800	Different fundraising strategies appeal to segments with particular demographic and psychographic profiles. Segmentation by activity and lifestyle profiles is possible for some specific fundraising strategies, but not for others.
Yavas et al. (1980)	Self-administered questionnaire	100	Donors appear to be more sympathetic, generous, loving and helpful than non-donors.

Altruism and self-interest

Authors such as Collard (1978) argue that all giving can be explained by reference to the benefits that will accrue to the donor as a consequence of their gift. In this sense the process is rational and the donor simply evaluates the costs and benefits of engaging in a particular donation. However, this fails to explain a large proportion of gifts where no direct benefit accrues to the individual and where perhaps the gift may be made anonymously (Walker and Pharoah 2002). Economists such as Andreoni (1989, 1990, 2001) have recently argued that the utility deriving from a gift can take a variety of different forms and have explained giving by reference to public good theory, exchange theory and the so-called 'warm-glow-effect' where the benefits of giving are purely psychological in nature. Other such benefits are considered in the discussion below.

Empathy

While empathy has been discussed as a personality trait above, with some individuals being more predisposed to prosocial and empathetic behaviour than others, it can also be viewed as a motive which drives giving behaviour. Empathy may be defined as an individual's emotional arousal elicited by the expression of emotion in another (Aronfreed 1968; Berger 1962; Shelton and Rogers 1981). While intuitively sound, the concept of empathy suffers from a lack of construct validity and a lack of clear measurement and manipulation techniques (Wispe 1986). Despite the difficulties of definition a number of studies have explicitly addressed the impact of empathy on giving behaviour and found a strong association between the level of empathy attained and the likelihood of providing help (e.g. Mount and Quirion 1988). To be effective, the psychology literature suggests manipulations must be powerful enough to arouse empathy, but not so powerful that they become personally distressing to the donor (Fultz *et al.* 1986).

However, Schaller and Cialdini (1988) argue that the presence of empathy can also increase feelings of sadness or personal distress. Separate analyses of empathy and sadness suggest it is actually *sadness*, not empathy that increases helping behaviour. Therefore, rather than empathy being an altruistic motive, individuals may be egoistically motivated to help so as to reduce the negative emotions from someone else's distress, known as the 'negative state–relief model' (Cialdini *et al.* 1987). These authors go on to propose that giving may occur to improve an individual's mood. When individuals were told that helping would not improve their mood because of a (placebo) drug they had taken, they were less motivated to help. However, others have provided evidence to the contrary (Batson *et al.* 1989; Schroeder *et al.* 1988).

Davis (1983) and Hoffman (1984) identified that a person is more likely to experience empathy when he/she has a high empathic ability, prior experience with the need and emotional attachment to the cause. Work by Davis *et al.* (1987) also established that in seeking to build empathy in fundraising communications, nonprofits should ask prospective donors to imagine how the beneficiary must feel, rather than asking the donor to imagine how they would feel in their place.

Sympathy

The motive 'sympathy' has also received attention in the literature, largely being viewed as a value expressive function, aiding individuals to conform to personally held norms (Clary and Synder 1991; Schwartz 1977). Again, there would appear to be a relationship between the degree of sympathy engendered and both the propensity to donate and the chosen level of support (Batson 1990).

Fear/pity/guilt

A variety of other potential motives for giving have been identified including fear, guilt and pity. These have been found to impact positively both on compliance and the extent thereof (Krebs and Whitten 1972; Pieper 1975). In general, the findings are similar to those reported above in the sense that the development of each motive in fundraising communications should be strong enough to demand action, but not so strong that it becomes personally distressing to the donor.

Social justice

Miller (1977) argued from social justice motivation theory (Lerner 1975) that if people witness undue suffering their belief in a just world will be threatened – consequently they will be motivated to respond to restore their faith in a just world. Thus as Bendapudi, Singh and Bendapudi (1996) note, donors motivated by social justice would be more likely to support breast cancer than lung cancer, since rightly or wrongly they might blame smokers for causing their own condition (see also Griffin *et al.* 1993). The organizational justice literature lends support for this proposition since it suggests that people asked to allocate resources will be concerned about the fairness of the allocation. Donors acknowledge injustice and act to reduce it (Greenberg 1987; Bies 1987; Tyler 1994).

Miller (1977) also identified that helping behaviour would be increased when the need is not widespread and the duration of the need (persistence) is short. It is interesting to note that most charity communications appear to be based on the exact opposite of this position. Appeals tend to stress the ongoing nature of the need for support and make much of the number of individuals currently being impacted with the affliction or cause for concern.

Prestige and 'making a difference'

Two newer and related motives for philanthropy have been identified as prestige (donors being motivated by the public recognition their contributions bring) and the desire to make a difference, known as impact philanthropy. These have not yet been empirically tested, but do suggest that certain fundraising techniques are better suited to each of these motivations, as will be discussed.

The prestige-based model proposed by Harbaugh (1998) is closely linked to the 'warm-glow' effect referred to earlier in this section, but rather than being about the internal satisfaction derived from charitable giving, prestige is the utility that comes from having the amount of a donation made publicly known. Being seen to give may enhance a donor's social status, or serve as a sign of wealth or reliability. Donors may wish to access a particular group, and thus desire to be defined by their philanthropic activity (Ostrower 1997). Prestige is clearly about recognition and is therefore also relevant to the feedback aspect of the giving-behaviour model presented in this chapter. To respond to the motive of prestige, charities can create gift categories and then disclose publicly donors who contribute to various categories. Categories may carry certain titles, such as 'patron' or 'founder', depending on the size of the gift. This type of motivation may be more relevant when addressing younger givers since Mathur (1996) has identified that for older adults, esteem enhancement motivations were negatively related to gift-giving.

Impact philanthropy, posited by Duncan (2004), is based on a donor's desire to personally make a difference. The defining assumption of this model is that donors give because they enjoy personally increasing the output of a good. For example, some donors prefer to give directly to a homeless person, rather than give to a charity for the homeless where their donation is distributed over a large number of recipients. An impact philanthropist prefers to target his or her gift as this increases the perceived impact on the cause or recipient. Sponsorship offers are therefore likely to attract individuals who value making a difference.

Tax

A number of studies have examined the relationship between income tax rates and charitable support and although findings vary, the responsiveness of individual giving to changes in taxation appears relatively great (Clotfelter 1985). Okten and Weisbrod (2000), for example, calculate that a change in the price of donating of a given percentage results in a 24 per cent greater percentage change in donations. A recent meta-analysis of previous work on the effects of changes in tax deductibility on charitable donations spanning forty years of literature (Peloza and Steel 2005) concluded that tax deductions are treasury efficient. That is, a decrease of $1 in the cost of giving can be expected to result in more than $1 being donated to charity. More specifically, their meta-analysis revealed that a 1 per cent reduction in the cost of charitable giving resulted in an average increase in donations of 1.44 per cent. Tax relief is therefore considered by many to be an important motive for charitable support (Ostrower 1987; Cermak et al. 1994) although as Sargeant and Jay (2004: 100) note, 'it is important not to overstate the influence of taxation . . . (since) . . . donors will always be better off not making a donation'.

Empirical studies pertaining to 'motives' are summarized in Table 7.7.

Table 7.7 Summary of empirical studies pertaining to motives

Author(s)	Method	N	Key findings
Batson *et al.* (1988)	Five experiments	80 + 120 + 88 + 60 + 48 (students)	Empathic emotion evokes altruistic motivation.
Coke *et al.* (1978)	Two experiments	44 (students)	Those subjects who experienced the most empathic emotion offered the most help.
Davis (1983)	Multiple questionnaires	1,354 (students)	A person is more likely to experience empathy when he/she scores highly on emotionality, shyness and a non-selfish concern for others.
Davis *et al.* (1987)	Experiment	144 (students)	Positive emotional reactions were affected primarily by cognitive empathy and negative emotional reactions were most heavily influenced by emotional empathy.
Eisenberg and Miller (1987)	Meta-analysis	N/A	Low to moderate relationships were found between empathy and pro-social behaviour.
Feldman and Feldman (1985)	Experiment	60 (students)	Telethons have a strong positive influence on the viewing public's perception of disabled persons. These attitudes do not impact significantly on donation behaviour.
Fultz *et al.* (1986)	Two experiments	22 + 32 (students)	Empathy evokes altruistic motivation to reduce victim's need.
Griffin *et al.* (1993)	Self-administered questionnaire	468	Causal attributions assigned to a victim lead to lower levels of empathy, personal distress and intentions to give.
Griffin *et al.* (1993)	Questionnaires	468	Under conditions where an audience is not captive, appeals should be designed to evoke maximum levels of empathy and minimum levels of distress.
Schaller and Cialdini (1988)	Experiment	90 (students)	Empathy produces sadness which is alleviated by enhanced helping behaviour, unless less costly means of bolstering mood are available.
Schroeder *et al.* (1988)	Experiment	128 (students)	When helping not personally costly, concern about another's distress rather than about one's own emotional state is the primary motive for helping.
Shelton and Rogers (1981)	Experiment	118 (Students)	Empathy-arousing appeals facilitate attitudinal change. Fear appeals can persuade individuals to protect themselves even through the mediation of social organizations.
Tyler (1994)	Two sets of telephone interviews	652 + 409	Distributive justice judgements are shaped by both resource and relational judgements. Procedural justice judgements are shaped by relational concerns.

Inhibitors

A number of factors have been shown to inhibit individual giving. Riecken *et al.* (1995) contend that lack of money, time or ego risks are the most notable of these. In respect of the latter Steffey and Jones (1988) concur that some donors may experience anxiety over ridicule that may result from the support of unpopular or 'fringe' causes (see also Yavas and Riecken 1985). A further notable barrier to giving has been shown to be doubts over the worthiness of the cause (Wagner and Wheeler 1969; Ford 1976; Mahatoo and Banting 1988) and in particular concerns in respect of how the donated resources will actually be used (Shuptrine and Moore 1980).

Feedback

Having decided to offer a donation to a nonprofit, donors will typically be thanked by the respective organization in the hope that this will be the first stage in building an ongoing relationship with the individual concerned. The literature suggests that there are two significant components of the feedback process that fundraisers should seek to address.

Labelling

In thanking donors for their gift, organizations often append labels to the donor such as kind, generous and/or helpful. Work by authors such as Swinyard and Ray (1977) has implied that this elicits a greater motivation to help and fosters favourable attitudes on the part of the donor (Moore *et al.* 1985). The impact of labels will be particularly potent when there are concrete prior behaviours to be labelled and when the label stresses the uniqueness of the donor's behaviour (McGuire and Padawer–Singer 1976). Consolidating donor self-perceptions via labelling thus furnishes an intrinsic motive to sustain behaviour (Kraut 1973). Repetitive labelling has been found to enhance efficacy (Tybout and Yalch 1980) and labels have been found to work only where the donor accepts the label (Allen 1982), emphasizing the need for the label to be credible and be supplied by a credible source.

Recognition/rewards

The fundraising literature is replete with references to the need for adequate donor recognition (e.g. Warwick and Hitchcock 2001; Irwin–Wells 2002; McKinnon 1999). Failure to provide adequate and appropriate recognition, it has been argued, will lead either to a lowering of future support or its complete termination (Boulding 1973). Sargeant *et al.* (2001) provide the first empirical support for this proposition indicating a link between the perception of adequate recognition and the level of gifts/lifetime value.

Conclusions

As the reader will by now appreciate there has been a plethora of different studies conducted in the realm of individual giving (albeit in many cases with student samples) in the disciplines of marketing, economics, clinical psychology, social psychology, anthropology and sociology. Academic interest in the marketing discipline has tended to focus on the characteristics of givers, distinguishing donors from non-donors and latterly in distinguishing high-value givers from low-value givers. There has also been considerable interest across the whole range of disciplines in the motives for the support of nonprofits and the links (if any) between these and different facets of giving and helping behaviour.

Other facets of giving behaviour have received less attention. There has been little interest, for example, in the use of particular fundraising techniques (with the notable exception of personal solicitations). There therefore remains a need to understand the factors that might drive giving in each key media (e.g. direct mail, direct response television, door to door, face to face, and so on). Many of the studies cited in this review talk of giving in general and fail to offer insight into how their findings might differ by the media employed. It would be particularly instructive to conduct work looking at the profiles of individuals who give through each fundraising medium and the promotional messages that might work best with each of these groups. An examination of demographic, lifestyle and geo-demographic characteristics would be warranted.

Allied to this there is a need for research to explore how new fundraising audiences could be identified and targeted. Some authors, such as Pharoah and Tanner (1997), have posited that the percentage of households electing to support nonprofits (and in particular younger households) may be in decline. Further empirical work is warranted to test both this assertion and identify how nonprofits can tailor their message to become more appealing to a broader percentage of society. Little work has been attempted with non-givers.

It would also be instructive to examine key 'output' variables such as lifetime value and donor loyalty. While a handful of studies has been conducted in this realm, there remains a significant opportunity to learn much more about the factors that drive donor loyalty and conversely give rise to attrition. Since many nonprofits now report attrition rates in the year immediately following acquisition of over 50 per cent (Sargeant and Jay 2004) this is becoming a major issue that nonprofits must address. It is interesting to note that academic interest has tended to focus around recruitment issues to date, rather than considering in detail how best to retain and develop individuals over time.

A further significant gap in the extant research pertains to the issue of cross-cultural comparisons. Individuals in the USA, for example, give approximately 2 per cent per annum of their household income to good causes (AAFRC 2005). In the UK it is less than 1 per cent (Walker and Pharoah 2002). Thus any attempt to understand why people give and how individuals might be encouraged to offer higher levels of support to the voluntary sector could be greatly informed through developing an understanding of why national differences in generosity might exist. The implications for public policy would be profound.

There is also a need for research around the issue of fundraising products. These have recently become popular in the UK and have been shown to be an aid to donor loyalty and retention. Fundraising products (e.g. Sponsor a Dog) have also been created with success in the USA, yet academic interest has been scant. While some research has been conducted into issues such as the portrayal of beneficiaries (particularly in the discipline of psychology), only Harvey (1990) has really addressed the components of the fundraising product and no researchers have to date explored issues pertaining to product design, portfolio management or the relationship between donor needs and the pattern of nonprofit responses.

Finally and allied to this there is a need to examine the take-up and perceptions of new or developing forms of giving, such as planned giving, committed or monthly giving and venture philanthropy. All three methods of giving have proved increasingly popular in recent years, yet the broad base of research continues to focus on the solicitation of one-off or cash gifts. This is particularly disappointing in relation to planned and legacy giving, which collectively is estimated to account for over 40 per cent of the voluntary income accruing to nonprofits in the USA (AAFRC 2005). Presently very little is understood about the motives for selecting such mechanisms for giving, perceptions of the fundraising communications designed to solicit these gifts and indeed most other dimensions of the model presented in this chapter as they apply to this context.

In the course of conducting this review it has been encouraging to note that there appears to be increasing interest in giving and fundraising on the part of marketing academicians. The emergence and success of two dedicated scholarly nonprofit journals has undoubtedly increased participation in the field but there nevertheless remain a number of highly significant gaps which need to be addressed. The authors consider this to be important not only for the sake of expanding knowledge, but also because unlike organizations in other sectors, nonprofits frequently do not have the resources to undertake detailed research of their own. Thus the view of the authors of this chapter is that the academic community has much to offer this increasingly hungry audience as they seek to inform and develop their professional practice.

References

AAFRC Trust for Philanthropy (2005) *Giving USA 2005*, Indianapolis, IN: AAFRC Trust for Philanthropy.

Aaker, J. L. (1997) 'Dimensions of brand personality', *Journal of Marketing Research*, 34(3): 347–56.

Abrams, B. A. and Schitz, M. D. (1978) 'The crowding-out effect on government transfers on private charitable contributions', *Public Choice*, 33(1): 29–39.

Adler, A. B., Wright, B. A. and Ulicny, G. R. (1991) 'Fundraising portrayals of people with disabilities: Donations and attitudes', *Rehabilitation Psychology*, 36(4): 231–40.

Aldrich, T. (2004) 'Do-it-yourself DRTV: A practical guide to making direct response television advertising work for charities', *International Journal of Nonprofit and Voluntary Sector Marketing*, 9(2): 135–44.

Allen, C. T. (1982) 'Self-perception based strategies for stimulating energy conservation', *Journal of Consumer Research*, 8(4): 381–90.

Amato, P. R. (1985) 'An investigation of planned helping behavior', *Journal of Research In Personality*, 19(2): 232–52.

Amos, O. M. (1982) 'Empirical analysis of motives underlying contributions to charity', *Atlantic Economic Journal*, 10(4): 45–52.

Andreoni, J. (1989) 'Giving with impure altruism: Applications to charity and Ricardian equivalence', *Journal of Political Economy*, 97(6): 1447–58.

—— (1990) 'Impure altruism and donations to public goods: A theory of warm-glow giving', *Economic Journal*, 100(401): 464–77.

—— (1993) 'An experimental test of the public goods crowding-out hypothesis', *American Economic Review*, 83(5): 1317–27.

—— (1998) 'Toward a theory of charitable fund-raising', *Journal of Political Economy*, 106(6): 1186–1213.

—— (2001) 'The economics of philanthropy', in N. J. Smelser and P. B. Baltes (eds) *International Encyclopedia of the Social and Behavioral Sciences*, London: Elsevier.

—— (2006) 'Leadership giving in charitable fundraising', *Journal of Public Economic Theory*, 8(1): 1–22.

—— and Payne, A. (2003) 'Do government grants to private charities crowd out giving or fundraising?', *American Economic Review*, 93(3): 792–812.

—— and Petrie, R. (2004) 'Public goods experiments without confidentiality: A glimpse into fund-raising', *Journal of Public Economics*, 88(7–8): 1605–23.

—— Brown, E. and Rischall, I. (2003) 'Charitable giving by married couples: Who decides and why does it matter?', *Journal of Human Resources*, 38(1): 111–33.

Aronfreed, J. (1968) *Conduct and Conscience: The Socialization of Internalized Control Over Behavior*, New York, NY: Academic Press.

Arrow, K. J. (1972) 'Gifts and exchanges', *Philosophy and Public Affairs*, 1(4): 343–62.

Ashton, M., Paunonen, S. V., Helmes, E. and Jackson, D. N. (1998) 'Kin, altruism, reciprocal altruism and the big five personality factors', *Evolution and Human Behaviour*, 19(4): 243–55.

Aune, R. K. and Basil, M. D. (1994) 'A relational obligations approach to the foot-in-the-mouth effect', *Journal of Applied Social Psychology*, 24(6): 546–56.

Auten, G. and Joulfaian, D. (1996) 'Charitable contributions and intergenerational transfers', *Journal of Public Economics*, 59(1): 55–68.

Bagnoli, M. and Lipman, B. (1989) 'Provision of public goods: Fully implementing the core through private contributions', *Review of Economic Studies*, 56(188): 583–601.

Batson, C. D. (1990) 'How social an animal? The human capacity for caring', *American Psychologist*, 45(3): 336–46.

—— (1991) *The Altruism Question: Towards a Social Psychological Answer*, Hillsdale, NJ: Lawrence Erlbaum.

—— Dyck, J. L., Brandt, R., Batson, J. G., Powell, A. L., McMaster, M. R. and Griffitt, C. A. (1988) 'Five studies testing two new egoistic alternatives to the empathy altruism hypothesis', *Journal of Personality and Social Psychology*, 55(1): 52–77.

—— Batson, J. G., Griffitt, C. A., Barrientos, J., Brandt, R., Sprengelmeyer, P. and Bayly, M. J. (1989) 'Negative–state relief and the empathy–altruism hypothesis', *Journal of Personality and Social Psychology*, 56(6): 922–33.

Bem, D. (1965) 'An experimental analysis of self-persuasion', *Journal of Experimental Social Psychology*, 1(3): 199–218.

—— (1972) 'Self-perception theory', in L. Berkowitz (ed.) *Advances in Experimental Social Psychology*, New York: Academic Press.

Bendapudi, N., Singh, S. N. and Bendapudi, V. (1996) 'Enhancing helping behavior: An integrative framework for promotion planning', *Journal of Marketing*, 60(3): 33–49.

Bennett, R. (2003) 'Factors underlying the inclination to donate to particular types of charity', *International Journal of Nonprofit and Voluntary Sector Marketing*, 8(1): 12–29.

—— and Barkensjo, A. (2005) 'Causes and consequences of donor perceptions of the quality of the relationship marketing activities of charitable organizations', *Journal of Targeting, Measurement and Analysis for Marketing*, 13(2): 122–39.

—— and Savani, S. (2003) 'Predicting the accuracy of public perceptions of charity performance', *Journal of Targeting, Measurement and Analysis for Marketing*, 11(4): 326–42.

Benson, P. L. and Catt, V. L. (1978) 'Soliciting charity contributions: The parlance of asking for money', *Journal of Applied Social Psychology*, 8(1): 84–95.

Berger, S. M. (1962). 'Conditioning through vicarious instigation', *Psychological Review*, 69(5): 450–66.

Berkowitz, L. and Daniels, L. R. (1962) 'Responsibility and dependency', *Journal of Abnormal and Social Psychology*, 66: 429–36.

Bies, R. J. (1987) 'The predicament of injustice: The management of moral outrage', in L. L. Cummings and B. M. Staw (eds) *Research in Organizational Behavior*, Greenwich, CT: JAI Press.

Blake, R. R., Rosenbaum, M. and Duryea, R. A. (1955) 'Gift giving as a function of group standards', *Human Relations*, 8(1): 61–73.

Bolton, G. and Katok, E. (1998) 'An experimental test of the crowding out hypothesis: The nature of beneficial behavior', *Journal of Economic Behavior and Organization*, 37(3): 315–31.

Boris, E. T. (1987) 'The values of the wealthy: Philanthropic attitudes as a reflection of political philosophy in American culture', in *The Constitution and The Independent Sector*, Washington, DC: Independent Sector, pp. 237–47.

Boulding, K. E. (1973) *The Economy of Love and Fear: A Preface To Grants Economics*, Belmont, CA: Wadsworth.

Brady, M. K., Doble, C. H., Utter, D. J. and Smith, G. E. (2002) 'How to give and receive: An exploratory study of charitable hybrids', *Psychology and Marketing*, 19 (11): 919–44.

Braus, P. (1994) 'Will boomers give generously?', *American Demographics*, 16(7): 48–52.

Brehm, J. W. (1966) *A Theory of Psychological Reactance*, New York: Academic Press.

Brehm, S. S. and Brehm, J. W. (1981) *Psychological Reactance: A Theory of Freedom and Control*, New York: Academic Press.

Brockner, J., Guzzi, B., Kane, J., Levine, E. and Shaplen, K. (1984) 'Organizational fundraising: Further evidence on the effects of legitimizing small donations', *Journal of Consumer Research*, 11(1): 611–14.

Brolley, D. Y. and Anderson, S. C. (1986) 'Advertising and attitudes', *Rehabilitation Digest*, 17(3): 15–17.

Brunetti, M. J. (2005) 'The estate tax and charitable bequests: Elasticity estimates using probate records', *National Tax Journal*, 58(2): 165–88.

Bryan, J. H. and Test, M. A. (1967) 'Models and helping: Naturalistic studies in aiding behaviour of crowding in on others', *Journal of Applied Social Psychology*, 6: 400–7.

Bryant, W. K., Jeon-Slaughter, H., Kang, H. and Tax, A. (2003) 'Participation in philanthropic activities: Donating money and time', *Journal of Consumer Policy*, 26(1): 43–74.

Burnett, K. (2002) *Relationship Fundraising*, San Francisco: Jossey Bass.

Callero, P. L., Howard, J. A. and Piliavin, J. A. (1987) 'Helping behavior as role behavior: Disclosing social structure and history in the analysis of pro-social action', *Social Psychology Quarterly*, 50(3): 247–56.

Cann, A., Sherman, S. J. and Elkes, R. (1975) 'Effects of initial request size and timing of a second request on compliance: The foot in the door and the door in the face', *Journal of Personality and Social Psychology*, 32(5): 774–82.

Cermak, D., File, K. and Prince, R. (1994) 'A benefit segmentation of the major donor market', *Journal of Business Research*, 29(2): 121–30.

Cialdini, R. B. (1984) *Influence: The New Psychology of Modern Persuasion*, New York: HarperTrade.

—— and Ascani, K. (1976) 'Test of a concession procedure for inducing verbal, behavioural and further compliance with a request to give blood', *Journal of Applied Psychology*, 61(3): 295–300.

—— and Schroeder, D. A. (1976) 'Increasing compliance by legitimizing paltry contributions: When even a penny helps', *Journal of Personality and Social Psychology*, 34(4): 599–604.

—— Reno, R. R. and Kallgren, C. A. (1990) 'A focus theory of normative conduct: Recycling the concept of norms to reduce littering in public places', *Journal of Personality and Social Psychology*, 58(6): 1015–26.

—— Schaller, M., Houlihan, D., Arps, K., Fultz, J. and Beaman, A. (1987) 'Empathy-based helping: Is it selflessly or selfishly motivated?', *Journal of Personality and Social Psychology*, 52(4): 749–58.

Clary, E. G. and Snyder, M. (1991). 'A functional analysis of altruism and pro-social behaviour: The case of volunteerism', *Review of Personality and Social Psychology*, 12: 119–48.

Clotfelter, C. T. (1985) *Federal Tax Policy and Charitable Giving*, Chicago: University of Chicago Press.

Cnaan, R. A. and Goldberg-Glen, R. S. (1991) 'Measuring motivation to volunteer in human services', *Journal of Applied Behavioral Science*, 27(3): 269–84.

Coke, J. S., Batson, C. D. and McDavis, K. (1978) 'Empathic mediation of helping: A two stage model', *Journal of Personality and Social Psychology*, 36: 752–66.

Coleman, J. S. (1990) *Foundations of Social Theory*, Cambridge, MA: Harvard University Press.

Coliazzi, A., Williams, K. J. and Kayson, W. A. (1984) 'When will people help? The effects of gender, urgency and location on altruism', *Psychological Reports*, 55: 139–42.

Collard, D. A. (1978) *Altruism and Economy: A Study in Non-selfish Economics*, New York: Oxford University Press.

Conley, A. (1999) 'Student organization membership and alumni giving at a public research university', unpublished doctoral dissertation, Indiana University.

Cutlip, S. M. (1990) *Fundraising in the United States: Its Role in America's Philanthropy*, New Brunswick, NJ: Transaction Publishers.

Davis, M. H. (1983) 'Measuring individual differences in empathy: Evidence for a multidimensional approach', *Journal of Personality and Social Psychology*, 44(1): 113–26.

—— Hull, J. G., Young, R. D. and Warren, G. G. (1987) 'Emotional reactions to dramatic film stimuli: The influence of cognitive and emotional empathy', *Journal of Personality and Social Psychology*, 52(1): 126–33.

—— Mitchell K. V., Hall, J. A., Lothert, J., Snapp, T. and Meyer, M. (1999) 'Empathy, expectations and situational preferences: Personality influences on the decision to participate in volunteer helping behaviours', *Journal of Personality*, 67(3): 469–503.

Dawson, S. (1988) 'Four motivations for charitable giving: Implications for marketing strategy to attract monetary donations for medical research', *Journal of Health Care Marketing*, 8(2): 31–7.

Desmet, P. and Feinberg, F. (2003) 'Ask and ye shall receive: The effect of the appeals scale on consumers' donation behavior', *Journal of Economic Psychology*, 24(3), 349–76.

Duncan, B. (2004) 'A theory of impact philanthropy', *Journal of Public Economics*, 88(9/10): 2159–81.

Eayrs, C. B. and Ellis, N. (1990) 'Charity advertising. For or against people with a mental handicap?', *British Journal of Social Psychology*, 29(4): 349–66.

Eisenberg, N. and Miller, P. A. (1987) 'The relation of empathy to prosocial and related behaviors', *Psychological Bulletin*, 101(1): 91–119.

—— Guthrie, I. K., Cumberland, A., Murphy, B. C. and Shepard, S. A. (2002) 'Prosocial development in early adulthood: A longitudinal study', *Journal of Personality and Social Psychology*, 82(6): 993–1006.

Elliot, T. R. and Byrd, E. K. (1982) 'Media and disability', *Rehabilitation Literature*, 43(11/12): 348–55.

Eysenck, S. B., Pearson, P. R., Esting, G. and Allsopp, J. F. (1985) 'Age norms for impulsiveness, venturesomeness and empathy in adults', *Personality and Individual Differences*, 6(5): 613–19.

Feinman, S. (1978) 'When does sex affect altruistic behavior?', *Psychological Reports*, 43: 1218.

Feldman, D. and Feldman, B. (1985) 'The effect of a telethon on attitudes toward disabled people and financial contributions', *Journal of Rehabilitation*, 51(3): 42–5.

Festinger, L. (1954) 'A theory of social comparison processes', *Human Relations*, 7(2): 117–40.

Ford, D. (1976) 'The marketing of non-profit making organizations: A preliminary report', *European Journal of Marketing*, 10(5): 266–79.

Fraser, C., Hite, R. E. and Sauer, P. L. (1988) 'Increasing contributions in solicitation campaigns: The use of large and small anchorpoints', *Journal of Consumer Research*, 15(2): 284–7.

Freedman, J. L. and Fraser, S. (1966) 'Compliance without pressure: The foot in the door technique', *Journal of Personality and Social Psychology*, 4(2): 195–202.

Frisch, M. and Gerrard, M. (1981) 'Natural helping systems: A survey of Red Cross volunteers', *American Journal of Community Psychology*, 9(4): 567–79.

Frumkin, P. and Kim, M. T. (2001) 'Strategic positioning and the financing of nonprofit organizations: Is efficiency rewarded in the contributions marketplace?', *Public Administration Review* 61(3), 266–275.

Fultz, J., Schaller, M. and Cialdini, R. B. (1988) 'Empathy, sadness and distress: Three related but distinct vicarious affective responses to another's suffering', *Personality and Social Psychology Bulletin*, 14(2): 312–25.

Fultz, J. C., Batson, D., Fortenbach, V. A., McCarthy, P. M. and Varney, L. L. (1986) 'Social evaluation and the empathy altruism hypothesis', *Journal of Personality and Social Psychology*, 50(4): 761–9.

Fundraising School (1999) *Principles and Techniques of Fundraising*, Indianapolis: Indiana University/Purdue University.

Gächter, S. and Fehr, E. (1999) 'Collective action as a social exchange', *Journal of Economic Behavior and Organization*, 39(4): 341–69.

Glaser, J. S. (1994) *The United Way Scandal – An Insider's Account of What Went Wrong and Why*, New York: John Wiley and Sons.

Goldberg, L. R. (1981) 'Language and individual differences: The search for universals in personality lexicons', in L. Wheeler (ed.) *Review of Personality and Social Psychology* (1st edn), Beverly Hills, CA: Sage Publications.

—— (1993) 'The structure of phenotypic personality traits', *American Psychology*, 48(1): 26–34.

Gorenflo, D. W. and Crano, W. D. (1998) 'The multiple perspectives inventory: A measure of perspective-taking', *Swiss Journal of Psychology*, 57(3): 163–77.

Graney, M. J. and Graney, E. E. (1974) 'Communications Activity Substitutions in Ageing', *Journal of Communication*, 24(4), 88–89.

Graziano, W. G. and Eisenberg, N. (1997) 'Agreeableness: A dimension of personality', in R. Hogan, J. Johnson and S. Briggs (eds) *Handbook of Personality Psychology*, New York, NY: Academic Press.

Greenberg, J. (1987) 'A taxonomy of organizational justice theories', *Academy of Management Review*, 12(1): 9–22.

Griffin, M., Babin, B. J., Attaway, J. S. and Darden, W. R. (1993) 'Hey you, can ya spare some change? The case of empathy and personal distress as reactions to charitable appeals', *Advances in Consumer Research*, 20(1): 508–14.

Grounds, J. and Harkness, J. (1998) 'Developing a brand from within: Involving employees and volunteers when developing a new brand position', *Journal of Nonprofit and Voluntary Sector Marketing*, 3(2): 179–84.

Gruder, C. L. and Cook, T. D. (1971) 'Sex dependency and helping', *Journal of Personality and Social Psychology*, 19(3), 290–4.

Halfpenny, P. (1990) *Charity Household Survey 1988/9*, Tonbridge, UK: Charities Aid Foundation.

Hall, H. (2004) 'Gender differences in giving: Going, going, gone?', *New Directions for Philanthropic Fundraising*, 2004(43): 71–81.

Hansler, D. F. and Riggin, D. L. (1989) 'Geo-demographics: Targeting the market', *Fundraising Management*, 20: 35–40.

Harbaugh, W. (1998) 'What do donations buy? A model of philanthropy based on prestige and warm glow', *Journal of Public Economics*, 67(2): 269–84.

Harris, R. M. (1975) 'The effect of perspective taking, similarity and dependency on raising funds for persons with disabilities', unpublished Master's thesis, University of Kansas, Lawrence, KS.

Harris, R. M. and Harris, A. C. (1977) 'Devaluation of the disabled in fundraising', *Rehabilitation Psychology*, 24: 69–78.

Harvey, J. (1990) 'Benefit segmentation for fundraisers', *Journal of the Academy of Marketing Science*, 18(1): 77–86.

Harvey, J. W. and McCrohan, K. F. (1988) 'Fundraising costs: Societal implications for philanthropies and their supporters', *Business and Society*, 27(1): 15–22.

Heider, F. (1958) *The Psychology of Interpersonal Relations*, Hillsdale, NJ: Lawrence Erlbaum.

Hibbert, S., Hogg, G. and Quinn, T. (2005) 'Social entrepreneurship: Understanding consumer motives for buying the *Big Issue*', *Journal of Consumer Behaviour*, 4(3): 159–72.

Hoffman, M. L. (1984) 'Interaction of affect and cognition in empathy', in C. E. Izard, J. Kagan and R. B. Zajonc (eds) *Emotions, Cognition and Behavior*, Cambridge, UK: Cambridge University Press.

Howard, D. J. (1990) 'The influence of verbal responses to common greetings on compliance behavior: The foot-in-the-mouth effect', *Journal of Applied Social Psychology*, 20(14): 1185–96.

Irwin-Wells, S. (2002) *Planning and Implementing Your Major Gifts Campaign*, San Francisco: Jossey Bass.

Isen, A. M. and Noonberg. A. (1979) 'The effects of photographs of the handicapped on donations to charity: When a thousand words may be too much', *Journal of Applied Social Psychology*, 9(5): 426–31.

Jackson, T. D. (2001) 'Young African Americans: A new generation of giving behavior', *International Journal of Nonprofit and Voluntary Sector Marketing*, 6(3): 243–54

Jay, E. (2002) 'The rise and fall? Of face to face fundraising in the United Kingdom', *New Directions for Philanthropic Fundraising*, 33 (autumn): 83–94.

Jenks, C. (1990) 'Varieties of altruism', in J. J. Mansbridge (ed.) *Beyond Self Interest*, Chicago: University of Chicago Press.

Jones, M. L. (1985) 'Words and images', *Independent Living Forum*, 2: 14–15.

Jones, A. and Posnett, J. (1991) 'Charitable giving by UK households: Evidence from the Family Expenditure Survey', *Applied Economics*, 23(2): 343–51.

Jones, M. and McKee, M. (2004) 'Feedback information and contributions to not-for-profit enterprises: Experimental investigations and implications for large-scale fundraising', *Public Finance Review*, 32(5): 512–27.

Kaehler, J. and Sargeant, A. (1998) 'Returns on fundraising expenditures in the voluntary sector', *Working Paper 98/06*, University of Exeter, UK.

Keating, B., Pitts, R. and Appel, D. (1981) 'United Way contributions: Coercion, charity or economic self-interest?', *Southern Economic Journal*, 47(3): 816–23.

Kelman, H. C. (1961) 'Processes of opinion change,' *Public Opinion Quarterly*, 25(1): 57–78.

Khanna, J. and Sandler, T. (2000) 'Partners in giving: The crowding-in effects of UK government grants', *European Economic Review*, 44(8): 1543–56.

Kingma, B. R. (1989) 'An accurate measurement of the crowd-out effect, income effect, and price effect for charitable contributions', *Journal of Political Economy*, 97(5): 1197–207.

Kotler, P. and Andreasen, A. (1987) *Strategic Marketing for Nonprofit Organizations* (3rd edn), Englewood Cliffs, NJ: Prentice Hall.

Kottasz, R. (2004) 'How should charitable organizations motivate young professionals to give philanthropically?', *International Journal of Nonprofit and Voluntary Sector Marketing*, 9(1): 9–27.

Kraut, R. F. (1973) 'Effects of social labeling on giving to charity', *Journal of Experimental Social Psychology*, 9(6): 551–62.

Krebs, D. (1982) 'Altruism – A rational approach', in N. Eisenberg (ed.) *Development of Prosocial Behaviour*, New York: Academic Press.

—— and Miller, D. T. (1985) 'Altruism and aggression', in G. Lindzey and E. Aronson (eds) *Handbook of Social Psychology* (2nd edn), New York: Random House.

—— and Whitten, P. (1972) 'Guilt edged giving', *Psychology Today*, 5: 50–60.

Latane, B. (1981) 'Psychology of social impact', *American Psychologist*, 36(4): 343–56.

—— and Nida, S. (1981) 'Ten years of research on group size and helping', *Psychological Bulletin*, 89(2): 308–24.

Lattin, D. (1977) 'Telethons: A remnant of the past', *Disabled USA*, 1(4): 18–19.

Lerner, M. J. (1975) 'The justice motive in social behavior', *Journal of Social Issues*, 31: 1–20.

Levis, W. C. (1990) 'Increased giving by investing more money in fundraising wisely', *Philanthropy Monthly*, April/May: 2.

Lindskold, S., Forte, A., Haake, C. S. and Schmidt, E. K. (1977) 'The effects in directedness of face-to-face requests and sex of solicitor on street corner donations', *The Journal of Social Psychology*, 101(1): 45–51.

List, J. A. and Lucking-Reiley, D. (2002) 'The effects of seed money and refunds on charitable giving: Experimental evidence from a university capital campaign', *Journal of Political Economy*, 110(1): 215–33.

Lohmann, R. (1992) 'The commons: A multidisciplinary approach to nonprofit organization, voluntary action and philanthropy', *Nonprofit and Voluntary Sector Quarterly*, 21(3): 309–24.

Macaulay, J. R. (1970) 'A skill for charity', in J. Macaulay and L. Berkowitz (eds) *Altruism and Helping Behavior: Social Psychological Studies of some Antecedents and Consequences*, New York: Academic Press.

Macaulay, J. R. (1975) 'Familiarity, attraction and charity', *Journal of Social Psychology*, 95(1): 27–37.

Mahatoo, W. M. and Banting, P. M. (1988) 'Breathing new life into the lung association', *European Research*, 16: 247–53.

Marx, J. D. (2000) 'Women and human services giving', *Social Work*, 45(1): 27–38.

Mathur, A. (1996) 'Older adults' motivations for gift giving to charitable organizations: An exchange theory perspective', *Psychology and Marketing*, 13(1): 107–23.

McClelland, R. and Brooks, A. C. (2004) 'What is the real relationship between income and charitable giving?', *Public Finance Review*, 32(5): 483–97.

McGuire, W. J. and Padawer-Singer, A. (1976) 'Trait salience in the spontaneous self concept', *Journal of Personality and Social Psychology*, 33(6): 743–54.

McKinnon, H. (1999) *Hidden Gold*, Chicago: Bonus Books.

McNair, I. (2005) 'International aid agencies wax while welfare wanes', *Fundraising and Philanthropy*, August: 24–5.

Mears, P. (1992) 'Understanding strong donors', *Fund Raising Management*, 23(2): 45–8.

Mesch, D. J., Rooney, P. M., Chin, W. and Steinberg, K. S. (2002) 'Race and gender differences in philanthropy: Indiana as a test case', *New Directions for Philanthropic Fundraising*, 37(fall): 65–78.

Midlarsky, E. (1971) 'Aiding under stress: The effect of competence, dependency, visibility and fatalism', *Journal of Personality*, 39(1): 132–49.

—— and Hannah, M. E. (1989) 'The generous elderly: Naturalistic studies of donations across the life span', *Psychology and Ageing*, 4(3): 346–51.

Milgram, S. (1970) 'The experience of living in cities: A psychological analysis', *Science*, 167(3924): 1461–68.

Miller, D. T. (1977) 'Altruism and threat to a belief in a just world', *Journal of Experimental Social Psychology*, 13(2): 113–24.

Millet, R. and Orosz, J. (2001) *Cultures of Caring: Philanthropy in Diverse American Communities*, The Kellogg Foundation.

Mitchell, H. E. and Byrne, D. (1973) 'The defendant's dilemma: Effects of jurors' attitudes and authoritari-ansim on judicial decisions', *Journal of Personality and Social Psychology*, 25(1): 123–9.

Moore, E. M., Bearden, W. O. and Teel, J. E. (1985) 'Use of labeling and assertions of dependency in appeals for consumer support', *Journal of Consumer Research*, 12(1): 90–6.

Morgan, J. N., Dye, R. F. and Hybels, J. H. (1979) *Results From Two National Surveys Of Philanthropic Activity*, Michigan: University of Michigan Press.

Mount, J. and Quirion, F. (1988) 'A study of donors to a university campaign', *Philanthropist*, 8(1): 56–64.

Mowen, J. C. and Cialdini, R. B. (1980) 'On implementing the door-in-the-face compliance technique in a business context', *Journal of Marketing Research*, 17(2): 253–8.

Nichols, J. E. (1992) 'Targeting older America', *Fund Raising Management*, 23(3): 38–41.

Nyborg, K. and Rege, M. (2003) 'Does public policy crowd out private contributions to public goods?', *Public Choice*, 115(3/4): 397–418.

Okten, C. and Weisbrod, B. (2000) 'Determinants of donations in private nonprofit markets', *Journal of Public Economics*, 75(2): 255–72.

Osgood, C. E. and Tannenbaum, P. H. (1955) 'The principle of congruity in the prediction of attitude change', *Psychological Review*, 62(1): 42–55.

Ostrower, F. (1997) *Why The Wealthy Give: The Culture of Elite Philanthropy*, Princeton, NJ: Princeton University Press.

Peloza, J. and Steel, P. (2005) 'The price elasticities of charitable contributions: A meta-analysis', *Journal of Public Policy and Marketing*, 24(2): 260–72.

Penner, L. A., Fritzsche, B. A., Craiger, J. P. and Freifeld, T. R. (1995) 'Measuring the prosocial personality', in J. Butcher and C. D. Spielberger (eds) *Advances in Personality Assessment Volume 10*, Hillsdale, NJ: Lawrence Erlbaum Associates.

Penner, L. A., Dovidio, J. F., Piliavin, J. A. and Schroeder, D. A. (2005) 'Prosocial behavior: Multilevel perspectives', *Annual Review of Psychology*, 56(1): 365–92.

Pharoah, C. and Tanner, S. (1997) 'Trends in charitable giving', *Fiscal Studies*, 18(4): 427–43.

Pidgeon, S. (2001) 'Using brands to build relationships', presentation to the Institute of Fundraising conference, Birmingham, UK, July.

Pieper, E. (1975) 'What price charity?', *Exceptional Parent*, 5(1): 35–40.

Piferi, R. L., Jobe, R. L. and Jones, W. H. (2006) 'Giving to others during national tragedy: The effects of altruistic and egoistic motivations on long-term giving', *Journal of Social and Personal Relationships*, 23(1): 171–84.

Piliavin, J. A. and Charng, H. W. (1990) 'Altruism: A review of recent theory and research', *Annual Review of Sociology*, 16(1): 27–65.

—— Piliavin, J. A. and Rodin, J. (1975) 'Costs of diffusion and the stigmatized victim', *Journal of Personality and Social Psychology*, 32(3): 429–38.

—— Dovidio, J. F., Gaertner, S. L. and Clark, R. D. (1981) *Emergency Intervention*, New York: Academic Press.

Potters, J., Sefton, M. and Vesterlund, L. (2005) 'After you – Endogenous sequencing in voluntary contribution games', *Journal of Public Economics*, 89(8): 1399–1419.

Radcliffe, R. (2002). 'Legacy fundraising', presentation to the Institute of Fundraising conference, Birmingham, UK, July.

Radley, A. and Kennedy, M. (1992) 'Reflections upon charitable giving: A comparison of individuals from business, "manual" and professional backgrounds', *Journal of Community and Applied Social Psychology*, 2(2): 113–29.

—— (1995) 'Charitable giving by individuals: A study of attitudes and practice', *Human Relations*, 48(6): 685–709.

Reeves, R. A., Macolini, R. M. and Martin, R. C. (1987) 'Legitimizing paltry contributions: On-the-spot versus mail-in requests', *Journal of Applied Social Psychology*, 17(8): 731–8.

Rege, M. (2004) 'Social norms and private provision of public goods', *Journal of Public Economic Theory*, 6(1): 65–77.

Rege, M. and Telle, K. (2001) 'An experimental discussion of social norms', discussion papers no. 310, *Research Department, Oslo, Statistics Norway.*

Reingen, P. H. (1978) 'On inducing compliance with requests', *Journal of Consumer Research,* 5(2): 96–102.

Ribar, D. C. and Wilhelm, M. O. (2002) 'Altruistic and joy-of-giving motivation in charitable behavior', *Journal of Political Economy,* 110(2): 425–57.

Riecken, G., Babakus, E. and Yavas, U. (1995) 'Facing resource attraction challenges in the nonprofit sector: A behavioristic approach to fund-raising and volunteer recruitment', *Journal of Professional Services Marketing,* 11(1): 45–70.

Roehler, G. A. (1961) 'Significance of public attitudes in the rehabilitation of the disabled', *Rehabilitation Literature,* 22: 66–72.

Roloff, M. E. (1987) *Interpersonal Communication: The Social Exchange Approach,* Beverly Hills, CA: Sage Publications.

—— Janiszewski, C. A., McGrath, M. A., Burns, C. S. and Manrai, L. A. (1988) 'Acquiring resources from intimate: When obligation substitutes for persuasion', *Human Communication Research,* 14(3): 364–96.

Rytting, M., Ware, R. and Prince, R. A. (1994) 'Bimodal distributions in a sample of CEOs: Validating evidence for the MBTI', *Journal of Psychology Type,* 31: 16–31.

Sargeant, A. (1996) 'Market segmentation in the UK charity sector', unpublished Ph.D. thesis, University of Exeter, UK.

—— (2001) 'Relationship fundraising: How to keep donors loyal', *Nonprofit Management and Leadership,* 12(2): 177–92

—— and Hudson, J. (2005) 'Nonprofit brand or bland: An exploration of the structure of charity brand personality', *Proceedings of EMAC,* Milan, Italy: Università Bocconi,, 24–7 May, CD-ROM.

—— and Jay, E. (2004) *Fundraising Management,* London: Routledge.

—— and Kaehler, J. (1998) *Benchmarking Charity Costs,* West Malling, Kent, UK: Charities Aid Foundation.

—— and Lee, S. (2004) 'Donor trust and relationship commitment in the U. K. charity sector: Determinants of donor behavior?', *Nonprofit and Voluntary Sector Quarterly,* 33(2): 185–202.

—— and McKenzie, J. (1998) *A Lifetime of Giving: An Analysis of Donor Lifetime Value,* West Malling, Kent, UK: Charities Aid Foundation.

—— Ford, J. B. and West, D. C. (2004) 'The perceptual determinants of charity giving', *Service Industries Journal,* 24(6): 19–36.

—— (2006) 'Perceptual determinants of nonprofit giving behaviour', *Journal of Business Research,* 59(2): 155–65.

—— and Woodliffe, L. (2005) 'The antecedents of donor commitment to voluntary organizations', *Nonprofit Management and Leadership,* 16(1): 61–78.

—— Radcliffe, R. and Jay, E. (2003) *Legacy Fundraising,* London: Smee and Ford.

—— West, D. C. and Ford, J. B. (2001) 'The role of perceptions in predicting donor value', *Journal of Marketing Management,* 17(3/4): 407–28.

Schaller, M. and Cialdini, R. B. (1988) 'The economics of empathic helping: Support for a mood management motive', *Journal of Experimental Social Psychology,* 24(2): 163–81.

Schervish, P. G. (1993) 'Philosophy as moral identity of caritas', in P. G. Schervish, O. Benz, P. Dulaney, T. B. Murphy and S. Salett (eds) *Taking Giving Seriously,* Indiana University, IN: Center on Philanthropy.

—— (1997) 'Inclination, obligation and association: What we know and what we need to learn about donor motivation', in D. Burlingame (ed.) *Critical Issues in Fund Raising,* Hoboken, NJ: Wiley.

—— and Havens, J. J. (1997) 'Social participation and charitable giving: A multivariate analysis', *Voluntas,* 8(3): 235–60.

Schlegelmilch, B. B. (1988) 'Targeting of fundraising appeals – How to identify donors', *European Journal of Marketing,* 22(1): 31–40.

—— and Tynan, A. C. (1989) 'The scope for market segmentation within the charity market: An empircal analysis', *Managerial and Decision Economics,* 10(2): 127–34.

Schroeder, D. A., Dovidio, J. R., Sibicky, M. E., Matthews, L. L. and Allen, J. L. (1988) 'Empathy, concern and helping behaviour: Egoism or altruism?', *Journal of Experimental Social Psychology*, 24(4): 333–53.

Schwartz, S. (1977) 'Normative influences on altruism', in L. Berkowitz (ed.) *Advances In Experimental Social Psychology*, volume 10, New York, NY: Academic Press, pp. 221–79.

Scott, C. A. (1977) 'Modifying socially conscious behavior: The foot-in-the-door technique', *Journal of Consumer Research*, 4(3): 156–64.

Shelton, M. L. and Rogers, R. W. (1981) 'Fear arousing and empathy arousing appeals to help: The pathos of persuasion', *Journal of Applied Psychology*, 11(4): 366–78.

Shuptrine, F. K. and Moore, E. M. (1980) 'The public's perceptions of the American Heart Association: Awareness, image and opinions', in J. H. Sumney and R. D. Taylor (eds) *Evolving Marketing Thought for 1980*, Atlanta, GA: Southern Marketing Association.

Shurka, E., Siller, J. and Dvonch, P. (1982) 'Coping behaviour and personal responsibility as factors in the perception of disabled persons by the non-disabled', *Rehabilitation Psychology*, 27: 225–33.

Silver, M. (1980) *Affluence, Altruism and Atrophy: The Decline of the Welfare State*, New York, NY: New York University Press.

Simmons, W. and Emanuele, R. (2004) 'Does government spending crowd out donations of time and money?', *Public Finance Review*, 32(5): 498–511.

Stark, O. (1989) 'Altruism and the quality of life', *American Economic Review*, 79(2): 86–90.

Staub, E. and Baer, R., 'Stimulus characteristics of a sufferer and difficulty of escape as determinants of helping', *Journal of Personality and Social Psychology*, 1974, 30: 279–284.

Steffy, B. D. and Jones, J. W. (1988) 'The impact of family and career planning variables on the organizational, career and community commitment of professional women', *Journal of Vocational Behavior*, 32(2): 196–212.

Steinberg, R. (1986) 'Should donors care about fundraising?', in S. Rose-Ackerman (ed.) *The Economics of Nonprofit Institutions: Studies in Structure and Policy*, New York, NY: Oxford University Press.

Stroebe, W. and Frey, B. S. (1982) 'Self-interest and collective action: The economics and psychology of public goods', *British Journal of Social Psychology*, 21(1): 121–37.

Swinyard, W. R. and Ray, M. L. (1977) 'Advertising–selling interactions: An attribution theory experiment', *Journal of Marketing Research*, 14(4): 509–16.

Tapp, A. (1996) 'Charity brands: A qualitative study of current practice', *Journal of Nonprofit and Voluntary Sector Marketing*, 1(4): 327–36.

Tybout, A. M. and Yalch, R. F. (1980) 'The effect of experience: A matter of salience?', *Journal of Consumer Research*, 6(4): 406–13.

Tyler, T. R. (1994) 'Psychological models of the justice motives: Antecedents of distributive and procedural justice', *Journal of Personality and Social Psychology*, 67(5): 850–63.

Venable, B. T., Rose, G. M., Bush, V. D. and Gilbert, F. W. (2005) 'The role of brand personality in charitable giving: An assessment and validation', *Journal of the Academy of Marketing Science*, 33(3): 295–312.

Wagner, C. and Wheeler, L. (1969) 'Model, need, and cost effects in helping behavior', *Journal of Personality and Social Psychology*, 12(2): 111–16.

Walker, C. and Pharoah, C. (2002) *A Lot of Give*, London: Hodder & Stoughton.

Wang, T., Brownstein, R. and Katzev, R. (1989) 'Promoting charitable behavior with compliance techniques', *Applied Psychology*, 38(2): 165–83.

Warwick, M. (1994) *Raising Money by Mail: Strategies For Growth and Financial Stability*, Berkeley, CA: Strathmoor Press.

—— and Hitchcock, S. (2001) *Ten Steps To Fundraising Success: Choosing the Right Strategy for your Organization*, San Francisco, CA: Jossey Bass.

Weyant, J. M. (1984) 'Applying social psychology to induce charitable donations', *Journal of Applied Social Psychology*, 14(5): 441–7.

—— (1996) 'Application of compliance techniques to direct-mail requests for charitable donations', *Psychology and Marketing*, 13(2): 157–70.

—— and Smith, S. L. (1987) 'Getting more by asking for less: The effects of request size on donations of charity', *Journal of Applied Social Psychology*, 17(4): 392–400.

Wilson, J. P. and Petruska, R. (1984) 'Motivation, model attributes and prosocial behavior', *Journal of Personality and Social Psychology*, 46(2): 458–68.

Wispe, L. (1978) *Altruism, Sympathy and Helping*, New York: Academic Press.

—— (1986) 'The distinction between sympathy and empathy: To call forth a concept, a word is needed', *Journal of Personality and Social Psychology*, 50(2): 314–21.

Yankelovich, D. (1985) *The Charitable Behavior of Americans, Management Survey*, Washington, DC: Independent Sector.

Yavas, U., Riecken, G. and Parameswaran, R. (1980) 'Using psychographics to profile potential donors', *Business Atlanta*, 30(5): 41–5.

Yavas, U. and Riecken, R. (1985) 'Can volunteers be targeted?', *Journal of the Academy of Marketing Science*, 13(2): 218–28.

Zuckerman, M., Iazzaro, M. and Waldgeir, D. (1979) 'Undermining effects of foot-in-the-door with extrinsic rewards', *Journal of Applied Social Psychology*, 9(3): 292–6.

8

Corporate philanthropy

Who gives and why?

Kym Madden and Wendy Scaife

Introduction

This chapter considers what we know, and what we might like to know about corporate philanthropy (CP) and community engagement (CE). This concern for corporate support cannot be underestimated. Giving may be increasing, but so too are nonprofit (NP) numbers and traditional government funding is waning. Currently corporate giving represents only a fraction of the funds feeding the NP sector and developing explicit ties with business is needed for nonprofit organizations (NPOs) to survive (Andreasen 2006).

Not all observers see corporate philanthropy as positive, however, and challenges exist from both the corporate and NP perspectives. From the corporate perspective, some suggest a relationship between corporations and NPOs diverts the corporation from its commercial objectives. Part of this argument is that collaboration makes more demands on business, even setting up NPOs as non-state regulators when corporations do not want more regulation. This school of thought asserts that NPOs are given an inappropriate power to direct the corporation, particularly when the NPO is an advocacy organization.

A similar criticism is levelled by NPOs that inappropriate power may be exercised by corporate partners and too much assumption of beneficial outcomes is made. As MacDonald and Chrisp highlight (2005: 305), the partnership literature tends towards the positive and prescriptive and the 'very vocabulary of partnership is saturated with sharing, caring words, poorly suited to rigorous analysis'. That this analysis and evaluation is usually carried out by those with a vested partnership interest proffers food for research thought.

NP–business alliances also provide an intriguing research environment. Not only are businesses now more savvy in using such alliances to achieve profits but willingness grows continually for business to collaborate across sectors to solve pressing community problems (Galaskiewicz and Colman 2006). Researchers from varying intellectual traditions are finding many unexplored issues, especially as the conventional boundaries of NPOs and governments are dissolving and innovative partnering opportunities are sought.

The chapter maps this diverse territory by first considering NP–business alliances as part of the tidal wave of studies in corporate social responsibility (CSR). Next, the chapter contemplates research on corporate philanthropy and corporate community involvement (CCI) from the perspective of business marketers, who are thinking 'strategically' about CE activities. Since the 1970s, an 'enlightened self-interest' paradigm has emerged, providing fresh impetus for business to deepen relationships with community organizations (Kotler and Lee 2005). The types and levels of NP support in which business engages is informed by what a business seeks to *achieve* through its activities – its motivations (the why) and its objectives at any given time (the what) – as well as by its perceived potential to engage. The chapter acknowledges research in the emerging area of community–business *partnerships* before turning to the vastly under-researched NP perspective. Chief concerns here include the challenge of adopting business marketing skills and orienting diverse stakeholders to business concepts for that NPO.

Interwoven are some theories that buttress understanding. While space precludes detailing the full array of these, the chapter primes researchers seeking to contribute to research and, in turn, practice. Where appropriate, we have taken the opportunity to complement the US studies that tend to populate the literature with other studies. The chapter concludes with possible research directions.

Before proceeding, we note that the term 'corporate philanthropy' is used in different ways by scholars: some exclude activities which bring advantages to business while others do not (see Bennett 1998; Bruch and Walter 2005). Moreover, businesses which support NPOs can grate at the suggestion of altruism in an era of escalating shareholder concerns for performance and accountability (Martin 1998). Burlingame (2001: 4) usefully observes the *evolution* of the term:

> [The notion of corporate philanthropy today] recognises multiple forms of giving by companies as vehicles for both business goals and social goals. In the current decade we are much more likely to find that corporate philanthropy, corporate sponsorship, corporate research support, volunteer time and CRM work together to achieve strategic corporate objectives.

This pressure for business to count its CP/CCI returns has existed for well over a decade (see Himmelstein 1997), although Adam Smith's 1776 writings show the longevity of the business–society relationship debate. However, we are seeing intensified efforts to justify these expenditures. As Bruch and Walter (2005: 50) emphasize the dual needs: 'Only philanthropic activities that both create true value for the beneficiaries and enhance the company's business performance are sustainable in the long run.'

In this chapter, then, corporate philanthropy and corporate community involvement will be terms used *together* (CP/CCI) to span the full collaboration spectrum. CCI is used to represent those alliances that benefit *both* businesses and society (the community), to a greater or lesser extent in different circumstances. While it may be argued that the term 'corporate philanthropy' thus is rendered redundant, it is retained in our discussion because it is a term relied upon by various scholars. The term 'community engagement' (CE) is also used interchangeably with CP/CCI as the latter can be cumbersome.

CSR as an overarching construct

CP/CCI (or CE) fits within the overarching business-centred construct of corporate social responsibility, a construct that could be likened to a main channel with many conceptual and practical tributaries (such as ethical business conduct, workplace diversity and well-being, environmental protection and corporate citizenship) (Clikeman 2004; Bruch and Walter 2005). More than twenty-five definitions of CSR exist (Godfrey and Hatch 2007) and in reviewing the literature, Gray *et al.* (1995: 47) conclude 'there is little about CSR which is not contestable – and contested'.

Researchers have explored links between CSR and customer loyalty, future purchases, new products, new markets and productivity gains. One of the strongest themes in the literature concerns CSR's link to corporate performance but Margolis and Walsh's (2003) review of more than 120 studies exploring this relationship between 1972 and 2002 showed mixed results. Despite inconclusive results of a positive *or* negative connection between corporate performance and CSR, however, stakeholder demand for CSR has continued to rise *and* companies themselves continue to invest in it (File and Prince 1998). CSR has attracted a raft of scholars but many aspects including CE remain underexplored (see Salzmann *et al.* 2005).

Godfrey and Hatch's 2007 framework for categorizing CSR theories and models helps to locate CE in the literature. Carroll's (1979) widely supported notion of business as a *hierarchy* of social responsibilities is also valuable. While CE sits relatively low in terms of this hierarchy, it is one of the oldest forms of corporate social performance (Mescon and Tilson 1987) and widely considered to be a vital element (Saiia 2001; Saiia *et al.* 2003). Moreover, it is commonly treated in the literature as a *measurable* manifestation of social responsibility (Wood 1991). Thus it is somewhat perplexing that relatively few CSR researchers have examined specific issues relating to CE. Corporate contributions run into billions of dollars not only in the USA and Europe but even in much smaller economies such as Australia (Bennett 1998; Sargeant and Crissman 2006).

Certainly some tension exists around the notion of CE. For example, while studies suggest businesses give high social desirability to such support (Buchholtz *et al.* 1999) individual managers may not regard it as an obligation for the business (Seifert *et al.* 2003). Moreover, CE may clash with business goals, with pressure to serve business self-interest (Varadarajan and Alcorn 1988; Paul and Lydenberg 1992). In these circumstances, CE can move out of the CSR function into marketing (File and Prince 1998).

The marketing perspective

Most obviously, business-giving activities overlap with the marketing function when they are deliberately designed to serve marketing purposes such as increasing sales, contributing to the firm's competitive positioning or attracting desired customers, employees or strategic partners. CE that is undertaken for the dual purpose of addressing community needs and helping a business to carve out a unique image for itself or its products, or even make direct sales, has been described as 'strategic philanthropy' (see e.g. Fry *et al.* 1982; Mescon and Tilson 1987; Wokutch and Spencer 1987; Saiia *et al.* 2003). McAlister and Ferrell (2002: 690) point to the carefully considered nature of CE when it meets marketing goals:

> Strategic philanthropy [is] the synergistic use of organizational core competencies and resources to address key stakeholders' interests and to achieve both organizational and social benefits.

To date, the literature suggests this effort can be fruitful: successful collaboration with NPOs is associated with strong brands and company reputation, as well as customer loyalty, employee commitment and productivity, and healthy stakeholder relations (see Sargeant and Stephenson 1997; McAlister and Ferrell 2002; Ricks 2005). Each of these contributes to a company's performance. For example, a strong brand is *crucial* for marketers facing unrelenting competitive pressure because it aids differentiation (Kotler and Lee 2005). Similarly, reputation is valuable as it involves the evaluation of the company behind the brand (Dowling 1994). While more research is needed to explain the contribution of CE (Collins 1993; McAlister and Ferrell 2002), and critics of CE for businesses exist (see e.g. Friedman 1970), the case for it to be treated as a marketing-mix element continues to build (Bennett 1998). In particular, some regard CE as a *product* that can be marketed to the public through the firm's communications (Murray and Montanari 1986; Mescon and Tilson 1987; Lowengard 1989; Collins 1994; Simon 1995). Others treat it as a resource *investment* for business sustainability (Bennett 1998). Both views encourage research into how and where corporate efforts should be made to create benefit or 'add value' for the firm. Ostergard (1994) observes this as an overall shift by business away from altruism towards an opportunity-seeking orientation.

This enthusiasm for mutual benefit is not *necessarily* shared by all. Much CE is underpinned by altruism, *not* by hopes of business advantage (Sargeant and Stephenson 1997; Brammer and Millington 2005; Cohen 2006). Moreover, corporate foundations commonly separate their grant-making from the marketing function of the firm (ACOSS 2005) although such virtuous distinction also signals the company's merits.

It can also be observed that while some firms are *content* with their current CE activity, regardless of whether they are motivated purely by altruism or some blend of self-interest, others strongly desire to *improve* their CE decision-making and impact (Porter and Kramer 2002; ACOSS 2005). A final group of businesses hold back on CE as they may not see it as the responsibility of business and do not want to impose their personal beliefs on their partners or the firm's owners (Lyons *et al.* 2006).

Theoretical foundations

Theories informing CP/CCI (or CE) draw most directly upon the CSR and marketing literatures, for example, branding and reputation. These, in turn, are informed by the economics, management, moral philosophy, psychology and sociology fields.

A range of theories have provided 'windows' through which CE can be understood, for example, stakeholder theory, legitimacy theory, social contract theory, agency theory and resource-dependency theory (Pfeffer and Salancik 1978; Gray *et al.* 1995; Froelich 1999). In stakeholder theory, emphasis is on management's addressing the expectations and demands of multiple, sometimes conflicting, stakeholder groups that support the firm's continued survival, rather than maximizing profit per se. The related arena of legitimacy theory recognizes that an organization's value system and activities sit within a larger social system, and must be studied within this interrelated political, social and institutional framework. Social contract theory also informs CP/CCI: it imagines a society without complex business entities and considers what conditions are needed for society to allow businesses to exist. A 'licence to operate' from society is exchanged for some societal benefits. Agency or stockholder theory, most notably associated with economist Milton Friedman (1962), suggests that CE is more likely to occur the greater a firm's cash resources (which finds support in the literature), yet it acts as a diversion that detracts from a firm's performance (not supported) (Seifert *et al.* 2003). Finally, the notion of strategic philanthropy is linked to resource-dependency theory which suggests that organizational behaviour is governed by its resource dependencies and that, to survive, organizations must adapt to the requisites of their key providers.

Other work has sought to explain engagement *styles*. For example, Galaskiewicz and Colman (2006) suggest four main types of NP–business collaboration: philanthropic ones, which mainly seek to generate social good and tend to be straightforward, and three types of collaboration where business benefits are sought. Strategic collaborations aim for a mix of firm and social outcomes, commercial collaborations aim for increasing revenues for both through joint ventures such as licensing and CRM and political collaborations focus on influencing the wider political environment to support both the business and NPO involved. NP marketers will be particularly drawn to research surrounding philanthropic, strategic and commercial alliances. Business marketers, seeking mutual benefit, may find strategic and commercial ones more relevant. However, no type of collaboration can be completely neglected as programmes are increasingly multilayered; even straightforward donations can signal responsiveness to one's community (Brammer *et al.* 2006). This four-model classification builds upon Burlingame and Young's (1996) approach of more than a decade ago. Their models suggest CE is motivated mainly out of a sense of corporate citizenship, desire to manage stakeholder relationships, the wish for profitability or to protect the business from government intervention.

Taking a different perspective, Bruch and Walter (2005) explain CE styles by the strength of a firm's orientation to either its external or internal environment. Drawing upon dependency theory, they hypothesize four alternative positions characterized by a strong/weak desire to meet external stakeholder/market expectations and a strong/weak desire to act out of core values and competencies. They argue that the high market/high competence orientation is optimal as it allows a firm to leverage its internal resources to systems to address real social issues, thus is low risk and high return.

Why businesses give

The enormous breadth of engagement activities in recent years (Wymer and Samu 2003) has prompted a variety of scholars to write about a *continuum* of CE activities (see Figure 8.1). This hypothetical continuum, based on business motivation, ranges from purely altruistic donations and in-kind gifts on the extreme left (Shaw and Post 1993) to innovative partnerships which deliver substantial societal *and* business benefit in the middle and ultimately to highly commercial alliances which also deliver some societal benefit (Varadarajan and Menon 1988; Kropp *et al.* 1999).

A continuum is useful because it suggests that a company may engage in activities at various points and oscillation over time can occur (Campbell *et al.* 2002; Seifert *et al.* 2003). It is shown also as a 'see–saw' to reflect the balance achieved overall, with tilting either towards community benefit, business or equilibrium across these two. For variations on the engagement continuum, see, for example, Collins' typologies of corporate response to global philanthropy (1993).

Taking a 'helicopter' view, businesses generally have come to embrace strategic philanthropy because they see it as contributing to the overall financial performance of the firm and thus can justify it as a business strategy. While academic findings on this positive relationship are inconclusive, evidence does exist of a direct association between profitability and the level of giving, and also that business *norms* influence corporate giving (Navarro 1988; Moore and Robson 2002). More research is needed in this area if the dynamics are to be understood, especially studies that 'drill down' into CE in *different* business contexts and industries to complement the macro studies conducted to date, longitudinal studies and efforts to tease apart currently aggregated measures and concepts (Godfrey and Hatch 2007).

From the business marketer's perspective, increased sales are the most tangible returns that may be sought from CE. However, it may be argued that quantified improvements in market reach and penetration, consumer awareness, attitudes including evaluations of the firm or its

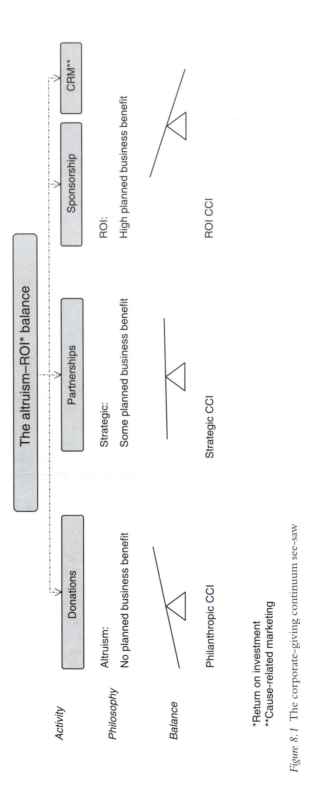

Figure 8.1 The corporate–giving continuum see-saw

products, or purchase intentions also are 'hard' returns. While consumers are a primary target for marketers, corporate strategies may also involve building understanding and cooperation with employees, suppliers and other partners in the delivery chain, communities and government for they provide indirect avenues to attract business (Turban and Greening 1997; Fombrun and Gardberg 2000; Greening and Turban 2000; Mohr *et al.* 2001; Backhaus *et al.* 2002). Global companies illustrate the strategic use of CE to mitigate operational risk in politically, economically or socially unstable countries such as Guinea and Nigeria (Porter and Kramer 2002). Multinationals spend up to 4 per cent of their annual in-country operating budgets on such activities (Barnes 2005).

Perhaps not surprisingly, research efforts in CE have largely focused upon returns to business from sponsorships (see O'Hagan and Harvey 2000; Miyazaki and Morgan 2001; Quester and Thompson 2001) and cause-related marketing (see File and Prince 1998; Bronn and Vrioni 2001). Yet these activities are not fully understood, particularly innovative associations at previously 'out of bounds' sponsorship sites such as hospitals, kindergartens, schools and universities, and within other core community activities like policing. Fresh aspects of CRM attracting research interest include the consumer perspective (Polonsky and McDonald 2000) and the division of resulting profits including share price increases (Wymer and Samu 2003).

However, some researchers place such commercial alliances outside the CE net altogether. For example, McAlister and Ferrell (2002) suggest that engagement with NPOs is not about immediate results but instead is a long-term investment for the firm.

For this reason, perhaps, *partnerships* are attracting more attention. The national Giving Australia survey of 2,700 businesses suggests that some 19 per cent of businesses in that country are now involved in community partnerships, up 6 per cent in the three years to 2004 with indications it is the fastest growing form of CE in that country (ACOSS 2005). These collaborative partnerships between business and NPOs occupy the middle ground of the CE continuum and commonly involve an association over time, mutually developed prosocial programmes and multidimensional resource support by the firm such as employee volunteering and mentoring, skills transfer, systems assistance and/or other in-kind support in addition to cash. In return, they offer individual businesses many staff-related and market benefits as well as helping the business sector more broadly to regain lost credibility as a result of scandals over the past decade, in particular (Lucas 2004).

The *relational* nature of partnerships opens up a large parcel of research issues not only for businesses but NPOs too, including optimal types of partnerships for different organizations, trust and power dynamics, how business and NP cultures might blend, and management issues such as partner selection, determining appropriate objectives, outcomes and evaluation, dealing with partner expectations, risk, even exit strategies (Samu and Wymer 2001; Mullen 2002; McQueen 2004; Todeva and Knoke 2005; Wholstetter *et al.* 2005). Unfortunately, despite growing interest in partnerships, little academic work has been done to date to understand, and assist, those experimenting with them. Scholars such as Kilpatrick and Silverman (2005), Robins (2005) and Wymer and Samu (2003) flag the importance of research that informs successful partnership formation, development and closure.

How much?

Different countries have their own history of corporate engagement with the NP sector, and their own unique social, political and economic web within which such activities currently exist and which shape their future direction. However, the overall trend has been for companies in western Europe, the USA and other countries to have *increased* their contributions since the

1980s, with some like Australia reporting a marked increase (see Campbell *et al.* (2002) for an analysis of UK and US trends). This rise parallels the growth of private wealth and generally strong business performance in such countries (Merrill Lynch/Capgemini 2006). Moreover, CP/CCI is expected to become increasingly important in world economies experiencing rapid growth, particularly China and India (Muirhead 2006).

In analysing how much businesses give, it is crucial to be aware of methodological variances and their implications. Different data collection methods muddy the tracking of change within any one country, as well as complicating international comparisons. Also, corporate giving statistics lend themselves to underreporting because they may exclude activities which involve NPOs and benefit the community but are funded by *marketing* budgets rather than corporate or community relations budgets (Burlingame 2001). There can be additional factors which influence corporate-giving statistics, too, and potentially distort tracking (ACOSS 2005). Several researchers have pointed out their *indicative* nature, and urge caution by researchers in using them (see e.g. Campbell *et al.* 2002). With this caveat in mind, giving by US businesses was estimated at US$13.77 billion in 2005 (Giving USA 2006), a substantial increase from $11.24 billion in 2004. This spike can be partly explained by urgent disaster relief appeals, especially the Asian tsunami; 59 per cent of US companies reported adding to their budgeted gifts for tsunami victims (Muirhead 2006).

In the UK, leading publicly traded companies recorded donations to NPOs of more than US$1.6 billion in 2003–4 – close to 1 per cent of pre-tax profits (Armstrong 2004). A year later, reporting in UK currency, the Community Foundation Network (2006) found that contributions by UK companies had risen some 15 per cent in real terms to stand at £1.1bn, taking into account both cash and in kind (although still representing a relatively low 0.8 per cent of pre-tax profit). In smaller countries such as Australia, recorded business giving has also risen markedly in recent years, from AUD$1.5 billion to $3.3 billion in the three years to 2004 (ACOSS 2005) and while this change may be somewhat inflated due to different measures, it is nevertheless remarkable. In the Netherlands, business giving accounts for 43 per cent of the total estimated giving of 2.27 billion euros in 2003 (Meijer *et al.* 2006).

Not all countries reflect this pattern. One example is Korea where corporate giving has remained steady in recent years and research suggests that the vast majority of smaller companies give at minimal levels. Overall, companies listed on the Korean stock exchange contributed approximately 0.42 per cent of their gross profit to NPOs in 2004, with average contributions of a mere 0.08 per cent of sales and 0.23 per cent of advertising and entertainment expenses (Beautiful Foundation 2007: 13).

The reasons for the general trend in increased CE are not clear. In the USA, corporate giving has reflected trends in profitability, prior giving, gross domestic product and corporate tax rates (Seifert *et al.* 2003). The link to profitability is highlighted by some researchers, who warn that as profits wane so too will corporate giving (Drucker 1984; Giving USA 2006). CSR has been highly publicized, too, and this may play a role.

Also, while aggregated corporate-giving figures are substantial in various countries, it does *not* represent a huge investment by individual companies – nor a substantial proportion of NP income in these countries. US corporate giving represented only 1.3 per cent of gross profits in the USA in 1999 (Hunt 2000) and a median figure of 1.6 per cent in 2004 (Muirhead 2006). As well, wide variations exist between individual businesses, and between industry sectors (Hunt 2000; Giving USA 2006).

Who gives?

In seeking to explain individual firm differences, some research has focused on the characteristics of managers (see e.g. Harvey 1990; Cermak *et al.* 1994). Walker (2002) found through a survey of top FTSE350 companies in the UK that two-thirds of senior executives gave time to charities. While only 44 per cent of finance directors were active, 89 per cent of chairpersons, 65 per cent of CEOs and 64 per cent of marketing and personnel directors volunteered. Often these personal contributions were long term and across a number of charities, suggesting corporate decision-makers can be strongly philanthropically inclined.

Others, such as Burnett and Wood (1988), have developed broader models of donor behaviour which incorporate, for example, giving antecedents such as personal and demographic characteristics (e.g. self-esteem, empathy, guilt, age, gender, education) as well as situational factors and perceived rewards.

Industry studies can also be revealing. For example, an analysis of IRS (Inland Revenue Service) claims for charitable giving highlights the generosity of the arts, entertainment and recreation sectors in the USA, where firms claiming contributions reported an average of 2.8 per cent of pre-tax income in 2003 compared with the average claim by contributing firms across all industries of 1.5 per cent of pre-tax income. Donors in the utilities, wholesale trade and healthcare/social assistance sectors also reported above average, at 2.2 per cent (Giving USA 2006).

Companies vary in expenditure treatment, with some activities seen as marketing, others community relations or corporate foundation grant-making. In one rare study where access to US treasury data was possible, Carroll and Joulfaian (2005) found that giving rose in line with firm income, tax rates and the amount spent on advertising. An additional obstacle for researchers can be identifying expenditure where record-keeping for such activity is poor; for example, small businesses may not keep consistent or detailed records of their contributions (ACOSS 2005). Indeed, the issue of firm size is of growing interest for researchers.

The sheer number of small to medium enterprises (SMEs) across many countries means that, collectively, SME giving dwarfs that of large corporations. At the firm level, however, as mentioned earlier, research shows that the greater the firm's assets (the larger the firm is), the more likely it is to engage in CCI and to give more (Wood and Jones 1995; Boatsman and Gupta 1996; Giving USA 2006). As Seifert *et al.* (2003) point out, the literature suggests a positive relationship between cash flow (having discretionary funds) and corporate giving (discretionary expenditure) and, thus, CE may be seen as a form of discretionary CSR. In this way, evidence exists in support of agency theory's assumption that corporate giving is linked to having available resources (Seifert *et al.* 2003).

File and Prince (1998) note that scant research exists for privately held companies, especially smaller ones in how they balance altruistic motivations with corporate self-interest. In such firms, giving can be seen as a *personal* decision not a business one which is forced on to business partners or owners (Madden *et al.* 2006). This Australian research suggests smaller businesses are driven by fewer motivations than is suggested for large business and their approach to CE, including decision-making and evaluation, is less systematic and strategic.

How businesses give

The traditional forms of CE – straightforward donations and in-kind gifts – still dominate corporate giving (Seifert *et al.* 2003; ACOSS 2005) although employee volunteering and payroll giving, use of facilities, and specialist advice and assistance are gaining in popularity. In-kind support equals at least one-third and up to one-half (depending on the study) of the value of cash contributions in the USA (Anonymous 1997; Giving USA 2006). Non-traditional activities such as community–business partnerships which allow business to join forces with NPOs in addressing social issues, CRM, licensing and joint ventures are also on the increase (Galaskiewicz and Colman 2006). In Australia, since the late 1990s, corporate resources being put into community–business partnerships have gathered pace while previously intense interest in sponsorships has levelled off (ACOSS 2005). The 1990s saw a dramatic rise in sponsorships and CRM in several countries including the USA (Himmelstein 1997; Weeden 1998). Tracking aggregated giving amounts can camouflage such fluctuations over time.

As well as direct contributions from business, support may come through corporate *foundations*, with many larger enterprises contributing both ways. In the USA, grants by corporate foundations totalled US$3.6 billion in 2005, according to the Foundation Center, adjusted to US$3.4 billion by Giving USA to avoid double-counting (Giving USA 2006).

In terms of recipients, US business overwhelmingly favoured health and human service recipients in 2004, winning 44 per cent of all corporate contributions, followed well behind by international aid and education which attracted 19 per cent and 14 per cent of funding, respectively (Muirhead 2006). In contrast, only 4 per cent of corporate funding in 2004 was directed at cultural and arts causes. With some variations across and within countries (for example, by industry and firm size), this pattern of robust support for welfare NPOs and low support for cultural, arts and the environment causes is replicated. There is some evidence that corporate foundations may support causes more equitably than do companies directly, for example US foundations directed 26.7 per cent of all grants to public–society benefit organizations. There is some evidence that corporate foundations may support causes more equitably than do corporations acting directly. For example, US foundations directed 26.7 per cent of all grants to public society benefit organizations (a broad category that includes social action and community development groups), 25.5 per cent to education and 18.8 per cent to human services (Giving USA 2006).

This scan of the literature reveals the range of efforts to understand the businesses most likely to engage in CE and the forms such giving takes. Yet many issues beg further investigation. One standout concern is the need to investigate the decision-making process for business, to appreciate better the 'why', the 'how' and the 'what' involved in corporate giving (Campbell *et al.* 2002; Saiia *et al.* 2003). Insight is also much needed into researching issues around variation within countries as well as across them. In particular, there is a gap in the literature for cross-cultural studies (Seifert *et al.* 2003; Madden *et al.* 2006). To put the relatively strong levels of corporate giving into perspective, they come at a time when globalization and other societal shifts have reframed traditional boundaries (Loza and Ogilvie 2005). Greater interdependence and shifts in resourcing have increased pressures on business to address more actively and collaboratively social needs, as well as look to their own sustainability. In turn, the NP sector is under pressure to reconceptualize its work and its support. We now turn to the NP marketing perspective to examine what we do know – and do not know – from research to date.

The nonprofit perspective

First, we consider marketing orientation issues. The seeming irony of *nonprofits* needing to *make* profits to fund their missions means they often mimic commercial marketing activities. With commercial sponsorships and CRM collaborations, for example, NPOs can be as keen as business to generate *income* as to increase community awareness for their organization or issue, or gain new supporters to lift their mission outcomes. At the same time, many grapple with the uncomfortable fit of a marketing orientation in a traditional NP culture (see Andreasen (2000) for a full discussion of the intersector transfer of marketing knowledge). Andreasen *et al.* (2005) posit resistance to change, and fear by internal and external stakeholders that a marketing view may contaminate mission focus as key obstacles to pursuing corporate/NPO engagements. An 'apparently thin line (exists) in the public's perception between being business–like and being a business' (Walker 2002: 14). Gaskin (1999) ties eroded public trust in charities to the increasing professionalization of the sector, particularly the use of commercial marketing tactics.

At a theoretical level, the business–NP dichotomy is also under discussion. Clarke and Mount (2001: 89), for instance, conclude that mainstream marketing's reliance on neo–classical methodology 'seems inappropriate, especially for the NP sector'. Others point to the dual constituency of donors *and* clients that NPOs must serve as problematic: they must know their funding market but not pander to it at the expense of their mission (McColl-Kennedy and Kiel 2000: 15).

Andreasen *et al.* (2005) point out that marketing plans and orientation are missing from most NPOs. This makes it difficult for NPOs to then reach into more sophisticated commercial tools such as demand forecasting, demographic segmentation and market share analysis and speak the same language as businesses. What are the implications of this generalized low level of marketing skills for nurturing corporate philanthropy and engagement?

Arguably the new return on investment 'opportunity-based paradigm' noted (Ostergard 1994; Sargeant and Stephenson 1997) has placed unprecedented pressure on NPOs to deliver marketing benefits and to act as quasi-businesses. This higher need for marketing savvy is intensified further by the move from 'armchair' philanthropy of writing a cheque to the more active partnership mode noted in the literature and empirical studies (see e.g. Staples 2004). The importance of marketing nous is even more pronounced when corporate CE is at the CRM end of the spectrum. Yet relatively few researchers to date have investigated marketing concepts which particularly apply to generating resources from the corporate market. As Walker (2002) suggests, despite the popularity of corporate fundraising, little contextual material is available in the voluntary sector literature.

One fertile future path for research is to replicate marketing-based studies undertaken to comprehend better and predict *individual* giving. Often a firm's charitable involvements are seen as 'partly personal, partly corporate' by those making the contribution (Walker 2002: 224).

Several interesting lines of enquiry impinge on our understanding of how NPOs use marketing skills to relate better to the corporate market including: market segmentation (Sargeant and Stephenson 1997) and NP branding (Polonsky and McDonald 2000; Hankinson 2001, 2002; Napoli 2006; Dickenson and Barker 2007). In addition, some research tries to track exchanges which actually happen and the outreach NPOs use to win support.

The gift of time and particularly leadership skills are commonly sought by NPOs. Notable patrons, names on letterhead, governance and other high-level volunteers add to a charity's reputation and level of public trust. A survey of the UK's top corporate donors found all of the top ten had at least one director serving as a charity trustee and some had as many as 75 per cent of directors with trustee appointments (CaritasData 2000). Walker (2002) considers the implications for charitable strategy of building relationships with corporate figureheads. Based on a survey of senior executives representing one-third of the FTSE350 companies in the UK and in-depth interviews, she established that a direct approach from a charity was the main mode of its becoming involved and that the personalized approach far outranked letters as a means of success. The second key avenue for involvement came through an approach on behalf

155

of the charity from someone within their formal or informal networks. This role of business champions was significant also for stimulating corporate volunteering.

Next, we consider market segmentation issues for NPOs looking for business support. Sargeant and Stephensen (1997) posited that market segmentation to target the right donor and send the right messages was crucial to tap corporate support. In this UK study, emphasis by business was on altruism rather than return on investment. Indeed less than 10 per cent of primary responsibility for giving sat with the marketing area in this study (and this breadth of location was confirmed in the Giving Australia study where, for instance, the human relations area was quite a popular site for CE staff (ACOSS 2005)). Sargeant and Stephensen confirmed the two clear segments that NP marketers need to target as: 'philanthropists', who give without looking for benefit and tend to give mainly through cash; and 'investors', who see opportunities emerging from their contributions, give in a variety of modes and monitor the success of this strategy. A third segment − non-donors − would benefit from similar marketing strategies to the investor group, as the main barriers to support were lack of financial capability and failure to consider the key benefits that could accrue.

What is known about these possible benefits from which NPOs may proffer? Research is evident on the fringes of this topic such as Drennan and Cornwell's (2004) case studies to consider the relevance of newer media such as the Internet as a means to both attract and deliver benefits to sponsors. However, one benefit which features more consistently in the literature is brand positioning. As canvassed in the corporate perspective that opened this chapter, the corporate is seeking better brand position through linking with a recognized charity or its work. This quest in turn has spotlighted the role of clear and appealing branding in the NP realm to attract corporate partners.

The challenge of branding for NPOs is significant. A range of studies address its importance to the NP sector, with reputation emphasized as a core NP asset to individual, corporate and other donors alike (for early work, see Roberts-Wray 1994; Tapp 1996). Ritchie et al. (2006) in their study of how NPOs might use brand for competitive advantage, highlight the basic premise that 'strong brand franchises make NPOs more desirable as businesses seek to develop their own goodwill through partnerships with NPOs' (29). As 'Current Brand Management . . .' concludes in considering the application of brand management theory to universities, there is a need for 'further evolution of the discipline of brand management and subsequent modelling of branding concepts to NPOs' (15). Some of this evolution is outlined below.

Most recently, Napoli (2006) found a positive correlation between NP brand orientation and organizational outcomes, and a high brand orientation in successful NPOs. Similarly, Hankinson (2002) considered the brand orientation of UK fundraising managers and its impact on their organizations' donations. This work built on Hankinson's prior explorative study of brand orientation levels in different sized charities where respondents acknowledged brand as a core tool for fundraising in a competitive market across statutory, voluntary and corporate sources of support (2002: 212). A key finding here was that such organizations generally did not *optimize* their brands, despite the charity brand being central to its donor and client outreach.

The trend toward co-branding alliances between corporate and NP groups has been examined by Dickenson and Barker (2007). Findings from their study indicate benefits to both entities hinge on the co-brand 'fit' being perceived as strong and logical, and the independent brands being familiar and well regarded. Brand alliances were found to impact significantly on brand attitudes to each of the entities, with NP and commercial partners benefiting equally.

In seeking to validate how brand personality works in NPOs and its impact on individual giving, Venable et al. (2005) found four dimensions of NP brand personality: integrity, nurturance, sophistication and ruggedness, and concluded that the intangibility of the services that NPOs often offer means the *organization* rather than the services becomes the brand focus.

Hyojin (2002) in considering the role of branding in building competitive advantage for NPOs adapts Brown and Dacin's (1997) model of corporate associations. This analysis raises the issues of 'uncontrolled branding' where the NP is branded as a result of partnering with a for-profit brand, often meaning risk if the for-profit brand becomes tainted through unethical practice.

Polonsky and Macdonald (2000) have added to the NP branding knowledge base in a different way, by considering how CRM programmes can shape an NP brand both positively or negatively. In similar vein, an empirical study in New Zealand (Chaney and Dolli 2001) found non-purchasers are likely to feel charities should exploit other fundraising methods, sending a message of discomfort with this form of marketing.

An area of perhaps equal discomfort for NP marketers is finding the right corporate partner (Hankinson 2001). Her study with UK charities found that matching the profiles of the corporation's consumer with the charity's donor was an important success factor. The literature has gone deeper into what makes a successful partnership.

The literature supporting partnerships is positive, with more interest shown by scholars in partnership strategy rather than seeking traditional donations (Austin 2000). Yet much that is written is anecdotal rather than empirical. Staples (2004), for instance, in questioning the implications of the CSR movement for charitable fundraising, concludes that a more mature relationship between business and the charitable sector and a focus on mutual benefit are needed to yield meaningful social change. He highlights the potential of exploring shared objectives. The studies represent a flow on from Burnett's (1992) application of relationship marketing to fundraising, based as it is on proactively developing the potential of each unique relationship rather than on the more transactional exchange of raising money.

The literature, while not voluminous, does highlight that the risk to both entities can be high if all aspects of the process are not well implemented (see Todeva and Knoke 2005).

The detail of the partnership agreement – including the care taken with partner selection – has been underlined (see Samu and Wymer 2001; McQueen 2004). Partnerships potentially can have adverse effects on the set goals as well as achieving respective benefits for the two parties (Martinez 2003). Both entities enter with expectations and at an early phase of mutual trust (Wholstetter *et al.* 2005). NPOs may lose out if seen as being 'owned' by the corporate partner and therefore unattractive to other companies or not in need of their support or that of traditional donors. The potential power differential is also an important factor (Mullen 2002) and commentators have called for more research on aspects such as blending the business–NP culture and achieving strong partnership management (see Wymer and Samu 2003; Kilpatrick and Silverman 2005; Robins 2005). The different work culture, objectives and operating styles of NPOs and corporations identified by Wymer and Samu (2003) can spell problematic management for partnership operatives.

Critics warn that interest in partnerships is fuelled by perhaps faulty assumptions that the NP sector is inefficient, ineffective and unaccountable (Mullen 2002; Lucas 2004), that businesses have relevant resources to assist with social problems (Gold 2004; Robins 2005) and that it is acceptable for businesses to shift from altruism to seek mutual returns (Lyons 1998).

The role of government

Public policy and government facilitation of NPO–business collaboration is an area attracting growing attention in the light of governments' interest in cross-sector efforts to meet community need (see Galaskiewicz and Colman 2006). Moreover, there is evidence from the rare studies that exist (Schwartz 1968; Arulampalam and Stoneman 1995; Moon 2004) that business *is* sensitive to the tax and policy treatment of giving options and that current policies do shape NPO–business collaborations.

Conclusion

In their valuable review of NPO–corporate collaboration, Galaskiewicz and Colman (2006) highlight the many newer forms of CE by business that have emerged in recent years to complement traditional giving practices. These opportunities will continue to unfold and it is only through rigorous research, as well as practical experimentation by the organizations themselves, that their potential to deliver efficiently successful outcomes will evolve. Scholarship is vital for the understanding it can bring to managers in both NPOs and businesses of the dynamics of corporate philanthropy and CCI – what is occurring, how, why and with what effect. Research is also needed to shift efforts to a higher level.

Current theoretical development in this arena is in many ways embryonic. Research is needed in wide-ranging areas, as this chapter identifies, and research from different perspectives informs the field (see Figure 8.2 for a summary of issues ripe for investigation).

The three *primary* areas deserving attention, we believe, are:

- International research – especially comparisons of giving patterns, motives and effects across countries (Seifert *et al.* 2003).
- Qualitative research – especially on the internal decision-making process employed by both businesses and NPOs, including but not limited to the process used to decide on engagement decisions and both internal and external influences on it, partner selection criteria, the ways that they decide to invest in relationships, and how they manage and evaluate engagement (Galaskiewicz and Colman 2006).
- NPO–business partnerships – especially initiating and 'growing' rich partnerships over time, from both NP and business perspectives, and even looking towards tripartite entities where governments of various tiers may form part of the equation and all parties – including society – benefit.

One of the biggest hurdles for research in this area involves access to quality data. First, just getting through the corporate door can present many challenges: data can be regarded as proprietary knowledge, and having a researcher's eye in a business may be threatening to both the business and personalities involved. Similar difficulties may also be experienced for researchers seeking to understand the NPO perspective: research participation is not necessarily a high priority for a sector grappling with stretching resources to fulfil its philanthropic and mission goals. Second, information may be scattered across the firm's operations in fragmented form. Comparisons between firms may be further hindered by inconsistent record-keeping.

Yet research in this area is pressing. Not only can appropriate corporate linkages bring urgently needed dollars and other resources to stabilize the delivery of NP programmes and increase the impact of its interventions (see Simpson 2005), alliances can contribute to NP brand image and reach for longer-term sustainability. For business, too, support of the NP sector holds a multitude of potential benefits, particularly strengthening corporate relationships with key stakeholders such as customers, employees and the community in which it operates.

Business needs encouragement to co-operate in research about its cross-sector alliances

Various scholars call for further research in this field. This synopsis captures this agenda and adds several other as yet unlit pathways for research (abbreviating corporate philanthropy and corporate community involvement to CP/CCI). As this list could be very long, these ideas are included to spark thought rather than be comprehensive of all research possibilities. The needs span theory building and testing, normative studies and critical debate.

Perspective	Research agenda
Cross-sector	Finding definitional clarity and cross-sector agreement for central terms such as CP and CCI Mutually-beneficial partnerships – formation, development or closure, the blending of cultures, managing needs and expectations, achieving optimal outcomes, evaluation, and characteristics of 'well-partnered' organizations
Corporate	The role of CP/CCI in a comprehensive CSR programme Differences between firms and industries on what constitutes meaningful social involvements Management practices – where the CP/CCI function is located, who fills roles and from what background, training and career paths CP/CCI decision-making processes Board role and understanding of CP/CCI, and factors that influence these Employee role and CP/CCI Brand-building – the role of CP/CCI Alignment of CP/CCI with business interests The impact of changing economies on CP/CCI budgets and activities Comparisons of CP/CCI among countries with mandated CSR and those with voluntary codes Studies of CP/CCI and other CSR activities in different business contexts and industries, including longitudinal studies and those that tease apart previously aggregated constructs Professional areas, e.g. PR and advertising, human resources management – applying underlying theories to CP/CCI Exploring innovative associations in previously 'out of bounds' sites Operational issues such as the criteria that might be used for dividing profits, including share price increases, and in selecting
Nonprofit	Conversion rate of corporate volunteers to long-term donors; applying aspects of the individual giving literature to CP/CCI, e.g. lifetime partner value; skills base of NP marketers managing their side of CP/CCI
Government	The effect on business behaviour of various kinds of tax deductions or other inducements in specific countries

Figure 8.2 Pathways for research

because, at its most fundamental, giving access to data is a core way to support the NP sector. For both sides, participation in research informs best practice in the long term. The onus is on researchers, too, to comply with the highest research standards and manage the informant relationship well not only to justify the trust placed in them by respondents but to advance future research interests.

References

ACOSS (2005) *Giving Australia: Research on Philanthropy in Australia. Summary of Findings*, Canberra: Prime Minister's Business Community Partnerships.

Andreasen, A. R. (2000) 'Intersector transfer of marketing knowledge', in P. N. Bloom and G. T. Gundlach (eds) *Handbook of Marketing and Society*, Thousand Oaks, CA: Sage Publications.

—— (2006) *Social Marketing in the 21st Century*, Thousand Oaks, CA: Sage Publications.

—— Goodstein, R. C. and Wilson, J. W. (2005) 'Transferring "marketing knowledge" to the nonprofit sector', *California Management Review*, 47:46–67.

Anonymous (1997) 'Corporate donations rise', *Philanthropy Journal*, 1.

Armstrong, M. (2004) 'Top 100 firms give less than 1 per cent of profits to charity', *Guardian*, 8 November.

Arulampalam, W. and Stoneman, P. (1995) 'An investigation into the givings by large corporate donors to UK charities 1979–86', *Applied Economics*, 27:935–45.

Austin, J. (2000) *The Collaboration Challenge*, San Francisco, CA: Jossey-Bass.

Backhaus, K. B., Stone, B. A. and Heiner, K. (2002) 'Exploring the relationship between corporate social performance and employer attractiveness', *Business and Society*, 41:292–318.

Barnes, S. T. (2005) 'Global flows: Terror, oil and strategic philanthropy', *African Studies Review*, 48:1–21.

Beautiful Foundation, the (2007) *Giving Korea 2005*, Seoul: Center on Philanthropy at the Beautiful Foundation.

Bennett, R. (1998) 'Corporate philanthropy in France, Germany and the UK', *International Marketing Review*, 15:458–75.

Boatsman, J. R. and Gupta, S. (1996) 'Taxes and corporate charity: Empirical evidence from microlevel panel data', *National Tax Journal (1986–1998)*, 49:193–213.

Brammer, S. and Millington, A. (2005) 'Corporate reputation and philanthropy: An empirical analysis', *Journal of Business Ethics*, 61:29–44.

—— Millington, A. and Pavelin, S. (2006) 'Is philanthropy strategic? An analysis of the management of charitable giving in large UK companies', *Business Ethics*, 15:234–45.

Bronn, P. and Vrioni, A. (2001) 'Corporate social responsibility and cause-related marketing: An overview', *International Journal of Advertising*, 20:207–22.

Brown, T. J. and Dacin, P. A. (1997) 'The company and the product: Corporate associations and consumer product responses', *Journal of Marketing*, 61:68–84.

Bruch, H. and Walter, F. (2005) 'The keys to rethinking corporate philanthropy', *MIT Sloan Management Review*, 49–55.

Buchholtz, A. K., Amason, A. C. and Rutherford, M. A. (1999) 'Beyond resources: The mediating effect of top management discretion and values on corporate philanthropy', *Business and Society*, 38:167–87.

Burlingame, D. (2001) 'Corporate giving', *International Journal of Nonprofit and Voluntary Sector Marketing*, 6:4–5.

—— and Young, D. R. (eds) (1996) *Corporate Philanthropy at the Crossroads*, Indianapolis: Indiana University Press.

Burnett, J. J. and Wood, V. R. (1988) 'A proposed model of the donation process', *Journal of Consumer Behaviour*, 3:1–47.

Burnett, K. (1992) *Relationship Fundraising: A Donor-based Approach to the Business of Raising Money*, London: White Lion Press Limited.

Campbell, D., Moore, G. and Metzger, M. (2002) 'Corporate philanthropy in the UK 1985–2000: Some empirical findings', *Journal of Business Ethics*, 39:29–41.

CaritasData (2000) *Investec Guinness Flight Who's Who in Charities*, London: CaritasData.

Carroll, A. B. (1979) 'A three-dimensional conceptual model of corporate performance', *Academy of Management. The Academy of Management Review (pre-1986)*, 4:17.

Carroll, R. and Joulfaian, D. (2005) 'Taxes and corporate giving to charity', *Public Finance Review*, 33:300–17.

Cermak, D. S. P., File, K. M. and Prince, R. A. (1994) 'A benefit segmentation of the major donor market', *Journal of Business Research*, 29:121–30.

Chaney, I. and Dolli, N. (2001) 'Cause-related marketing in New Zealand', *International Journal of Nonprofit and Voluntary Sector Marketing*, 6:156–63.

Clarke, P. and Mount, P. (2001) 'Nonprofit marketing: The key to marketing's "mid-life crisis"?', *International Journal of Nonprofit and Voluntary Sector Marketing*, 6:78–91.

Clikeman, P. M. (2004) 'Return of the socially conscious corporation', *Strategic Finance*, 85:22–7.

Cohen, T. (2006) 'Doing good can be good business', *Philanthropy Journal*, 22 November.

Collins, M. (1993) 'Global corporate philanthropy – Marketing beyond the call of duty?' *European Journal of Marketing*, 27:46–58.

—— (1994) 'Global corporate philanthropy and relationship marketing', *European Management Journal*, 12:226–33.

Community Foundation Network (2006) 'CFN ebulletin no. 49', 31 August.

Dickenson, S. and Barker, A. (2007) 'Evaluations of branding alliances between non-profit and commercial brand partners: The transfer of affect', *International Journal of Voluntary Sector Marketing*, 12:75–89.

Dowling, G. R. (1994) *Corporate Reputations: Strategies for Developing the Corporate Brand*, Melbourne: Longman Professional.

Drennan, J. C. and Cornwell, T. B. (2004) 'Emerging strategies for sponsorship on the Internet', *Journal of Marketing Management*, 20:1123–46.

Drucker, P. F. (1984) 'Converting social problems into business opportunities: The new meaning of corporate social responsibility', *California Management Review (pre-1986)*, 26:53–63.

File, K. M. and Prince, R. A. (1998) 'Cause-related marketing and corporate philanthropy in the privately held enterprise', *Journal of Business Ethics*, 17:1529–39.

Fombrun, C. J. and Gardberg, N. A. (2000) 'Opportunity platforms and safety nets: Corporate citizenship and reputational risk', *Business and Society Review (1974)*, 105:85–106.

Friedman, M. (1962) *Capitalism and Freedom*, Chicago, IL: University of Chicago.

—— (1970) 'The social responsibility of business is to increase its profits', *New York Times Magazine*, 13 September.

Froelich, K. A. (1999) 'Diversification of revenue strategies: Evolving resource dependence in nonprofit organizations', *Nonprofit and Voluntary Sector Quarterly*, 28:246–68.

Fry, L. W., Keim, G. D. and Meiners, R. E. (1982) 'Corporate contributions: Altruistic or for-profit?', *Academy of Management Journal*, 25:94–106.

Galaskiewicz, J. and Colman, M. S. (2006) 'Collaboration between corporations and nonprofit organizations', in W. Powell and R. Steinberg (eds) *The Non-profit Sector: A Research Handbook*, New Haven, CT: Yale University Press.

Gaskin, K. (1999) 'Blurred vision: Public trust in charities', *International Journal of Nonprofit and Voluntary Sector Marketing*, 4:163–78.

Giving USA (2006) *Giving USA: A Publication of Giving USA Foundation*, Indiana: Centre on Philanthropy, Indiana University.

Godfrey, P. C. and Hatch, N. W. (2007) 'Researching corporate social responsibility: An agenda for the 21st century', *Journal of Business Ethics*, 70:87–98.

Gold, M. E. (2004) 'Making the business–nonprofit partnership a win–win', *Nonprofit World*, 22:7–8.

Gray, R., Kouhy, R. and Lavers, S. (1995) 'Constructing a research database of social and environmental reporting by UK companies', *Accounting, Auditing and Accountability Journal*, 8:78–101.

Greening, D. W. and Turban, D. B. (2000) 'Corporate social performance as a competitive advantage in attracting a quality workforce', *Business and Society*, 39:254–80.

Hankinson, P. (2001) 'Brand orientation in the charity sector: A framework for discussion and research', *International Journal of Nonprofit and Voluntary Sector Marketing*, 6:231–42.

—— (2002) 'The impact of brand orientation on managerial practice: A quantitative study of the UK's top 500 fundraising managers', *International Journal of Nonprofit and Voluntary Sector Marketing*, 7:30–44.

Harvey, J. W. (1990) 'Benefit segmentation for fundraisers', *Academy of Marketing Science Journal*, 18:77–86.

Himmelstein, J. L. (1997) *Looking Good and Doing Good: Corporate Philanthropy and Corporate Power*, Bloomington: Indiana University Press.

Hunt, A. R. (2000) 'Charitable giving: Good but we can do better', *Wall Street Journal*, 21 December.

Hyojin, K. (2002) 'Branding nonprofit organizations: A potential solution for a competitve market', *LBJ Journal of Public Affairs*, 14:47–57.

Kilpatrick, A. and Silverman, L. (2005) 'The power of vision', *Strategy and Leadership*, 33:24–6.

Kotler, P. and Lee, N. (2005) *Corporate Social Responsibility: Doing the Most Good for Your Company and Your Cause*, Hoboken, NJ: John Wiley & Sons Inc.

Kropp, F., Holden, S. J. S. and Lavack, A. M. (1999) 'Cause-related marketing and values in Australia', *International Journal of Nonprofit and Voluntary Sector Marketing*, 4:69–80.

Lowengard, M. (1989) 'Community relations: New approaches to building consensus', *Public Relations Journal*, 45:24–30.

Loza, J. and Ogilvie, S. (2005) *Corporate Australia Building Trust and Stronger Communities? A Review of Current Trends and Themes*, Canberra: Prime Minister's Community Business Partnership, Department of Family and Community Services.

Lucas, T. (2004) 'The emerging practice of corporate citizenship in Australia', *The Journal of Corporate Citizenship*, 28–40.

Lyons, M. (1998) 'The history of philanthropy and nonprofits: A comment', *Third Sector Review*, 42:23–5.

—— McGregor-Lowndes, M. and O'Donoghue, P. (2006) 'Researching giving and volunteering in Australia', *Australian Journal of Social Issues*, 41:385–97.

Macdonald, S. and Chrisp, T. (2005) 'Acknowledging the purpose of partnership', *Journal of Business Ethics*, 59:307.

Madden, K., Scaife, W. and Crissman, K. (2006) 'How and why small to medium size enterprises (SMEs) engage with their communities: An Australian study', *International Journal of Nonprofit and Voluntary Sector Marketing*, 11:49–60.

Margolis, J. D. and Walsh, J. P. (2003) 'Misery loves companies: Rethinking social initiatives by business', *Administrative Science Quarterly*, 48:268–305.

Martin, N. (1998) 'A natural progression', *Corporate Philanthropy Report*, 13:2–6.

Martinez, C. V. (2003) 'Social alliances for fundraising: How Spanish nonprofits are hedging the risks', *Journal of Business Ethics*, 47:209–309.

McAlister, D. T. and Ferrell, L. (2002) 'The role of strategic philanthropy in marketing strategy', *European Journal of Marketing*, 36:689–743.

McColl-Kennedy, J. R. and Kiel, G. C. (2000) *Marketing: A Strategic Approach*, Melbourne: Nelson ITP.

McQueen, M. (2004) 'Us and them: Decoding the language of nonprofit–business partnerships', *Nonprofit World*, 22:21–3.

Meijer, M-M., de Bakker, F. G. A., Smit, J. H. and Schuyt, T. (2006) 'Corporate giving in the Netherlands 1995–2003: Exploring the amounts involved and the motivations for donating', *International Journal of Nonprofit and Voluntary Sector Marketing*, 11:13–28.

Merrill Lynch/Capgemini (2006) *The World Wealth Report, 10th Annual Report*, New York, NY: Merrill Lynch & Co, Inc. and Capgemini Global Financial Services.

Mescon, T. S. and Tilson, D. J. (1987) 'Corporate philanthropy: A strategic approach to the bottom line', *California Management Review*, 29:49–61.

Miyazaki, A. and Morgan, A. (2001) 'Assessing market value of event sponsoring: Corporate Olympic sponsorships', *Journal of Advertising Research*, 41:9–16.

Mohr, L. A., Webb, D. J. and Harris, K. E. (2001) 'Do consumers expect companies to be socially responsible? The impact of corporate social responsibility on buying behavior', *Journal of Consumer Affairs*, 35:45–72.

Moon, J. (2004) *Government As A Driver of Corporate Social Responsibility*, Nottingham, UK: University of Nottingham, International Centre for Corporate Social Responsibity.

Moore, G. and Robson, A. (2002) 'The UK supermarket industry: An analysis of corporate social and financial performance', *Journal of Business Ethics*, 11:25–39.

Muirhead, S. A. (2006) *Philanthropy and Business: The Changing Agenda*, New York, NY: Conference Board.

Mullen, J. (2002) 'Nonprofits must take the lead in business alliances', *Nonprofit World*, 20: 5–12.

Murray, K. B. and Montanari, J. R. (1986) 'Strategic management of the socially responsible firm: Integrating management and marketing theory', *Academy of Management Review*, 11:815–27.

Napoli, J. (2006) 'The impact of nonprofit brand orientation on organizational performance', *Journal of Marketing Management*, 22:673–94.

Navarro, P. (1988) 'Why do corporations give to charity?', *Journal of Business*, 61:65.

O'Hagan, J. and Harvey, D. (2000) 'Why do companies sponsor arts events? Some evidence and a proposed classification', *Journal of Cultural Economics*, 24:205.

Ostergard, P. M. (1994) 'Fasten your seat belts', *Fundraising Management*, 36–8.

Paul, K. and Lydenberg, S. D. (1992) 'Applications of corporate social monitoring systems; Types', *Journal of Business Ethics*, 11:1–10.

Pfeffer, J. and Salancik, G. R. (1978) *The External Control of Organizations: A Resource Dependence Perspective*, New York, NY: Harper & Row.

Polonsky, M. and Macdonald, E. (2000) 'Exploring the link between cause-related marketing and brand building', *International Journal of Nonprofit and Voluntary Sector Marketing*, 5:46–57.

Porter, M. E. and Kramer, M. R. (2002) 'The competitive advantage of corporate philanthropy', *Harvard Business Review*, 80:56–68.

Quester, P. and Thompson, B. (2001) 'Advertising and promotion leverage on arts sponsorship effectiveness', *Journal of Advertising Research*, 41:33–47.

Ricks, J. M., Jr. (2005) 'An assessment of strategic corporate philanthropy on perceptions of brand equity variables', *Journal of Consumer Marketing*, 22:121–34.

Ritchie, R. J. B., Swami, S. and Weinberg, C. B. (2006) 'A brand new world for nonprofits', *International Journal of Nonprofit and Voluntary Sector Marketing*, 4:26–42.

Roberts-Wray, B. (1994) 'Branding, product development and positioning the charity', *Journal of Brand Management*, 1:3–370.

Robins, F. (2005) 'The future of corporate social responsibility', *Asian Business and Management*, 4:95–115.

Saiia, D. (2001) 'Corporate citizenship and corporate philanthropy: Strategic philanthropy is good corporate citizenship', *Journal of Corporate Citizenship*, 1:1–19.

—— Carroll, A. B. and Buchholtz, A. K. (2003) 'Philanthropy as strategy when corporate charity "begins at home" ', *Business and Society*, 42:169–201.

Salzmann, O., Ionescu-Somers, A. and Steger, U. (2005) 'The business case for corporate sustainability: Literature review and research options', *European Management Journal*, 23:27–36.

Samu, S. and Wymer, W. W. J. (2001) 'Nonprofit–business alliance model: Formation and outcomes', *Journal of Nonprofit and Public Sector Marketing*, 9:45–62.

Sargeant, A. and Crissman, K. (2006) 'Corporate giving in Australia: An analysis of motives and barriers', *Australian Journal of Social Issues*, 41:477–92.

—— and Stephenson, H. (1997) 'Corporate giving: Targeting the likely donor', *Journal of Nonprofit and Voluntary Sector Marketing*, 2:64–79.

Schwartz, R. A. (1968) 'Corporate philanthropic contributions', *Journal of Finance*, 23:479–97.

Seifert, B., Morris, S. A. and Bartkus, B. R. (2003) 'Comparing big givers and small givers: Financial correlates of corporate philanthropy', *Journal of Business Ethics*, 45:195–211.

Shaw, B. and Post, F. (1993) 'A moral basis for corporate philanthropy', *Journal of Business Ethics*, 745–51.

Simon, F. L. (1995) 'Global corporate philanthropy: A strategic framework', *International Marketing Review*, 12:20–37.

Simpson, J. (2005) 'Setting a strategy for social investment at Shell Australia', *Corporate Responsibility Management*, 1:26.

Staples, C. (2004) 'What does corporate social responsibility mean for charitable fundraising in the UK?', *International Journal of Nonprofit and Voluntary Sector Marketing*, 9:154–8.

Tapp, A. (1996) 'The use of brand management tools in charity fundraising', *The Journal of Brand Management*, 3:400–10.

Todeva, E. and Knoke, D. (2005) 'Strategic alliances and models of collaboration', *Management Decision*, 43:123–48.

Turban, D. B. and Greening, D. W. (1997) 'Corporate social performance and organizational attractiveness to prospective employees', *Academy of Management Journal*, 40:658–72.

Varadarajan, P. R. and Alcorn, D. S. (1988) 'Cause-related marketing: A new direction in the marketing of corporate responsibility', *Journal of Marketing*, 52:58–74.

—— and Menon, A. (1988) 'Cause-related marketing: A coalignment of marketing strategy and corporate philanthropy', *Journal of Marketing*, 52:58–74.

Venable, B. T., Rose, G. M., Bush, V. D. and Gilbert, F. W. (2005) 'The role of brand personality in charitable giving: An assessment and validation', *Academy of Marketing Science Journal*, 33:295–312.

Walker, C. (2002) 'Philanthropy, social capital or strategic alliance', *International Journal of Nonprofit and Voluntary Sector Marketing*, 7(3):219–28.

Weeden, C. (1998) *Corporate Social Investing: The Breakthrough Strategy for Giving and Getting Corporate Contributions*, San Francisco, CA: Berrett-Koehler Publishers.

Wholstetter, P., Smith, J. and Malloy, C. L. (2005) 'Strategic alliances in action: Toward a theory of evolution', *Policy Studies Journal*, 33:424–42.

Wokutch, R. E. and Spencer, B. A. (1987) 'Corporate saints and sinners: The effect of philanthropic and illegal activity on organizational performance', *California Management Review*, 29:62–77.

Wood, D. J. (1991) 'Corporate social performance revisited', *Academy of Management. Academy of Management Review*, 16:691–718.

—— and Jones, R. E. (1995) 'Stakeholder mismatching: A theoretical problem in empirical research on corporate social performance', *International Journal of Organizational Analysis*, 3:229–67.

Wymer, W. W., Jr. and Samu, S. (2003) 'Dimensions of business and nonprofit collaborative relationships', *Journal of Nonprofit and Public Sector Marketing*, 11:3–23.

9

Why the wealthy give

Factors which mobilize philanthropy among high net-worth individuals

Paul G. Schervish

Introduction

Why the wealthy give is both a commonplace and a distinctive matter. It is commonplace because the motives that generate philanthropic giving are for the most part what prompt people across the economic spectrum. Inquire of any individual, rich or poor, just why he/she gives and we will hear a similar array of factors that inspire his/her philanthropy, mainly identification or empathy with the fate of others, and gratitude for blessings in his/her life. There is, too, for all people the deep and reinforcing satisfaction that accompanies meeting directly the true needs of others.

Why the wealthy give is also a distinctive matter, for there are several factors that mobilize philanthropy, which are particular to those with substantial means. In particular are the motives of financial security, a desire to limit the amount of inheritance to heirs, and what I call hyperagency. The truly wealthy are those who are financially secure, having settled the economic problem of achieving indefinitely a desired standard of living for themselves and their heirs, and are now looking for an additional outlet for the productive use of their money. They, of course, provide substantial inheritances to their heirs, but have in mind a plan to allocate only an amount that will be a positive force in the life of their heirs, rather than the goal of simply transferring to heirs as much as possible. Hyperagency is the combination of psychological and material capacity to not just contribute to or support causes, but to relatively single-handedly produce new philanthropic organizations or new directions in existing ones.

There are, of course, many other motivations which are important, but I do not address them here. First there are tax incentives – which may, but not necessarily, affect wealth holders more, but advance giving by the non-wealthy, as well. There are also religious and spiritual obligations, family traditions, guilt and prestige to name just a few. Name any motivation and it will induce philanthropic giving by someone, somewhere, in some circumstance. A book by Theresa Lloyd, *Why Rich People Give* (2004) covers some of the same ground I review here and should also be useful for those interested in her focus on giving by wealth holders in the UK.

In the end, all giving is motivated by an array of factors, some of which we might consider nobler than others. But I have learned that it is rarely possible for people who do not intimately know the hearts of others to draw hard conclusions about what compendium of motives are in play and which determine any gift. We may be able to criticize attitudes and behaviours. But when it comes to motives, it is far more difficult to discern from the outside whether any individual is imbued with nobler or baser ones. In order to avoid as much as possible the notion of motivation as an ultimate inner disposition which is either lofty or low, I will speak of motivations and motives in the sense of their Latin root, *movere* – to move. As such, motives are the *mobilizing forces* of purpose and aspiration that animate activity.

In this chapter I will address just some of the motivations that spawn philanthropic giving by wealth holders. Nevertheless, in my view, these are among what can be called the major motives of major donors (Schervish 1997). I begin by setting out the conceptual and theoretical context for understanding how motivations come into play as wealth holders allocate their resources to philanthropy in the light of their aspirations. I call this the moral biography of wealth. In the second section, I give an overview of the emerging new directions in philanthropy and discuss how this allows for emphasizing the positive and voluntary motivations revolving around the discovery rather than the outside imposition of responsibility for the care of others. In the third to eighth sections, I review both the key motivations which our years of research on this topic indicate are rather universal, such as identification, gratitude and strategic friendship, as well as those motivations which tend to be peculiar to wealth holders, such as financial security, limiting the amount of inheritances allocated to heirs, and hyperagency. I conclude by returning to the notion of moral biography in order to draw out the biographical and historical implications of the international turn towards philanthropy. Throughout the chapter, I draw heavily on my previous writing, in places incorporating only slightly revised sections of text (Schervish 1997, 2005; Schervish and Havens 1997, 2002, 2004; Schervish et al. 2001).

The moral biography of wealth

The context for discussing the motivations for charitable giving among wealth holders is what I call the moral biography of wealth (see Schervish 2006a). The term moral biography refers to the way that individuals conscientiously combine in daily life two elements: personal capacity and moral compass. Capacity is simply the set of resources we have at our disposal to accomplish our goals, and includes our financial assets, intellectual capital and physical talents. Moral compass is the array of purposes or aspirations to which we devote our capacity. Living a moral biography is something as simple as leading a good life and something as profound as following Aristotle's teaching that happiness comes from making wise decisions in our daily life. What creates a moral biography is not merely the existence of financial, intellectual, physical, creative or other personal capacities, but the presence of a moral compass which identifies and strives to accomplish the nobler aims of life for which finances – and one's other capacities – serve as instruments; that is, to combine prosperity and purpose in a spiritually fulfilling, culturally formative and socially consequential way.

If the intersection of capacity and purpose constitutes the general nature of a moral biography, carrying out social relations of care constitutes the moral sentiments and behaviours of that biography in practice. In our age of affluence, the major material capacity for choice takes the form of financial wherewithal, while purpose, or moral wherewithal, takes the form of an orientation to care. The notion of financial or material wherewithal is straightforward enough, and does not require further discussion here. The notion of care, however, is not so clear-cut and needs further elucidation.

Jesuit philosopher Jules Toner systematically formulates a notion of care grounded in a phenomenological analysis of *radical love*. Toner defines radical love as the affection by which a lover 'affirms the beloved for the beloved's self (as a radical end)' (1968: 183), as one that is to be unconditionally regarded as an end and never as a means. Going further, Toner says that care is the implemental or instrumental aspect of love; it is love in concrete practice. As such, for Toner, care is love directed at meeting the true needs of others.

Philanthropy is one of the primary ways that individuals pursue care. As such, philanthropy is also a central dimension of the moral compass, by which wealthy individuals allocate their financial resources for the care of others. In carrying out philanthropy, wealth holders carry out their moral biography imbued with substantial financial capacity. To explore the motivations of philanthropy, then, is to examine the motivations of care and, more broadly still, to examine some of the key motivations for living a moral biography.

Before turning to the motivations that generate a commitment to philanthropy as part of one's moral biography, I review what I call the new physics of philanthropy as a second context for understanding just why the wealthy give.

The new physics of philanthropy

The distinctive trait of wealth holders in all eras is that they enjoy the fullest range of choice in determining and fulfilling who they want to become and what they want to do for themselves, their families and the world around them. Today, increasing numbers of individuals are approaching, achieving or even exceeding their financial goals with respect to the provision for their material needs, and doing so at younger and younger ages. A level of affluence which before this time was the province of a scattering of rulers, generals, merchants, financiers and industrialists has come to characterize large groups and even whole cultures. For the first time in history, the question of how to align broad material capacity of choice with spiritual capacity of character has been placed before so many of a nation's people.

Today, many changes in capacity and purpose are taking place on the supply (or donor) side of philanthropy and on the demand (or beneficiary and fundraising) side. Taken together, the financial and personal factors we have uncovered in the course of research (Schervish and Herman 1988; Havens and Schervish 1999; Schervish and Havens 2001a, 2001b, 2002; Schervish *et al.* 2001) constitute what I call the new physics of philanthropy. The new physics entails an innovative way of thinking, feeling and acting in regard to philanthropy. In the new physics, wealth holders:

- are becoming more numerous, have higher net worth at a younger age, and increasingly recognize their financial security;
- seek out rather than resist greater charitable involvement;
- approach their philanthropy with an entrepreneurial disposition;
- move their giving towards *inter-vivos* involvements;
- plan to limit the amount of inheritance for heirs;
- understand that caring for the needs of others is a path to self-fulfilment;
- make philanthropy a key and regular ingredient of the financial morality that they observe and impart to their children; and
- view philanthropy as a way to achieve simultaneously the happiness of themselves and others.

167

When speaking about motivations for philanthropy by wealth holders, we are addressing more and more what motivates individuals to carry out the new physics of philanthropy as a moral biography.

Motives for philanthropy

The next question is just what motivations mobilize wealth holders to carry out the new physics of philanthropy and to make charitable giving an important dimension of a moral compass of care? What factors motivate high net-worth individuals to allocate substantial portion of their wealth to philanthropy rather than to other worthwhile endeavours? As stated, the motivations of identification, gratitude and strategic friendship, which are common to all who engage in philanthropy, join financial security, a desire to limit bequests to heirs and hyperagency as motivations which are distinctive to wealth holders. I discuss the motivation of identification most at length because it is the cornerstone of all care.

Identification

The key to care and philanthropy, as I have written elsewhere (e.g. Schervish *et al.* 1993), is not the absence of self that motivates charitable giving, but the presence of self-identification with others. This is what Thomas Aquinas teaches as the convergence of love of neighbour, love of self and love of God. In its civic expression, it is what de Tocqueville meant by 'self-interest properly understood' (1966) [1835]: 526), and what Harriet Martineau, a contemporary of Tocqueville who wrote six volumes on her travels in the USA, calls the 'spirit of fraternity'. Such a spirit of fraternity, she maintains, arises 'from the movers feeling it their own concern that any are depressed and endangered as they would themselves refuse to be' (1989 [1838]: 218).

Such empathetic identification animates the giving of wealth holders that I have interviewed over the years. In order to protect confidentiality, all names attributed to wealth holders are pseudonyms. For the same reason, references to their professions, businesses, organizational affiliations and philanthropic enterprises have been changed, but in a way that preserves the general character of their activities.

Washington industrialist Dean Ehrlich expresses this connection in personalistic terms as his and his wife's attraction to those causes 'we can be identified with in order to give part of ourselves to'. Recognizing the unity of self-development and community development has become the touchstone for Malcolm Hirsch's modest assessment of his giving which he charac-terizes as 'no big deal' and 'not particularly generous'. Rather, says the Tacoma environmental activist, 'giving was just a front for figuring out who I was'.

Given the strength of identification as the wellspring of charitable giving, it is not surprising that donors contribute the greatest bulk of their charitable dollars to causes from whose services the donors directly benefit. It is not by coincidence that schools, health and arts organizations, and especially churches attract so much giving. For it is here that donors, because they are also recipients, most identify with the individuals – namely themselves, their families and people much like them – whose needs are being met by the contributions. Although, describing this form of giving as *consumption philanthropy* (Schervish 2000) may seem to discount its value, my intention is just the opposite. Within the identification model, consumption philanthropy is an honourable prototype of motivation to be emulated rather than a regrettable stereotype to be eschewed. Consumption philanthropy mobilizes charitable giving so formidably because it is here that identification between donor and recipient is strongest.

The question for generating generosity is how to expand those very same sentiments of identification to human beings in wider fields of space and time. That is, to extend the sentiments of family feeling to the realms of fellow feeling. This is the key to adoption philanthropy (see Schervish 1992) where donors support individuals on the basis of a feeling of surrogate kinship. Again, it is not by coincidence that the golden rule entreats us to love our neighbour as ourselves.

'I listen and I go where I'm needed', says New York philanthropist, Laura Madison. 'The only thing I'm interested in in the world is the health of humanity. To be human is to be a spiritual person as well as a physical, mental, emotional person. This means to really relate to other human beings all over the world – whoever they are, wherever they are', she explains, highlighting how she extends her identification beyond her immediate sphere. Her goal is 'making a oneness in every way that's there but isn't seen by most people – healing the earth, healing the rifts between people, all that sort of thing: that's what I'm really interested in. And wherever I see any chance or see that I'm supposed to be doing something about it, that's what I'm interested in.'

While for Madison, the sentiments of identification derive from her perception of being needed, for Chicagoan Nancy Shaw they derive from her humanistic rendition of the golden rule that she 'professes' as her only religion. 'I feel that you have a certain debt to society, and if you are comfortable, you pay it. And this is my way of doing it. I treat people as I would like to be treated. And that's as close to a religion as I can get.'

New York philanthropist Janet Arnold traces her empathy for the least advantaged to her childhood when she and her siblings 'were exposed to a wide variety of people and taught by both our parents the dignity of the human being'. 'I think that was the foundation of my attitudes', she explains. The people who worked for her parents were always treated well. When she was young, her father took her along on his Latin American travels where her father would 'go into the villages and talk to the people: He loved going into the villages. He was wonderful with these people. He used to take us on trips. He worked in Latin America, and because of that, we were exposed to people who were not wealthy. We didn't move in a very narrow circle the way most people of wealth do, but a much wider circle through travel and because of my father's constantly reaching out to the people. And all of us, my brothers and sisters and I, worked in Latin America in summer jobs.'

Arnold also spent years living among the poor and disguising her wealth on the east side of Detroit: 'I loved being there and I loved working with those people. I guess I discovered that I had a very abiding belief in the potential of human beings, and that was something I wanted to affirm in my philanthropic work', she recalls. To this day, Arnold grounds her substantial philanthropic efforts on these formative experiences and has come to direct all of her endeavours to 'enabling people to grow and to achieve their potential'. Again, being put face to face with those in need becomes the occasion for developing the necessary knowledge and desire for her to initiate small beginnings. 'There are people who do small entrepreneurial things in their neighborhoods and they could use help', she explains. 'To make their lives somehow successful in its own terms seems to me to be very important. You know, having better schools for children so that the children who grow up in Detroit or in Harlem, so their lives won't be circumscribed because they can't read.'

Identification also turns out to be the school of care for Boston condominium builder Walter Adams, who purposefully guides his charitable giving by the maxim that 'charity begins at home'. He is grateful to his Alma Mater for making him conscientious, and to his employees for making him prosperous. So he directs his wealth to improving their fortunes. His major conventional charity is Boston College. But even closer to home and more worthy of Adams's attention are his workers, especially those at the lower end of the pay scale. He tells how instead of giving $100,000 to the United Way, he prefers to allocate the sum in order 'to help some of [my] people who are in the lower end. Give them a bonus, I mean, or take $100,000 and hire a couple of truly non-employables.'

Taking a gift with gratitude

The motivation of identification is complemented by a particularly strong sense of gratitude for unmerited advantages or, as some say, 'blessings' in reaching financial success. Over the course of two decades, my colleagues and I have interviewed over 250 individuals from across the economic spectrum about their motivations for care. A virtually universal disposition which we encountered is the propensity that many summarize by the simple yet heartfelt phrase 'to give back'. It turns out, however, that upon probing we unearth an impetus that is even more vital than this salutary phrase suggests. Invariably, beneath the desire to give back is a sense of gratitude, and behind that gratitude is an appreciation of blessing, grace, gift, luck or fortune. Gratitude is an active, mobilizing sentiment; a discerning encounter with blessing animates a response of care for others.

Theologian Robert Ochs remarked in a lecture years ago that there are three ways to take a gift. It may be taken for granted, taken with guilt or taken with gratitude. We find that one of the most positively formative dispositions of philanthropic consciousness and conscience involves taking the gifts of fortune with gratitude. Those who take their gifts with gratitude approach the world with a more emotionally abundant, secure and gracious disposition. They recognize their material and personal capacities as dependent on the providence of God, people or circumstances. And they discern from experience more than from tenet that because so much has been given to them, so much can be given by them.

For instance, in our High-Tech Donors study (Schervish et al. 2001), we found that most participants do not credit their wealth solely to their own efforts and skills. They understand that at various points in their careers there was always risk of failure. Thus, some credit their wealth at least in part to luck and good fortune, or if they are religiously inclined, to God's will or God's blessing. Such experience of blessing and gratitude further animates them to seek ways to help individuals and causes with which they identify.

The dynamics of gift and gratitude leading to care for others is precisely what David Hendricks describes as motivating his concern for the vocation of education as a 'noble thing'. 'The other piece of it', he continues, moving from identification to gratitude:

> is I personally got so much out of my education. It has enriched me beyond measure. Not only the practical aspects of it, for instance in my career, [but also] to have a sense of irony, and to build an intellectual richness in life that for me has just meant so much as a gift: The gift of knowledge you might say – the gift of how to think, how to write, how to communicate, how to analyse, as well as the gift of all the touchstones that an education gives you – the building of commonality in a community. You know, if everybody has read Shakespeare, there's a commonality that comes out of that which makes for better life. I do believe in having touchstones – that communities have points of reference that are rich and deep which can be commonly held and therefore allow people to not feel alone and to have confidence in the like-mindedness of their fellows.

This motivation of gratitude is at the heart of what I call the spiritual secret of wealth. Those who are prosperous invariably recognize that their success derives from a confluence of effort, merit and dedication, on the one hand, and of luck, blessings and breaks, on the other. Those who are self-reflective come to the conclusion that if their fortune was not due completely to their own efforts, then the misfortune of others cannot be due in all cases to their lack of effort. This softens the heart and places wealth holders and those in need into a common human family where positive, thoughtful intercessions for the benefit of others are an appropriate way to bring increased advantage to them.

In a perceptive way, this brings us back full circle to identification. Those who experience such blessing and gratitude also formulate the moral logic by which a spiritual experience of blessing engenders a pragmatic practice of care. The most consequential corollary of apprehending one's life as imbued with gift is the generative recognition that just as my fortune is not due entirely to my own merit, others' misfortune may not be completely attributable to their own failure. Such an insight forges identification between donors and recipients as the offspring of a common heritage of unmerited positive and negative fortune, and as the source of a common destiny. Those who have been dealt a friendly hand care for those who have been dealt an inauspicious one. Blessing breeds gratitude and gratitude breeds identification and, again, identification breeds generosity. There is one other mobilizing factor that affects all givers – namely, the satisfaction of directly caring for others. I will discuss this factor below as the motivation that leads those who are financially secure to focus on philanthropy rather than other productive uses for their wealth.

Financial security

In addition to identification and gratitude, which motivate all givers including the wealthy, key mobilizing forces that lead major wealth holders to make major gifts include the mobilizing factors of financial security, a desire to limit the amount of bequests to heirs, and the world-constructing disposition of hyperagency.

Financial security is the self-perceived ability, despite general financial downturns, to provide a desired standard for oneself and one's family. Our research has offered some suggestive empirical evidence which indicates a positive relation between financial wealth and both *inter-vivos* giving and charitable bequests. For every category of high net worth, controlling for income, those who understand themselves as financially secure contribute a higher percentage of their wealth, a higher percentage of their income and a higher dollar amount to charity. For the non-wealthy, those who express economic confidence in the future, controlling for income, contribute a higher dollar amount and a higher percentage of income to charity (Schervish and Havens 2004). But what is the inner nexus by which financial security leads to greater charitable giving? What is the decision-making logic whereby those who are financially secure tend to allocate their wealth to charity to a greater extent than those who are not financially secure?

Murphy (2001), an actuary, business owner and wealth holder, has conceptualized the formal or informal reckoning that wealth holders make to determine how much of the quantity of resources to donate to charity. The process is one in which wealth holders determine a stream of resources; a stream of expenditures for self, family and investment; and a stream of truly discretionary resources which is the positive difference (if any) between the stream of resources and the stream of expenditures:

Given the generally accepted assumption that one provides first for oneself and one's family and does so at some level of lifestyle, philanthropy enters into the decision-making process [in a more formidable manner] when the difference between the expected level of income, current and future, and expected level of expense, current and future, to maintain and enhance one's standard of living is substantial and relatively permanent as measured by the subjectively determined criteria of the decision maker . . . The extent to which this difference (discretionary income) between income and expense is positive quantifies the financial resources available for philanthropic activities. The extent to which this difference is perceived as permanent strengthens the case for allocating some of the resources for philanthropy. The extent to which the difference is positive, permanent and growing in magnitude enhances the philanthropic allocation.

(34–5)

This decision-making scenario described by Murphy regarding the meaning of financial security and how it translates into charitable transfers reflects what we have repeatedly heard wealth holders describe in their intensive interviews. Reviewing in some detail the transition from accumulation to charitable allocation by 45-year-old David Hendricks confirms Murphy's analysis and demonstrates how and why we believe a substantial behavioural sea-change is taking place in the decision-making dynamics of the very wealthy in regard to charitable involvement. Hendricks, a now cashed-out equity partner of a venture capital firm, is typical and articulate about the way that he has defined financial security, calculated its amount, and has come to devote his redundant resources and intellectual capital to charity. Hendricks defines financial security as:

basically having a very, very low chance that you will go broke even if you don't have a job, given an acceptable lifestyle. I have a computer model that I built that reaches out to when we're [he and his wife] ninety years old that factors in inflation and that plays out all this growth stuff and what the random fluctuations of the stock market could possibly be. And it lays out a thousand versions of the way the world might play out and in only one time out of a thousand will we go broke given the lifestyle that we've chosen. And that's financial independence.

He goes on to explain that as a mathematician and computer programmer, and as one who is exceptionally risk averse when it comes to long-term financial independence, he constructed an elaborate model that:

randomly simulates the way the stock market will play out over the years, using history as a guide for what numbers you should put in there. And the question for me was, do you have enough squirreled away so that basically we can maintain the lifestyle that we've chosen through our old age and have a very low probability of having either inflation or a lack of appreciation in the stock market make us go broke?

For Hendricks, the amount designed for financial security is a present-value resource stream of $6 million, net of prospective taxes, net of inflation and net of potential negative stock-market shocks. Hendricks makes it clear that a serious pursuit of philanthropy would have only been pursuing a 'romantic' rather than a 'pragmatic' ideal had he not first achieved financial independence:

You need wealth to actually act on that ideal because, I'm sorry, I enjoy so much the lifestyle you can achieve with wealth. The pragmatist in me, like the squirrel, says, 'save your chestnuts' and the sooner you get that done, the sooner you can rise up a Maslovian level and do the other things. And beware trying to rise up the Maslovian level before you are ready to do it. Be very, very sure that you are ready to do it because it is tough to turn back.

It is instructive that even with financial security in hand the transition to a sharper focus on philanthropy is not an automatic step either for Hendricks or for his financial peers. Financial security leads to philanthropy only in combination with other motivational vectors. This array of motivations for Hendricks and his peers includes identification, gratitude, the prospect of entrepreneurial effectiveness and the desire to limit bequests to heirs. For Hendricks, the identification with the needs of schoolchildren striving to get ahead as he did in his youth and his gratitude for the advantages of his own education parallel what I gleaned from other wealth holders whom I quoted when discussing identification and gratitude.

Limiting transfers to heirs

For the high net-worth individuals, the allocation of wealth to heirs is regularly limited by considerations such as the potentially negative effects of large inheritances on children; and allocations to philanthropy are more frequently occurring via a family foundation or through the involvement of the wealth holder and heirs in philanthropy, as a good way to resolve the moral dilemmas that surround the best use of excess wealth.

In the *Wealth With Responsibility* study (Deutsche Bank 2000), 112 respondents worth $5 million or more were asked about the effect of the estate tax on their allocation of wealth between charitable bequests and heirs. The distribution of responses indicated that if taxes were eliminated as a consideration, wealth holders would give more to charity rather than giving all the tax savings to heirs. For example, when asked how they expected to and how they would like to allocate their estates to heirs, taxes and charity, on average the respondents *expected* 47 per cent of assets from their estates to go to heirs, 37 per cent to go to taxes and 16 per cent to go to charities. Their *desired* allocation, however, was to see 64 per cent of their assets go to heirs and 26 per cent to charity, with taxes unsurprisingly trailing a distant third priority at 9 per cent (unspecified other purposes made up the remaining 1 per cent). In other words, in their ideal scenario, their 76 per cent reduction in taxes would result in a 63 per cent increase in bequests to charity. This study also showed that the desire to reallocate money from taxes to charity is even stronger at the upper levels of wealth: respondents with a net worth at or above $50 million envisioned an even greater shift to charity than those with a net worth below that amount.

Additional evidence for this trend in the USA is provided by the estate filings data provided by the Internal Revenue Service (IRS) each year. We adjust the tables provided by the IRS to approximate final estates, the states for which there is no surviving spouse and from which most distributions to non-spousal heirs, charity and taxes are made. We find (for instance, Schervish and Havens 2006) that:

1   As the value of the estate goes up, a larger portion of the estate goes to charity, with estates valued at $20 million or more bequeathing 40 per cent of their value to charity.
2   As the value of the estate increases, a smaller portion of the estate flows to heirs, with estates valued at $20 million or more bequeathing just 30 per cent to heirs.
3   As the value of the estate increases, a larger portion of the estate is allocated to taxes, with

the exception of the estates valued at $20 million or more, which reduce their tax bill with substantially larger charitable bequests.

For out considerations here, the major point of the previous findings is that those who are financially secure do not maximize the total amount they could transfer to heirs. They limit such bequests to heirs to an amount they deem appropriate and instead make substantial gifts to charity through charitable bequests from their estates.

Some personal evidence is provided by high-tech entrepreneur Greg Yancey. He speaks for the majority of those that we interviewed in citing his fear that the burden of wealth would overwhelm his children. He plans to limit the financial resources he will transfer to his heirs because he views an overly abundant inheritance as an extravagance, if not a downright injury. Although he is just 35 years old and has four children under the age of eight, he is already concerned about ensuring their financial virtue. Yancey grew up fending for himself with several small entrepreneurial ventures and struck it rich when a larger firm bought his Connections To company that developed software to link stored data. The fact that his children will grow up affluent is 'a bitch', something that is 'really scary' and 'haunts' him. Recalling his own upbringing, 'you had to make your own way . . . There wasn't some rich uncle somewhere who would keep bailing you out of university or anything like that. There's decisions you make and consequences to each one of them and that's really frightening.' Turning to his kids, he wonders aloud how he should eventually talk to them about 'all the challenges that wealth is going to bring to them'. Although he is 'damn well going to' teach his kids how to handle wealth responsibly, he remains clearer about the difficulties than the solutions tied to such training. Educating the children about wealth is 'really a difficult area for us to think about and we are only a year into this and we certainly don't have the answers there yet'. One thing Yancey does know is that he 'just can't see anything beneficial' from simply transferring all of his wealth to his kids. That would turn out to be 'just mostly downside for them, more complexities'. At the same time, Yancey has begun to think that involving his kids in philanthropy offers some 'practical' potential for teaching his kids how to handle their wealth:

> I think the Social Venture Partners Fund [my wife and I founded] is a good example. If we build this thing right our kids are going to grow up knowing us as people that took our own unique gifts and got back involved in the community. Not someone that just kind of got a wing of the music college named after them for a couple million dollars or something easy like that. But that we rolled up our sleeves and took our unique gifts and tried to build something where something didn't exist.

Neither the survey nor ethnographic evidence just presented *proves* that financial security changes the decision-making dynamics for those who have solved 'the economic problem' for themselves and their families. However, the foregoing statistical and interview evidence does indicate that the allocation of wealth between family and philanthropy may take on a different character for the financially secure, one that does not depend primarily upon estate-tax avoidance, but depends more upon a logic that inclines the very wealthy to view philanthropy as both a positive alternative to bequeathing wealth to heirs and a way to combine philanthropy with the transmission of financial morality through the creation of foundations and philanthropic trusts that will involve the next generation.

The satisfactions of philia

Even with financial security and a disposition to limit the inheritance to heirs, the question remains, just why philanthropy is such an attractive venue for allocating wealth instead of, say, to more investments. Why is philanthropy such an appealing outlet for allocation of wealth? The beginning to the answer is found in Aristotle's discussion of *philia*.

For Aristotle, the essence of philanthropy is to be found in friendship love or *philia*, which in turn is the basis for community. *Philia* is first encountered in the family where family members learn to love others as they love themselves. Friends become 'a sort of other selves' (2002: VIII.12). A person is 'related to a friend as he is to himself (since the friend is another self)' (IX.4). The upshot is that 'Every sort of friendship, then, is in a community'. It extends beyond the family to companions, fellow citizens, and so forth, wherever the relationship is extended towards 'something good and superior' (VIII.12). It is for this reason that I have now come to refer to philanthropy as strategic friendship, and strategic friendship as the foundation of civil society, or what I call the moral citizenship of care (see Schervish and Havens 2002).

In commercial and political relations, the goal to achieve 'something good and superior' may be actively present. But it is subordinated to market relations wherein the provision of goods and services to meet the needs of others occurs only to the extent that others voice their needs through dollars for purchases, in the commercial realm, and campaign contributions and votes in the political realm.

In the philanthropic realm of strategic friendship and the moral citizenship of care, the telos of the moral biography is oriented directly to the well-being of the other as a friend (even at a distance). A friend, says Aristotle, is 'someone who wishes for and does good things . . . for the sake of the other person, or who wants the friend to be and to live for the friend's own sake' (2002: XI.4). The moral vision that directs philanthropy is the recognition that 'life is difficult for one who is alone', and that 'a human being is meant for a city and is such a nature as to live with others', that 'it is necessary for a happy person to have friends' because happiness is an activity that requires contact with others. The content of that contact is the mutual benefit of friendship which when extended to broader horizons of kinship, time and space, makes strangers into friends. 'A friend, who is another self', says Aristotle, 'supplies what someone is incapable of supplying by himself' and, conversely, 'the excellent person will need people for him to benefit' (2002: IX. 9).

Returning to David Hendricks, we hear him enunciating the attraction of direct care for others through a strategic friendship of care extended into the community. What Aristotle refers to as the attraction of *philia*, Hendricks talks about as becoming engaged in a non-commercial relationship that enables him to 'do something that is unambiguously socially positive':

> I've always kind of rolled my eyes a little bit when I hear about do-gooders because I have this image in my mind – not grounded at all on any experience – they will be lightweight type of stuff, full of petty politics. So I've always steered away from the world of philanthropy or non-profit and pooh-poohed it somewhat. But there is a side of me that says that maybe I can tune in a little bit more and do something that is unambiguously socially positive and see how that feels. I would like to see how that feels and if I find myself getting up in the morning very excited about how I am spending my time, if indeed I do find something that is unambiguously socially positive. This is something that struck me really very profoundly: those simple pleasures of being a contributor and being able to map how those contributions fit into the larger scheme of things. Kind of the social welfare, if you will.

The moral compass of a moral biography, then, is one that is inherently communal and attends directly, and not just through the market, to the needs of others. Such a moral biography is the building block of the moral citizenship of care, that array of intersecting relationships of care by which individuals respond to the needs of others, not through commercial or political markets, but directly because of the tie of *philia*, or friendship love, that one wishes to carry out effectively and strategically.

Individuals who are financially secure and those who are not both have an inclination towards extending the mutual nourishment to others directly. They are inclined and find it fulfilling to participate in the direct care of others by creating and carrying out a relationship of *philia*. Those with great resources have the fullest ability in the financial realm to extend the satisfactions of *philia*, first found in the family, to others distanced from them in time, space and kinship. When discretionary resources are available for the non-wealthy, the attractive aspiration of *philia* induces choices to care for others rather than provide some increased consumption for themselves. For the financially secure, who have no need to reduce desired consumption and have the fullest choice to do what is naturally rewarding, the benefits of *philia* extending the friendship of mutual nourishment outward enter as a gratifying world-building impetus.

Hyperagency: the capacity and great expectations to be world-builders

In one of his more famous statements, Marx argued that while people do indeed make their own history, they are not able to choose the conditions under which they do so. Although Marx was referring to collective action, the same dictum holds for individual actors as well. However, the capacity to 'make history' is not equally distributed. Some, including wealth holders, make more history than others. I call this history-making capacity of individuals 'hyperagency'. For sure, not every hyperagent is wealthy. Some financially common folk make history by virtue of being profound, creative or spiritual. But in the material realm, every wealth holder is at least potentially a hyperagent, and all of those who start businesses or set directions in philanthropy certainly are.

The desire to make a difference in philanthropy is one outlet for exercising the entrepreneurial disposition of hyperagency. Coupled with the motives of identification, gratitude, financial security, the desire to limit inheritances to successors and the attractive call of *philia*, the ability to exercise hyperagency and change the world becomes an especially strong motivation for philanthropy.

Hyperagency refers to the enhanced capacity of wealthy individuals to establish or control substantially the conditions under which they and others will work and live. For most individuals, agency is limited to choosing among and acting within the constraints of those situations in which they find themselves. As monarchs of agency, the wealth holders can circumscribe such constraints and, for good or for ill, create parts of the world according to their own design. As everyday agents, most of us strive to *find* the best possible place to live or job to hold within a given field of possibilities. As hyperagents, the wealthy – when they choose to do so – can *found* a broad array of the field of possibilities within which they and others will live and work.

Whenever someone we interview is asked to identify the most important attribute of wealth, the answer is invariably the same: *freedom*. Such freedom is both a negative release *from* constraint and a positive capacity *to* secure desire. Negative freedom refers to the loosening or negation of constraints, especially from the immediate pressures surrounding the stable provision of material well-being.

West-coast Attorney Rebecca Austin who is also independently wealthy expresses this duality of freedom in her assessment of how wealth 'smoothes out' the everyday toils of life and enables her to set her 'own agenda':

> Everything is easier when you have money. It's a shame because it's such a hard thing to get. It is the one item that smoothes out what everyone is struggling for: security, good health, fitness, good relationships, taking care of your children. Work choices are easier. Life is easier. You can do anything you want. You can take a vacation whenever and wherever you want. And even though I have a job, it's the kind of job that I can get there when I want to get there, because I want to be there rather than having to be there. The reason I work at [the public interest firm] Citizen Law is that I can integrate my life. It allows me to focus on issues and do things that can become all encompassing in terms of things that I care about. I don't work on anything I don't care about. I don't take assignments from anybody else. I set my own agenda.

To set one's own agenda, especially where others usually set it, is the fundamental endowment of wealth. Wealth enables individuals to conceive freely of and choose among a constellation of alternatives. It would, of course, be foolish to assert that the possession of wealth dissolves all the fetters of time, health and social constraint. The wealthy do indeed face constraints and rightly feel bounded in certain ways by obligation and responsibility. They have concerns with the continued and expanded accumulation of wealth, the organizational pressures of business, strategies of investment, the generational reproduction of family wealth, the preservation of a congenial political and economic climate, and the moral and social responsibilities of philanthropy. Such concerns do indeed demand their time, money and consciousness. As Norman Stryker, a Houston-born heir to an oil fortune, says, being granted an inheritance is a surprisingly alien burden. Without quotidian necessity to shape his life, he is forced to 'carve out every goddamn day'. Still, we find that even those who first flounder about with an inheritance overcome the obstacles and eventually learn the advantages of carving out rather than receiving their daily round.

The definition of wealth holders as hyperagents with personal determination and institutional dominion directly applies to their activity in the realm of philanthropy. Self-construction and world-building do not stop at the doors to their homes or their businesses. It extends to all of their involvements including, for those who choose, politics, community, religion and philanthropy. The wealthy are by dint of personality no more egoistically myopic or socially responsible than anyone else. Great expectations and grand aspirations occupy people across the financial spectrum. What is different for wealth holders is that they can legitimately be more confident about actualizing their expectations and aspirations because they are able to directly effect the fulfilment of their desires. It's a matter of realizing 'how much a little money can make a difference', as Californian Francis Toppler puts it.

Hyperagency in philanthropy does not mean that the wealthy always and everywhere conceive or achieve major innovative interventions. It means they tend to think more about doing so, and to partake more in bringing them about. Entrepreneurs, said respondent Brendan Dwyer, are investors who have two characteristics. First, they have a creative idea. They discern an area of output for which demand outstrips supply. Second, entrepreneurs are investors who affect actively the rate of return on their investment by directly commanding production. Correspondingly, venture capitalists are investors who bolster the capacity for others to be entrepreneurs. In business, wealth is an output. In philanthropy, wealth is an input. As such, wealth holders are the entrepreneurs and venture capitalists of philanthropic endeavours.

The distinctive class trait of the wealthy in philanthropy is the ability to bring into being and not just support particular charitable projects. Hyperagency in the field of philanthropy assigns financial resources to fabricating major outcomes. When exercising this capacity, wealth holders are *producers* rather than supporters of philanthropy, underwriters rather than just contributors. Finding neglected social niches where needs are great and resources scarce is precisely Janet Arnold's craft. 'I am involved in human rights and I tend to be more involved with the American Indian, at this particular time, than I am with other minorities', says the third-generation guardian of a Detroit fortune. She contributes to many other causes, but her 'main focus is on the American Indian' and other 'unpopular' issues. 'I gravitate to areas that have need and have no access to support', she says, because it is especially there 'I feel like I can make a difference'.

In common parlance we regularly speak of large and small contributors. Distinguishing between producers and supporters of philanthropy is a more functional distinction. Each philanthropic enterprise pursues resources in order to produce outcomes in response to social needs and interests. Most individuals respond to appeals for contributions in a manner parallel to how a consumer responds to the products or services of a business. That is, they are consumers or supporters rather than creators or architects of the enterprise whose goods and services they wish to receive. Only as a group acting formally or informally in concert, can consumers and contributors determine the fate of a charitable endeavour. Because it is the accumulated support of many individuals, rather than of any particular single individual, that determines the existence and direction of a venture, each separate individual is at most a joint or collateral producer.

It is a different story altogether, however, when a wealthy contributor provides a sizeable enough gift to actually start a new philanthropic direction or shape the agenda of a charity. In this instance, the contributor may be termed a direct producer or architect. Such direct production, of course, is Janus faced, and so it is always important to discern the conditions under which philanthropic hyperagency produces care rather than control (see Schervish 2006b).

Laura Madison clearly appreciates the productive potential of her charitable giving. 'Because I have a large amount of money to put in,' she explains, 'I have an opportunity to really make a difference if I see something that a large amount of money could do more for than a small amount of money could.' The extreme case of direct production is the personal founding of an original philanthropic organization or project. Such hyperagency gets exercised formally through the creation of a private or working foundation, or through the contribution of enough resources to establish a novel direction within an existing organization, such as a clinic, endowed chair or hospital wing. Less formally, individuals of means can directly produce philanthropic outcomes by 'adopting' specific individuals (including family members), organizations or causes that they assist in a sufficiently large manner as to 'make a difference'.

It is precisely the possibility and practice of 'making a difference' that undergirds the determination and dominion of hyperagency that marks Brendan Dwyer's charitable giving. 'Whatever success I've got, and whatever I've learned, and whatever I get my satisfaction from come from being able to make a difference,' says Dwyer. 'That's what makes me happy. When I've felt I've made a difference in a beneficial way.' Establishing a personal foundation as one vehicle for his charitable giving is only a small part of his institution-shaping philanthropy. He also contributes substantially enough to be considered a producer of the work of two university-based research institutes, a metro Detroit prison rehabilitation programme, an inner-city charter school and an inner-city church-based community organization. In the end, Dwyer counsels, there are two fairly straightforward questions that, if answered in the affirmative, mark the path of inclination that leads to philanthropy: 'Is there something valuable you want to do that needs to be done in society? And can you do it better than Uncle Sam?'

Conclusion

In his 1930 essay, 'Economic possibilities for our grandchildren', John Maynard Keynes wrote about the growth in financial wealth and its implications for the growth in moral wealth. According to Keynes, 'The *economic problem* [of scarcity] may be solved, or at least within sight of solution, within a hundred years. This means that the economic problem is not – if we look into the future – *the permanent problem of the human race*' (1930 [1933]: 366, italics in the original). 'I look forward,' he continues, 'to the greatest change which has ever occurred in the material environment of life for human beings in the aggregate . . . Indeed, it has already begun. The course of affairs will simply be that there will be ever larger and larger classes and groups of people from whom problems of economic necessity have been practically removed' (372). The consequence of lifting economic necessity will be that 'for the first time since his creation man will be faced with his real, his permanent problem – how to use his freedom from pressing economic cares, how to occupy the leisure, which science and compound interest will have won for him, to live wisely and agreeably and well' (367).

It is Keynes's aspiration that '[t]he love of money as a possession – as distinguished from the love of money as a means to the enjoyments and realities of life – will be recognized for what it is, a somewhat disgusting morbidity, one of those semi-criminal, semi-pathological propensities which one hands over with a shudder to the specialists in mental disease' (369).

Even when individuals are in the accumulation phase of their life, acquiring wealth is seldom the ultimate end of life. But it is usually a high-priority intermediate end. When individuals reach a level of subjectively defined financial security, there is the potential for a shift in moral purpose and values whereby the accumulation of wealth ceases to be an end and becomes more fully a means to achieve other ends. Such ends may be retirement, providing an inheritance, pursuing a hobby or enjoying more leisure. But Keynes singles out one specific prospect, namely, a change in 'the nature of one's duty to one's neighbour. For it will remain reasonable to be economically purposive for others after it has ceased to be reasonable for oneself' (372).

The shift of wealth from an end to a means, then, is arguably the most significant transformation of capacity and character for individuals who have solved or are close to solving the economic problem. In other words, the cultural context is ultimately a personal and moral context in which generous and innovative allocation becomes a way of life. Increasing numbers of wealth holders and at an earlier age are seeking to understand the creative moral purpose and not just the quantitative prospects of their wealth. In essence, they are capable of asking and seeking answers about how to deploy their wealth as a tool to achieve the deeper purposes of life when achieving a higher standard of living or acquiring more wealth ceases to be of high importance. They face the question about how to live and impart to their children a moral biography of wealth while, at the same time, expanding the quality and quantity of care for the moral biography of others. Clarifying and drawing on the motivations that mobilize the allocation of wealth for philanthropy will help individuals make care simultaneously for neighbour and self a path to greater happiness, which I define as the confluence of effectiveness and significance.

References

Aristotle (2002) *Nicomachean Ethics*, 2nd edn, trans. Joe Sachs, Newburyport, MA: Focus Publishing.

Deutsche Bank Group (2000) *Wealth With Responsibility/2000*, P. G. Schervish and J. J. Havens, Center on Wealth and Philanthropy, Boston College, Deutsche Bank Group, New York: Bankers Trust Private Banking.

Keynes, J. M. (1930) [1933] 'Economic possibilities for our grandchildren', in *Essays in Persuasion*, London: Macmillan and Co, pp. 358–73.

Lloyd, T. (2004) *Why Rich People Give*, London: Association of Charitable Foundations.

Martineau, H. (1989) [1838] *How to Observe Morals and Manners*, New Brunswick, NJ: Transaction.

Murphy, T. B. (2001) 'Financial and psychological determinants of donor's capacity to give', in *New Directions in Philanthropic Fundraising. Understanding the Needs of Donors: The Supply-Side of Charitable Giving*, E. R. Tempel and D. F. Burlingame (eds), 28: 33–49.

Schervish, P. G. (1992) 'Adoption and altruism: those with whom I want to share a dream', *Nonprofit and Voluntary Sector Quarterly*, 21(4): 327–50.

—— (1997) 'Major donors, major motives: The people and purposes behind major gifts', in *New Directions for Philanthropic Fundraising*, 16: 85–112.

—— (2000) 'The modern Medici: Patterns, motivations and giving strategies of the wealthy', paper presented on the panel The New Philanthropists at the inaugural forum, 'What is "new" about new philanthropy', of the University of Southern California Nonprofit Studies Center, Los Angeles, 20 January.

—— (2005) 'The sense and sensibility of philanthropy as a moral citizenship of care', in *Good Intentions: Moral Obstacles and Opportunities* (ed.) David H. Smith, Bloomington, IN: Indiana University Press, pp. 149–65.

—— (2006a) 'The moral biography of wealth: Philosophical reflections on the foundation of philanthropy', *Nonprofit and Voluntary Sector Quarterly*, 35(3): 477–92.

—— (2006b) 'Philanthropy's Janus-faced potential: The dialectic of care and negligence facing donors', in *Taking Philanthropy Seriously: Beyond Noble Intentions to Responsible Giving*, W. Damon and S. Verducci (eds) Bloomington, IN: Indiana University Press, pp. 218–36.

—— Benz, O., Dulany, P., Murphy, T. B. and Salett, S. (1993) *Taking Giving Seriously*, Indianapolis, IN: Indiana University Center on Philanthropy.

—— and Havens, J. J. (1997) 'Social participation and charitable giving: A multivariate analysis', *Voluntas: International Journal of Voluntary and Nonprofit Organizations*, 8(3): 235–60.

—— — (1999) *Millionaires and the Millennium: Prospects for a Golden Age of Philanthropy*, Center on Wealth and Philanthropy, Boston College.

—— — (2001a) 'The mind of the millionaire: Findings from a national survey on wealth with responsibility', *New Directions for Philanthropic Fundraising: Taking Fundraising Seriously*, 32: 75–107.

—— — (2001b) 'The new physics of philanthropy: The supply-side vectors of charitable giving – Part 1: The material side of the supply side', *The CASE International Journal of Higher Education Advancement*, 2(2): 95–111.

—— — (2002) 'The new physics of philanthropy: The supply-side vectors of charitable giving – Part 2: The spiritual side of the supply side', *The CASE International Journal of Higher Education Advancement*, 2(3): 221–41.

—— — (2004) 'The meaning and motives of financial security: A new model of philanthropic decision-making among the wealthy', presentation to the 2004 annual meeting of the Association for Research on Nonprofit Organizations and Voluntary Action, Los Angeles, 20 November.

—— — (2006) 'New findings and trends on the relationship of wealth and income and philanthropy', presentation to the 2006 annual meeting of the Association for Research on Nonprofit Organizations and Voluntary Action, Chicago, 16 November.

—— and Herman, A. (1988) *Empowerment and Beneficence: Strategies of Living and Giving Among the Wealthy*,

Final report: The study on wealth and philanthropy, Center on Wealth and Philanthropy, Boston College.

—— O'Herlihy, M. A. and Havens, J. J. (2001) *Agent-animated Wealth and Philanthropy: The Dynamics of Accumulation and Allocation Among High-tech Donors*, Center on Wealth and Philanthropy, Boston College and the Association of Fundraising Professionals, Washington, DC, April.

Tocqueville, Alexis de (1966) [1835] *Democracy in America*, trans. George Lawrence, and (ed.) J. P. Mayer, New York: Harper Perennial.

Toner, J. (1968) *The Experience of Love*, Washington, DC: Corpus Books.

10

Issue and trends in foundation fundraising

Diana Leat

Introduction

This chapter looks at issues and trends in the foundation-funding market in the UK, largely from the viewpoint of foundations themselves. It begins by briefly sketching the outlines of the UK foundation sector, identifying numbers, key types and patterns of spending. The second section outlines some key phases in the history of foundation approaches, some cultural characteristics and common criticisms. The third section looks at current issues and developments, and speculates about future trends likely to affect foundation funding. These issues are of importance to fundraisers in understanding the shape and nature of the foundation market and the ways in which they engage in that market.

The UK foundation sector

For the purposes of this chapter a charitable grant-making foundation is defined as an endowed charitable organization whose primary activity is making grants to other organizations in pursuit of its mission.

Foundations are unusual within the world of organizations in general in that they are resource independent; they do not have to raise or earn money from others and are thus free, in theory at least, from the constraints of donors (within the confines of the trust deed), customers and constituents. However, there are degrees of resource independence and thus degrees of freedom.

Grant-makers' independence

Very broadly, we might categorize grant-makers as follows:

1 Grant-makers with independent funds derived from a permanent endowment.
2 Grant-makers dependent on funds raised annually from non-government sources.

3 Grant-makers dependent on non-government funds but accountable to government (e.g. lottery distributors).
4 Grant-makers dependent on government funding.

Although in theory only those in the first category above are 'real' foundations, as discussed below organizations commonly known as foundations straddle categories 1 and 2.

Some figures

In the first category there are around 7,500 grant-making charitable foundations in Britain giving away approximately £2 billion each year. However, grant-seekers are likely to know about, at best, only the a fraction of these – the top 500 trusts and foundations estimated to give more than three-quarters of all grants by value, or the even smaller group of super-rich trusts within the top 500. This super-rich group includes Wellcome, giving £350 million per annum, Wolfson, Gatsby, Garfield Weston, Esmee Fairbairn, Tudor, Henry Smith Charity, Lloyds TSB Foundation, and others, each giving away more than £20 million per year (*www.acf.org.*) In addition to foundations whose main business is giving grants there is a small proportion of large operating charities who also make some grants.

Categories 3 and 4 above contain other bodies that give grants to charities and other voluntary organizations. These include the lottery distributors and government-funded foundations spending around £352 million per annum (CAF and CaritasData Ltd 2005), as well as various government departments giving both grants and contracts.

Distinguishing between types

For grant-seekers, the distinction between the four categories above may often be of little interest. Getting the grant is what matters, not whether Big Lottery Fund is properly described as a 'foundation' or not. However, the distinction between 'foundations' and other grant-makers, as well as other distinctions within the category of foundations, does have important implications for the sector now and, perhaps even more so, in the future. Foundations are the only source of funds independent of both government and popular support. Foundations can fund the truly, madly, deeply unpopular without worrying about future votes or fundraising. Foundations can fund the truly, madly, deeply risky without worrying about the questions asked when the project fails.

In many respects the key distinction is between charitable grant-makers that have an independent, permanent endowment – foundations – and those that do not. Having a permanent or long-term endowment means that foundations are free to do whatever they like within their trust deed and the law. Unlike all other institutions in society, they do not have to please anyone in order to survive.

Although it is conventional to reserve the term 'foundation' for endowed, independent foundations, if we look more closely at categories 1 and 2 above we find various differences between foundations. In addition to obvious differences in age, size and interests, there are differences in sources of income with implications for degree of independence discussed above:

(a) Fully endowed foundations deriving all of their income from a permanent or semi-permanent endowment. Endowed foundations vary radically in size and level of grant-making activity and have very different histories and original sources of income. Some

183

are run solely by family members; others include non-family members on their boards. The key characteristic is that they live solely on income from endowment.

(b) Corporate foundations derive their income from a company. Corporate foundations straddle categories 1 and 2 above in that only a minority of corporate foundations are endowed. More commonly, corporate foundations have no permanent endowment but rather receive regular transfers from the associated companies. Yet again, corporate giving is very unevenly distributed – after the top-ten company givers, the percentage of pre-tax profit donated drops dramatically.

(c) Community foundations also straddle categories 1 and 2 above. Community founda-tions exist to raise and manage a permanent endowment of charitable donations from which they make grants to local and community projects. Community foundations restrict their grant-making and much (though not all) of their fundraising to a specific geographical area. In a sense, community foundations are 'endowed foundations in the making'. Community foundations have grown rapidly in the last decade. By 2001–2 there were thirty-one community foundations (with another thirty-three aspiring community foundations, with a total endowment of £90 million making grants to the value of £28.1 million (Community Foundation Network 2002). As in so many areas of the foundation world, these overall figures conceal huge variations between individual community foundations. Community foundations have found a special place in the new policy environment acting as an 'agent' for some large central government grant-making programmes to local areas.

(d) Other fundraising grant-makers have increased in recent years. Fundraising grant-makers include, among others, broadcast appeals on radio and television. A conservative estimate of the annual amounts given in grants from broadcast appeals might be £40–£50 million.

Patterns of spending

Figures on patterns of grant-making are, for various reasons, sometimes misleading. Broadly speaking, however, foundations show a distinct preference for funding social services, health and education with a total of 45 per cent of all foundation funding going to these causes. By contrast, arts and culture, for example, receive only 9 per cent of all foundation funding, and the environment around 4 per cent (for further details, see CAF and CaritasData Ltd 2005).

The past is not always a good guide to the future. The discussion in the final section of this chapter raises the possibility that patterns of foundation funding may change in favour of, for example, spending on the environment. Data on current patterns of spending are useful not so much as a guide to the future but as an indication of how far things would have to change if, say, civil rights were to become a key issue.

A history of foundations in two-and-a-half phases

Foundations are relatively conservative organizations, lacking many of the usual pressures that force organizations to change. Over the last century, however, some have moved with the times, and that change has accelerated in recent years.

The charity/service approach was the original model, developed throughout the world in different guises and going by different names. Originally the charity/service approach was rooted in religious beliefs such as alms giving and tithing on the one hand, and moral codes such as *noblesse oblige* on the other. Its later nineteenth- and early twentieth-century application by charitable foundations was linked in some countries to the secularization of giving and the growing role of the industrial elite and urban middle class in philanthropy (Smith and Borgmann 2001).

The charity approach was in many ways well suited to its social and political context. Without adequate provision by church and state, foundations provided services to those unable to care for themselves. As governments increasingly began to provide some services for some groups, foundations adapted the service approach to provide services complementary to those of government or to fill gaps in statutory provision. Foundations began to stress their roles as innovators, risk–takers and funders of unpopular causes. At certain periods in many societies, foundations added a 'demonstration' or 'pump-priming' element to the charity approach. Foundations innovated or spotted as yet unacknowledged needs, in effect doing the initial 'R&D', in the expectation that some other funder (often government) would pick up the project, method or need, and make it more widely known and available. In the mid-twentieth century in particular this service demonstration effect was probably very effective (Anheier and Leat 2006).

The major weakness of a charity/service approach, still arguably the dominant approach in the UK, is that, although it makes a difference to beneficiaries, it addresses symptoms rather than causes and changes very little. This was the key criticism of the charity approach that led to the rise of the philanthropic/science foundation approach.

Although the terms 'charity' and 'philanthropy' tend to be used interchangeably today, originally 'philanthropic' foundations distinguished themselves from charitable foundations in their emphasis on dealing with causes rather than symptoms of problems.

This was the approach adopted by the Rockefeller, Carnegie and Russell Sage foundations, among others, in the USA in the early twentieth century, and by, for example, the Joseph Rowntree trusts in the UK. Rowntree captured the new philosophy of these foundations when he wrote in his original trust deed that the foundations should distinguish themselves from current philanthropic effort by searching out underlying causes rather than 'remedying the more superficial manifestations of weakness or evil' (Joseph Rowntree Charitable Trust 2000–2002).

Again, the rise of the philanthropic foundation was a product of its time. Belief in the power of a 'scientific approach' was riding high, as was the notion of social engineering. The assumption was that social, medical and economic problems could all be solved once their causes were understood and 'scientific' solutions applied (Bulmer 1999). Foundations adopting a philanthropic approach undoubtedly did, and continue to do, hugely important work, including establishment of the research university and other higher-education institutions. But for all the achievements of the philanthropic approach, it too suffers from some weaknesses when viewed from a twenty-first-century perspective.

In the last quarter of the twentieth century, foundations entered a new phase – or perhaps subphase: the scientific–managerialist. The rapid accumulation of new wealth by entrepreneurs and the run-up of the stock market in the 1990s enabled many individuals to increase their giving or to engage in formal, institutionalized giving for the first time. Many of these young, confident venture capitalists for social change viewed charitable organizations as lacking management capacity and capitalization; they saw charitable actions as investments and demanded a demonstrable 'return' on their investment (Letts *et al.* 1997). The new philanthropists are generally results oriented; they want to see the impact and the results of their giving relatively quickly.

These new kids on the block are, in many respects, modern descendants of the philanthropy approach. While they have stimulated healthy debate, they share some fundamental weaknesses stemming, in part, from their fundamentally instrumentalist assumptions. First, they tend to focus on foundation processes rather than roles. They do not address the question of the unique value of foundations in a democracy. Second, they apply managerialist business models to foundation practices. The assumption is that if only foundations, and their grantees, were run more like businesses, all would be well. As Sievers has remarked, the emphasis on technical interventions in systems to improve performance: 'reflects the fix-it character of American social improvement – agnostic on values but committed to improved performance' (Sievers 1997).

These two-and-a-half phases are only sequential for some foundations. In practice, the 'charity', 'philanthropy' and 'scientific–managerial' approaches co-exist in the UK today.

Characteristics and criticisms

Running alongside the approaches above are some enduring, cross-cutting criticisms of foundation funding. These are important in understanding the current and future challenges for foundations and the degree of change that may be required.

One frequent criticism of foundations is that they are elitist and out of touch with real social issues. So, for example, Odendahl (1990: 27) charges that: 'The rich do not give to the poor but to institutions they use and cherish – the charity of the wealthy doesn't just begin at home, it stays there.'

A second criticism is that, despite the rhetoric of innovation and risk-taking, foundations follow rather than start things. For example, in the USA the civil rights movement began in 1955 with the Montgomery bus boycott, but foundation grants were not significant until 1962 (McIlnay 1998: 11): 'Foundation grants to organizations directly serving women and minorities have been minuscule, dispelling the myth that foundations are crusaders for social change and contradicting the descriptions that foundations have given of themselves' (ibid.). Similarly, Vincent and Pharoah (2000) in the UK suggest that grant-makers as a whole tend to approach problems similarly, indicating a considerable degree of conformity in the way foundations address needs. Grant-making reveals strong patterns of 'fashion' across foundations.

Another criticism of foundations is that grant size tends to be determined by general principles within foundations, rather than the needs of the project or proposal. In other words, grant size is related not to what is needed to achieve the goals of the grant but to foundations' own organizational needs (for risk control, spread of grant distribution, etc.). For example, some foundations operate with predetermined rules that they do not give grants above $£x$ or for more than y years.

Various commentators have criticized mainstream foundation practices for their focus on small short-term grants. Skloot makes the point most colourfully when he criticizes foundations for behaving 'like gamblers playing the two-dollar slots in Vegas. We sit staring straight ahead, holding our little bucket of metal coins. Repeatedly, we drop in small change, hoping for a big pay-off'; 'We put large dreams on small coins', 'we almost always feed the slots more than we win' (Skloot 2001). The complaint that foundations are ineffective because they spread their money too wide and too thinly is closely related to the criticism that they are ineffective because they fail to make choices and lack focus (see e.g. Covington 1997; Schumann 1998).

Foundations have typically seen their lack of predefined focus as a virtue, demonstrating their democracy and responsiveness. But 'Whilst some might argue that this "let 1,000 flowers bloom" approach is inherently democratic, normal (and typically American), I suggest it is autocratic, ineffective and willful – (and typically American)' (Skloot 2001: 3; my parentheses – we might substitute British).

Ask any nonprofit organization what they most need and want and the reply will be 'more core funding/operational support'. But what mainstream foundations most often give is (short-term) project funding. Again this is said to be one reason why mainstream foundations are less effective than they might be. Both Bothwell (2002) and Burkeman (1999) relate the apparent preference for project funding to mainstream foundations' lack of trust in grantees and thus their reluctance to engage in the loss of control entailed in core funding.

Criticism of foundations' overemphasis on project funding is related to the claim that mainstream foundations have been ineffective in building sustainable change because they have funded in traditional policy and programme silos. This may not only hamper the emergence of new, creative ideas and solutions to old problems, but also create, or perpetuate, 'barriers to permeation and cross-issue connections' among nonprofits (Bothwell 2002: 40).

Most foundations have a very narrow view of their potential grantees. They appear to operate on the assumption that: (a) what nonprofit organizations choose to do accurately reflects social needs and problems of society; and (b) nonprofit organizations are the major locus of new thinking and innovation generally. These assumptions persist despite numerous studies which demonstrate that the existence of nonprofit organizations is very imperfectly related to social need (see Anheier and Kendall 2001; Flynn and Hodgkinson 2002; Perrow 2001), and that nonprofit organizations are not particularly innovative (Kramer 1990). The important point, however, is that foundations seem somehow locked into funding nonprofit organizations and find it more difficult to fund individuals or groups other than tax-exempt entities. This is a highly compartmentalized world with clear sector boundaries.

Foundations are sometimes criticized for being overly individualistic, poor at collaboration, sharing and learning. Skloot, continuing his gambling analogy, suggests: 'We sit straight ahead, rarely pulling our eyes away from the spinning icons. We don't interact with the other players on our left or right. If we did, we wouldn't learn much anyhow – they're behaving in just the same way' (2001: 3). Much of philanthropy, Skloot argues, 'especially at the largest 100 foundations',

> works in isolation, rarely sharing the task or the results. We make grants based on inadequate due diligence, partially relevant information, or simple intuition. After a grant is made we rarely share what we really know – the good, the bad and the ugly – with grantees or with our own colleagues. We are novices at cross-program collaboration and rarely buddy-up for mutual gain . . . there are no incentives in philanthropy to do that. Finally, we don't measure our successes, course-correct and learn intentionally.
>
> (2001: 3–4)

Foundations appear generally unwilling to challenge the widespread assumption that they should spend next to nothing on their own management. Some so-called overhead costs may indeed be wasteful and inefficient. Others are simply the costs of making good grants and of achieving sustainable change, and are more like investments and R&D expenditure than overhead costs proper.

While some foundations abhor planning; for others making and sticking to a plan has become a sort of holy grail that will make everything right. The value of planning is just one of the rationalist assumptions which implicitly or explicitly underlie grant-making policies and practices. Most obviously these theories include the assumption that 'good and successful' projects are a function of good ideas, well-thought-through plans, and good organization. Organizational structures and processes, management and financial resources are major determinants and predictors of the likely success of the project; clear objectives, planning and control processes are taken as important indicators of the 'good' or capable organization.

Underlying many of the criticisms above is a deeper weakness: foundations' lack of an adequate theory of social change. Foundations say that they want to make a difference but often fail to think through what or who would have to change in order for that to happen and how those people/institutions might be reached. For example, many foundations have aimed to address child poverty without making the link to either low wages in many predominantly female occupations or inadequacies of child support payment systems.

Although foundations often (wrongly) cite legal restrictions as the reason for avoidance of involvement in policy issues, another reason may be lack of any realistic theory of social change. Foundations often fail to realize that sustainable change happens only rarely without government involvement of some sort and at some level – whether as policy innovator, funder, implementor or champion.

The foundation world tends to rank its members by the size of their assets and income; money is the currency foundations give and by which they account for their activities (i.e. size and number of grants given). Underlying this focus on money, there are some complex assumptions about the power of money alone to solve problems. Money is the root of all solutions, and more money to make more grants makes foundations more effective. The assumption is that we know what needs to be done; money is all that is missing.

The review above suggests a sector that finds it difficult to:

- keep in touch;
- set rather than follow fashion;
- focus/be proactive;
- think and fund across silo boundaries;
- see beyond clear sector boundaries;
- collaborate and learn;
- accept that real life is complex, messy and irrational;
- identify what has to change and follow through;
- address policy issues; and
- focus on assets other than money (for a more general discussion of foundations' structural limitations, see Anheier and Leat 2002).

Underlying these difficulties there are some clear themes related to foundations' structural location in society. First, foundations find it hard to stay in touch because they suffer from 'weak signals'; they do not have the usual sources of market information – whatever they choose to fund, grantees will respond. Second, their somewhat anomalous position in a democracy makes them reluctant to 'play God' – hence they stress their responsiveness to voluntary organizations and acceptance of conventional silos. Third, the fact that they have independent resources, and can survive no matter what, means that they have no strong incentives to collaborate or to learn how to do better.

And, more speculatively, constantly subject to the random demands of grant-seekers, foundations seek to impose some order on a messy world by creating rules and procedures to structure their experiences and to make sense of grant-making.

Future issues and trends

This is a time of change for foundations – probably the greatest in the last fifty years. Philanthropic giving and foundation formation is on the policy and wider public agenda. Political parties of all persuasions are keen to encourage giving and to harness private action for public benefit. Proposed legal changes will extend the definition of charitable purposes from four to twelve heads. New philanthropists, including Gates, Buffett and Branson, are raising the profile and the bar in giving. New philanthropists are adopting new approaches and requiring greater control. But just as philanthropic giving and foundation formation is increasing it is also declining relative to the problems it seeks to address. For example, Andrew Carnegie could afford to build a library in every town in Britain; few, if any, UK foundations today could afford to build more than a couple.

Policy change is creating new roles for philanthropy – and new demands and challenges. Foundations are increasingly expected to demonstrate their contribution to public benefit, and to be more accountable and transparent in what they do. Contracting has created new complications in both the role of foundations and the nitty-gritty of assessing applications. When is a grant an indirect subsidy to government provision/responsibility?

Although there is no pay-out requirement in the UK (as there is in the USA), foundations are increasingly aware of the need to consider not just where they give grants but also how they invest their assets in ways consistent with their missions.

Many of the old foundation mantras – innovation, risk-taking, doing what the state does not do – have been seriously undermined by the redefined role of government. Government increasingly sees itself as the innovator, the gap filler, and contracts out to others much of what it used to do. So, how are foundations responding and what are the likely challenges ahead?

A recent study of foundations in the UK (Leat, 2006) revealed that foundations generally found it difficult to articulate any distinctive role. Some noted that there were various formulaic answers to the question of foundations' roles but these did not really say anything. The majority of foundations emphasized that they saw their roles as complementing those of others, including government.

Although most foundations were keen to avoid substituting for government, most also commented that this was more difficult in practice. It was felt that government had 'changed the rules', cutting back on services, involving the voluntary sector in providing services on contract, and taking on the role of experimenter. In this situation, foundations argued that 'avoiding substitution is no longer viable'. The issue of substitution and relationships with statutory funding was for many foundations the most difficult current issue.

Innovation was the single most common term used, by foundations and others, to describe the roles of foundations. Foundation representatives identified a wide range of innovations which they attributed to foundations. But some foundations questioned what the term really meant and whether foundation grant-making actually reflected this role. There were also questions regarding the viability of innovating in the light of an interventionist government creating innovation fatigue with a flow of 'new' programmes and initiatives.

A minority of foundation staff saw the major role of the foundation in terms of social change and policy influence, providing new ideas, acting in some respects like, or with, think-tanks. A small number of others were exploring this type of role 'as part of searching for ways to have more impact'. But there were problems in adopting this role: foundations' traditional emphasis on being apolitical, combined with 'a history and culture of reticence'; trustees' tendency to equate policy and politics, and to shy away from developing networks for policy influence; lack of research and knowledge: 'Why would anyone listen to us? We aren't service providers so we don't have that sort of knowledge, and the knowledge we do have we don't really organize or use properly'.

More generally, the majority of foundations did not see themselves as having much, if any, policy influence. In part, this was attributed to politicians' lack of understanding and knowledge of foundations. But some foundations questioned whether foundations encourage people – politicians or others – to understand them and/or try to influence policy. Some foundations, as well as commentators, were unhappy with any notion of social change and policy influence. Despite this, some foundations saw greater policy relevance and involvement as one of their ideal roles.

Foundations generally saw their proper or ideal relationship with government as one of complementing government. But some wanted a more equal and involved, but still distanced, relationship with government in which foundations capitalized on their resource independence and knowledge to contribute to agenda-setting and policy development. In addition, some foundations wanted to see more risk-taking, more idiosyncracy, more learning and foundations being more outward-looking and cooperative.

In terms of emerging issues almost all foundations were grappling with monitoring and evaluation. No one saw the pressures for monitoring and evaluation diminishing over the coming years, and some, especially those outside the foundation world saw those pressures as likely to increase. Monitoring and evaluation were seen as linked to accountability. But founda-tions, and others, generally had problems defining accountability: 'We all keep repeating this mantra but what does it mean?'

With one exception, the foundations giving internationally did not typically fund in Europe, and there was much more emphasis on funding in the Third World. The possibility of getting better value for money was pinpointed as a particular opportunity presented by international giving, and some foundations already giving internationally were considering expanding such giving.

UK foundations appear to adopt a highly pragmatic approach to wider European involve-ment. Where there are easy mechanisms for involvement and/or where there are tangible benefits, UK foundations seem to become involved in wider European fora and issues. There are, however, signs of change. Some foundations noted a desire to engage with wider European colleagues in discussions on specific policy and practice issues. But issues to do with costs, time and overheads were cited as potential barriers.

Foundations varied in what they saw as the most important policy issues in the coming years. However, responses clustered under four broad headings: demonstrating effectiveness; relating to government; legal and tax frameworks; responding to new needs in the light of reduced public spending. So what? If effectiveness continues to be a major pressure on and concern for foundations what might this mean for both grant-makers and grant-seekers?

Emphasis on demonstrable effectiveness is likely to lead to more foundations expecting grant-seekers to specify performance measures, targets, outputs and outcomes and plans for evaluation in their applications. At worst, this may lead to pressure for counting; at best, it may lead to rethinking performance measures and recognizing the complexity and uncertainty of outcomes.

Concern with demonstrable effectiveness may lead foundations to become more focused, to adopt a smaller number of priorities and to be more selective/proactive about the areas in which they believe they can really make a difference. Funding for effectiveness may also lead to a focus on funding organizations which have a demonstrable track record in getting things done, fewer risks and thus less real innovation. This in turn may advantage the larger, more established organizations (or perhaps simply those capable of presenting themselves in the most positive light), and what Cohen (2005) has referred to as a new 'ice age' for smaller organizations.

The better news may be that in their search for demonstrable effectiveness foundations will become more concerned and more realistic about sustainability. The trend towards giving larger and longer-term grants may be heightened – but this will raise new issues about when and how to exit and about 'silting up' foundations' funds. Will some foundations make no new grants in some years because their funds are already fully committed?

Concern with effectiveness is likely to lead to foundations attempting to exert more control over use of their funds. The days of the 'end of term' report may be numbered. Instead grantees may be expected to produce more regular reports and keep in close touch with funders throughout the grant period. Some grant-makers may want to be even more involved, sitting on project steering groups or offering other support. This trend towards greater hands-on involvement is already apparent among some new donors.

Foundations may look for ways of overcoming the 'weak signals' noted above. Intermediary organizations such as New Philanthropy Capital, and somewhat differently Guidestar, may increase in number and become more influential.

Concerns with effectiveness and sustainability may have other effects. One might be that foundations will drop their traditional emphasis on innovation and start focusing more on replication of what has already been shown to work. Another effect may be that broad 'fashions' in funding become much more tightly specified. For example, instead of talking about funding for 'capacity building', foundations may start to ask 'capacity building for what?', and begin to question how this may be most effectively achieved.

Issues of sustainability may lead to more searching analysis of how change is achieved, more questioning of the assumption that change follows in some magical way from 'demonstration', and greater resources devoted to marketing and dissemination of ideas and innovations. Insofar as a concern with sustainability leads foundations to take a greater interest in systemic/structural change, this may raise new issues in foundations' relationships with campaigning organizations and with government.

Demands that foundations demonstrate effectiveness may lead beyond focus on grantees to questions about what value foundations add over and above their 'cash machine' functions (Porter and Kramer 1999). One effect of questions about the value added by foundations might be greater emphasis on using all of the foundation's resources – their knowledge, reputation, independence, networks, and so on. This in turn might lead to more emphasis on learning, knowledge dissemination, collaborative working, mergers and partnerships. Focusing on their non-financial resources might also lead foundations to adopt new roles as knowledge and social issue entrepreneurs and convenors (de Borms 2005; Anheier and Leat 2006).

A related, but somewhat different, scenario might be that some foundations move away from grant-making (and all the uncertainty and loss of visibility and control involved) and capitalize on their own unique knowledge and reputation resources, and independence, to run some of their own projects; or to add value by very clearly branding work they fund (as, in some respects, the Joseph Rowntree Foundation, for example, already does; on operating foundations more generally, see Toepler 1999; Smith 1999, 2002).

Finally, questions about foundations' own added value may underline trends towards critical consideration of how foundations use not just their income but also their assets (Emerson 2004). Mission-related investment (i.e. where foundations invest their assets not merely to maximize income but also to best pursue their missions) may become more widely practised.

The wider context

Concerns around effectiveness and value added will be played out in a wider social–political context. This wider context will include factors affecting the size, structure and regulation of philanthropy, as well as the issues that philanthropy is called upon to address. How these factors will develop and interact is anyone's guess. The following discussion lays out some guesses, looking first at factors directly affecting foundations and then at wider social issues.

Intergenerational transfer of wealth

If the much heralded intergenerational transfer of wealth creates a boom in new foundation formation, what might be the consequences? Much will depend on the number, size and, crucially, the degree of control required by new foundations. The upside of new foundation formation from the viewpoint of grant-seekers may be new and diverse sources of funding. The downsides might include reduced government provision and funding, muddle, duplication and/or increasing inequality between different geographical regions and causes.

On the other hand, the intergenerational transfer of wealth may be delayed or reduced by new developments in medicine and healthy living enabling people to live ever longer.

Increased demands for accountability and regulation of foundations

The longer-term effects of greater transparency of foundations (via SORP requirements) may be to increase media and wider public awareness of and interest in foundations' activities and expenditures. This in turn may lead to pressures on foundations to concentrate their (tax-exempt) funds on more popular causes. The sort of tabloid pressure currently experienced only by grant-makers such as Big Lottery Fund and the Diana, Princess of Wales Memorial Fund may become the norm for a wider range of foundations.

Greater public scrutiny, and more onerous reporting requirements, could reduce foundation formation and/or lead to greater concentration of foundation funds on a smaller number of safer grants.

Insofar as greater direct and indirect regulation of non-profit organizations in general leads to rising costs for grant-seekers, foundations may decide to concentrate more of their funding abroad where costs are lower and, some might argue, needs greater or results more dramatic. Overseas funding may, however, be complicated by the trend to tie official overseas aid to 'good government' requirements – what governments require today foundations may require tomorrow.

Public benefit, public responsibility and blurring of sector roles

Notions of public benefit and public responsibility straddle the line between philanthropy-specific trends and wider social issues. New charity legislation requires that foundations demonstrate their contribution to public benefit. A focus on public benefit, combined with changing notions of public responsibility, further privatization of responsibility and provision, as well as a blurring of sector roles, could lead foundations radically to rethink who and what they fund.

On the one hand, foundations may cease focusing on the voluntary sector and look instead at whoever is most likely to deliver maximum public benefit. Voluntary organizations may become only one category of potential partners/grantees for foundations.

On the other hand, as noted above, foundations are deeply concerned about acting as substitutes for government. If, as seems likely, the trend towards privatization continues, foundations may stop trying to plug the gaps and instead start trying to hold back the wave. Relationships with some larger service-providing voluntary organizations could change as foundations stand out against the colonization of the voluntary sector and the blurring of sector boundaries. Organizations that work to remind, not to relieve, government of its responsibilities may find new favour with some foundations.

Increasing social diversity and fragmentation

Various factors look set to increase diversity and fragmentation within society. Increasing economic inequality and the possibility of development of a permanent underclass, combined with migration and religious and racial intolerance, would have obvious effects on integration and social harmony; the search for scapegoats would only exacerbate such tensions. This scenario would present new challenges for foundations. One response from foundations might be to make more use of their independence and interstitial position to take on a brokering, convening role, making connections between issues and parties. Another response might be for foundations to take clearer stands on values and the promotion of social justice and human rights.

The ongoing tension between security and freedom

The tension between security and freedom does not look likely to lessen in the foreseeable future. One response would be for foundations to become increasingly careful about funding any group or activity which could possibly be regarded as a threat, real or imagined, to security. Alternatively, or even additionally, foundations may become more concerned to defend existing civil rights – especially, perhaps, if they see their own autonomy threatened.

Simultaneous pressures for devolution/localism and globalism

Foundations will also face new challenges from the simultaneous pressures in society for both localism and globalism. These challenges will be exacerbated by the related turmoil in our sense of, and search for, identity. What does it mean for, and do to, individuals when they have multiple, possibly conflicting, identities? What happens to everyday life and interaction when identity has little to do with (temporary) residency? What does it mean to be a UK foundation addressing issues that are European, or global, in nature?

Global warming

There are those who argue that none of the problems above are of great consequence unless we address issue of global climate change. Aside from apocalyptic visions of planetary meltdown, in the shorter term environmental changes are likely to create a raft of new problems; for example, energy and water poverty within and between countries creating new distributions/patterns of wealth.

One scenario is that environmental issues come to dominate foundation agendas, leaving little money for anything else. Another scenario is that a debate emerges around prioritization and effectiveness of different types of problem and intervention; for example, does Aids present a greater, more immediate threat than global warming, and can we use scarce resources more effectively to address the former rather than the latter? Another scenario is that as global warming (temporarily) slows down, new forms of energy are used, and the issue is delayed until tomorrow.

Conclusion

The underlying message of this chapter has been that the past may not be a wholly reliable guide to the future. What foundations have done in the past is worth reviewing insofar as it tells us something about where they are, and to that extent gives us some pointers to how they might react to new issues and challenges. What no one knows is what those challenges will be. Some challenges seem worth a bet at least in the short term (pressures for effectiveness, for example) but how foundations will react is not entirely predictable. Any one issue or challenge may have positive and/or negative effects, and issues and their effects may exacerbate/support each other, or may cancel each other out.

In addition, we need to acknowledge the effects of 'shocks' that are not predicted (even if, in retrospect, they were predictable); shocks may introduce whole new strands and/or they may underline and amplify an existing trend. But none of this makes the exercise of thinking about possible future trends worthless. The point is not to predict the future but to be fore-armed and maybe to 'talk about how to improve the trends we don't like' (Robert Wood Johnson Foundation, quoted in Curtis 1999).

References

Anheier, H. K. and Daly, S. (2006) *Foundations in Europe: Roles and Visions*, London: Routledge.
—— and Kendall, J. (eds) (2001) *Third Sector Policy at the Crossroads: An International Nonprofit Analysis*, London: Routledge.
—— and Leat, D. (2002) *From Charity to Creativity, Philanthropic Foundations for the 21st Century*, London: Comedia.
—— — (2006) *Creative Philanthropy*, London: Routledge.
de Borms, L. T. (2005) *Foundations Creating Impact in a Globalised World*, London: John Wiley and Sons.
Bothwell, R. O. (2002) 'Trends in self-regulation and transparency of nonprofits in the US', *International Journal of Not-for-Profit Law*, 2(3).
Bulmer, M. (1999) 'The history of foundations in the United Kingdom and the United States: Philanthropic foundations in industrial society', in H. K. Anheier and S. Toepler (eds) *Private Funds and Public Purpose, Philanthropic Foundations in International Perspectives*, New York, NY: Kluwer Academic/ Plenum.
Burkeman, S. (1999) 'An unsatisfactory company?', The 1999 Allen Lane lecture, London: Allen Lane Foundation.
CAF and CaritasData Ltd (2005) *Charity Trends – 25th Anniversary Edition 2004*, London: CAF and CaritasData Ltd.
Cohen, R. (2005) 'What can and should philanthropy do in the future?', *Dialogues on Civic Philanthropy*. www.civicphilanthropy.net/event1opeds.html (accessed 21 August 2007).
Community Foundation Network (2002) *Review of the Year 2001–2*, London: Community Foundation Network.
Covington, S. (1997) 'Moving a public policy agenda: The strategic philanthropy of conservative foundations', USA: National Council for Responsive Philanthropy.
Curtis, J. (1999) 'The future of philanthropy', *Foundation, News and Commentary*, March/April, www.foundationnews.org/CME/article.cfm?ID=756 (accessed 21 August 2007).

Emerson, J. (2004) 'The blended value proposition: Tracking the intersects and opportunities of economic, social and environmental value creation', www.blendedvalue.org.

Flynn, P. and Hodgkinson, V. (eds) (2002) *Measuring the Impact of the Nonprofit Sector*, New York, NY: Plenum/Kluwer.

Heifetz, R. A., Kania, J. V. and Kramer, M. R. (2004) 'Leading boldly', *Stanford Social Innovation Review*, 1:21–32.

Joseph Rowntree Charitable Trust (2000–2002) 'Triennial Report', York: London: Joseph Rowntree Charitable Trust.

Kramer, R. (1990) 'Change and continuity in British voluntary organizations, 1976 to 1988', *Voluntas* 1(2): 33–60.

Leat, D. (2006) 'Britain', in Anheier, H. K. and Daly, S. (eds) (2006) *Foundations in Europe: Roles and Visions*, London: Routledge.

Letts, C., Ryan, W. and Grossman, A. (1997) 'Virtuous capital: What foundations can learn from venture capitalists', *Harvard Business Review*, 75(2): 36–44.

McIlnay, D. P. (1998) *How Foundations Work*, San Francisco, CA: Jossey Bass.

Odendahl, T. (1990) *Charity Begins at Home*, New York, NY: Basic Books.

Perrow, C. (2001) 'The rise of nonprofits and the decline of civil society', in H. K. Anheier (ed.) *Organisational Theory and the Non-profit Form*, London: Center for Civil Society, Report 2, London School of Economics.

Porter, M. E. and Kramer, M. R. (1999) 'Philanthropy's new agenda: Creating value', *Harvard Business Review*, 77(6): 121–30.

Schlueter, A., Then, V. and Walkenhorst, P. (eds) (2001) *Foundations in Europe: Society, Management and Law*, London: Directory of Social Change.

Schumann, M. (1998) 'Why do progressive foundations give too little to too many?', *The Nation*, 12(19), www.tni.org/detailpage.phtml?page=archiveshumannation (accessed 21 August 2007).

Sievers, B. (1997) 'If pigs had wings', *Foundation News and Commentary* November/December.

Skloot, E. (2001) 'Slot machines, boat building and the future of philanthropy', address to Waldemar Nielsen lectures on philanthropy, Georgia, GA: Georgetown University, Surdna Foundation.

Smith, J. A. (1999) 'The evolving role of American foundations', in C. Clotfelter and T. Ehrlich (eds) *Philanthropy and the Nonprofit Sector in a Changing America*, Bloomington, IN: Indiana University Press.

—— (2002) 'Foundations and public policy making: A historical perspective', www.usc.edu/philanthropy.

Smith, J. and Borgmann, K. (2001) 'Foundations in Europe: The historical context', in A. Schluter, V. Then and P. Walkenhorst (eds) *Foundations in Europe, Society, Management and Law*, London: Directory of Social Change.

Toepler, S. (1999) 'Operating in a grantmaking world: Reassessing the role of operating foundations', in H. K. Anheier and S. Toepler (eds) *Private Funds, Public Purpose: Philanthropic Foundations in International Perspective*, New York, NY: Kluwer Academic/Plenum.

Vincent, J. and Pharoah, C. (2000) *Dimensions 2000, Volume 3: Patterns of Independent Grantmaking in the UK*, West Malling, Kent, UK: Charities Aid Foundation.

www.acf.org.

e-Philanthropy

Leveraging technology to benefit charities and donors

Ted Hart

Professional fundraisers are typically familiar with a wide range of fundraising techniques, while some have developed specialized skills. The growth of e-Philanthropy has required even the most seasoned professionals to learn new skills and to re-evaluate how they approach nearly every aspect of fundraising. This is not to suggest that e-Philanthropy has taken the place of any traditional fundraising methods; actually the opposite. These tools add a new dimension of efficiency and require higher levels of integration for nearly every 'offline' approach to attracting philanthropic support. While some would relegate e-Philanthropy as a specialty area to be administered separately from other fundraising methods, much in the way some offices might have a prospect research specialist on staff, doing so would diminish the overall effectiveness and deny the opportunity to benefit fully from these tools. This chapter will provide an overview of e-Philanthropy techniques which nonprofits can use to cultivate and steward relationships, invite advocacy for their cause and solicit contributions online.

Defining e-Philanthropy

e-Philanthropy is a set of efficiency-building Internet-based techniques that can be employed to build and enhance relationships with stakeholders interested in the success of a nonprofit organization.

e-Philanthropy is the building and enhancing of relationships with volunteers and supporters of nonprofit organizations using the Internet. It includes the contribution of cash or real property or the purchase of products and services to benefit a nonprofit organization, and the storage and usage of electronic data and services to support relationship-building and fundraising activities.

e-Philanthropy is born: September 11

Is there a date we can refer to that marked the beginning of direct mail or planned giving? If there is, I do not have it circled on my calendar. After more than two years of strong growth in both its effectiveness and its infrastructure, e-Philanthropy came of age on 11 September 2001.

In the days and weeks following the terrorist attacks on the USA, the world turned to the Internet as a vehicle for its charitable response to the tragic events. The level of online philanthropic activity in the weeks following these events was so amazing that the experience has become a defining moment in US philanthropy.

In the two months following the disaster, more than 1.3 million contributors donated over $128 million online. Contributors were aided by several for-profit websites which quickly linked their online credit-card-processing systems to create an opportunity for millions of their visitors to make a contribution. The prior relationship that online customers already had with the for-profit websites provided both the comfort level and mechanism donors needed to create an unprecedented outpouring of online giving. The online movement was massive; the American Red Cross reported that for the first time in its history online, donations had outnumbered those given via their 800 number, by a 3:1 margin. As a Red Cross spokesperson, Devora Goldberg commented in a *New York Times* article, 'clearly, the power of the Internet is huge' (Christensen 2001).

Since 2001 scores of new for-profit companies have been created offering a wide array of services specifically geared towards the charitable sector, while fundraising online in the USA has soared past $4.5 billion annually (2005) and more than $9.0 billion globally (2005), as estimated by the ePhilanthropy Foundation (http://ephilanthropy.org).

Engaging the donor

The true powers of e-Philanthropy-based methods lie in their ability to do more than function simply as a novel way to raise money. They lie in the areas of communication and relationship building. In fact, these are the real drivers of fundraising success both offline and online. The Internet is an ideal platform from which to reach, inform and engage potential donors, many of which may be beyond the reach of normal fundraising channels. Communication and relationship building are key components to the successful use of these techniques.

Social-networking techniques online have become one of the strongest and most important differences between what is traditionally practical offline and what is now possible for charities to access online.

Giving donors the chance to participate and to contribute to the success of a charity beyond the gift online is proving to be successful for nonprofits. While proving a serious area of growth, *the use of these new techniques challenges* the traditional top-down, ask–give relationship charities have traditionally had with their supporters.

Along with these changes in the way that a charity interacts with a donor come more demands from donors for transparency and disclosure. e-Philanthropy is a transformative force that is propelling charities around the world towards a new way of doing business characterized by donor participation, openness and social networking.

Charities should approach the Internet as a communication and stewardship tool first and as a fundraising tool second. Any seasoned fundraiser will tell you that when you can build and enhance a relationship with a prospective donor, you have a much higher chance of successfully soliciting a gift.

e-Philanthropists must be asked

Apart from tragedies around the world which from time to time capture the attention of the global community, and inspire donors to give of their own volition in response to great suffering, nonprofit organizations must still ask for support if they expect to receive it. Over the past several years, many millions, who previously had never considered making a gift online, have done so. Wise charities are reaching out to these experienced e-Philanthropists offering them experiences and opportunities to connect with causes they care about. However, if support is to be earned *they must still be asked*!

Local, national and global charities which do not offer their supporters the opportunity to communicate and contribute online fail to do so at their peril. Every nonprofit now has unprecedented ability to reach out to more donors and prospects than they could ever afford to using traditional methods of direct mail, telephone or personal visits, but they must cultivate an online relationship before asking for support.

While a focus on building online capacity is a central message of this material, it must be noted that no online effort will meet its potential without integration with its more traditional offline counterparts. Successful e-Philanthropy strategy does not exist in isolation.

Back to the future

This is not the first time that nonprofit organizations and fundraisers have adapted to new technologies. The radio, television, newspapers, telephone, fax machine, computers, electronic databases and direct mail have all affected the ways we raise money. Some of the new methods that have evolved are more successful than others, and not all of them have been used with equal success by all nonprofits. This is the case for e-Philanthropy as well.

Each new advance in technology has created a particular set of challenges for nonprofits and their donors; each has triggered a corresponding set of fundraising norms. For nonprofit organizations, the Internet provides an unprecedented and cost-effective opportunity to build and enhance relationships with supporters, volunteers, clients and the communities they serve. Connecting with supporters online provides a new means for converting interest in a mission to direct involvement and support.

In March 2001, Harvard's Professor James Austin wrote,

> make no mistake; the ePhilanthropy revolution is here to stay, and it will transform charitable giving in as profound a way as technology is changing the commercial world. Charities that have dismissed ePhilanthropy as a fad, or run from it in confusion, will sooner or later, need to become reconciled to it. If they don't, they risk losing touch with donors and imperiling the vitality of their work
>
> (Cited in Clohesy and Reis 2001: 30)

In order to harness the power of e-Philanthropy, nonprofit organizations must remember three things:

1 e-Philanthropy should be seen as a set of relationship-building tools first and fundraising tools second;
2 nonprofit websites and use the of email for promotional purposes will succeed when integrated into every other form of communication used by the nonprofit

(i.e. direct mail, brochures, planned giving, newsletters, telephone, radio, print media, etc.); and

3 the ability to inspire current and known supporters to reach out to their own networks of family, friends and colleagues, often unknown to the charity, is the single most powerful and often untapped resource that a charity has.

Taming the World Wide Web

As new forms of media have been introduced into our culture, appropriate regulation has followed. As Mike Johnston points out, 'lawmakers are only now coming to grips with the legal ramifications of Internet tools such as email and the Web' (Johnston 2002: 47).

The Internet challenges existing charitable regulation. As a set of tools, e-Philanthropy crosses the boundaries of traditional jurisdictions by offering even the smallest of organizations the ability to communicate and solicit support on a global scale. In the absence of specific regulation related to the Internet, many regulators are attempting to apply current laws to online activities. Scores of states and local municipalities are attempting to require registration of every charity that has online donation opportunities accessible via the web by citizens of those jurisdictions.

If all charities were required to register in all states, provinces, counties and municipalities, the cost in both money and time to maintain such registration would extinguish the use of the Internet for philanthropic purposes. The National Association of State Charity Officers (www.NASCOnet.org) has issued a document known as the Charleston principles, which call for a fair and equitable approach to online charity registration. While not law, it is a set of guidelines which all states are urged to consider enacting. In addition to this important effort, the ePhilanthropy Code of Ethics was established by the ePhilanthropyFoundation.Org, which Clohesy and Reis (2001: 19) referred to as 'the first of, hopefully, more organizations tackling the challenge of monitoring and setting e-philanthropy practice standards'. Nonprofits that follow these principles can be confident that their online efforts are consistent with sound ethical practices – and, more importantly, they will send a signal to donors that the nonprofit is knowledgeable of and committed to the ethical use of the Internet in its cultivation and solicitation of support.

New opportunities

The Internet gives donors easy access to numerous philanthropic choices. More and more people have turned to the web to fulfil their charitable intentions. As e-Philanthropy has emerged, organizations have discovered that consistent and deliberate email communication driving traffic to the organization's well-organized and informative website has become the key to success, but then inspiring these supporters to do more than just give but to encourage others to give as well is the ultimate prize of e-Philanthropy strategy.

Privacy and security

Years of experience in the offline world have taught fundraisers that attention to detail, privacy, security of information, honesty in reporting, while building a case for support are key components to any successful solicitation of support, whether that support comes in the form of volunteerism, advocacy or contributions. Through the appropriate use of permission-based email, a nonprofit can provide its donors with increased access to information and more timely details regarding the stewardship and solicitation of their charitable support. This increased access and detailed information help to strengthen the relationship and trust between the nonprofit and supporters. To earn this trust, nonprofit organizations must become accustomed to increased levels of scrutiny and demands for evidence that the charity is well managed and provides service consistent with its mission.

Building a website is not enough

Success on the Internet requires an integrated strategy that embraces standards for protecting and preserving donor relationships. For-profit vendors have developed a wide array of services to help 'power' nonprofits' websites. Many of these services are catalogued on the Global Nonprofit Resource Center at http://ephilanthropy.org/gnrc.

As charities look at various services, they should start by understanding the strategic objectives for their website. It is not necessary to have all the 'bells and whistles' before engaging prospects and donors online. It is advisable to start small and build slowly. Begin with collecting email addresses, communicating via email and offering the opportunity to give online via an encrypted web page.

Taking the time to plan ahead can often mean the difference between the use of the Internet and development of a successful e-Philanthropy strategy. The exact mix of strategies and techniques is as varied as the number and types of nonprofits that deploy them.

e-Philanthropy techniques fall into six categories:

1 communication/education and stewardship
2 online donations and membership
3 event registrations and management
4 prospect research
5 volunteer recruitment and management
6 relationship building and advocacy.

Organizations should always evaluate options and test assumptions. Incremental improvements and additions of services will help supporters and staff to become accustomed to using the new technology and communicating via the Internet. Only by testing can the organization learn which techniques perform the best.

Communication/education and stewardship

The first step towards building online donations, volunteer base and to better communicate the organization's mission with a larger audience using the power of the Internet is to identify who you want to reach, what you want them to do and what will inspire them to accept the organization's invitation to take action, volunteer or give.

Use of the Internet as a standalone solution is not effective. While some have predicted that e-Philanthropy will replace many traditional approaches to soliciting support, this will not be the case. Just as television failed to kill radio, yet changed it significantly, so too the Internet changes traditional forms of fundraising, not by eliminating them but by changing their utility and increasing their effectiveness.

While there are no short cuts to long-term success offline, there are similarly no short cuts online. e-Philanthropy methods permit an organization to communicate and engage supporters not only through a website, but directly through email, which can direct attention back to the organization.

As part of an integrated communication and fundraising strategy, e-Philanthropy offers effective and efficient opportunities for nonprofits to communicate with a much wider audience than they might otherwise have the resources to do. Direct mail, telephone, radio, television, personal visits and other traditional means of communication with supporters all have significant personnel, printing, postage or other costs associated with them.

The organization's website should reflect the mission of the organization; outdated content on a website indicates there is nothing new to share. The website must be a true resource for information relating to the charity's mission, and provide ample opportunities to support and communicate with the charity.

Supporters who begin or maintain an online relationship with an organization have expectations of communication different to their 'offline' counterparts. In most cases, those who communicate via the Internet will expect to receive an automatic electronic response; or, where such a response is inappropriate, they expect a response in less than 36 hours.

Integration

Promotion of online resources and services through integration with traditional marketing and communication channels enables organizations to increase significantly the effectiveness of overall operations, while providing additional options to supporters:

- Direct mail/telemarketing: every direct mail and telephone appeal should provide the opportunity for supporters to give by mailing in the response form or by making a gift or pledge online. In the case of telemarketing, those who might be at their computer when the call is placed could be directed to an online audio or video message that can enhance the telemarketer's message, thereby prompting them to give online.
- Print material and literature: every publication and printed item should include the organization's web address. Any place where the address and/or phone number for the nonprofit is printed should include the web address. Large and expensive to produce publications, like an annual report, can be posted on a website as a pdf (www.Adobe.com). Directing donors and supporters to download and print the file not only saves money but also expands the number of people who can access the report.
- Brand building: promotional opportunities: public service announcements (PSAs) and paid advertising and marketing efforts on television, radio and in print are often ways which organizations share their message to a wider audience. By directing those hearing or viewing these messages to a website, the nonprofit is able to make a more comprehensive appeal for support of its mission.
- Press: press conferences, television and radio appearances, and public-speaking engagements are prime opportunities to promote online resources. Nonprofits should establish an 'online' press room, providing in a downloadable format background information, press releases, photos and other material of interest to the media. This will give the press an opportunity to learn about the organization at any time, day or night.

Getting the word out

The online environment offers several opportunities to communicate with potential supporters. Essential aspects to getting the word out online are:

- Email: this is the most powerful and cost-effective online communication tool available to nonprofit organizations. In accord with the e-Philanthropy code of ethics, it is important that supporters 'opt in' to nonprofit email lists. This means that they give permission to receive email from the nonprofit; permission should never be assumed. Even after permission is granted, the supporter must also be given the option to have his/her name removed from the email list at any time, known as 'opt out'.

- Search engines: each has its own criteria for cataloguing the resources of the Internet, yet no single search engine provides reference to more than 20 per cent of the Internet. Therefore it is important to register the organization's website with several of the leading search engines (i.e. Google, Lycos, Alta Vista, Yahoo!, etc.).

- Search engine/keyword advertising: increasingly, search engines are paid to attach relevant advertising to search engine results. Nonprofits can increase their visibility and reach new markets for their services and charitable efforts by purchasing these services. In some cases grant support is available, such as Google Adwords Grants for charities. Find out more information by searching at Google.com.

- 'Pass-along' marketing: while it is highly unlikely that anyone receiving a direct mail appeal from a charity will make several copies, address envelopes to their friends and family, and mail copies of the letter urging that they also support the organization; it is very likely this activity will take place online. Also known as viral marketing, it is a method of asking the recipient of an email to send the message along to other people they know of who might be interested. Within a few seconds, the message can be sent along to scores of people on their personal email list. Very important to the success of this method is the fact that the message is now being sent by a friend or family member, thereby increasing the chances of it being read.

- Send to a friend: those who visit a nonprofit organization's website are often looking for expert information relating to the mission of that organization. By offering the option to 'send-to-a-friend' an article or link to a web page on the site, the utility of the website's content is further enhanced. Once again, the power of this feature is that the recommendation is coming from a trusted friend or family member.

Online donations and membership

Most visitors to a website go there because they know or care something about an organization or its mission, and they are seeking information. Effective sites offer multiple opportunities for visitors to support the organization through advocacy, volunteerism or donations often on each page of the website.

William Park, the chief executive of marketing firm Digital Impact, talking about e-mail marketing in an interview with the the *New York Times*, noted: 'it's the most measurable marketing vehicle of all time'. Response rates are more quickly and accurately measured than in other media. This combination of price and response makes email, particularly email newsletters, very attractive to nonprofits (Stellin 2000).

E-campaigns

Several vendors have developed services that make it easy for organizations to use email and the Internet for soliciting donations, outreach, education and advocacy strategies. The integration of the organization's website (content and encrypted online donor forms) and e-mail (pushing the message to supporters) along with direct mail/telephone and other campaigns, not only provide additional options for donors, but give them the opportunity to become more informed and engaged donors.

Planned giving online

Planned giving is often complicated to both donors and nonprofits. For donors, education is the first step towards matching their charitable intentions with their estate plans. Nonprofit organizations are faced with the challenge of identifying those who may support their missions with planned gifts – and provide them with the details that they need for choosing the correctly planned giving vehicle. For both large and small nonprofits, and for donors and prospects, the Internet is increasingly becoming both a strong marketing tool for planned giving and a great resource for information. The Internet can be an effective vehicle to promote and enhance planned giving efforts, allowing nonprofits to provide detailed information regarding tax-wise giving to more of their donors and prospects. These online resources provide information related to various planned giving vehicles:

- It is relatively easy for most nonprofits to put planned giving information on their websites; keeping the site updated and legally accurate is more difficult. Several services provide Internet-ready tools which are regularly updated and kept compliant with changing tax laws. These tools represent a cost-effective way to provide compelling and effective planned giving content.
- Many donors are turning to the Internet to investigate for themselves how a planned gift would work, instead of calling an adviser or asking a charity for a planned giving illustration.
- To meet the needs of these donors, charities can include online tools and a gift-planning calculator on their websites. This information makes available to donors information and resources which had once been the exclusive purview of accountants, lawyers and planned giving professionals. Providing these tools gives another reason for donors to visit the website.

Marketing using planned giving

Once planned giving information is available on the charity's website, it is time to invite donors and prospects to visit. Most board members and staff members hesitate to discuss planned giving with donors and prospects for fear that they will be asked questions that they cannot answer. The website provides a valuable tool in reaching out to these donors by providing self-explanatory planned giving pages. Local lawyers, financial planners and other advisers should be contacted and made aware of the content and services available. These advisers are often asked by their clients if they know of reputable organizations which they might support via the will or planned giving vehicle. Advisers not wanting to appear to have a conflict of interest will often offer several options. They are much more likely to advise in favour of organizations which they feel are prepared, and whose concepts and topics they understand.

Event registration and management

e-Philanthropy special-event management makes event registration easier for nonprofits and event attendees. Online services are available to send event invitations, organize volunteer activities, maintain income and expense records and provide high-quality registration and donor relations' services. Golf tournaments, walks, silent and live auctions each have specialized registration and item organization needs. Several online services have been developed to address one or more of these specific requirements.

Event evaluation

Surveying the participants from the prior year's event can enhance special-event planning. An online survey form can easily be distributed via e-mail and website to participants to obtain feedback.

Prospect research

While an incredible amount of information about fundraising prospects is available online, it is important to pay close attention to the management and use of information gathered. Whether you subscribe to the Association of Professional Researchers for Advancement (APRA) (www.aprahome.org) code of ethics, or develop your own privacy policy, it is important to protect sensitive and confidential information.

Some Internet resources regarding online privacy issues include:

- ePhilanthropy Foundation: www.ephilanthropy.org/ethics
- Online Privacy Alliance: www.privacyalliance.org
- Electronic Frontier Foundation: www.eff.org/privacy
- Electronic Privacy Information Center: www.epic.org

Manual prospect research

While it is estimated that the Internet comprises more than one-half trillion web pages (growing daily), the challenge is to wade through all of the information identified and determine what is most likely to support fundraising. Indexed websites offer an easier approach to finding helpful databases. These sites have been developed to aid access to information databases and websites.

Internet Prospector (www.internet-prospector.org) (see Figure 11.1) is a roadmap to resources that have direct bearing on gathering information on prospects. Staffed by a national network of volunteers, this nonprofit site provides a unique service that 'mines' the Internet to report on resources of use to prospect researchers.

Several university development programmes have developed websites, which catalogue useful websites, and resources for use by their own fundraising staffs, and many of these sites are open to the Internet public. Some of the better sites are: NETSource@USC, (www.usc.edu/dept/source), maintained by the University of Southern California Development Research Department, Michigan State University (www.lib.msu.edu/harris23/grants/prospect.htm), and Northwestern University Development Research, (www.development.northwestern.edu/research/bookmark.html), maintained by Northwestern University Development Office.

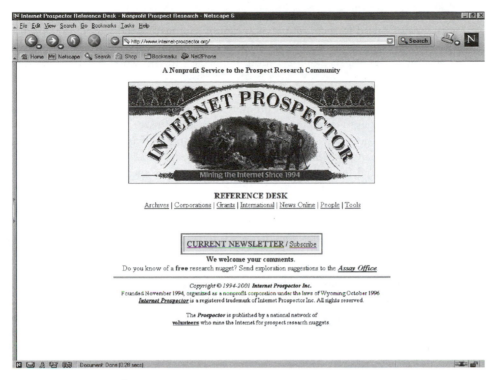

Figure 11.1 Home page for Internet Prospector

Electronic screening

The Internet makes it possible for charities of all sizes to obtain helpful information regarding the capacity of their key prospects to make a major gift. There are several free and paid access databases available to nonprofits seeking to identify prospects with wealth. Several companies have developed services that make it possible to match a charity's prospect database to specific information about known persons with private wealth, philanthropists, inside stock traders, private company owners, high net-worth professionals, as well as corporate and foundation executives and trustees.

Volunteer recruitment and management

Volunteers are important to any successful nonprofit programme or fundraising endeavour. The Internet provides tools which can enhance relationships and improve communication. Recruiting volunteers online is an excellent way to reach non-traditional volunteers, including populations which might be underrepresented in an organization's volunteer ranks (seniors, ethnic minorities, people with disabilities, etc.).

There are several online resources available which can help with technical assistance, resource sharing, training and consultation. Organizations interested in posting volunteer opportunities online have several options to obtain help in locating volunteers, tracking them and managing their activities. One of the largest is ServeNet (www.servenet.org).

Virtual volunteer management

The Internet can be used to increase communication, coordination education and collaboration with and among volunteers. The Internet can help volunteers, particularly those who work away from direct supervision, feel more connected to the work and mission of the organization. For example:

1　Email is an easy and free way to communicate with volunteers quickly and provide them opportunities to communicate easily with nonprofit staff.
2　An online 'ask a peer' discussion group for your volunteers is an ideal tool to help them to collaborate, share what they have learned and increase teamwork.
3　Regular email updates on important organizational news and volunteer activities can help in volunteer retention.
4　Volunteer manuals, guidelines, statistics and other information which volunteers may find helpful to their service can all be posted online, making them available any time.
5　Online calendars can help volunteers to remember important assignments and deadlines.

According to the Virtual Volunteering Project (www.serviceleader.org/vv), 'virtual volunteering means volunteer tasks completed, in whole or in part, via the Internet'. This combines technology with offline volunteer recruitment and management efforts. Organizations can expand their reach by attracting volunteers from new areas and increasing their level of participation.

Online donations

The technical details of establishing and owning a secure e-commerce server are easy enough; however, with so many vendors and several free services available for processing online gifts in accord with ethical and security standards, it is inadvisable that most nonprofits undertake the creation of a 'home-grown' online donation solution.

Privacy concerns

When an organization asks donors or members for demographic and personal contact information, it is implicitly asking them to trust that it will not misuse the information they provide. Organizations must address privacy concerns. Information will not be given and donations will not be made online if the donors or members do not trust that their information will be used responsibly.

To increase the likelihood that the trust that supporters have for the charity will be transferred to the online environment, charities should:

1　Publish their privacy policy on the website and at other places where such data is requested or required.
2　Review and strengthen internal security and use of confidential data.
3　Ensure that supporters can control the information collected about them, including removing their name from lists for future online communication and/or solicitation.
4　Respond promptly to complaints and all forms of electronic communication.
5　Consider seeking certification from one of the well-known privacy trustmarks, such as Truste or BBB Online.

Shopping and bidding

Shopping sites, auction sites, and others can give supporters an opportunity to show their support by encouraging them to shop or bid to benefit the charity of their choice. Few of these options raised significant revenue for charities. The appropriate allocation of staff time would place an emphasis on improving the website, developing an effective email communication programme and integrating these efforts into traditional forms of fundraising. Even though such services have failed to generate quick and easy money for nonprofits, it is appropriate to use these services as additional options on a charity's website only when the items being sold or the auction event is somehow tied to the mission of the organization.

Learn and share online

The Internet provides many opportunities to reach out to colleagues and professionals who share an interest in almost any topic relative to e-Philanthropy. There are several services that allow others to learn from colleagues and share experiences.

PRSPCT-L features discussion of prospect research issues, developments, sources and techniques. To subscribe, go to http://charitychannel.com/collaborate/wa.exe?SUBED1=-PRSPCT-L&A=1. In addition, Charity Channel (www.charitychannel.com), hosts over fifty discussion groups on a wide range of topics including annual giving, planned giving and e-Philanthropy.

Relationship building and advocacy

For some organizations the promotion of their mission through emailing an elected official, signing an electronic petition, receiving electronic 'action alerts' or forwarding email messages to friends, co-workers and family serves an important role in building and enhancing online relationships.

An online advocacy campaign can serve as a successful way to rally support and an excellent way to build an email database. Making effective use of an organization's website and email database requires careful planning. The messages in the 'action alerts' should match those of print media and the website. It is important to identify specific goals for online advocacy.

Follow-up to these prospects or donors through traditional direct mail or other methods should refer to the initial email contact. An example might be: 'Last month you joined with 75,000 other dedicated Americans who are joining the fight for tougher drunk driving laws. Today, we are writing to ask for your help.'

Since their initial contact was on the occasion of an advocacy campaign, it is important to provide appropriate follow-up. Charities might consider proposing additional advocacy activities, an invitation to volunteer or a suggestion to make a charitable gift to support ongoing efforts relating to the initial advocacy request. The purpose is to turn potential donors acquired during an online activism campaign into donors.

Conclusion

e-Philanthropy techniques have brought to the nonprofit world an unprecedented opportunity to leverage technology for the benefit of the charity and convenience of the donor. In every organization, time and resources are spent on recruiting and retaining charitable support. This support is based on relationships built and missions fulfilled. Hundreds of options exist to develop solutions for each of the six categories of e-Philanthropy outlined in this chapter. Use of the Internet enhances these efforts by providing efficient and effective communication tools tied to robust, secure online services. These services empower donors to utilize information and support charitable causes anytime and anywhere.

References

Austin, J. E. (2001) 'The e-philanthropy revolution is here to stay', *Chronicle of Philanthropy*, 8 March, 16.

Christensen, J. (2001) 'Tools for the aftermath: Relief agencies retool to handle online flood', *New York Times*, 26 September, H1.

Clohesy, S. J. and Reis, T. K. (2001) *e-Philanthropy v2.001: From Entrepreneurial Adventure to an Online Community*, 1 April, http://www.wkkf.org/DesktopModules/WKF.00_DmaSupport/ViewDoc. aspx?LanguageID=0&CID=2&ListID=28&ItemID=20661&fld=PDFFile.

http://ephilanthropy.org.

Johnston, M. (2002) 'Regulating online fundraising', in *Fundraising on the Internet: The ePhilanthropy Foundation.Org's Guide to Success Online*, (eds) Mal Warwick, Ted Hart and Nick Allen, pp. 47–53, San Francisco, CA: Jossey-Bass.

Stellin, S. (2000) 'E-commerce report: Advertisers are turning to specialists to handle their e-mail marketing campaigns', *New York Times*, 21 August, C6.

www.serviceleader.org/vv.

12

Social entrepreneurship

Advancing research and maintaining relevance

Gillian Mort and Jay Weerawardena

Sophia Khatoon, a 22-year-old highly skilled furniture-maker in the tiny village of Jobra in Bangladesh, worked seven long days a week, looked twice her age and lived in abject poverty. She made stools and chairs out of bamboo, which she had to sell to a moneylender who provided the credit to buy the raw material. The price she received barely covered the costs. Dr Yunus – Professor of Economics at the University in the Southern port city of Chittagong who later founded the Grameen Bank – calculated that effectively Sophia was paying interest at the rate of 10 per cent a day, more than 3,000 per cent a year. Yunus could not reconcile the fact that a woman with such excellent skills, who worked so hard, produced such beautiful bamboo furniture and created wealth at such a high rate was earning so little.

In fact, the poor all over the world are trapped in such exploitation. While they work extremely hard and create enormous wealth, the middle-men, moneylenders and employers keep the fruits of their labour. The poor have no access to 'institutional credit', which you and I have, because they cannot provide a collateral. The system keeps them firmly trapped in debt, poverty and exploitation.

With a loan of 50 taka (a few dollars), it took Sophia only a few months to establish her own little self-employment, increase her income sevenfold and repay the loan (Grameen Bank – Banking on the Poor 2006).

Introduction

The concept of social entrepreneurship can be succinctly captured as a paradigm where business principles and methods are applied not for individual gain and profit, but for group or social gain and for social change. Philosophically, the late twentieth and early twenty-first centuries may be identified as an era of the primacy of capitalism as a model for economic development and management, following the decline of prominent superstates organized around the communist system through dissolution or marketization and a growing globaliza-tion of markets and free trade. Perhaps it was thus simply a natural evolution for the 'ideaware' of the successful capitalist model, business principles and methods, to begin to be applied to what is often termed areas where there is market failure (Dart 2004). Thus there has developed a growing interest and application of social entrepreneurship as an alternative model for social change, for social and economic development, particularly as an approach that avoids welfare dependency (Pearson 2002). One of the most well-known social entrepreneurship models is that of M. Yunus and the Grameen Bank concept profiled above, where access to banks, bank loans and finance through the provision of micro-credit provided an innovative solution allowing the poorest of the poor to break out of poverty through their own initiative and resourcefulness. This model has been widely influential and adopted throughout the world, clearly exemplifying the power of social entrepreneurship to have great effect for positive social value creation.

A current definition of social entrepreneurship, focusing on the social enterprise, generally enterprises founded with the motive of social value creation but including profit-generating initiatives, identifies social entrepreneurship as:

> any attempt at new social enterprise activity or new enterprise creation, such as self-employment, a new enterprise, or the expansion of an existing social enterprise by an individual, teams of individuals or established social enterprise, with social or community goals as its base and where the profit is invested in the activity or venture itself rather than returned to investors.
>
> (Harding 2006, emphasis added)

An alternative definition with the more customary emphasis on the themes of entrepreneurship and social change is also widely available:

> Social entrepreneurship is the work of a social entrepreneur. A social entrepreneur is someone who recognizes a social problem and uses entrepreneurial principles to organize, create, and manage a venture to make social change. Whereas business entrepreneurs typically measure performance in profit and return, social entrepreneurs assess their success in terms of the impact they have on society and often work through nonprofits and citizen groups.
>
> (Wikipedia 2006)

Social entrepreneurship can be distinguished from other forms of social action, advocacy, philanthropy and non-profit organizations more generally. Several researchers, prominently among them Dees (1998a) and also Sullivan et al. (2003), argue that social mission is explicit and central for social entrepreneurial organizations. Dees (1998b) also argues that similar to a for-profit firm, the purpose of which is to create superior value for its customer, the primary purpose of social entrepreneurship is to create superior social value. He argues that a social entrepreneur's ability to attract resources (capital, labour, equipment, etc.) in a competitive marketplace is a good indication that venture represents a more productive use of these resources than the alternative it is competing against. On the funding side, social entrepreneurs look for innovative ways to assure that their ventures will have access to resources, including creating profitable social ventures, accessing grants and providing public goods as an agent of governments, as long as they are creating social value.

Paralleling the centrality of the social mission, there is a corresponding emphasis on innovation as a defining characteristic of social entrepreneurship (Nicholls 2006). Dees (1998b) speaks of the role of engaging in a process of continuous innovation. Prabhu (1998), and Sullivan Mort et al. (2003) identify the three factors of innovativeness, proactiveness and risk-taking (from Covin and Slevin 1989) as central to social entrepreneurship. Similarly, Borins

(2000) identifies innovation as crucial for social entrepreneurs in the public domain. Recently in a seminal contribution to clarifying the conceptualization of social entrepreneurship, Weerawardena and Sullivan Mort (2006) conducted empirical research identifying social entrepreneurship as possessing the core attributes of entrepreneurship – proactiveness, innovativeness and risk-taking – within a constrained optimization framework bounded by the environment, the social mission and the need for organizational sustainability. This conceptualization resolves the controversy of whether social entrepreneurial nonprofits should simply be run as businesses; with business models transparently adopted from the for-profit sector implemented by a cadre of experienced business professionals. Based on empirical case studies, Weerawardena and Sullivan Mort (2006) found that successful entrepreneurial nonprofits thrive by offering superior value to their clients and can sustain their competitive advantage in increasingly competitive markets while retaining their focus on achieving their social mission. The study finds that social entrepreneurship is a bounded multidimensional construct which is deeply rooted in an organization's social mission, its drive for sustainability and highly influenced and shaped by the environmental dynamics.

Social entrepreneurship: the history of an idea

The terms social entrepreneur and social entrepreneurship were first used in the literature on social change in the 1970s in relation to values orientations (Banks 1972). The terms came into widespread use in the 1990s, with attention from leading business academics and practitioners (Rosabeth Moss Kanter and Bill Drayton, the founder in 1981 of Ashoka, the organization devoted to fostering social entrepreneurship (www.ashoka.org/)). Michael Young, a prominent thought leader in the field, founded the Institute of Community Studies in 1953 and established a number of significant organizations and initiatives including the School for Social Entrepreneurs (UK) in 1997. Dees et al. (2001, 2002) have provided significant leadership in conceptualizing the field with Bornstein (2004) profiling many compelling examples of social entrepreneurship in practice.

The year 2006 provided a number of important milestones in social entrepreneurship. In the research domain three important publications have appeared. A special issue on social entrepreneurship appeared in the influential business journal *Journal of World Business*, marking attention to the field by a prominent business journal. Second, the publication by Oxford University Press of an edited volume by Nicholls (2006) on social entrepreneurship, including chapters from leading practitioners and academics in the field highlighted social entrepreneurship as providing new models of sustainable social change. Third, Palgrave Macmillan (2006) published a book edited by Mair et al. specifically addressing social entrepreneurship theory and research. These publications indicate the legitimization of social entrepreneurship as a field of academic enquiry. Significantly, 2006 also saw the award of the Nobel Peace Prize to Muhammad Yunus and the Grameen Bank for the social entrepreneurial practice of providing micro-credit to people previously denied access to funds through traditional banking systems, thereby providing an innovative model for impacting positively on the lives of people living in extreme poverty. The Nobel Peace Prize is likely to increase significantly the acceptance of the idea of social entrepreneurship by individuals, organizations, governments and business. Indeed social entrepreneurship has already been identified by some as a twenty-first-century revolution (Skoll 2004).

Advancing research in social entrepreneurship: literature review and research agenda

Emergence of a research field

Social entrepreneurship as a focus of academic enquiry has a relatively brief history, although it has grown markedly in the last few years. We observe that the emergence of any new field of research will be characterized by several stages: identification and observation of a loosely identified phenomenon, closely followed by expository and exploratory case studies aimed at providing 'slice of life' insight into the phenomenon and its context. The contributors at this stage will come from various backgrounds, including advanced practitioners and consultants. Next, more in-depth case studies emerge using comparative theoretical frameworks relying on existing well-tested or established theories in an attempt to better understand antecedents and performance outcomes of the phenomenon. This will be immediately followed by definitions seeking to capture operational characteristics and the contextual domain. Next a conceptualization of the phenomenon results in the identification of dimension constituting the construct – allowing for a deeper, more nuanced understanding of the available definitions and paving the way for subsequent stages of measurement development and the testing of theoretical relationships. The optimum final stage is a consistent body of knowledge and a limited domain theory. We identify that the domain of social entrepreneurship has rapidly passed through the stages of identification of the phenomenon and exploratory case study and has advanced towards concluding the stage of expository definition and conceptualization. This section proceeds as follows. First, an attempt has been made to collate the growing literature in the field of social entrepreneurship (Table 12.1). The literature was reviewed to identify preoccupations and themes which are then matched with the manifestation of the development of a field of research outlined above. Finally, emerging research directions are identified and an agenda for research is developed.

Civic, for-profit or government: what is the domain of social entrepreneurship?

An 'unprecedented wave of growth in social entrepreneurship [has been identified] globally over the last ten years' (Nicholls 2006: 3). An early theme of research continuing to the present is the concern about the appropriate domain of social entrepreneurship. Reinventing government initiatives leading to smaller government and a user-pay orientation to provision of services, growth in need for public goods and greater competitive stance by businesses competing aggressively in globalized markets has led to changing relationships among the market, the state and civil society. It is in this context that social entrepreneurship has emerged in clearer focus. Some researchers (Cook et al. 2001; Wallace 1999) suggest that social enterprises which carry out for-profit activity to support other nonprofit activities can be viewed as social entrepreneurs. Others have argued that for-profits that may take some innovative action towards building social capital can be considered as being socially entrepreneurial (Thompson et al. 2000; CCSE 2001). Providing some clarity Thompson (2002) identifies social entrepreneurship as possibly occurring in profit-seeking businesses which have some commitment to doing good, in social enterprises set up for a social purpose but operating as businesses and in the voluntary or nonprofit sector. However, he concludes that the 'main world of the social entrepreneur is the voluntary [NFP] sector', in the domain of civil society (Thompson 2002: 413). Not every NFP is a social entrepreneurial organization. Social entrepreneurship reflects initiatives in NFPs undertaken to 'increase organizational effectiveness and foster long term

Table 12.1 Summary of social entrepreneurship literature

Author(s)	Focus or objective(s) of the paper/book	Domain	Empirical research (cases or survey)	Definition of social entrepreneurship	Comments (if any)
Banks (1972)	Social movements	Civic/not for profit (NFP)	Not applicable (n/a)	First mention – related to values	
Waddock and Post (1991)	To define who SEs are and what they do	Public Sector	Two case studies	Creating or elaborating a public organization to alter greatly the existing pattern of allocation of scarce public resources	
Campbell (1997)	Prescription for developing new social purpose business ventures (focus on healthcare industry)	Social enterprises	n/a	Social purpose ventures provide communities with needed products or services and generate profit to support activities that cannot generate revenue	Article summarizes talk given by James Thalhuber at a conference
Leadbetter (1997)	Investigate the use of SE to provide services that the UK welfare state cannot or will not	Nonprofit/social action	Five case studies	Identification of underutilized resources which are put to use to satisfy unmet social needs	Sees SE occurring in the public, private and voluntary sectors
Cornwall (1998)	Describing the social impact of entrepreneurs in low-income communities	NFP	n/a	Entrepreneurs have social responsibility to improve their communities	
Dees (1998)	Definition of social entrepreneurship	Public and NFP	n/a	Social entrepreneurs play the role of change agents in the social sector	Definitions based on the work of Schumpeter, Say, Drucker and Stevenson
Prabhu (1998)	Investigation of concept of social entrepreneurial leadership	NFP/social action	n/a	Entrepreneurial organizations whose primary mission is social change and the development of their client group	

Continued

Table 12.1—continued

Author(s)	Focus or objective(s) of the paper/book	Domain	Empirical research (cases or survey)	Definition of social entrepreneurship	Comments (if any)
Ryan (1999)	Looks at impact of the entry of large for-profit corporations on the operations of nonprofit organizations	NFP	n/a	Not really defined	Primarily looks at the need for NFPs to adopt a more business like approach
Wallace (1999)	Examines role of social purpose enterprise in facilitating community development	NFP	n/a	Entrepreneurs have social responsibility to improve their communities – derives from social and political cohesion in a community	Similar in approach to Cornwall paper, but more comprehensive
Borins (2000)	Studies two sets of entrepreneurial public leaders to assess characteristics of public entrepreneurship: are they rule–breakers or positive leaders?	Public sector	Survey – given to two sets of innovative public managers – second survey used to validate results of initial survey	Leaders that innovate in public sector organizations	
Thompson et al. (2000)	Review of private sector SE	For profit	6 very brief case studies	The process of adding something new, something different for the purpose of building social capital – focuses on actions taken by private sector actors	
Canadian Centre for Social Entrepreneur-ship (2001)	General review of social entrepreneurship, in particular looking at the impacts of globalization and the rise of dual-bottom-line reporting	NFPs	n/a	Innovative dual–bottom–line initiatives emerging from the private, public and voluntary sectors. 'Dual bottom line' refers to generating both economic and social rates of return	

				Extremely influential
Dees et al. (2001, 2002)	Practical skills books for social entrepreneurs	NFP	n/a	n/a
Hibbert et al. (2001)	Measures the attitudes of consumers to a social entrepreneurial initiative (the *Big Issue* – a UK magazine that supports the homeless)	NFPs	Qualitative – 2 focus groups with 13 people to identify major issues followed by quantitative – survey of 645 purchasers of the magazine	The use of entrepreneurial behaviour for social ends rather than for profit objectives; or an enterprise that generates profits that benefit a specific disadvantaged group
Cook et al. (2001)	Attacks the idea that SE can replace welfare state initiatives as misguided and dangerous	Social enterprises	n/a	Social partnerships between public, social and business sectors designed to harness market power for the public interest
Shaw et al. (2002)	Comprehensive review of social entrepreneurs – looks at characteristics, objectives, actions, and prescriptions for encouraging them	NFP	Interviews with 80 social entrepreneurs	Bringing to social problems the same enterprise and imagination that business entrepreneurs bring to wealth creation
Thompson (2002)	Outline of the scope of SE – looks at who SEs are, what they do and what support is available to them	NFP	2 case studies	The process of adding something new and something different for the purpose of building social capital
Sullivan Mort et al. (2003)	To develop a conceptualization of SE as a multidimensional construct	NFP	None	Searching for and recognizing opportunities that lead to the establishment of new social organizations and continued innovation in existing ones
Alvord et al. (2004)	Identify factors associated with successful social entrepreneurship	NFP	Empirical/cast studies	A catalyst for social transformation

Continued

Table 12.1—continued

Author(s)	Focus or objective(s) of the paper/book	Domain	Empirical research (cases or survey)	Definition of social entrepreneurship	Comments (if any)
Eikenberry and Kluver (2004)	Marketization trends in the nonprofit sector	NFP and public sector	Conceptual and analytical	Nonprofit executives who pay attention to market forces without losing sight of the social mission	
Boschee (2004)	Useful ideas, tips and cautions for starting a social enterprise and making it work	Social enterprise/social venture	Sourcebook – practical	Earned income ventures to financially support an organization's mission	Social ventures
Heilbrunn (2005)	Effect of culture on entrepreneurship in community settings	NFP	Empirical/survey	Not social entrepreneurial by identification	
Hemingway (2005)	Relationship between personal values, moral agency and corporate social entrepreneurship	For-profit	Conceptual	Defined on a matrix of personal values and corporate culture	
Roper and Cheney (2005)	Historical development and current usages of the social entrepreneurship concept	Cross domains	Theoretical/conceptual	Not defined	Suggested parallel to sustainability
Seelos and Mair (2005)	New business models to serve the poor	NFP	Expository	Combines resourcefulness of traditional entrepreneurs with a mission to change society	
Anderson et al. (2006)	Social entrepreneurship in collective culture of indigenous communities	NFP/land rights	Empirical/case studies	Having a dual-nature strategy, including a degree of cohesion of indigenous people, as well as financial success	

Reference	Focus	Sector	Method	Definition	Notes
Harding (2006)	To monitor social entrepreneurship activity in the UK	NFP	Empirical/survey	Any attempt at new social enterprise activity or new enterprise creation, such as self-employment, a new enterprise, or the expansion of an existing social enterprise by an individual, teams or established social enterprise, with social or community goals as its base and where the profit is invested in the activity or venture itself rather than returned to investors	Second survey
Korosec and Berman (2006)	How cities help social entrepreneurship	Public sector/NFP	Empirical/survey	Individuals or private organizations that take the initiative to identify and address important social problems	
Light (2006)	Social entrepreneurship – broaden focus	NFP	Expository	Risk-taking individuals who create social change	
Mair and Marti (2006)	A comprehensive picture of social entrepreneurship	NFP	Conceptual	Synthesis of previous definitions	Need for unified paradigm of entrepreneurship
Mair et al. (2006) (edited book)	Collection conference proceedings on social entrepreneurship research	NFP	Conceptual and empirical (qualitative)	Varied	Proceedings from inaugural research conference; European–North American conference
Mosher-Williams (2006) (edited book)	Research papers	NFP	Empirical and conceptual	Varied	Recent research report from ARNOVA – Association for Research on Nonprofit Organizations and Voluntary Action – Occasional Paper Series; US based

Continued

Table 12.1—continued

Author(s)	Focus or objective(s) of the paper/book	Domain	Empirical research (cases or survey)	Definition of social entrepreneurship	Comments (if any)
Nicholls (2006) (edited book)	Comprehensive approach covering research, praxis and policy on social entrepreneurship	Largely NFP	Conceptual, analytical	Varied	Comprehensive and up-to-date treatment from advanced practitioners, researchers and policy analysts; mainly UK
Peredo and McLean (2006)	Gauge success of social ventures	Social ventures	Conceptual	When some person or group aims . . . to create social value . . . exploiting opportunities; employing innovation; tolerating risk; declining to accept limitations on current resources	Social entrepreneurship not the sole domain of an individual but also of a team of people
Sharir, M. and Lerner, M. (2006)	To develop generalizable inductive theoretical contributions	New social ventures	Empirical	Change agent creating social value – not limited by resources in hand	
Weerawardena and Sullivan Mort (2006)	Conceptualization of entrepreneurship	NFP	Empirical	Constrained optimisation model bounded by social mission, environment and sustainability	Data collected in Australian NFPs

sustainability' (CCSE 2001: 1). However, Roper and Cheney (2005) have studied social entrepreneurship across domains. Recently, Battle Anderson and Dees (2006) have put the case for framing research on social entrepreneurship in a context-neutral way; that is, in research that does not depend on a particular organizational context or form, be it for profit, not for profit or government. They suggest that organizational form is often adopted by social entrepreneurs as a convenience to advance their social impact agenda, not as a subscription to denying or accepting profit as a central ethos. Further questions also arise from the delineation of the changing relationships among the three sectors. Does social entrepreneurship provide not only an innovative model for NFPs but also for corporate philanthropy? Corporates are increasingly being called upon to donate money to good causes. However, perhaps a more salient question lies in addressing the other side of the coin in corporate terms: is social entrepreneurship the equivalent of the corporation volunteering? Is the formation of partnerships and the active transfer of knowledge across the sectors a neglected component of social entrepreneurship? Austin et al. (2006) have recently proposed an extension to the field in corporate social entrepreneurship. Similarly, in an era of renegotiated relationship between the citizen and the state that rather than emphasizing citizen rights tends to emphasize mutual obligation, is social entrepreneurship with its emphasis on risk-taking and innovation a preferred model for the social policy initiatives and funding by government? (e.g. Korosec and Berman 2006). These concerns map to the early issues of identification and observation of a loosely identified phenomenon in the development of a new field of enquiry.

Social entrepreneurship: description of diversity

Case study-based research has contributed strongly to our appreciation of the social entrepreneurship domain. Many case studies are available through organization websites such as www.ashoka.org and www.grameen-info.org. Published social entrepreneurship case studies have not only been useful for practitioners but have also provided insight for researchers in an emerging field. In the public sector/government domain, case studies have focused on leadership of public organizations (e.g. Lewis 1980) and the development of public policy (e.g. King and Roberts 1987). In the public domain, researchers argued that social entrepreneurs possess several leadership characteristics, namely, significant personal credibility and ability to generate followers' commitment to the project by framing it in terms of important social values, rather than purely economic terms (Lewis 1980; Waddock and Post 1991). We identify that case research on social entrepreneurship in the public sector domain has mainly been directed towards conceptualization of the construct in terms of individual qualities of leadership.

Case study research provided description and identified much diversity in the field, including coverage of social enterprises, profitable ventures often established to provide for social needs or a separate income stream for an existing nonprofit. Leadbeater (1997) in a series of in-depth case studies investigated social enterprises in the provision of welfare services and provided a large number of specific policy recommendations designed to increase social enterprises in the UK. Thompson et al. (2000) examined six case studies using the envisioning, enacting and enabling framework to identify the process of adding something new and something different for the purpose of building social capital. Their work focused on actions taken by private sector actors. Thompson (2002) used case studies to understand the scope of social entrepreneurs and looked at who they are, what they do and what support is available to them. Shaw et al. (2002) conducted in-depth interviews with social entrepreneurs in the UK using a type of case study approach identifying psychological characteristics of vision, creativity and personal satisfaction as important for social entrepreneurs. They emphasized the diversity of the social initiatives and the economic and social impact. Hibbert *et al.* (2001) examined the issue of support of consumers for social enterprise initiatives – specifically the *Big Issue*. They used qualitative and quantitative methods and identified very positive attitudes overall by consumers. Bornstein (2004) profiled an exciting group of social entrepreneurs in an influential book entitled *How to Change the World: Social Entrepreneurs and the Power of New Ideas*. The best-practice case study approach profiled social entrepreneurs from around the world as a transformative force for systematic change. Overall, in the NFP sector, case studies have provided rich descriptions of social entrepreneurial initiatives and contexts, with again emphasis on leadership constructs with emerging application of comparative theoretical frameworks from entrepreneurial studies.

Social entrepreneurship: establishing conceptualization

Much of the literature in the last five years has been concerned with the transition between establishing comprehensive definitions of social entrepreneurship and moving towards rigorous conceptualizations of the construct. It is evident that the field of social entrepreneurship is consolidating the conceptualization of the phenomenon (e.g. Mair and Marti 2006; Peredo and McLean 2006; Nicholls and Cho 2006; Weerawardena and Sullivan Mort 2006). This has resulted in substantial convergence in the meaning of the construct around the dimensions of innovation, social impact, opportunity recognition/market orientation and risk management within the broader boundary of social mission and sustainability. The distinction between social entrepreneurship and social ventures or social enterprises – organizations supported primarily by an independent for-profit revenue stream – has also been established (Nicholls 2006; Harding 2006).

The conceptualizations of social entrepreneurship provide remarkably consistent insights to future researchers embarking on the development of psychometric measures enabling the testing of relationships. There is emerging consensus that social entrepreneurship is a multidimensional construct, implying the ability to operationalize the construct using higher-order factor models and supporting quantitative studies in the field. As yet, there has been little attempt to move to a psychometrically valid measurement of the construct, a necessary next step in the research agenda, apart from work by Korosec and Berman (2006) who operationalized a divergent conceptualization of social entrepreneurship.

Social entrepreneurship: an agenda for future research

Beyond the need to develop sound measurement of the social entrepreneurship construct, Mulgan (2006) has suggested a number of research topics which appear to hold promise, as have Weerawardena and Sullivan Mort (2006) and Mair *et al.* (2006). We identify seven high-priority research areas and one where there is need for caution. The review identifies a potential controversy in the social entrepreneurship literature paralleling that of the for-profit entrepreneurship literature, and that is the issue of level of analysis of future research. The research field is divided between an approach which views social entrepreneurs as 'one special breed of leaders' (Dees 1998b) or reflect individual traits (Prabhu, 1998; Shaw *et al.*, 2002) and one that focuses on capturing the behavioural characteristics of entrepreneurship, in particular how social entrepreneurs achieve their organizational objectives by enacting the social mission, and striving for operational efficiency while responding to environmental dynamics. While some suggest particular attention to the issue of the characteristics of social entrepreneurs (Mulgan 2006), caution should be exercised in pursuing this issue lest it hinder other research initiatives.

The role of environmental dynamics is the first area that appears to warrant further attention. CCSE (2001) state that it is no coincidence that social entrepreneurship is receiving increased attention when the competitive environment is undergoing rapid change and the traditional boundaries between profit and nonprofit sectors, both public and private, are changing. Ryan (1999) identified a new competitive landscape for NFPs in the light of a market which rewards discipline, performance and organizational capacity rather than simply not-for-profit status and mission. Sullivan Mort *et al.* (2003) also argue the effect of environmental changes with increased globalization, 'reinventing government' initiatives and the increasing entry of for-profit organizations into markets traditionally served by nonprofits as the context for social entrepreneurship. Boschee (2006) has linked this to the development of earned-income strategies, providing a starting point for research in this area.

Market orientation provides a valuable input in social entrepreneurial organizations, differentiating them from other social organizations; indeed, some (Nicholls and Cho 2006) have advanced that it is central to the social entrepreneurship conceptualization. This issue warrants focus in the research agenda. The value of market orientation is that it gives primacy to efficient and effective deployment of resources to achieve social goals. Market orientation may operate by allowing optimization of entrepreneurial drive within the constraints of social mission, sustainability and the environment (Weerawardena and Sullivan Mort 2006). However, many social entrepreneurial organizations do not operate in 'markets' in the classical sense, but, in fact, in areas often under conditions of market failure; that is, while needs can be identified, the basis for exchange is non-monetary. While there has been some work on this issue (Sargeant *et al.* 2002; Gainer and Padanyi 2005), further work is necessary in this area.

An important area for further investigation (Mulgan 2006; Mair *et al.* 2006) is the need to understand establishment and growth in social entrepreneurial ventures. Little is known about the establishment and sustainability of socially entrepreneurial organizations, but it is likely that they are at least as vulnerable as for-profit start-ups, and that probably leads to significant loss for the social economy. Research on this topic is already under way in the Australian context (Douglas *et al.* 2007).

Governance issues (Mulgan 2006), specifically, the inherent tension between entrepreneurship and risk-taking on the one hand and the traditional roles of trustees acting as guardians of values who are therefore almost constitutionally risk averse, will require specific research in this context. Specific attention, it has been suggested (Mair *et al.* 2006), should be given to the role of governance in achieving organizational sustainability. In parallel there is an emerging consensus that socially entrepreneurial organizations must operate in an increasingly competitive environment requiring them to adopt a competitive posture (Weerawardena and Sullivan Mort 2001). This requires research to focus on sources of competitive advantage, particularly understanding the role of innovation (Mulgan 2006), marketing-mix factors (Mottner and Ford 2005) as well as market orientation (Nicholls and Cho 2006).

The issue of success in social entrepreneurship (Alvord *et al.* 2004) and performance outcomes of social entrepreneurship is another area requiring attention. There is agreement that social entrepreneurship should lead to superior social value creation, but there is little clarity in what constitutes social value and then how this can be measured. Indeed, as Young (2006) has identified, social value remains a fuzzy goal. There is much necessary work to be done in conceptualizing social value more clearly before the issue of research on performance metrics (Mair *et al.* 2006), and allied research topics, can validly be undertaken.

Finally, though some work has already begun (Anderson *et al.* 2006), the issue of cross-national study, application and validation of social entrepreneurial initiatives is worthy of

221

research (Mulgan 2006). Research in this area would allow better understanding of the effects of cultural contexts on successes and failures in social entrepreneurship, and also assist in understanding the effects of local legal and government contexts on social value creation in an allied manner to that undertaken in international business research.

Conclusion

Social entrepreneurship has quickly established itself as a dynamic field of practice and academic enquiry. Located at the interstices of the nonprofit, for-profit and government sectors, it appears to draw substantial expertise, commitment and energy from a diverse set of contributors facilitating the rapid advancement of the field. A strong interplay between theory and practice is characteristic, also contributing to the rapid growth and sustained interest in this research. After a period of reflexive description, maturing conceptualization of the social entrepreneurship construct has allowed researchers to advance to address issues of measurement, validation across cultures and contexts and the testing of complex sets of relationships examining the relationship of social entrepreneurship to the creation of superior social value. The field promises to continue an accelerated forward momentum with significant commitment from the academic community of researchers and institutions, practitioners, social change agents and policy planners.

References

Alvord, S. H., Brown, L. D. and Letts, C. (2004) 'Social entrepreneurship and societal transformation', *Journal of Applied Behavioral Science*, 40(3): 260–82.

Anderson, R. B., Dana, L. P. and Dana, T. E. (2006) 'Indigenous land rights, entrepreneurship, and economic development in Canada: "Opting-in" to the global economy', *Journal of World Business*, 41(1): 45–55.

Ashoka: 'Innovators for the public' (2006) www.ashoka.org/ (accessed 24 December).

Austin, J. E., Leonard, H. B., Reficco, E. and Wei-Skillern, J. (2006) 'Social entrepreneurship: Is it for corporations, too?', in A. Nicholls (ed.) *Social Entrepreneurship: New Models of Sustainable Social Change*, Oxford: Oxford University Press.

Banks, J. (1972) *The Sociology of Social Movements*, London: Macmillan.

Battle Anderson, B. and Dees, J. G. (2006) 'Rhetoric, reality and research: Building a solid foundation for the practice of social entrepreneurship', in A. Nicholls (ed.) *Social Entrepreneurship: New Models of Sustainable Social Change*, Oxford: Oxford University Press, pp. 144–68.

Borins, S. (2000) 'Loose cannons and rule breakers, or enterprising leaders? Some evidence about innovative public managers', *Public Administration Review*, 60(6): 498–507.

Bornstein, D. (2004) *How to Change the World: Social Entrepreneurs and the Power of New Ideas*, Oxford: Oxford University Press

Boschee, J. (2004) *The Social Enterprise Sourcebook: Profiles of Social Purpose Businesses Operated by Nonprofit Organizations*, Minneapolis: Northland Institute.

—— (2006) 'Social entrepreneurship: The promise and the perils', in Nicholls, A. (ed.) *Social Entrepreneurship: New Models of Sustainable Social Change*, Oxford: Oxford University Press, pp. 356–90.

Campbell, S. (1997) 'Social entrepreneurship: How to develop new social-purpose business ventures', *Health Care Strategic Management*, 16(5): 17–18.

CCSE (Canadian Centre for Social Entrepreneurship) (2001) Social entrepreneurship discussion paper no.1, February.

Cook, B., Dodds, C. and Mitchell, W. (2001) *Social Entrepreneurship: False Premises and Dangerous Forebodings*, Newcastle, UK: Centre of Full Employment and Equity, University of Newcastle, working paper no. 01–24.

Cornwall, J. (1998) 'The entrepreneur as building block for community', *Journal of Developmental Entrepreneurship*, 3(2): 141–8.

Covin, J. G. and Slevin, D. P. (1989) 'Strategic management of small firms in hostile and benign environments', *Strategic Management Journal*, 10(1): 75–87.

Dart, R. (2004) 'The legitimacy of social enterprise', *Nonprofit Management and Leadership*, 14(4): 411–24.

Dees, J. G. (1998a) The meaning of social entrepreneurship. www.gpnnet.com/perspective/social_-entrepreneurship.htm. Visited 21 June, 2001.

—— (1998b) 'Enterprising nonprofits', *Harvard Business Review*, 76 (January–February): 55–67.

—— Emerson, J. and Economy, P. (eds) (2001) *Enterprising Nonprofits: A Toolkit for Social Entrepreneurs*, New York: Wiley.

—— — (eds) (2002) *Strategic Tools for Social Entrepreneurs: Enhancing the Performance of Your Enterprising Nonprofit*, New York: Wiley.

Douglas, H., Sullivan Mort, G. and Cuskelly, G. (2007) 'Analysing elements affecting the survival of new nonprofit organizations in the context of social entrepreneurship ventures', Brisbane, Australia: Fourth AGSE International Research Exchange, 6–9 February.

Eikenberry, A. M. and Kluver, J. D. (2004) 'The marketization of the nonprofit sector: Civil society at risk', *Public Administration Review*, 64(2): 132–40.

Gainer, B. and Padanyi, P. (2005) 'The relationship between market-oriented activities and market-oriented culture: Implications for the development of market orientation in nonprofit service organizations', *Journal of Business Research*, 58(6): 854–62.

Grameen Bank – Banking on the Poor (2006) www.rdc.com.au/grameen/home.html (accessed 23 December).

Harding, R. (2006) 'Social entrepreneurship monitor', London: London Business School, Global Entrepreneurship Monitor, 2005. www.gemconsortium.org/download/1168007763984/Gem%-20Soc%20Ent%20web.pdf (accessed 22 December 2006).

Heilbrunn, S. (2005) 'The impact of organizational change on entrepreneurship in community settings', *Journal of Small Business and Enterprise Development*, 12(3): 422–36.

Hemingway, C. A. (2005) 'Personal values as a catalyst for corporate social entrepreneurship', *Journal of Business Ethics*, 60: 233–49.

Hibbert, S. A., Hogg, G. and Quinn, T. (2001) 'Consumer response to social entrepreneurship: The case of the *Big Issue* in Scotland', *International Journal of Nonprofit and Voluntary Sector Marketing*, 7(3): 288–301.

King, P. J. and Roberts, N. C. (1987) 'Policy entrepreneurs: Catalysts for policy innovation', *Journal of State Government*, 60(July–August): 172–8.

Korosec, R. L. and Berman, E. M. (2006) 'Municipal support for social entrepreneurship', *Public Administration Review*, 66(3): 448–62.

Leadbeater, C. (1997) *The Rise of the Social Entrepreneur*, London, UK: Demos.

Lewis, E. (1980) *Public Entrepreneurship: Toward a Theory of Bureaucratic Power*, Bloomington, IN: Indiana University Press.

Light, P. C. (2006) 'Reshaping social entrepreneurship', *Stanford Social Innovation Review*, 4(3): 47–51.

Mair, J. and Marti, I. (2006) 'Social entrepreneurship research: A source of explanation, prediction and delight', *Journal of World Business*, 41(1): 36–44.

Robinson, J. and Hockerts, K. (eds) (2006) *Social Entrepreneurship*, Basingstoke, UK and New York: Palgrave Macmillan.

Mosher-Williams, R. (ed.) (2006) *Research on Social Entrepreneurship: Understanding and Contributing to an Emerging Field*, Indianapolis, IN: ARNOVA, occasional paper series (vol. 1, no. 3).

Mottner, S. and Ford, J. B. (2005) 'Measuring nonprofit marketing strategy performance: The case of museum stores', *Journal of Business Research*, 58(6): 829–40.

Mulgan, G. (2006) 'Cultivating the other invisible hand of social entrepreneurship: Comparative advantage, public policy and future research directions', in Nicholls, A. (ed.) *Social Entrepreneurship: New Models of Sustainable Social Change*, Oxford: Oxford University Press, pp. 74–96.

Nicholls, A. (ed.) (2006) *Social Entrepreneurship: New Models of Sustainable Social Change*, Oxford: Oxford University Press.

—— and Cho, A. H. (2006) 'Social entrepreneurship: The structuration of a field' in Nicholls, A. (ed.) *Social Entrepreneurship: New Models of Sustainable Social Change*, Oxford: Oxford University Press, pp. 99–118.

Pearson, N. (2002) 'Social entrepreneurship network conference – Dinner address', Carlton Crest, Melbourne, Australia, March, www.partnerships.org.au/Library/sen_conf_dinner_address.htm (accessed 23 December 2006).

Peredo, A. M. and McLean, M. (2006) 'Social entrepreneurship: A critical review of the concept', *Journal of World Business*, 41(1): 56–65.

Prabhu, G.N. (1998) 'Social entrepreneurial management', in '*Leadership in management*', www.mcb.co.uk/services/conferenc/sept98/lim/paper_a2.htm (accessed 21 June 2001).

Roper, J. and Cheney, G. (2005) 'Leadership, learning and human resource management: The meanings of social entrepreneurship today', *Corporate Governance*, 5(3): 95–104.

Ryan, W. P. (1999) 'The new landscape for nonprofits', *Harvard Business Review*, 77(1): 127–36.

Seelos, C. and Mair, J. (2005) 'Social entrepreneurship: Creating new business models to serve the poor', *Business Horizons*, 48(3): 241–9.

Sargeant, A., Foreman, S. and Liao, M-N. (2002) 'Operationalizing the marketing concept in the nonprofit sector', *International Journal of Nonprofit and Voluntary Sector Marketing*, 10(2): 41–54.

Sharir, M. and Lerner, M. (2006) 'Gauging the success of social ventures initiated by individual social entrepreneurs', *Journal of World Business*, 42(1): 6–20.

Shaw, E., Shaw, J. and Wilson, M. (2002). *Unsung Entrepreneurs: Entrepreneurship for Social Gain*, Durham, UK: University of Durham Business School, Barclays Centre for Entrepreneurship.

Skoll, J. (2004) 'Social entrepreneurship: The twenty-first century revolution', Oxford, UK: address Said Business School, March.

Sullivan Mort, G., Weerawardena, J. and Carnegie, K. (2003) 'Social entrepreneurship: Towards conceptualization', *International Journal of Nonprofit and Voluntary Sector Marketing*, 8(1): 76–88.

Thompson, J. L. (2002) 'The world of the social entrepreneur', *International Journal of Public Sector Management*, 15(4/5): 412–31.

—— Alvy, G. and Lees, A. (2000) 'Social entrepreneurship: A new look at the people and the potential', *Management Decision*, 38(5/6): 328–38.

Waddock, S. A. and Post, J. E. (1991) 'Social entrepreneurs and catalytic change', *Public Administration Review*, 51(5): 393–407.

Wallace, S. L. (1999) 'Social entrepreneurship: The role of social purpose enterprises in facilitating community economic development', *Journal of Developmental Entrepreneurship*, 4(2): 153–74.

Weerawardena, J. and Sullivan Mort, G. M. (2001) 'Learning, innovation and competitive advantage in not-for-profit aged care marketing: A conceptual model and research propositions', *Journal of Nonprofit and Public Sector Marketing*, 9(3): 53–73.

—— — (2006) 'Investigating social entrepreneurship; A multidimensional model', *Journal of World Business*, 41(1): 21–35.

Wikipedia (2006) 'Social entrepreneurship', http://en.wikipedia.org/wiki/Social_entrepreneurship (accessed 23 December 2006).

Young, R. (2006) 'For what it is worth: Social value and the future of social entrepreneurship', in Nicholls, A. (ed.) *Social Entrepreneurship: New Models of Sustainable Social Change*, Oxford: Oxford University Press.

Part 3

Arts marketing

13

Implications of government funding and support for marketing programmes of nonprofit performing-arts organizations

John B. Ford and Theresa A. Kirchner

Introduction

This chapter concentrates on the implications of government support for the marketing of nonprofit performing-arts organizations to income-contributing external stakeholders: private donors, performance attendees and governments. It presents a detailed discussion of the implications of cultural economics for government support of arts organizations. It then examines the characteristics and implications of government subsidies for the arts, such as the nature of government subsidies, the funding process, the various granting organizations and individuals, the different levels of funding available, and the expectations and requirements associated with receiving funds. Finally, marketing for the performing arts in the context of government support is examined, including marketing tools and techniques which can help arts organizations to acquire funding in order to grow and thrive. The chapter concludes with high-level managerial implications related to the topic of nonprofit performing-arts marketing, and opportunities for future research from both the practitioner/consultant and academic perspectives.

The performing arts are a unique and significant global sector. For example, revenues from admissions for performing arts organizations in the USA reached $10.6 billion in 2001, with a consumption figure of $37.20 per person (Nichols 2003). However, these organizations have historically been viewed as unable to survive relying solely on ticket sales to cover expenses, requiring them to turn to contributions from public as well as private sources (Schulze and Ursprung 2000). Government support has therefore traditionally been acknowledged as a necessity for the survival of performing-arts organizations (Baumol and Bowen 1966). More recently, other economic-related views of the desirability and importance of public support have emerged. One such view involves crowding theory, the concept that government support for the arts may actually be harmful as well as helpful to the extent that, as a source of income, it can 'crowd out' or stifle the inherent motivation of organizations to engage aggressively in marketing to achieve earned or privately contributed income. Another view of the economics of arts organizations involves the bottom-line recognition, by governments and their publics, that the arts are a good public investment and can contribute substantially to all levels of the economy, for example, through the ripple effects of arts organizations salaries; entertainment taxes; and positive effects on complementary organizations, such as restaurants patronized by arts attendees in conjunction with performances (Frey 2003). A primary source of funding for performing-arts organizations in a variety of countries is the government, which supports the performing arts at national, regional and local levels. Although governments, in general, recognize the desirability of supporting the arts, the nature and focus of that support has shifted in recent years. Competition, from other arts and non-arts organizations, for available funding and other support is fierce. Constantly changing governmental spending priorities, including requirements for matching support by private funders for arts support, are forcing an increasing reliance by arts organizations upon private funding (Brooks 2003). In addition, governments in a number of western countries have implemented requirements for arts organizations to show evidence of long-term viability in order to justify subsidizations (McDonald and Harrison 2002).

Marketing in nonprofit performing-arts organizations has traditionally concentrated on current and potential ticket buyers and season subscribers. Those organizations are increasingly addressing the traditional financial issues associated with the sector with the realization that doing so may require marketing to those and other stakeholders with more sophisticated strategic marketing tools and techniques (Arnold and Tapp 2003). For those organizations, continued governmental support and long-term viability may depend upon the appropriate use of marketing research, marketing strategy development, implementation and ongoing assessment to prove that financial subsidies are warranted (Rentschler *et al.* 2002).

Figure 13.1 provides a heuristic of the scope of nonprofit arts marketing in the context of government support and a high-level overview of material covered in the chapter. As the top level indicates, there is a growing consensus that nonprofit arts organizations can benefit from the implementation of strategic management and marketing concepts and tools that have traditionally been applied to for-profit companies. Strategic planning begins with development of strategic and business plans with specific, measurable goals and objectives. A detailed,

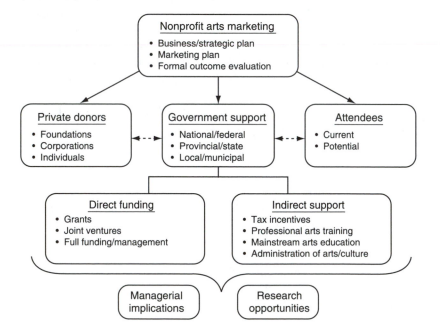

Figure 13.1 The scope of nonprofit arts marketing, with emphasis on government support

comprehensive, marketing plan should then be built based on those higher-level plans, with periodic assessment of results, relative to both organizational and marketing goals and objectives (Byrnes 2003).

Marketing tools and techniques can be applied to arts organization fundraising from private donors. However, in most arts organizations, marketing (e.g. advertising, public relations, ticket sales) and fundraising are looked at and worked on as two separate organizational functions, despite the typically significant overlap between attendees and donors. We propose that, as the second level of Figure 13.1 indicates, a comprehensive marketing plan should include a non-profit's arts marketing programme triangle which integrates not only marketing to private donors and attendees, but also to providers of government support at all levels: national/federal, regional/provincial/state and local/municipal.

The arrows between the groups of income-contributing external stakeholders outlined on the second level of Figure 13.1 suggest both that there are opportunities for integrated market-ing to different types of stakeholders, and that success in marketing to one type of stakeholder has implications for marketing results for other stakeholders. For example, Brooks's (1999) research indicates that government funding does not negatively impact on, or 'crowd out', private donations for arts organizations. In fact, a positive implication for recipients of govern-ment funding is that private donors may view that funding as validation of the merits of those organizations and may therefore donate more readily to them. In addition, receipt of private donor support and/or healthy attendance may be viewed by government support agencies as indications of organizational health and viability, which are increasingly important factors in government-funding decisions.

The concept of marketing to governments to obtain or maximize support is a relatively new one, and few arts organizational marketing programmes include the integration of specific marketing goals, objectives and activities targeting governments for either direct funding or indirect support. As indicated at the third level of Figure 13.1, direct funding includes grants, joint ventures and, in some cases, full funding or management by the government. Indirect support can take the form of tax incentives, professional arts training, mainstream arts education and administration of arts/culture.

Implications of cultural economics for government support of arts organizations

The study of governmental support for the arts is facilitated by the relatively recent emergence of cultural economics as a field of study, which focuses on the application of economic theory to the arts. The first application of economic thinking in a cultural arts context was found in the work of Baumol and Bowen (1966), which involved an examination of government funding for the arts in the USA and noted that a basic dilemma is that arts organizations face continu-ously rising resource and operating expenses due to inflation but are limited in their ability to demonstrate significant productivity gains because of fixed human resource requirements for performers. Research in the area of cultural economics was later extended to the UK by Peacock in 1969. Netzer (1978) studied twenty years of policy creation and suggested that governmental policy involving the arts is predicated upon two concerns: the potential for market failure (inefficient allocation of resources) and the desire for social/cultural equality. According to market failure theory, the performing arts generally have no opportunity to achieve productivity improvements over time; therefore, market failure is a near certainty.

Baumol (1995) referred to the productivity problem as a 'cost disease', noting that the perform-ing arts do not lend themselves to automation or to downsizing. This cost–disease problem is often compounded by inflation, as inflationary pressures on the arts outstrip those of other industries. Baumol reported that arts costs have risen more than seven hundred times higher than the general rate of inflation since the Second World War, largely due to the inflation-driven rising human resource costs for performers as well as operations and administrative personnel. As a result, government support for the arts is a necessity for survival of the arts as an industry.

Other economic factors related to government support of the arts have emerged in recent years. First, several related 'crowding theories' have emerged, which suggest that: (a) donations from one contributing stakeholder may be either positively or negatively affected by contri-butions of other stakeholders; (b) government support can 'crowd out' or negatively impact on the perception by arts organization managers of the need to market to and solicit from other potential funding sources in an assertive way; and (c) from an artistic standpoint, performing arts may be negatively affected by public support in terms of 'crowding out' of intrinsic motivation and creativity (Frey 2003; Brooks 1999). Another factor favouring government intervention in terms of support is the resulting significant direct and indirect economic impact, with spillover benefits to externalities (e.g. business and society) that are both financial and cultural (Heaney and Heaney 2003). There are many stakeholders that may be negatively affected by the loss of government funding, such as arts organizations, individual artists, corporate donors, local communities, foundations, society and governments themselves (Radbourne 1998). Offerings by arts organizations provide perceived social and cultural advantages for citizens which spur government intervention to keep those organizations functioning (Frey 2003; Schuster 1999). A serious concern is that without government support, the arts will regress to amateur status in terms of both quality and variety, which would leave society in a poorer state (Baumol 1995).

Characteristics and implications of government subsidies for the arts

Government subsidies traditionally have comprised a large percentage of the operating budgets for performing-arts organizations. In terms of arts spending by the government as a percentage of gross domestic product, Canada is at the highest relative position in terms of English-speaking countries, followed by the UK and Australia percentages (NEA 2000). The USA lags far behind, due largely to the proportionally small size of public sector direct support relative to support by the private sector. The USA supports the arts, in large part, by forgoing taxes from nonprofit organizations and allowing tax-free contributions to nonprofit organizations from private citizens and corporations (Schuster 1987).

A serious issue facing US arts organizations is the fairly steady decline in government funding experienced over the last ten to fifteen years. Funding provided by the US National Endowment for the Arts dropped a staggering 40 per cent from 1992 to 1996, and this trend appears to be continuing. The UK has faced similar pressures, but Canada and Australia have experienced actual increases in government subsidization for the arts as a whole. It is important to note that while Australia has experienced overall funding increases, these have been offset by an increasing number of recipient firms, thereby reducing the amount given to each firm as a proportion of the overall Australian government budget (Arts Council of England Policy Research and Planning Department 1998).

Government support for the arts typically takes three forms: direct, indirect and induced subsidies. Direct subsidies involve direct cash payments to arts organizations (Netzer 1978).

Indirect support takes the forms of tax deductions for private contributors and government expenditures for arts-related needs such as professional training, formal educational pro-grammes, and administration of the arts (Feist *et al.* 1998). Finally, induced subsidies include such spillover benefits as enhancing the well-being of society, preserving civilized values (Gainer 1989) and the use of the arts to attract tourists (Peacock 2000).

Who are the recipients of governmental support? Both arts organizations and individual artists can receive direct funds from the government. These typically involve traditional grants for which the receiving firm or individual develops a funding proposal, outlining how the objectives for the granting agency will be fulfilled through the monies awarded. Company personnel or individual artists can also scan available research funding proposals (RFPs) to see which could apply to the particular organization in question. In terms of indirect subsidies, both individual and corporate donors can share in government support in terms of being exempt from taxes on contributions made to nonprofit arts organizations. Communities can also receive benefits through induced subsidies allowing the arts to provide a better quality of life for citizens and attractions for visitors.

What are typical levels of governmental funding? Funding can be provided at one or more of three different levels (Gainer 1989). First, and most importantly, subsidies can be provided from national or federal agencies. As previously mentioned, the National Endowment for the Arts is the most significant provider of governmental funding for arts organizations in the USA, and similar organizations exist in other countries. Western countries have long provided sub-sidies for the arts, and a number of countries have established clear policies governing support for the arts, with national agencies created to oversee these subsidizations. The first national agency, the Ministry of Culture, was founded in France in 1959, and was later followed by the USA with the National Endowment for the Arts (NEA), the UK with the forerunner for the Department of Culture, Media and Sport (DCMS), and the Netherlands with the Ministry of Culture, Recreation and Social Work in 1965. Sweden and Germany created similar organiza-tions in 1974. Since then, many other countries have developed their own national/federal agencies to oversee the development of culture/the arts. These types of governmental agencies are founded on the perceived need for government support for the arts, based on the cultural economics concepts previously discussed in this chapter. They are concerned with improving the quality of life for their citizens while preserving cultural arts and heritage. The emphasis placed on arts funding differs. France, Sweden and Germany place the burden on public entities for the administration of arts organizations, while the USA places greater emphasis on the arts as a private responsibility. The NEA does not have permanent funds. Each fiscal year the US Congress allocates a certain amount to the NEA to accomplish its mission. NEA grants often require matching funds from private organizations. The DCMS falls in between the emphases of public responsibility in France and Germany and the US focus on private support. The DCMS typically provides funds through some kind of intermediary for arts organizations other than national museums and art galleries (Peacock 2000). Along with differing levels of private versus public support of the arts, there are varying degrees of control applied by the govern-ments regarding what is presented/displayed. The USA, with its hands-off approach, does little to control artistic offerings, while France and Germany exert far more pressure on recipient organizations (Schulze and Ursprung 2000).

A second level of government support is found at provincial/state levels. Where provinces (e.g. Canada) and states (e.g. the USA) have their own separate governmental structures, many of the same concerns that affect national funding may also be found. Again, cultural economics can be seen to affect the decision-making of governmental officials even at this more focused level of responsibility. Often, these types of agencies are established to supplement the work done by national funding agencies, since the needs of the individual states and provinces are typically better understood by local legislators than by more disconnected national regulators. In the USA, each separate state has its own arts funding organization. For example, the New York State Council on the Arts offers grants to statewide arts organizations through its grant proposal process, which takes place on 1 March of each year. This organization also provides a series of resources that are readily available for both arts organizations and individual artists that reside within the state boundaries. Canada and Australia have similar organizations (e.g. the British Columbia Arts Council and the Queensland Arts Council). These organizations provide additional funding and resource support to various statewide/provincial arts organizations and individual artists.

The lowest level of governmental funding organization can be found at the local/municipal level, where there often is a governmental structure, in the form of a local arts commission or council, responsible for the well-being of the local population. These organizations have much narrower funding scopes and provide funding and resource support for local arts organizations and individual artists. Typically, the broader the scope of the governmental agencies, the fewer the organizations that receive needed funding, resulting in a hierarchy of funding prospects for the arts. National agencies want to achieve the greatest good for the greatest number of citizens, which often precludes the funding requests of small organizations and forces proposals to be sent to lower agencies in the hierarchy.

Given the emphasis on private donations in the USA, the types of organizations that are targeted for funding relief are usually private donors, in the form of foundations, corporations and individual citizens. Foundations, such as the Ford Foundation or the Aspen Institute, provide funding for projects that coincide with their altruistic goals for the community, including the improvement of the living conditions of its citizens. For foundation funding, the applying organization needs to show how money received will not only alleviate its financial needs but also contribute to the accomplishment of key goals of the funding foundation. Corporations, on the other hand, are often focused on key image-enhancement initiatives which result in making them perceived as good community citizens. As with government funding, the larger the corporation, the more important the arts organization or project may need to be to warrant significant donations. A particularly important factor is that even large corporations have branch offices in local communities, and often there is a corporate policy to foster community giving and involvement for purposes of image and reputation enhancement. The need for visible presence in the community presents even the smallest arts organizations with opportunities for funding. Finally, arts organizations can also obtain smaller funding grants from individuals. This normally involves funding drives in local communities to support particular arts organizations. Fundraising might include telemarketing efforts to reach individuals/ families who are potential donors. The focus of these efforts should consider the past arts contributions of those individuals. Usually these types of givers look for tax advantages related to their gifts and give to nonprofit arts organizations to both alleviate the organization's financial burdens and acquire a resulting good feeling of charitable responsibility and preferential status (Sargeant et al. 2006).

What do funding agencies expect in return for their grants? There is increasing demand from private and public donors for recipient arts organizations to show financial responsibility. Continued viability of the receiving organization is an indication that the money being provided by the government agency is not wasted or squandered. Recipient organizations typically must account for how funding was spent and demonstrate that they have used the money to improve their positions in the marketplace. The failures of various nonprofit arts organizations that were once believed to be financially viable raise the need for tight controls and accountability, the achievement of meaningful and measurable goals, and efficiencies gained through the proper use of newer technologies, including innovative marketing techniques (Rentschler and Potter 1996).

Another expectation is that artistic works presented reflect quality and integrity. This may preclude the performance of questionable works and require feasibility studies to enhance the chances of success. What specific performance measures could be used to demonstrate success? Typical performance criteria include audience attendance numbers, theatre occupancy rates and subscription revenues. However, it should be noted that these types of measures do not indicate the actual financial health and viability of the arts organization. Increasingly, arts organization executive directors are concentrating on the 'bottom line' in terms of measures like annual surplus/deficit.

Marketing for the performing arts in the context of government support

Laczniak and Murphy (1977) suggested, thirty years ago, that development of marketing objectives, strategies and campaigns enables nonprofit arts organizations to achieve both financial and artistic objectives. Improved performance can be achieved with the evolution of management from an 'impresarial' to a structured administration and the introduction of sound business practices and marketing savvy (Peterson 1986).

Marketing concepts, tools and techniques should be adopted and supported in the context of strategic planning to enhance the chances of success in terms of acquiring government financial support as well as improving performance with both existing patrons and donors (individuals, corporations and foundations) and new ones. While this section addresses marketing for nonprofit arts organizations in a general way, an organization's detailed marketing programme should be developed to include marketing to all external income-contributing stakeholders, including government funders. Specific marketing strategies, tools and techniques should be applied individually and targeted to the specific government, private donor or individual ticket-buyer or season ticket-buyer involved. Figure 13.2 provides a model of important components of the marketing process that must be adopted and effectively utilized to achieve optimal results.

For nonprofit performing arts organizations, the use of marketing is not a luxury – it is a necessity. Until relatively recently, for many arts organizations, 'marketing' typically was limited to relatively rudimentary public relations and advertising activities (Byrne 2003). Kaali-Nagy and Garrison first proposed, in 1972, that for performing arts organizations to be successful in terms of expanding audiences and raising revenues, they must use demographic and arts/cultural activity analyses to develop appropriate target markets and effective marketing strategies. Studies indicate that educational level and income are the two most important variables in this type of segmentation analysis (Dimaggio et al. 1978; Hoffman and Fritschner 1984). Other important factors include the reputations of performers and artistic directors (Belk and Andreason 1980; Currim et al. 1981), age of attendees, and the time necessary to travel to the performance venue (Fitzhugh 1983; Garbarino and Johnson 1999). What makes marketing even more vital are the elusive aesthetic and intangible aspects of the performing arts, since without effective marketing, there is little to help the consumer to tangibilize the artistic offering. As with all services organizations, making what is intangible as close to tangible as possible is necessary in order for an organization to differentiate itself from the competition and enable the consumer to see the benefits associated with its offerings.

For performing-arts organizations, the nature of competition is increasingly intense as new forms of entertainment become relevant substitutes, such as cable TV, the Internet, movies

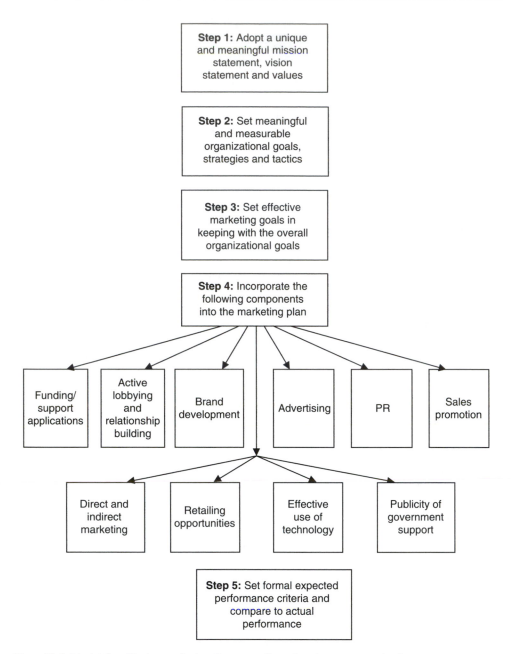

Figure 13.2 Model for effective marketing for nonprofit performing-arts organizations

(cinema) and sporting events. A problem currently faced by performing-arts organizations is confusion as to exactly what marketing entails and how it should be utilized by nonprofit arts organizations (Scheff and Kotler 1996). McDonald and Harrison (2002) noted that, until relatively recently, many performing-arts organizations were guilty of using traditional public relations and advertising almost exclusively, neglecting other marketing opportunities. Advertising and public relations are only pieces of the overall marketing puzzle, and companies choosing not to go further and utilize strategic marketing and management techniques have not reached their potential. Adopting sophisticated marketing tools and techniques can be important for success, and those organizations which adopt a market orientation are more likely to create a market-oriented organizational culture, which should directly lead to increased resources, greater customer satisfaction and enhanced image and brand reputation (Gainer and Padanyi 2002). Sargeant *et al.* (2002) suggested that the concept of market orientation, while developed in the context of large national and multinational firms, can effectively be adapted for nonprofit organizations, taking not the form of a traditional market orientation so much as a 'societal orientation'. McDonald and Harrison (2002) identified the following relevant components of marketing for nonprofit organizations: (a) market assessment; (b) customer segmentation; (c) product development; (d) pricing; (e) distribution; (f) servicing; (g) sales force (for purposes of ticket sales and donor identification/development); (h) sales promotion (incentives to help with ticketing and donors); and (i) advertising. They then delineated relevant aspects of public relations which should be added to marketing efforts: (a) publications (brochures, programmes, etc.); (b) event creation; (c) news items; (d) community relationship building and development; (e) media identification; (f) lobbying; and (g) social initiatives and investment. They proposed a series of items that are representative of a hybridization of marketing and public relations for use by nonprofits: (a) image assessment; (b) customer satisfaction; (c) perceptual surveys; (d) media strategy; (e) corporate advertising; and (f) internal marketing (employee attitude assessment).

In keeping with previous findings, Arnold and Tapp (2003) proposed that performing-arts organizations should utilize those activities which aid in the building of relationships with customers and donors (including governments), which facilitate the conversion to a truly market-oriented entity, and which involve direct marketing to reach carefully selected target customers. We propose three key factors in the achievement of those goals: (a) the building of a market orientation; (b) the use of relationship marketing; and (c) the careful use of direct marketing tools and techniques. These factors comprise a synergistic combination which is invaluable for performing-arts organizations. Each of these components will now be discussed in greater detail.

First, market orientation is necessary, because it focuses the firm's efforts on being customer-centred. Mechanisms are put in place which allow access to customers to collect information about their particular wants and needs and then disseminate it to those within the organization who need it in order to develop artistic offerings that meet the expectations of the customers. This market orientation requires that the firm be skilled at the identification of proper target segments which is vital for success. Information can be gathered from the identified segments and the offerings shaped accordingly. For performing-arts organizations, this should involve the careful analysis of patron attendance patterns and contribution efforts (Andreason and Belk 1980). Rentschler (1998) reported that performing-arts organizations which do these types of analyses may often use the information primarily for political reasons rather than using it strategically to shape their offerings to competitive advantage by building greater loyalty in patrons and donors. Andreasen (1985) also suggested the use of environmental scanning to determine social and cultural changes that may affect patron behaviour and preferences. Database management systems, combined with seasonal attendance forecasting, and promotional and fundraising strategies, can be particularly helpful in enabling nonprofit arts organizations to develop optimal audiences and adapt their offerings to satisfy attendees (Desai *et al.* 2001).

Relationship-marketing tools and techniques can also significantly improve nonprofit performing arts organizations' results. Relationship marketing has been embraced by many major for-profit corporations, and the benefits associated with relationship building and maintenance also apply to the nonprofit sector as well. It focuses on the creation of intimate relationships between the company and its customers/donors, and this requires an assessment of the lifetime value of each customer/donor group so that the most important ones are catered to, and fewer resources are spent on unprofitable customers. McCort (1994) highlighted the usefulness of relationship marketing to build ticket sales and donor development, which can then allow for the development of catered offerings and unique pricing to enhance long-term profitable relationships being built with both audience patrons and individual/corporate donors (Bhattacharya et al. 1995). Rentschler et al. (2002) found that relationship marketing is well suited to the arts, since the products/performances involved are highly experiential and require emotional investments. They proposed the development of a loyalty ladder for arts patrons which involves mutual exchange and fulfilment of promises to move individuals and corporations to higher levels of the loyalty ladder and improve financial results. This concept is also supported by Garbarino and Johnson (1999), who noted that the firm must treat individual ticket-buyers differently from season-ticket buyers. Satisfaction is a concern for the individual ticket-buyer, while trust and commitment keep the season-ticket subscriber involved. If the performing arts organization does its relationship building well, it may be possible to convert the single ticket-buyer into a season-ticket subscriber. Treating all customers in the same way would not be an effective way to accomplish that transition, especially since industry research indicates that, with increasing choices and options, patrons are increasingly less interested in buying season-ticket subscriptions which lock them into a fixed number of performances. Scheff (1999) suggested that strategic opportunities for converting the single ticket-buyer to a subscriber could include offering extended payment options and liberal ticket-exchange programmes.

The third group of strategic marketing tools and techniques involves direct marketing through avenues such as personal letters, e-mail and home and mobile telephones, which offer unique opportunities to reach both existing and potential audience patrons and givers. As Sargeant et al. (2006) found, communications are an important mechanism for motivating donors to continue to give to a nonprofit. Direct marketing should be used to facilitate two-way communication between the performing-arts organization and its various audiences/targets with the end goal of building loyalty and long-term profitable relationships (Bhattacharya et al. 1995). Simmel and Berger (2000) proposed that ideal mechanisms for doing this are one-on-one telefundraising and telemarketing, when combined with well-written scripts for use by fundraisers/contact personnel. While research indicates that, generally, performing-arts organizations have been slow to adopt marketing tools and techniques, Desai et al. (2001) suggested that they have been relatively quick to adopt the use of database marketing, which, when combined with sound strategic planning, should aid greatly in developing competitive advantage, which can ensure not only survival but success.

Will the application of marketing tools and techniques be sufficient to make the organization successful? While it appears to be clear from the research that nonprofit performing-arts organizations which have chosen to adopt appropriate marketing tools and techniques have tended to achieve improvements in their performance, achieving long-term competitive advantage and success will take more than that. Adopting a market orientation and the necessary accompanying customer focus requires a change in organizational culture. The firm cannot just go through the motions of saying that it is customer focused. It has to live this out in its values and practices. What helps to make this happen is a top-down organizational push to change the culture, with the executive director and all management embracing the philosophy underlying the new cultural change. It also requires the effective use of new technologies. Kirchner et al. (2006) found that, in a study of US symphony orchestras, organizations that invested in the implementation of marketing tools and techniques were more likely to receive governmental resources. Of course, just spending money for the sake of spending money does not ensure that governmental agencies will continue funding nonprofit performing arts organizations, but being able to demonstrate how those monies have improved performance will make a strong case for relevance and viability. Kirchner *et al.* (2006) raise an interesting question in their study: is it not possible that firms which spend less on marketing activities can perform better financially without those additional expenses? The intuitive answer is that while that may give the appearance of solvency in the short term, it may lead to disaster in the long run, as the firm finds itself offering and publicizing less and less of what the patrons want and expect. Sound marketing, strategic information gathering and strategic plan development and implementation are the keys to competitive advantage.

Managerial implications

So, what does the information outlined above mean for managers of performing-arts organizations? First, the idea that marketing in nonprofit performing-arts organizations should take the form of a comprehensive organizational programme which integrates efforts to maximize resources obtained from all income-contributing external stakeholders to meet organizational goals is a powerful one (Byrnes 2003). Managers of arts organizations should leverage strategic management and marketing concepts found in the for-profit corporate environment and apply them appropriately. They should review their marketing programmes to ensure that they address marketing goals, objectives and results in terms of both fundraising and ticket sales, and that they target and leverage support from private donors and government support, as well as event attendees. Important synergies can be achieved by recognizing opportunities for support from a variety of sources, and increasingly, arts organizations are successfully developing joint projects and related funding requests and appeals, which both donors and attendees at various levels often find interesting and worthy of support.

From the standpoint of publicity, advertising and public relations, organizations should be aware of the potential benefits of publicizing all support received in a variety of ways, to both external and internal stakeholders. While managers may instinctively fear that news of grants, awards and significant contributions may contribute to a perception that the organization is not in need of additional support, research indicates that 'crowding out' of new support by previous support is probably not an issue for nonprofit arts organizations (Brooks 1999).

Nonprofit performing arts organizations should seek to avoid rewarding major donors or politically powerful individuals with important marketing-related positions. Marketing programme development and responsibility should go to those properly trained and experienced in the subject area. Responsible, trained professionals may seem to be a luxury for NPOs, but the improper placement of untrained individuals can be disastrous (Ford and Mottner 2003).

Managers should also evaluate their marketing programme components in terms of the model outlined in Figure 13.2, to ensure that key factors such as marketing-mix elements, market segmentation and technology investments reflect an integrated stakeholder orientation. They may want to consider combining traditional marketing, fundraising and funding-application functions under a single marketing executive rather than have those areas function in a conventional stove-piped organizational structure.

In terms of developing or enhancing a highly effective marketing programme, managers should adopt a top-down approach. The strategic planning process should drive the marketing programme, beginning with adoption of a mission statement, vision statement and values. Meaningful and measurable organizational goals, strategies and tactics should be derived from the mission and vision statements and values of the organization. Marketing goals, objectives and strategies should be developed to achieve organizational goals, and they should provide a framework for achieving desired results for all stakeholders. Finally, criteria for performance outcome evaluation should be established in conjunction with development of marketing objectives, and actual performance should be assessed in terms of expected performance (Byrnes 2003).

Opportunities for future research

From a micro-marketing standpoint, arts organizations and consultants can use market research techniques to explore implications of the integrated stakeholder marketing approach outlined in this chapter for their organizations and environments. They may want to band together with other arts organizations in their sectors or geographic areas to optimize the results of research efforts and investments.

Arts organizations can also take advantage of larger-scale opportunities for industry or sector-oriented research, which may be funded and supported by governments, private foundations and/or corporations. An example is the 2005 Knight Foundation research project, which explored the conceptual and practical possibilities related to cooperative marketing initiatives with the potential to produce collective benefits, strategies and cooperative structures. Fifteen symphony orchestras took part in this project, which was 'the largest discipline-specific study of arts consumers ever undertaken in the US' (Wolf 2005: 5–6). Funded by the foundation, it produced significant lessons learned for the organizations and their funders.

From an academic standpoint, the concept of a comprehensive and deeply integrated performing-arts organizational marketing programme is one that has not specifically been explored in depth. Research to evaluate the nature and characteristics of arts industry marketing programmes, structures, organizations and results is needed, not only to establish their current state but also to propose, from a normative perspective, how arts organizations can improve their ability to obtain and fully leverage resources from all of their income-contributing external stakeholders, including private donors, audience attendees and governments.

Academic research might also concentrate on exploration of cross-national commonalities and differences. This is likely to be a difficult undertaking, since underlying economic and social factors and data related to the arts and arts marketing are significantly different in composition and reporting, even across countries which share a common language and similar cultures and arts heritage, such as the UK, the USA, Canada, New Zealand and Australia.

References

Andreasen, A. R. (1985) 'Marketing or selling the arts: An orientational dilemma', *Journal of Arts Management and Law*, 15(1): 9–20.
—— and Belk, R. W. (1980) 'Predictors of attendance at the performing arts', *Journal of Consumer Research*, 7(2): 112–20.
Arnold, M. and Tapp, S. (2003) 'Direct marketing in nonprofit services: Investigating the case of the arts industry', *Journal of Services Marketing*, 17(2): 141–60.
Arts Council of England Policy Research and Planning Department (1998) 'International data on public spending on the arts in eleven countries', research report no. 13.
Baumol, W. J. and Bowen, W. G. (1966) *Performing Arts: The Economic Dilemma*, New York: Twentieth Century Fund.

—— —— (1995) 'The case for subsidizing the arts', *Challenge*, 38(5): 50–6.

Belk, R. W. and Andreasen, A. R. (1980) 'The effects of family life cycle on arts patronage', *Journal of Cultural Economics*, 6(2): 25–36.

—— Semenik, R. J. and Andreasen, A. R. (1980) '*De gustibus non est disputandum*: A study of the potential for broadening the appeal of performing arts', *Advances in Consumer Research*, 7: 109–13.

Bhattacharya, C. B., Rao, H. and Glynn, M. A. (1995) 'Understanding the bond of identification: An investigation of its correlates among art museum members', *Journal of Marketing*, 59(4), 46–58.

Brooks, A. C. (1999) 'Do public subsidies leverage private philanthropy for the arts? Empirical evidence on symphony orchestras', *Nonprofit and Voluntary Sector Quarterly*, 28(1): 32–45.

Byrnes, William J. (2003) *Management and the Arts*, Boston, MA: Focal Press.

Currim, I. S., Weinberg, C. B. and Wittink, D. R. (1981) 'Design of subscription programs for a performing arts series', *Journal of Consumer Research*, 8(1): 67–75.

Desai, C., Fletcher, K. and Wright, G. (2001) 'Drivers in the adoption and sophistication of database marketing in the services sector', *Service Industries Journal*, 21(4): 17–32.

Dimaggio, P. J., Useem, M. and Brown, P. (1978) *Audience Studies of the Performing Arts and Museums: A Critical Review*, Washington, DC: National Endowment for the Arts.

Feist, A., Fisher, R., Gordon, C., Morgan, C. and O'Brien, J. (1998) 'International data on public spending on the arts in eleven countries', Arts Council of England Policy Research and Planning Department, research report no. 13.

Fitzhugh, L. (1983) 'An analysis of audience studies for the performing arts in America, part I: The audience profile', *Journal of Arts Management and Law*, 13(2): 49–85.

Ford, J. B. and Mottner, S. (2003) 'Retailing in the nonprofit sector: An exploratory analysis of church-connected retailing ventures', *International Journal of Nonprofit and Voluntary Sector Marketing*, 8 (4): 337–48.

Frey, B. S. (2003) *Arts and Economics*, Berlin: Springer-Verlag.

Gainer, B. (1989) 'The business of high culture: Marketing the performing arts in Canada', *The Services Industries Journal*, 9(4): 43–162.

—— and Padanyi, P. (2002) 'Applying the marketing concept to cultural organizations: An empirical study of the relationship between market orientation and performance', *International Journal of Nonprofit and Voluntary Sector Marketing*, 7(2): 182–93.

Garbarino, E. and Johnson, M. S. (1999) 'The different roles of satisfaction, trust and commitment in customer relationships', *Journal of Marketing*, 63(2): 70–83.

Heaney, J. and Heaney, M. F. (2003) 'Using economic impact analysis for arts management: An empirical application to a music institute in the USA', *International Journal of Nonprofit and Voluntary Sector Marketing*, 8(3): 251–66.

Hoffman, M. K. and Fritschner, L. M. (1984) 'Art and art audiences: Testing the market', *The Journal of Arts Management and Law*, 14(2): 5–19.

Kaali-Nagy, C. and Garrison, L. C. (1972) 'Profiles of users and nonusers of the Los Angeles Music Center', *California Management Review*, 15(2): 133–43.

Kirchner, T. A., Markowski, E. P. and Ford, J. B. (2006) 'Relationships among levels of government support, marketing activities, and financial health of nonprofit performing arts organizations', *International Journal of Nonprofit and Voluntary Sector Marketing*, 12(2): DOI 10.1002/nvsm.285.

Laczniak, G. R. and Murphy, P. E. (1977) 'Marketing the performing arts', *Atlanta Economic Review*, 27(6): 4–9.

McCort, J. D. (1994) 'A framework for evaluating the relational extent of a relationship marketing strategy: The case of nonprofit organizations', *Journal of Direct Marketing*, 8(2): 53–66.

McDonald, H. and Harrison, P. (2002) 'The marketing and public relations practices of Australian performing arts presenters', *International Journal of Nonprofit and Voluntary Sector Marketing*, 7(2): 105–17.

NEA (2000) 'International data on government spending on the arts', *National Endowment for the Arts*. Available at: www.nea.gov/research/ResearchNoteschrono.html (accessed 20 August 2007).

Netzer, D. (1978) *The Subsidized Muse*, Cambridge, UK: Cambridge University Press.

Nichols, B. (2003) 'The arts in the GDP, consumers spent $10.6 billion on performing arts events in 2001', *National Endowment For The Arts*, research note no. 83. Available at: www.nea.gov/research/Notes/83.pdf (accessed 29 January 2007).

Peacock, A. T. (2000) 'Public financing of the arts in England', *Fiscal Studies*, 21(2): 171–205.

Peterson, R. A. (1986) 'From impresario to arts administrator: Formal accountability in nonprofit cultural organizations', in P. D. DiMaggio (ed.) *Nonprofit Enterprise in the Arts: Studies in Mission and Constraint*, New York: Oxford University Press.

Radbourne, J. (1998) 'The role of the government in marketing the arts', *Journal of Arts Management, Law and Society*, 28(1): 67–82.

Rentschler, R. (1998) 'Museum and performing arts marketing: A climate of change', *Journal of Professional Services Marketing*, 28(1): 83.

—— and Potter, B. (1996) 'Accountability versus artistic development: The case for nonprofit museums and performing arts organizations', *Accounting, Auditing and Accountability Journal*, 9(5): 100.

—— Radbourne, J., Carr, R. and Rickard, J. (2002) 'Relationship marketing, audience retention and performing arts organization viability', *International Journal of Nonprofit and Voluntary Sector Marketing*, 7(2): 118–30.

Sargeant, A., Ford, J. B. and West, D. C. (2006) 'Perceptual determinants of nonprofit giving behavior, *Journal of Business Research*, 59(2): 155–65.

—— Foreman, S. and Liao, M. (2002) 'Operationalizing the marketing concept in the nonprofit sector', *Journal of Nonprofit and Public Sector Marketing*, 10(2): 41–65.

Scheff, J. (1999) 'Factors influencing subscription and single-ticket purchases at performing arts organizations', *International Journal of Arts Management*, 1(2): 16–27.

—— and Kotler, P. (1996) 'Crisis in the arts: The marketing response', *California Management Review*, 39(1): 28–52.

Schulze, G. G. and Ursprung, H. W. (2000) '*La donna e mobile* – or is she? Voter preferences and public support for the performing arts', *Public Choice*, 102(1–2): 131–49.

Schuster, J. M. D. (1987) 'Making compromises to make comparisons in cross-national arts policy research', *Journal of Cultural Economics*, 11(2): 1–36.

—— (1999) 'The other Side of the subsidized muse: Indirect aid revisited', *Journal of Cultural Economics*, 23(1): 51–70.

Simmel, L. L. and Berger, P. D. (2000) 'The art of the ask: Maximizing verbal compliance in telefundraising', *Journal of Interactive Marketing*, 14(3): 12–40.

Wolf, T. (2005) *The Search for Shining Eyes*, Miami, FL: John S. and James L. Knight Foundation Publications.

14

Relationship marketing in the arts

The new evoked authenticity

Ruth Rentschler and Jennifer Radbourne

Introduction

Relationship marketing and audience retention have implications in terms of authenticity. The importance of this matter is predicated on the view that the search for authenticity is one of the main drivers for building relationships and retaining audiences in cultural organizations. It is also predicated on the view that the arts represent a dynamic and increasingly important arena for expressing identity. It is audiences which provide the basis for building relationships. Audiences can be formed from local and tourist segments of the market. Building relationships with cultural audiences can have major impacts on audience retention. However, it is an area little researched in the arts, although recognized as important in tourism research.

There are three key assumptions about the arts and about consumer experiences on which relationship marketing research rests. First, arts audiences desire authentic experiences (Cohen 1988; Prentice 2001). Authenticity is defined as a higher level of cultural experience for the audience provided by spiritual fulfilment and self-actualization through participation in arts events and experiences. In other words, audiences are taken 'back stage' rather than relying on only 'front stage' views. Authenticity is evident in the object, the consumer experience of brand essence and in identity construction and confirmation through physical attributes. Object authenticity is when objects have a link to the special world and when they physically resemble something that is authentic, whereas staged authenticity presents the audience with a controlled experience. Some argue that museums, heritage centres and cultural performances provide a controlled and hence 'staged' experience (Higham and Hinch 2004), while others see these organizations as providing an 'evoked' authenticity (Prentice 2001). We follow Prentice (2001) in arguing that the arts generally and museums particularly provide evoked authenticity.

As the provenance of the word 'authenticity' is in the museum, where objects are what they appear to be, it is appropriate to use the words 'evoked authenticity' for cultural experiences (Cohen 1988). Here audiences participate in a less contrived experience. Consumers' participation is perceived to be authentic when the object and its ownership have provenance, thus providing an ideal standard and preservation of brand heritage (Leigh *et al.* 2006). This has been argued particularly strongly in relation to museum audiences (Prentice 2001), but is equally true for other types of arts audiences, such as in the performing arts and at festivals and events

(Urry 1991). Evoked authenticity is seen to be offering an experience that has provenance in that it is providing knowledge and liminal experiences of the world, whether old or modern, such that a true engagement with a culture is evoked in audience members.

This leads to the second point. Marketing strategy in arts organizations is in a period of major reassessment. Until recently, the focus of both organizational energies and funding support was directed at product development. While this focus has allowed the development of a world-class product, creativity and innovation need to be extended to the managerial realm for further organizational development. Since the late 1990s, there has been a shift in focus to relationship marketing in arts organizations. This change in focus is being encouraged to ensure the long-term sustainability of arts organizations. Attention is being directed at building new audiences and at consolidating existing audiences. While attention has been directed at developing loyalty ladders for arts audiences (Rentschler et al. 2002), little work has been done in identifying the types of experiences that arts organizations desire.

Third, authenticity is contrasted with commodified experiences which lack depth, originality and a sense of place. Commodification is seen to destroy the authentic and replace it with contrived, staged authenticity (Cohen 1988). Commodification in this chapter implies cultural activities spoiled by commercial relationships. In contrast, authentic experiences are seen to be true to the experience intended. For example, in the museums' literature, Disneyland is often cited as a commodified experience, but, in the marketing and tourism literature, there is now recognition that Disneyland has developed to the point of becoming an authentic experience which is representative of North American culture (Higham and Hinch 2004; Wang 1999).

Relationship marketing is not enough any more. Authenticity is the way to go. This scan of the literature, while enlightening, is far too scant in relation to a new dimension to relationship marketing. Future research needs to examine in more depth the authentic arts experience. Are there differences in the art authenticity experience of museum and gallery visitors, art investors, cultural tourists, orchestral music or theatre *aficionados*? Do youth market segments differ from more mature audience segments? Is authenticity affected by the experience, information, knowledge of arts audiences or the context of the arts experience? Does authenticity only occur at the satisfaction of higher-level needs? Or is it an experience that can occur with satisfying lower-level needs? Is authenticity exhibited in audience values or audience experiences? This new field of knowledge is deserving of further research.

This chapter explores the theme of *evoked* authenticity through relationship marketing – the development of audiences. The chapter applies authenticity to the arts organization context, identifying the changing environment which has led to recognition of the importance of marketing. It then explains the concepts of relationship marketing and its pertinence to authenticity. Finally, the chapter presents a new model of relationship marketing, not simply a loyalty ladder. The structure is modelled as a dynamic conceptualization of the relationships between audience needs and artists' needs to assist audience retention outcomes and the sustainability of arts organizations.

Background

Relationship marketing is defined as an association or connection between two parties which benefits both of them by creating trust in the quality of services offered (Garbarino and Johnson 1999; Shirastava and Kale 2003). Its focus is on long-term relationships rather than short-term transactions. With particular relevance for the arts, building relationships is about creating links between producers, distributors and consumers of art – whether contemporary art, performance art or event (Chong 2005). Importantly, Chong argues that art consumption is inherently experiential and that the relationship between consumer and product has a cumulative effect on future consumption: 'The more you know, the more you appreciate it. This is to say that a self-reinforcing system exists: arts consumption increases with the ability to appreciate art, which is a function of past arts consumption. *Satisfaction* from arts consumption rises over time' (2005: 87).

According to Chong, the arts consumer has a relational bond to both the current product(s) and to the future production and consumption of like products. This is rationalized through personal taste and is realized through the stakeholder advantage: 'Collectors of contemporary art, who are buying on personal taste, can have an impact on shaping the permanent collections of museums of modern art, which may represent national views of taste through donations of art works' (Chong 2005: 99).

Experience suggests that managers in arts organizations are very interested in the concept of audience retention but need tools to judge its impact on their own organization. This view is reinforced by government interest in arts organization sustainability, as in many western countries the funding dollar is being spread across more nonprofit arts organizations and those organizations are being asked to find a greater amount of money by means other than direct government grants.

The important feature of relationship marketing, according to Petkus (2004), is its memorability in experience-based consumption. This point links relationship marketing to authenticity. Following Cohen (1988) Leigh *et al.* (2006) situate authenticity as a personalized and experiential phenomenon for consumers. We call it evoked authenticity after Prentice (2001). They call it existential authenticity. With particular relevance to the performing arts, Leigh *et al.* outline Wang's (1999) evoked authenticity as 'activity based', arguing that it shares important links with Urry's (1991) proposition that, for postmodern consumers, the 'staged experience' represents the most authentic experience, as they recognize that authenticity now only *appropriates* a sense of reality.

Leigh *et al.* summarize Urry's evoked authenticity as follows (but name it existential authenticity, as explained above):

> Existential authenticity is activity driven and coincides with postmodern consumers' quest for pleasure and fun. This form of authenticity involves personal or subjective feelings activated by the liminal process of activities [. . .] In such liminal experiences, consumers feel more able to express and be true to themselves than in everyday life.
>
> (Leigh *et al.* 2006: 483)

According to the authors, consumers' desire for authenticity stems from a drive for self-actualization, self-creation and self-realization: 'Hence, in the context of existential authenticity, individuals feel they are in touch both with a "real" world and with their "real" selves.'

This is further emphasized in the work of Lewis and Bridger (2001) who described the process of consumer need for self-actualization and quest for authenticity. They used four elements of the new consumers – individualistic, involved, independent and informed – to build a new model of authentic loyalty based on authenticity. Authenticity is defined as a product or service considered authentic if it can be trusted to do what is claimed for it (Lewis and Bridger 2001: 194). Importantly they described the personalization of authenticity arising out of each individual's personal experience and response. 'One cannot mass produce authenticity. Rather, it has to be introduced on an almost person-to-person basis, with individual needs, desires, expectations and interests being fully accounted for' (Lewis and Bridger 2001:

194). Audiences are consumers, and arts audiences clearly represent Lewis and Bridger's 'new consumer'. They have moved up Maslow's pyramid of human needs, seeking personal fulfilment in artistic experiences. They are intent on closing the gap between the person they are (the real self), and the person they want to be (the ideal self). This self-actualization is the outcome of the quest for authenticity. Lewis and Bridger claim that if the producer can meet the needs of consumers with authentic experiences (products and services), then authentic loyalty is achieved, which transcends the pseudo-loyalty given by other consumers, easily tempted by better offers. The shift in the analysis of authenticity reflects a shift in focus from the authenticity of objects to the authenticity of subjects, and to the links between these two fields of relationship marketing and authenticity. This model of relationship marketing is proved in research for this chapter.

Critics argue that authentic experience is destroyed by staged experience, allowing audiences only to experience 'commodified culture' (MacCannell 1973). This argument has been echoed many times, particularly in the heritage and museums sector (e.g. Macdonald and Alsford 1995). It is often heard that museums are being 'Disneyfied', always used as a negative term to denote a staged authenticity which degrades the real purpose of museums that is to deal in the collection and exhibition of authentic objects. The performing arts parallel is manifested in unwelcome breaks from tradition, especially in relation to contemporary or abstract art breaking previous 'rules' of performance or painting. There have been particularly robust arguments on the authenticity of indigenous art, which has broken away from tradition and thus moved from anthropological object to high art, using ancient symbols but modern techniques (Myers 2002). These changes in relation to indigenous Australian art provide one example of more flexible interpretations of authenticity where it is appreciated that change can occur and objects can remain authentic, often through negotiation. This view is supported by research on tourism and authenticity (Higham and Hinch 2004). This view is consistent with Cohen's (2000) view that authenticity may be 'emergent', thus reflecting the gradual growth of authenticity through the eyes of the audience. Higham and Hinch (2004) give the example of Disneyland, used as a term so disparagingly in museums, becoming an 'emergent' form of authentic US culture. Museologists would be appalled to consider views on emergent authenticity as being paralleled in both indigenous art and in Disneyland!

With tourism initiatives encouraging the development of authentic experiences, with a shift in focus to the importance of marketing for artistic success, and with Disney-style theme shows and blockbusters overtaking subscription activity, the need to review arts organizations' approaches to building audience loyalty through evoked authenticity is urgent (Gill 1996; McLean 1995; Prentice 2001). Blockbuster entertainment shows have customer care and entertainment values at the forefront of their ethos, even if significant authors do not consider their entertainment as authentic. Arts organizations are competing with these events for the leisure dollar of their audiences, and while the leisure environment is expanding and developing, competition is also increasing (McLean 1995).

This chapter offers a perspective on relationship marketing for arts organizations which may be a solution to the issues identified above. Using qualitative and quantitative research methods, the authors surveyed over 500 audience members and held three discussion groups in Melbourne and four in Brisbane, Australia, in 2006. These interviews were in the performing arts, with audiences, artists, producers, curators, administrators and industry stakeholders, such as consulates and government representatives. An overview of the results discussed below highlights strategies identified from the research in the field.

Research from the field

Arts organizations, such as orchestras, performing-arts centres and small performing companies, are facing financial pressures threatening their survival. This is a worldwide phenomenon. For example, performing arts centres cannot be sustained as venues for hire and are seeking to reinvent themselves to counter competition in the environment from other entertainments, be that a day at a tennis grand slam, viewing a new film or walking in botanical gardens.

The usual response by nonprofit arts boards and managers is to bemoan reduced government funding, suggesting that this funding is a responsibility of government for the purpose of maintaining the cultural integrity of the community. They also point to declining audiences as the traditional arts audience is ageing. But the marketing strategies adopted are usually flexible subscription packages, partnerships with non-classical music groups and non-traditional performers to attract new and younger audiences, and sending a reduced company on tour to attract regional audiences. None of these recognize the demands of the new consumer for authenticity and closer engagement. Our research outlines four significant challenges facing performing-arts organizations in the twenty-first century. It demonstrates how these challenges can be resolved through an enlightened approach to relationship marketing.

The four challenges are the reconfiguration of repertoire, competition from cinema and stadium rock concerts, technology-driven distribution channels, and the need for commercial business models based on new approaches to marketing.

The first is the challenge of repertoire. In the nineteenth century, access to concerts by a professional orchestra was very limited for most people (Philip 2004). It was highly unusual to have the opportunity to hear a work more than a few times in one person's lifetime. Thus the repertoire was not well known by most people. This pattern changed with the growth of classical recordings, especially during the second half of the twentieth century. In these early years of the twenty-first century, audiences are faced with the opposite problem, a well-known but tired and overexposed repertoire, with many of the great works available in hundreds of versions. This homogeneity of interpretation is stultifying the artform and limiting musico-logical development. As performing-arts audiences get older, there has been a decline in attendance numbers (Kotler and Scheff 1997; Kolb 2001). The temptation therefore is to offer an ageing audience the product they want, and to increase attendance in a minor way from this same demographic segment. Similar patterns of change and development have necessitated new ways of working in other performing-arts areas such as theatre, ballet and the venues themselves. Theatre companies present modern and challenging interpretations of classical works, modern dance companies partner with classical ballet companies and share choreographers and repertoire. Venues are opening up concert halls and proscenium theatre spaces for alternative arts product and audiences.

This has made the marketing for performing-arts organizations increasingly difficult. One success in the classical repertoire has been the Australian opera ensemble the *Ten Tenors* and the Italian *Il Divo* which have focused on the attractiveness of the tenor singer, by investigating and testing ways of changing and reconfiguring the repertoire, while maintaining the essence of the tenor voice.

This leads to the second challenge: new competition. This performing-arts audience dilemma has taken place at a time when competition from other 'art' forms has been fierce: the large movie screen, the stadium rock concert, or both combined, can often give an audience a high-quality experience with musical substance. The didactic approach of the custodians of the orchestral and ballet tradition, for example, has resulted in a culture that is highly demanding of an audience. Incomprehensible scores, stark listening conditions and strict behaviour rules

245

entice too few to make the experience viable economically. This does not mean that the only solution is to commercialize classical music or other performing arts as entertainment, but rather to seek multiple and nuanced solutions which will surprise and enthuse live and mediated audiences. The *Ten Tenors* international success derives from enveloping the new repertoire, presentation and distribution with a comprehensive audience development strategy (Arthurs 2004).

The third challenge is technology, which has opened up new possibilities in all areas of art and entertainment. It enables more spectacular events to reach more people while paradoxically producing work that can be more customized to individuals. In 2007 music can be broadcast to the world, yet pressed as small runs of CDs to suit a particular audience. It is anticipated that creative technological solutions to presentational modes will be fully embraced. This includes looking to other artform successes, such as film, where enveloping the audience in an immersive environment has proved irresistible (Arthurs and Vella 2003). Further innovative uses of technology, such as the use of projected live, recorded, preprogrammed and interactive images around the space and fully spatialized 3D audio will impact on music performance. There is also room for more theatrical experiences using technology, with better staging, lighting and stagecraft in both live and DVD environments (Arthurs and Vella 2000).

The fourth challenge is the development of new business models. New solutions need to be explored if the artform is to survive, artistically and economically. Research on cultural sustainability and productivity in the arts shows that sustainability is the point where the artistic effort is sufficiently supported by audiences such that the arts organization or artform is sustained for the next generation (Radbourne 2003). The challenge of globalization is a positive in terms of sustainability. The potential audience for performing arts has increased through the ability to distribute across the world. But it cannot be done merely by using the old product development and product extension models. Further research is required to investigate ways of presentation, direction of repertoire, medium of distribution, social patterns and future audience needs, including what is happening globally (Harding and Robinson 1999). Global markets themselves pose challenges for relationship marketing.

Case study 1: new audiences for new orchestras

As a process of developing a new orchestral model for the twenty-first century that embraced these four challenges, a test orchestra called Deep Blue was created. The experiment in Brisbane, Australia, explored new product development models in music which link the development of new repertoire in a responsive strategy to expressed audience needs and desires, guaranteeing a sustainable product. Deep Blue presented an eclectic selection of existing works and new compositions with projected visual images, player involvement and audience involvement, no conductor, no music stands and a shared performance and audience space.

Primary research through focus groups with the audience and the Deep Blue musicians, and through an audience survey, showed that the audience enjoyed the interaction between the performers and themselves, positively describing the experience of no barriers, the live enthusiasm, the feeling of engagement and stretching the boundaries of their relationship with music. The performance mirrored the changes and challenges of life in the early twenty-first century. Participants talked about the animation of the musicians generating energy, and the appeal of the physical staging. However, the audience felt that the repertoire in the test orchestra was not innovative, as it included familiar elements of classical repertoire and rock performances. The survey revealed that music is a personal experience provoking an emotional experience, yet participated in with friends. This audience claimed that they would not buy a

CD of the performance, but that the venue, ambience and audience behaviour were strong contributors to the experience.

The Deep Blue musicians enjoyed the freedom, innovation, diversity and audience inter-activity of this orchestral performance model. They wanted to be able to share intellectually, emotionally and physically with the audience, as the response factor was needed for their best performance. They revealed a lack of interaction with the other performers which was necessary to heighten their interaction with the audience. The musicians also wanted some ownership of, and involvement in, the production process. This calls for new thinking on the issues of intellectual property and content development. The findings from this early research pointed to some form of connectivity as critical to a new orchestral model.

Further audience research using the same survey questions and focus group questions was conducted with orchestral concert performances by the established Queensland Orchestra (TQO) in their classic 'Maestro' concert series presented in the state's major concert hall, and in the early evening contemporary music series (sci-fi) presented at the city hall. There is an important difference between the TQO concert audiences and the Deep Blue audience in regard to their preferred style of music. While the Deep Blue audience had classical music as the highest selection, there was also a large number of people preferring jazz and rock music, while the TQO audiences predominantly preferred classical music. This shows that a choice of polystylistic music repertoire would be more of a success in a Deep Blue concert than in a TQO concert, given their different target audiences.

In all concerts, the musicians or performers were considered the best element of the per-formance. This indicates that irrespective of the different audience demographics, it was important for people to connect and engage with the performing artists. In fact, the TQO concerts had a higher percentage than the Deep Blue concert, which shows that traditional classical audiences still need to relate to the performers and this supports the attraction of attending a live event. If classical musicians were able to demonstrate a greater connection with their audience, rather than being hidden behind their music stands, this may help to increase audience numbers. This is also supported by the high popularity of well-known musicians/soloists and their ability to attract an audience. The fact that the Deep Blue concert did not score higher in this area is disappointing, as the role of the musicians was one of the main elements promoted in this concert.

Buying a CD/DVD of the performance was not a very high priority for the audiences of all concerts, highlighting that attending a live performance provides more of an 'experience'. The data showed that the importance of context (venue, ambience, behaviour of audience) on the meaning of a performance was high for all the concerts, and can contribute to building loyalty for performances, orchestral or otherwise. Audiences attend concerts not just for the music, but for the holistic experience. There was a good response for all concerts concerning performer and audience interaction, supporting the need by audiences for authenticity and involvement. In fact, the Maestro audience scored highest for this question, indicating that interaction can be more fully developed for a traditional audience, as well as for the Deep Blue-style concert.

The influence of the audience's social network was demonstrated by the way people find out about a concert and also in the way they attend a concert. Data suggested that the information need of the new performing arts consumer can be captured in the shared experience. Attending the concert with friends was the most popular way for all concert audiences and this informa-tion can be used to build relationship-marketing strategies.

One of the highest-rating questions was in relation to the role of the audience. Most partici-pants indicated that they were an 'emotional listener'. Although all the concert repertoire, venues and productions were quite different, it appears that an emotional connection was

Table 14.1   Orchestral audience responses to experiential authenticity

Question	Maestro concert $n = 45$	Deep Blue concert $n = 220$	Sci-Fi concert $n = 24$
Role of the audience in a musical performance nominated 'emotional listener'.	73.8%	64%	77%
A musical performance evokes an emotional response in the audience (mean score on scale 1–5).	4.49	4.05	4.41

established with the audience, irrespective of the style of music and performance. Self-actualization was therefore common for all music attendees. Respondents were asked to nominate the role of the audience in a musical performance from a list of six roles: spectator, emotional listener, passive listener, co-producer, active participant, or other. The highest response for every concert, that is, type of orchestral performance surveyed, was 'emotional listener'. Question 10 in the survey presented a series of statements with which respondents rated their agreement, from strongly disagree to strongly agree. Statements covered the use of visual images in the performance, the influence of a person's musical background and experience, pre-performance information, the venue and ambience, the emotional response of the audience, and the interaction between audience and performers. The emotional response statement received significantly higher agreement than all the others (see Table 14.1)

These responses have been selected for this research because they directly explore authenticity. Musical preference, repertoire, age, education or occupation had no significant influence on responses.

Overall, all the concerts were a success based on the response that most participants would come again to such a performance. This suggests that all the concerts were correctly targeted for their respective audiences. A conclusion that can be drawn from this data is that different audience demographics provide niche markets with different expectations for authenticity. Relationship-marketing strategies which reflect this are most likely to sustain audiences and the company.

Case study 2: new and diverse audiences for traditional venues

A second case which embraced the four challenges is the creation of Mix It Up at the Arts Centre in Melbourne, Australia, in 2006, a partnership in creating new repertoire and new and diverse audiences with Multicultural Arts Victoria. Mix It Up was a diversified programme of local, national and international artists (800 in total) from 23 nationalities over 96 events. It attracted 160,000 visitors to the Arts Centre – 47,000 to major events plus a further 113,000 to the free exhibition Meeting Place Keeping Place. The innovative and successful repertoire led to two state government awards for leadership in public programmes and excellence in multicultural affairs. The research project that led to this case study was funded by the Australia Council for the Arts, the federal government's arts funding and advisory body. The strategy entailed seeking to meet audience needs through both product and audience development, guaranteeing a new approach for an organization which was seeking to diversify its activities (Rentschler 2006).

Research entailed interviews, focus groups and surveys with the musicians, artists, curators, administrators, wider stakeholders and audiences. Results showed that the audiences enjoyed the participation in the events and performances, the freedom to dance in theatres where seats had been removed for this purpose and the representation of ethnic foods and wares in theatre foyers, things that had never been done before in the Arts Centre. Audiences positively described the sense of 'theatre coming alive' and 'rocking' to the music, breaking boundaries from the traditions of quiet audiences sitting in seats and clapping politely. Performances paralleled the changed tempo of life in the twenty-first century. Artists and other musicians talked about the enthusiasm, the full houses and the energy of the performances. Curators talked about the risks taken and the successes achieved: 'the Arts Centre took a risk and I bless them for it' said a music programme curator. Another said: 'it [Mix It Up] brought a lot of young people into the Arts Centre who had never been before and that was a huge success.'

Mix It Up enabled international and local artists in diverse performance programmes to engage and excite new audiences and regular visitors alike. The programme was an organic, participatory learning experience for people from the Arts Centre and Multicultural Arts Victoria, their communities and stakeholders that addressed the need to confront competition in the performing arts.

In all performances and exhibitions, Mix It Up demonstrated the need to move beyond traditional methods and marketing channels to draw ethnic and minority audiences to the Arts Centre. Once there, audiences were delighted by experiencing the high-quality venues and production and the innovations used by the performers to entertain them. People commented on the connections made between performers and audience, irrespective of audience segment surveyed, illustrating the importance of connectivity with audience for authentic experiences.

Global markets themselves pose challenges for relationship marketing. This was certainly the case with Mix It Up. New ways of working and new marketing models emerged from the project by moving beyond the traditional channels used to market events, thus drawing in new audiences. As an administrator at the Arts Centre stated: 'What we were agile enough to do in particular in the music was fairly quickly understand that the sort of marketing strategies that we had in place weren't going to work for this market.' Consequently, the large institution of the Arts Centre interacted with loosely assembled 'business' networks, linked by strategic alliances between partners. Expressed another way, the core institution was surrounded by satellite units to which functions were outsourced. Such arrangements allow small creatives to benefit from the superior management know-how of large institutions and conversely, large institutions to benefit from the flexibility and entrepreneurship of small creatives. The large institution has access to greater capital investment and distribution to mainstream markets. The small creatives have access to new ideas and grass-root networks, useful for a new type of street marketing.

One of the questions in the research asked audience members to rate their emotional response to performances attended. Interestingly, the emotional connection with the performances was significantly higher for the Mix It Up performances than for other Arts Centre performances. A challenging audience development argument is that it is about removing barriers to attendance to create audiences of the future. Creating an authentic experience to which people respond emotionally is part of meeting that challenge. The concerts, foyer entertainment and exhibition were unique in content and approach for Arts Centre events. Irrespective of whether the performance was from Africa, Brazil or Taiwan, or the style of performance, self-actualization through 'exhilaration' was approximated through Mix It Up events. Participants were asked to nominate how exhilarated they were at the events on a five-point scale (see Figure 14.1).

The graph shows that 82 per cent of audiences for the total performances were 'very' or 'somewhat' exhilarated on a five-point scale. The Canadian circus-cum-physical performance event, 7 Fingers, had audiences significantly more likely to have been left feeling very exhilarated (69 per cent), while Vive La Fiesta (26 per cent) and Cariba (22 per cent) audiences

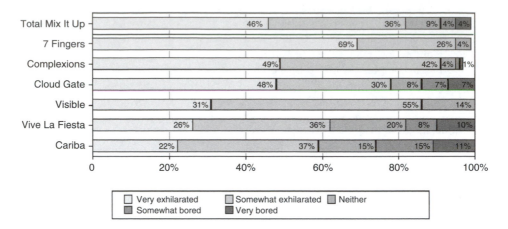

Figure 14.1 How did the performance make them feel?

had a lower propensity to have provided this rating. Indeed, audiences for Vive La Fiesta reported higher levels of feeling neither exhilarated nor bored (20 per cent) and somewhat or very bored (18 per cent). Feelings are very strongly linked with the impact that the performance had on audiences – those left feeling very exhilarated significantly more likely to consider the performance authentic overall. Of interest, females had a higher propensity than males to indicate they felt very exhilarated (51 per cent versus 37 per cent).

It was shown that the importance of context (venue, ambience, behaviour of audience) on the meaning of a performance was high for all the concerts, so this is an element that needs to be considered when judging authenticity of performances by audiences. Audiences attend performances not just for the music or acrobatics, but for the holistic experience. There was a strong response for all performances concerning performer and audience interaction, given the lively and engaging events that took place in the Arts Centre foyers, removing barriers between audience and performer, leading to rowdy, fun interaction between the two groups. Audience members surveyed said that the foyer 'rocked'. This supports the need by audiences for authenticity and involvement.

Overall, Mix It Up was a resounding success with a new round of performances planned for 2007. The results suggest that the performances were correctly pitched for the audiences targeted. Conclusions drawn from this case study suggest that different levels of involvement engage audiences to different levels of authenticity at different performances. Relationship-marketing strategies that reflect these differences are more likely to be successful with such a complex programme testing new ground.

Conclusions and implications

What has emerged from the research is that audiences are demanding, but discerning, and prepared to take risks if they can be involved. They want to participate and be free to express their engagement. They value creativity, innovation and the new technologies. But they want new repertoire and new musical and sensory experiences. They do not want to be removed from the production process. This directly represents Lewis and Bridger's definition of

Table 14.2 Model of relationship marketing in arts organizations

Inputs	Relationships	Outputs	Outcomes
Audience needs →	Immersive → Participation	Spiritual Emotional fulfilment	→ Audience retention Loyalty
Artists' needs →	Engagement → Connectivity	Artistic fulfilment New roles and responsibility	→ Sustainability of the arts

authenticity: the desire to be involved in the process of production and consumption, wanting their own individual experience, making the decision to engage independently, and seeking information when making the decision to attend. The search for authenticity is a search for an original, unique and personal experience, that fulfils a spiritual quest for actualization which is the 'emotional response' role attributed to and by the audience.

The authors propose the following new definition of authenticity in relationship marketing as it applies to the arts. Authenticity in arts marketing is the evoked experience of each audience member engaged by artists and arts marketers to enable self-actualization.

Relationship marketing can influence sustainability if the audience is at the core of the production model. Audiences should not be removed from the development process. Musicians, actors, dancers and the other creative artists (director, composer, conductor, sound technician, lighting technician, film and image maker, projectionist, editor) are at once producers and consumers, and are also core to the business model. The research with models of twenty-first-century performance has established that without audience and performer connectivity, the performance does not work, nor is content created. Likewise, the distribution is multidimensional, serving a multidimensional space inhabited by multidimensional consumers.

A new model of relationship marketing in the arts is based on the flow of inputs and outputs for an outcome of audience retention. This new model of relationship marketing is not a simple loyalty ladder. It requires effort in the relationship-building to create the conditions for evoked authenticity. The effort requires immersive participation in the production and consumption of the performing-art event, as well as engagement bringing fulfilment to artists. Satisfying both needs provides the outcome of audience loyalty and artistic sustainability.

Acknowledgements

The authors thank the Australian Research Council, as well as the Victorian Arts Centre, the Australia Council and Multicultural Arts Victoria for their support of these two important projects. Without their support, these valuable studies could not have been conducted.

References

Arthurs, A. (2004) (producer/composer) *Larger Than Life, The Ten Tenors*, CD/DVD, USA and Germany: Warners.
—— and Vella, R. (2000) *Musical Environments*, Sydney: Currency Press.
—— — (2003) *Sounds in Space, Sounds in Time*, London and New York, NY: Boosey and Hawkes.
Chong, D. (2005) 'Stakeholder relationships in the market for contemporary art', in I. Robertson (ed.) *Understanding International Art Markets and Management*, London: Routledge, pp. 84–102.

251

Cohen, E. (1988) 'Authenticity and the commoditization of tourism', *Annals of Tourism Research*, 15:371–86.

—— (2000) 'A phenomenology of tourist experiences', in Y. Apostolopoulos, S. Leivadi and A. Yiannakis, London: Routledge, pp. 179–99.

Garbarino, E. and Johnson, M. (1999) 'The different roles of satisfaction, trust and commitment in customer relationships', *Journal of Marketing*, April: 70–87.

Gill, R. (1996) 'VSO reaches out to a younger audience', *The Age*, 21 June: A15.

Harding, A. and Robinson, M. (1999) *Forecasting the Characteristics of Consumers in 2010*, University of Canberra, Australia: National Centre for Social and Economic Modelling.

Higham, J. and Hinch, T. (2004) *Sport Tourism Development*, Clevedon: Channel View.

Jackson, S., Batty, R. and Scherer, J. (2001) 'Translational sport marketing at the global/local nexus: The Adidasification of the New Zealand All Blacks', *International Journal of Sports Marketing and Sponsorship* 3(2):185 (17).

Kolb, B. (2001) 'The decline of the subscriber base: A study of the Philharmonia Orchestra Audience', *International Journal of Arts Management*, 3(2):51–9.

Kotler, P. and Scheff, J. (1997) *Standing Room Only: Strategies for Marketing the Performing Arts*, Boston, MA: Harvard Business School Press.

Leigh, T. W., Peters, C. and Shelton, J. (2006) 'The consumer quest for authenticity: The multiplicity of meanings within the MG subculture of consumption' *Journal of the Academy of Marketing Science*, 34(4):481–93.

Lewis, D. and Bridger, D. (2001) *The Soul of the New Consumer*, London: Nicholas Brealey Publishing.

MacCannell, D. (1973) 'Staged authenticity arrangements of social space in tourist settings', *American Journal of Sociology*, 79(3):589–603.

Macdonald, G. F. and Alsford, S. (1995) 'Museums and theme parks: Worlds in collision?', *Museum Management and Curatorship*, 14:129–47.

McLean, F. (1995) 'Future directions for marketing in museums', *European Journal of Cultural Policy*, 1(2):355–68.

Myers, F. R. (2002) *Painting Culture*, USA: DUP.

Petkus, E. Jr. (2004) 'Enhancing the application of experiential marketing in the arts', *International Journal of Nonprofit and Voluntary Sector Marketing*, 9(1):49–56.

Philip, R. (2004) *Performing Music in the Age of Recording*, New Haven and London: Yale University Press.

Prentice, R. (2001) 'Experiential cultural tourism: Museums and the marketing of the new romanticism of evoked authenticity', *Museum Management and Curatorship*, 19(1):5–26.

Radbourne, J. (2003), 'Regional development through the enterprise of arts leadership', *Journal of Arts Management, Law and Society*, 33(3):211–27.

Rentschler, R. (2006) *Mix It Up Project Report: Working in New Ways*, Deakin University, Melbourne: Evaluation report for the Australia Council for the Arts.

—— Radbourne, J., Carr, R. and Rickard, J. (2002) 'Relationship marketing and performing arts organization viability', *International Journal of Nonprofit and Public Sector Marketing*, 7(2):118–30.

Shirastava, S. and Kale, S. H. (2003) 'Philosophizing on the elusiveness of relationship marketing theory in consumer markets: A case for reassessing ontological and epistemological assumptions', *Australasian Marketing Journal*, 11(3):61–71.

Urry, J. (1991) *The Tourist Gaze: Leisure and Travel in Contemporary Societies*, London: Sage Publications.

Walker-Kuhne, D. (2005) *Invitation to the Party: Building Bridges to the Arts, Culture and Community Theater*, New York: Communications Group.

Wang, N. (1999) 'Rethinking authenticity in tourism experience', *Annals of Tourism Research*, 26(2):349–70.

Part 4

Education marketing

15

Applying the marketing concept in higher education

A stakeholder approach

Mei-Na Liao

Introduction

During the past four decades, there has been a constant move from an elite system to a mass system in the higher-education (HE) sector in developed countries, in particular, the UK and the USA (Bargh *et al.* 1996; Bekhadnia 2001; Dearing 1997; Thomas 2001). Compounded by a decrease in government funding (per student), this movement has created an increasingly competitive environment for higher-education institutions (HEIs). Consequently, these institutions are now placing far greater emphasis on marketing. Marketing activities have become important within universities, and many authors now write widely about the application of marketing techniques in the HE sector. However, the application of the marketing concept *per se* in HE received little attention, and it remains an area of challenge (Brookes 2003; Maringe 2005; Sargeant 2004). The extant literature tends to adopt the market orientation construct, which was developed within large multinational organizations, as the operationalization of the marketing concept for all sectors. However, many authors in nonprofit marketing have questioned the appropriateness of this approach, in terms of its terminology and its components (Frerris 2002; Liao *et al.* 2001; Maringe 2005; Sargeant *et al.* 2002; Siu and Wilson 1998). Furthermore, as it is argued in this chapter, if universities strictly apply market orientation, it could compromise their societal role and charitable status. The subsequent parts of this chapter provide an overview of the extant studies on marketing in HE, review literature on the development of the operationalization of the marketing concept, critically evaluate the adoption of market orientation in HEIs and identify the main issues faced, propose a societal orientation model and discuss the implications for the implementation of the societal orientation construct. The model was developed from my earlier works with Adrian Sargeant (Liao *et al.* 2001; Sargeant *et al.* 2002) on nonprofit organizations. Because most of the HEIs are essentially nonprofit organisations, the societal orientation model would fit the HEIs better than other for-profit models, such as customer orientation and market orientation models.

Marketing in HE

Marketing is becoming one of the main operational activities within universities. Most universities now have a marketing director and/or an independent marketing department, rather than or in addition to a recruitment officer/department. Marketing issues are now well cited in education management journals, such as the *International Journal of Education Management* and the *Journal of Educational Administration*. Indeed, the adoption of marketing techniques in HEIs is not a new phenomenon. Kotler and Levy (1969) were the first to argue the relevance of the marketing concept to nonprofit organizations, which include most educational institutions. Since then many authors have written widely on the application of marketing HEIs (e.g. Heist 1995; Kotler 1976; Kotler and Fox 1995; Sargeant 2004; Sargeant and Liao 2000). In particular, much of the literature has focused on one of the following areas: student recruitment and decision-making (Cubillo *et al.* 2006; Maringe 2006); student retention and relationship management (Armstrong 2003; Farr 2003; Klayton 1993; Seeman and O'Hara 2006;); marketing mix in HE (Bingham 1987; Stewart 1991); international education marketing (Cubillo *et al.* 2006; Hemsley-Brown and Oplatka 2006; Mazzarol *et al.* 2003); marketing strategy, segmentation and positioning in HE (Bakewell and Gibson-Sweet 1998; Maringe 2006; Trim 2003); students' corporate brand identification (Balmer and Liao 2006); or student satisfaction and services quality (Abdullah 2006; Adee 1997; Ivy 2001; Mai 2005). Despite the extended interests of HE marketing demonstrated in the literature, the application of the marketing concept per se in HE has received little attention (Brookes 2003; Maringe 2005; Sargeant 2004).

There is a consensus in the literature that market orientation represents the operationalization of the marketing concept and indeed some authors adopted the market orientation construct to represent the operationalization of this business philosophy in the HE sector. However, this approach has been criticized for its inadequate representation of the reality and for providing limited guidance for implementation (see e.g. Liao *et al.* 2001; Maringe 2005; Sageant *et al.* 2002). Indeed, Maringe (2005) points out that HE marketing has not adequately domesticated itself and continues to rely on imported wisdom from the business sector, which in turn has contributed to the resistance of marketing practices among academic staff in the HE sector.

Market orientation

The early works on the operationalization of the marketing concept were instructive and normative in nature; they were largely reports of consultants' and practitioners' personal experience (Felton 1959; Keith 1960). For example, based on his professional experience at Pillsbury, Keith (1960) illustrated the evolution of the marketing concept, from product orientation, to sales orientation, to marketing orientation, and finally to marketing control (which subsequent literature referred to as market orientation, in terms of achieving an integrated marketing company). The subsequent works considered the philosophy of marketing and developed descriptive accounts of how to achieve a market orientation (McNamara 1972), delineate the benefits of achieving it (Viebranz 1967), broaden its scope (Kotler and Levy 1969), define its boundaries (Houston 1986; Levitt 1969), or focus primarily on implementation issues (Felton 1959). Kohli and Jaworski (1990) and Narver and Slater (1990) were among the first to develop empirically the market orientation construct, that is, to operationalize the marketing concept.

Over the many years of debate on the meaning and scope of market orientation, there has been considerable confusion in terms of both the components, its construct and the terminology that should be used (Shapiro 1988). Indeed, many different terms have been used in the literature for what is essentially the same concept, namely, market driven, customer driven, market led, customer led, customer orientation, marketing orientation and market orientation (Chang and Chen 1993; Kohli and Jaworski 1990; Shapiro 1988; Webster 1994). There is now a consensus in the literature that the term 'market orientation' is preferred to denote the implementation of the marketing concept.

Given these discrepancies, it is perhaps not surprising that a variety of different meanings have been attributed to the construct (Kohli *et al.* 1993). These include involving marketing executives in strategic decisions (Felton 1959; McNamara 1972), emphasizing customer concerns over those of the production function (Konopa and Calabro 1971), integrating activities within the marketing function (Felton 1959; McNamara 1972), and determining the extent to which marketing can be afforded a leadership role (Viebranz 1967). Among these, the literature has particularly emphasized the necessity for organizations to adopt a focus on their customers (Levitt 1969; Piercy 1997) if they are to survive in the long run. Piercy (1997) provides several practical insights into how this might be accomplished. A variation on this theme that emphasizes the importance of the interaction with the customer emerged from the services marketing literature (Grönroos 1981), and from the theory of relationship marketing (Gummesson 1987). It has been argued that, particularly in services contexts, the role of the employee is paramount. In cases in which production and consumption occur simultaneously, the employee is the service, and therefore the development of a 'customer consciousness' among staff is essential (Grönroos 1981).

In addition to the dimensions of customer and employee orientations, Kohli *et al.* (1993) note that other relatively consistent themes emerged from the literature. These include coordinated marketing and a focus on profitability. Indeed, these critical dimensions have been reflected in more recent definitions of the market orientation construct. For example, Kohli and Jaworski (1990) emphasize the activities on which organizations should focus, namely, organization–wide generation and dissemination of market intelligence pertaining to current and future customer needs, and organization–wide responsiveness to it. In contrast, Narver and Slater (1990: 21) define market orientation as '[t]he organization culture that most effectively and efficiently creates the necessary behaviors for the creation of superior value for buyers and, thus, continuous superior performance for the business'. The authors considered several behavioural dimensions, including a cultural perspective (see also Deshpandé *et al.* 1993), and assumed the view that specific activities (e.g. intelligence generation) are a product of market orientation, rather than market orientation per se. They viewed market orientation as being composed of customer orientation, competitor orientation and interfunctional coordination and developed a set of measurement items to capture each dimension.

However, both sets of authors agreed that market orientation should be regarded as a multidimensional organizational phenomenon, in which each dimension represents a different feature of market orientation. To date, the empirical studies have been based on the extent or degree to which market orientation attained by companies has been measured as an overall average of these various dimensions. Much of the subsequent research conducted in this field has mirrored one or the other conceptualization of the construct (see e.g. Caruana *et al.* 1998; Deng and Dart 1994; Deshpandé *et al.* 1993; Greenley 1995).

Nonprofit market orientation

Many studies have examined the extent to which the market orientation construct might have relevance for nonprofit organizations. The findings show an overwhelming body of evidence to support the significance of the construct but, more importantly, point out that some adaptations may be required. For example, Siu and Wilson (1998) argue that to apply market orientation to the setting of further education colleges, it is necessary to drop the concepts of profit and competition and to replace them with what authors refer to as 'employ orientation' and a 'long term survival requirement'. Stewart (1991) illustrates market orientation through the management of the marketing mix in the universities examined and concludes that this construct enables institutions to attract and retain students (see also Berry and Allen 1977; Blackburn 1980; Kotler 1976; Kotler and Fox 1995). However, the marketing-mix construct represents only the functional elements of the marketing concept but it neglects the philosophical aspect of the concept, which market orientation represents (Grönroos 1989; Gummesson 1987). Caruana et al. (1998) apply the abridged market orientation instrument (MARKOR) to the public and university sectors and find a positive relationship between the level of market orientation and the various measures of performance they adopted. In a study of market orientation in healthcare, Hayden (1993) distinguishes between customers and con-sumers and examines the organization's orientation towards both. Also in the healthcare sector, George and Compton (1985) emphasize the role of personnel in the context studied and include this dimension in their definition of the construct.

These studies perceived the construct of market orientation as the embodiment of the marketing concept for all sectors regardless of their specific context and thus they have the predisposition to overlook the development of the concept itself. Kotler and Levy (1969: 7) define the marketing concept quite differently when they apply it to the nonprofit sector. Thus, it would seem more appropriate to begin from such a definition – namely 'sensitively serving and satisfying human need' – and work from this to an appropriate measure of the extent to which a given organization embodies this philosophy. Sargeant et al. (2002) termed this a 'societal orientation'. It could also be argued that the terminology of market orientation developed from the for-profit context does not transfer unequivocally to the nonprofit context, because it implies an orientation towards markets. Although it could be argued that nonprofits have a market for resource acquisition and a market for resource allocation, these are often not true markets in the economic sense of the term. Indeed, as Hansmann (1980) notes, nonprofits can often be a response to a particular form of market failure. It has been argued that nonprofits are the most appropriate category of organization to supply goods and services under (certain) circumstances in which the market mechanism fails. It therefore seems clear that if nonprofits are a reasonable response to the breakdown of the discipline of the market, the term 'market' orientation is a misnomer.

The *components* of market orientation are also problematic in the nonprofit context. The consensus now emerging from the literature in respect to the importance of a customer focus was highlighted previously. In the nonprofit context, organizations are often less concerned with customer satisfaction per se, than they are with the notion of longer-term benefit to society. For example, arts organizations may also forgo customer satisfaction and elect to show particular forms of art, which they know will not appeal to the majority of their existing customers. They do so, however, because they believe that the promotion of such art forms will be good for society and worthwhile overall, even if a loss should result. Such organizations are actively engaged in the furtherance of their mission, often to the detriment of short-term customer satisfaction. In general, it is agreed that placing service users' needs in the centre of the concern when designing new services is important (Bruce 1998). However, although customer satisfaction is important, it is not the only consideration for nonprofit organizations.

Harding (1998: 35) points out that from the perspective of a 'non-distribution constraint', the focus on satisfying customers' needs and wants is not a logical goal. First, nonprofits are far from being able to serve customers well; this type of enterprise simply reduces the incentive to serve customers poorly. Second, nonprofits exist precisely because no one group's needs can be preferred. Third, a focus on the end user (e.g. customers, students) is not going to bring in all the incomes that a nonprofit organization needs. Therefore, nonprofits need to satisfy a much wider group of stakeholders than do commercial firms (Lovelock and Weinberg 1984).

Societal orientation in the HE context

In many countries, such as in the UK, HEIs are part of public services, as well as nonprofit organizations; thus, the sector as a whole must fulfil its societal role and provide equal access to HE for all socioeconomic groups (Dearing 1997). Therefore, the economic model cannot be applied unambiguously in the HE context for several reasons. First, HEIs provide education services that have a high level of credence value and are intangible in nature (i.e. students rely on universities to tell them what they need, and it can be difficult for them to obtain accurate comparison among competing offers). Second, the price of services is not entirely determined by the level of demand; for example, in the UK, the government sets a fixed upper-price limit (at the time of writing, the UK universities were allowed to charge students up to £3,000 for fees, which is called a top-up fee) and universities still rely heavily on government funding to subsidize the full cost required. As a result, universities at the top end have their pick of students, while less well-known universities struggle to fill up empty seats in many classes. The latter face the dilemma of whether to charge the top end of the fee. If a university decides to lower its tuition fee, it may give the impression that its programme is of low quality and value, but if it adopts the upper limit, it might not be able to fill its space and consequently might need to take students with lower grades (Baty 2001). Third, in many cases, agreements of service delivery (e.g. university policies, quality standards, regulations) are set by universities and quality-assurance bodies, not by students. Students can choose only to agree to the policy or to decide to withdraw from the university. Fourth, universities set admission criteria to select students according to their intellectual abilities, not their ability to pay a higher price. Indeed, many concerns are raised regarding the effect of 'marketization' in the HE sector on the equality of access to HE. Recently, the *Economist* (2006) cited the writings of Daniel Golden in the *Wall Street Journal* about the admissions practices of US elite universities, which suggested that they are not so much engines of social justice as bastions of privilege. Applying an economic model could mean the end of equal access to HE. Finally, students cannot insist on guarantees of service outcome, even if they are willing to pay an extra price. The outcome of the education services not only depends on universities, but also relies heavily on students' intellectual ability and the efforts made in their learning.

Furthermore, it might be argued that universities are being driven by their mission and value to fulfil societal needs rather than being market driven to satisfy customer needs. This can be clearly identified from most universities' mission statements, in which, to a certain extent, they all reflect their societal responsibilities and values. Two examples of mission statements from UK universities are as follows:

The University of Oxford aims to achieve and sustain excellence in every area of its teaching and research, maintaining and developing its historical position as a world-class university, and enriching the international, national and regional communities through the fruits of its research and the skills of its graduates.

(University of Oxford, 2006)

The University of Bristol is a world-class institution that contributes to society by advancing knowledge and developing creative graduates, and through its cultural, social, economic and environmental activities.

(University of Bristol, 2006)

These mission statements focus on creating, advancing and disseminating knowledge in order to benefit society as a whole, through the achievement of researches and their graduates and their interactions with the industry and society at large. It is clear that the term 'market orientation' is not appropriate in a context in which organizations exist for the betterment of society, as opposed to the generation of shareholder wealth. A societal orientation would seem more appropriate because it implies an organization's aim to satisfy societal needs rather than market needs.

The societal orientation construct

The societal orientation construct consists of four major components: stakeholder focus, competitor focus, collaborative focus and interfunctional coordination (Liao *et al.* 2001). These four components represent an HEI's focus of actions towards its environments, when it adopts the marketing concept. A university's efforts on these four dimensions will enhance its efficiency and effectiveness as a result (see Figure 15.1).

Stakeholder focus

Stakeholder theory was first mentioned by name in a Stanford Research Institute memorandum in 1963 (Freeman 1984). Since then, it has gained increasing use in strategy development literature (see e.g. Donaldson and Preston 1995; Freeman 1984). Much of this literature has suggested that stakeholder theory allows the organization to consider a wider range of influencers when developing strategy and that previous theories of the firm do not consider all the 'groups' that influence organizational activities. Freeman (1984: 46) defines a stakeholder in an organization as follows: '*A stakeholder in an organization is (by definition) any group or individual who can affect or is affected by the achievement of the organization's objective.*'

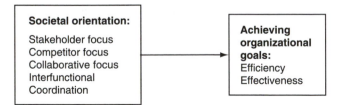

Figure 15.1 The societal orientation construct

Marketing authors, especially in the areas of social marketing and green marketing, have suggested that it is inadequate to focus only on customers and shareholders, and that a broader range of stakeholders should be considered (Polonsky 1995). Polonsky (1995) observes that to some extent, stakeholder theory has implicitly been a core component of marketing theory, since the development of modern marketing philosophy. The stakeholder concept comes into the marketing perspective by addressing the dynamics between the marketing function and the external environment, because it recognizes that an organization is dependent upon multiple publics (e.g. the government, consumers, employees, suppliers, the host community and the general public) for support (Kotler 1972). Lusch and Laczniak (1987) point out that the stakeholder concept is the continuance of an evolutionary marketing process and is the key to the management of an organization's relationships with its broader stakeholders.

As discussed previously, HEIs have a much wider group of stakeholders than a typical for-profit firm; thus, they are arguably the most logical type of organization to require a stakeholder approach in marketing. A review of the literature suggests that by applying a marketing concept, a firm is much more likely to understand the needs of various stakeholders in order to satisfy them most effectively. An emphasis on the collection and dissemination of stakeholder information is crucial in achieving organizations' goals (Kohli and Jaworski 1990). However, there are two fundamental questions that need to be addressed: (a) who are the organization's stakeholders?; (b) how should organizations prioritize their different needs should a conflict arise between them?

To assess properly the extent to which the marketing concept has been operationalized within an HE context, it would be necessary to examine the organization's orientation towards such groups as individual students, alumni, faculties, industry, research funders, local communities, local/national government and society in general.

Competitor focus versus collaboration focus

It is apparent that competition has become an inevitable trend in the HE sector. However, the term 'competitor orientation' implies a direct competitive relationship with other service providers in the sector. In reality, however, although universities compete for sources of finding and student recruitment, in many cases, HEIs collaborate among themselves. For example, the HE sector often collaborates with other nonprofits institutions in teaching, student exchange, student placement and in research. Indeed, one of the main purposes of an HE institution is knowledge-sharing, to make knowledge accessible to everyone. Universities' mission statements seldom encourage outperforming competitors; rather, they encourage excellence in teaching and/or research. The desire to attain excellence does not necessarily come from competitive pressure (as economic theories tend to suggest), but rather from the mission and value of the institution that drives the integrated efforts. Excellence cannot be achieved by being competitive alone; rather, it often requires effective and meaningful collaborations with other organizations. Therefore, to assess the extent to which the marketing concept has been operationalized within an HEI, it would be necessary to examine its attainment of competitive focus and collaborative focus.

Being competitive focused means a university is aware of the competition in its environment, including competitors' offering (i.e. other universities' course design, facilities and staff recruitment), strategies, student demands, industry employment requirements and academic preferences. The constant generation of marketing intelligence is now critical for universities. It is important to note that the quality standard of a university depends heavily on the quality of its faculty and students. Thus, the ability to attract high-quality academics and students is critical for maintaining university success. In many cases, universities will no longer be able to sustain both high standards of teaching and research (*The Times* 2006). There is now a scope and need for universities to differentiate themselves, to define their own institutional portfolio, and identify what they can do best to achieve their mission. A university needs to identify its position in the market and focus on its core business.

Collaborative focus is crucial to a university. Collaboration is an essential part a university's mission, as most activities in knowledge creation, advancement, dissemination and sharing require certain levels of collaboration with individuals and/or organizations. Being collaborative focused means a university is actively exploring opportunities for collaboration with other organizations for research, knowledge transfer and teaching. This includes encouraging and supporting its academic members to collaborate with other institutions for research and teaching and to participate in international conferences and forums. Universities have a responsibility to support and maintain scholarly communities. Furthermore, collaborative activities and research projects are rated highly by government research agencies when they consider funding. A collaborative focus is also important for enhancing student learning; for example, many international collaborative networks provide opportunities for students to explore international learning experiences, as well as scholarly collaboration for academics. When a university is part of these networks (e.g. Universitas 21, Worldwide University Network), it is often perceived as prestigious and a good-quality institution.

Interfunctional coordination

A consensus has emerged in the literature supporting the idea that interfunctional coordination is essential for an organization to achieve its goals (Kohli and Jaworski 1990). Indeed, Keith (1960) argued that the final stage of the evolution of the marketing concept is to achieve an integrated marketing organization in which each department within an organization co-ordinates to satisfy market needs. Narver and Slater (1990) include this element as one of their three behavioural components; they argue that the coordinated utilization of company resources enables a firm to create superior values for target customers. Siu and Wilson (1998) allude to this as organizational coordination and investigated it at three different levels of coordination (i.e. the individual level, intergroup level and infrastructure level). Interfunctional coordination is particularly supported in the services-marketing literature, in which the important role of individuals in marketing their organization is emphasized (Grönroos 1981; Gummesson 1991). The success of service delivery depends on an organization's ability to coordinate every department involved in the process. In HEIs, interfunctional coordination is paramount. Because HEIs are service organizations, every staff member and department have direct or indirect impact on students' experience of the service encounter. Furthermore, universities tend to have diverse departmental objectives (e.g. between research and teaching, between academic and administrative departments), which can cause conflicting interests and affect staff efficiency and working morale. The attainment of interfunctional coordination depends on the extent to which different university departments share a common goal and work together synergistically.

Societal orientation and HE performance

Since the 1950s, the link between the extent to which the marketing concept has been operationalized within an organization and its performance has attracted tremendous interest among researchers and practitioners. Most studies have taken the readily attainable financial criteria, such as profitability, turnover, market share and return on investment. Indeed, for a commercial company profitability is its bottom line, and any measure related to such would be considered germane. However, for a nonprofit HEI, assessing its performance is more complex than measuring profitability alone (Drucker 1990; Kanter and Summers 1987). Liao *et al.* (2002) argue that in a nonprofit context, in which the impact of a societal orientation on performance is assessed, it is desirable to consider both efficiency (in using its resources) and effectiveness (mission directiveness).

Further research

Marketing in the HE sector is relatively underdeveloped and would benefit from more academic attention on theory-building and empirical research. A direct departure from this chapter would be to test empirically the societal orientation model, derived from nonprofit literature, in HEIs and to establish an instrument for measuring the extent to which an HEI has implemented societal orientation. This would potentially verify the proposed model and provide more detailed implications for implementing societal orientation. Further research on universities' relationships with their various stakeholder groups, such as students, academics faculty, local business communities and residences, would also be fruitful. This coincides with the increasing importance of corporate social responsibility for HEIs in their changing environment.

Conclusion

To respond to the increasing competition in the environment, universities have begun to put more emphasis on their marketing activities. There has been an increasing interest in applying market orientation in the HE sector. The review of literature shows that market orientation developed from for-profit context is inadequate for implementation in nonprofit organizations, such as HEIs. Here it is argued that the terminology of market orientation is inappropriate, because it indicates a focus on market needs. If an HEI applies market orientation without adapting to the context, it could neglect its societal role. In addition to the limitation of the terminology, the components of the market orientation construct are not all suitable for application in the HE context. For example, the term 'customer focus' is a narrow and partial representation of the relationship between the university and the student. Thus, it could prevent a university from viewing its responsibility towards its students beyond the transactional relationship. By viewing students as customers, a university may fail in its educational responsibility to them (Frerris 2002) and lose the opportunity to build a strong brand affiliation among them, which in turn may cause it to lose the potential opportunities to benefit from such a unique, lifelong relationship (e.g. many US universities rely heavily on their alumni donations). Furthermore, as do most nonprofit organizations, universities have multiple constituencies with different interests and needs that must be addressed. It would be more appropriate to adopt a stakeholder approach when managing their multiple constituencies (Liao *et al.* 2001). Although universities must increasingly compete for students and fundings, it is also critical for them to collaborate with other organizations to fulfil their mission. Therefore to operationalize the marketing concept in this context, the societal role of the HE sector must be taken into account. The societal orientation model, which was developed from a nonprofit context, is more appropriate for the HE sector because it addresses contextual factors (Liao *et al.* 2001;

Sargeant *et al.* 2002). Herein, the four components of the societal orientation construct – namely, stakeholder focus, competitor focus, collaboration focus and interfunctional coordination – are discussed in relation to HEIs. In addition, directions for further research are identified.

References

Abdullah, F. (2006) 'Measuring service quality in higher education: HEdPERF versus SERVPERF', *Marketing Intelligence and Planning*, 4(1):31–48.
Adee, A. (1997) 'Linking student satisfaction and service quality perceptions: The case of university education,' *European Journal of Marketing*, 37(7):528.
Armstrong, M. J. (2003) 'Students as clients: A professional services model for business education', *Academy of Management Learning and Education*, 2(4):371–4.
Bakewell, C. J. and Gibson-Sweet, M. F. (1998) 'Strategic marketing in a changing environment: – Are the new UK universities in danger of being "Stuck in the Middle"?', *International Journal of Educational Management*, 12(3):108.
Balmer, J. M. T. and Liao, M. (2006) 'Issues of identification: Corporate brand/identity affinity among overseas-based students of Bradford University. An exploratory case study', 2nd Annual Colloquium: Academy of Marketing's Brand and Corporate Reputation SIG, 7–8 September.
Bargh, C., Scott, P. and Smith, D. (1996) *Governing Universities: Challenging the Culture*, Buckingham: SRHE and the Open University Press.
Baty, P. (2001) 'No A levels? No problem . . .', *Times Higher Education Supplement*, 7 September.
Bekhadnia, B. (2001) 'Widening participation and lifelong learning 2', keynote speech, Institute for Access Studies, Staffordshire University, 19 September.
Berry, L. L. and Allen, B. H. (1977) 'Marketing's crucial role for institutions of higher education', *Atlanta Economic Review*, 27:24–31.
Bingham, F. B. Jr. (1987) 'Distribution and its relevance to educational marketing efforts', *Journal of Professional Services Marketing*, 2(4):137–43.
Blackburn, J. C. (1980) 'Marketing and selective admissions', *National ACAC Journal*, 24:25–8.
Brookes, M. (2003) 'Higher education: Marketing in a quasi-commercial service industry', *International Journal of Nonprofit and Voluntary Sector Marketing*, 2(2): 134–42.
Bruce, I. (1998) *Marketing Need*, Hemel Hempstead: ICSA Publishing.
Caruana, A., Ramaseshan, B. and Ewing, M. T. (1998) 'The marketing orientation performance link: Some evidence from the public sector and universities', *Journal of Nonprofit and Public Sector Marketing*, 6(1): 63–82.
Chang, T. Z. and Chen, S. (1993) 'The impact of market orientation on total offering quality and business profitability', in Varadarajan, R. and Jaworski, B. (eds) *AMA Winter Educators' Conference: Marketing Theory and Applications*, vol. 4, Chicago: American Marketing Association.
Cubillo, J. M., Sánchez, J. and Cervino, J. (2006) 'International students' decision-making process', *International Journal of Educational Management*, 20(2): 101–15.
Dearing, R. (1997) 'Higher education in the learning society', UK: National Committee of Inquiry into Higher Education, Stationery Office.
Deng, S. and Dart, J. (1994) 'Measuring market orientation: A multifactor, multi-items approach', *Journal of Marketing Management*, 10:725–42.
Deshpandé, R., Farley, J. U. and Webster, F. E. Jr. (1993) 'Corporate culture, customer orientation and innovativeness in Japanese firms: A quadrad analysis', *Journal of Marketing*, 57 (January): 23–7.
Donaldson, T. and Preston, L. E. (1995) 'The stakeholder theory of the corporation: Concepts, evidence and implications', *Academy of Management Review*, 20:65–91.
Drucker, P. (1990) *Managing the Nonprofit Organisation*, Oxford: Butterworth-Heinemann.
Economist, the (2006) 'Poison ivy', 21 September.

Farr, M. (2003) ' "Extending" participation in higher education: Implications for marketing', *Journal of Targeting, Measurement and Analysis for Marketing*, 11(4):314–25.

Felton, A. P. (1959) 'Making the marketing concept work', *Harvard Business Review*, July–August:55–65.

Freeman, R. E. (1984) *Strategic Management: A Stakeholder Approach*, Boston, MA: Pitman.

Frerris, W. P. (2002) 'Students as junior partners, professors as senior partners and B-school as the firm: A new model for collegiate business education', *Academy of Management Learning and Education*, 1(2):185–93.

George, W. R. and Compton, F. (1985) 'How to initiate a marketing perspective in a health services organization', *Journal of Health Care Marketing*, 5(1):29–37.

Greenley, G. E. (1995) 'Forms of market orientation in UK companies', *Journal of Management Studies*, 32(1):47–66.

Grönroos, C. (1981) 'Internal marketing: An integral part of marketing theory', in Donnelly, J. H. and George W. R. (eds) *Marketing of Services*, Proceedings Series, Chicago: American Marketing Association, pp. 236–8.

—— (1989) 'Defining marketing: A market-oriented approach', *European Journal of Marketing*, 23(1):52–60.

Gummesson, E. (1987) 'The new marketing: Developing long-term interactive relationships', *Long Range Planning*, 20(4): 10–20.

Hansmann, H. B. (1980) 'The role of nonprofit enterprise,' *Yale Law Journal*, 89(April): 835–98.

Harding, S. (1998) 'The marketing orientation and nonprofits: The concept revisited', *Social Marketing Quarterly*, summer: 35–9.

Hayden, V. (1993) 'How to increase market orientation', *Journal of Management in Medicine*, 7(1):29–46.

Heist (1995) *The Role of Marketing in the University and College Sector*, Leeds: Heist.

Hemsley-Brown, J. and Oplatka, I. (2006) 'Universities in a competitive global marketplace: A systematic review of the literature on higher education marketing', *International Journal of Public Sector Management*, 19(4):316.

Houston, F. S. (1986) 'The marketing concept: What it is and what it is not', Journal *of Marketing*, 50(April): 81–7.

Ivy, J. (2001) 'Higher education institution image: A correspondence analysis approach', *International Journal of Educational Management*, 15(6/7): 276–82.

Kanter, R. M. and Summers, D. V. (1987) 'Doing well while doing good: Dilemmas of performance measurement in nonprofit organizations and the need for a multiple constituency approach', in Powell, W. W. (ed.) *The Nonprofit Sector*, Newhaven, CT: Yale University Press, pp. 55–64.

Keith, R. J. (1960) 'The marketing revolution', *Journal of Marketing*, 24(January): 35–8.

Klayton, M. A. (1993) 'Using marketing research to improve university programs', *Journal of Professional Services Marketing*, 9(1): 105–15.

Kohli, A. K. and Jaworski, B. J. (1990) 'Market orientation: The construct, research propositions and managerial implications', *Journal of Marketing*, 54(April): 1–18.

—— Jaworski, B. J. and Kumar, A. (1993) 'MARKOR: A measure of market orientation', *Journal of Marketing Research*, 57(November): 467–77.

Konopa, C. J. and Calabro, P. J. (1971) 'Adoption of the marketing concept by large northeastern Ohio manufacturers', *Akron Business and Economic Review*, 2:9–13.

Kotler, P. (1972) 'A generic concept of marketing', *Journal of Marketing*, 36(2):46–54.

—— (1976) 'Applying marketing theory to admissions', in *A Role For Marketing in College Admissions*, New York, NY: College Entrance Examination Board, pp. 54–72.

—— and Fox, K. (1995) *Strategic Marketing for Educational Institutions*, Englewood Cliffs, NJ: Prentice Hall.

—— and Levy, S. (1969) 'Broadening the concept of marketing', *Journal of Marketing*, 33(January): 10–15.

Levitt, T. (1969) *The Marketing Mode*, New York, NY: McGraw Hill.

Liao, M., Foreman, S. and Sargeant, A. (2001) 'Market versus societal orientation in the nonprofit context', *International Journal of Nonprofit and Voluntary Sector Marketing*, 6(3): 254–69.

Lovelock, C. H. and Weinberg, C. B. (1984) *Marketing for Public and Non-Profit Managers*, New York, NY: John Wiley.

Lusch, R. F. and Laczniak, G. R. (1987) 'The evolving marketing concept, competitive intensity and organizational performance', *Journal of the Academy of Marketing Science*, 15(3):1–11.

Mai, L. (2005) 'A comparative study between USA and UK: The student satisfaction in higher education and its influential factors', *Journal of Marketing Management*, 21(7):859.

Maringe, F. (2005) 'Interrogating the crisis in higher education marketing: The CORD model', *International Journal of Educational Management*, 16(6/7): 564–78.

—— (2006) 'University and course choice: Implications for positioning, recruitment and marketing', *International Journal of Educational Management*, 20(6):466.

Mazzarol, T., Soutar, G. N. and Seng, M. S. Y. (2003) 'The third wave: Future trends in international education', *International Journal of Educational Management*, 17(2):90–9.

McNamara, C. P. (1972) 'The present status of the marketing concept', *Journal of Marketing*, 36 (January):50–7.

Narver, J. C. and Slater, S. F. (1990) 'The effect of a market orientation on business philosophy', *Journal of Marketing*, 54(October):20–35.

Piercy, N. (1997) *Market-led Strategic Change*, 2nd edn, Oxford: Butterworth-Heinemann.

Polonsky, M. J. (1995) 'A stakeholder theory approach to designing environmental marketing strategy', *Journal of Business and Industrial Marketing*, 10(3):29–46.

Sargeant, A. (2004) *Marketing Management for Nonprofit Organisations*, 2nd edn, Oxford: Oxford University Press.

—— and Liao, M. (2000) 'Operationalizing the marketing concept: Just what can be achieved when you get it right?', *CASE International Journal of Educational Advancement*, 1(1):24–39.

—— and Foreman, S. (2002) 'Operationalizing the marketing concept in the nonprofit sector', *Nonprofit and Public Sector Marketing*, 10(2):41–65.

Seeman, E. D. and O'Hara, M. (2006) 'Customer relationship management in higher education: Using information systems to improve the student–school relationship', *Campus-Wide Information Systems*, 23(1):24–35.

Shapiro, B. P. (1988) 'What the hell is market oriented?', *Harvard Business Review*, 6(November–December): 119–25.

Siu, N. Y. M. and Wilson, R. M. S. (1998) 'Modelling market orientation: An application in the education sector', *Journal of Marketing Management*, 14:293–323.

Stewart, K. L. (1991) 'Applying a marketing orientation to a higher education setting', *Journal of Professional Services Marketing*, 7(2): 117–24.

The Times, (2006) 'Universities to get extra money for giving places to the poor', 21 November.

Thomas, L. (2001) 'The current widening participation environment', Widening Participation: The Marketing Dimension, Birmingham, 22 November.

Trim, P. R. J. (2003) 'Strategic marketing of further and higher educational institutions: partnership arrangements and centres of entrepreneurship', *International Journal of Educational Management*, 17(2): 59–70.

Viebranz, A. C. (1967) 'Marketing's role in company growth', *MSU Business Topics*, 15(autumn):45–9.

Webster, F. E. Jr. (1994) *Market-driven Management*, New York, NY: John Wiley.

16

Decision-making within higher education

Yvonne Moogan

Introduction

As higher education (HE) is rapidly shifting from being product driven to being market driven, it is becoming more crucial to understand the behaviour and actions of potential customers (prospective students). This is because the HE marketplace is operating within an increasingly competitive environment with many institutions all trying to attract the best possible candidates from a decreasing pool of potential students. This is partly due to changes in the structure of government funding, the introduction of tuition fees with a decline in the real value of maintenance grants and a fall in the birth rate.

The university selection (decision-making) process concerns the behaviour of potential students as they absorb, store and make rational decisions concerning the 'best' course to undertake and at the 'best' institution for them. However, with the complexities involved, the time and risk associated with making such choices, one would classify this decision-making as extensive problem-solving (Kotler and Armstrong 2007) or high involvement. By using all the information that is available, they will collect it, assess/analyse it, evaluate it and make the most optimal selection. Like most services, which are associated with higher levels of intangibility, simultaneity of production and consumption (Zeithaml 1981; Zeithaml *et al.* 1985), there is some element of risk but with university decision-making this is elevated even higher. This is because the majority of prospective HE students at undergraduate level are allowed to select a maximum of five institutions approximately a year in advance of the consumption process. This consideration set then has to be reduced to an evoked set of two institutions (firm offer and insurance offer) approximately six months later. As examinations do not take place until after both of these decision-making periods with the results not being known until several months later, there is much uncertainty involved. In addition, students do not have the opportunity to 'test drive' their future HE course, which may last between three and four years, hence the risk of making the wrong choice (with regard to the programme of study or the institution itself) is important, particularly as it can affect the students' lives in the foreseeable future. Consequently, potential HE students are making very important investment decisions which are of a long-term nature. Finally, annual tuition fees (introduced from September 2006) make it a costly experience if the outcome becomes unfavourable and again this increases the level of potential risk.

There is evidence that more pre-purchase information is being acquired by potential students and their parents in order to gain as much information as possible and that an increasing number of potential HE students are choosing a local institution whereby they stay at home and commute daily. Financial considerations are frequently the reason for staying at home to continue one's studies. Further investigation is needed since comprehension of the decision-making process by potential HE students is especially important for policy makers, marketers and institutions. For example, which attributes are viewed to be significant in deciding what to study and where to attend needs discussing. Then institutions can offer exactly what their customers are demanding and to a satisfactory level.

As universities are influenced by other factors, such as political decisions, economic conditions, the desirability of a degree and its value or even perceived value, they must be aware of the factors that influence students throughout the whole of the decision-making period so taking notice of the magnitude of change over time. For example, some attributes may become more or less important over time, meaning that some potential HE students may value these differently as they make their decisions. With the aid of conjoint analysis, research has been conducted on measuring the relative importance of the key decision-making variables over a fourteen-month period covering two academic school years. However, once the evoked set had been reached (two offers: the firm and insurance offer) no further research was performed, as the researcher left the participants before their examinations took place. Consequently research is limited to the pre-purchase stages only.

This chapter therefore examines the university selection decision-making process by drawing on and empirically testing ideas from the broader literature on consumer behaviour and service marketing with a discussion of the influential characteristics of HE institutions and the decision-making variables. By tracking potential HE students over the long period and measuring the attributes at different periods in time (from problem recognition to the pre-purchase stage) this piece of research is relatively unique.

The literature

Problem recognition is where a gap exists between the ideal state and the actual state. The ideal state refers to the position consumers would like to be in and the actual state is the consumer's current perception of their present situation. Consumers must therefore decide whether to proceed and consume a product/service in order to fill this gap, or not. The larger the disparity between these two states with the greater the level of enthusiasm, capability and opportunity, then the more likely the consumer will act. With regard to potential HE students, they will first have to decide whether or not they wish to continue studying with HE only being a possible option if it appears to be worthwhile to them. For instance, they may decide to enter a particular profession which demands a university education or to have a career with a decent salary or they may even choose to work instead and not enter the decision-making process at all. If they plan to continue studying, they will then move into the second stage of information search whereby searching for university information will occur.

During this stage, consumers may search for information internally from within their memory (from past experience) and/or externally from outside. However, the majority of potential HE students will have little or no experience of higher education, so in order to make the best possible choice they will research the 'educational market' by whatever means present. As they may not have a well-defined choice criteria nor any knowledge of the brands available they may utilize marketing literature such as prospectuses, UCAS guidebooks, electronic sources of information, or they may consult informative personnel such as subject teachers, careers officers, friends and family (Moogan *et al.* 1999). Parental pressure can exert considerable effect upon potential HE students' awareness and this can be especially lacking within 'deprived' areas (Moogan and Baron 2003) where there can be little supportive guidance or influence in general. With all service decision-making, perfect information is often lacking and education in particular, which is an extremely pure and intangible service, is even more difficult to gain full knowledge on. Word of mouth can therefore be especially useful in such circumstances and, as with most services, personal recommendation is particularly important where the source is trustworthy.

After each 'brand' is searched, the consumer must then decide if he/she is going to continue further. If he/she ceases searching, he/she will choose the brand with the maximum utility (value) to date with the selected brand being viewed as superior. However, should the consumer wish to carry on searching, he/she must select the next brand to be searched, pay the unit cost of doing so and wait for the result (Moorty *et al.* 1997). During this stage potential HE students may consider some options as being suitable, while ignoring others which are deemed to be inappropriate. Evidence does show that consumers can make mistakes, especially if there is information overload or if it is difficult to obtain relevant information in the first place. If perfect knowledge did exist, potential HE students would keep the most suitable institutions in their choice set and disregard those which are unknown or inappropriate to them.

The potential HE student now progresses to evaluate the alternatives present. Through the potential HE student assessing various institutions' characteristics and by visiting them to learn about their environments, the student will learn about the competing sets of brands and their features. This is referred to as the buyer's evoked set. He/she will allocate a level of importance to each alternative which will be affected by individual differences (such as proximity to home) as well as environmental differences. Student characteristics such as socio-economic factors and level of aptitude together with influence from significant personnel (teachers and family) can also impact during this stage (Moogan and Baron 2003).

Previous research by the author showed that selecting a university is a complex procedure due to its high level of involvement and the uncertainty incurred. Nevertheless, potential students did stress that course specifics (content, structure, method of assessment of the degree programme) was the most popularly stated variable, followed by location (distance from home, rural/urban place, atmosphere of the campus, facilities of the city/town of the university) and then reputation (league tables, recognized name or department, 'old' red-brick universities in comparison to 'new' universities) of the institution (Moogan *et al.* 1999). Further research on another and very different sample of potential HE students (containing a variety of ethnic backgrounds) was asked the same question: 'what criteria are you using in deciding which university to consider?', and again they included the same three variables of course content, location and reputation (Moogan *et al.* 2001). Research work may highlight the key university decision-making attributes affecting student choice to be course content, location and reputation, but work performed in this area relates to these in absolute terms only. Consequently potential HE students may trade one attribute for another with some being willing to choose an ideal programme of study (more relevant, interesting or better structure) at a highly reputable institution (well established), in exchange for a less favourable location (too far away from home or too close, too urban or too rural).

Interestingly, student choice environments can be affected by the existing alternative brands, the format and layout of information with the number of attributes which characterize the institution. Decision effectiveness is also affected by the quality of information (usefulness to

269

the consumer) and the quantity of information (number of items describing the alternative) (Keller and Stealin 1987). Consequently, like most consumers involved in extensive or high-involvement decision-making, the potential student is faced with a huge amount of data leading to a rather daunting processing task, unless he/she decides to employ simplifying heuristics. Heuristics are what Coupey (1994: 83–99) terms 'as short-cuts retrieved from memory, for acquiring and evaluating information' and by simplifying the task at hand, (for example, using an elimination procedure) these 'rules of thumb' will reduce the information load on memory. This is particularly essential with services. According to Blythe and Buckky (1997) there are three types of heuristics: search heuristics (rules developed for finding information); evaluation heuristics (judging of the product/service); and choice heuristics (comparing the alternatives). In the case of potential HE students searching for information and making those decisions, the Internet is becoming increasingly popular in gathering data efficiently, with parents being more involved throughout the whole process of contrasting and comparing the alternatives due to the complexities (personal risk and financial risk) concerned. As parents increasingly have to support their offspring with the multitude of fees and costs associated with HE, they tend to take a more interactive role.

Purchasing a service can be complicated which is why consumers may be described as 'cognitive misers' exerting as little remembering effort as possible and retrieving just enough information to complete the task (Costley and Brucks 1992). Evidence does show that people have restricted limits to the amount of information they process during a given amount of time which if they go beyond, overload will occur (Jacoby 1984; Malhotra et al. 1983). This is probably more so with potential HE students who are at relatively young and inexperienced phases of their lives yet making investment decisions from a huge array of possible institutions and other options available to them.

The application of conjoint analysis

By making a trade-off judgement (having more of one characteristic, but less of another) on a hypothetical product/service, consumers will examine the good and the bad features of the product/service in order to construct a preference (Herrmann and Huber 1997; Ostrom and Iacobucci 1995). Much conjoint work has been performed in the area of consumer goods and in particular services but the researcher is not aware of performance in the HE sector. Conjoint analysis allows the assessment of preferences from individual buyers through measuring the relative impact of each of the components contributing to those preferences. They can be employed to stimulate a variety of market scenarios and to make market share predictions across a complete latitude of service characteristics, both at individual and aggregate levels. While conjoint analysis retains a large amount of realism, it allows the researcher to perceive the composition of consumer preferences. The great advantage of this tool is that the respondent is providing very sensitive information which can often uncover many hidden traits such as which attribute is considered to be of prime importance and why. According to Aaker et al. (1996), conjoint analysis has two main objectives: the first motivation is that of prediction and the second is that of understanding relationships.

By attempting to measure the relative weightings of key variables or attributes it may be better to understand potential HE students' decisions, especially as they may move from being 'novices' to becoming more informed 'experts', and marketers need to recognize that their efforts will have to adapt to the current situation. For example, there are two critical points in time: the initial selection of the five institutions followed by the later choice of the evoked set to just two institutions. If the relative importance of the choice attributes differs at these points in time, institutions' marketing efforts need to reflect this difference.

It needs to be noted that there are a few problems associated with the practical application of conjoint analysis. First, selecting the relevant attributes which are to be included in the model in the first instance can be difficult, although the investigation of secondary data with subsequent primary research can provide realistic and relevant attributes to be considered. Second, it is essential that the respondents can absorb a large volume of facts/information, so comprehending the various scenarios and yet avoiding any boredom or fatigue. Despite the full-profile procedure requiring complete cooperation and attention from the respondent, with good interviewer techniques, it is possible to administer it successfully. Consequently, the researcher invested much time and effort throughout the fourteen-month period but more so at the onset of the research.

The objectives

The three key variables (course content, location and reputation) selected for the conjoint-analysis exercise will create a scenario which will establish trade-offs which potential HE students will exchange when selecting their chosen universities. The researcher met with the potential HE students from a high school (11 to 18 year olds) fortnightly over a period of fourteen months during their free-study periods, as they progressed from lower sixth form (first year of college) into upper sixth form (second and final year of college). Again, focus groups and individual interviews together with the delivery of two separate conjoint questionnaires were the methods of data collection. The researcher was able to follow the pupils throughout the various decision-making processes (from first realizing that HE existed, to deciding which two institutions to keep in their evoked set), so identifying any movements in pupils' intentions and assessing any variations over time.

By performing a conjoint test on a longitudinal basis, differences can be investigated and recommendations given to personnel regarding their recruitment policies and in particular the timing of these programmes. By using a relatively small sample size (n=37), not only could the researcher establish a personal relationship with all individuals, but anticipate more easily any problems with regard to pupil participation. Seeing the pupils every two weeks over the fourteen months allowed the researcher to obtain in-depth understandings as to each respondent's current developments. As a starting point, those pupils who were not planning on attending university were immediately eliminated from the sample. The profile of the sample is shown in Table 16.1.

All (thirty-seven) pupils at the high school agreed to participate in the study, but only those (thirty-two) planning to enter HE were eligible, so comprising a high response rate (86 per cent). With the exception of two pupils who left before the end of the study, the researcher maintained direct contact with all of the respondents.

Table 16.1 Profile of the sample group (Project One)

	Male		Female	
	N	%	N	%
(Stages 1 and 2)	10	31	22	69
(Stage 3)	9	30	21	70

Methodology

The first visit (stage 1) occurred when all the pupils were searching through UCAS guide-books and prospectuses, as well as having compulsory careers meetings during the summer term. (There is a school policy that all pupils must speak with a careers officer towards the end of the lower sixth form.) At this point in time, none of the pupils had attended any university open days individually, although they had visited some university information sessions, as attended by the sixth form college as a whole. During stage 1, potential HE students were informally interviewed prior to the focus group sessions with an aim to developing an affiliation with them. The focus sessions comprised two to four pupils and conversations were tape-recorded. The researcher tried to build the relationship with each individual so that further visits would be informal and friendly. Although the first questionnaire (general questions) helped to create a structured interview, the questions were open-ended in order to encourage unrestricted discussions. Comments were noted during all sessions and documented immediately afterwards. Subsequent visits incorporated the gathering of conjoint data (conjoint questionnaire) via individual interviews with the researcher. Again, prior to each meeting, an update and informal chat took place. An example of the first page only of the questionnaire can be seen in Table 16.2.

The model

A simple regression model using dummy variables was employed to administer the conjoint procedure. All the pupils were individually asked to rate the key variables of *location, reputation* and *course content*, for the three levels of: 'worse/less than what they wanted', 'exactly/equal to what they wanted' and 'greater/better than' what they wanted, with regard to their HE choices. This created twenty-seven possible profiles ($3 \times 3 \times 3$) each varying from a minimum value of 1 (least likely to attend – 'worse than what you wanted') to a maximum value of 7 (definitely likely to attend – 'greater than what you wanted'). Hence the dependent variable is the intention to attend a particular university. The 'conjoint' questionnaire therefore incorporated the full profile method. Using Microsoft Excel, parameters for each beta value (b1 to b6) were totalled and averaged to be obtained in aggregate (Table 16.3). Given the dummy variable coding in which level three is the base rate, these coefficients were related to the

Table 16.2 First page of the questionnaire used

If university location was what you expected (equal) how likely would you be to attend, if . . .

	Less						High
	1	2	3	4	5	6	7
Reputation & Course were both less than what you wanted?							
Reputation & Course were both equal . . .							
Reputation & Course were both better . . .							
Reputation was less but Course was better . . .							
Reputation was less but Course was exactly . . .							
Reputation was exactly but Course was less . . .							
Reputation was exactly but Course better . . .							
Reputation was better but Course exactly . . .							
Reputation was better but Course was less . . .							

part-worths. These were then placed in simultaneous equations and values to be assigned to each attribute's levels were ultimately calculated. These part-worths (Table 16.4) symbolize the utility (level of preference) that respondents will attach to the attribute levels of location, reputation and course specifics/content. The final result of conjoint analysis (Table 16.6) consisted of the relative importance weights in terms of percentages, which have been used to construct the stimuli (course specifics, location and reputation) that the pupils have evaluated in terms of desirability. These importance weights highlighted which attributes were most significant and important in affecting student decision-making.

The second visit, pre-open day (stage 2) took place in the autumn term of the upper sixth form (September to November). With a view to obtaining the current position of each pupil's progress, detailed yet informal meetings were held before the main interviews and remarks were recorded. The majority of pupils were still deciding either what course to study or where to apply to, although a few had already submitted their UCAS forms prior to the college deadline of 21 October. Again pupils had yet to attend university open days individually. The sample size remained the same at thirty-two. Since the questionnaire involved complicated trade-off scenarios with pupils ranking the twenty-seven stimuli (course content, location and reputation) in terms of suitability, it was performed in the presence of the interviewer. Consequently the interviewer related each of the respondents' individual circumstances to the various questions. Introducing some realism into each pupil's scenario helped to accentuate levels of understanding. For verification purposes, each pupil signed their own questionnaire upon completion.

The third visit, post-open day (stage 3) occurred in the final summer term (April to May) prior to the pupils' A-level examinations. Since the last stage, all pupils had attended interviews and/or open days for some or all of their UCAS choices. Two pupils had also left the sixth form college during the last six months. Consequently, the sample size decreased to thirty (81 per cent) pupils. The process from the previous visit was repeated with the same questionnaire being administered, on a one-to-one basis in the presence of the interviewer. Again in order to elevate the level of understanding, a recap discussion occurred with the interviewer relating the respondent's most recent circumstances to the tasks at hand. Pupils were not allowed to see their previously completed questionnaires from stage 2.

Findings

The values from the respondents of both stage 2 (thirty-two pupils) and stage 3 (thirty pupils) were aggregated and then averaged for the pre-open day (autumn 1997) and post-open day (spring/summer 1998) periods respectively. The results were analysed mathematically (Tables 16.3 to 16.6) and are presented graphically (Figures 16.1 and 16.2).

Stage 1

These initial and introductory sessions seemed to highlight that most pupils were uncertain of which university to choose with many showing limited knowledge about the institutions' reputations. Only a few were more concerned in attending an institution with a good reputation and this was often dictated by their parents. Consequently, many viewed reputation according to the necessary entrance grades and whether or not an interview was compulsory. The pupils did, however, have predetermined ideas of what courses to undertake and the subjects that they were generally interested in studying at degree level. The majority (84 per

273

Table 16.3   Aggregate average beta results

	Beta values	
	Stage 2: Pre-open day	*Stage 3: Post-open day*
b1	−1.63	−2.60
b2	−0.28	−1.10
b3	−1.36	−1.07
b4	−0.59	−0.71
b5	−2.74	−2.23
b6	−0.89	−1.06

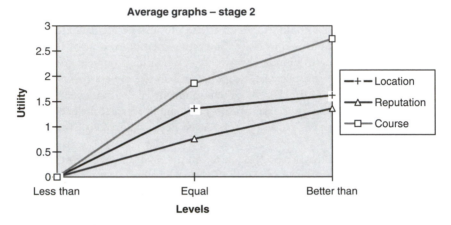

Figure 16.1 Pre–open day (stage 2)

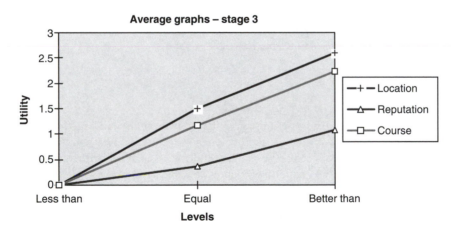

Figure 16.2 Post-open day (stage 3)

cent) wanted to participate on a degree programme similar to that of their current studies. Course content was rated most frequently in terms of the selection criteria being employed. Although social factors (big city, night life, clubs, bars, and so on) were formally recorded from previous research work, prior responses do confirm the present sample's replies in that course specifics was still the most popular variable.

Over two-thirds of the pupils (69 per cent) had made up their minds to leave home, with 31 per cent wishing to stay at home and commute daily. Of the 69 per cent, ten pupils (31 per cent) stated the requirement of remaining fairly close to their parents' house, either within a one-hundred-mile vicinity or less than two hours' drive away, but twelve pupils (38 per cent) did not consider distance from home to be an issue. Many of the respondents holding general views of their interests in programmes of study with possible places to attend, were wholly undecided as to their futures in HE. Despite the pupils finding the university information sessions/days to be useful, none of the thirty-two pupils had definite consideration sets at this stage. Nevertheless, there were still over two months remaining before the pupils would have to start applying through UCAS, upon their return from the summer break.

Stage 2 (pre-open day)

Five months later into the research project, pupils were in the process of selecting their choices via UCAS. The graph in Figure 16.1 shows a rapid increase in utility for the attribute course content at all three levels ('A11 = less than what you want', 'A12 = equal to what you want' or 'A13 = greater than what you want'), a steady rise for the attribute reputation and an initial increase but gradual levelling out for the attribute location. There is little difference between 'equal to' and 'better than' for this latter attribute. Consequently, as long as location is at least 'equal to' in the scenario, pupils are still willing to attend. The level of 'better than' only then becomes marginally more attractive. In contrast, course content and reputation become substantially more preferred, as the curves increase from the level of 'equal to' until the level of 'better than'.

Table 16.4 (part-worths), for example, shows respondents at stage 2 having a greatest preference at 'A13' and 'A23' and 'A33' (better than what one expects) for all of the attributes, location (0.64), reputation (0.65) and course content (1.21) respectively. Therefore pupils wish to obtain entry into the most reputable institution, on to the best programme of study in the most ideal place.

Table 16.4 Aggregate average part-worths for all attributes

Part-worth values	Stage 2 (1997) (pre-open day)	Stage 3 (1998) (post-open day)	% Change
Location:			
A11	−0.99	−1.37	38
A12	+0.36	+0.14	62
A13	+0.64	+1.23	94
Reputation:			
A21	−0.71	−0.48	32.5
A22	+0.06	−0.12	101
A23	+0.65	+0.60	8
Course content:			
A31	−1.53	−1.13	26
A32	+0.33	+0.03	90
A33	+1.21	+1.10	9

Stage 3 (post-open day)

Eleven months on into the research study, pupils were now in the process of selecting their two conditional offers to retain for UCAS. The majority were currently justifying their two conditional choices via their UCAS form and the minority were still in the process of visiting university departments for interviews and/or attending open days. Figure 16.2 illustrates graphically the difference between the utilities at 'less than' and 'equal to' for each of the attributes being smaller in stage 3, when compared to that of stage 2, with the exception of the attribute location which rises at an accelerating rate above the curves of course content and reputation.

Table 16.4 (part-worths) shows for stage 3, that the greatest preferences are again at 'A13' and 'A23' and 'A33' for all of the attributes location (1.23), reputation (0.60) and course content (1.1). The highest part-worth values in stage 2 belong to course content (1.21), yet in stage 3 it belongs to location (1.23). The final column showing percentage change calculates the movement from stage 2 (pre-open day) to stage 3 (post-open day). Hence the largest change for location is 94 per cent (from A12 to A13), for reputation it is 101 per cent (from A21 to A22) and course content is 90 per cent (from A31 to A32).

Table 16.5 includes the average utility values (levels of satisfaction) in stages 2 and 3 at 'better than' for all the attributes, location (1.63 and 2.60), reputation (1.36 and 1.07) and finally course content (2.74 and 2.23). Hence it shows mathematically, that at a level of 'equal to', the attribute of location has a lower utility value (1.35) in stage 2 (pre-open day), than in stage 3 (1.51) after the open day. However, the difference in utility from 'equal to' until 'greater than' for location, rises substantially from (1.63) stage 2 to (2.6) stage 3. The variable of location seems to have become a more important consideration in these later days prior to leaving school. Pupils, having seen the location (distance from home, the logistics of returning home, type of environment the university is in – conurbation/rural – and so on) aspect of the institution through attending open days or interviews, obtain a 'feel' for what they want. If the place is viewed to be unsuitable, they will prefer to go elsewhere, especially if their chosen degree programme is similar at an alternative institution. Although course content remains predominantly essential throughout stage 2, it is overtaken by location in stage 3, as the pupils are approaching the final steps of the decision-making process.

Table 16.6 shows location and course content in stage 2, having a relative importance of 28.4 per cent and 47.9 per cent respectively. In stage 3, location becomes more influential and the relative importance increases to 44.1 per cent, with course content becoming less preferable and decreasing to 37.7 per cent.

Table 16.5 Aggregate average utility values for all attributes

Attribute levels		Stage 2 (pre-open day)	Stage 3 (post-open day)
Location:	'Less than'	0	0
	'Equal to'	1.35	1.51
	'Better than'	1.63	2.60
Reputation:	'Less than'	0	0
	'Equal to'	0.77	0.36
	'Better than'	1.36	1.07
Course content:	'Less than'	0	0
	'Equal to'	1.85	1.16
	'Better than'	2.74	2.23

Table 16.6   Aggregate average relative importance for all attributes (as percentages)

Attributes	Stage 2 (1997) (pre-open day)	Stage 3 (1998) (post-open day)
Location	28.4	44.1
Reputation	23.7	18.2
Course content	47.9	37.7

Discussion

There seemed to be two main clusters developing: first, those pupils wanting to remain at home and attend an institution locally started to prioritize according to the location (distance from home) of the university, followed by the courses on offer. Second, and in contrast, those wishing to study away from home looked at all the possible courses first and then the location (geographic place, type of campus – city/rural – local attractions, and so on) of where these programmes were available. Location was therefore viewed differently for each cluster. Since the majority of pupils were choosing degree courses similar to their present A-level studies, they carefully analysed the structure of the degree course and the content of the modules, looking at the methods of assessment, and so on. Reputation seemed to be determined by the perception of entry grades or by tutors stating particular institutions ('old' universities) offering certain courses (usually where they attended as a student) as being superior. 'New' universities (established post-1992) were viewed to offer more degrees relevant to industry with modern ideas and updated resources. Reputation was considered to be lower at 'new' universities compared to 'old' universities, but this did not affect the majority of potential HE students from applying.

When in the process of choosing their five options for UCAS (stage 2), pupils viewed the degree programme (course content) as being of prime importance. This was their starting point in the decision–making process. However, eleven months later (stage 3), pupils seemed to be using other variables to justify their strategies of eliminating their alternatives, into their chosen two. During this period, students are corresponding with institutions, discussing matters with teachers and friends, as well as visiting universities to see for themselves what the environment and the location is like. Location therefore becomes more important as time passes with location during the pre-open day being categorized as distance from home with a rural or urban site but during the post-open day it is assessed for its city attractions with night life and shops. Consequently, many pupils valued the importance of attending university open days, particularly with regard to obtaining first impressions such as the campus layout or the general social scene of the university. Matching requests for such information besides communicating knowledge on the content of the degree programme is what potential students want. Therefore open days that were well organized, informative, pleasurable, yet covering such topics of inter-est, helped students to make their selections more easily. Consequently, upon deciding which two institutions to retain on their UCAS forms, pupils regarded the social atmosphere of the campus, the entry grades and in particular the university's location to be the domineering factors.

Since the potential student decision–making process is complicated and long, it was sug-gested that the relative weights given to the key attributes may alter over the extended period and this should be reflected in the marketing strategies of the institutions.

Conclusion

The conjoint work (Figures 16.1 and 16.2) clearly shows an increase in importance of the variable location over the period of study. Location seemed to be categorized by the pupils into two segments as follows: some pupils were looking for a cosmopolitan city (shops, entertainment attractions), within or outside a certain distance from home, while others clearly wanted to live at home and choosing a local institution was the only option. Although variations in the pupils' decisions were generally caused by changes in family and personal commitments (considerations relative to their partners) the financial pressure of fees was frequently mentioned. Consequently, staying at home and attending a local university was viewed to be a more economical option and a solution for many.

In this article, the focus was on establishing whether the importance weighting, given by potential HE students of key institutional attributes, changes over the long period when decisions are being made. Findings do suggest that these weightings do change for there is a demand for course-specific information during the earlier period of the process which becomes less important later on. The findings provide an impetus for institutions to assess their marketing strategies and examine the level and timing of the information that they are disseminating. For example, is the information readable, informative, appropriate and understandable as students move from being relative novices to becoming experts?

Limitations

In choosing to apply only three variables within the conjoint analysis project, the researcher has attempted to provide a parsimonious set of issues that reasonably reflects choice criteria. However, this may lead to a sacrifice of important distinctions and in particular the interpretation of the construct location may vary according to the timing of the data collection. Although the sample was relatively small (n = 30), one-to-one attention could be given to the respondents throughout the study, so that the complex questionnaire could be completed as accurately as possible with maximum understanding and minimum fatigue. However, such a small sample may limit the inferences that can be made.

For instance, the respondents may have understood the conjoint questionnaire and related it to their individual needs as explained by the interviewer, but was the whole project pragmatic and would the pupils reciprocate their replies to the scenarios again? Although this school covers a large catchment area with ethnic minorities present, it failed to capture mature students. Mature students account for a large proportion of university scholars and work needs to be performed on this cohort, as well as pupils who are attending other further education institutions such as colleges, private and public schools. It also included a large percentage (70 per cent) of female pupils (Table 16.1).

Furthermore, although the investigative period was taken over two academic years, comprising a duration of fourteen months, it did not continue into the purchase stage whereby the students actually enrol at their chosen institution. Continuation throughout the whole of Kotler and Armstrong's (2007) model would have been enlightening and research in this area and of a longitudinal nature is also limited. For example, potential students of HE may decide not to take up their firm or insurance offer for whatever reason and either apply somewhere else or not at all.

Validity

The simple model applied in this study provides regression coefficients which indicate the 'goodness of fit' of the evaluations. For instance, if dummy variable regression is employed, the value of r^2 will indicate the extent to which the model fits the data. A low correlation may mean that the model does not fit the data well. Models with poor fit are suspect (Malhotra *et al.* 1982). In stage 2, the average correlation coefficient of the sample of thirty-two pupils was 0.93 and in stage 3 with thirty pupils it had increased to 0.96. Again, such a high correlation does prove statistical reliability.

References

Aaker, D. A., Kumar, V. and Day, G. (1996) *Marketing Research*, 5th edn, Part 4, Chapter 21, p. 629, New York, NY: John Wiley & Sons.

Blythe, J. and Buckley, A. (1997) *The Essence of Consumer Behaviour*, Chapter 11, pp. 166–78, New York, NY: Prentice-Hall.

Costly, C. L. and Brucks, M. (1992) 'Selective recall and information use in consumer preferences', *Journal of Consumer Research*, 8(1):464–74.

Coupey, E. (1994) 'Restructuring: Constructive processing of information displays in consumer choice', *Journal of Consumer Research*, 21(1):83–99.

Herrmann, A. and Huber, F. (1997) 'Utility-orientated product distribution', *International Review of Retail, Distribution and Consumer Research*, 7(4):369–81.

Jacoby, J. (1984) 'Perspective on information overload', *Journal of Consumer Research*, 10(1):432–5.

Keller, L. K. and Staelin, R. (1987) 'Effects of quality and quantity of information on decision-effectiveness', *Journal of Consumer Research*, 14(2); 200–13.

Kotler, P. and Armstrong, G. (2007) *Principles of Marketing*, New York, NY: Prentice-Hall.

Malhotra, N. K., Jain, A. K. and Lagakos, S. W. (1982) 'The information overload controversy: An alternative viewpoint', *Journal of Marketing*, 46(1):27–37.

Moogan, Y. J., Baron, S. and Harris, K. (1999) 'Decision-making behaviour of potential higher education students', *Higher Education Quarterly*, 53(3):211–28.

—— (2003) 'An analysis of student characteristics within the student decision-making process', *Journal of Further and Higher Education*, 27(3):271–87.

—— and Bainbridge, S. (2001) 'Timings and tradeoffs in the marketing of higher education courses: A conjoint approach', *Marketing Intelligence and Planning*, 19(3):179–87.

Moorty, S., Ratchford, B.T. and Talukdar, D. (1997) 'Consumer information search revisited: Theory and empirical analysis', *Journal of Consumer Research*, 23(1):263–77.

Ostrom, A. and Iacobucci, D. (1995) 'Consumer trade-offs and the evaluation of services', *Journal of Marketing*, 59(1):17–28.

Zeithaml, V. A. (1981) 'How consumer evaluation processes differ between goods and services', in Donnelly, J. H. and George, W. R. (eds) *Marketing of Services*, Chicago, IL: American Marketing Association, pp. 186–90.

—— Parasuraman, A. and Berry, L.L. (1985) 'Problems and strategies in services marketing', *Journal of Marketing*, 49(2):33–46.

17

The promise of marketing in higher education

Where we have been, where we are and where we are going

Charles S. Madden

For the majority of the history of modern higher education (HE) there has been a largely Darwinian view of what should happen to institutions when they encounter competition, declining demand or other problems that we frequently associate with a need for strategic marketing thinking. Hundreds of colleges and universities have ceased to exist because of economic shortfalls over the past two hundred years in the USA and Europe (Mulnix 1989: 124). Usually because of fluctuations in student applications or because of new start-up institutions, both new and established colleges have cut costs, eliminated programmes or sought emergency funding to continue to survive during difficult times. Because 'selling' or otherwise employing 'commercial' approaches to save colleges was considered beneath the dignity of the leaders of those institutions, many schools have perished or merged through the years. It was thought that ceasing to exist was preferable to 'debasing' the institution by using marketing techniques to address problems. Frankly, the very idea of using marketing was rarely considered because the arenas of learning and commerce were far apart in the thinking of institutional leaders.

Bringing marketing to the academy

Although small incidents of using advertising and personal selling are reported over the years in recruiting students for some post-secondary schools thought of as proprietary 'business colleges' and 'trade schools' (Mulnix 1989: 126), the strategies for keeping colleges and universities financially sound have, historically, been relegated to controlling expenses. The best institutions for HE typically have kept their sizes small, so that demand would always exceed supply for their enrolled positions in their classes.

A major turning point in thinking about marketing came with the publication of Kotler and Levy's article, 'Broadening the concept of marketing' (1969). In this chapter the radical idea that marketing strategies and techniques could be applied to the problems of most nonprofit organizations, particularly those of healthcare and education, was put forward. As academic marketing had been a part of university instruction for only about sixty years, there was some disagreement as to whether attention should be diverted from commercial enterprises to nonprofits. Despite this discussion though, there was agreement from other scholars that marketing had much to offer the nonprofit sector.

Around the same time that the application of marketing to higher education and healthcare was being discussed, a major turning point in the growing trend of the US population came along. After the Second World War, government support of HE in the form of the 'GI Bill' put a large number of students in colleges and universities in the USA. Immediately on the heels of that programme came the 'baby boom' generation of those born after the Second World War who began to swell the numbers of college-age students from the mid-1960s until the early 1970s. The inevitable down turn of both population and enrolled students following the Second World War came in the wake of most public colleges' and universities' efforts to accommodate the largest entering classes in history (Shumar 1997). While institutions were straining to deal with record numbers of students in the 1950s, 1960s and 1970s, the real challenge, however, came when applications began to diminish after the population boom in the late 1970s (Doyle and Newbould 1980; Bingham 1988).

The realization that their institutions were not so excellent that they would draw more than their share of enrolments slowly dawned on administrators of many colleges and universities. Pyke, in a paper published in 1977, raised the issue of whether private universities could survive in the USA. The question was based on the observation that the number of public institutions was growing at a time of diminishing student enrolments. While Pyke, who was the coordinator of academic planning at the University of Southern California, a private institution, made the case that some private schools would survive, he also predicted a major decline in such institutions.

Around that same time, the leadership of many colleges and universities began to embrace the idea that their institutions could benefit from public relation activities. This idea was suggested both in support of fundraising and to enhance the public awareness of public colleges with state legislators. The 'news bureau' model of public relations was mostly used by colleges and universities. Producing a large number of news releases that would be sent to public media with hopes of publication or broadcast, schools expected to 'tell their story' and thereby become prominent among the many available institutions of the day. While this was not traditional marketing as such, it was a step in the direction of understanding that nonprofit and public institutions could benefit from strategies and techniques that were normally associated with private businesses.

Around the time that Kotler and Levy (1969) and Shapiro (1973) made a case for using strategic marketing in HE, Krachenberg (1972) proposed directly how marketing could strengthen educational institutions. He pointed out that many schools were already using some aspects of marketing thought in such areas as student recruitment, pricing tuition and raising money from alumni. He further suggested that marketing was not being used in a comprehensive and intentional way. He made a compelling case for using marketing research and institutional differentiation along with the managerial tools of promotion, distribution and price. He was perhaps the first and for several years the most articulate voice for using a total marketing programme in colleges and universities.

Several other authors proposed a comprehensive use of strategic marketing to different audiences in the HE community (Johnson 1989; Schmidt 1988; Brooker and Noble 1985). Each of these authors created 'how to' guides for college administrators who wanted to undertake the strategic marketing process for their institutions.

Over the next decade, two textbooks were introduced to guide administrators in the process of introducing a managerial marketing approach for their schools (Gray 1991; Kotler and Fox 1995). Gray presented a basic discussion of the major factors of a marketing programme, while

Kotler and Fox put forth a managerial marketing framework for using strategic marketing. While a limited amount of research and publishing had been done at the time of the introduction of these books, their presence in the marketplace had a very positive and encouraging effect on the HE market.

Barriers to the diffusion of HE marketing

Despite much progress, there were several significant factors that worked against the adoption of comprehensive marketing strategies by administrators of colleges and universities. A feeling within the faculty culture persisted in the belief that marketing was not necessary and was having a cheapening effect on the institutions of HE that were embracing the strategic marketing framework. In 1980, Riesman suggested that the adoption of marketing was a result of consumerism among students. Since then some authors characterized marketing in higher education as a 'fad' along with many other short-run quick-fix solutions (Birnbaum 2000). Other authors suggest that marketing has limited possibilities as a management framework because it has a 'commmoditization' effect on the educational product (Gibbs 2001). Gibbs also harks back to the belief held many years ago that marketing serves the lowest common denominator of students and restricts the creative process among colleagues. Fortunately, many authors of that era have rejected that position and made a compelling case for trying to overcome the barriers to marketing in HE institutions.

Even in schools that have a commitment to embracing marketing, there are several other barriers that have impaired the fulfilment of a promise of a comprehensive marketing system. An article in the mid-1970s warned that marketing may have more of a negative impact on some schools than positive (Hugstad 1975). Several schools that tried to adopt a marketing framework in the early years found the following problems when adopting a marketing approach:

1 The marketing functions had been built in several fragmented organizational areas of the university. Enrolment management, public relations, fundraising and alumni relations were all frequently found in different areas of the school. Each area presented the potential of a turf battle.
2 Functions, such as pricing and product management, were usually completely removed from marketing decision-making. Finance and administration decision-makers frequently controlled tuition and other pricing decisions. Product management was usually under the auspices of the provost/chief academic officer.
3 In many institutions marketing and public relations were considered synonymous. While the public relations function was a significant portion of the marketing function in any nonprofit organization, there were many other marketing factors as well.
4 In far too many institutions, marketing was seen as an unnecessary expenditure of resources.
5 Some marketing expenditures were made in areas where outcomes were difficult to measure without spending further money for field research. The temptation of asking for less money while not measuring outcomes frequently would put managers in a position of not being able to justify the original marketing expenditure.
6 Many public institutions had their hands tied with regard to marketing tactics such as pricing, product and the distribution of educational programmes.

Even more recently, some authors have raised the question of whether marketing was being used properly in HE institutions (Goldgehn 1990). However, despite the barriers facing college administrators in adopting marketing for their institutions, a number of marketing strategies and tactics have produced a rich stream of research that has improved the management of such schools (Michael *et al.* 1993).

Where are we more recently in using marketing in HE?

In the 1950s and 1960s, as marketing management was emerging as a decision-making paradigm, a number of concepts and tactics were introduced, such as marketing research, market segmentation, the marketing mix, consumer behaviour and the marketing concept. The 1970s and 1980s brought marketing to HE following a similar path of tactical ideas. Perhaps one of the most helpful papers published in the early days was another article by Philip Kotler who suggested strategies for successfully introducing marketing into nonprofit organizations (1979). The research agenda after that time began to focus on using marketing ideas to solve practical problems facing colleges and universities (Wasner and Bruner 1999). For example, the knowledge in the field enabled a series of researchers to explore the processes used by prospective students to choose a college (Cook and Zallocco 1983; Chapman 1981; Hossler and Gallagher 1987; Clinton 1989). Through the past twenty years, probably the most common subject of papers for marketing in HE continued to focus on how student choice can be better understood and influenced (Dixon and Martin 1991; Flint 1992; Galotti and Mark 1994; Coccari and Javalgi 1995; Canale and Dunlap 1996; Broekemier and Seshadri 1999; Dawes and Brown 2002; Dawes and Brown 2004; Parmar 2004). Even the role of marketing services and the quality of service providers was explored as a positive application to HE education (Johnson 1987–8; Canterbury 1999; Brooks 2003).

Perhaps one of the most useful and practical areas of research for the decision-making college administrator has been the stream of work in institutional image measurement and enhancement. The introduction of the topic as a management tool came from a few authors in the late 1980s and the early 1990s (Hayes 1993; Riesman 1980). Other work explored how typical communication vehicles such as the campus view book could be powerful image techniques (Klassen 2000), and institutional positioning could be undertaken through showing the campus social life (Capraro *et al.* 2004). Later studies suggested the importance of comprehensive image management to the sustainability of a college or university (George 2000; Finley *et al.* 2001).

Some of the more recent and useful streams of research have focused on institutional brand images among colleges and universities (Bulotaite 2003). Over several years the mutual support of marketing and public relations has been explored as many colleges and universities have had their marketing functions controlled by the public relations department (Walle 1990). While marketing and public relations are not interchangeable, the introduction of marketing frameworks has brought about conversations over the last several years among marketing and public relations scholars concerning the integration of marketing communications (Sands and Smith 1999; George 2000). These discussions have served the HE marketing community very well, in that many administrators were already committed to departments of communications or public relations when the needs of an institutional marketing strategy became apparent. Bringing that support of marketing to the broader HE community was a natural extension of the process of integrating each piece of the promotional process into a comprehensive and meaningful strategy (Morris 2003).

As is commonly the case in the diffusion of any managerial innovation, marketing ideas both in the literature and in professional meeting discussions have preceded practice by as much as a decade. It must also be realized that like distributions of many other organizations HE institutions have primarily paid lip-service to marketing idea frameworks. Even among schools that pride themselves on their progressiveness in implementing marketing, most schools have only adopted marketing frameworks piecemeal. In a 2002 study by Newman, a sample of HE institutions reported that among the highest-ranking members of each school's administrations responsible for one or more marketing functions carried a title of director or dean (36 per cent or 26.7 per cent respectively), and another 19.6 per cent carried titles of vice-president or assistant/associate chancellor. Of the various responsibilities assigned to the highest-ranking marketing officers in the reporting institutions, enrolment management was the most common with 93.2 per cent, financial aid was 46.6 per cent, publications was 34.6 per cent, registration/records followed with 24.3 per cent and the last responsibility listed was public relations with 10.0 per cent. All responding institutions were asked what marketing and planning activities they were currently using. In order of frequency, the respondents listed strategic planning (90.2 per cent), advertising (87.7 per cent), marketing planning (85.0 per cent), target marketing (84.5 per cent), marketing research (76.8 per cent), market segmentation (64.0 per cent), self-audits of marketing (61.9 per cent), and positioning (56.9 per cent). Newman also compared her 2002 findings with a comparable study that had been conducted by Goldgehn in 1989. The comparison showed that every marketing and planning activity had increased in frequency with the exception of target marketing and market segmentation which had regressed from 91 per cent in 1989 to 84 per cent in 2002 and from 78 per cent in 1989 to 64 per cent in 2002. While specific marketing tools, like target marketing and market segmentation were used with less frequency, most of the broader activities were embraced by a larger percentage of respondents.

Another use of marketing planning that has been observed in the literature looked at the relationship between marketing planning and national rankings (LeBlanc 1997). Many ranking criteria in the *US News and World Report*'s annual rankings issue of the publication can be strategically addressed with a marketing planning process. Included among those criteria would be student recruitment (quality of test scores and class ranks, student retention, etc.), peer institution evaluation of image and alumni giving. Investment in targeted communications can not only affect those criteria, but can also improve a ranking, thereby making such criteria and other attributes that are easier to affect because of the resulting rank.

Could we do better in using marketing?

The history of HE over the past forty years has shown that colleges and universities tend to embrace marketing when forced to by environmental conditions, such as population or enrolment declines. There seems to be more of a willingness to use marketing strategies when the institutional status quo is challenged, such as enrolment revenue declines, than when great opportunities present themselves. One way of looking at how marketing has diffused into the HE community is to compare it with the rate at which the healthcare industry accepted marketing as a strategic framework over the past thirty years. The difference between the two may be attributed to the healthcare community's combination of a highly competitive industry and the infusion of a great deal of private capital in the 1990s. Dozens of nonprofit hospital organizations were sold to three or four national 'chain' healthcare corporations in that era. The motive for such sales was the belief that many hospitals could not survive without the infusion of a great deal of private capital to enable them to embrace cutting-edge technologies. These two converging trends gave healthcare institutions both a motive and an opportunity to embrace strategic marketing. The corporate management teams that had experience in other industrial settings pushed hospitals towards a commitment to marketing. There was no such parallel to the conditions in healthcare existing in HE. Despite that, however, today there seem to be some emerging environmental conditions that may spur a regeneration of interest in using marketing in the HE community.

What could energize a new era of marketing?

Zusma (1999) predicted that some factors are aligning which may prod colleges and universities to re-examine the role that marketing strategies could play in coping with emerging environmental and market difficulties. Among the pressures that Zusma identified were: (a) declining public support for state colleges and universities; (b) subsequent shrinking financial resources made available by state legislatures; (c) uncertain federal research funding; (d) unstable student grant and loan support from the state and federal governments; (e) impending de facto privatization of public HE institutions; and (f) shifting size and quality of today's college-aged student populations available to enrol.

If history is any predictor of the reaction of HE institutions to environmental change, we are coming face to face with a new wave of strategic marketing interest (Newman et al. 2004). Much like the earlier days of the diffusion of marketing in HE, enrolment fluctuations will drive some interest in enrolment marketing, tuition-setting and student financial aid. This coming phase may be more intense because of the growing dependency of schools on student tuition (Zemsky et al. 2001). Additionally, with the more pervasive use of student tuition-discounting and leverage, we can expect a more sophisticated use of marketing in these areas (Kronholz 2002). As the trends cited above come to fruition, we will also see an attempt to use and understand more broadly marketing in areas which have not formally been a part of the institutional strategies of colleges and universities (Paul 2005). We must never underestimate the survival instinct present in HE. In 1977, Pyke wrote an article entitled 'The future of higher education: Will private institutions disappear in the US?'. Although he concluded that private universities would not disappear, his point was that large, state-funded, land grant institutions were a threat to private schools because they were more of a bargain. We have now reversed the argument by tentatively predicting (Zusma 1999) that public institutions will be 'privatized' because of a loss of public political support for state colleges and universities. It must be noted that by privatizing these schools, it puts them in a position of competing for both students and private funding, thereby needing marketing more than ever before.

What form will the next wave of marketing take?

There are several opportunities available to HE in using marketing to solve immediate problems such as enrolment shortages, but there are also broader and richer frameworks available to schools to embrace opportunities for branding, positioning and building collaborative communities which exceed the future expectations of faculty, staff, students and alumni (Levine 2000).

Institutions have sought to use marketing to solve immediate and incremental problems such as the need for awareness (bringing about public relations), the need for funding (bringing about development), the need for enrolment (bringing about enrolment management and student financial aid) and the need to improve relations with alumni and state government. In church-related schools, relations with denominations or churches (bringing about alumni rela-tions, governmental relations and church relations) other areas are sure to emerge as needed. Each area, though, while needed, has frequently become unrelated 'turfs' that have not enjoyed the synergism possible in an organized cooperative marketing effort. While many of the departments listed above exist in a large number of colleges and universities, the real opportun-ities for using marketing in the future lie in finding ways to weave the efforts together and build integrative strategic frameworks for the future (Stewart 1991).

Marketing's next likely contributions

We know far more about marketing than we can effectively use in HE because of political and organizational barriers. Institutions of HE will continue to implement additional facets of marketing as problems arise. There are, however, some areas in marketing knowledge that promise institutional improvement and competitive advantage. The foremost opportunities for contributing to the future of HE exist for the use of marketing in the following areas: (a) the use of a strategic marketing plan offers to align market needs with the mission and vision of the college or university; (b) choosing a college is one of the most consequential and complex consumer choices that most people ever make. Marketing offers an opportunity for a college to create an institutional profile that can attract the best students available with aspirations served by that institution (Spiegler 1998); (c) while for-profit businesses select markets that are ready and willing to pay the highest acceptable price for a product, HE institutions must select markets for many reasons other than ability to pay. The creation of the transaction between a university and a prospective student is based on varying prices that result from scholarship discounting balanced against the talent (intellectual, athletic, musical, etc.) and other potential that the student brings to the exchange. Consumer behaviour as a part of the marketing decision framework offers a way to better understand each side of that transaction (Hoffman and Kretovics 2004); (d) a large part of the success of a college or university is rooted in the quality of service provided by the faculty, staff and administration (Aldridge and Rowley 1998). A marketing framework offers a way for the university service community to both understand and better serve students; (e) much of the customer satisfaction research stream offers HE institutions a better way to build an environment conducive with greater student retention; (f) marketing research offers universities insight into the way students, alumni and other prospective donors view the school. This enables the university decision-maker to raise the probabilities that students will choose to attend and that donors may willingly give; (g) the creation of new HE products, such as a new major field of study, can improve the probability of the programme's survival by using a demand analysis framework. Many new programmes of study fail because they are driven by faculty desire to study and teach in an area that has not been analysed for strength of student demand. Matching a creative proposal with an objective demand analysis can either strengthen the course offered or eliminate the programme before it fails; (h) the analysis of market size for the various market segments that provide students to the university can stabilize and optimize the resulting size of the university student body. Many universities, especially state-supported schools, grow above their sustainable size for political reasons and are sometimes unable to maintain both size and quality over time. Other schools may be unable to offer high-quality and synergistic programmes because they are reluctant to grow the institution to a reasonable and market sustainable size; (i) if pricing decisions concerning tuition and scholarship leverage are approached using the best practices available, net revenue and available resources can be used to support a higher-quality institution. Many schools still set tuition based on the needs of a current institutional budget. In trying to increase the quality of students or to seek more tuition revenue, some institutions have raised their scholarship discount rate to unsustainable levels. Pricing the college experience strategically can provide both adequate support for the educational institution and make a school reasonably affordable to its student markets; (j) HE institutions can improve their sustainability in the long run by building a differentiated brand. The homogenization of universities and colleges has resulted from attempts to meet accreditation standards, national ranking standards and to emulate larger, older and more prestigious schools. That lack of differentiation has yielded the perception that colleges are offering an educational commodity in the classroom. While some similarity is expected and reasonable in quality among colleges, the ability of an institution to show its strengths and to set itself apart from the other two thousand or more schools of HE is essential; (k) marketing has recently offered a 'customer relationship management' framework to those charged with raising resources from both alumni and other stakeholders of the university (Black and Miller 1991). Many schools have directed their fundraising efforts towards mass appeals, framed in impersonal direct mail requests. While this technique can be appropriate as a beginning point to identify sincere future supporters of the college, substantial gifts are hard to acquire without building sophisticated databases and strategies to cultivate major givers; (l) enrolment management has contributed to growing institutions and has enabled many schools to enhance their student quality. Now many of the same marketing techniques offer schools the opportunities of shaping the student characteristics of classes; (m) as many institutions shift their attention from only the traditional student to the various markets of non-traditional students, the marketing-mix element of 'place', also called distribution, may become increasingly important. Obvious implications may include locating classes in such places as office buildings, locations convenient to older students and putting more course content on the Internet; (n) the idea of 'internal marketing' has typically in the past meant marketing the need of producing quality services from the faculty and staff. Other uses of internal marketing are many and may include such areas as persuading the faculty to support the student recruitment programme or convincing the administration that budget support for a sophisticated marketing initiative is a good investment, not just an expense; (o) some initial uses of 'customer relationship management' have been made in identifying and cultivating relationships with alumni and other relevant external stakeholders with the objective of raising resources. Other applications of the relationship management framework promise a much broader and richer contribution of money, volunteering and influence for the benefit of the university or college.

Marketing's future in HE: a promise that will be kept?

Each of the areas listed above offer substantial progress in the contribution of marketing to the future of HE. While the list is probably not exhaustive, each area can be explored by marketing managers in HE administrative positions to the benefit of their institutions.

Strategic marketing planning

Institutions that use a strategic marketing planning format will find that their stakeholder markets can more easily align with the schools' mission and vision. Additionally, a strategic marketing approach offers probable institutional growth and long-term strengthening of the university community (Naude and Ivy 1999). The typical strategic planning format offers a vehicle for bringing very diverse members of the university community into a meaningful discussion concerning the future of the institution. While financial planning can strengthen an institution, strategic marketing planning offers a market-driven plan which is more likely to yield both revenue and institutional opportunities over time (Pabedinskaite and Friman 2003; Sevier 2001).

Consumer behaviour for college choice

Marketing managers who use the best empirical findings concerning the college choice process find that their institution has a major advantage in selecting and enrolling the 'best of the best' from the available student pool. Understanding the extent research literature also encourages administrators to attempt to influence the choice process much earlier than ever before (Martin and Dixon 1991). Programmes that expose high-potential young students (middle school, junior high school and high school) to the university years before they begin to consider and ultimately make a college decision offers great dividends in attracting high-quality students (Stupak 2001). Marketing also offers opportunities for colleges to create institutional profiles which can attract the very best students that aspire to success in the targeted programmes (Murphy 1981).

Complex choices of students after matriculation

While most uses of consumer behaviour understanding by university marketing administrators are committed to the way choices are made in selecting a college by students, other applications such as choosing majors, making housing choices and deciding about enrolling in overseas programmes can also be understood and enhanced by the use of consumer decision-making research. Other student choice processes can be improved and better understood, including employment searches and the choice of attending summer school sessions, for example.

Service quality in the university enterprise

The overall satisfaction of students with their college experiences is largely rooted in the ability of the various on-campus service units to deliver what is perceived by students as high-quality service encounters. A strong research tradition has emerged over the past twenty years regarding the components of quality services. Understanding students' needs for quality services in such varied contexts as dining services, telephone services and access to university computer systems can make a great difference in the ways students perceive an overall quality university experience. This overall perception of services at the university can substantially contribute to the long-term willingness of a student to become a supportive alumni or active volunteer.

Student satisfaction and student retention

Previous research in student retention has focused on the day-to-day connections that are made by students when they begin their college careers. Later drop-out problems can best be understood by using student satisfaction models. Properly understood, the factors that affect students' persistence can inform student academic advisers in advance of seeing the student drop out. The research on customer satisfaction encourages marketing managers to set carefully and monitor customer expectations (Verhoef 2003; Blasco and Saura 2006). Students' expectations are frequently affected by written communications and other interactions that lead to enrolment and other student choices (Shank *et al.* 1995). By simply understanding students' expectations, advisers and university marketing administrators can have a chance to enhance student satisfaction. Although students' roles as customers are controversial (Brennan and Bennington 1999; Clayson and Haley 2005; Obermiller *et al.* 2005), their complex roles in the university context can be understood by using what we know about customer satisfaction.

Viewing student needs through the lens of marketing research

Every group of stakeholders in the university can be better understood with a consistent programme of marketing research (Madden 2000). Prospective students and their families, current students, alumni, faculty, staff and university boosters in all areas (athletic teams, arts, academic programmes, etc.) have specific ways of viewing the university that cannot be imagined by marketers without objective research techniques. Marketing decision-makers think about the issues pertinent to stakeholders far too much and frequently to remain objective. The actual stakeholder groups have different, diverse and competing activities in their lives, and consistent, longitudinal research helps bring the thoughts and perceptions of these stakeholders into realistic focus. Benchmarks of stakeholders' market segments can be used as a point of comparison with future studies to understand changes in each market.

Ascertaining new programme success with market demand studies

Each year hundreds of new academic programmes are launched, based on the interest of faculty. Many of them fail and represent a waste of scarce resources. Further, other needed and potentially successful programmes are viewed with scepticism because of the frequency with which other programmes fail. By using demand analysis of both students' interest in the programmes and practical market acceptance by employers or others (graduate programmes, licensing boards, etc.), the probable success of programmes can be expected. Even existing programmes can be improved by researching the demand of students and others who are needed for future student success with the improved programmes.

Achieving sustainable equilibrium in the size of the student body

Every institution has to deal with the question of what its 'natural size' is as a school. By understanding the market segments that are likely to be sources of student demand, a proper institutional size can be projected, given the size of endowment, career aspirations of students and the student segments' available resources to pay tuition, fees and other costs of education. Being able to project sustainable size for the institution requires a very sophisticated understanding of markets and market segments to which the institution has access. Advantages of being able to accurately estimate an appropriate size for the school include being able to project accurately tenured faculty needs, constructing only buildings that are needed and that can be maintained and projecting needed scholarship funds. The ability to project sustainable size of an institution also provides the foundation for long-range strategic planning and visioning. Understanding the dynamics of this process also contributes to attracting institutional funding, including endowment and buildings.

Setting prices by understanding student demand and overall value

Institutions have realized in recent years that tuition rates are, at best, a 'sticker price' for students and their families to compare colleges generally. Many students do not pay the full tuition rate because of the availability of scholarship discount leveraging (Hoverstad *et al.* 2001). Schools frequently divide their total market into several market segments that differ because of varying levels of price elasticity of demand and their ability to pay. Schools that try to set a tuition rate that is affordable to all students leave a great deal of money on the table. Tuition can best be set as a result of understanding the perceived value of the college when compared to other peer institutions. Again, understanding the demand function of the school's market is fundamental.

Building a brand helps a college to differentiate itself and all of its programmes

National academic ranking systems such as *US News and World Report* place value on several quantitative factors in their annual published evaluations. Despite denying the importance and influence of such rankings, most schools have allowed them to influence institutional decision-making and therefore exerting a similarity levelling on choices made by the various administrations. A second homogenizing influence on universities is the accreditation process. Meeting standards of university accreditation as well as having internal schools and college units seeking accreditation tends to make institutions more similar than different. The work that has been done in the for-profit arena has shown that building a brand for an institution can have many advantages, the least of which is not that organizations that are differentiated can attract many supporters that subscribe to their values and goals (Naddaff 2004; McAlexander *et al.* 2004). The advantages for an institution of HE in having a well-known and differentiated brand are numerous. Prospective students will be aware of and include the school in their evoked set of prospective enrolment choices. Alumni and other supporters will take pride in the prominence of the institution and peer schools will recognize and positively evaluate the college when opportunities arise for colleague interaction.

Using customer relationship management to identify and cultivate donors

In the last few years a major paradigm shift has occurred in marketing that has only recently been applied to colleges and universities (Harrison 1995). Customer relationship management (CRM) has shifted the focus of marketing activities from mass markets and even market segments to individuals within the market segments. To support this approach, databases and depth information about individual stakeholders are used to match individuals with institutional opportunities. The first and most developed application for CRM in HE has been fundraising. In the past the best strategy for fundraising was to seek wealthy alumni who were capable of giving a significant gift and then cultivate them and hope that their memories of their college experience were positive enough to support the giving of a significant gift to the university. With CRM, the university development division can learn enough about the potential givers and develop strategies to cultivate relationships with each prospect over time. Through the use of CRM models that predict giving using relationship factors, the university fundraisers can improve the likelihood that a potential giver would take an interest in specific philanthropy projects. The use of this framework, although it may take many years to yield some significant gifts, promises much larger giving from donors, over time. Some experts in the application of CRM to raising HE gifts have compared the old fundraising paradigm to 'hunting and gathering' while CRM techniques are more like 'planting and harvesting'.

Moving from 'recruiting' classes to 'shaping' classes

One of the most successful applications of marketing in HE for the past twenty years has been enrolment management. The focus of that practice has been to generate more students in times of population decline or qualified prospective student decline. A more recent use of enrolment management has been relegated to leveraging student scholarship discounting. While many institutions have not developed a full use or appreciation for those applications, some schools have moved beyond that to 'shaping' classes. Shaping the characteristics of an entering class for a university can be focused on such goals as improving the size of the minority student enrolment, improving the male–female ratio or enhancing the proportion of out-of-state students (Shank and Beasley 1998). Especially in schools that have a large number of applications, the opportunity to build an entering class of high quality and significant diversity can be greatly improved by using class-shaping techniques (Tapp *et al.* 2004). Once a school has attracted a large number of applicants that have high test scores, the next opportunity to improve the student body is through the use of student attribute selection or 'shaping' (Shah and Laino 2006; Moogan *et al.* 1999).

Building non-traditional student programmes by offering convenience

Within the next five years the number of traditional college-aged students in North America will begin to fall for the first time in over a decade. Many institutions will have to rethink their opportunities in the non-traditional market for HE. If non-traditional students are to be successfully reached, institutions will have to put educational opportunities at convenient locations and at convenient times (Emil 1994; Raisman 1999). Some programmes will need to be integrated into the workplace, near the workplace or near home. Other programmes will have to be reframed towards online alternatives (Dunn 2000). Again, the success of these programmes will be dependent on the willingness of colleges and universities to offer courses and programmes to students in both time- and distance-appropriate forms.

Using 'internal marketing' to improve faculty and staff support

Perhaps, though, the most underused marketing tool in HE is 'internal marketing' (Mobley and Ibrahim 1989). Treating the faculty, staff and administration as markets for efforts and initiatives can help those who are implementing such programmes by gaining cooperation and support. As with any other marketing process, each of the internal markets must be researched and understood before any programmes are launched. Properly executed, faculty and staff can be encouraged to help with student recruitment or retention efforts. Staff can be shown better ways to serve the student community and to adopt innovations on the campus that must be implemented from time to time. The use of internal marketing can also offer a higher level of communication and cooperation from students, too. Many schools depend on current students for help with student recruiting efforts, guiding alumni around campus on special event days or raising student scholarships from supporters.

Building a broader community with customer relationship management

As already stated, customer relationship management (CRM) techniques are being used by many schools in fundraising. A broader application of the CRM paradigm for colleges and universities is possible by integrating all stakeholders into a database starting when individuals are first encountered as children, when they become prospective students, when they matriculate as students, or when they become alumni (Arnett *et al*. 2003). As various individuals move through a lifetime of interactions the college or university collects data about them and implements strategies that enhance and intensify their relationships (Madden 2006). By committing to the stakeholders for their entire lifetimes, the institution needs to identify areas in which it must contribute to the stakeholders' future success (Reinartz and Kumar 2003). Among the possible foci of contributing to the life of a stakeholder could be: enhancing college preparation of young people (students with high academic potential or legacies) through camps in the summer on the college campus (science, debate, engineering, music, environmental studies, leadership, etc.); bringing prospective freshman applicants to campus to interact with students and meet with faculty in their areas of interest; building a service culture towards the university community as an undergraduate student; offering students who are about to graduate opportunities for service and leadership in the alumni association; offering senior undergraduate students opportunities for interaction with alumni in their prospective career interests; asking new graduates to mentor and help undergraduates in the same field; asking older alumni to connect senior undergraduates with career opportunities in their companies; asking new graduates to volunteer in going on recruiting assignments for the university; offering career counselling for graduates who have been out of school for three to five years; offering continuing education directed at subjects that address current life needs, such as raising children, investing and changing careers; offering alumni travel opportunities; asking alumni to take leadership roles in the alumni association. The three basic building blocks of stakeholder relationships are: (a) offer programmes or other opportunities that can meet career or family needs to the stakeholder; (b) ask for volunteer service, personal influence and financial contributions to the university; and (c) offer a place in the university community that grows, evolves and matures throughout the stakeholder's life (Heckman and Guskey 1998; Bingham *et al*. 2001). A stakeholder relationship with the university is mutually beneficial, based on a growing appreciation by both parties (university and stakeholder) and contributes to the long-run quality of life in the university community (Madden 2001).

Using marketing to enhance the university of the future

The various initiatives mentioned in this chapter offer universities ways that the application of marketing can improve the quality of any institution. Over time colleges and universities will integrate their various marketing efforts, broaden the use of marketing tools to solve problems and set strategies and see marketing as a way of building communities that are richer and offer all members an enhanced life. Using brand management, customer relationship management and strategic marketing frameworks will be the basic price of competing within the HE markets of the future. In the recent past, universities have been able to seize great advantage by using marketing tools to make their institutions competitive. Most of these applications will not be enough in the future to make a school competitive. The promise of marketing in HE will be kept and expanded over time to the benefit of all members of university communities. Schools that do not take advantage of this promise will do so at their organizational peril.

References

Aldridge, S. and Rowley, J. (1998) 'Measuring customer satisfaction in higher education', *Quality Assurance in Education*, 6(4):197–204.

Arnett, D. B., German, S. D. and Hunt, S. D. (2003) 'The identity salience model of relationship marketing success: The case of nonprofit marketing', *Journal of Marketing*, 67(2):89–105.

Bingham, F. G. (1988) 'Background and practices related to educational marketing efforts', *Journal of Marketing for Higher Education*, 1(1):3–13.

—— Quigley Jr. C. J. and Murray, K. B. (2001) 'A response to beyond the mission statement: Alternative futures for today's universities', *Journal of Marketing for Higher Education*, 11(4):19–27.

Birnbaum, R. (2000) 'The life cycle of academic management fads', *Journal of Higher Education*, 71(1):1–16.

Black, D. R. and Miller, S. D. (1991) 'What makes small colleges successful?', *Fundraising Management*, 22(5):23–5.

Blasco, M. F. and Saura, I. G. (2006) 'Segmenting university students on the basis of their expectations', *Journal of Marketing for Higher Education*, 16(1):25–45.

Brennan, L. and Bennington, L. (1999) 'Concepts in conflict: Students and customers – an Australian perspective', *Journal of Marketing for Higher Education*, 9(2):19–40.

Broekemier, G. M. and Seshadri, S. (1999) 'Differences in college choice criteria between deciding students and their parents', *Journal of Marketing of Higher Education*, 9(3):1–13.

Brooker, G. and Noble, M. (1985) 'The marketing of higher education', *College and University*, 60(3):191–200.

Brookes, M. (2003) 'Higher education: Marketing in a quasi-commercial service industry', *International Journal of Nonprofit and Voluntary Sector Marketing*, 8(2):134–42.

Bulotaite, N. (2003) 'University heritage: An institutional tool for branding and marketing', *Higher Education in Europe*, 18(4):449–54.

Canale, J. R. and Dunlap, L. (1996) 'The relative importance of various college characteristics to students in influencing their choice of a college', *College Student Journal*, 30(2):214–16.

Canterbury, R. M. (1999) 'Higher education marketing: A challenge', *Journal of Marketing for Higher Education*, 9(3):15–24.

Capraro, A. J., Patrick, M. L. and Wilson, M. (2004) 'Attracting college candidates: The impact of perceived social life', *Journal of Marketing for Higher Education*, 14(1):93–105.

Chapman, D. W. (1981) 'A model of student college choice', *Journal of Higher Education*, 52(5): 490–505.

Clayson, D. E. and Haley, D. A. (2005) 'Marketing models in education: Students as customers, products or partners', *Marketing Education Review*, 15(1):1–10.

Clinton, R. J. (1989) 'Factors that influence the college prospect's choice of schools: Methodology, analysis and marketing implications of a recent study', *Journal of Marketing for Higher Education*, 2(2):31–41.

Coccari, R. L. and Javalgi, R. G. (1995) 'Analysis of students' needs in selecting a college or university in a changing environment', *Journal of Marketing for Higher Education*, 6(2):27–39.

Cook, R. W. and Zallocco, R. L. (1983) 'Predicting university preference and attendance: Applied marketing in higher education administration', *Research in Higher Education*, 19(2):197–211.

Dawes, P. L. and Brown, J. (2004) 'The composition of consideration and choice sets in undergraduate university choice: An exploratory study', *Journal of Marketing for Higher Education*, 14(2):37–59.

Dixon, P. N. and Martin, N. K. (1991) 'Measuring factors that influence college choice', *National Association of Student Personnel Administrators Journal*, 29(1):31–6.

Doyle, P. and Newbould, G. D. (1980) 'A strategic approach to marketing a university', *Journal of Educational Administration*, 18(2):254–70.

Dunn, S. L. (2000) 'The virtualizing of education,' *Futurist*, 34(2):34–9.

Emil, B. B. (1994) 'Customers, costs, and context: An integrated approach to funding university outreach programs and services', *Journal of Nonprofit and Public Sector Marketing*, 2(2):91–114.

Finley, D. S., Rogers, G. and Galloway, J. R. (2001) 'Beyond the mission statement: Alternative futures for today's universities', *Journal of Marketing for Higher Education*, 10(4):63–82.

Flint, T. A. (1992) 'Parental and planning influences on the formation of student college choice sets', *Research in Higher Education*, 33(6):689–708.

Galotti, K. M. and Mark, M. C. (1994) 'How do high school students structure an important life decision? A short-term longitudinal study of the college decision-making process', *Research in Higher Education*, 35(5):589–607.

George, A. M. (2000) 'The new public relations: Integrating marketing and public relations strategies for student recruitment and institutional image building – a case study of the University of Texas at San Antonio', *Journal of Nonprofit and Public Sector Marketing*, 7(4):17–31.

Gibbs, P. (2001) 'Higher education as a market: A problem or solution?', *Studies in Higher Education*, 26(1):85–94.

Goldgehn, L. A. (1989) 'Admissions standards and the use of key marketing techniques by United States' colleges and universities', *College and University*, 65(1):44–55.

—— (1990) 'Are US colleges and universities applying marketing techniques properly and within the context of an overall marketing plan?', *Journal of Marketing for Higher Education*, 3(1):5–28.

Gray, L. (1991) *Marketing Education*, Philadelphia, PA: Open University Press.

Harrison, W. B. (1995) 'College relations and fundraising expenditures: Influencing the probability of alumni giving to higher education', *Economics of Education Review*, 14(1):73–84.

Hayes, T. J. (1993) 'A higher education dialog image and the university', *Journal of Marketing for Higher Education*, 4(1/2):423–5.

Heckman, R. and Guskey, A. (1998) 'The relationship between alumni and university: Toward a theory of discretionary collaborative behavior', *Journal of Marketing Theory and Practice*, 6(2):97–112.

Hoffman, K. D. and Kretovics, M. A. (2004) 'Students as partial employees: A metaphor for the student–institution interaction', *Innovative Higher Education*, 29(2):103–20.

Hossler, D. and Gallagher, K. S. (1987) 'Studying student college choice: A three-phase model and the implications for policymakers', *College and University*, 62(3):207–21.

Hoverstad, R., Sylvester, R. and Voss, K. E. (2001) 'The expected monetary value of a student: A model and example', *Journal of Marketing for Higher Education*, 10(4):51–62.

Hugstad, P. S. (1975) 'The marketing concept in higher education: A caveat', *Liberal Education*, 61(4):504–12.

Johnson, B. (1987–88) 'Marketing: It's not everything', *College Board of Review* (winter),146:14–15, 25–6.

Johnson, W. C. (1989) 'Marketing in higher education: The brave new world', *Journal of Marketing for Higher Education*, 2(1):69–77.

Klassen, M. L. (2000) 'Lots of fun, not much work, and no hassles: Marketing images of higher education', *Journal of Marketing for Higher Education*, 10(2):11–26.

Kotler, P. (1979) 'Strategies for introducing marketing into nonprofit organizations', *Journal of Marketing*, 43(1):37–44.

—— and Fox, K. F. A. (1995) *Strategic Marketing for Educational Institutions*, 2nd edn, Englewood Cliffs, NJ: Prentice-Hall.

—— and Levy, S. J. (1969) 'Broadening the concept of marketing', *Journal of Marketing*, 33(1):10–15.

Krachenberg, A. R. (1972) 'Bringing the concept of marketing to higher education', *Journal of Higher Education*, 43(5):369–80.

Kronholz, J. (2002) 'On sale now: College tuition – discounting for top students hits new heights; only the "real unlucky" pay full price', *Wall Street Journal*, 16 May, p. D1.

LeBlanc, P. J. (1997) 'College ranking time: It's like finals', *Christian Science Monitor*, 9(228):819.

Levine, A. E. (2000) 'The future of colleges: Nine inevitable changes', *Chronicle of Higher Education*, 47(9):10–13.

McAlexander, J. H., Koenig, H. F. and Schouten, J. W. (2004) 'Building a university brand community: The long-term impact of shared experiences', *Journal of Marketing for Higher Education*, 14(2):61–79.

Madden, C. S. (2000) 'The case for integrated marketing in higher education', *CASE International Journal of Educational Advancement* (October):117–19.

—— (2001) 'Piece by piece', *Case Currents*, (March):21–5.

—— (2006) 'Building university community: A customer relationship management lifecycle approach', Symposium for the Marketing of Higher Education, Chicago: American Marketing Association: 1–2.

Martin, N. K. and Dixon, P. N. (1991) 'Factors influencing students' college choice', *Journal of College Student Development*, 32(3):253–7.

Michael, S. O., Holdaway, E. A. and Young, H. C. (1993) 'Administrators' perceptions of institutional marketing', *Journal of Marketing for Higher Education*, 4(1/2):3–25.

Mobley, M. F. and Ibrahim, N. A. (1989) 'Fragmentation within the university setting: An internal marketing response', *Journal of Marketing for Higher Education*, 2(1):79–85.

Moogan, Y. J., Baron, S. and Harris, K. (1999) 'Decision-making behaviour of potential higher education students', *Higher Education Quarterly*, 53(3):211–28.

Morris, L. M. (2003) 'Integrated marketing: The process and challenge of implementing this evolving concept at three private universities', unpublished Ph.D. dissertation, Texas Tech University, Lubbock, Texas.

Mulnix, M. (1989) 'College students as consumers: A brief history of educational marketing', *Journal of Marketing for Higher Education*, 2(2):123–49.

Murphy, P. E. (1981) 'Consumer buying roles in college choice: Parents' and students' perceptions', *College and University*, 56(2):140–50.

Naddaff, A. (2004) 'Branding by design: How nonprofits can fight for dollars with a strong visual presence', *Communication World* (September–October):18–21.

Naude, P. and Ivy, J. (1999) 'The marketing strategies of universities in the United Kingdom', *International Journal of Educational Management*, 13(3):126–33.

Newman, C. M. (2002) 'The current state of marketing activity among higher education institutions', *Journal of Marketing for Higher Education*, 12(1):15–29.

Newman, F., Couturier, L. and Scurry, J. (2004) 'Higher education isn't meeting the public's needs', *Chronicle Review*, 51(8):B6.

Obermiller, C., Fleenor, P. and Raven, P. (2005) 'Students as customers or products: Perceptions and preferences of faculty and students', *Marketing Education Review*, 15(2):27–36.

Pabedinskaite, A. and Friman, M. (2003) 'Marketing as efficient innovation in higher education institutions', *Management of Organizations: Systemic Research*, 27:101–12.

Parmar, A. (2004) 'Student e-union: Colleges write textbook on internet marketing', *Marketing News*, 38(6):13–14.

Paul, D. A. (2005) 'Higher education in competitive markets: Literature on organizational decline and turnaround', *Journal of General Education*, 54(2):106–38.

Pyke, D. L. (1977) 'The future of higher education: Will private institutions disappear in the US?', *Futurist* (December):371–4.

Raisman, N. A. (1999) 'Leave the field of dreams! Successful strategies for marketing the community college', *Community College Journal* (February–March):14–19.

Reinartz, W. J. and Kumar, V. (2003) 'The impact of customer relationship characteristics on profitable lifetime duration', *Journal of Marketing*, 67(1):7–99.

Riesman, D. (1980) *One Higher Education: The Academic Enterprise in an Era of Rising Student Consumerism*, San Francisco, CA: Jossey-Bass.

Sands, G. C. and Smith, R. J. (1999) 'Organizing for effective marketing communications in higher education: Restructuring for your competitive edge in marketing', *Journal of Marketing for Higher Education*, 9(2):41–58.

Schmidt, S. L. (1988) 'Marketing higher education: Past, present and future,' *Journal of Marketing for Higher Education*, 1(2):3–14.

Sevier, R. A. (2001) *Thinking Outside the Box*, Hiawatha, IA: Strategy Publishing.

Shah, A. and Laino, H. (2006) 'Marketing a U.S. university to international students: Which approach is best – standardization, adaptation or contingency? An investigation of consumer needs in seven countries', *Journal of Marketing for Higher Education*, 16(1):1–24.

Shank, M. D. and Beasley, F. (1998) 'Gender effects on the university selection process', *Journal of Marketing for Higher Education*, 8(3):63–71.

Shank, M. D., Walker, M. and Hayes, T. (1995) 'Understanding professional service expectations: Do we know what our students expect in a quality education?', *Journal of Professional Services Marketing*, 13(1):71–89.

Shapiro, B. P. (1973) 'Marketing for nonprofit organizations', *Harvard Business Review*, 51(5):223–32.

Shumar, W. (1997) *College for Sale: A Critique of the Commodification of Higher Education*, London: Falmer Press.

Spiegler, M. (1998) 'Have money will matriculate', *American Demographics* (September):51–6.

Stewart, K. L. (1991) 'Applying a marketing orientation to a higher education setting', *Journal of Professional Services Marketing*, 7(2):117–24.

Stupak, R. J. (2001) 'Perceptions management: An active strategy for marketing and delivering academic excellence at liberal arts colleges', *Public Administration Quarterly*, 25(2):229–46.

Tapp, A., Hicks, K. and Stone, M. (2004) 'Direct and database marketing and customer relationship management in recruiting students for higher education', *International Journal of Nonprofit and Voluntary Sector Marketing*, 9(4):335–45.

Verhoef, P. C. (2003) 'Understanding the effect of customer relationship management efforts on customer retention and customer share development', *Journal of Marketing*, 67(4):30–45.

Walle, A. H. (1990) 'Beyond advertising and public relations: An agenda for the marketing of higher education', *Journal of Marketing for Higher Education*, 3(1):1–4.

Wasmer, D. J. and Bruner, G. C. (1999) 'The antecedents of the market orientation in higher education', *Journal of Marketing for Higher Education*, 9(2):93–104.

Zemsky, R., Shaman, S. and Shapiro, D. B. (2001) *Higher Education as Competitive Enterprise: When Markets Matter*, San Francisco, CA: Jossey-Bass.

Zusma, A. (1999) 'Issues facing higher education in the twenty-first century', in P. G. Albach, R. O. Berdahl and P. J. Gumport (eds) *American Higher Education in the Twenty-first Century*, Baltimore, MD: Johns Hopkins University Press, pp. 109–12.

Part 5

Political marketing

18

Marketing politics . . . saving democracy?

Jenny Lloyd

Introduction

It might be said that in the UK and USA, politics is suffering something of an image crisis. In the UK, the initial euphoria that followed the election of 'New Labour' in 1997 appears to have been replaced by an atmosphere of distrust and disillusionment. This is evidenced by an Ipsos MORI poll for the newspaper the *Sunday Times* which suggested that 64 per cent of the British public felt that their politicians were 'all spin and no substance' (Anonymous 2006). Similarly in the USA, having been the first US President to win an election with over 50 per cent of the vote since his father, George Bush Senior, President George W. Bush's popularity has plummeted to an all-time low according to an ABC News/Washington Post poll which recorded a 65 per cent disapproval rate.

While in the USA, it might be possible to dismiss such discontent as a phenomenon attached to a single political figure, in the UK, the problem appears much more long-term and endemic to the field of politics as a whole. Indeed, in the UK, high levels of disaffection have been cited as one potential reason for the poor turnout at both local and national elections with the 61 per cent turnout in the 2005 UK general election only a slight improvement upon the record low of the 58 per cent achieved in 2001 (Electoral Commission 2005). Gosschalk *et al.* (2002) found that British voters had often disengaged from the political process as a result of their disillusionment with politicians' failure to deliver on electoral promises, apparent dishonesty and general self-interest. According to Mortimore (2003), this degree of negativity poses a real danger not only for the politicians and parties themselves, but also for the credibility of the democratic process as a whole. Poor levels of voter turnout raise issues of legitimacy and public mandate when, as in the case of the current UK New Labour government, it is elected on the basis of just over 20 per cent support of the total potential electorate.

Having highlighted this danger to democracy, Mortimore (2003) calls for a coherent programme of marketing to resuscitate the public enthusiasm for politics and repair its damaged reputation. In reply, this chapter highlights some of the challenges faced by marketers in the political field and proposes a systematic and more 'consumer'-focused response to rescue politics' ailing reputation.

The challenges facing political marketers

It might be said that the main challenge facing today's political marketers is the re-engagement of the voting public through the restoration of their faith in politicians' competence and honesty. The importance of this is highlighted by Van den Berg (2005) who suggests that perceived poor performance on the part of the institution of government is likely to undermine the public's perception of its legitimacy. Indeed, Curtin and Meijer (2006) concur but go further to identify a perceived lack of transparency as also being severely damaging.

Unfortunately, political marketers find themselves hindered on three fronts. In the first instance, they face the challenge of overcoming the uncomfortable relationship that sometimes exists between politics and marketing, particularly in the UK. While it is perhaps surprising that, in light of today's wide acceptance and use of marketing tools within the field of politics, this relationship has been so fraught, it is also understandable as each field tries to preserve what they see to be their underlying values.

From the political perspective, the main cause for concern relates to the potential for con-tamination by the commercialism associated with the marketing field. This was first reflected in post-revolutionary USA, where political campaigning activity was regarded with distaste in the newly formed democracy (Perloff 1999). Perloff (1999: 20) quotes one New Jersey critic who stated that a political candidate should be considered a 'detestable and dangerous wretch when his popularity has been "sought after" by daylight and candlelight'. Even to the present day, political marketing is viewed with suspicion. Harris (2001) and Egan (1999) both warn that there exists significant unease both inside and outside of politics concerning its potential impact upon the maintenance of ethical standards and ideological integrity.

In a similar way, those in marketing expressed concern as to the extent to which any extension of marketing outside the commercial sphere might dilute it to a point of extinction (Luck 1969). However, with the passage of time, these fears appear to have been allayed. Henneberg (2004) suggests that now much of current concern relates to the applicability of marketing theory to the field of politics. In particular, he cites the often raised question as to the extent to which the marketing concept can be applied to a product that has an unquantifiable value and a system in which non-economic exchange takes place. Such concerns echo those previously voiced by O'Shaughnessy (2001: 1047):

> Marketing is a business discipline whose relevance lies primarily in business: we should not assume that political contexts are invariably analogous to business to the extent that methods can be imported and used with equal effect.

The second obstacle relates to the way that political marketers are often hindered by the complex and multifaceted structures associated with the political machine that lend themselves to the generation of ethically 'grey' areas. A good example and a source of some disquiet is the practice of 'lobbying', defined as 'the practice of trying to influence governmental decisions, particularly legislative votes, by agents who serve interest groups' (Starling 1984: 363). A long-established and accepted element within western democracies, it appears both loved and loathed in equal measure. According to Grunig and Hunt (1984), there is a continuum in which, on one side, lobbying may be seen as a highly positive addition to the political process in that its main objective is the provision of sufficient information to the legislature to allow them to vote on the basis of informed decisions, and on the other, it is corrupt, using money or favours to buy votes. Whichever may prove to be the case, the influential presence of the political 'lobby' is both undeniable and unavoidable. In the USA, almost every one of the

Fortune 500 companies has some form of political representation in Washington either directly or through the establishment of specialized 'issue networks' (Coen 1999).

Finally, the behaviour of politicians individually, and collectively, often makes it difficult to successfully market politics, parties and politicians. Lloyd (2006) found that repeated instances of apparently unethical behaviour by politicians in their public and private lives negatively impacted not only on the perception of them as individuals but of the political sector as a whole.

Yet while these challenges are not new, increasing levels of public disengagement suggest that existing strategies are floundering. Therefore, to halt this arrest and safeguard existing democratic processes, it is time to revisit current political-marketing practices in search of a more efficacious approach. A logical first step in this direction is an examination of the platform used by voters to compare the various alternatives on offer; something that might be conceptualized within marketing terminology as a 'market'.

Examining the political 'market'

The conceptualization of the political arena as a 'market' is one that some find troublesome. According to Egan (1999), there are those who feel it to be inappropriate and trivializing to reduce the field of political science to the level of a commercial transaction. Yet it appears that there are strong parallels to be drawn between political and commercial 'markets'. Typical dictionary definitions of a 'market' describe it as the location at which potential buyers and sellers meet to exchange goods or services, ideally to their mutual benefit. On such a basis, conceptualization is not incompatible with the political scenario in which voters choose between the various political 'brands' on offer on the basis of which best satisfies their needs.

It is through Levitt's (1960) classic treatise on 'marketing myopia' that we can appreciate the relevance of the concept of the 'market' in today's political sphere. His warning of the dangers associated with defining one's product too narrowly has certainly been evidenced in recent times, as voters turn away from conventional political parties in search of other organizations, such as the Make Poverty History or anti-globalization movements that they feel more effectively meet their needs (Lloyd 2006). Therefore it is only through a thorough understanding of both the multiplicity of consumer needs and their speed of evolution that a political party can fully understand the true structure and dynamics of the market within which it operates and, most importantly, its consumer base and who its competitors really are.

The centrality of consumer need is a perspective which is endorsed by Lees-Marshment (2001b). She draws parallels between political campaigning and the concept of 'sales orientation'; a situation in which an organization focuses upon 'selling' its argument to the public and using opinion research to gauge a response. Instead, she strongly advocates the adoption of a market orientation by political parties which identifies consumer needs and then developing and modifying their product offering in response. Following from this, she suggests that such a strategy is likely to generate satisfaction among the voting public, or political 'consumers', and is the best way of achieving success within the political 'market'.

Consumer need and political brands

Alongside the adoption of a 'marketing orientation' comes the imperative for political agents first to identify their consumers, and then clearly ascertain the nature and variety of needs that

301

they seek to satisfy when making their political choices. From this informed position, they are able to modify their product offering and differentiate themselves clearly from their political competitors through the creation of distinct political brands.

However, at the outset it is important to distinguish between the concept of political 'customers' and political 'consumers'. According to the American Marketing Association (AMA 2006), 'customers' differ from 'consumers' in that while a 'customer' is seen as the potential or actual purchaser of a good or service, the consumer is the ultimate end user. It is the case that in most democratic countries, the population as a whole may be seen to be 'consumers' of the political product with a smaller proportion also assuming the mantle of 'customers' because they are in possession of the right to vote. The criteria that determine who is entitled to vote vary from country to country and often region to region. In the case of the UK, individuals under 18 and prisoners are exempt from taking part in elections although this might change following concern over falling participation levels and a 2005 ruling in the European Court of Human Rights that such exemptions might run counter to prisoners' human rights. Similarly in the USA individuals under the age of 18 are exempt, plus those who do not comply with the residency requirements imposed by each individual state and virtually all incarcerated felons and many non-incarcerated felons.

On this basis, one might assume that the focus of marketing activity should be on the political 'customer' as he or she is in possession of the vote that may determine which party or politician would take office. Indeed, it would concur with the current emphasis of the AMA's definition of marketing which states that:

> Marketing is an organizational function and a set of processes for creating, communicating, and delivering value to customers and for managing customer relationships in ways that benefit the organization and its stakeholders.
>
> (AMA 2006)

Yet it is the position of this author that the term 'consumer' is much more appropriate and strategically much more important. First, it has been identified in previous work (Lloyd 2003) that, unlike almost any other type of product, those domiciled within a country consume the 'product' generated by government whether they voted for the governing political party or not. In most cases a country's residents may be seen to consume the 'product' of it in one form or another (e.g. management of the economy, defence of the country's borders, provision of basic education, etc.) both passively and actively from the moment they are conceived until the day they die.

In addition, the concept of 'consumer' recognizes the fact that individuals not only make choices between products, they actively use products not only to satisfy their functional needs but also to satisfy less tangible, symbolic needs (Belk 1988). Through what Firat and Venkatesh (1995) define as self-productive consumption practices, political consumers make a contribution to the totality of the political 'product', endowing it with values and attributes that may be quite different to those intended by the original brand owner. A good example of this is cited in research by Lloyd (2006) who found that some of her respondents said that the main reason they had supported the Communist Party in their youth was as a form of rebellion against authority figures (usually parental), while one or two also saw such action as a fashion statement.

From this perspective, there can be no doubt that consumers use political parties as political 'brands'. In his consideration of political parties as 'brands', Smith (2003) cites Aaker's (1991: 7) definition of a brand as being particularly pertinent:

> A brand is a distinguishing name and/or symbol (such as a logo) intended to identify the goods or services of either one seller or a group of sellers and to differentiate those goods or services from those of competitors.

The benefit of conceptualizing political parties as brands is that it lends insight into the variety of ways they are used to satisfy political consumers' needs. For instance, it is clear that the political 'brands' not only act as differentiators but also function as a form of shorthand reflecting de Chernatony and Dall'Olmo Riley's (1998) proposition that consumers use brands to simplify the decision-making process. In this way, a political 'brand' may be seen as a representative entity which embodies an individual party's array of policies, propositions and values.

Further, according to de Chernatony and Dall'Olmo Riley (1998), a central role of the brand is to provide 'added value' to the consumer, over and above the functionality of the product. Within the field of politics, this 'added value' can take a number of forms. It has often been stated that political parties in the UK are converging on the middle ground with the result that factors other than policy must be seen as a differentiator. These factors might take the form of a 'relationship' (Fournier 1998) either with a politician, party or with a community, virtual or real, that supports that party (Muniz Jr. and O'Guinn 2001; Schouten and McAlexander 1995). Alternatively, affiliation with a specific party may provide more of a symbolic benefit to individuals in their attempt to establish their identity (Belk 1988) or their place in society (Bourdieu 1984).

Such an idea corresponds with the proposition behind Campbell et al.'s (1960) party identification theory and Tajfel's (1978) subsequent and highly influential social identification theory which identifies that individuals use their affiliation to groups such as political parties to develop their self-concept and support their self-esteem. Butler and Stokes (1974) concur, suggesting that while at its most basic level party identification could be seen as simply an individual's predisposition for one party over another, the presence of strong emotional, expressive and apparently irrational components could not be denied.

This proposition has been supported more recently by Lloyd (2006) whose research found that association with groups either formal or informal often fulfilled one or more of a variety of consumer needs, taking both functional and symbolic forms. In this way, the choice of one political 'brand' over another might not only offer the political consumer the chance of satisfying functional needs such as a stable economy or secure national boundaries but affiliation with a specific political party may also satisfy symbolic needs such as the social desire for friendship and belonging while supporting psychological needs such the maintenance of self-esteem and the establishment and communication of social identity.

Finally, a clearly branded political party offers the 'added value' of acting as a risk reducer in the minds of voters. Bauer (1960) identifies that when consumers make a choice between products and services, they perceive a degree of risk. Solomon et al. (2002) identify five kinds of risk faced by consumers: monetary, functional, physical, social and psychological. A political party or candidate functioning as a brand can reassure voters that their economic status, their personal security or their social position would be secure if elected successfully. New Labour successfully capitalized on the desire for risk reduction in the 1997 general election when they had ten election pledges, originally printed in their manifesto, printed on cards and handed out to the general public. These pledges addressed every type of risk, either directly ('We will be tough on crime, tough on the causes of crime') or indirectly ('We will give Britain the leadership in Europe which Britain and Europe need'), thereby offering voters what appeared to be a safe choice.

Taking all of this into account, the importance of establishing a clearly branded political offering in response to political consumers' needs is clear. Further, having identified the multifaceted nature of political consumer–political brand interaction, it falls to political agents to re-examine their products to create an offering that uniquely satisfies the needs of political consumers.

Creating a political 'product' which satisfies consumer need

In line with many other 'intangibles', a difficulty that has long faced political marketers when analysing the political product is the lack of consensus as to exactly what it is. Indeed, the precise nature of the political 'product' has long been a source of debate among academics. One school of thought posits that politicians as a body might be seen to be the political 'product' (Posner 1992 cited by O'Cass 1996) while others adopt a more narrow focus upon the party leaders themselves (Foley 1993; Crew and King 1994; O'Shaughnessy 2001). Alternatively, others describe the political 'product' in terms of elements more closely linked to the political parties themselves, for example, 'policy' (O'Shaughnessy 2001), 'policy commitments' (Harris 2001) and 'party behaviour' (Lees-Marshment 2001a), yet interestingly the one element that is obvious by its absence is that of 'ideology' (Lloyd 2003).

Yet while there is little agreement as to precisely what the political product is, a general acceptance has emerged as to its characteristics. There appears to be a consensus that the political 'product' possesses very similar features to those identified by Shostack (1977) and Cowell (1984) as typical of the service sector: intangibility, perishability, heterogeneity, inseparability and lack of ownership (Butler and Collins 1994; Henneberg 2004; Lloyd 2003, 2005b). Further agreement is found in the statement by O'Shaughnessy (2001) who submits that analogies may be drawn with the promise-based offers found in the insurance or finance industries. This, together with Harrop's (1990) proposition that the main objective of all political marketing activity is the projection of belief in a party's ability to govern supports the idea that the political 'product' is not so much an 'output' from a particular activity as an 'outcome'. This being the case, the political 'product' may be defined as the expertise that enables the successful generation of 'outcomes' through the processes associated with the institution of government. In real terms, within democratic political systems, this might be seen as the expertise that enables the successful management of national security, social stability and economic growth on behalf of the electorate.

Yet when defining the political 'product' on the basis of such 'outcomes', there is the tendency to take the perspective that its main purpose is to satisfy the functional needs of political consumers. Yet it has been already established that political consumers 'consume' politics on the basis of both functional and symbolic values. Therefore, as can be seen in Figure 18.1, when conceptualizing the political product it is essential that both the functional and symbolic elements must be taken into account and, most importantly, not only those outcomes generated by the political parties, but also those whose origins come from the political consumers themselves.

Despite many misgivings cited within conventional marketing literature (O'Malley and Patterson 1998), hand in hand with any definition of the 'product' usually comes the concept of the 'marketing mix'; those aspects of a 'product' that are deemed to be controllable with the implication that marketers can manipulate them in order to achieve their objectives (Brassington and Pettitt 1997). Political-marketing literature is no different and, despite similarly voiced concerns as to its relevance and applicability, there is still frequent citation of

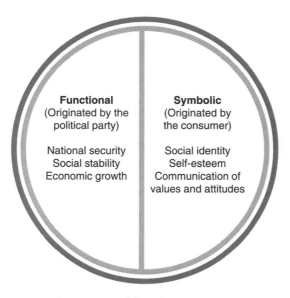

Figure 18.1 The composition and origination of the political product

the most iconic of these models, the classic '4Ps' (product, place, price and promotion), advocated by Borden (1962) and McCarthy (1964).

Inconsistency does exist, however, as despite politics' acknowledged similarity to the service industry, there has been only limited reference to Booms and Bitner's (1981) service marketing mix that also incorporated the additional 'Ps' of 'people', 'process' and 'physical evidence' (Lloyd 2003, 2005). In this light and the ongoing realization that analytical frameworks cannot simply be superimposed from one type of market to another (Beaven and Scotti 1990; Butler and Collins 1994; Lock and Harris 1996; O'Cass 1996), a product mix has been advocated by Lloyd (2005a) in response to what she believed to be the unique circumstances faced by those functioning within the political 'market'.

Figure 18.2 Components of the political 'marketing mix' (Lloyd 2003, 2005b)

According to Lloyd (2003, 2005b), there are five components that comprise the political marketing mix, depicted in Figure 18.2. While this mix exhibits some of the characteristics proposed by Borden (1962), McCarthy (1964), Booms and Bitner (1981) and Beaven and Scotti (1990), it also takes into account the unique nature of the political market.

Component 1: The services offering

This is the first component of the political marketing mix. From the perspective of the political party, this involves having the expertise to manage the whole range of 'services' associated with government; for example, national security, social stability and economic growth. These 'services' take two forms, the first of which is that of 'consultant'. As a 'consultant', the relationship that political parties have with the electorate may be seen to be similar to that which some organizations have with their consumers; that of doctor–patient (Kaldor 1971). Such a perspective is not at odds with the organizational adoption of a marketing orientation (Lees-Marshment 2001b) in that it assumes that a political party's expertise allows it to assess a situation and address needs that might not have been articulated by the consumer. Indeed, in some cases, the consumer might not even be aware of these needs. In this way, Houston's (1986: 86) analogy may be seen to be reflective of the situation:

> the patient does not specify the treatment; it is the doctor's task to assess the specific product needs of the patient. Yet, this does not mean that the doctor is not addressing the needs and wants of the patient; the doctor's unique offering is that special capability to identify and satisfy the patient's needs.

The second form of 'services offering' is that of 'project management' and is particularly important for those political parties that achieve electoral success. Having used their expertise to diagnose the country's needs, it is then necessary for the party in government to possess the skills to manage their delivery. It is certainly the case that electors judge the suitability of a party not only on their electoral policies, but also as to whether they feel they have the ability to fulfil their responsibilities (Butler and Collins 1994; Wring 2005). Consequently, political parties must ensure that they have appropriate management skills and expertise to fulfil both roles adequately.

Component 2: Representation

This is the second component of the political marketing mix. In contrast to the definition that is usually cited when considering concepts associated with democracy (i.e. that of working on behalf of a particular part of the electorate), in this instance the term 'representation' is seen to relate to the presentation of the political party and all that might be connected with it. It relates to the representation of the political party in the eyes of the electorate. From this perspective, the term 'representation' goes further than purely 'communication' or 'promotion' because it takes into account both the controllable aspects of political activity such as policy statements and briefings, public appearances and political advertising and PR, and the uncontrollable elements such as media coverage and word of mouth. It recognizes the indirect route that communications take between political parties and the voters and the role that consumers play in the political communication process and the construction of political brands. This process was outlined by Lloyd (2006) who, based upon her own research, combined elements of the

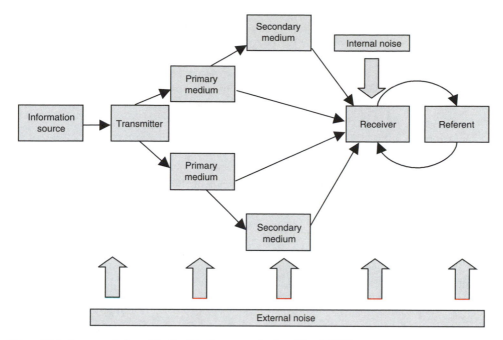

Figure 18.3 An amended model of political communication (Lloyd 2006)

classic models proposed by Shannon and Weaver (1947) and Westley and MacLean (1957) to produce an amended model of political communication (Figure 18.3).

According to the Lloyd (2006) model, the 'transmitter' of the message party is rarely the original source, the political party. For example, while the party hierarchy or a specific policy–making unit might formulate new policy, they rarely 'transmit' it direct to the public, but instead announce it using press officers at a press conference or other form of media briefing, or, alternatively, they will issue a policy document. This is then reported through a set of primary media, for example, the television or radio news, which may or may not be received directly by the political consumer or 'receiver'. If a 'receiver' does not receive a message directly from the primary media, he or she might receive it from secondary media, for example, political commentators.

As with Shannon and Weaver's (1947) classic model, the message is subject to interference or corruption throughout the transmission process by distorting factors such as media bias (external noise) or human emotion (internal noise). When received, the message may then be passed to somebody or something known as a 'referent' that, in the eyes of the receiver, has credibility. In this way, the 'referent' can help the receiver gain a sense of perspective and has a strong influence over how the party representation is read. Electors then consult their mental 'scripts' to match expectation to representation. These 'scripts' are histories based upon voters' past experiences, real and vicarious, that form their expectations. If a match occurs, the representation will serve to reinforce the existing perception of the political 'product'. In contrast, a mismatch will result in dissonance and a resulting alteration of the mental 'script'. Given the nature of the composition of this process, it is not difficult to understand why it is often the case that the representation offered by a political party is quite different from the one that is read by the voter.

The representational element of the political marketing mix has three important implications for political parties. First, and most importantly, it is not enough to be in possession of the expertise and the ability to govern, it is essential that they should be *seen* to possess such ability. This offers a serious challenge for opposition parties such as the Liberal Democrats in the UK who have a strong record in local government but are yet to achieve similar success to gain a parliamentary majority. Without a previous record in government, their aim must be to shift consumers' focus on to those aspects of their work that offer visible demonstrations of both their competence and their efficacy in the eyes of the electorate.

That being said, it is essential that political parties paint representations of themselves that are both realistic and believable. There can be no doubt that parties will seek to depict themselves as positively as possible, particularly when in the throes of an electoral campaign. However, if voters are allowed to acquire unrealistic expectations, any inability to deliver will only result in disappointment and distrust. This has certainly been the case with New Labour and the former British Prime Minister Tony Blair and in the USA with the US President George Bush.

However, nine years later, the New Labour image appears to have become somewhat tarnished by allegations of discord between the two main protagonists of the New Labour movement, Tony Blair and Gordon Brown, and a number of high-profile 'scandals', fuelled by continuous media pressure. Issues such as the 'Ecclestone affair', in which Formula One's exemption from the ban on tobacco advertising was linked to a million-pound donation to New Labour, Peter Mandelson's apparent receipt of a 'secret' £373, 000 house loan from ministerial colleague Geoffrey Robinson together with allegations of misconduct over passport applications made by supporters of the Millennium Dome, the Hinduja brothers, and accusations, later disproved, of offering peerages in exchange for loans appear to have inflicted severe damage upon the image of the party. A public backlash ensued, reflected in a YouGov opinion poll which reported 69 per cent of those questioned believed that New Labour under Tony Blair looked sleazy compared with the 63 per cent who, nine years previously, felt the same about the Conservative Party under John Major (King 2006). Worryingly, this disillusionment appears to have poisoned the public view of politicians as a whole. Ipsos MORI's (2007) survey on behalf of the UK's Sun newspaper suggested that the electorate held little hope of improvement in Blair's successor Gordon Brown or the leader of the Opposition, the Conservative Party's David Cameron.

Component 3: Accommodation

This is the third component of the political marketing mix; the requirement on the part of political parties to understand the needs of the electorate and be able to 'accommodate' them appropriately with an appropriate response. As has been previously stated, political consumers 'consume' politics to satisfy a variety of needs, both functional and symbolic. Therefore it is only through a constant programme of research that parties can attain a thorough understanding of public priorities and therefore place themselves in a position to address them. In addition, the Beaven and Scotti (1990) definition of 'accommodation' as 'something supplied for convenience' reflects the political imperative to make the democratic process more accessible to the electorate.

It should be noted, however, that while political parties should aim to be more accommodating to the needs of the electorate, it does not mean that the priorities of the political parties should become focus-group led. Instead, parties should attain an understanding of public priorities and public interest and be prepared to address these topics on the basis of their political ideology. During the 2001 UK general election, the Conservative Party made a major strategic error when it decided to focus its attention on what it saw to be a Labour Party weakness, the issue of Europe when the focus of the electorate was on issues that had greater impact on the electorate's day-to-day lives, such as the National Health Service and education. By taking this decision, the Conservative Party could only appear as one of two things to the electorate: ignorant (of the priorities of those it sought to represent) or incompetent (unable to understand the priorities of those it sought to represent). Either way, this strategic error made it unelectable in the eyes of many, a fact that was reflected in the response of one caller to a BBC Radio 5 general election phone-in programme who suggested that they had simply 'lost the plot'.

In addition, when considering 'accommodation' within the political market, the electorate must be able to gain access and participate within it with some degree of ease. Public representatives and members of the government should be seen as accessible and open, while participation at all levels should be both encouraged, and seen to be encouraged, across all sections of the community. Central to this notion is the requirement that those participating should feel that they have (and be seen to have) some degree of influence. Without this, potential participants will question the point of expending time and effort doing so. At a time when most western democracies are experiencing a fall in levels of participation, the need to accommodate public participation in every way possible becomes all the more acute.

Components 4 and 5: Investment and outcome

The fourth and fifth components of the political marketing mix, 'investment' and 'outcome', are inextricably linked. In contrast to the concept of 'outlay' used by Beaven and Scotti (1990) or 'price' by Borden (1962), McCarthy (1964) and Booms and Bitner (1981), the term 'investment' more closely reflects the stakeholder-type relationship that the electorate has with its political representatives. 'Investment' on the part of political consumers can take many forms. First and most obviously it can take the form of direct financial payment such as subscriptions or donations to political parties or candidates. Alternatively, it can also take the form of a delayed financial 'investment' such as the promise of changes in tax or welfare benefits or changes in the standard of living. Finally, 'investment' can also take the form of factors which are difficult to quantify in monetary terms; for example, the time and effort to participate (Beaven and Scotti 1990) and the emotional and experiential aspects (Dermody and Scullion 2001) attached to participation within the political process.

Whatever forms these investments take, those who invest in some aspect of the political system usually expect to see a return or 'outcome'; either tangible or intangible, functional or symbolic. Certainly the ability to deliver upon policy issues and election promises is one of the most tangible ways by which electors judge the performance of political parties. However, because of the symbolic as well as functional aspect of the political product, consumers also have the ability to use political brands to support their self-concept or satisfy other personal needs.

Further, it is not just the final outcome that counts, but also how that outcome is achieved. Research by Seawright (2001) and Lloyd (2006) suggests that while voters are suspicious of politicians' motives and honesty, the possession of integrity is an important trait within the field of politics. That being the case, they take a dim view of those politicians and parties who behave dishonestly. This being the case, politicians and the political parties they represent should not only be seen to deliver on their promises effectively and efficiently but also ethically and with integrity.

Ultimately, if politicians and political parties fail to provide the electorate with the 'outcomes' they desire, they are likely to take their 'investment' elsewhere. Further, because of the wide variety of different needs and functions fulfilled by the political product, there are a similarly wide variety of substitutes. Gordon (2003) observes that, in the USA, concern over the public provision of services has resulted in the growth of private government in the form of 'common interest developments' (CIDs) which, in turn, has been linked with falling levels of political participation. These developments, which include condominiums, planned developments, cooperatives and business improvement districts, promise high levels of service and, in return, levy 'taxes' upon their members to cover the provision of such services such as waste collection, snow clearance, security and street cleaning that had previously been provided by local government.

Similarly, in the UK, electors also appear to be taking the initiative where political parties and candidates appear to have failed. At a time when participation in national and local elections has fallen consistently for many years, Lloyd (2006) found that individuals often sought personal political empowerment through participation in non-conventional political organizations such as environmental charities or campaigning organizations that they felt offered tangible results in response to their commitment. Ultimately, if it appears that conventional political organizations fail to provide an acceptable return upon 'investment' in whatever form it takes, it is clear that political consumers have few qualms about looking elsewhere or even taking matters into their own hands.

This being the case, the onus falls upon political parties to design and produce their own unique brand of political product that responds to the needs of political consumers. Further, having created a branded political product that satisfies the needs of its consumers, they must enter into an ongoing system of political brand management to ensure that they maintain their relevance and distinctiveness.

Managing political brands

The aim of an effective political brand management system is to ensure that the political brand in question achieves sufficient longevity to maximize its chances of achieving successive election victories. This, in turn, will provide them with sufficient time in government to implement long-term proactive strategies which will satisfy the needs of their consumers. Henneberg (2004) distinguishes between the term 'political marketing' which relates to the micro-management of individual elements of the product mix and branding and 'political marketing management' which he describes as the overarching and strategic processes that underpin the successful management of the political exchange process. The importance of achieving longevity in government was reflected in a speech by former British Prime Minister Tony Blair, following a second, successive New Labour General Election victory in 2001:

> I believe in the last four years we have laid foundations. I believe our victory in this election shows the British people understand we have laid foundations but now is the time to build upon them.
>
> (*Guardian*, 8 June 2001)

Yet despite the practical acknowledgement of the need for continuity, limited attention has been paid to strategic political-marketing management processes (Butler and Collins 1996). Indeed, it has long been acknowledged that the field of political marketing has yet to achieve a consensus upon a precise definition as to what they encompass (Scammell 1999). The complexity of the field may be partially responsible for this. Harrop (1990) suggested that central to

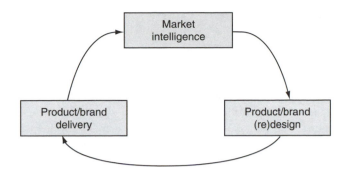

Figure 18.4 A simple model of political-marketing management process

the role of political-marketing management was the positioning of political parties; a concept that encompassed far more activities and processes than the electoral speeches, party political broadcasts and political advertising that were usually associated with it.

The highly generalized definitions of political marketing that have emerged in recent years may also have hindered the development of political-marketing management models. For example, while Henneberg's (2004: 226) definition of political marketing as a function that facilitates 'the societal process of political exchange' may allude to the field's complexity through its lack of specificity, a danger that arises from generality is that such definitions offer little direction and the attribution of processes associated with the field can be rather arbitrary.

One of the few political-marketing management models in existence is that proposed by Lees-Marshment (2001b). She suggests a linear eight-step marketing process which includes market intelligence, product design, product adjustment, implementation, communication, campaigning, election and, finally, delivery. However, being linear, this process infers that there is a distinct 'beginning' and 'end' to the process; an idea that runs counter to Sparrow and Turner's (2001) proposition that political parties are now engaged in a 'permanent campaign'.

This being the case, a political-marketing management system based upon a simple, circular model, such as that to be found in Figure 18.4, may be used to give direction as to the nature of the processes required. The first stage in the process, 'market intelligence', requires a wide-ranging analysis of the political 'market', an environmental analysis and an understanding of the nature and structure of the various consumer and stakeholder segments that operate within it. Certain models developed to analyse commercial markets may be seen to be of use here. For example, Porter's (1980) classic five forces model identifies potential threats posed by new entrants, substitute products, suppliers, direct competitors and consumers themselves. Further, Dean and Croft (2001) have identified Christopher *et al.*'s (1991) six markets model as leading particular insight into the nature and variety of the political consumer base. Ultimately, the aim of the market intelligence stage of the management process should be to understand the needs of the various consumer groups together with the relative ability of the variety of political agencies within the market to satisfy them.

Having identified where consumer needs are not being fulfilled, political brand owners must then redesign their products using the political-marketing-mix framework to meet those unmet needs. On delivery of the political product, the circular process continues as an ongoing programme of market intelligence must then be implemented to ensure consumers' needs are being fulfilled and any further changes that might be required.

Conclusion

Mortimore's (2003) proposition that the future of democracy is endangered by the current public disengagement with conventional politics is not an idle comment but currently visible in the UK. The fact that the public are still engaged with politics in the wider sense has become clear with the increasing popularity of campaigning movements such as the 'Make Poverty History' campaign or the anti-globalization movement. It appears that they have simply turned away from what they saw as the ignorance, disinterest or inability on the part of conventional political parties towards undemocratic entities that appear to understand and are willing to address their needs and concerns in a direct fashion. At the same time, falling participation on the part of voters in elections has opened the door to political parties previously unseen as, for example, the radical right-wing British National Party (BNP) who, according to BBC Online (2002), made a gain of twenty seats in local elections when commanding only 0.7 per cent of public support nationwide.

In response to the falling participation rates, in the UK, the response of the government has been to try to improve turnout by improving access with proposals to hold elections on public holidays, to hold them over a two-day weekend, to have 'special' polling stations in locations such as supermarkets, the introduction of advanced voting, and the implementation of constituency transfers. However, as the limited success of postal voting demonstrated, facilitation of the process is not really the answer. It is more important to create political products and brands that the electorate will be happy to buy into – both literally and metaphorically – with their votes.

This can only be achieved when conventional political parties are seen by the electorate as being responsive to their needs. To this end, the conceptualization of the political arena as a 'market' provides an excellent vehicle to do this. A 'political market orientation' (Lees-Marshment 2001b) acknowledges the centrality of the political consumer and with it the complex nature of the needs they wish to satisfy. It is therefore no longer sufficient for political parties to churn out their 'product' without first identifying that the 'mix' they have adopted responds to political consumers' concerns and addresses both their functional and symbolic needs. Further, having addressed these needs, it behoves political parties to manage their brands so that not only do they continue to deliver their product consistently, but they are in a position to modify it as the occasion arises.

This being said, it must again be restated that this does not mean the 'product' offered by the respective political parties should be reactively determined by the results from focus groups. What it does mean is that, through an acknowledgement of the electorate's concerns and the production of a response, a dialogue is generated between the processes of government and the electorate which in turn may regenerate a level of political engagement that itself is the lifeblood of a healthy democracy.

References

Aaker, D. A. (1991) *Managing Brand Equity*, New York and London: Free Press.

American Marketing Association (2006) 'Marketing definitions', available online at: www.marketingpower.com (accessed 12 December 2006).

Anonymous (2006) The *Sunday Times*, Ipsos MORI poll, 20 August.

Bauer, R. (1960) 'Consumer behaviour as risk taking', in R. S. Hancock (ed.) *Dynamic Marketing for a Changing World*, Chicago, IL: American Marketing Association.

Beaven, M. H. and Scotti, D. J. (1990) 'Service-oriented thinking and its implications for the marketing mix', *Journal of Services Marketing*, 4:5–19

Belk, R. (1988) 'Possessions and the extended self', *Journal of Consumer Research*, 15:139–69.

Booms, B. H. and Bitner, M. J. (1981) 'Marketing strategies and organization structures for service firms', in J. Donnelly and W. R. George (eds) *The Marketing of Services*, Chicago, IL: American Marketing Association.

Borden, N. (1962) 'The concept of the marketing mix', in G. Schwartz (ed.) *Science in Marketing*, New York, NY: Wiley & Sons.

Bourdieu, P. (1984) *Distinction: A Social Critique of the Judgment of Taste*k, trans R. Nice, London: Routledge.

Brassington, F. and Pettitt, S. (1997) *Principles of Marketing*, London: Pitman Publishing.

Butler, D. and Stokes, D. (1974) *Political Change in Britain: The Evolution of Electoral Choice*, London: Macmillan.

Butler, P. and Collins, N. (1994) 'Political marketing: Structure and process', *European Journal of Marketing*, 28:19–34.

—— (1996) 'Strategic analysis in political markets', *European Journal of Marketing*, 30:25–36.

Campbell, A., Converse, P., Miller, W. E. and Stokes, D. (1960) *The American Voter*, New York, NY: Wiley.

Christopher, M., Payne, A. and Ballantyne, D. (1991) *Relationship Marketing*, Oxford: Butterworth-Heinemann.

Coen, D. (1999) 'The impact of US lobbying practice on the Europen business–government relationship', *California Management Review*, 41:27–44.

Cowell, D. (1984) *The Marketing of Services*, Oxford: Heinemann Professional Publishing.

Crew, I. and King, A. (1994) 'Did Major win? Did Kinnock lose? Leadership effects in the 1992 British general election', in A. Heath (ed.) *Labour's Last Chance?*, London: Dartmouth.

Curtin, D. and Meijer, A. J. (2006) 'Does transparency strengthen legitimacy?', *Information Polity: The International Journal of Government and Democracy in the Information Age*, 11(2):109–22

de Chernatony, L. and Dall'Olmo Riley, F. (1998) 'Defining a "brand". Beyond the literature with experts' interpretations', *Journal of Marketing Management*, 14:417–43.

Dean, D. and Croft, R. (2001) 'Friends and relations: Long-term approaches to political campaigning', *European Journal of Marketing*, 35:1197–1216

Dermody, J. and Scullion, R. (2001) 'Delusions of grandeur? Marketing's contribution to "meaninful" western political consumption', *European Journal of Marketing*, 35. 1085–98.

Egan, J. (1999) 'Political marketing: Lessons from the mainstream', *Journal of Marketing Management*, 15:495–503.

Electoral Commission, the (2005) 'Engaging the public in Great Britain', available online at: www.electoralcommission.org (accessed 1 January 2007).

Firat, A. F. and Venkatesh, A. (1995) 'Liberatory postmodernism and the reenchantment of consumption', *Journal of Consumer Research*, 22:239–67.

Foley, M. (1993) *The Rise of the British Presidency*, Manchester, UK: Manchester University Press.

Fournier, S. (1998) 'Consumers and their brands: Developing relationship theory in consumer research', *Journal of Consumer Research*, 24:343–64.

Gordon, T. M. (2003) 'Crowd out or crowd in?: The effects of common interest developments on political participation in California', *Annals of Regional Science*, 37:203–34.

Gosschalk, B., Marshall, B. and Kaur-Ballagan, K. (2002) 'Non-votors, political disconnection and parliamentary democracy', *Parliamentary Affairs*, 55: 715–30.

Grunig, J. and Hunt, T. (1984) *Managing Public Relations*, Orlando, CA: Harcourt Brace Jovanovich.

Guardian, the (2001) 'Tony Blair's victory speech', 8 June, available online at http://politics.guardian.co.uk/speeches/story/0. . .590671.00.html.

Harris, P. (2001) 'To spin or not to spin, that is the question: The emergence of modern political marketing', *Marketing Review*, 2:35–53.

Harrop, M. (1990) 'Political marketing', *Parliamentary Affairs*, 43:277–91.

Henneberg, S. (2004) 'The views of an *advocatus dei*: Political marketing and its critics', *Journal of Public Affairs*, 4:225–43.

313

Houston, F. S. (1986) 'The marketing concept: What it is and what it is not', *Journal of Marketing*, 50:81–7.

Kaldor, A. G. (1971) 'Imbricative marketing', *Journal of Marketing*, 35:19–25.

King, A. (2006) 'It began with Tony Blair's promise that "things can only get better". They haven't,', *Daily Telegraph*, 15 July.

Kotler, P. (2003) *Marketing Management*, New Jersey, NJ: Prentice Hall.

—— and Levy, S. J. (1969) 'Broadening the concept of marketing', *Journal of Marketing*, 33:10–15.

Lees-Marshment, J. (2001a) 'The marriage of politics and marketing', *Political Studies*, 49:692–713.

—— (2001b) *Political Marketing and British Political Parties: The Party's Just Begun*, Manchester, UK: Manchester University Press.

—— and Lilleker, D. (2001b) 'Political marketing and traditional values: "Old Labour" for "few times"?', *Contemporary Politics*, 7:205–16.

—— and Quayle, S. (2000) 'Spinning the party or empowering the members? The Conservative Party reforms of 1998', presented at the Annual Conference of the Political Studies Association, London.

Levitt, T. (1960) 'Marketing myopia', *Harvard Business Review*, 38:45–56.

Lloyd, J. (2003) 'Square peg, round hole?: Can marketing-based concepts such as the "product" and the "marketing mix" have a useful role in the political arena?', Paper presented at the PSA Conference, 'Democracy and Diversity', Leicester, England.

—— (2005a) 'Horses to water? Marketing concepts and the problem of falling electoral participation in the UK', paper presented at the Academy of Marketing Conference, University of Gloucestershire, Cheltenham, England.

—— (2005b) 'Square peg, round hole?: Can marketing-based concepts such as the "product" and the "marketing mix" have a useful role in the political arena?', in W. Wymer and J. Lees Marshment (eds) *Current Issues in Political Marketing*, London: Haworth Press.

—— (2006) 'A dynamic model of consumer brand conceptualization within the political market', doctoral thesis (unpublished).

Lock, A. and Harris, P. (1996) 'Political marketing – *vive la différence!*', *European Journal of Marketing*, 30:14–24.

Luck, D. J. (1969) 'Broadening the concept of marketing too far', *Journal of Marketing*, 33:55–63.

McCarthy, E. J. (1964) *Basic Marketing: A Managerial Approach*, Homewood, IL.

McKenzie, R. and Silver, A. (1968) *Angels in Marble*, London: Heinemann Educational Books.

Mortimore, R. (2003) 'Why politics needs marketing', *Journal of Nonprofit and Voluntary Sector Marketing*, 8(2):117–21.

Muniz Jr., A. M. and O'Guinn, T. C. (2001) 'Brand community', *Journal of Consumer Research*, 27:412.

O'Cass, A. (1996) 'Political marketing and the marketing concept', *European Journal of Marketing*, 30:37–53.

—— (2002) 'A micromodel of voter choice: Understanding the dynamics of voter characteristics in a federal election', *Psychology and Marketing*, 19:1025–46.

O'Malley, L. and Patterson, M. (1998) 'Vanishing point: The mix management paradigm re-viewed', *Journal of Marketing Management*, 14:829–52.

O'Shaughnessy, N. (2001) 'The marketing of political marketing', *European Journal of Marketing*, 35:1047–57.

Perloff, R. M. (1999) 'Elite, popular and merchandised politics – historical origins of presidential campaign marketing', in B. Newman (ed.) *The Handbook of Political Marketing*, California, CA: Sage Publications.

Porter, M. E. (1980) *Competitive Strategy – Techniques for Analysing Industries and Competitors*, New York, NY: Free Press.

Posner, M. (1992) 'Repositioning the right honorable', *Canadian Business*.

Scammell, M. (1999) 'Political marketing: Lessons for political science', *Political Studies*, 47:718–39.

Schouten, J. W. and McAlexander, J. H. (1995) 'Subcultures of consumption: An ethnography of new bikers', *Journal of Consumer Research*, 22(1):43–62.

Seawright, D. (2001) 'Landslide II or trauma II? The national results', *The Journal of Marketing Management*, 17:1019–33.

Shannon, C. and Weaver, W. (1949) *The Mathematical Theory of Communication*, Illinois, IL: University of Illinois Press.

Shostack, G. L. (1977) 'Breaking free from product marketing', *Journal of Marketing*, 41(2):73–80.

Smith, G. (2003) 'Assessing brand personality of UK political parties: An empirical approach', Paper presented at the Academy of Marketing Political Marketing Conference, London.

Solomon, M., Bamossy, G. and Askegaard, S. (2002) *Consumer Behaviour – A European Perspective*, Prentice Hall, London.

Sparrow, N. and Turner, J. (2001) 'The permanent campaign', *European Journal of Marketing*, 35:984–1002.

Starling, G. (1984) *The Changing Environment of Business*, Boston, MA: Kent Publishing Company.

Tajfel, H. (1978) 'Social categorization, social identity and social comparisons' in H. Tajfel (ed.) *Differentiation Between Social Groups*, London: Academic Press.

Troy, G. (1996) *See How They Ran: The Changing Role of the Presidential Candidate*, Cambridge, MA: Harvard University Press.

Van den Berg, C. (2005) 'The crisis of public authority', *Brown Journal of World Affairs*, 12(2):223–37.

Westley, B. and MacLean, M. (1957) 'A conceptual model for communication research', *Journalism Quarterly*, 34:31–8.

Wring, D. (2005) *The Politics of Marketing the Labour Party*, Basingstoke, UK: Palgrave Macmillan.

19

Comprehensive political marketing

Global political parties, strategy and behaviour

Jennifer Lees-Marshment

Introduction

Political marketing is a new, fast-developing area of nonprofit marketing, and like all other areas of non-commercial activity enjoys its fair share of academic debates, ethical issues and practical problems. The study of political marketing historically suffered from the same fate of early business marketing: too much focus on the selling of politics rather than the design of the political product. In the last decade, however, new scholars have applied wider marketing theory to politics in a more effective and illuminating manner. This chapter will set out a comprehensive approach to political marketing, a model of political marketing behaviour for political parties alongside examples of global practice and raise a number of issues and debates within political marketing.

Comprehensive political marketing

Political marketing, like marketing, previously suffered from the common misconception that it was all about spin doctors and soundbites and political advertisements. Academic study was narrowly focused on election campaigns rather than how parties behave in the years before an election (see Lees-Marshment 2003 for detailed review of this literature as well as Henneberg 2005). More recently, political marketing has been viewed more broadly. Political marketing is about political organizations adapting techniques (such as market research) and concepts (such as the desire to satisfy voter demands) originally used in the business world to help them to achieve their goals (Lees-Marshment 2001a). Like commercial marketing, it is not just about how organizations sell their product. Political marketing is not just concerned with how parties use advertising to persuade voters to support them, or what they do in the official election campaign in the weeks prior to voting day. It is concerned with the influence of marketing concepts (product, sales and market orientation) on behaviour and can be applied to a wide range of political organizations.

In order to ensure that we understand that political marketing is more than just selling, we can take five principles to research. This approach is more comprehensive and enables political

1	CPM applies marketing to the whole behaviour of a political organization, not just communication.
2	CPM uses marketing concepts, not just techniques: the product, sales and market orientation as well as direct mail, target marketing and market intelligence.
3	CPM integrates political science literature into the analysis.
4	CPM adapts marketing theory to suit the differing nature of politics.
5	CPM applies marketing to all political organizational behaviour: interest groups, policy, the public sector, the media, parliament and local government as well as political parties.

Figure 19.1 Comprehensive political marketing: key principles

marketing to have a broader scope and greater utility to political practitioners. Comprehensive political marketing has five main principles (from Lees–Marshment 2003, building on Lees–Marshment 2001a): see Figure 19.1.

With this broader definition comes many more issues and scope for debate. While the selling of political ideas is an interesting topic, it is when discussion moves to how marketing may influence what those ideas are, and therefore policy-making at governmental level, that the democratic implications become more evident. More recent work by scholars has discussed the nature of the political product, strategy, internal political marketing and local political marketing (see e.g. Lloyd 2003, 2006; Ormrod 2006b; Henneberg 2005; Lilleker and Negrine 2002, 2004; Bannon 2002, 2005).

The Lees-Marshment (2001) political party marketing model

Taking this comprehensive approach, Lees–Marshment developed a model of party behaviour in political marketing. Seeing political marketing more as a *way of thinking* for political parties: how they view the needs and views of voters, and how they behave in relation to that. Although political parties may be argued to be office-seeking, and marketing viewed as a potential means to gain that power, political marketing is concerned with the strategies parties use to develop a political product they offer to voters to win that election and maintain support in office. Comprehensive political marketing is less about how they sell that product, and more about how they design that product in relation to market intelligence, for if you develop the right product that suits voter demands, they will support it without the need for aggressive selling.

The product is basically its behaviour, which encompasses many characteristics, is ongoing, and is offered at all times (not just elections) and at all levels of the party (for a more marketing-led definition and exploration of the political product, see Lloyd 2003, 2006). The product includes aspects such as those listed below, although this will vary from one country to another:

- leadership: powers, image, character, appeal, relationship with the rest of the party organization and with the media;
- Members of Parliament (existing or candidates);
- membership: powers, recruitment, loyalty and behaviour;
- staff: researchers, professionals, advisers, and so on – their role, influence, office powers and relationship with other parts of the party organization;
- symbols: name, logo and anthem;
- constitution: formal, official rules;
- activities: party conferences, rallies and meetings; and
- policies: those proposed for when in office and those enacted once in office.

317

Parties using comprehensive political marketing change their product to suit the nature and demands of their market: they become market oriented.

The market-oriented party

Combining an understanding of marketing as being about behaviour, product development and strategy rather than just selling, and the knowledge that political parties are complex, evolving organizations which need to win elections but also maintain long-term relationships with their voters and members, led to the development of the concept of the market-oriented party (Lees-Marshment 2001). Applying the commercial marketing philosophy of putting satisfying customers at the heart of the business operation, in politics, political parties can also become market oriented. A market-oriented party, therefore, uses party views and political judgement to design its behaviour to respond to and satisfy voter demands in a way which meets their needs and wants, is supported and implemented by the internal organization, and is deliverable in government.

Using this definition, political marketing is used to understand the public, rather than manipulate it. While practice may differ, if marketing is to be used most effectively, parties will seek less to manipulate and persuade opinion, and more to follow it. It places the power in the hands of the masses, rather than elites – but by enabling elites to understand the public more effectively it provides the potential for them to use this understanding to be responsive and representative of the public will. Parties may use their ideology as a means to create effective solutions to public demands, but party elites try to respond to market demand, rather than trying to shape opinion. The distinction is therefore in how politicians respond to the intelligence, by following rather than leading public opinion.

This diverges from more traditional views of political parties as organizations who seek to pursue their ideological vision, and who therefore campaign to persuade voters to support their policies. Traditionally, parties were seen to try to change voter opinion to suit what the party offered, rather than change what the party does to suit the voters. Where marketing was used it was in creating the most effective communication to persuade voters to change their minds. Market-oriented politics is about the party changing, rather than the public.

Nevertheless it is not as simple as merely promising to do what the median voter wants. The market is complex and includes members, related think-tanks and politicians. Needs, not just wants, must be considered, in the long as well as the short term. A market orientation is not about simply giving people what they want, because a party needs to ensure that it can deliver the product on offer. It also needs to ensure that the new product will be accepted within the party and so needs to adjust its product carefully to take account of this. Market-oriented parties (MOPs) should not all become the same, or assume the characteristics of catch-all parties, or simply move to the Downsian centre-ground.

In order to ensure this, there is a process of activities – known as the market-oriented party political marketing process – which parties should carry out to achieve a market orientation: see Figure 19.2.

In order to illustrate how this model differs or is similar to practice, we will discuss the example of UK leader Tony Blair in 1997.

UK New Labour market-oriented party

The best example of an MOP is New Labour in the 1997 UK election. After losing three successive general elections employing approaches which were more elite, party driven and

Stage 1: market intelligence
The party aims to understand and ascertain market demands. Informally it 'keeps an ear to the ground', talks to party members, creates policy groups, meets with the public. Formally it uses methods such as polls, focus groups and segmentation to understand the views and behaviour of its market, including the general public, key opinion-influencers, MPs and members. It uses market intelligence continually and considers short-term and long-term demands.

Stage 2: product design
The party then designs 'product' according to the findings from its market intelligence, before adjusting it to suit several factors explored in Stage 3.

Stage 3: product adjustment
The party then develops the product to consider:
• achievability: ensures promises can be delivered in government;
• internal reaction: ensures changes will attract adequate support from MPs and members to ensure implementation, taking into account party ideology and history, retaining certain policies to suit the traditional supporter market where necessary;
• competition: identifies the opposition's weaknesses and highlights own corresponding strengths, ensuring a degree of distinctiveness; and
• support: segments the market to identify untapped voters necessary to achieve goals, and then develops targeted aspects of the product to suit it.

Stage 4: implementation
Changes are implemented throughout the party, needing careful party management and leadership over an appropriate timeframe to obtain adequate acceptance, to create party unity and enthusiasm for the new party design.

Stage 5: communication
Communication is carefully organized to convey the new product, so that voters are clear before the campaign begins. Not just the leader, but all MPs and members send a message to the electorate. It involves media management but is not just about spindoctoring; it should be informative rather than manipulative, and built on a clear internal communication structure.

Stage 6: campaign
The party repeats its communication in the official campaign, reminding voters of the key aspects and advantages of its product.

Stage 7: election
The party should win not just votes but attract positive perception from voters on all aspects of behaviour including policies, leaders, party unity and capability, as well as increased quality of its membership.

Stage 8: delivery
The party then needs to deliver its product in government.

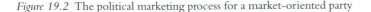

Figure 19.2 The political marketing process for a market–oriented party

only used marketing to sell an unwanted product, the party accepted the need to follow rather than try to educate, persuade or lead public opinion. The party elected a brand-new leader, Tony Blair, who fully accepted the need for a market orientation. Full-scale market intelligence was conducted and many aspects of the product altered to suit voters' demands. The new product was communicated so effectively that by the time of the election campaign the party had little to sell: voters already knew what they had to offer. The approach had extremely positive results: Labour won the election with a majority of 179, taking seats normally considered unwinnable and attracting a wide base of support. An overview of the activities involved in the process is provided in Figure 19.3.

Sales-oriented party

The Lees-Marshment (2001) model does however acknowledge that not all parties follow the market-oriented model, and many are prone to adopt a sales orientation. Sales-oriented parties aim to sell what they decide is best for the people, utilizing effective political marketing communication techniques. Market intelligence is used not to inform the product design, but to help the party to persuade voters it is right: see Figure 19.4.

In proportional representation (PR) electoral and multiparty political systems there is a greater tendency for parties to be sales oriented, especially for minor parties. Minor parties, with little chance of winning power, will predominantly want to influence the agenda and potential coalition partners, and therefore a sales orientation is a rational option to use marketing to present their argument most effectively to the segments most open to persuasion.

Like any approach, the use and effectiveness of political marketing depends on the goals of the organization and the nature of the environment.

Product-oriented party

Parties may also opt for a more old-fashioned approach and be product oriented, whereby they maintain their elite-driven beliefs and policies but do not put effort into trying to sell this; they simply hope electors will see the merit of their argument. In some rare cases this may be effective for new, single-issue-dominated, short-lived political movements which capture the public mood and respond to a concern other established parties are ignoring. However the desire for long-term survival encourages parties to be sales or market oriented.

The market-oriented party as the winner

The current research view, as with business marketing, remains that major parties generally need to adopt a market orientation in order to win control of government, regardless of the system, because being responsive to and satisfying voters is the best way to gain and maintain their support. This differs from more traditional views of party behaviour as being about leading and changing public opinion, or more conventional views of political marketing.

Practice varies however: while the UK Labour 1997 case fits the model well, as do other examples such as Clinton's New Democrats in 1992 in the USA, and the German SPD (see p. 323), clearly not all parties follow this approach. The George W. Bush–Karl Rove strategy from 2000 to 2008 might be viewed as a more manipulative, sales-oriented approach where market intelligence is used to understand and then persuade voters. Nevertheless, despite the Republican Party's ability to win and maintain control of the presidency, it has suffered losses in Senate and Congress, and public satisfaction with the government declines alongside growing

Stage 1: market intelligence
- post-election analysis was conducted, focusing on traditional Labour supporters who had voted Tory;
- internal discussion occurred through policy groups;
- NOP conducted surveys and polls and focus groups were run; and
- proposed policies were even pre-tested.

Stage 2: product design
- the new leader, Tony Blair, had less links to traditional labour movement; pro-change; a strong leader; popular with voters;
- MPs and candidates were under strict leadership;
- members' rights were increased; one member, one vote achieved; the party distanced from trade unions;
- increased use was made of staff with professional expertise, especially those closest to the leader (e.g. Alastair Campbell);
- clause IV of the constitution was altered to remove unpopular commitment to state ownership;
- the slogan *New Labour, New Britain* was adopted;
- specific pledges were made in issue areas most important to voters (e.g. education, health service; general commitment to fiscal prudence, low government spending and income tax); and
- a mini-manifesto was launched a year before election to pre-test policies; the final manifesto was popular.

Stage 3: product adjustment
- specific pledges for delivery were short and limited; included details on how it would achieve them (e.g. cutting waiting lists in the NHS by reducing money spent on bureaucracy);
- internal members were consulted on changes to Clause IV and balloted on manifesto;
- past weaknesses were removed (e.g. reduction of link with trade unions and reassurances made on income tax and economic management; Conservative weaknesses exploited); and
- 'Middle England' voters were targeted especially in communications.

Stage 4: implementation
- a strong leadership style ensured high party unity; public accepted the party had changed.

Stage 5: communication
- communications were tightly run from new centre in Millbank Tower;
- a strategy to gain positive relationship with press was pursued;
- the media were fed positive stories;
- party figures who stepped outside official product designed were reprimanded; and
- the product was well communicated to voters before campaign even started.

Stage 6: campaign
- this was tightly run and well planned; good communication within party organization;
- repeated the message Labour had changed;
- a rebuttal unit dealt with criticism;
- campaigning on ground focused on target seats needed to win; and
- posters reinforced party's pledges; photo-opportunities used.

Stage 7: election
- Labour won with 419 seats and 43% of the popular vote; membership also rose.

Stage 8: delivery
- party focused on delivery; issued annual reports on its performance; delivered on constitutional reform but their ability to achieve voter satisfaction with quality of public services is more questionable.

Figure 19.3 UK Labour's marketing in 1997 (based on Lees–Marshment 2001)

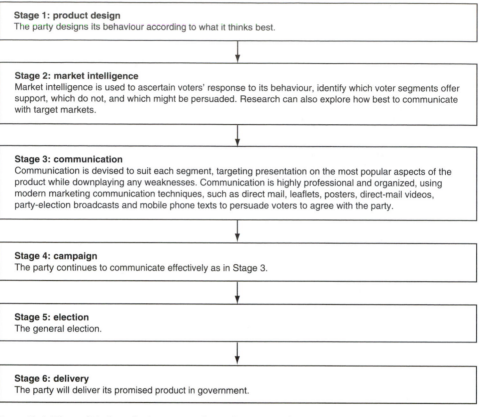

Stage 1: product design
The party designs its behaviour according to what it thinks best.

Stage 2: market intelligence
Market intelligence is used to ascertain voters' response to its behaviour, identify which voter segments offer support, which do not, and which might be persuaded. Research can also explore how best to communicate with target markets.

Stage 3: communication
Communication is devised to suit each segment, targeting presentation on the most popular aspects of the product while downplaying any weaknesses. Communication is highly professional and organized, using modern marketing communication techniques, such as direct mail, leaflets, posters, direct-mail videos, party-election broadcasts and mobile phone texts to persuade voters to agree with the party.

Stage 4: campaign
The party continues to communicate effectively as in Stage 3.

Stage 5: election
The general election.

Stage 6: delivery
The party will deliver its promised product in government.

Figure 19.4 The political marketing process for a sales-oriented party

criticism. A more responsive, market-oriented strategy would arguably create more productive voter satisfaction and a more positive appraisal of the Bush presidency.

Criticisms of the model

As with any models, this is not a 100 per cent foolproof explanation and depiction of party behaviour at all times. It has naturally attracted its fair share of criticism (see Ormrod 2006a and Lees-Marshment 2006a for details). One solid weakness is the lack of empirical operationalization of the Lees-Marshment model (see Henneberg 2004). It would be very complex to do this; to test it fully would require a long-scale, well-funded project with access to internal behaviour within a political party, as well as full-scale statistical analysis of all public data about voter perception: access and resources which are not easily obtained. Larger-scale, deeper statistical analysis is needed to provide any sense of 'proof' but even then analysis would need to use the final election-study data available after the final vote and therefore be open to the criticism of still fitting the data to suit the theory. A second fair criticism was that the model was not comparative in its origin: it was very much developed to suit the British context. In politics, just as in business, each country has different rules, systems and organizations which affect the way that marketing is used. However, political marketing in the market-oriented form is happening all around the world, even in countries we might not expect.

Global political party marketing

Global New Labour

Centre-left parties seem almost to have not only adopted a market orientation, but utilized the same product design developed during that process. First, Tony Blair's UK Labour design was in large part modelled on, or adapted from, the New Democrat strategy espoused first by Bill Clinton in the USA in 1992. Ingram and Lees-Marshment (2002) argue that Clinton used marketing in a market-oriented manner. They relaunched Clinton following the market research carried out in May and June 1992 where findings had indicated that voters viewed Clinton as a slick and privileged politician: the short bio film *A Man from Hope* was developed to counteract this negative perception. Clinton focused on policy concerns of target middle-class voters and traditional Democrat supporters, such as the economy and healthcare. In terms of achievability, considerable effort was put into reducing the number of Clinton's spending pledges and other promises, including his plans for infrastructure spending and deficit reduction, in order to make them more feasible. Clinton adopted the market-oriented concept and produced a responsive, targeted New Democrat design which won control of both the presidency and Congress in 1992.

This model was then adapted by Tony Blair in the UK in 1997, and the German SPD/ Schroder (Lees 2005) and New Zealand Labour/Helen Clark (Rudd 2005). Lees studied the transformation of the German Social Democrats' (SPD) marketing 1995–8, noting the use of market intelligence, professional consultants, direct marketing and target marketing. The SPD made changes in terms of leadership and policy, at least at an overall thematic level, designed convey perceptions of competence and leadership, restored credibility in the party and retained its comparative advantage within social justice. Market intelligence identified four positive aspects that the party then communicated: political change; leadership; innovation; and justice.

In the New Zealand Labour Party, Rudd (2005) noted how the party engaged in internal market intelligence and external quantitative polling (e.g., UMR Insight), utilized management consultants to create strategic plans and subsequently assessed performance against objectives. It responded to market intelligence in policy development, especially in key areas identified as of particular importance to voters, such as health, pensions, jobs, and law and order, as well as the general desire for positive vision and achievable proposals. Copying Tony Blair and the UK Labour Party in response to voter desire for credibility and believable promises, Clark offered clear-cut policy pledges appearing on a 'credit card' in 1999. Like Blair, Clark's pledges were created to suit the target market middle-income New Zealanders and focused on the issues that voters cared most about. The New Zealand Labour Party also copied the UK in making vigorous efforts to tell the electorate that it was keeping its election promises, issuing progress reports and lists of achievements in government. The pledge card was used again by UK Labour and New Zealand Labour in the most recent election in 2005 (Lees-Marshment 2006b).

Clearly, the market-oriented party model has been used around the world by labour parties extremely successfully. A key question will be whether this success can continue – for example, whether the US Democrats can make a return to power by developing a secure, balanced and responsive market-oriented product. There were concerns that the Clinton period in the 1990s left the party with a vacuum of policies, lacking a clear vision or ideology. When Tony Blair left office in July 2007 many questions were asked about the legacy he had left behind, with criticisms that New Labour had not made much of a difference. With the new leader, Gordon Brown, comes a chance to refresh the product. However, despite an initial increase in polling support, if he is in office for more than a year the public will expect to see either evidence of substantial improvement in delivery of 2005 promises, and/or a fresh proposal for the future. In

323

government, parties need to maintain their responsive market orientation by re-engaging in the process to formulate new products for each election.

Copying conservatives

The left-of-centre parties are not the only ones engaged in a game of copying or adapting ideas from each other. More recently we can see examples of parties who reach out to new target markets and balance ideology with the need to reach out to new external target markets. Although an assessment of the Republican Party in its second term, post-Iraq era suggests a more manipulative, sales-oriented approach, George W. Bush did make use of the market-oriented approach to win. Analysis by Knuckey and Lees-Marshment (2005) showed that they employed research to understand the voting behaviour of key segments, as well as voter attitudes towards the parties and candidates. The significant market intelligence endorsed the candidature of George W. Bush whose product as state governor, developed in response to public demands and criticisms of other Republican approaches, set the foundations for a market-oriented strategy which guided the 2000 presidential campaign. Bush was a popular candidate because he portrayed himself as a different type of Republican – a compassionate conservative – and as a different type of politician – a uniter not a divider. He focused on issues which opinion polls showed to be of paramount concern for most Americans in the 2000 election, including where Democrats traditionally had an advantage: education, social security and healthcare. Bush incorporated these with traditional Republican themes: tax cuts, smaller government and a stronger military, but by talking about public services he emphasized new Republicanism. Implementation during the primaries and long campaign involved adjustment in leadership and symbolism as well as policies to respond to internal reaction, competition analysis, public perception of achievability and analysis of the segments he needed to win. Communication was long term, positive advertising was designed to appeal to target groups (women, moderates and independents) because market intelligence indicated they were repelled by negative advertising.

This approach was also copied. Iain Duncan-Smith, who was leader of the UK Conservative Party from 2001 to 2003, adopted many of the concepts used by George W. Bush in 2000 (Knuckey and Lees-Marshment 2005) in the USA, such as 'No child left behind, Compassionate Conservatism' and focusing on the vulnerable. However, he was not able to maintain internal support and had to resign as leader in 2003 and this strategy was abandoned. Other recent examples suggest conservative parties are moving away from the market-oriented model. In 2005 the New Zealand National Party's campaign appeared very similar to that run by the Australian Liberal Party in 2004 and the UK Conservatives in 2005 in terms of its focus on right-wing and negative issues and therefore a sales, not market-oriented approach (see Lees-Marshment and Rudd 2006a, 2006b). As already discussed, George W. Bush's second election campaign in 2004 and second term in office also suggest a move away from a market orientation to a leadership-driven policy on war and a focus on using marketing purely as a sales method to get voters to vote Republican, rather than using it to develop policies to suit its wants and needs.

Comparative analysis

In terms of the extent to which political parties follow the more specific and complex market-oriented party model, this was first analysed in *Political Marketing in Comparative Perspective* (Lilleker and Lees-Marshment 2005), which illustrated the extent to which political marketing is being used by parties to determine their behaviour around the world. The Lees-Marshment model was applied to a range of countries (Germany, Austria, Brazil, Peru, Canada, Scotland, Ireland, New Zealand, the UK, the USA) successfully, utilizing all three party types in the market-sales-product-oriented party framework and thereby adding considerably to our understanding of political marketing around the world.

A surprising result was the extent to which new democracies such as Brazil and Peru showed signs of utilizing a market orientation. Cotrim Maciera (2005)'s study of Brazil focused on the Brazilian left-wing party PT – Partido dos Trabalhadores (Workers Party), led by Luiz Inácio Lula da Silva. The analysis showed how the PT changed its behaviour in order to win the 2002 presidential election. Using the recent electoral record to press for change, it employed professionals and utilized quantitative and qualitative research and created a mini-campaign to convey Lula's new approach from the results of survey analysis. Lula dropped more radical lines to become more moderate. Communication avoided radicalism and confrontation, accompanied by subtle but significant changes to his personal appearance. The PT also moved to the centre, its manifesto became less ideological, and together with its coalition partner, PL, its policies became more pragmatic. There was some internal opposition but change was justified due to losing so many elections. Effective support analysis, segmentation and targeting were carried out, developed from market intelligence. Lula had previously alienated female voters, but in 2002 he targeted the female vote, with Lula's wife accompanying her husband on the campaign rallies. The PT also exercised careful competition analysis, learning that, although the Brazilian population was dissatisfied with the government and welcomed change, it would not accept the opposition discrediting everything Cardoso had achieved.

International political marketing: differences in practice

The comparative party marketing book did note a number of differences between countries, however (see Lilleker and Lees-Marshment 2005). One of these had been predicted: a PR electoral system, by requiring coalition governments, enables smaller parties to adopt a sales-oriented approach and still have influence in coalition. The power of the leader and strength of the party is also an issue – some UK party leaders have tried but failed to follow a market orientation, as they are blocked by internal culture, but in the US presidential system, where there is a separation of powers, that is not an issue. The availability and regulations of funding for political parties affects their ability to conduct market intelligence and utilize professional staff (see Marland 2005). Looking comparatively, it is also important to note that in Stage 7, election, if a market orientation is successful, it will achieve its goals which may be to gain control of government, either solely or in coalition; or just to make advances in seats or an aspect of the policy agenda. For Stage 8, delivery, this may be achieved for smaller parties by delivering greater representation to their members and supporters by entering into coalition, or purely by continuing to influence government through pressure while retaining their radical character. Nevertheless, the Lees-Marshment model was still found to be a useful means of investigating its presence and effectiveness in relation to a range of systemic features and potential causal factors, as noted by Strömbäck and Nord (2005). A forthcoming book entitled *Global Political Marketing*, edited by Lees-Marshment, Rudd and Strömbäck to be published by Routledge in 2009 will attempt to explore the systemic features using more scientifically selected countries: established democracies will include the USA, the UK, Australia, New Zealand, Sweden, Germany, Japan and Greece. Emergent democracies include the Czech Republic, Russia, Hungary, Turkey, Peru, Taiwan, South Korea and South Africa.

Overall, while academics may debate the detail, variance and effectiveness of political marketing, there is no doubt that political parties across the world are using marketing in a comprehensive form. However, political marketing raises many concerns and objections, both from practical and ethical perspectives.

Ethical concerns: political marketing and democracy

Political marketing in the form of a market-orientated party raises many issues. On the one hand, listening and responding to voters' concerns may be democratic. A market orientation may develop into a form of deliberative democracy and market intelligence becomes a new form of political participation. However, others such as Savigny (2004) and Washbourne (2005) are more critical, arguing that there is a need to distinguish between wants, desires, interests and needs; and responsiveness, listening and responding; and to develop the difference between market oriented and market driven (see also Lilleker 2006). If all parties adopt a market orientation and follow public opinion this can reduce the opportunity for new product development, more radical but beneficial policy ideas, and the input of professional, expert (if elite) opinion to develop and produce the best public services and management of the country. The other common criticism, relative to UK New Labour, is that political marketing will always get rid of political ideology. However, UK New Labour can be seen as more of a market-driven rather than market-oriented party: Blair neglected internal analysis and careful implementation, alienating traditional supporters in the process. He also adopted many policies similar to the Conservative Party without making the contribution of Labour ideology clear. A fully market-oriented party engages in a complex balance of different demands (see Stage 3 and Stage 4 of the model). Although identifying voter demands is crucial, any product design needs to be achievable, take into account a party's ideology and history, retaining certain policies to suit the traditional supporter market where necessary; identify the opposition's weaknesses while highlighting its own corresponding strengths, ensuring a degree of distinctiveness in order to segment the market to identify untapped voters necessary to achieve goals, and then develop targeted aspects of the product to suit them. A market-oriented party is not about removing all ideology, or just following public fashion, but about being responsive; respecting voters and reflecting on the party's own behaviour. A market orientation in politics should incorporate judgement, leadership, professionalism and ideologies, so long as they are executed in response to voter concerns. If adopted and utilized comprehensively, it can be a positive force for democracy.

Practical issues: delivery and internal management

Delivery is one of the key potential flaws in the political marketing model. The definition of a market-oriented party is that a party should design its product to suit voter satisfaction. It is an ideal, which is difficult to achieve in practice. It could be that parties do deliver, but voters are not aware of success. Delivery needs to be communicated as well as actioned; for example, when I interviewed Alastair Campbell (2005) he argued that the media deliberately obstruct the link between government and hospitals/the NHS and when government has delivered 'they don't credit the government for it'. My interviews with UK media practitioners have, naturally, defended the media. Gareth Butler (2006), deputy editor of the BBC's Politics Show noted:

> what [we] do is spend several minutes analysing the story or the problem, and then have a
> politician on to talk about it . . . [b]ut they don't want to talk about policy – we don't get

them to talk about the detailed policy that they're in charge of, that they spend all those hours every day doing. They don't come on for this and believe me we've tried.

Another issue is that parties often fail to manage the introduction of a market orientation: they fail in the implementation stage. The British Conservative Party has battled with the issue twice under William Hague and Iain Duncan-Smith (Lees-Marshment 2004b, 2005b). As one MP said:

> William Hague, for the first four years of that Parliament, is a classic example of where he didn't achieve a breakthrough, then the party went back into its comfort zone and appealed to its own traditional supporters. It is not irrational, because William was in a terrible situation where their group that might have supported him felt he was being too left-wing with them and the left-wing press was never going to support him anyway. So he just had no friends at all in the media, and that's a very lonely place. So he went back to the people he could make friends with, but by doing so drove away potential voters.
>
> (Green 2006; see also Lees-Marshment 2001d for further detail)

Here, the differences between politics and business are profound. Will Harris, a business marketer, was director of political marketing for the Conservative Party for one year in 2003. He said that politics is 'utterly, utterly different'; in business you 'spend the whole time trying to get people to write about you; in politics you need to try to stop negative things being written; have to be cagey about what you say' (Harris 2004). 'In politics it's about getting elected once every five years. In business, you get elected every day. Otherwise, you go out of business, and so you think in very different ways. In a political party you could spend the whole day with the administration and not do a single bit of marketing. In politics it is very easy to focus on the wrong things' (Harris 2006). Similarly Archie Norman, a successful businessman who was chief executive of the Conservative Party from 1998 to 1999, said, 'it was a big change coming to this world'; 'had I known I'd have been much more cautious' because politics is a 'management free zone' (Norman 2001). Political marketing in practice is not as easy as in theory, and further work needs to be conducted to investigate the barriers and opposition that get in the way of those who try to make it happen.

Conclusion

Political party marketing is used by political parties all around the world. It is used to understand the electorate and to inform communication, but more importantly, to inform the political product that parties offer to voters. It is much more than public relations or campaigning. Political marketing involves the use of market intelligence results to formulate a strategy that is responsive to voter demands. If parties adopt the marketing philosophy, they become a market-oriented party, and respond to voter demand, using marketing to decide what policies to offer, rather than sell an unwanted product. This suggests a change in the way parties behave: from leading to following public opinion. The type of marketing used in the commercial world, which places customer satisfaction at the heart of business endeavour as a means to obtain and maintain consumer support, is now being developed within the political arena. This raises many debates as to whether market-oriented politics is good or bad for democracy. This depends largely on whether you think politicians should have more of a leadership role and seek to persuade the public of their point of view, or seek to elevate the voter to the role of a consumer and represent citizens' views without persuasion or manipulation – and that, of course, depends on your view of democracy as much as political marketing.

References

Bannon, D. (2004) 'Marketing segmentation and political marketing', UK PSA conference paper.

—— (2005) 'Internal marketing and political marketing', UK PSA conference paper.

Butler, G. (2006) Deputy editor of the UK BBC Politics Show, interviewed by Jennifer Lees-Marshment, London (April).

Campbell, A. (2005) interviewed by Jennifer Lees-Marshment 6 October, London.

Cotrim Maciera, J. (2005) 'Change to win? The 2002 general election PT marketing strategy in Brazil', in D. Lilleker and J. Lees-Marshment (eds) *Political Marketing: A Comparative Perspective*, Manchester: Manchester University Press, pp. 148–64.

Green, D. (2006) Conservative MP, UK; interviewed by Jennifer Lees-Marshment (April).

Harris, W. (2004) Interviewed by J. Lees-Marshment (March).

—— (2006) Interviewed by J. Lees-Marshment (April).

Henneberg, S. C. M. (2004) 'The views of an *Advocatus Dei*: Political marketing and its critics', *Journal of Public Affairs*, 4(3):225–43.

Ingram, P. and Lees-Marshment, J. (2002), 'The anglicisation of political marketing: How Blair out-marketed Clinton', *Journal of Public Affairs*, 5/6.

Knuckey, J. and Lees-Marshment, J. (2005) 'American political marketing: George W. Bush and the Republican Party', in D. Lilleker and J. Lees-Marshment (eds) *Political Marketing: A Comparative Perspective*, Manchester: Manchester University Press, pp. 39–58.

Lees, C. (2005) 'Political marketing in Germany: The case of the SPD', in D. Lilleker, and J. Lees-Marshment, *Political Marketing: A Comparative Perspective*, Manchester: Manchester University Press.

Lees-Marshment, J. (2001a) *Political Marketing and British Political Parties*, Manchester: Manchester University Press.

—— (2001b) 'The marriage of politics and marketing', *Political Studies*, 49(4):692–713.

—— (2001c) 'The product, sales and market-oriented party and how Labour learnt to market the product, not just the presentation', *European Journal of Marketing*, 35(9/10):1074–84.

—— (2001d) 'Marketing the British Conservatives 1997–2001', *Journal of Marketing Management*, 17:929–41.

—— (2003) 'Political marketing: How to reach that pot of gold', *Journal of Political Marketing*, 2(1):1–32.

—— (2004a) *The Political Marketing Revolution: Transforming the Government of the UK*, Manchester: Manchester University Press.

—— (2004b) 'Mis-marketing the Conservatives: The limitations of style over substance', *Political Quarterly*, 75(4)(October–December):392–7.

—— (2005a) 'Political marketing and the UK election: The triumph of the political consumer or a return to salesmanship?', British General Election 2005, London School of Economics Conference (April).

—— (2005b) 'The marketing campaign: The British general election of 2005', special issue of the JMM, 21 pages.

—— (2006a) 'Political marketing theory and practice: A reply to Ormrod's critique of the Lees-Marshment market-oriented party model', *Politics*, May.

—— (2006b) 'Political marketing', in Raymond Miller (ed.) *New Zealand Government and Politics*, 4th edn, Oxford: Oxford University Press.

—— and Lloyd, J. (2005) 'It's their party and they'll cry if they want to. A political marketing assessment of the state of the Labour and Conservative product from the eye of the voter', presentation to the 2005 PSA PM Conference, Political Marketing and the UK Election, 24–25 February, Grange Hotel, Holborn, London.

—— and Roberts, J. (2005) 'Why it didn't work for Labour . . . political marketing and the 2005 election: The importance of thinking before you target', Charted Institute of Marketing online paper available at: www.cim.co.uk/mediastore/Election_2005/Election_2005_–_Why_it_did_not_work_for_Labour_article.pdf

—— and Rudd, C. (2006a) 'Anglocisation, Americanisation and Australiasisation of campaigning in NZ', paper presented at the New Zealand Political Studies Association Conference, Christchurch (August).

—— — (2006b) 'Marketing New Zealand politics: Following or leading the rest of the world?', round-table seminar, Auckland University, together with Steven Joyce, former general manager, National Party and Mike Williams, Labour Party president.

Lilleker, D. (2006) 'Political marketing: The cause of an emerging democratic deficit in Britain?', in J. Lees-Marshment and W. Wymer (eds) *Current Issues in Political Marketing*, Haworth Press.

—— and Lees-Marshment, J. 2005 (eds) *Political Marketing: A Comparative Perspective*, Manchester: Manchester University Press.

—— and Negrine, R. (2002) 'Marketing techniques and political campaigns: The limitations for the marketing of British political parties', PSA conference paper.

—— — (2004) 'Not big brand names but corner shops: Marketing politics to a disengaged electorate', *Journal of Political Marketing*, 2(1):55–74.

Lloyd, J. (2003) 'Square peg, round hole?: Can marketing-based concepts such as the "Product" and the "marketing mix" have a useful role in the political arena?', Paper presented at the UK Political Studies Association Conference.

—— (2006) 'Square peg, round hole?: Can marketing-based concepts such as the "Product" and the "marketing mix" have a useful role in the political arena?', in J. Lees-Marshment and W. Wymer (eds) *Current Issues in Political Marketing*, Haworth Press.

Marland, A. (2005) 'Canadian political parties: Market-oriented or ideological slagbrains?', in D. Lilleker and J. Lees-Marshment (eds) *Political Marketing: A Comparative Perspective*, Manchester: Manchester University Press, pp. 59–78.

Norman, A. (2001) Interview by Jennifer Lees-Marshment, Porticullis House (18 October).

Ormrod, R. P. (2006a) 'A critique of the Lees-Marshment market-oriented party model', *Politics* (May).

—— (2006b) 'A conceptual model of political market orientation', in J. Lees-Marshment and W. Wymer (eds) *Current Issues in Political Marketing*, Haworth Press.

Rudd, C. (2005) 'Marketing the message or the messenger? The New Zealand Labour Party, 1990–2003', in D. Lilleker and J. Lees-Marshment (eds) *Political Marketing: A Comparative Perspective*, Manchester: Manchester University Press.

Savigny, H. (2004) 'Political marketing: A rational choice?', *Journal of Political Marketing*, 3(1):21–38.

Strömbäck, J. and Nord, L. (2005) 'Political marketing: The road to electoral success or to electoral backlash?', Paper presented at the Political Marketing Group Conference, London, 24–25 February.

Washbourne, N. (2005) '(Comprehensive) political marketing, expertise and the conditions for democracy', paper presented at the PSA/PMG Conference.

Part 6

Social marketing

20

Critical issues in social marketing

A review and research agenda

Ross Gordon, Laura McDermott and Gerard Hastings

Introduction

Social marketing has enjoyed a period of evolution and growth in recent years. It has matured as a discipline and is currently a key contributor to social and health behaviour change efforts globally (Andreasen 2003). Now is an opportune time to take stock of social marketing's progress and review its current challenges. This chapter provides a review of social marketing and offers a research agenda for the future. It begins by examining the evolution and growth of social marketing before addressing key contemporary issues and challenges within the social marketing field. These include:

- defining and conceptualizing social marketing;
- building an evidence base and creating a research agenda;
- identifying new areas in which social marketing can be applied;
- considering how to market social marketing; and
- ensuring the sustainability and durability of social marketing.

Social marketing: evolution and growth

The term 'social marketing' was first coined by Kotler and Zaltman in 1971 to refer to the application of commercial marketing techniques to the resolution of social and health problems. The idea dates back to the early 1950s, when Wiebe asked the question: 'Can brotherhood be sold like soap?'. For the first time, people seriously contemplated whether techniques used successfully to influence behaviour in the commercial sector might transfer to the nonprofit sector. During the late 1950s and early 1960s, marketing academics considered the potential and limitations of applying marketing to the political and social arenas.

Social marketing evolved in parallel with commercial marketing. The expansion of marketing itself combined with a shift in public health policy towards disease prevention paved the way for the development of social marketing. Over the next two to three decades, marketing academics and public health experts developed and refined social marketing thinking, learning particularly from international development efforts, where social marketing was used for disease control programmes and family planning (Manoff 1985). By the 1980s, academics were no longer asking *if* marketing should be applied to social concerns, but rather *how* should this be done? During this period, practitioners shared their experiences and made suggestions for the development of social marketing theory and practice (Ling *et al.* 1992; Fox and Kotler 1980; Bloom 1980). In 1981, Bloom and Novelli reviewed the first decade of social marketing and advocated more research to dispel criticism that social marketing lacked theory or rigour. They identified a need for research to examine audience segmentation, choosing communications channels and designing message appeals, implementing long-term positioning strategies, and organizational and management issues (Bloom and Novelli 1981). Lefebvre and Flora (1988) and Hastings and Haywood (1991, 1994) then gave social marketing widespread exposure in the public health field, generating lively debates about its applicability and contribution. The publication of these papers was followed by a widespread growth in social marketing's popularity (Lefebvre 1996). Centres of expertise began to emerge, including the Centre for Social Marketing at Strathclyde University (now the Institute for Social Marketing at Stirling at the Open University).

Social marketing is now located at the centre of health improvement in numerous countries. In the USA, social marketing is increasingly being touted as a core public health strategy for influencing voluntary lifestyle behaviours such as smoking, drinking, diet and drug use (CDC 2005). Recently in the UK the potential of social marketing was recognized in the white paper on public health, which talks of the 'power of social marketing' and 'marketing tools applied to social good' being 'used to build public awareness and change behaviour' (Department of Health 2004: 21). The National Social Marketing Centre, led by the National Consumer Council and the Department of Health, has been established to 'help realise the full potential of effective social marketing in contributing to national and local efforts to improve health and reduce health inequalities' (NCC/DH 2005). It is leading a national review of social marketing and developing the first national social marketing strategy for health in England. Similarly, the Scottish Executive recently commissioned an investigation into how social marketing can be used to guide health improvement. Australia, New Zealand and Canada, as well as the USA, all have social marketing facilities embedded high within their health departments. The *British Medical Journal* has also already responded to this growing interest by publishing a series of articles on social marketing (Hastings and McDermott 2006; Evans 2006).

Current challenges in social marketing

Defining and conceptualizing social marketing

This growth and development is extremely welcome, but as social marketing increases in visibility and acceptability, funders and policy-makers are increasingly asking for hard evidence of its effectiveness. Providing this evidence is challenging, not least because it is difficult to 'prove' that many kinds of complex social interventions work. But there is a particular difficulty in the case of social marketing, and that is that social marketing remains poorly understood, not only by the outside world but even within its own field (Maibach 2002). In part, there are too many definitions which conflict in both major and minor ways. There is also insufficient differentiation from competing behaviour change approaches and social marketing has often been confused with related – but quite distinct – marketing concepts such as societal marketing, socially responsible marketing and nonprofit marketing (MacFadyen *et al.* 2003). The term social marketing is also commonly erroneously used to refer simply to social communications or advertising. As social marketing experiences significant growth, it is imperative to ensure that it is correctly understood.

A recent definition, offered by the National Social Marketing Centre in the UK, describes social marketing as 'the systematic application of marketing concepts and techniques to achieve specific behavioural goals relevant to the social good' (French and Blair-Stevens 2005). Here the emphasis is on the unique, defining feature of social marketing – taking learning from the commercial sector and applying it to the resolution of social and health problems. Another useful definition was proposed by Lazer and Kelley (1973: ix) during the early days of the discipline:

> Social marketing is concerned with the application of marketing knowledge, concepts, and techniques to enhance social as well as economic ends. It is also concerned with analysis of the social consequence of marketing policies, decisions and activities.

This definition too captures the essence of social marketing as well as highlighting both sides of the social marketing 'coin'. On the one hand, social marketing encourages the use of marketing skills and insights to progress social good. On the other, it facilitates the control and regulation of commercial marketing through critical studies of its impact on the health and welfare of society.

Like commercial marketing, social marketing is not a theory in itself. Instead, it is a framework that draws upon several other disciplines, including psychology, sociology and communications theory, in an effort to understand human behaviour and how we might influence it (Kotler and Zaltman 1971). Like generic marketing, social marketing offers a strategic planning process which utilizes conventional marketing techniques. Over the past thirty or so years, social marketers have systematically applied concepts from commercial marketing – concepts like consumer research, segmentation and targeting, the marketing 'mix', competitor analysis and, more recently, branding and stakeholder marketing – to topics as diverse as domestic recycling, cancer prevention, sexual health and road safety. Several other key features characterize the social marketing approach. The first is a focus on *voluntary* behaviour change: social marketing isn't about enforcement or coercion. It is based on the voluntary exchange of costs and benefits between two or more parties (Kotler and Zaltman 1971). Social marketers try to bring about change by applying the principle of *exchange* – the recognition that there must be a clear benefit for the customer if change is to take place (Housten and Gassenheimer 1987). In addition, the *end goal* of social marketing is to improve individual welfare and society, not to benefit the organization doing the social marketing. This is what distinguishes social marketing from other forms of marketing (MacFadyen *et al.* 2003). The emphasis on society as well as the individual illustrates another key point about social marketing: it can apply not only to the behaviour of individuals, but also to that of professionals, organizations and policy-makers. Good social marketing embraces this idea of going 'upstream' (Lefebvre 1996; Goldberg 1995). Encouraging retailers to stock healthy foods as opposed to confectionary at checkouts, or policy-makers and legislators to ban junk-food advertising to children, are just two examples of upstream social marketing.

Several key departures from commercial marketing also suggest that undertaking social marketing may be a more challenging task (MacFadyen *et al.* 2003). For example, the social marketing product is often inherently more complex than a commercial product. It may be intangible (e.g. a change in beliefs); it may require considerable involvement and effort on the part of the target audience (e.g. visiting the gym regularly or using a condom); or it may represent a change in behaviour to which people are resistant, such as quitting smoking.

Furthermore, the benefits may not always be immediate or direct (e.g. recycling to protect the environment).

Bearing these key principles and characteristics in mind can help to ensure a shared and coherent view of what is (and hence what is *not*) social marketing. However, for academics and policy-makers charged with the task of answering the question 'is social marketing effective?' a more precise yardstick is required against which to decide whether an intervention is a legitimate application of social marketing. A recent series of systematic reviews of social marketing effectiveness sought to identify such a yardstick. The reviews, undertaken on behalf of the National Social Marketing Centre (NSMC) at the Department of Health and the National Consumer Council, evaluated the effectiveness of social marketing in improving diet and physical activity and tackling substance misuse (McDermott *et al.* 2006; Gordon *et al.* 2006; Stead *et al.* 2006). As a means of identifying legitimate examples of social marketing for inclusion in the reviews, Andreasen's (2002) six essential benchmarks of a 'genuine' social marketing intervention were used (see Table 20.1). The benchmarks were used as a set of criteria against which potentially eligible interventions could be assessed. If an intervention was judged to meet all six criteria, it was defined as having adopted a social marketing approach, regardless of the label that the author used to describe the programme.

The reviews represent the first systematic test of Andreasen's benchmarks as a concrete method for identifying social marketing programmes. The approach worked well in practice and overall the benchmarks proved workable. However, several key challenges were met. For example, it was often difficult to make judgements based on the amount of information provided in the papers and, as anticipated, some criteria were easier to judge than others (e.g. identifying whether research was undertaken to formulate the strategy versus determining whether a meaningful exchange was being offered). It is also possible that Andreasen's benchmarks fail to capture fully some of the recent thinking in social marketing (e.g. the use of

Table 20.1 Andreasen's benchmark criteria (based on McDermott *et al.* 2005)

Benchmark	Explanation
1 Behaviour change	Intervention seeks to change behaviour and has specific measurable behavioural objectives.
2 Consumer research	Intervention is based on an understanding of consumer experiences, values and needs.
	Formative research is conducted to identify these.
	Intervention elements are pre-tested with the target group.
3 Segmentation and targeting	Different segmentation variables are considered when selecting the intervention target group.
	Intervention strategy is tailored for the selected segment/s.
4 Marketing mix	Intervention considers the best strategic application of the 'marketing mix'. This consists of the four Ps: 'product', 'price', 'place' and 'promotion'. Other Ps might include 'policy change' or 'people' (e.g. training is provided to intervention delivery agents). Interventions which only use the promotion P are social advertising, not social marketing.
5 Exchange	Intervention considers what will motivate people to engage voluntarily with the intervention and offers them something beneficial in return. The offered benefit may be intangible (e.g. personal satisfaction) or tangible (e.g. rewards for participating in the programme and making behavioural changes).
6 Competition	Competing forces to the behaviour change are analysed. Intervention considers the appeal of competing behaviours (including current behaviour) and uses strategies that seek to remove or minimize this competition.

branding and relationship marketing). Despite these limitations, the reviews represent the first attempt to translate systematically a generalized definition of the social marketing approach into a set of precise measures against which potential interventions can be assessed. This kind of work is crucial because it helps us to move towards a consensus on the key defining and recognizable features of social marketing. More vigorous debate among academics and funding bodies is needed on, for example, the merits and limitations of the Andreasen model and any possible alternatives.

Creating an evidence base and research agenda

The rise of social marketing has led many to ask for evidence that it actually works. The evidence base to support the use of social marketing to improve health and tackle social problems is gradually growing. A number of reviews have examined social marketing effectiveness in an international development context, particularly in the promotion of family planning (Family Health International 2004; Price 2001). However, these have been somewhat limited by their narrow definition of social marketing (which in the reviews is often taken to mean, principally, the free distribution of condoms) and by their use of non-systematic methods.

More recent research has improved this situation. A series of literature reviews commissioned by the NSMC provides a systematic account of social marketing and its effectiveness in improving a range of health behaviours and, as discussed earlier in this chapter, has brought a more consistent approach to assessing the effectiveness of social marketing. The first of these was a full-scale systematic review of the effectiveness of social marketing nutrition interventions (McDermott *et al.* 2006). The review found that social marketing nutrition interventions were strongly and equally effective at influencing nutrition behaviour, knowledge and psychosocial variables such as self-efficacy and perceptions of the benefits of eating more healthily. Social marketing appeared to be less, but still moderately, effective at influencing stages of change in relation to diet, and to have a more limited effect on diet-related physiological outcomes such as blood pressure, body mass index and cholesterol. This latter finding might be expected, as these kinds of outcomes are arguably more difficult to influence, and changes are likely to take a much longer time to occur and be detected. The review also found that social marketing interventions could achieve both narrower and broader goals. Social marketing interventions which sought to target nutritional behaviours in several domains at once (for example, increasing fruit and vegetable intake, reducing fat intake) could be just as effective as those concerned with change in just one domain (for example, fruit and vegetable intake only). This suggests that social marketing interventions can produce changes across a relatively wide spectrum of behaviours, rather than only working, or working better, when they have a narrow behavioural focus. There are clear cost-effectiveness implications if it is possible to design social marketing interventions which can produce changes in several behaviours and risk factors at once.

Two additional reviews examined the use of social marketing in increasing physical activity and tackling tobacco, alcohol and illicit drug use. The reviews found reasonable evidence that interventions developed using social marketing principles can be effective (Gordon *et al.* 2006).

A majority of the interventions which sought to prevent youth smoking, alcohol use and illicit drug use reported significant positive effects in the short term. Effects tended to dissipate in the medium and longer term, although several of the tobacco and alcohol interventions still displayed some positive effects two years after the intervention. These results are broadly comparable with systematic reviews of other types of substance use prevention interventions (e.g. Foxcroft *et al.* 2002; Sowden and Arblaster 1998; Thomas 2002). The evidence is more mixed for adult smoking cessation, although small numbers of programmes were nonetheless effective in this area. There is modest evidence of impact on levels of physical activity and psychosocial outcomes, with an apparently weaker effect on physical activity-related physiological outcomes. The interventions seem also to have had some effects on the behaviour of retailers, and to have encouraged adoption of policies and other environmental-level changes, although the data on these are less robust and it is often difficult to attribute changes to the interventions rather than to other events and trends in the community. The reviews also imply that the quality of implementation of the intervention may have a bearing on effectiveness, though this needs to be more directly researched.

As discussed earlier, social marketing is also concerned about the impact of commercial marketing practices on the health and welfare of society. These effects have been examined in numerous studies. Several decades of international research have shown that advertising and other forms of tobacco marketing encourage young people to take up smoking and adults to continue smoking (Hastings and MacFadyen 2000; Aitken *et al.* 1987, 1991; Aitken and Eadie 1990; Pollay *et al.* 1996; Pierce *et al.* 1998), and there is a growing body of evidence to suggest that alcohol marketing plays an important role in encouraging and sustaining drinking (Hastings *et al.* 2005; Atkin *et al.* 1984, 1988; Grube and Wallack 1994). One of the most systematic examinations of the effect of marketing on health behaviour is a recent review into the effects of food promotion on children's diet for the Food Standards Agency (Hastings *et al.* 2003). Using rigorous and systematic review procedures, this research found convincing evidence that food promotion has an effect on children, particularly in the areas of food preferences, purchase and consumption behaviour.

In the coming years, social marketers must endeavour to continue to develop and expand the social marketing evidence base in a systematic and rigorous way. Evidence of social marketing's effectiveness in improving health in other areas, such as sexual risk behaviours and taking care in the sun, is needed. On the critical marketing side, similarly rigorous evidence is needed to identify the impact of commercial marketing on the health and welfare of society. Through this kind of work, social marketers can help to get the balance right by ensuring that the potential for harm is monitored and controlled. Burgeoning areas of commercial marketing activity require particular attention – for example, the promotion on prescription-only medicines and the marketing of gambling and betting practices.

Identifying new areas in which social marketing can be applied

Rothschild (1999) distinguished marketing as an alternative to education and the law for effecting social change, with education sufficient in situations in which information alone will achieve the desired behaviour change, and the law intervening where consumers are reluctant to act. Everything else can be prospectively covered by social marketing (Andreasen 2003). Therefore the areas and opportunities for the application of social marketing are almost limitless. However, as discussed previously, the process of applying social marketing also involves making clear distinctions of the approach – how it differs from other behaviour change approaches and being consistent in doing so (Andreasen 2003).

Social marketing is traditionally regarded as being restricted to a particular arena and client base: nonprofit organizations, public health bodies and government agencies. Undeniably these are often the areas in which social marketers work and in which social marketing principles and practices are applied. However, the aim of effecting positive behaviour change in society is not restricted to these arenas, the corporate sphere is ripe with opportunities for the application of social marketing ideas, particularly with the increased focus on ethical behaviour and corporate social responsibility in the commercial world. Indeed Andreasen (2003) has suggested that we be bolder in suggesting ways in which social marketing lessons can be transferred back to the private sector, such as to influence the behaviour of personnel (e.g. Neiger *et al.* 2001), franchisees, channel partners and other stakeholders.

Given the long-standing trend of voter apathy and disengagement in politics, there is an opportunity for social marketing interventions to build upon efforts to improve citizen engagement (McKenzie Mohr 1999; Bhattacharya and Elsbach 2002) especially among younger age groups. Mass-media campaigns carried out by organizations such as 'Rock the vote' have already attempted to get people to engage in politics and such efforts could be developed using social marketing principles. Social marketing interventions could also be developed to encourage financial solvency, which is especially topical given the growing concern over personal debt in the UK (BBC News Online 2006). Interventions such as the 'Sorted' campaign in New Zealand which encourages young people to save for retirement have demonstrated the applicability of such programmes.

Social marketing has already been applied to a number of environmental issues (Altman and Petkus 1994; Geller 1989; Shrum *et al.* 1994) and this is an area with opportunity for expansion given the huge focus on such issues currently. For example, campaigns to encourage recycling (Herrick 1995) have emerged but there is capacity to increase such efforts. Exploratory research has examined whether social marketing could encourage composting (McDermott *et al.* 2004) and also play a part in improving carbon efficiency by encouraging people to change a range of carbon-emitting behaviours (Marcell *et al.* 2004). The field of land management has also experienced social marketing in action. For example, a study in Australia advocated the application of social marketing strategies to assist in the management of pest control in Victoria (Binney *et al.* 2003). However, these are areas in which social marketing has merely 'dipped a toe in the water' and there are many opportunities for development and expansion.

In the critical marketing arena attention has rightly focused on tobacco (MacFadyen *et al.* 2001), food (Hastings *et al.* 2003) and alcohol marketing (Hastings *et al.* 2005). Yet doubts remain over the effect if any of alcohol marketing on drinking behaviour (Prime Minister's Strategy Unit 2004). Despite recent longitudinal research suggesting a causal link (Stacy *et al.* 2004; Ellickson *et al.* 2004; Snyder *et al.* 2006) further research is needed to assess the impact of the full range of alcohol marketing communications. Research has commenced in the UK (Gordon *et al.* 2006) and New Zealand which will add to the evidence base but more research would strengthen the case for regulatory decisions.

Recently there has been concern expressed over car marketing, especially in relation to SUVs and an obsession with speed and inefficient, pollutant vehicles (Hastings in press). This is an area in which research could evaluate the effect on behaviour and inform the development of interventions designed to limit car use or change the types of cars driven by people to reduce road accidents and pollution. Demarketing the car has been suggested (Wright and Egan 2000) and the possibilities of marketing clean and efficient vehicles has been examined (Kurani and Turrentine 2002). Encouraging the use of public transportation could be achieved using social marketing methods. Other areas in which social marketing has been suggested as a behaviour change approach include the illegal marketing of weapons (Goldberg 1995), the illicit drugs market and issues surrounding the homeless (Hill 1991) and gambling (Byrne *et al.* 2005).

Upstream social marketing is an area which would benefit for development and increased prominence (Andreasen 1995; Goldberg 1995). Although social marketing's primary niche is at the individual level, efforts to effect social change at the wider societal level can be made (Wallack 1990). This involves a focus on media advocacy, policy change, regulation and law-making. Upstream application of social marketing can influence communities, regulators, managers, policy and law-makers. Critical marketing research to inform regulation such as in tobacco control, food and alcohol marketing, or community interventions designed to effect policy changes are examples of where upstream social marketing can be applied. Debate has raged over whether social marketers should become politically active or merely let their research speak for itself (Goldberg 1995; Wells 1997), however the insights that such research can offer to society can be valuable.

Marketing social marketing

Recent years have witnessed the emergence and growth of a number of training courses and educational programmes in social marketing and this section will examine some of these, the importance they hold and discuss ways in which social marketing can be further disseminated to practitioners and academics alike.

Social marketing conferences are a good way for people to meet, debate and discuss issues within the field. Indeed there are now three annual social marketing conferences, one of which has been established for over a decade (Andreasen 2003). However, attendance at such events should not be restricted to social marketers but should also encourage people from other fields and disciplines who might benefit from gaining an understanding of social marketing. Professional training courses in social marketing are also a good way to expand knowledge and understanding and such courses are already offered to health professionals in the UK, USA, Canada, Australia and New Zealand.

Social marketing has also been expanding in higher education with modules offered in universities in several countries. Efforts are being made to start an M.Sc. in social marketing at universities in Stirling in the UK and Wollongong in Australia, and the Open University in the UK is to launch an online social marketing course in 2007. Social marketing textbooks are becoming increasingly common; several textbooks have already been published (Andreasen 1995; Kotler *et al.* 2002) with more in the pipeline (Hastings in press). Chapters on social marketing are now appearing in nonprofit and critical marketing books and these all help in bringing social marketing to a wider audience. The university environment is a key arena for targeting the social marketers of the future. Student access to good teaching and textbooks on social marketing are vitally important. Yet although there have been promising developments in this area, social marketing still lacks academic stature – it is rarely taught as a standalone subject and there is a lack of recognized academic qualifications in social marketing (Andreasen 2002).

Wide dissemination is also required to keep social marketing on the map. This requires social marketers to make efforts continually to hold well-publicized dissemination events for their research findings and by submitting articles to journals with both high-impact scores and large readerships. Social marketing has its own journal, *Social Marketing Quarterly*, and efforts should continue to improve its contribution and readership base. Interdisciplinary collaboration and dissemination is also an important consideration, and research, seminars and events involving other disciplines will help broaden the base and appeal of social marketing. Traditionally there has been a tendency for social marketing to be promoted to those working in the public health or marketing arenas, but other disciplines such as psychology, sociology and political science may benefit and welcome input and ideas from the social marketing field. As Andreasen highlights, social marketing must understand better and then advocate how it can complement other approaches to social change (Andreasen 2003). These suggestions are very much compatible with the current drive to encourage interdisciplinary collaboration in universities.

Social marketers must also embrace media and technology to market the discipline effectively to the general public. Media training and management are important skills for social marketers to develop and it is important for those working in the field to seize opportunities to gain publicity for their research or the wider discipline when they present themselves. There-fore social marketing agencies and organizations should include such training in their staff development programmes where possible.

Sustainability and durability of social marketing

Social marketing has become a fairly fashionable concept among policy-makers. This section will discuss the sustainability and durability of social marketing and ways to ensure it does not merely become a flash in the pan idea among decision-makers.

It has taken a lot of time, effort and persistence to bring social marketing into adulthood (Andreasen 2003) and on to the political landscape, getting decision-makers to think about it when forming policy or interventions. Recent years have witnessed increasing acknowledge-ment of social marketing and its applications among politicians and government, albeit if sometimes the principles and definitions are a little misunderstood. However, it must not be taken for granted that social marketing will always be on decision-makers' radars and efforts must be taken to avoid social marketing becoming another public policy fad (Andreasen 2002). Other public policy approaches have been fashionable and then fallen by the wayside and the dangers of this happening have been well documented (Hilmer and Donaldson 1996; Adams and Hess 2001). In the political world there is an issue attention cycle (Hogwood and Gunn 1984, 1999) in which certain issues are brought on to the agenda by the media, experts, the public or the government, or by a combination of these sources. It can be difficult to set the agenda and this is an area in which social marketers must work hard to ensure that the issues discussed earlier are brought on to the agenda and that the power of social marketing to offer solutions is accentuated. There is a requirement for social marketing to be self-confident (Andreasen 2003) and become a trusted concept to utilize when making policy decisions and this can be achieved in a number of ways.

As discussed at several points within this chapter, there is also a need to agree on social marketing concepts and definitions and unify the field behind them. It must be made easier for people to understand what social marketing is and what it can do. As social marketing has matured there have been calls for less of a dogmatic reliance on commercial marketing principles; replacing products with social propositions, price for costs of involvement, place for accessibility, promotion for social communication, exchange for interaction and framing competition in terms of competing ideas and the need to win attention and acceptance to effect behaviour change (Peattie and Peattie 2003). This is in line with the call from conver-gents (Altman and Petkus 1994; Gilder et al. 2001) who argue for an interdisciplinary approach to social marketing generating ideas for progression in the field. Indeed it has been argued that social marketing's future development will be enhanced by creating its own unique tools, theories and vocabulary. Traditionalists are more focused on retaining the neoclassical theoretical basis of social marketing adopted from commercial marketing theory (Black and Farley 1979; Zimmerman 1997). These are issues that must be developed and conclusions reached to enable social marketing to move forward.

First-class research needs to be carried out and continued into the effectiveness of social marketing interventions and also in critical marketing studies. This means considerable effort to raise and secure funding, carry out good-quality research and disseminate findings effectively. Research into social marketing effectiveness can be problematic (Pavia 1995; Hornik 2002), though not insurmountable (McDermott et al. 2005; Stead et al. in press) and efforts must be continued to make measurement easier. Furthermore, there is a need to ensure that the findings of such research are acknowledged and lessons learned and the necessary changes effected. For example, research into the effectiveness of social marketing interventions has shown us that certain conditions can boost the likelihood of an intervention succeeding. Therefore these must be adopted when designing and implementing social marketing interventions.

Implementation is a key issue here and an area in which many social marketing interventions can fail. Adequate resources, training and focus must be provided on the proper implementation of social marketing interventions for them to have a greater chance of succeeding. Appropriate funding is vital, as often interventions can have a short-term impact and then fade into obsolescence or do produce instant results and are then terminated. There is a requirement for a more long-term view and a realization that social marketing interventions must be given adequate time and resources to make a measurable impact on behaviour.

In commercial marketing, brand loyalty and recognition are key facets of any successful brand; Coca-Cola has been established as a brand for over a hundred years. However, in the public sector the political and social landscape often results in regular reorganization, rebranding, expansion and retrenchment of brands. For example, in Scotland the Public Health Board has been rebranded four times in the last twenty years, preventing an established brand from being formed over a period of time which can help brand recognition and customer loyalty. Branding concepts and principles can and should be applied to social marketing programmes as required to allow interventions to go beyond advertising and create a brand image, awareness and attitudes for campaigns (Keller 1998). This is a clear area for improvement; if social marketing campaigns are delivered using recognized, trusted and successful brands this can only help their chances of success.

There is also a requirement for building and maintaining good working relationships with other stakeholders including decision-makers. Efforts at collaboration with other academic disciplines should be encouraged, broadening the level of understanding and allowing for a pooling of resources and expertise. Furthermore, relationships with government bodies should be maintained at a workable level. Although it is often a requirement to 'shout loudly' and often critically achieving the required outcomes involves forming effective partnerships. Yet there is a danger in losing independence and academic integrity, and credibility should be maintained at all times. Often it can be easy to succumb to political pressure to make recommendations that are preferable to the client but do not actually reflect the reality of what is required. Herein lies a careful balancing act of working in partnership but remaining at arm's length.

Social marketers must also work hard to keep abreast of what is going on around them, keeping their eyes open and their ears to the ground as to what issues are on the agenda in society and watching out for trends and emerging concerns. Furthermore, diversification is paramount and forming a review and research agenda such as this aids the discipline by focusing minds, stimulating debate and offering ideas about how social marketing can continue to expand and branch out. This involves rethinking how social marketing can be applied to new areas and problems – an area that has already been discussed. Finally, social marketing must prove its adaptability to changing conditions by demonstrating an ability to alter strategies and tactics caused by changes in the marketplace.

If the above requirements are met, then the likelihood of social marketing maintaining its position as a mainstream concept on the social change landscape will be greatly increased.

Conclusions

For social marketing to reach its full potential it must continue to expand and develop, and the discipline must exude confidence in its ability to effect social change. Here we have outlined some of the ways in which this can be achieved by offering a review and research agenda. It is now up to social marketing students, academics and practitioners alike to accept these challenges and progress the discipline into a long and successful future.

References

Adams, D. and Hess, M. (2001) 'Research and evaluation community in public policy: Fad or foundation?', *Australian Journal of Public Administration*, 60(2):13–23.

Aitken, P. P. and Eadie, D. R. (1990) 'Reinforcing effects of cigarette advertising on underage smoking', *British Journal of Addiction*, 85:399–412.

—— — Hastings, G. B. and Haywood, A. J. (1991) 'Predisposing effects of cigarette advertising on children's intentions to smoke when older', *British Journal of Addiction*, 86:383–90.

—— — O'Hagan, F. J. and Squair, S. I. (1987) 'Children's awareness of cigarette advertisements and brand imagery', *British Journal of Addiction*, 92:615–22.

—— — and Scott, A. C. (1988) 'Ten- to-sixteen-year-olds' perceptions of advertisements for alcoholic drinks', *Alcohol*, 23(6):491–500.

Altman, J. A. and Petkus, E. Jr. (1994) 'Toward a stakeholder-based policy process – An application of the social marketing perspective to environmental-policy development', *Policy Sciences*, 27(1):37–51.

Andreasen, A. R. (1995) *Marketing Social Change*, San Francisco, CA: Jossey-Bass.

—— (2002) 'Marketing social marketing in the social change marketplace', *Journal of Public Policy and Marketing*, 21(1):3–13.

—— (2003) 'The life trajectory of social marketing: Some implications', *Marketing Theory*, 3(3):293–303.

Atkin, C., Hocking, J. and Block, M. (1984) 'Teenage drinking: Does advertising make a difference?', *Journal of Communications*, 34:157–67.

Bhattacharya, C. B. and Elsbach, K. D. (2002) 'Us versus them: The roles of organizational identification and disidentification in social marketing initiatives', *Journal of Public Policy and Marketing*, 21(1):26–36.

Black, T. R. L. and Farley, J. U. (1979) 'The application of market research in contraceptive social marketing in a rural area of Kenya', *Journal of the Market Research Society*, 21(1): 30–43.

BBC News Online (2006) 'Britons face a lifetime of debt', available online at: http://news.bbc.co.uk/1/hi/business/5009510.stm.

Binney, W., Hall, J. and Shaw, M. (2003) 'A further development in social marketing: Application of the MOA framework and behavioural implications', *Marketing Theory*, 3(3):387–403.

Bloom, P. N. (1980) *Evaluating Social Marketing Programs: Problems and Prospects*, the 1980 Educators' Conference Proceedings, Chicago: American Marketing Association.

—— and Novelli, W. D. (1981) 'Problems and challenges in social marketing', *Journal of Marketing*, 45:79–88.

Byrne, A., Dickson, L., Derevensky, J., Gupta, R. and Lussier, I. (2005) 'An examination of social marketing campaigns for the prevention of youth problem gambling', *Journal of Health Communication*, 10:681–700.

Centers for Disease Control and Prevention (2005) Communication at CDC, Practice Areas: Social Marketing, available online at: http://www.cdc.gov/communication/practice/socialmarketing.htm (accessed October 2006).

Department of Health (2004) *Choosing Health: Making Healthier Choices Easier*, Public Health White Paper, Series No. CM 6374, London: Stationery Office.

Ellickson, P. L., Collins, R. L., Hambarsoomians, K. and McCaffrey, D. F. (2004) 'Does alcohol advertising promote adolescent drinking? Results from a longitudinal assessment', *Addiction*, 100:235–46.

Evans, W. D. (2006) 'How social marketing works in health care', *British Medical Journal*, 332(7551):1207–10.

Family Health International (2004) 'Promoting reproductive health for young adults through social marketing and mass media: A review of trends and practices', available online at: www.comminit.com/evaluations/steval/thinking-1046.html (accessed October 2006).

Fox, K. F. A. and Kotler, P. (1980) 'The marketing of social causes: The first ten years', *Journal of Marketing*, 44:24–33.

Foxcroft, D. R., Ireland, D., Lowe, G. and Breen, R. (2002) 'Primary prevention for alcohol misuse in young people', *Cochrane Database of Systematic Reviews*, Issue 3. Art. No.: CD003024. DOI: 10.1002/14651858.CD003024.

French, J. and Blair-Stevens, C. (2005) *Social Marketing: A Pocket Guide*, London: National Consumer Council.

Geller, E. S. (1989) 'Applied behavior analysis and social marketing: An integration for environmental preservation', *Journal of Social Issues*, 45(1):17.

Glider, P., Midyett, S. J., Mills-Novoa, B., Johannessen, K. and Collins, C. (2001) 'Challenging the collegiate rite of passage: A campus-wide social marketing media campaign to reduce binge drinking', *Journal of Drug Education*, 31(2):207–20.

Goldberg, M. E. (1995) 'Social marketing: Are we fiddling while Rome burns?', *Journal of Consumer Psychology*, 4(4):347–70.

Gordon, R., Eadie, D., Hastings, G., Harris, F. and MacKintosh, A. M. (2006) 'Assessing the cumulative impact of alcohol marketing communications on young people's drinking', London: (July) Academy of Marketing Conference.

—— McDermott, L., Stead, M., Angus, K. and Hastings, G. (2006a) *A Review of the Effectiveness of Social Marketing Physical Activity Interventions*. Report prepared for the National Social Marketing Strategy for health. Stirling: Institute for Social Marketing.

—— McDermott, L., Stead, M. and Angus, K. (2006b) 'The effectiveness of social marketing interventions for health improvement: What's the evidence?', *Public Health*, 120(12):1133–9.

Grube, J. W. and Wallack, L. (1994) 'Television beer advertising and drinking knowledge, beliefs and intentions among schoolchildren', *American Journal of Public Health*, 84(2):254–9.

Hastings, G. (in press) *The Potential of Social Marketing: Or Why Should The Devil Have All the Best Tunes*, London: Elsevier.

—— and Haywood, A. J. (1991) 'Social marketing and communication in health promotion', *Health Promotion International*, 6(2):135–45.

—— and Haywood, A. J. (1994) 'Social marketing: A critical response', *Health Promotion International*, 9(1):59–63.

—— and MacFadyen, L. (2000) 'A day in the life of an advertising man: Review of internal documents from the UK tobacco industry's principal advertising agencies', *British Medical Journal*, 321:366–71.

—— and McDermott, L. (2006) 'Putting social marketing into practice', *British Medical Journal*, 332:1210–12.

—— Anderson, S., Cooke, E. and Gordon, R. (2005) 'Alcohol marketing and young people's drinking: A review of the research', *Journal of Public Health Policy*, 26:296–311.

—— Stead, M., McDermott, L. *et al.* (2003) *Review of Research on the Effects of Food Promotion to Children*, London: Food Standards Agency, available online at: www.food.gov.uk/news/pressreleases/foodtochildren.

Herrick, D. (1995) *Taking it to the Stores: Retail Sales of Recycled Products*, Resource Recycling.

Hill, R. P. (1991) 'Homeless women, special possessions and the meaning of "home": An ethnographic case study', *Journal of Consumer Research*, 18:298–310.

Hilmer, F. G. and Donaldson, L. (1996) *Management Redeemed: Debunking the Fads That Undermine Our Corporations*, New York, NY: Free Press.

Hogwood, B. W. and Gunn, L. A. (1984, 1999) *Policy Analysis for the Real World*, Oxford: Oxford University Press.

Hornik, R. (ed.) (2002) *Public Health Communication: Evidence for Behavior Change*, Mahway, NJ: Lawrence Erlbaum Associates.

Housten, F. S. and Gassenheimer, J. B. (1987) 'Marketing and exchange', *Journal of Marketing*, 51:3–18.

Jones, D. B. (2001) 'Marketing psychological services: Using client problem and solution perceptions to design help offering promotional appeals', *Psychology and Marketing* 18(3):261–79.

344

Keller, K. L. (1998) 'Branding perspectives on social marketing', *Advances in Consumer Research*, 28: 299–302.

Kotler, P., Roberto, E. and Lee, N. (2002) *Social Marketing: Strategies for Changing Public Behavior*, Thousand Oaks, CA: Sage Publications.

—— and Zaltman, G. (1971) 'Social marketing: An approach to planned social change', *Journal of Marketing*, 35:3–12.

Kurani, K. S. and Turrentine, T. S. (2002) *Marketing Clean and Efficient Vehicles: A Review of Social Marketing and Social Science Approaches*, Davies, CA: Institute of Transportation Studies, University of California, research report.

Lazer, W. and Kelley, E. J. (1973) *Social Marketing: Perspectives and Viewpoints*, Homewood, IL: Richard D. Irwin.

Lefebvre, R. C. (1996) 'Twenty-five years of social marketing: Looking back to the future', *Social Marketing Quarterly*, special issue: 51–8.

—— and Flora, J. A. (1988) 'Social marketing and public health intervention', *Health Education Quarterly*, 15(3):299–315.

Ling, J. C., Franklin, B. A. K., Lindsteadt, J. F. and Gearion, S. A. N. (1992) 'Social marketing: Its place in public health', *Annual Review of Public Health*, 13:341–62.

Maibach, E. W. (2002) 'Explicating social marketing: What is it, and what isn't it', *Social Marketing Quarterly*, 8(4):7–13.

Manoff, R. K. (1985) *Social Marketing: New Imperative for Public Health*, New York, NY: Praeger.

Marcell, K., Agyeman, J. and Rapport, A. (2004) 'Cooling the campus', *International Journal of Sustainability in Higher Education*, 5(2):169–89.

MacFadyen, L., Stead, M. and Hastings, G. (1999). 'A synopsis of social marketing', available at: www.ism.stir.ac.uk/pdf_docs/social_marketing.pdf (accessed 15 November 2006).

—— Hastings, G. B. and MacKintosh, A. M. (2001) 'Cross-sectional study of young people's awareness of and involvement with tobacco marketing', *British Medical Journal*, 322(3 March):513–17.

—— Stead, M. and Hastings, G. B. (2003) 'Social marketing', 27 in M. J. Baker (ed.) *The Marketing Book*, 5th edn, Oxford: Butterworth-Heinneman.

McDermott, L., Stead, M. and Hastings, G. (2005) 'What is and what is not social marketing: The challenge of reviewing the evidence', *Journal of Marketing Management*, 21(5):545–53.

—— Stead, M., Gordon, R., Angus, K. and Hastings, G. (2006) *A Review of the Effectiveness of Social Marketing Nutrition Interventions*. Report prepared for the National Social Marketing Strategy for Health, Stirling, UK: Institute for Social Marketing.

—— Stead, M., Hastings, G. B., Banerjee, S. and Kent, R. (under review) 'Social marketing interventions for changing nutrition behaviour: A systematic review', Prepared for Preventive Medicine.

—— Eadie, D., Peattie, K., Peattie, S., Hastings, G. and Anderson, S. (2004) 'Domestic composting: Challenges and opportunities for social marketing', Academy of Marketing Conference, Gloucester, UK.

McGinnis, J. M. and Foege, W. H. (1993) 'Actual causes of death in the United States', *Journal of the American Medical Association*, 270(18):2207–12.

McKenzie-Mohr, D. (1999) *Fostering Sustainable Behaviour – An Introduction to Community-based Social Marketing*, Gabriola Island: New Society Publishers.

National Consumer Council and Department of Health (2005) *Realising the Potential of Effective Social Marketing*, London.

Neiger, B. L., Thackeray, R., Merrill, R. M., Miner, K. M., Larsen, L. and Chalkley, C. M. (2001) 'The impact of social marketing on fruit and vegetable consumption and physical activity among public health employees at the Utah Department of Health', *Social Marketing Quarterly*, 7:9–28.

Pavia, T. M. (1995) 'Issues in identifying performance measures for social marketing programs', *Advances in Consumer Research*, 22(1):713–16.

Peattie, S. and Peattie, K. (2003) 'Ready to fly solo? Reducing social marketing's dependence on commercial marketing theory', *Marketing Theory*, 3(3):365–86.

Pierce, J. P., Choi, W. S., Gilpin, E. A. (1998) 'Tobacco industry promotion of cigarettes and adolescent smoking', *Journal of the American Medical Association*, 279:511–15.

Pollay, R. W., Siddarth, S., Siegal, M. (1996) 'The last straw? Cigarette advertising and realized market shares among youths and adults 1979–1993', *Journal of Marketing*, 60:1–16.

Price, N. (2001) 'The performance of social marketing in reaching the poor and vulnerable in AIDS control programmes', *Health Policy and Planning*, 16(3):231–9.

Prime Minister's Strategy Unit (2004) *Alcohol Harm Reduction Strategy for England*, London: Stationery Office.

Rothschild, M. (1999) 'Carrots, sticks and promises: A conceptual framework for the management of public health and social issue behaviors', *Journal of Marketing*, 63(4):24–37.

Shrum, L. J., Lowrey, T. M. and McCarty, J. A. (1994) 'Recycling as a marketing problem: A framework for strategy development', *Psychology and Marketing*, 11(4):393–416.

Sirgy, M., Morris, M. and Samli, A. C. (1985) 'The question of value in social marketing: Use of quality-of-life theory to achieve long-term life satisfaction', *American Journal of Economics and Sociology*, 44(2):215–28.

Snyder, L. B., Milici, F. F., Slater, M., Sun, H. and Strizhakova, Y. (2006) 'Effects of alcohol advertising exposure on youth drinking', *Arch. Pediatr. Adoles Med.*, 160:18–24.

Sowden, A. J. and Arblaster, L. (1998) 'Mass media interventions for preventing smoking in young people', *Cochrane Database of Systematic Reviews*, Issue 4. Art. No.: CD001006. DOI: 10.1002/14651858.CD001006.

Stacy, A. W., Zogg, J. B., Unger, J. B. and Dent, C. W. (2004) 'Exposure to televised alcohol ads and subsequent adolescent alcohol use', *American Journal of Health Behavior*, 28(6):498–509.

Stead, M., Gordon, R., Angus, K. and McDermott, L. (in press) 'A systematic review of social marketing effectiveness', *Health Education*.

—— McDermott, L., Gordon, R., Angus, K. and Hastings, G. (2006) *A Review of the Effectiveness of Social Marketing Alcohol, Tobacco and Substance Misuse Interventions*, report prepared for the National Social Marketing Strategy for Health, Stirling, UK: Institute for Social Marketing.

Thomas, R. (2002) 'School-based programmes for preventing smoking', *Cochrane Database of Systematic Reviews*, Issue 2. Art. No.: CD001293. DOI: 10.1002/14651858.CD001293.

Wallack, L. (1990) 'Media advocacy: Promoting health through mass communication', in K. Glanz, F.M. Lewis and B.K. Rimer (eds) *Health Behavior and Health Education*, San Francisco, CA: Jossey-Bass Publishers, 370–86.

Wells, W. D. (1997) 'Comment on social marketing: Are we fiddling while Rome burns?, *Journal of Consumer Psychology*, 6(2): 197–201.

World Health Organization (2006) *Largely Preventable Chronic Diseases Cause 86 per cent of Deaths in Europe: 53 WHO Member States Map a Strategy to Curb the Epidemic*, Copenhagen: WHO.

Wright, C. and Egan, J. (2000) 'De-marketing the car', *Transport Policy*, 7(4):287–94.

Zimmerman, R. (1997) *Social Marketing Strategies for Campus Prevention of Alcohol and Other Drug Problems*, Massachusetts: Higher Education Center for Alcohol and Other Drug Prevention, Education Development Center.

21

Marketing AIDS prevention

An application of social marketing

Michael Basil

History of AIDS

In 1981, five cases of a rare pneumonia were diagnosed and almost immediately identified as a potential public health threat. During the next few years the Centers for Disease Control and Prevention (CDC) followed this 'gay pneumonia'. While the early research demonstrated that the disease was primarily associated with homosexual or bisexual males, the disease also made occurrences in intravenous (IV) drug users and Haitians. As the CDC pursued this outbreak, it eventually led to the identification of Acquired Immune Deficiency Syndrome (AIDS) as a unique disease that was very fatal (Stall and Mills 2006). Randy Shilts' (1987) book *And the Band Played on* documents the identification of AIDS in the early 1980s. After it was identified as a communicable disease, much of the response to AIDS was biomedical research attempting to understand the disease and its transmission.

Just a year after its identification, the CDC had identified 593 cases of AIDS which resulted in 243 deaths (MMWR 1982). In 1984 it was recognized that a virus, HIV, was responsible for the disease and that it was a potential epidemic that threatened to be a substantial public health burden around the world (Gallo and Montagnier 2003). By 1985 there were more stories about heterosexual transmission (including the Haitians), but these were still seen as isolated incidents (Check 1985). Subsequently, however, the infection rates began to grow at a much higher rate, especially among heterosexual women (MMWR 2006). Just twenty-five years later, in 2006, it was estimated that 40 million people around the world had AIDS (Stall and Mills 2006).

Because of its importance, its communicable nature, and the variety of means which could be applied to prevent the disease, AIDS is an excellent example of where social marketing can and should be applied. Public health practitioners have probably helped to slow the spread of the disease. Yet the potential of social marketing has not yet been fully achieved in the fight against AIDS. This chapter will demonstrate that the history of AIDS prevention efforts reveals that a number of factors have prevented social marketing from achieving its full potential.

The social marketing approach

In 1969, Kotler and Levy suggested that the ideas of commercial marketing could be employed not only to help us to market commercial products, but also services, ideas and social needs. Only a slightly broader conceptualization of products and consumers was needed to include intangible products and other forms of consumption. Kotler (1972) went on to suggest that the marketing approach can be seen in many situations where one entity is trying to elicit a voluntary behaviour from the other entity by offering something of value (an exchange) to the other party. After a couple of uses of the term 'social marketing' seems to have caught on. Bagozzi (1975) proposed that 'social marketing' requires the creation and resolution of these voluntary exchanges.

Although none of these initial efforts mentioned applications to public health, many others have explained how the marketing approach can be used to improve public health (e.g. Andreasen 1995). Public health is probably the area that has been the most receptive to social marketing. In fact it was the application to public health that inspired Rothschild (1999) to further define what social marketing is by contrasting it with education and law. Rothschild argued that the educational approach is to get people to change their behaviour voluntarily by teaching or creating awareness without providing any reward or punishment. The legal approach tries to get people to behave by coercing them with a threat of punishment. Meanwhile, social marketing is the use of rewards, and attempts to minimize barriers to the desired behaviour. For example, making safer sex easier, more attractive or more available, and making unsafe activities harder, less attractive and less available would all be possible ways to alter sexual behaviour.

With regard to the issue of AIDS prevention, there have been many domestic educational campaigns employed, but considerably fewer legal or social marketing efforts. Next we will review the history of AIDS and some of the strategies that have been used to try to prevent, or at least reduce, the spread of HIV and AIDS in the USA. This will also be an opportunity to discuss some of the barriers to social marketing prevention programmes.

US domestic developments

Probably the most observable issue that arises from looking at the issue of AIDS is the storm that arose because of the fact that AIDS is tied to sexual behaviour. This context caused people to focus more on morality issues about sex than the public health aspects. Instead of developing a concerted effort to reduce people's risk, the sexual nature of the disease caused fight over what was the 'right' approach to trying to change people's sexual behaviour.

One outcome of AIDS being initially identified as a gay disease is that the homosexual community began getting active in AIDS education and prevention almost as soon as the disease was initially diagnosed (Shilts 1987). As early as 1982, gay men in San Francisco and New York began grass-roots preventative activities that were generally based on education that explained what the disease was, its means of transmission and how to prevent it (Dearing and Rogers 1992; MMWR 2006). Given the identification as a gay disease, this response should not be surprising. This immediate effort can be seen as evidence of the importance of self-interest and community ties. As Adam Smith would say, people typically act in their own self-interest. Because AIDS was initially identified with gays, that community was responsible for some of the first efforts. These efforts usually involved education about the disease and prevention through the use of condoms.

The news media gave some coverage to AIDS in the early 1980s (Dearing and Rogers 1992). We know that news coverage does reach people and can sway public opinion through opinion leaders, so this was somewhat promising in educating people about AIDS. However, because the disease was most often identified with homosexuals, its effect was probably limited. First, we also know that people often make a distinction between personal risk and risk to others – called the 'impersonal impact hypothesis' (Tyler and Cook 1984). So just because the overall rates to the public were rising did not necessarily lead to people feeling personally at risk. Second, we know that people will often find ways to minimize their own risk levels, through processes such as attribution theory (Heider 1958). Attribution theory has found that people tend to blame the problems of others on internal factors (such as not being cautious enough) but see them as better able to protect themselves (because they are straight or by being better able to select partners). Because the news media generally identified AIDS as a disease among gay men (Dearing and Rogers 1992), it likely enabled people to use the fundamental attribution error and other means to minimize their own risk estimates (Heider 1958; Ross 1977). That is, people were able to think that AIDS was a risk to very sexually active gay men and ignored calls for their own action. In what is known as a 'fear control' process (Witte 1992), people found ways to minimize their own risk, largely by distancing themselves from the disease in the ways mentioned above.

In 1985, US actor Rock Hudson was diagnosed with AIDS. As a result, the number of news articles in mainstream media made a jump from fourteen stories per month to 143, a tenfold increase. Clearly, a celebrity with AIDS garnered considerably more coverage for the issue (Dearing and Rogers 1992). While this event markedly increased the number of stories about AIDS, and likely increased awareness of it, the fact that Rock Hudson was gay may have also limited the impact of this story on the general public directly. (Interestingly, however, it is possible that Rock Hudson's diagnosis affected the way a former actor colleague named Ronald Reagan perceived the disease. Since Ronald Reagan was, at the time, president of the USA, this may have had secondhand effects on the general public.) Even though the medical evidence at the time was that the disease could be spread to heterosexuals, there is evidence that the public still engaged in fear control by distancing themselves from the disease and minimizing their own risk. Again, because the initial identification of AIDS was primarily as a gay disease, this allowed heterosexual Americans to feel safe (e.g. Check 1985). Again, the fundamental attribution error, impersonal impact and fear control may have been operating to allow people to minimize their perceptions of risk, and therefore not change their behaviour (Anonymous 1987).

By 1987, the public health community noticed that the epidemic was not changing the straight community as much as they would have liked. So mainstream public health prevention efforts kicked in with a National AIDS Clearinghouse and in 1988 with the surgeon general's 'Understanding AIDS' brochure (MMWR 2006). One of the main messages was that AIDS was a sexually transmitted disease that could affect anyone, regardless of sexual orientation. The brochure was mailed to every home in the USA. Both efforts were primarily educational, explaining what the disease was, the means of transmission, and the ways in which transmission could probably be prevented, largely through abstinence or the use of condoms. However, several groups began to suggest that advocating the use of condoms encouraged sexual activity and infidelity, and perhaps even encouraged the spread of AIDS. So while his surgeon general was advocating the use of condoms, President Reagan was putting forth a message of monogamy and abstinence (*Ottawa Citizen* 1987). At the same time the US Department of Education put out a guide for parents and teachers which suggested abstinence was the only effective means of preventing AIDS (Bennett 1987). As a result, the use of condoms became a

349

bit of a political football and the use of condoms was not as strongly advocated as it could have been.

In the late 1980s, despite the dilution of the condom message, there is evidence of increasing condom sales over this period (Moran *et al.* 1990). This is probably an instance of commercial marketing meshing with social marketing to increase people's ability to cope with the concern. Most of these studies tended to focus on comparing sales at the same outlets before and after these educational efforts. However, it is likely that additional channels of distribution were employed (e.g. Cohen *et al.* 1999), and therefore these studies likely underestimate the effects of these educational efforts on condom sales. Around the same time, HIV screening of the US blood supply was very effective in reducing the transmission rate from blood transfusions to about one in two million (MMWR 2006). In the case of blood transfusions, the application of a single structural change enabled by biomedical technology had a large and almost immediate effect on one form of HIV transmission.

In 1991, another important point in the story of AIDS was Earvin 'Magic' Johnson's announcement that he had HIV. Johnson was a basketball player and celebrity. Since Magic denied any homosexual activity, the public may have seen this as proof that HIV could be spread by heterosexual activity, as the surgeon general had claimed. Research suggests that this single event led to a considerable increase in calls to the AIDS hotline, from 3,000 to 40,000, a thirteenfold daily increase, and an increase in HIV tests from 30 to 146, almost a fivefold increase (Harris and Chavez 1991). In addition, the news of this story was quickly spread, largely by word of mouth (Basil and Brown 1994). Evidence suggests that men were more likely to pass this story on than were women (Basil and Brown 1994). Evidence suggests that celebrity patients result in press coverage and public awareness (Lerner 2006). In studying this phenomenon, Basil and Brown found that people identified with Magic Johnson; the notion that people felt that they knew him as a friend, led to their concern about the risk of HIV and AIDS to themselves (Basil 1996; Basil and Brown 1995, 1997). Left with a feeling of vulnerability, many people were tested for HIV. This was also an opportunity for social marketing interventions to offer the types of exchanges that Rothschild (1999) advocates to ensure safer behaviour. Later research on identification has shown that a similar feeling of identification was also important in determining people's reactions to the death of Princess Diana (Brown *et al.* 2003a) and their desire to emulate the opinions and behaviours of Mark McGwire (Brown *et al.* 2003b).

Another important time was in 1994; at an AIDS day conference, then-US Surgeon General Jocelyn Elders suggested that sexual education classes should suggest masturbation as alternative sexual outlet. An immediate negative response from religious groups erupted, and led to her resignation (Frankel 1994). This added more fuel to the fiery debate on whether abstinence or condoms should be the focus of prevention efforts and further stoked the storm still raging over what was the 'right' way to alter people's sexual activities. This fight was at least partly responsible for framing abstinence and condoms as an either–or proposition, with only one 'right' approach.

By 1996, another biomedical advance, the use of antiretroviral drugs, became common. Survival rates began to increase markedly (MMRW 2006). Again, because it did not require a change in sexual activity, this advance had a large direct impact on AIDS. While some suggest that this also may have reduced the potential threat of the disease (Kippax and Race 2003), the fact that the disease was still fatal meant that the threat could not be seen as completely ameliorated. But the face of the disease was changing. The diagnosis rates began to grow in the heterosexual community while the number of new cases actually fell in male-to-male and injection drug transmission (MMWR 2006). Another important development in AIDS prevention was the use of HIV testing to prevent the transmission from mother to child (MMWR 2006). Evidence shows a significant increase in HIV testing, especially among pregnant women between 1994 and 1999 (Lansky *et al.* 2001). The process of testing, coupled with antiretroviral therapy is purported to have dropped the cases of transmission from mother to child from 1,650 to a range of 144 to 236, a tenfold decrease (MMWR 2006).

In 2001, the CDC proposed a new prevention strategy which focused on reducing the number of new infections in the USA by 50 per cent (Linas *et al.* 2006). One important aspect of this effort involves increasing the number of people tested, so that people will know their HIV status. Increased federal funding was shown to result in increased levels of testing (Linas *et al.* 2006), and this finding is consistent with social marketing approaches which suggest that increasing the availability of testing or reducing the costs would lower the barriers to testing and increase compliance. If people had been more aware of testing, and that the results were anonymous, it is likely that more people would have known their HIV status, and, in theory, would have acted accordingly.

Summary of US social marketing efforts

The main debate in the USA was based on the controversial aspects of sexual behaviour. It centred on whether abstinence, limiting the number of sexual partners, or use of condoms was the 'right' approach. Some of this debate may have distracted people from the point that any and all of these behavioural changes were effective in AIDS control. In addition, most of the US interventions continued to focus on education, even though there was considerable awareness and knowledge. This means we missed other social marketing options to provide exchanges for risk reduction behaviours and disincentives for risky behaviours (DeJong 1989). The focus on education may reflect the fact that education is sometimes easier than social marketing – just putting together a brochure, information session or poster classifies as education. In addition, the news media in the West is an existing structure that is eager to seek out celebrity stories to fill its pages and attract an audience. Educational approaches were also probably less controversial than trying to alter people's sexual behaviour. It is also possible that this reflects cultural biases where we believe our own citizens are more rational or perhaps that our consumer culture is better able to deliver commercial products such as condoms to the marketplace (Ciszewski and Harvey 1995). But for whatever reasons the USA has focused more effort on educational approaches to AIDS prevention that involved information but not incentives or exchanges.

Perhaps the main reason that social marketing has been employed at all in the USA arises from the fact that AIDS initially appeared in marginalized communities and gained higher rates of prevalence in those communities (Stall and Mills 2006). The USA tends to think of social marketing approaches for people who are more marginalized. Yet it is a bit disconcerting that while educational approaches do have their use, there is plenty of evidence that people act in their own self-interest. Making condoms more available and other means of reducing the barriers to their use does result in increased use. So perhaps ethnocentrism has done the most harm, by limiting the ways in which the USA has tried to prevent the spread of HIV and AIDS to primarily educational approaches.

Yet there are some examples of social marketing programmes in the USA. One example is a programme in Louisiana which made condoms more available in clinics and in businesses in neighbourhoods with high rates of sexually transmitted diseases (STDs) (Cohen *et al.* 1999). Another is a word-of-mouth campaign for minority gay men (Silvestre *et al.* 2006). Both of these approaches were found to be successful.

Another social marketing campaign which got some attention was the calls for abstinence among teenagers (Thomas 1999; Zipperer 1999). In addition to education efforts around social norms, the abstinence campaign asked young people to sign pledges affirming their desire to remain abstinent and by building communities where abstinence was supported. Silver rings were added as symbols. The effort, however, was met with some resistance from the American Civil Liberties Union who claimed that the financial support of the movement constituted government promotion of religion (Anonymous 2005). By delaying intercourse or reducing the number of partners this approach had potentially positive outcomes. There was some 'told-you-so' outside the religious community when research revealed that many abstinence pledges were broken (Akst 2003). More critical to the effectiveness of the programme, however, was that more than half of the pledges reported oral sex during their pledge and, further, when the pledges eventually did have sex they were not likely to use condoms (Akst 2003). Overall, the promise of the campaign was probably not as large as hoped, and ultimately may have been discredited.

Overall, then, the political and religious polarization of the issue led to competing messages about what should be done. The philosophical battle distracted from an effort that could have resulted in unified HIV prevention efforts (Rifkin 2004). Unfortunately, this can best be seen as a missed opportunity, and a lesson for social marketers to pay head to cultural norms, especially for any behaviours with strongly felt beliefs.

International efforts

While the diagnosis of AIDS arose from cases identified by the CDC in the USA, there is evidence that human retroviruses first appeared in Africa, even before AIDS was first diagnosed in the USA in 1981. Perhaps partly because of its earlier start in Africa, sub-Saharan Africa is probably the most severely affected area in the world, with six million cases, and almost a 30 per cent seroprevalance rate (Pawinski and Lalloo 2006). In Botswana this rate is an even higher 39 per cent (White 2006).

Yet for many of the same reasons that people try to deny their risks, other countries also tried to find ways to distance themselves from AIDS and HIV and this delayed their own action (Stall and Mills 2006). Typically, the first reaction was for countries to deny any cases of AIDS, or explain that it was limited to homosexuals and foreigners (Watts 1999). A typical second reaction was to control AIDS by limiting visits of people who may be HIV positive. This delay likely led to cases of HIV infection that might have been avoided. It took several years of increasing seroprevalance (blood test) before many countries confronted AIDS and HIV prevention among their own citizens (Watts 1999).

From the beginning, AIDS in Africa was primarily a heterosexual disease (Riche 1988). Perhaps this is another explanation as to why US domestic approaches have focused on educational efforts, while the rest of the world was more likely to employ social marketing approaches. When AIDS is seen primarily as a 'gay disease' or one of promiscuity (as in the USA), this may have been seen as an opportunity by many groups to 'educate' people about problems with these lifestyles. But when AIDS is primarily a heterosexual disease, people may feel less need to try to change others, and instead look to other ways of making existing sexual behaviour safer. One piece of evidence for the acceptance of social marketing can be seen in the United Nations pamphlet 'Social marketing: An effective tool in the global response to HIV/AIDS' (UNAIDS 1998). The pamphlet documents several success stories in selling condoms to low-income consumers.

The debate on whether condoms promote promiscuity also arose in the international forum, including Canada (Byfield 2002) and the Sudan (Moszynski 2006). However, there was much greater success in combining the basic strategies of prevention into a unified 'A–B–C (abstinence, be faithful and use condoms) approach' (Rifkin 2004).

Meanwhile, the UN and the WHO have been promoting a behavioural intervention of 'no condom, no sex'. The evidence for the 'no condom, no sex' approach comes from Cambodia and Thailand where research has shown 80 per cent and 95 per cent drops in the rates of new infections (UNFPA/WHO 2006). Similar effects were found in Mozambique (Agha *et al.* 2006). So there was a considerable level of success with this approach.

Other countries have also attempted to increase the availability of condoms; back in 1991 heavily Catholic Ireland decided to lower the age limits on condom sales to make them more available to people (Anonymous 1991). China also allows sales of condoms via vending machines (Anonymous 2000). France, reversing a previously increasing trend of oral contraceptive use, increased their use of condoms (Toulemon and Leridon 1998). In Japan oral contraceptives were not legal, so baseline condom use was already high, but still showed signs of increase from concern about AIDS (Concar 1993).

Research has also demonstrated that the price of condoms affects sales (Ciszewski and Harvey 1995). So, overall, the evidence suggests that it is not just a matter of condom availability, but also price that determines the sales and frequency of use. The evidence is clear – making condoms more available and less expensive will generally increase their use. But in 2006 the USA, under the Bush administration, limited this approach by withdrawing financial support for condom distribution because of the claim that condoms may encourage promiscuity (Jack 2006).

It is interesting to note that the idea of focusing on condom availability and price is somewhat at odds with the educational approach that was seen in the USA. By some measures Africa would benefit from education. Evidence can be seen in reports that girls in Tanzania had low levels of knowledge about AIDS and that only 12 per cent of people in Botswana can explain how its transmission could be prevented (White 2006). Of course there is no reason that interventions need to be *limited* to education when other aspects of social marketing can either add to that effort or provide an additional contribution. Each approach appears to have its own contribution to behaviour (Rothschild 1999).

Other opportunities in reducing the spread of HIV and AIDS

It is clear that public health practitioners have done a good job of informing people in the West about AIDS. News stories and other information have resulted in good awareness. There is some evidence that education may have increased efforts to avoid HIV/AIDS (Moran *et al.* 1990). However, the perception of being personally at risk is harder to convey. The media may help accomplish this when a celebrity is diagnosed and his or her story is told in the press (Dearing and Rogers 1992; Lerner 2006). This appears to activate interpersonal networks of communication (Basil and Brown 1994) and result in people feeling at greater personal risk. The perception of personal risk appears to hinge on the feeling of identifying with a celebrity who has HIV (Brown and Basil 1995). This appears to affect people as if a real friend has been diagnosed (Basil and Brown 1997). Therefore it appears that efforts of personalizing the risk with the use of affected celebrities might have lasting effects.

The fight over whether condoms promoted promiscuity was also a lost opportunity. Perhaps less fighting between church and state might have led to a more cohesive integrated programme which did not derogate either abstinence or condoms as a viable approach. The way this was eventually combined as an A–B–C (abstinence, be faithful and use condoms) approach in the African community might also have been beneficial in other parts of the world (Rifkin 2004). Of course, this approach benefited from having evolved only in 2004. But had various factions spent less time fighting and more time reaching a compromise solution it is possible that this would have saved lives in the meantime by allowing people to use whatever risk reduction strategy suited them best.

With regard to the question of whether people have changed their behaviour, research has found that education and knowledge about AIDS are predictive of condom use. Other research has examined the barriers to condom use, yet few of these insights appear to have been fully tapped into improving the product or countering these concerns. Yet the evidence that social marketing programmes which have helped to make condoms more available result in increased use is promising (Agha *et al.* 2001; Cohen *et al.* 1999). It suggests that even with factors working against condom use, if they are available they are more likely to be used (Moran *et al.* 1990). But building a better condom, or doing a better job of destigmatizing their use could have been done. For example, some attempts at getting women to refuse sex with an unprotected partner have been tried and may have been more successful if combined with other options such as a female condom.

Despite some evidence of increased condom use, there is less evidence of other changes in people's sexual behaviour. Yet many of these other efforts might have been used to slow down the spread of HIV/AIDS. One critique of the educational approach is that previous health outbreaks have been successfully contained by interrupting the chain of transmission (Dannemeyer and Franc 1989). So another potential opportunity was to increase testing. With other diseases, positive STDs tests are required to be reported to authorities. However, HIV testing in the USA was initially done anonymously. Despite this limitation, though, some voluntary-testing efforts have been successful. The testing of pregnant women was voluntary, and yet the results of the mother-to-child interventions have been remarkably effective in lowering this means of transmission (MMWR 2006).

One of the reasons for voluntary testing is to avoid stigmatization of victims, and another is to protect their health coverage. Because the USA has a private healthcare insurance system, individual carriers can drop high-risk or high-cost individuals, and can exclude existing conditions. Because retroviral therapy can be relatively expensive (especially in the early days), being dropped from coverage was a very serious risk. Therefore it was this structural factor that effectively eliminated the possibility of tests being mandatory. For mandatory reporting to be more viable, it would have been necessary to alter the laws around the insurance industry in the USA. This was probably seen as too interventionist for US lawmakers. As a result, the mandatory reporting, though potentially effective, was not used.

Another attempt to slow down the chain of transmission is laws that require the disclosure of a known positive HIV status to potential sexual partners. Failure to disclose is often framed as fraud or assault. There have been some prosecutions of people who did not disclose their HIV status to sexual partners (Wikipedia 2007).

Are there other ways we might have changed sexual behaviour to reduce AIDS risks? Because sexual behaviour is rooted in physiological needs, shaped by experience, and played out in the context of culture, attempting to alter it may be difficult and require a great deal of consideration of viable alternatives. One of the advantages of condoms is that people could still engage in their normal sexual behaviour, but do it more safely. Trying to reduce or change people's sexual behaviours raises more difficulties. One possibility was raised by former US Surgeon General Jocelyn Elders' pragmatic suggestion that sex education classes should mention masturbation as an alternative activity. But this comment offended religious groups who found the suggestion ran afoul of their fundamental principles (Frankel 1994). One approach that was acceptable to religious groups was the idea of abstinence. The silver ring programme attempted that, but perhaps by trying to delay and stigmatizing sex may have inadvertently raised desire, and the result appears to have resulted in unsafe alternatives. But there is some evidence that there were some spontaneous changes in sexual behaviour as a result of AIDS. This can be seen in an increase in erotic material including romance novels, pornography and sex toys (Harlib 1993). So a better consideration of the importance of sexuality to individuals, and how low-risk alternatives could be made as equivalent as possible, might have helped to design a combination of social marketing interventions that afforded the possibility of abstinence, being faithful, condoms *and* different types of safe activities.

References

Agha, S., Karlyn, A. and Meekers, D. (2006) 'The promotion of condom use in non-regular sexual partnerships in urban Mozambique', *Health Policy and Planning*, 16(2):144–51.

Akst, L. (2003, September/October) 'Like a virgin: Abstinence pledges are usually broken', *Psychology Today*, 18.

Andreasen, A. R. (1995) *Marketing Social Change*, San Francisco, CA: Jossey Bass.

Anonymous (1987) 'Facts don't back alarms about AIDS spread', *Vancouver Sun*, 6 February, B5.

Anonymous (1991) 'Condom sales in Ireland', *Lancet*, 20 April, 337:970.

Anonymous (2000) 'Thriving campus college sales upsets parents and teachers', *China Today*, 49(7):1–2.

Anonymous (2005) 'ACLU v. silver ring thing', *Contemporary Sexuality*, 39(7):8.

Anonymous (2006) 'Back to prevention', *Economist*, 15 August, 1.

Bagozzi, R. P. (1975) 'Marketing as exchange', *Journal of Marketing*, 39(4): 32–39.

Basil, M. D. (1996) 'Identification as a mediator of celebrity effects', *Journal of Broadcasting and Electronic Media*, 40: 478–95.

—— and Brown, W. J. (1994) 'Interpersonal communication in news diffusion: A study of "Magic" Johnson's announcement', *Journalism Quarterly*, 71: 305–20.

—— —— (1997) 'Marketing AIDS prevention: The differential impact hypothesis versus identification effects', *Journal of Consumer Psychology*, 6:389–411.

—— —— and Bocarnea, M. C. (2002) 'Differences in univariate values versus multivariate relationships: Findings from a study of Diana, Princess of Wales', *Human Communication Research*, 28:501–14.

Bennett, W. (1987). *AIDS and the Education of our Children: A Guide for Parents and Teachers*, US Department of Education, Washington, DC.

Brown, W. J. and Basil, M. D. (1995) 'Media celebrities and public health: Responses to "Magic" Johnson's HIV disclosure and its impact on AIDS risk and high-risk behaviors', *Health Communication*, 7: 345–70.

—— —— and Bocarnea, M. (2003a) 'Social influence of an international celebrity: Responses to the death of Princess Diana', *Journal of Communication*, 53:587–605.

—— —— —— (2003b) 'The influence of famous athletes on health beliefs and practices: Mark McGwire, child abuse prevention and androstenedione', *Journal of Health Communication*, 8:41–57.

Byfield, J. (2002) 'Bishops for free choice? A spokesman for Canada's Catholic episcopacy fudges the teaching of condoms', *Report Newsmagazine*, 29(5):50.

Check, W. (1985) 'Public education on AIDS: Not only the media's responsibility', *Hastings Center Report*, 15(4):27–31.

Ciszewski, R. L. and Harvey, P. D. (1995) 'Contraceptive price changes: The impact on sales in Bangladesh', *International Family Planning Perspectives*, 21:150–4.

Cohen, D. A., Farley, T. A., Bediom-Etame, J. R., Scribner, R., Ward, W., Kendall, C. and Rice, J. (1999) 'Implementation of condom social marketing in Louisiana', *American Journal of Public Health*, 89(2):204–8.

Concar, D. (1993) 'Love me tender (Japanese condom industry)', *New Scientist*, 140:43.

Dannemeyer, W. E. and Franc, M. G. (1989) 'The failure of AIDS-prevention education', *Public Interest*, 96:47–60.

Dearing, J. W. and Rogers, E. M. (1992) 'AIDS and the media agenda', in T. Edgar, M. A. Fitzpatrick and V. S. Freimuth (eds) *AIDS: A Communication Perspective*, Hillsdale, NJ: Erlbaum, pp. 173–94.

DeJong, W. (1989) 'Condom promotion: The need for a social marketing program in America's inner cities', *American Journal of Health Promotion*, 3(4):5–10.

Frankel, D. (1994) 'US surgeon general forced to resign', *Lancet*, 344:1695.

Gallo, R. C. and Montagnier, L. (2003) 'The discovery of HIV as the cause of AIDS', *New England Journal of Medicine*, 349:2283.

Harlib, L. (1993) 'Erotica booms in a dangerous era', *American Demographics*, 15(11):14–15.

Harris, S. and Chavez, S. (1991) 'Calls floods AIDS hot lines, clinics after announcement', *Los Angeles Times*, 1.

Heider, F. (1958) *The Psychology of Interpersonal Relations*, New York, NY: John Wiley & Sons.

Jack, A. (2006) 'US AIDS chief denies morality comes before life', *Financial Times* (London), 17 August, 4.

Kippax, S. and Race, K. (2003) 'Sustaining safe practice: Twenty years on', *Social Science and Medicine*, 57:1–12.

Kotler, P. (1972) 'A generic concept of marketing', *Journal of Marketing*, 36:46–54.

—— and Levy, S. J. (1969) 'Broadening the concept of marketing', *Journal of Marketing*, 33:10–15.

Lansky, A., Jones, J. L., Frey, R. L. and Lindegren, M. L. (2001) 'Trends in HIV testing among pregnant women: United States, 1994–99', *American Journal of Public Health*, 91:1291–3.

Lerner, B. H. (2006) *When Illness Goes Public: Celebrity Patients and How We Look at Medicine*, Baltimore, MD: Johns Hopkins University Press.

Linas, B. P., Zheng, H., Losina, E., Walensky, R. P. and Freedberg, K. A. (2006) 'Assessing the impact of federal HIV prevention spending on HIV testing and awareness', *American Journal of Public Health*, 96:1038–43.

Moran, J. S., Janes, H. R., Peterman, T. A. and Stone, K. M. (1990) 'Increase in condom sales following AIDS education and publicity', *American Journal of Public Health*, 80:807–8.

Morbidity and Mortality Weekly Report (MMWR) (1982) 'Current trends update on Acquired Immune Deficiency Syndrome (AIDS)', 31(37): 513–14, DHHS; CDC.

Morbidity and Mortality Weekly Report (MMWR) (2006) 'Twenty-five years of HIV/AIDS – United States 1981–2006', 55(21), DHHS; CDC.

Moszynki, P. (2006) 'Sudanese health minister's advocacy of condoms sparks protests', *British Medical Journal*, 332:1233.

Ottawa Citizen (1987) 'Reagan stresses monogamy, abstinence in fight against AIDS', 2 April, A14.

Pawinski, R. A. and Lalloo, U G. (2006) 'Multisectoral responses to HIV/AIDS: Applying research to policy and practice', *American Journal of Public Health*, 96:1189–91.

Riche, M. F. (1988) 'Getting the data on AIDS', *American Demographics*, 10(4):8.

Rifkin, W. (2004) 'Strategies in HIV prevention: The A–B–C approach', *Lancet*, 364:1033.

Ross, L. (1977) 'The intuitive psychologist and his shortcomings: Distortions in the attribution process', in L. Berkowitz (ed.) *Advances in Experimental Social Psychology* (Vol. 10), New York, NY: Academic Press.

Rothschild, M. L. (1999) 'Carrots, sticks and promises: A conceptual framework for the management of public health and social issue behaviors', *Journal of Marketing*, 63:24–37.

Shilts, R. (1987) *And the Band Played on*, New York, NY: St Martin's Press.

Silvestre, A. J., Hylton, J. B., Johnson, L. M., Houston, C., Witt, M., Jacobsen, L. and Ostrow, D. (2006) 'Recruiting minority men who have sex with men for HIV research: Results from a 4-city campaign', *American Journal of Public Health*, 96:1020–7.

Stall, R. and Mills, T. C. (2006) 'A quarter century of AIDS', *American Journal of Public Health*, 96:959–61.

Thomas, G. (1999) 'Where true love waits', *Christianity Today*, 43(3):40–6.

Toulemon, L. and Leridon, H. (1998) 'Contraceptive practices and trends in France', *Family Planning Perspectives*, 30:114–20.

Tyler, T. R. and Cook, F. L. (1984) 'The mass media and judgments of risk: Distinguishing impact on personal and societal level judgments', *Journal of Personality and Social Psychology*, 47:693–708.

UNAIDS (1998) *Social Marketing: An Effective Tool in the Global Response to HIV/AIDS*, United Nations: Joint United Nations Programme on HIV/AIDS.

UNFPA/WHO (3 October 2006) Press release: Joint UNFPA/WHO meeting on 100 per cent condom use programme, United Nations, available online at: www.wpro.who.int/media_centre/press_releases/pr_20061003.htm.

Watts, J. (1999) 'Japanese face reality about sexually transmitted diseases', *Lancet*, 354:2059.

White, D. (2006) 'Rate of decline fails to match huge efforts HIV/AIDS', *Financial Times* (London), 20 June, 2.

Wikipedia (2007) R._v._ Cuerrier, available online at: http://en.wikipedia.org/wiki/R._v._Cuerrier.

Witte, K. (1992) 'Putting the fear back in fear appeals: The extended parallel process model', *Communication Monographs*, 59:329–49.

Zipperer, J. (1999) ' "True love waits" now worldwide effort', *Christianity Today*, July 18, 38(8):58.

Part 7

Volunteer recruitment, management and retention

22

Volunteer recruiting, retention and development

Paul Govekar and Michelle Govekar

Introduction

The nonprofit sector is an important, though little recognized, sector of the economy, growing faster than either the for-profit or the government sectors. Further, the nonprofit sector is a major economic force internationally (Anonymous 1997). Since 1977, paid employment as a percentage of US employment rose from 5.5 to 9.5 per cent (Independent Sector 2006) and total numbers of organizations grew to 837,027 million with expenditures at almost 9 per cent of US GDP.

With cutbacks in government funding and decentralization of government programmes, private nonprofits assume greater importance in many vital areas of society. Reduced government support brings increased demands for nonprofit services, making increased efficiency and effectiveness essential for their future (Drucker 1990). That the growing social need creates increased demand for trained motivated volunteers is seen throughout the USA (Zimmerman *et al.* 2003). Even the 2006 election will not change this, as current analysis suggests lesser cutbacks but at the same time it is unlikely to provide increased support at the cost of ballooning government deficits (Schwinn 2006). These same forces are increasingly at work in other geographic areas, such as Australia and the UK as well (Greenslade and White 2005; Bussell and Forbes 2002).

Nonprofit organizations depend heavily on volunteer labour to perform essential functions which allow these organizations to meet their goals. At $15.40 per hour an estimated 83.9 million volunteers contributed the equivalent of $239 billion worth of labour in 2001 to the US economy alone (The Nonprofit World Its Size and Scope 2006). Had they paid for this labour, no nonprofit organization could have fulfilled its mission. This is not new. Generally, the not-for-profit sector sees a decline in volunteers during economic downturns. However, shifting promotional emphasis based on volunteer workforce needs could result in an increase in volunteers during economic downturns in addition to retention and further suggest volunteer development avenues.

In order to understand marketing's role in increasing the availability of volunteers, we must first understand why individuals volunteer. This chapter next explores the recent marketing literature concerning the acquisition, retention and development of volunteers. Finally, we offer a review of recommendations to increase the role of marketing in the volunteer lifecycle, suggest areas for future research and provide some concluding remarks.

Why individuals volunteer

Those who contribute their time, skills and labour (i.e. volunteers) are involved in most aspects of nonprofit operations (Gallagher and Weinberg 1991). Previous research on determinants of volunteer participation has been conducted across several social science disciplines. Volunteering is of interest to many disciplines because of the importance of volunteerism to volunteers, the associations they serve and society in general (Smith 1994). Much of the research on volunteers is demographic in nature. This research is commonly known. Regular national surveys by the Independent Sector, the Census Bureau and the Bureau of Labor Statistics consistently find that voluntary participation is overly represented by white, middle-class, well-educated, middle-aged adults in families with at least one child (Gerard 1985). The latest analysis of the US Census Bureau and Bureau of Labor Statistics data conducted by the Corporation for National and Community Service updates these findings. This analysis finds that volunteerism rates have exploded in the past thirty years. This is especially true for older Americans. Key findings of this analysis include: people aged 45 to 65 volunteer at higher rates than previous generations; the portion of Americans volunteering at educational or your-service organizations has increased by 63 per cent since 1989; and teenagers 16 to 19 years of age spend more than twice as much time volunteering as did young people in 1989 (Barton 2007). While these studies are interesting and tell us who is doing the volunteer work, they do not tell us why these individuals volunteer or how to retain them once they do volunteer. To understand this, we must better understand what influences people to undertake volunteer work.

Since today's volunteers are educated people who often hold important positions, it is not likely that the overall number of volunteers will increase. Additionally, it is unlikely that the number of hours that these individuals contribute will increase significantly. In times of increased demand, it is essential that the nonprofit sector apply marketing ideas to recruit and retain volunteers. What causes these talented individuals to volunteer, what outside influences can cause the supply of volunteer labour to shift (Greenslade and White 2005) and how to keep and develop volunteers (Farmer and Fedor 1999; Leviton et al. 2006; Starnes and Wymer 2001) are questions that must be answered.

Bussell and Forbes' (2002) literature review identified the what, where, who and why of volunteering; noting that little work existed on local variations. Starnes and Wymer (2001) found that changes may result in volunteers quitting short term but these changes eventually merge identity with organizational goals and reactivate past volunteers.

Empirical research on volunteerism has been limited due to challenges of securing data. Data on volunteering come from the Independent Sector series of surveys (Independent Sector 1999), currently continued by the Urban Institute (2006). These surveys, conducted biennially since 1988, report volunteer time from May of each year based on a representative national sample of 2,500 or more individuals, adjusted for adequate representation of African-Americans, Hispanics and affluent Americans with incomes over $70,000. The sample is weighted to insure representation by age, race/ethnicity, education, marital status, size of household, region of the country and household income. The error rate is +/− 3 per cent (Saxon-Harrold 1999: 16).

French (2006) finds that many professionals volunteer to build their work skills beyond what is possible in their own job (see also this premise reflected in the model of USA Leadership Corps 2006). Sharir and Lerner (2006) mention the importance of past volunteer services in the role of social entrepreneurship, or starting new nonprofits. Mueller (2006) notes the lure for professionals of working for less powerful causes where these individuals can make a real difference. Miller (2005) finds professional volunteers facilitated through associations and collaborative volunteer networks. Hibbert *et al.* (2003) discovered a growing recognition of enhanced skills, self-esteem and self-confidence that developed over time for volunteers at community food cooperatives. Their study relied on Dwyer *et al.*'s (1987) phases of marketing relationships in order to develop marketing tactics to recruit and keep volunteers. Gladney (2006) focuses on the mixed motives that may involve professionals' volunteering, which in turn can bring the professional business. He brings up ethical issues associated with profiting by doing good works. The conflict of interest involves marketing oneself personally, rather than marketing the nonprofit. Orr (2005) provides the example of Taproot, a professional network providing slick marketing services to nonprofits who gained in both income and clients. Volunteers sensed that their contribution was valuable and directly aimed at using their expertise to improve the project. James (2000) noted that *pro bono* work by marketers can benefit nonprofits while building marketing skills and improving personal networks for those who volunteer. Volunteering is not limited to the USA. Volunteering is in its early development stages in Spain. Beerli *et al.* (2004) explored differences in images portrayed by charitable and ecological organizations and noted that individual self-concepts impact upon individuals' choice of volunteering targets, suggesting that nonprofits could use social marketing tactics to build volunteering.

Much volunteerism research focuses on values, attitudinal and behavioural factors which may motivate individuals to volunteer for a particular position or organization. Inglis and Cleave (2006) explored the motivations of board volunteers and found six components: enhancement of self-worth, learning through community, helping the community, developing individual relationships, unique contributions to the board and self-healing. These cluster into two groups, one personal and one more altruistic. They suggest application of these findings to recruitment, training, development and retention. Callow (2004) suggests retirees' motives for volunteering are not homogeneous, but contain considerable variability. Perceived motives for volunteering among seniors include the feel-good factor, a need for socialization, and a search for structure and purpose. Dutta–Bergman (2004) suggests developing a dialogue which highlights the nonprofit organization's responsible commitment to the community and incorporating communication strategies that appeal to different aspects of a responsible lifestyle such as exercising, consumerism, healthy eating and an environmental consciousness. Govekar (2004) suggests highlighting the social networking aspects of volunteering, using current volunteers to gain other volunteers through facilitation. Other suggestions include:

1. Self-esteem: volunteers have positive self-images, feel capable and competent (Okun 1994; Gerard 1985). Feeling in control of their lives is also important (Miller 1985). Wymer (2003) noted that literacy volunteers reported a need to be productive.
2. Moral/civic duty: volunteers frequently report a sense of moral responsibility or a sense of duty as a motive (Gerard 1985; Okun 1994). The Austin Mini used cause-related marketing to build upon this motive by encouraging their car owners to participate communally in National Volunteers' Week (Kurylko 2006). Gaschen (2005) relates the experience of Susan Hager, a PR professional who built a career by making a difference. Mintzberg and Westley (2000) characterize nonprofits as social-value achievers.

3   Religious beliefs: opportunities to express religious beliefs and values are provided in many volunteer situations (Wood and Hougland 1990). Leviton *et al.* (2006) noted that church congregations can encourage their members to help others in need, particularly in caring for the chronically ill, a particularly difficult but vital area for volunteer recruitment and retention.

4   Facilitation: rather than volunteers' behaviour, others asking them to volunteer can be important (Wymer 1997; Govekar 2004). McDermott *et al.* (2000) found that health research organizations apply personal selling techniques to recruit board members and regular volunteers.

5   Social benefits: social benefits are yet another need mentioned by Hibbert *et al.* (2003). Hayes and Slater (2001) studied 'friends' schemes which are also known as membership schemes and societies. Saxton and Benson (2005) looked into the role of social capital in the formation of new nonprofit organizations and found that trust was not as significant a factor as they posited it would be.

Marketing's role

Marketing concepts are not foreign to nonprofits. Initial application of marketing ideas to nonprofits originated almost forty years ago (Kotler and Levy 1969). An early specific application to volunteerism is also twenty years old (Yavas and Reicken 1985) applying basic demographic and attitude-related marketing techniques to differentiate donors of time in an offshoot of fundraising research. This work set in motion a serious practical marketing analysis of volunteers (Schlegelmich and Tynan 1989) and ignited nonprofit organizations' use of marketing tactics to obtain volunteers (Wilkinson 1989). On the organizational side, nonprofits have used the concepts of market segmentation (e.g. geo-demographics, relationship marketing, database marketing) for many years. Until fairly recently, the primary emphasis of these efforts was aimed at increasing either the amount of money donors give, or the number of donors giving the money. Some performing-arts organizations also use market segmentation concepts in an effort to improve the size of their audience (Scheff 1996). Bruce (1995) proposed dividing constituents into beneficiaries, supporters, stakeholders and regulators with intermediary groups in each case to trace channels to reach the final constituent. He blames both nonprofits and marketing professionals for failing to project the benefits a marketing approach brings to better serve their constituents. One key to a nonprofit organization's marketing success may be in adapting to internal and external environments to reposition themselves in creative and dramatic ways (Scheff 1996). For example, the Sacramento Symphony remade itself after its 1992 bankruptcy by emphasizing inclusiveness, outreach and community education.

Bennett and Sargeant (2005) and Bennett and Barkensjo (2005) both found that employment of marketing techniques to attract volunteers has received 'much' attention. Bennett and Kottasz (2000) found in studying affective, cognitive and connative characteristics that both less and more altruistically (egoistical) motivated targets responded more positively to recruitment advertisements that emphasized the material and emotional benefits of volunteering. Also those longer-serving individuals most often reported egoistical motives, mostly resulting in emotional satisfaction.

Leviton *et al.* (2006) present many cases of private foundations coming forward to involve church groups in providing critical elder care. They consider how faith motivates particularly for the 'hard' social service delivery positions. Hankinson and Rochester (2005) explore whether negative perceptions of volunteering are suitable for reshaping through 'branding' to increase volunteerism; they find that different areas of volunteering may be developed as 'sub-brands' and argue that UK national-level programmes are best able to use brand to this effect. Ratje (2003) explained how well-trained volunteers can be the carriers of an individual nonprofit organization's brand.

Wymer and Samu (2002) found that male and nonworking volunteers spend more time, while female and working volunteers are more empathetic and also distinguished different values reported by men and women for volunteering. Wymer (2003) followed Smith's (1994) lead in investigating segmentation of literacy volunteers to identify subgroups' motives and perceived benefits. He also differentiated motives of high-performing and poor-performing volunteers. Nonprofits can use this differentiation to determine what to say and where to say it to recruit, screen, place, use, manage and retain volunteers.

Market segmentation techniques, then, are familiar to nonprofit managers, developed and applied mostly for fundraising. Similar techniques help find, develop and retain the right volunteers for the organization.

Other research proposes that relationship-marketing practices, including friends' programmes carry benefits beyond cashflow, extending to volunteer retention (Hayes and Slater 2003). They develop social-club frameworks, public members and integrated membership schemes reflecting strategic directions of alignment, convergence and unification which can drive organizational marketing activities which retain volunteers.

Bussell and Forbes (2003) applied a relationship-marketing perspective to develop a 'volunteer lifecycle' model, linking various marketing tactics to volunteers' needs at each stage in their organizational involvement, recruitment, retention and reactivation. Bennett and Barkensjo (2005) address retention with their research on internal marketing programmes. They argue that applying marketing communications affected commitment; the volunteers' experience, job attributes, personal affect, stress, motivations and recognition all affect job satisfaction and organizational commitment, thus retention and performance. Mitchell and Taylor (2004) present a seven-step internal marketing process to build long-term relationships with volunteers. Leviton et al. (2006) find that good supervision is associated with growth in volunteers and that regular contact between volunteers and their supervisor engenders satisfaction and loyalty as well as a willingness to continue to serve.

Wymer and Starnes (2001) focus their review on recruitment, but preface it with the idea that retention is key. They present a model of volunteer behaviour including personal influence (such as self-esteem and empathy, values, personal experience and life stage), interpersonal influences (mainly facilitation, social norms and parental volunteering), attitudes and situational factors (such as time and income); then develop a complete marketing programme which draws on these factors.

Kaufman et al. (2004) present a Soviet Union example of volunteer retention, supporting the contention of Govekar et al. (2000) that a volunteer-centred orientation requires comprehensive social support, organizational commitment to goals and using the potential volunteer's professional skills in the recruitment and placement effort. Such a programme results in decreased costs, and enhanced benefits to support volunteers and volunteer recruitment. In times of strong GDP levels and low unemployment levels nonprofits grow and enjoy a stable supply of volunteers (Saxton and Benson 2005). These volunteers want to build social capital and feel psychologically content in helping society through the nonprofit organization of their choice. Nonprofits can use this analysis to build campaigns which support volunteers' natural desires (Houle et al. 2005).

Retention is the key to Starnes and Wymer (2001) who begin by defining volunteer turnover. They suggest that volunteer screening, matching programmes, tenure systems, offering leadership roles and organizational support can significantly reduce turnover. Their suggestions provide academically sound support to Morley and Rossman's (1997) report for the Urban Institute on community initiatives. In this report the authors recommend that programme managers put energy and creativity into volunteer recruitment, screen and train volunteers, match volunteers and clients, provide ongoing support and monitoring and recognize volunteer efforts in both small and large ways. A more direct take on retention comes from Self (2001) who points out the application of promotional materials to support commitment through volunteer recognition and retention.

The nonprofit literature has been enhanced over the past forty years by explaining how a volunteer organization might benefit by using various corporate marketing practices (Herman 1994). Bradner (2001) argues that promotional messages must emphasize the need that non-profit programmes hope to remedy. This traditional approach attracted volunteers using the social good that would be done by the organization. This works fairly well. Bradner (2001) further argues that the promotional message must also speak to the needs of those people who could most effectively fill the job. This strategy has the potential to be very effective. Such a distinction in promotional campaigns calls for a strategy to analyse the needs of potential volunteers and, as suggested above, for volunteer agencies to respond accordingly. The marketing concept of Perreault and McCarthy (1999) suggests that nonprofits know the needs of their volunteers and respond accordingly. The changing needs of potential volunteers cannot be satisfied if volunteer organizations do not adapt to dynamic economic conditions. Wymer (1999) applied this same logic in suggesting that nonprofits view their volunteers as customers.

Another alternative vision of marketing strategies resonates with the concept of the product lifecycle. It suggests that every product offered to consumers, no matter how successful, will eventually lose popularity due in part to the changing needs of the consumers who have been buying it (Herman 1994). The theory suggests that an organization must be dynamic and adjust its offerings or create new ones. Wasson (1978) used this idea to remind nonprofit managers that the way their organization successfully served its target market in the past may not work in the future. We argue that this can also impact upon an organization's desired and even its current volunteers.

Managerial process and volunteer lifecycle

As discussed above, market segmentation techniques can assist in these areas. As Drucker (1990) indicates, a nonprofit organization has multiple vitally important key relationships and constituencies to be addressed. Market segmentation is a two-step process of: (a) *defining* broad product markets; and (b) *segmenting* these broad product markets in order to select target markets and develop suitable marketing mixes. Real-world market segmentation studies generally follow one of two designs: (a) an a priori design where management decides the basis for segmentation; or (b) a clustering design where segments are determined by clustering external or internal customers on a set of relevant variables (Wind 1978).

A nonprofit organization is trying to 'sell' its mission and its volunteer opportunity to individuals with many choices of how to spend their time. More and more, volunteers are educated people with specific skills and knowledge that they can offer and needs they might fulfil through volunteer work. They demand that a nonprofit has a clear mission that drives everything the organization does (Drucker 1990).

An a priori segmentation design could concentrate on what volunteers want. One thing that volunteers demand is training, training and more training (Drucker 1990). Volunteers want to feel qualified and to know that the organization will ensure they can succeed. Can the organization fulfil this need through the training that it provides? Nonprofits have other means to fulfil volunteers' wants. Even their mission and culture can draw volunteers who share these goals (Mitchell and Yates 2002). Lysakowski (2002) points up the crucial role of mission in attracting capital campaign volunteers. Malloy and Agarwal (2003) noted that nonprofits' organizational climates perceived as 'individual caring' had a clear impact on relationship-marketing tactics and also impacted on how staff and volunteers would behave. Rangan (2004) suggested systematic methods connecting this idea of a calling to their programmes using mission to draw volunteers through emotional appeal. Volunteers should be considered much more than helpers, as they directly influence the organization's norms. Marketing is important both externally and internally.

Nonprofit organizations must value their internal and external customers to capture those constituencies described by Drucker (1990) or Bruce (1995). They must address difficult situations and volunteer diversity. Finding volunteers to work with troubled teenagers may be difficult in an area. One way to fill this gap is to determine what needs this work fulfils to identify persons who might volunteer. Likewise, recruiting black and Hispanic volunteers may be problematic. Research suggests 'black volunteers are more motivated by altruistic impulses than white volunteers' (McCurley 1994: 521). For each special challenge, volunteer managers must develop a logical combination of needs and determine how the organization's mission meets them. Some potential volunteers' needs may fit multiple clusters; these should be combined if necessary, and some overlap is expected. If clusters overlap too much, specific needs should be redefined (Wind 1978).

Current volunteers' affinity networks should be used to find new volunteers. 'The most effective marketers are satisfied volunteers already working for your organization' (Mitchell and Yates 1996: 47). Berkshire (2005) recommends using word-of-mouth marketing. They describe a case where 'buzz-agents' worked to identify appropriate people to talk to. This worked better than other marketing techniques because the messages were delivered by someone familiar who has already developed some trust with the message target. Hibbert et al. (2003) found this strategy worked best for the initial-awareness stage of the volunteer relationship. Hart (2002) suggested using the Internet for building and keeping up relationships with donors and volunteers.

Chiagouris (2005) notes that nonprofits need a coherent branding message to facilitate success in all appeals. In an increasingly tight charitable market, successful Internet presence requires a strong brand. For nonprofits the lead brand element is the mission. The mission statement must be specific and realistic, providing a unique selling proposition and reason to believe. These should intersect with the needs mentioned above to communicate strongly and persuasively with potential volunteers. They argue that the nonprofit brand image is even more important than in the for-profit sector. In related research, Bennett and Barkensjo's (2005) study of the impact of negative experiences on retention of volunteers highlights matching volunteer roles to the targets' emotionality, vulnerability to stress, and core motivation but not to job characteristics.

Both paid staff and key volunteers must devote considerable time and energy to understanding the wants and needs of potential volunteers and clustering these into homogeneous market segments. More aggressively marketing the organization and its brand to new volunteers clearly affects the nonprofit's long-term course. Bennett and Barkensjo (2005) contend that there is a positive and significant connection between instituting an internal marketing programme and subsequent improvement in volunteer's satisfaction and commitment. Developing and implementing such a programme, however, requires the expenditure of resources that are always in demand for other uses. Mitchell and Taylor (2004) suggest that such a programme involves seven steps to improve individual performance and create long-term relationships with volunteers. Developing an internal marketing programme would involve analysing the current organizational culture, deciding on the benefits that volunteers want, recruiting people whose values match, designing an internal programme to cultivate the desired culture, planning a socialization process, structuring ceremonial activities to support the desired culture and maintaining a feedback mechanism.

A more targeted campaign brings in more, better-qualified volunteers. Interviewing and matching, orientation and training, and supervision and motivation (McCurley 1994) will require additional effort but provide enhanced contribution opportunity. Today's volunteers are not satisfied with being helpers. They are knowledge workers, and they want to be knowledge workers as they contribute to society (Drucker 1990). Like Taylor and Mitchell's (1996) donors, it is much more expensive to get new volunteers than it is to keep good ones that are found. Better volunteers require more work from managers and paid staff as well as other volunteers.

Areas for future research

Starnes and Wymer (2001) suggest researchers explore the notions of managing volunteers like employees with job descriptions, interviews and written performance standards and wonder whether volunteer programme managers will do the extra work necessitated by treating volunteers more like employees. They further suggest exploring whether fallen-away former volunteers will return if they are asked.

Callow (2004) suggests further research to examine the relative importance of benefits and costs associated with volunteering among senior citizens. He also suggests researchers explore the steps that occur when seniors are deciding whether or not to volunteer. Further, building a better understanding of the cognitive and affective behaviour of potential volunteers would assist in formulating a more marketing-based approach to the recruitment and retention of volunteers.

Hayes and Slater (2003) suggest that further research is needed to benchmark and plot membership schemes from subsectors of the cultural sector. They further recommend better identifying subgroups within what they call the 'social club group' and the 'integrated membership scheme' groups.

Saxton and Benson (2005) suggest that future research is needed to investigate the role of interpersonal trust on community-level outcomes. This research could build on the social trust work done by Fukuyama (1999) and the 'weak ties' identified by Granovetter (1973).

As can be seen, future research on the determinants of volunteer participation will continue to be conducted across several social science disciplines. Marketing's role in this research is undeniable.

Conclusion

Recruiting, developing and retaining volunteers are complex tasks. These tasks are, however, essential if nonprofit organizations are to continue meeting client needs. Informed marketing techniques have a significant role to play in this process. While the application of marketing techniques to nonprofit organizations has a long history, much work still needs to be done. This is especially true of the application of these techniques to the management of volunteers. This continues to be an area where research can truly inform and assist practising managers.

References

Anonymous (1997) 'Nonprofit sector becomes worldwide economic force', *Nonprofit World*, 15(2):10.

Barton, B. (2007) 'Older people lead jump in volunteerism, 30-year study finds', *Chronicle of Philanthropy*, 1 November: 37.

Beerli, A., Díaz, G. and Martín, J. D. (2004) 'The behavioural consequences of self-congruency in volunteers', *International Journal of Nonprofit and Voluntary Sector Marketing*, 9(1):28–48.

Bennett, R. and Barkensjo, A. (2005) 'Internal marketing, negative experiences and volunteers' commitment to providing high-quality services in a UK helping and caring charitable organization', *Voluntas: International Journal of Voluntary and Nonprofit Organizations*, 16(3):251–74.

—— and Kottasz, R. (2000) 'Advertisement style and the recruitment of charity volunteers', *Journal of Nonprofit and Public Sector Marketing*, 8(2):45–63.

—— and Sargeant, A. (2005) 'The nonprofit marketing landscape: Guest editors' introduction to a special section', *Journal of Business Research*, 58(6):797–805.

Berkshire, J. C. (2005) 'Passing on a charity's message', *Chronicle of Philanthropy*, 18(2):65–8.

Bradner, J. H. (2001) 'Volunteer management', in T. D. Connors (ed.) *The Nonprofit Handbook*, New York, NY: John Wiley & Sons, pp. 751–84.

Bruce, I. (1995) 'Do not-for-profits value their customers and their needs?', *International Marketing Review*, 12(4):77–84.

Bussell, H. and Forbes, D. (2002) 'Understanding the volunteer market: The what, where, who and why of volunteering', *International Journal of Nonprofit and Voluntary Sector Marketing*, 7(3):244–57.

—— —— (2003) 'The volunteer life cycle: A marketing model for volunteering', *Voluntary Action*, 5(3):61–79.

Callow, M. (2004) 'Identifying promotional appeals for targeting potential volunteers: An exploratory study on volunteering motives among retirees', *International Journal of Nonprofit and Voluntary Sector Marketing*, 9(3):261–74.

Chiagouris, L. (2005) 'Non profit brands come of age', *Marketing Management*, 14(5):30–3.

Drucker, P. F. (1990) *Managing The Nonprofit Organization*, New York, NY: Harper Business.

Dutta-Bergman, M. J. (2004) 'Describing volunteerism: The theory of unified responsibility', *Journal of Public Relations Research*, 16(4):353–69.

Dwyer, F. R., Schurr, P. H. and Oh, S. (1987). 'Developing buyer seller relationships', *Journal of Marketing*, 51:11–27.

Farmer, S. M. and Fedor, D. B. (1999) 'Volunteer participation and withdrawal', *Nonprofit Management and Leadership*, 9(4):349–68.

French, J. (2006) 'The good-cause bonus', *Sales and Marketing Management*, 158(1):51.

Fukuyama, F. (1999) 'Social capital and civil society', paper presented at the International Monetary Fund Conference Second Generation Reforms, available online at: www.imf.org/external/pubs/ft/seminar/1999/reforms/fukuyama.htm (accessed 9 February 2007).

Gallagher, K. and Weinberg, C. B. (1991) 'Coping with success: New challenges for nonprofit marketing', *Sloan Management Review*, 33(1):27–42.

Gaschen, D. J. (2005) 'From Alaska to the Washington, DC Beltway', *Public Relations Tactics*, 12(5):8.

Gerard, D. (1985) 'What makes a volunteer?', *New Society*, 74:236–8.

Gladney, R. J. (2006) 'The ethics of volunteering', *Advisor Today*, 101(2):24–5.

Govekar, M. A., Govekar, P. L. and Ewing, R. L. (2000) 'Nonprofit volunteer recruiting: Applying market segmentation', proceedings of the 2000 Atlantic Marketing Association, pp. 287–95.

Govekar, P. L. (2004) 'Are you making it hard to volunteer?', *Nonprofit World*, 22(5):24–5.

Granovetter, M. (1973). 'The strength of weak ties', *American Journal of Sociology*, 78:1360–80.

Greenslade, J. H. and White, K. M. (2005) 'The prediction of above-average participation in volunteerism:

A test of the theory of planned behavior and the volunteers functions inventory in older Australian adults', *Journal of Social Psychology*, 145(2):155–72.

Hankinson, P. and Rochester, C. (2005) 'The face and voice of volunteering: A suitable case for branding?', *International Journal of Nonprofit and Voluntary Sector Marketing*, 10(2):93–105.

Hart, T. R. (2002) 'ePhilanthropy: Using the Internet to build support', *International Journal of Nonprofit and Voluntary Sector Marketing*, 7(4):353–60.

Hayes, D. and Slater, A. (2003) 'From "social club" to "integrated membership scheme": Developing membership schemes strategically', *International Journal of Nonprofit and Voluntary Sector Marketing*, 8(1):59–75.

Herman, R. D. (1994) *The Jossey-Bass Handbook of Nonprofit Leadership and Management*, San Francisco, CA: Jossey-Bass.

Hibbert, S., Piacentini, M. and Al Dajani, H. (2003) 'Understanding volunteer motivation for participation in a community-based food cooperative', *International Journal of Nonprofit and Voluntary Sector Marketing*, 8(1):30–42.

Houle, B. J., Sagarin, B. J. and Kaplan, M. F. (2005) 'A functional approach to volunteerism: Do volunteer motives predict task preference?', *Basic and Applied Social Psychology*, 27(4):337–44.

Independent Sector (1999) 'Key findings', Giving and Volunteering in the United States: Findings from a National Survey 1999, available online at: www.independentsector.org/GandV/s_volu.htm (accessed 24 November 2006).

Independent Sector (2006) 'Employment in the nonprofit sector', *Nonprofit Almanac Facts and Findings*, available online at: www.independentsector.org/PDFs/npemployment.pdf (accessed 24 November 2006).

Inglis, S. and Cleave, S. (2006) 'A scale to assess board member motivations in nonprofit organizations', *Nonprofit Management and Leadership*, 17(1):83–101.

James, D. (2000) '*Pro bono* marketing a winning deal', *Marketing News*, 34(17):13–14.

Kaufman, R., Mirsky, J. and Avgar, A. (2004) 'A brigade model for the management of service volunteers: Lessons from the former Soviet Union', *International Journal of Nonprofit and Voluntary Sector Marketing*, 9(1):57–68.

Kotler, P. and Levy, S. J. (1969) 'Broadening the concept of marketing', *Journal of Marketing*, 33(1):10–15.

Kurylko, D. T. (2006) 'Mini advertising promotes good works, good news', *Automotive News*, 80(6194):49.

Leviton, L. C., Herrera, C., Pepper, S. K., Fishman, N. and Racine, D. P. (2006) 'Faith in action: Capacity and sustainability of volunteer organizations', *Evaluation and Program Planning*, 29(2):201–7.

Lysakowski, L. (2002) 'The importance of volunteers in a capital campaign', *International Journal of Nonprofit and Voluntary Sector Marketing*, 7(4):325–32.

Malloy, D. C. and Agarwal, J. (2003) 'Factors influencing ethical climate in a nonprofit organization: An empirical investigation', *International Journal of Nonprofit and Voluntary Sector Marketing*, 8(3):224–53.

McCurley, S. (1994) 'Recruiting and retaining volunteers', in R. D. Herman and Associates (eds) *The Jossey-Bass Handbook of Nonprofit Leadership and Management*, San Francisco, CA: Jossey-Bass, pp. 511–34.

McDermott, D. R., Tuckman, H. P. and Urban, D. J. (2000) 'Assessing the marketing and development of health research organizations', *Marketing Health Services*, 20(1):28–31.

Miller, E. K. (2005) 'Good deeds in the city of brotherly love: The community design collaborative', *Journal of Housing and Community Development*, 62(6):30–2.

Miller, L. E. (1985) 'Understanding the motivation of volunteers: An examination of personality differences and characteristics of volunteers' paid employment', *Journal of Voluntary Action Research*, 14(2–3):112–22.

Mintzberg, H. and Westley, F. (2000) 'Sustaining the institutional environment', *Organization Studies*, 21:71–94.

Mitchell, M. A. and Taylor, S. (2004) 'Internal marketing: Key to successful volunteer programs', *Nonprofit World*, 22(1):25–6.

—— and Yates, D. (1996) 'How to attract the best volunteers', *Nonprofit World*, 14(4):47–8.

—— — (2002) 'How to use your organizational culture as a competitive tool', *Nonprofit World*, 20(2):33–4.

Morley, E. and Rossman, S. B. (1997) *Helping At-risk Youth: Lessons From Community-based Initiatives*, Washington, DC: Urban Institute Press.

Mueller, G. (2006) 'Cause and effect', *Adweek*, 47(13):18.

Okun, M. A. (1994) 'The relation between motives for organizational volunteering and the frequency of volunteering by elders', *Journal of Applied Gerontology*, 13(2):115–26.

Orr, A. (2005) 'Attracting attention', *Stanford Social Innovation Review*, 3(1):55–6.

Perreault, W. D. and McCarthy E. J. (1999) *Basic Marketing: A Global Approach*, Boston MA: Irwin/ McGraw-Hill.

Rangan, V. K. (2004) 'Lofty missions, down-to-earth plans', *Harvard Business Review*, 82(3):112–19.

Ratje, J. M. (2003) 'Well-prepared volunteers help the brand image', *Marketing News*, 37(8):17–18.

Saxon-Harrold, S. K. E. (1999) *Giving and Volunteering in the United States: Findings from a National Survey 1999 Edition, Executive Summary*, Washington, DC: Independent Sector.

Saxton, G. D. and Benson, M. A. (2005) 'Social capital and the growth of the nonprofit sector', *Social Science Quarterly*, 86(1):16–35.

Scheff, J. (1996) 'Crisis in the arts: The marketing response', *California Management Review*, 39(1):28–52.

Schlegelmilch, B. B. and Tynan, C. (1989) 'Who volunteers?: An investigation into the characteristics of charity volunteers', *Journal of Marketing Management*, 5(2):133–51.

Schwinn, E. (2006) 'Congress' new outlook', *Chronicle of Philanthropy*, 23 November 2006:25–9.

Self, D. R. (2001) 'Promotional products: Adding tangibility to your nonprofit promotions', *Journal of Nonprofit and Public Sector Marketing*, 9(3):205–13.

Sharir, M. and Lerner M. (2006) 'Gauging the success of social ventures initiated by individual social entrepreneurs', *Journal of World Business*, 41(1):6–20.

Smith, D. H. (1994) 'Determinants of voluntary association participation and volunteering: A literature review', *Nonprofit and Voluntary Sector Quarterly*, 23(3):243–64.

Starnes, B. J. and Wymer Jr., W. W. (2001) 'Conceptual foundations and practical guidelines for retaining volunteers who serve in local nonprofit organizations: Part II', *Journal of Nonprofit and Public Sector Marketing*, 9(3):97 and 118.

Taylor, S. L. and Mitchell, M. A. (1996) 'Building donor relations: Enter database marketing', *Nonprofit World*, 14(6): 22–4.

Udry, R. J. (1994) 'The nature of gender', *Demography*, 31(4): 561–73.

Urban Institute (2006) 'Nonprofit sector in brief 2007', available online at: www.urban.org/ url.cfm?ID=311373 (accessed 27 November 2006).

'USA Leaderships Corps assists nonprofits with problem solving' (2006) *Associations Now*, October, 2(11):23.

Wasson, C. R. (1978) *Dynamic Competitive Strategy and Product Life Cycles*, Austin, TX: Austin Press.

Wilkinson, G. W. (1989) 'Getting and using information, the united way', *Marketing Research*, 1(3):5–12.

Wind, Y. (1978) 'Issues and advances in segmentation research', *Journal of Marketing Research*, XV:317–37.

Wood, J. R. and Hougland, Jr., J. G. (1990) 'The role of religion in philanthropy', in J. van Til and Associates (eds) *Critical Issues in American Philanthropy*: 29–33, San Francisco, CA: Jossey-Bass.

Wymer, Jr., W. W. (1997) 'Segmenting volunteers using values, self-esteem, empathy and facilitation as determinant variables', *Journal of Nonprofit and Public Sector Marketing*, 5(2):3–28.

—— (1999) 'Hospital volunteers as customers: Understanding their motives, how they differ from other volunteers and correlates of volunteer intensity', *Journal of Nonprofit and Public Sector Marketing*, 6(2/3):51–76.

—— (2003) 'Differentiating literacy volunteers: A segmentation analysis for target marketing', *International Journal of Nonprofit and Voluntary Sector Marketing*, 8(3):67–85.

—— and Samu, S. (2002) 'Volunteer service as symbolic consumption: Gender and occupational differences in volunteering', *Journal of Marketing Management*, 18(9/10):971–89.

—— and Starnes, B. J. (2001) 'Conceptual foundations and practical guidelines for recruiting volunteers to serve in local nonprofit organizations: Part I', *Journal of Nonprofit and Public Sector Marketing*, 9(3):63–96.

Yavas, U. and Riecken, G. (1985) 'Can volunteers be targeted?', *Journal of the Academy of Marketing Science*, 13(2):218–28.

Zimmermann, J. A. M., Stevens, B. W., Thames, B. J., Sieverdes, C. M. and Powell, G. M. (2003) 'The DIRECTIONS nonprofit resource assessment model: A tool for small nonprofit organizations', *Nonprofit Management and Leadership*, 14(1):79–91.

23

Implications of sexual dimorphism on volunteer recruitment and retention

Walter Wymer

Introduction

Sexual dimorphism refers to any difference, morphological (i.e. form and structure) or behavioural, between males and females of the same species. The following discussion will be limited to human male and female differences. These differences refer to average differences between the sexes. For example, men, on average, are taller than women, although an individual woman may be taller than an individual man. Some women are taller than some men, but, on average, men tend to be taller than women. The following discussion refers to average differences between the sexes, not absolute differences between all members of either sex.

There are other human sexual dimorphic examples. Men's skin is thicker and oilier than women's skin. Women tend to have smaller waists in comparison to their hips than do men. In men, the second digit (index finger) tends to be shorter than the fourth digit (ring finger), while in females the second tends to be longer than the fourth. Women tend to have lower blood pressure and tend to live longer than men (Gender Differences 2007). Among the differences between males and females, the following discussion is limited to those that may have implications for researchers examining issues pertaining to recruiting and retaining volunteers in the various types of nonprofit organizations.

Sex has long been used by commercial marketers as a segmentation variable for target marketing purposes (Putrevu 2001; Voss and Cova 2006). Consumer-behaviour researchers have produced a stream of research examining sex differences in consumer-information processing (Kempf *et al*. 2006; Meyers–Levy 1989) and consumer–choice criteria (Fischer and Arnold 1994; Holbrook 1986).

Nonprofit marketers are giving more attention to sex as a segmentation variable for target marketing purposes. In the area of fundraising, early exploratory research in the telemarketing context found that females tend to pledge more often, while males tend to pledge greater amounts. Also, male fundraisers calling male donors were most productive while female fund-raisers calling female donors were least productive (Smith 2006). In other areas of fundraising, greater awareness of sex differences is generating interest (Capek 2001; Newman 1995).

In regards to volunteering, females generally volunteer in greater numbers than males (Wymer and Samu 2002). There are other sex differences in volunteering with regards to the amount of time volunteering, the frequency of volunteering, motives for volunteering, interest in volunteering, the nature of the volunteer organization and volunteer commitment (Mesch *et al.* 2006; Wymer and Samu 2002).

There are several reasons to believe that sex differences in volunteer behaviour is an especially timely and important topic.

1   Females are participating in the paid labour force in ever greater numbers, decreasing their availability for volunteer participation (Wymer and Samu 2002).
2   Females are more likely to care for elderly relatives. As the population ages, females' discretionary time will be further consumed by elder care (Taniguchi 2006).
3   Voluntary participation is declining, especially among young adults and teenagers and especially for females (even though, overall, females still volunteer in greater numbers) (Bureau of Labor Statistics 2007).
4   Male voluntary participation in traditionally male emergency services, like volunteer firefighting, is declining, and localities are searching for ways to recruit more females into these roles (Wood 2002).

While the research of sex differences on consumer behaviour has progressed slowly, and at a rudimentary level, this has not been the case in other fields. Subdisciplines of biology, psychology, endocrinology and especially neuroscience have greatly added to our understanding of human sexual dimorphism in the past fifteen years (Baron–Cohen 2003; Brizendine 2006; Kimura 2000; Sax 2005).

The discussion that follows will serve to highlight those sex differences that: (a) have received strong research support (i.e. robust and replicated studies) in various scientific fields; and (b) may have implications for nonprofit marketers and researchers in the various areas of nonprofit marketing, with an emphasis on volunteer recruitment and retention.

Before proceeding, however, it should be pointed out that nothing written in this work is intended to imply that sex differences are absolute, all-inclusive and categorical. As stated previously, sex differences as used in the following discussion refer to average differences between males and females. Some sex differences are greater than others. Some sex differences are quite small (Kimura 2002). There is overlap between sexes, just as two normal bell curves may have different means, but will overlap at the leading and lagging tails (Baron–Cohen 2003, 2004; Hines 2004). The brains of males and females are more similar than different. However, these differences may enhance our understanding of cognitive and behavioural sex differences (Onion 2005). Sex differences may demonstrate that males and females are not the same, on average, on various characteristics, but never that they are not equal (Pool 1994). Nothing that follows in this work is intended to imply, nor should it be inferred by the reader, that females or males are better or superior, worse or inferior, in any respect.

The biology of sexual dimorphism

Sexual differences begin at conception. Each cell in the developing foetus has a nucleus. Each nucleus has twenty-three pairs of chromosomes. The twenty-third pair is the sex chromosome. If the twenty-third pair is coded X and Y, the cell is male; if it is coded X and X, the cell is female (DNA Tutorial 2007). The presence of a Y chromosome in the twenty-third pair means that the foetus will develop testes; while two Xs means that the foetus will develop an ovary (Maddox 2003).

The first crucial event shaping sex differences occurs *in utero* to the developing foetus. Early in the second trimester, male foetuses' testicles begin producing large quantities of testosterone. This masculinizes male foetuses' genitalia and their brains, affecting their brain's neural structure. The surge of male hormones triggers cell death in some regions of the brain and fosters cell development in other regions (Onion 2005; Spratt 1999). By the third trimester, males and females have some different brain structures. For the female foetus, the much less quantity of testosterone (a small quantity comes from the mother's blood through the placenta) is not available to influence the development of genitalia or the brain. The effect of foetal testosterone reorganizes the brain permanently (Kimura 2000; Udry 1994). This structural brain difference between males and females influences cognition and behaviour (Kimura 2002).

The second crucial period shaping sex differences occurs during puberty. Sex hormone surges cause the well-known anatomical changes, and also cause changes in neural structures begun during the prenatal period. These two periods produce sexual dimorphism and sex-dimorphic behaviour. Of the two periods shaping sex dimorphism, prenatal exposure to testosterone is the most influential (Baron-Cohen 2005; Brizendine 2006; Moir and Jesel 1991; Udry 1994).

More disclaimers

The preceding discussion presents facts that substantiate a biological basis for sexual dimorphism. This is not to say that social influences have no influences on male/female behaviour. While biology is the basis for sex differences, social influences interact with and reinforce sex dimorphic behaviours and influence them throughout a lifetime (Baron-Cohen 2003; Hines 2004; Mealey 2000; Rhoads 2004).

Brain structure and brain function

The prior discussion briefly described the biological origins of structural differences between the brains of the average male and the average female. The sculpting of the brain *in utero* by hormonal influences and resulting morphological (structural) differences are widely documented in the scientific literature (Cahill 2005; Sabbatini 1997; Tyre and Scelfo 2006; Wizemann and Pardue 2001). The purpose of this chapter is to propose how sex differences may provide insights to nonprofit marketers and nonprofit marketing researchers. Therefore, the following discussion shall focus upon functional differences derived from sexual dimorphic structural differences. Some examples of these functional differences are that females tend to be higher in empathy, verbal skills, social skills and security-seeking while males tend to be higher in independence, dominance, spatial and mathematical skills and rank-related aggression (Wilson 2000). The following organization of this chapter will present sexual dimorphic functional differences and their potential managerial implications. A series of propositions will be embedded in the chapter to stimulate further research into this promising area of inquiry.

Functional differences

General sex differences: systemizing and empathizing

The female brain is organized for empathy. The male brain is organized for understanding and building systems (Baron-Cohen 2003). Empathizing is the drive to identify another person's emotions and thoughts, and to respond to them with an appropriate emotion. Baby girls, as young as 12 months old, respond more empathetically to the distress of other people than boys. Women also show more comforting behaviour than men (Baron–Cohen 2003, 2005; Zahn-Waxler *et al.* 1992).

There are two components of empathy: the cognitive component and the affective component. The cognitive component of empathy deals with understanding other people's feelings and being able to take their perspective. The affective component of empathy deals with controlling the observer's appropriate emotional response to another person's emotional state (Baron–Cohen 2003).

Systemizing is the drive to analyse, explore and construct a system. The systemizer intuitively figures out how things work, or extracts the underlying rules that govern the behaviour of a system (Baron–Cohen 2003). Not all males have the typical male brain type. Not all females have the typical female brain type (Baron–Cohen 2003, 2004). About 15 per cent of women have typical male brains and about 15 per cent of males have typical female brains (Moir and Jessel 1991). Baron–Cohen (2005) provides different proportions. He estimates that about 20 per cent of males have female brain types and about 40 per cent of females have male brain types, and Baron–Cohen also proposes that some individuals have a balanced male–female brain. The point is that one cannot determine an individual's brain type by only knowing his or her sex.

Females are better at discerning when it is appropriate to suppress the expression of an emotion, to avoid hurting someone else's feelings. Females have been found to be better at judging emotion from facial expressions than males, in different types of tests and with subjects in different cultures (Kimura 2000). In terms of valuing social relationships, females tend to value altruistic, reciprocal and supportive relationships. Males tend to value power, politics, competition and affirmation of their social status (Baron–Cohen 2003).

Specific sex differences: language, memory, emotions, vision and hearing

The most significant differences between male and female brains occur in regions involved in language, memory, emotion, vision, hearing and navigation (Cahill 2005). Since navigational differences do not have a clear implication for volunteer programme managers or nonprofit scholars, they will not be discussed further.

Females, on average, are more socially interested than males. Females' brains are structured to be interested in faces and interpreting expressions (Sax 2005). The female visual system is optimized to discern colours and textures. Females also have wider peripheral vision (Pease and Pease 2000; Sax 2005). Females tend to hear better than males, with brains having the ability to categorize sounds and differentiating tone changes in voice volume and pitch (Moir and Moir 1996; Pease and Pease 2000).

Males tend to be interested in things. Females tend to be interested in people. In studies examining what newborns and toddlers attend to, males' attention is drawn to objects and shapes. Females' attention is drawn to faces (Baron–Cohen 2005; Wizemann and Pardue 2001). Baron–Cohen (2003) conducted experiments with newborn infants using mobiles placed above each infant's head; one mobile was the image of a human face, and the other mobile was a geometric shape. Trained observers, without knowing the sex of the infants, monitored the infants' observation of the mobiles. Male infants observed the geometric shape. Female infants observed the human face.

In another study, mothers and their toddlers (male or female) were put in a room with several toys. Before the experiment, mothers were instructed to prevent the toddler from picking up a toy, non-verbally if possible. Before the girls picked up the toy, they would look at their mothers, who would look at their daughters disapprovingly. None of the toddler females picked up the toy. When the boys noticed the toy, they did not look at their mothers, and, even after their mothers verbally warned them, all of the boys picked up the toys. This experiment highlights the verbal fluency and empathy of females as well as the more impulsive and self-directed behaviour of males (Sax 2005).

Females tend to have superior language abilities and verbal dexterity than males (Cahill 2005; Rhoads 2004). When conversing, females tend to provide more facial expressions and more reactions (Glass 1992; Hall 1990). Coupled with the average female language superiority, female brains are structured in a manner that allows for more accessible emotional processing and greater emotional integration with discourse (Brizendine 2006; Pease and Pease 2000). The superior female language skills and emotional acuity demonstrates itself in the daily difference of communication intensity between males and females. Each day, the average female utters 6,000 to 8,000 spoken words (males, 2,000 to 4,000), makes 2,000 to 3,000 vocal sounds (males, 1,000 to 2,000) and uses 8,000 to 10,000 gestures, facial expressions, head movements and other body language signals (males, 2,000 to 3,000). In total, the average female communicates each day about 16,000 to 21,000 verbal, vocal and body messages; whereas the average male sends out about 5,000 to 9,000 signals (Hall 1990; Moir and Moir 1996; Pease and Pease 2000).

In regards to emotions, it is more difficult for females to separate emotion from reason because of the way in which the female brain is organized. The female brain has emotional capacities on both sides of the brain, plus there is more information exchanged between the two sides of the brain (thicker corpus callosum, giving more connections between the two sides of the brain). The emotional side is more integrated with the verbal side of the brain (Moir and Jessel 1991). Males have their emotional responses residing in the right side of the brain (Cahill 2005; Moir and Jessel 1991).

In summary, on average, women are more able than men to perceive minor variations in facial expressions, tone of voice, body language and other types of interpersonal communication (Hall 1990; Moir and Jessel 1991). The typical female brain is organized such that emotions are accessible to language centres and processed at a higher-order level than in the typical male brain. Females tend to be more aware of their emotions and their discourse is more often influenced by emotions and concerned with emotions than male discourse (Kimura 2000; Moir and Jessel 1991).

Propositions

1 Volunteer recruitment appeals targeting females would be more effective if using video and audio elements which take advantage of greater female perceptual abilities.

2 Prospective female volunteers are likely to be more influenced by appeals that use facial close-ups so that actors' facial expressions can be used to communicate more emotional and non-verbal information to female audience members.

3 Radio spots targeted to females should use more emotive tonal voice qualities and discourse so that females' tendencies towards more discerning hearing, emotional sensitivity and greater empathizing will derive more information, attend more closely, and be more influenced than more bland, more monotone and more rational messages.

4 Since females tend to have greater empathy than males, they are more likely to be influenced by appeals showing human distress.

5   Since males have less ability than females to discern subtle facial expressions and non-verbal messages, recruitment appeals targeting males should make their appeals focused and direct. For males, the message should be explicit.

Stress, aggression and risk-taking

Different levels of oestrogen, cortisol and dopamine may cause females to be more stressed by emotional conflict than males (Brizendine 2006). 'A few unpaid bills can set off a cascade of hormones in a woman that can catapult her into a fear of impending catastrophe, a reaction triggered in men only by physical danger' (Tyre and Scelfo 2006: 46).

As a result of testosterone exposure *in utero*, the orbital frontal cortices are larger in males than in females. This brain region is known to be connected with aggressive behaviour (Stein 2002). Males tend to be more aggressive across cultures (Hines 2004). Males are more physically aggressive than females because they are less able to control those impulses resulting from anger (Campbell 2002). The amygdala, a part of the brain which responds to emotionally arousing information, is larger in males than in females. The orbitofrontal cortex, a region of the brain associated with regulating emotions, is larger in females than in males (Cahill 2005). Male brains are structured to react more to emotional-evoking stimuli (increased adrenalin), while males are less able to process and monitor emotions (smaller orbitofrontal cortex), and, with much higher testosterone levels, are more likely to respond physically and aggressively to the evoked stress. This is not to suggest that males cannot control their behaviour, but that it requires more effort because males have a greater tendency towards aggression and impulsivity.

While the negative effects of a male brain structure and proportionally high (compared to females) levels of testosterone are apparent by such characteristics as aggression and impulsivity, there are also positive effects. For example, males respond to stress differently than females. Females' response to stress is directed by the parasympathetic system which causes unpleasant, nauseated feelings. Males' response to stress is directed from the sympathetic system, giving a 'thrill' feeling (Sax 2005). Males take greater risks than females. They take even more risks in the presence of other males. Boys are more likely to do something dangerous in the presence of other boys (Sax 2005). Boys like challenges from their peers and seek them out (Baucom *et al.* 1985; Maccoby 1998). Of child pedestrians killed or injured on the roads, boys outnumber girls by two to one (Pease and Pease 2000).

Males enjoy risk-taking more than females. Males find the thrill of risk-taking pleasurable; females do not. For males, danger is exhilarating. For females, danger makes them fearful (Sax 2005). Males are more likely than females to assume risk, especially physical risk (Rhoads 2004). Levels of testosterone are correlated with fearlessness (Navarro 2001). Males prefer and respond well to difficult challenges (Browne 1995). Males are more likely than females to risk their lives to rescue others (Johnson 1996; Morin 1997). The following propositions ensue from this:

6   Males are more likely than females to attend to and respond more favourably to volunteer recruitment appeals that emphasize physical risk and danger in volunteering.
7   Males are more likely than females to prefer volunteer roles which assume some level of risk-taking and danger.
8   Males are more likely than females to respond to a volunteer appeal for a potentially risky or dangerous volunteer task when asked in the presence of others of the same sex.

Infants and children

Compared to men, women tend to be more motivated to reproduce (Hrdy 1999; Rhoads 2004). Reproducing refers to the conception and parenting of a child. Numerous studies have found that females are more attracted to infants and children, they are more motivated to spend more time caring for infants and children, and females are more likely to feel that infants and children are important to their personal happiness (Rhoads 2004).

Oxytocin, a hormone linked to nurturing behaviour, promotes a calm, relaxed emotional state. In men, oxytocin is released during orgasm. In women, it is released in large quantities during pregnancy and breastfeeding (Rhoads 2004). In a study of virgin female monkeys, injection of oxytocin resulted in maternal behaviour (Hrdy 1999). Human females have more neural receptors for oxytocin than men and this number increases further during pregnancy (Hrdy 1999; Moir and Moir 1996).

In addition to the stronger desire for parenthood (Rhoads 2004), females are also more likely than males to seek out contact with infants (Maccoby 1998). Females are more likely to look after a baby (Sax 2005). Progesterone is released when a woman sees a baby. Progesterone is a hormone that releases parental and nurturing feelings. Men do not have this experience (Pease and Pease 2000). Females find it more pleasurable to care for infants (Ehrensaft 1990).

Among children, girls prefer more play parenting. They, like women, are typically more responsive to infants and young children than males (Sax 2005; Geary 1998). Boys, in play behaviour, prefer inanimate mechanical objects (Geary 1998).

Mothers spend more time with their children than do fathers (Rhoads 2004). These sex differences in nurturing behaviours occur very early, before socialization could influence behaviour (Blum 1997; Fisher 199; Geary 1998). Increases in oestrogen and progesterone, which do not occur in males, are linked to females' interest in infants (Fisher 1999; Maccoby 1998). Bonding and nurturing instincts in males are weaker than in females (Hrdy 1999). Mothers of young children tend to be more involved in their children's lives and feel a stronger bond with their young children than do fathers (Ambert 1999; Tooley 2002). The following propositions ensue from this:

9   Females will be more attentive than males to volunteer recruitment appeals which use sights and sounds of infants.
10 Females will have more favourable attitudes and better recall than males for recruitment appeals that use sights and sounds of infants.
11 Females will have a stronger preference than males for volunteer roles involving the care of infants and children.
12 Females will have a stronger preference than males for volunteer roles in organizations with missions that help infants and children.

Social differences

Sexual dimorphism with respect to social relationships will be discussed in this section. The social relationships of children will be presented, followed by a discussion of adult social relationships.

At the earliest ages in which boys and girls are developmentally mature enough to engage in social play, girls prefer to play with girls; boys prefer to play with other boys (Geary 1998; Hines and Kaufman 1994).

Boys engage in more physical, rough-and-tumble play. Boys are more competitive and enjoy group-level competitive play. Boys enjoy playing in a larger physical space which allows for the physicality of types of play that they enjoy. Boys prefer inanimate mechanical objects (vehicles and weapons) in their play. They enjoy taking things apart and putting them back together (experimental manipulation). The male brain's spatial ability helps boys excel at motor skills. Their targeting, throwing and intercepting abilities are benefited (Kimura 2000). The sociodramatic play of boys focuses more on themes associated with power, dominance and aggression (Geary 1998; Hines 2004). Males' rough play as boys teaches them the rules of male social behaviours and makes them less likely to be violent as adults (Sax 2005).

Girls engage in less competitive, more socially interactive play. Girls prefer dolls, dolls' clothes, cosmetics, dress-up items and household toys (Berenbaum and Hines 1992; Hines and Kaufman 1994). Girls enjoy play parenting; they are more responsive to infants and young children than males. Sociodramatic play of girls focuses on family-related themes, such as taking care of children (Geary 1998). Generally speaking, boys are interested in things and how they work. Girls are interested in people and relationships (Pease and Pease 2000).

In addition to play behaviour, social relationships also differ. Females are more consistently communal, manifesting greater empathy, more concern for the well-being of other girls, more nurturing, greater intimacy and greater social–emotional support. Males are more consistently instrumental, manifesting more concern for the establishment of dominance, control of group activities, task orientation and greater risk-taking. Males are more concerned with the establishment and maintenance of social dominance. Females are more concerned with a reciprocal and socially stable system of interpersonal relationships. Although males tend to organize their social groups into dominance hierarchies, male social groups tend to be more stable across situations and time than female social groups, which tend to splinter into status cliques based on various attributes (such as popularity, beauty, athletics and sociability). Females are more likely to use language as a socially binding process. Females compete by using language to disrupt the social relationships of their competitors (Geary 1998).

Male awareness is concerned with getting results, achieving goals, status, power, beating the competition and getting efficiently to the bottom line. Female awareness is focused on communication, cooperation, harmony, love, sharing and interpersonal relationships (Pease and Pease 2000). Men value work. Women value relationships. Research in the 1990s showed that 70 to 80 per cent of men reported work to be most important in their lives; 70 to 80 per cent of women said their families were most important (Pease and Pease 2000).

Males' substantially higher testosterone levels are associated both with their stronger interest in competitive sports and with their stronger interest in demanding careers (Navarro 2001). As noted previously, males tend to be more competitive than females (Rhoads 2004). Males are more competitive; females more cooperative (Maccoby 1998; Browne 2002).

In terms of valuing social relationships, females tend to value altruistic, reciprocal and supportive relationships. Males tend to value power, politics, competition and affirmation of their social status (Baron-Cohen 2003). Men seek to dominate other men through moving up in hierarchical groups. Women seek influence, but they place greater value on reciprocal relationships. Females value group-oriented and group-facilitating acts more than males. Female groups are more cohesive, but less structured and less hierarchal than men's groups (Browne 1995; Golombok and Fivush, 1994; Lips 2001; Rhoads 2004). In prison, women say they miss relationships and intimacy; men say they miss their lost power and sense of masculinity (Rasche 1991).

A study conducted in five western countries asked men and women to describe the kind of person they would ideally like to be. Men chose adjectives such as bold, competitive, capable, dominant, assertive, admired and practical. Women chose warm, loving, generous, sympathetic, attractive, friendly and giving (Pease and Pease 2000).

These sexually dimorphic social differences have interesting implications for volunteer recruitment and retention. It is reasonable to expect that individuals would prefer to volunteer for and remain as volunteers for organizations in which they can be part of a social community they enjoy. The following propositions ensue from this:

13 Males prefer to volunteer in organizations which are goal and achievement oriented, emphasizing efficiency and practicality in meeting clearly defined objectives.
14 Females prefer to volunteer in organizations which are people oriented, emphasizing consensus, communication and cooperation.
15 Males prefer to volunteer in organizations with a clearly defined hierarchy.
16 Females prefer to volunteer in organizations which are less structured and less hierarchal than do men.
17 Males prefer volunteer tasks that involve team competition.
18 Females prefer volunteer tasks which emphasize group orientation, group facilitation and reciprocal relationships.
19 Males will remain longer in volunteer roles in which they feel dominant, and derive a sense of efficacy.
20 Females will remain longer in volunteer roles in which they feel a sense of intimacy and belonging with others in the organization.

Sexual dimorphism and age

Female oestrogen production increases during puberty, remains high during peak reproductive years, and then declines sharply after the menopause. In males there are two types of testosterone: total and free (biologically active) testosterone, whose levels peak in late adolescence and decrease slowly thereafter, especially after the age of 50 (Cranton 1997). Due to a series of endocrine changes in ageing men, free testosterone is especially reduced by an enzyme conversion of testosterone to oestrogen known as aromatase. As men age, then, their total testosterone declines slowly, their oestrogen levels rise and their free testosterone levels decline even more. This condition is known as andropause. It is surprising to learn that the average 60-year-old male has more circulating oestrogen in his bloodstream than the average 60-year-old female (Andropause 2007; Merck 2005).

Since hormonal differences between men and women narrow with age, and especially the reduction of testosterone and increase of oestrogen in older men, it is reasonable to expect behavioural sex differences to narrow. Legato (2005) has observed that the communication differences between men and women narrow with age. Hyde (2005) conducted a meta-analytic study of sex difference studies and found that the magnitude of differences between males and females was less during childhood and increased in adolescence. Prepubescent girls and boys have similar testosterone levels until puberty, at which time girls' testosterone levels double while boys' levels increase by a factor of ten to twenty (Rhoads 2004). The following proposition ensues from this:

21 Behavioural differences between males and females increase with a rise in sex hormones and decline with a decrease in sex hormones.

Testosterone levels are correlated with confidence, aggression and several of the typical male behaviours discussed previously. Therefore, as free testosterone levels decline and oestrogen levels rise in males as they age, it is reasonable to expect a lessoning of these behaviours. For example, males become more empathetic, more cooperative, placing a greater importance on relationships and intimacy. The following propositions ensue from this:

22 Older males are more likely than younger males to volunteer in roles emphasizing helping and nurturing of others.
23 Older males are more likely than younger males to volunteer for and remain it organizations in which relationships among volunteers are cooperative (not competitive) and reciprocal (not hierarchical).
24 Older males are more likely than younger males to volunteer in roles helping children.
25 Older males are less likely than younger males to volunteer in risky, potentially dangerous roles.

Sexual dimorphism and marriage

The magnitude of sex differences appears to be mediated through sex hormones (Kimura 2000). In the previous section, the effect of age on sex hormones was discussed. In the scientific literature, the influence of testosterone on aggression and violence has been studied. One study, which pertains to this work, examined the effect of marriage on male testosterone levels. Mazur and Booth (1998) conducted a ten-year longitudinal study of 2,100 men, finding that testosterone levels began to decline slowly after marriage as men made the transition from bachelor to husband, and remained low after men remained stably married. Among men who divorced, testosterone levels rose just before and after the separation. In a subsequent study of fifty-eight Boston-area men, the investigators examined the testosterone levels of single men, married men with children and married men without children. Whether or not a man was a father was not a significant predictor of testosterone levels. However, single men had significantly higher testosterone levels than married men (Cromie 2002).

As discussed in the previous section, it is reasonable to expect sex differences to narrow with the narrowing of sex hormonal differences. The following propositions ensue from this:

26 Married males are more likely than single males to volunteer in roles emphasizing helping and nurturing of others.
27 Married males are more likely than single males to volunteer for and remain in organizations in which relationships among volunteers are cooperative (not competitive) and reciprocal (not hierarchical).
28 Married males are more likely than single males to volunteer in roles helping children.
29 Married males are less likely than single males to volunteer in risky, potentially dangerous roles.

Conclusion

The intensive multidisciplinary interest in sex differences has produced a substantive body of work. The remarkable increase in the knowledge of sex differences has largely been overlooked in voluntary action research. This chapter has presented sex differences which: (a) had the most scientific support through robust studies and replications; and (b) had managerial implications for volunteer programme managers. For voluntary action researchers, a number of testable propositions were offered to stimulate future investigations. Indeed, researchers in related areas such as fundraising, nonprofit marketing, social marketing, cause marketing, Internet marketing, healthcare marketing and higher-education marketing can adjust these propositions to their contexts for future research in their fields.

Researchers investigating implications of sex differences should always keep in mind that men and women are more alike than different. Sex differences are referring to average differences between males and females. For example, on average, men are taller than women. Obviously, some women are taller than some men, so if two normal distributions of height measures were placed side by side on a chart, the mean for males' height would be greater than the mean for females' height, but there would be overlaps on the leading and lagging tails of the distributions. However, in scientific inquiry, explaining variation in a phenomenon is the focus, and, as such, sex differences offer a rich opportunity to understand more about recruiting and retaining male and female volunteers in a variety of nonprofit organizations.

References

Ambert, A. M. (1999) 'The effect of male delinquency on mothers and fathers: A heuristic study', *Sociological Inquiry*, 69(4):621–40.

Andropause (2007) 'Andropause', available online at: http://collegepharmacy.com/menshealth/andropause.asp (accessed 18 February 2007).

Baron-Cohen, S. (2003) *The Truth About the Male and Female Brain: The Essential Difference*, New York, NY: Basic Books.

—— (2004) *The Essential Difference: Men, Women and the Extreme Male Brain*, New York, NY: Gardners Books.

—— (2005) 'The essential difference: The male and female brain', *Phi Kappa Phi Forum*, 85(1):23–6.

Baucom, D. H., Besch, P. K. and Callahan, S. (1985) 'Relation between testosterone concentration, sex role identity and personality among females', *Journal of Personality and Social Psychology*, 48(5):1218–26.

Berenbaum, S. A. and Hines, M. (1992) 'Early androgens are related to childhood sex-typed toy preferences', *Psychological Science*, 3(3):203–6.

Blum, D. (1997) *Sex on the Brain*, New York, NY: Viking Press.

Briton, N. J. and Hall, J. A. (1995) 'Beliefs about female and male nonverbal communication', *Sex Roles*, 32(1–2):79–90.

Brizendine, L. (2006) *The Female Brain*, New York, NY: Broadway Books.

Browne, K. R. (1995) 'Sex and temperament in modern society: A Darwinian view of the glass ceiling and the gender gap', *Arizona Law Review*, 37(3):973–1106.

—— (2002) *Biology at Work: Rethinking Sexual Equality*, New Brunswick, NJ: Rutgers University Press.

Bureau of Labor Statistics (2007) 'Volunteering in the United States, 2006', US Department of Labor, available online at: www.bls.gov/news.release/volun.nr0.htm (accessed 5 February 2007).

Cahill, L. (2005) 'His brain, her brain', *Scientific American*, 292(5):40–7.

Campbell, A. (2002) *A Mind of Her Own*, New York, NY: Oxford University Press.

Capek, M. E. (2001) *Women and Philanthropy: Old Stereotypes, New Challenges* (Volume 1), Women's Funding Network.

Cranton, E. (1997) *Resetting the Clock: Five Anti-aging Hormones that Improve and Extend Life*, M. Evans and Company, Inc.

Cromie, W. J. (2002) 'Marriage lowers testosterone: Hormones range less on the homestead', *Harvard Gazette*, available online at: www.news.harvard.edu/gazette/2002/09.19/01-testosterone.html (accessed 18 February 2007).

Darlington, C. (2002) *The Female Brain*, CRC.

DNA Tutorial (2007) 'DNA Tutorial', available online at: www.dnatutorial.com (accessed 7 February 2007).

Ehrensaft, D. (1990) *Parenting Together: Men and Women Sharing the Care of Their Children*, University of Illinois Press, Urbana, IL: Illini Books.

Fischer, E. and Arnold, S. J. (1994) 'Sex, gender identity, gender role attitudes and consumer behaivor', *Psychology and Marketing*, 11(2):163–82.

Fisher, H. (1999) *The First Sex: The Natural Talents of Women and How They Are Changing the World*, New York, NY: Random House.

Geary, D. C. (1998) *Male, Female: The Evolution of Human Sex Differences*, Washington, DC: American Psychological Association.

Gender Differences (2007) available online at: www.wikipedia.org (accessed 31 January 2007).

Glass, L. (1992) *He Says, She Says: Closing the Communication Gap Between the Sexes*, New York, NY: Putnam.

Golombok, S. and Fivush, R. (1994) *Gender Development*, Cambridge: Cambridge University Press.

Hall, J. A. (1990) *Nonverbal Sex Differences: Communication Accuracy and Expressive Style*, Baltimore, MA: Johns Hopkins University Press.

Hines, M. (2004) *Brain Gender*, New York, NY: Oxford University Press.

—— and Kaufman, F. R. (1994) 'Androgen and the development of human sex-typical behavior: Rough-and-tumble play and sex of preferred playmates in children with congenital adrenal hyperplasia (CAH)', *Child Development*, 65(4):1042–53.

Holbrook, M. (1986) 'Aims, concepts, and methods for the representation of individual differences in esthetics responses to design features', *Journal of Consumer Research*, 13(3):337–48.

Hrdy, S. B. (1999) *Mother Nature: A History of Mothers, Infants and Natural Selection*, New York, NY: Pantheon Books.

Hyde, J. S. (2005) 'The gender similarities hypothesis', *American Psychologist*, 60(6):581–92.

Johnson, R. C. (1996) 'Attributes of Carnegie medalists performing acts of heroism and of the recipients of these acts', *Ethology and Sociobiology*, 17(5):355.

Kempf, D. S., Laczniak, R. N. and Smith, R. E. (2006) 'The effects of gender on processing advertising and product trial information', *Marketing Letters*, 17(1):5–16.

Kimura, D. (2000) *Sex and Cognition*, Massachusetts, MA: MIT Press.

—— (2002) 'Sex differences in the brain', *Scientific American*, 12(1):32–7.

Legato, M. J. (2005) *Why Men Never Remember and Women Never Forget*, Rodale Inc.

Lips, H. M. (2001) *Sex and Gender*, Mountain View, CA: Mayfield Publishing Co.

Lovejoy, D. (2005) *Neuroendocrinology: An Integrative Approach*, New York, NY: John Wiley & Sons.

Maccoby, E. E. (1998) *The Two Sexes*, Cambridge, MA: Harvard University Press.

Maddox, L. (2003) 'Men and women: Like chalk and cheese. sex differences in brain and behavior', *Physicspost.com*, available online at: www.physicspost.com/printpage.php?articleId=159 (accessed 7 February 2007).

Mazur, A. and Booth, A. (1998) 'Testosterone and dominance in men', *Brain and Behavioral Sciences*, 21(3):353–63.

Mealey, L. (2000) *Sex Differences: Development and Evolutionary Strategies*, New York, NY: Academic Press.

Merck (2005) 'Male reproductive endocrinology: Introduction', available online at: www.merck.com/mmpe/sec17/ch227/ch227a.html (accessed 18 February 2007).

Mesch, D. J., Rooney, P. M., Steinberg, K. K. and Denton, B. (2006) 'The effects of race, gender and marital status on giving and volunteering in Indiana', *Nonprofit and Voluntary Sector Quarterly*, 35(4):565–87.

Meyers-Levy, J. (1989) 'Gender differences in information processing: A selectivity interpretation', in Cafferata, P. and Tybout, A. (eds) *Cognitive and Affective Responses to Advertising*, Lexington MA: Lexington Press, pp. 219–60.

Moir, A. and Jessel, D. (1991) *Brain Sex: The Real Difference Between Men and Women*, New York, NY: Carol Publishing Group.

—— and Moir, B. (1996) *Why Men Don't Iron: The Fascinating and Unalterable Differences Between Men and Women*, London: HarperCollins.

Morin, R. (1997) 'Is there a heroism gender gap?', *Washington Post*, 6 August.

Navarro, M. (2001) 'Women in sports cultivating new playing fields', *New York Times*, 13 February.

Newman, R. H. (1995) 'Perception of factors relating to gender differences in philanthropy', unpublished Ph.D. dissertation, University of San Francisco.

Onion, A. (2005) 'Scientists find sex differences in brain', *ABC News*, 19 January, available online at: http://abcnews.go.com/Technology/print?id=424260 (accessed 8 February 2007).

Pease, B. and Pease, A. (2000) *Why Men Don't Listen and Women Can't Read Maps*, New York, NY: Welcome Rain Publishers.

Pool, R. (1994) *Eve's Rib: The Biological Roots of Sex Differences*, New York, NY: Crown Publishers.

Putrevu, S. (2001) 'Exploring the origins and information processing differences between men and women: Implications for advertisers', *Academy of Marketing Science Review*, Vol. 10, available online at: www.amsreview.org/articles/putrevu10–2001.pdf (accessed 18 February 2007).

Rasche, C. E. (1991) *Special Needs of the Female Offender: A Curriculum Guide for Correctional Officers*, Tallahassee, FL: Florida State Department of Education.

Rhoads, S. (2004) *Taking Sex Differences Seriously*, San Francisco, CA: Encounter Books.

Sabbatini, R. M. E. (1997) 'Are there differences between the brains of males and females?', *Mind and Behavior*, available online at: www.cerebromente.org.br/n11/mente/eisntein/cerero-homens.html (accessed 7 February 2007).

Sax, L. (2005) *Why Gender Matters: What Parents and Teachers Need to Know About the Emerging Science of Sex Differences*, New York, NY: Doubleday.

Smith, N. (2006) 'Fundraising: Gender testing finds whopper of a difference', *DM News*, 14 July, available online at: http://www.dmnews.com/cms/dm-sectors/nonprofits-fundraising/37488.html (accessed 5 February 2007).

Spratt, D. (1999) 'Neuro-endocrinology briefings 7: Sex differences in the brain', British Neuroendocrine Group, available online at: www.neuroendo.org.uk/content/view/17/11/ (accessed 9 February 2007).

Stein, R. (2002) 'Do men have anger in mind?', *Washington Post*, 30 September.

Taniguchi, H. (2006) 'Men's and women's volunteering: Gender differences in the effects of employment and family characteristics', *Nonprofit and Voluntary Sector Quarterly*, 35(1):83–101.

Tooley, J. (2002) *The Miseducation of Women*, London: Continuum Publishing Group.

Tyre, P. and Scelfo, J. (2006) 'Why girls will be girls', *Newsweek*, 31 July: 46–7.

Udry, R. J. (1994) 'The nature of gender', *Demography*, 31(4): 561–573.

Voss, Z. G. and Cova, V. (2006) 'How sex differences in perceptions influence customer satisfaction: A study of theatre audiences', *Marketing Theory*, 6(2):201–21.

Wilson, E. O. (2000) *Sociobiology: The New Synthesis, Twenty-fifth Anniversary Edition*. New York, NY: Belknap Press.

Wizemann, T. M. and Pardue, M. (2001) *Exploring the Biological Contributions to Human Health: Does Sex Matter?* New York, NY: National Academic Press.

Wood, L. (2002) 'A sociological exploration of the occupational culture of the fire service and women's place within it', Masters of Sociology thesis, Graduate School of Social and Political Studies, University of Edinburgh.

Wymer, W. W. and Samu, S. (2002) 'Volunteer service as symbolic consumption: Gender differences in volunteering', *Journal of Marketing Management*, 18(9–10): 971–89.

Zahn-Waxler, C., Radke-Yarrow, M., Wagner, E. and Chapmen, M. (1992) 'Development of concern for others', *Developmental Psychology*, 28(1):126–36.

Part 8

Public sector marketing

24

Improving service quality in the new public sector

Christine S. Williams and Mark N. K. Saunders

Introduction

Public sector reform movements around the world in the 1990s, codified as new public management (NPM) have been aimed at 'fostering a performance-oriented culture in a less centralised public sector' (OECD 1995). Such reforms are characterized by key elements including increasing use of markets and competition in the provision of public services (e.g. contracting out and other market-type mechanisms) and increasing emphasis on performance, outputs and customer orientation. One consequence of these reforms has been the reorientation of public services towards their consumers. This has brought with it pressure for better-quality public services, from service users as their needs change and their expectations rise in respect of how well services can be performed (Flynn 1995). Furthermore, increased service user choice, such as that occurring in the UK National Health Service (Vidler and Clarke 2005) forces public service providers to consider how to deliver high-quality public services both efficiently and effectively, generating best value (Martin 2002). In some instances this requirement is underpinned by statutory guidance. For example, the UK government's 'Best Value' policy was designed to 'secure improvements in quality as well as in cost' (Department of Environment, Transport and the Regions 1998: 57). As a result, high-quality service is a priority for public service providers worldwide (Borins 2000) and service quality improvement has become a very real issue for new public management (Edvardsson and Enquist 2006).

The resulting focus on service quality improvement has forced public service managers to engage with the measurement of service quality. They have had to become involved increasingly in assessing satisfaction of both external and internal customers – service users as well as deliverers of services (Farnham and Horton 1993). This has resulted in the extensive use of satisfaction surveys in the public sector (Wisniewski and Donnelly 1996). However, while it is clear that performance measurement of economy and efficiency is well developed in the public service context, there is less evidence of performance indicators relating to effectiveness or quality (Black *et al.* 2001), or measures that fully reflect the constructs of service quality (Wisniewski and Donnelly 1996). Furthermore, although there is no shortage of views on survey-based instruments such as SERVQUAL (Parasuraman *et al.* 1985) for measuring service quality and customer satisfaction, there is disagreement over whether the prime purpose of such instruments is to provide an accurate measure of service quality (their predictive ability) or identify specific reasons for quality issues (their diagnostic ability) (Robinson 1999). Indeed, Brysland and Curry (2001) question the applicability of such instruments specifically in relation to quality improvement within a public service context.

In this chapter we report on an alternative qualitative approach to the measurement of service quality, the Extended Service Template Process (ESTP) (Williams and Saunders 2006) and evaluate its ability to enable agendas for service quality improvement in a public service context. The ESTP not only allows the views of the users and deliverers of a service to be captured separately in their own words and recorded visually but also enables them to be explored, understood and owned, as a precursor to joint development of an improvement agenda.

This chapter commences with a brief review of the context for approaches to measuring service quality in public services, highlighting issues associated with use and interpretation of generic quantitative measures such as the questionnaire to service users. The ESTP is outlined and its application evaluated in relation to three distinct UK-based public service situations: the main reception service of a large multisite organization; the provision of funding to develop social housing and dissertation supervision in a new university business school. Within the evaluation, particular attention is given to the extent to which facets of the service encounter or relationship considered important by service users and deliverers are measured, the development of shared understandings and the process's utility in enabling quality improvement. The chapter concludes with observations on the value of the ESTP in relation to the drivers for quality improvement in public services.

The new public management and the context for service quality improvement

Pollitt (2002) acknowledges that new public management reforms around the world are underpinned by some common aims and features. These include the production of effective, efficient and responsive services by public service organizations which are close to their customers, a commitment to continuous quality improvements and the empowerment of staff to innovate. More recently, government modernization agendas place growing emphasis on collaboration and partnerships as means by which such aims can be realized (Newman 2002). Indeed, Entwistle and Martin (2005: 236) propose that partnerships 'designed to bring together competencies from different sectors' are the basis for transformational approaches to service quality improvement in public services.

Quantitative approaches to measuring service quality

Quantitative survey-based approaches to measuring service quality such as SERVQUAL (Parasuraman et al. 1985) measure the gap between service users' perceptions and expectations across a series of standardized dimensions characterizing the service. Each of these dimensions (e.g. in the case of SERVQUAL: tangibles; reliability; responsiveness; assurance and empathy: Parasuraman et al. 1988) is measured using generic questions, data being collected from a statistically representative sample via a survey instrument such as a questionnaire. Although the disconfirmation approach is reported widely in the literature (e.g. Brysland and Curry 2001;

Donnelly *et al.* 2006; Parasuraman 1995), there has also been considerable debate with regard to the generic standardized nature of dimensions.

A number of authors (e.g. Babakus and Boller 1992; Carman 1990; Robinson 1999) argue that, rather than being based upon standardized dimensions, a service's quality is a function of that particular service and the industry within which it is located. Furthermore, the use of generic dimensions to measure a particular service's quality is unlikely to provide the details necessary to define specific causes of a problem rather than its symptoms (Killmann 1986). Standardized dimensions may therefore provide insufficient focus or detail to account for the uniqueness and realities of specific services or service relationships, and how these are expressed, assessed and interpreted by the both service users and deliverers (Rosen and Suprenant 1998). Where these measures are used only from the perspective of the service user or deliverer, any symptoms identified are unlikely to reflect fully the dyadic nature of service encounters (Svensson 2001).

For service quality measurement to enable improvement, data collected must be useful. In this context, usefulness can be viewed from the three interrelated perspectives. As highlighted in the discussion above, in order to ensure construct validity, those used need to be able to capture perceptions of reality considered important by each party involved within the specific service (Chi Cui *et al.* 2003). Second, these constructs must incorporate sufficient detail to allow a clear understanding of the particular service situation, thereby ensuring content validity. Finally, the measurement process must enable the meanings of the data collected to be understood and explored and quality improvement agendas derived.

Data collected using quantitative measures of service quality are usually subject to interpretation by third parties, such as consultants or managers. The meanings ascribed to such data by a third party may differ from those given by service users or deliverers leading to problems of second-order interpretation (Yin 2003). For example, a manager evaluating a service may explain the finding that 75 per cent of users were unhappy with the responsiveness of service providers as due to the poor attitudes of the people providing the service when, in reality, this is due to there being insufficient people to deliver the service at the required standard. The manager has added her or his own interpretation to the answers offered and emphases placed by respondents, rather than these being understood and interpreted as intended (Foddy 1994). Consequently, meanings in the data are misreported or, at worst, unrecognized. Furthermore, such quantitative measures rarely require respondents to indicate the relative importance of quality constructs (Pitt *et al.* 1995). Rather, the person undertaking the inquiry judges what is important and consequently those aspects about which data should be collected. Attention is therefore focused on those areas that she or he believes are of critical concern (Foddy 1994; Krueger and Casey 2000). Consequently, service users' and deliverers' perceptions about which characteristics are key to the quality of service may not form the basis for analysis and future action.

A user- and deliverer-focused approach: the Extended Service Template Process

The ESTP is a process in which separate groups of service users and deliverers generate their own visual (qualitative) representations or service templates of a defined service. Each group records separately the characteristics of the service or service relationship they identify as important by creating their own service template. For each characteristic, perceptions and expectations are measured against a group-defined Likert-type scale anchored by 'ideal' and

Table 24.1   The Extended Service Template Process

Phase	Stage	Description
I		**Participant selection**
II		**Service quality measurement and data validation (for each group)**
	1	Preparation
	2	Explore service characteristics
	3	Plot perceptions and expectations against identified characteristics on service template
	4	Interpret and validate issues
III		**Improvement agenda development**
	1	Brief participants, surface concerns and refamiliarise
	2	Explore and learn
	3	Generate agenda for improvement

'worst' descriptors (Figure 24.1). Developed over the last decade, through a series of consultancy interventions, the ESTP not only measures perceptions of service quality, but also reflects the dyadic nature of service encounters and the need to promote action to improve service quality. For a full account of its development, see Williams and Saunders (2006). The process incorporates three phases (Table 24.1).

Participant selection

This is phase I, in which discrete purposive samples are drawn from groups of service users and service deliverers (the parties) involved in a service. Individuals are selected for each non-probability sample on the basis of their criticality to that service or service relationship, rather than to ensure statistical representativeness of those involved. Each party therefore provides their own, in-depth account of the service in question from which logical rather than statistical generalizations can be developed. Together these represent the diversity of views regarding those dimensions which users and deliverers consider are key to the service.

Service quality measurement and data validation

This is phase II (see Table 24.1), which allows the independent collection of qualitative data from users and deliverers involved in the service. Separate meetings of approximately two hours' duration are organized with each party, the number of participants (six to ten) being informed by Krueger and Casey's (2000) work on focus groups. Each meeting is managed by a facilitator and progresses through the four stages outlined in Table 24.1. In the preparation stage, the purpose and nature of the process is explained and meanings of terms clarified. The service situation being considered is displayed prominently to help to maintain focus. The characteristics of this situation are then elicited and displayed in the order they emerge, by the facilitator using the group's words, through a thought-shower-type process (stage 2). Clarification of meanings is sought to help to ensure that participants have both a similar frame of reference and the same understanding. Subsequently, the list of characteristics is refined and ideal and worst situation descriptors (bipolar adjectives) generated for the extremes of each characteristic (Figure 24.1). Perceptions and expectations of the service and variations within these are then measured and plotted for each characteristic relative to the extremes using a ten-point scale, the value ten representing the ideal and the value one, the worst case (stage 3).

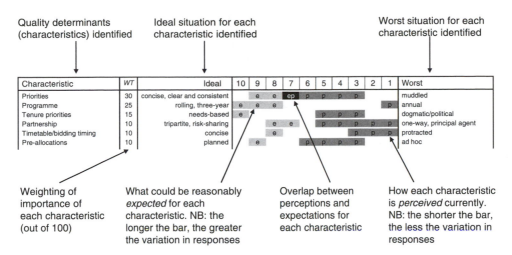

Quality determinants (characteristics) identified

Ideal situation for each characteristic identified

Worst situation for each characteristic identified

Characteristic	WT	Ideal	10	9	8	7	6	5	4	3	2	1	Worst
Priorities	30	concise, clear and consistent		e	e	ep	p	p	p	p			muddled
Programme	25	rolling, three-year	e	e	e							p	annual
Tenure priorities	15	needs-based	e					p	p	p			dogmatic/political
Partnership	10	tripartite, risk-sharing			e	e		p	p	p	p	p	one-way, principal agent
Timetable/bidding timing	10	concise				e			p	p	p	p	protracted
Pre-allocations	10	planned			e			p	p	p	p		ad hoc

Weighting of importance of each characteristic (out of 100)

What could be reasonably *expected* for each characteristic. NB: the longer the bar, the greater the variation in responses

Overlap between perceptions and expectations for each characteristic

How each characteristic is *perceived* currently. NB: the shorter the bar, the less the variation in responses

Figure 24.1 Annotated extract from service template reflecting registered social landlord development managers' views on the provision of funding to develop social housing

The resultant service template (Figure 24.1), typically including between twenty and thirty characteristics, is then discussed with participants to help confirm internal validity. Finally (stage 4) participants identify and weight those characteristics they consider most important by allocating 100 points between them.

Improvement agenda development

In the final phase (see Table 24.1, phase III), service users and deliverers who have generated their templates separately meet and explore jointly each other's views of the service and develop an improvement agenda. The meeting commences with the facilitator reminding participants of the process to date and the purpose of the meeting, namely to share, explore, learn and identify possible actions (phase III, stage 1). The service templates created in phase II are used as visual catalysts for these users and deliverers to explore and learn about each other's perceptions and expectations (phase III, stage 2). Service users and deliverers are facilitated to share their templates, prior to them establishing and understanding jointly which characteristics are important for the service's quality and explaining why by offering rich in-depth accounts. The composition of facilitated groups and the content of their discussions are determined by the service users and deliverers to help to maintain their ownership of the process. Finally, they are asked to reflect on the meeting and focus upon actions needed to improve service quality (phase III, stage 3). To help to provide structure, feedback from participants is sought by the facilitator adopting the role of confrontive enquirer (Schein 1999). Through this, participants identify and own an agenda to improve service quality.

The ESTP addresses several of the shortcomings of quantitative approaches to measuring service quality. The constructs (characteristics) against which service quality is measured are neither generic nor pre-specified. Rather, as part of the process, users and deliverers involved in the service determine separately those characteristics they consider important, resulting in service templates that reflect their specific language, terminology, detail and priorities. Furthermore, organizational development research (for example, Schein 1999) has highlighted the importance of problem ownership for those developing appropriate solutions. Phase III of the ESTP helps to encourage ownership of the process and its outcomes by the participants, enabling service users and deliverers to understand and, where necessary, reconcile their own and others' views, prior to jointly generating a service quality improvement agenda.

Following a description of the research method, the remainder of the chapter evaluates the ESTP, paying attention to both measurement and the utility of the process in enabling the development of a service quality improvement agenda.

Evaluation of the ESTP: method

Evaluation of the ESTP focuses upon two interrelated aspects: provision of rich in-depth accounts of service quality and the process's utility to develop an improvement agenda. Data were therefore collected in three distinct UK public service situations during and after the application of the ESTP. These were the provision by reception staff and their manager of a reception service to internal users on the main site of a large multisite public sector organization; the delivery by supervisors of dissertation supervision to final-year undergraduate students at a new university business school; and the provision by the housing corporation managers of funding to registered social landlord (housing association) development managers to develop social housing to meet needs identified by local authorities' development managers. For each case, data were collected during and after the application of the ESTP from the purposive samples of service users and deliverers involved in the process (Table 24.2).

Data collection incorporated a combination of research diaries, participant observation, follow-up interviews and written feedback from participants. Consent was obtained in each of the three cases to use the data for research purposes and ESTP evaluation. For each of the cases, one researcher acted as facilitator and the other as observer. The former recorded secondary observations in a research diary and the latter noted primary observations such as participants' interactions, comments and the extent to which they appeared involved, as well

Table 24.2 Sample organizations

Organization(s)	Service quality issue	Purposive samples
Large, multi-site public service	**Main reception**: improvement to main reception service on the organization's main site	**Service users**: 6 internal staff representing key users of reception services **Service deliverers**: 3 reception staff; 1 departmental manager
New university business school	**Dissertation supervision**: improvement to undergraduate business management dissertation supervision	**Service users**: 8 level III undergraduates **Service deliverers**: 6 dissertation supervisors
Housing corporation, local authorities, registered social landlords	**Provision of funding to develop social housing**: improvement in the service relationship between the housing corporation, local authorities and registered social landlords	**Service users**: 8 registered social landlord development managers **Service deliverers**: 6 housing corporation managers; 7 local authorities' enabling officers

as any amendments to the process. At each meeting, participants were introduced to the facilitator and observer and assured of anonymity and confidentiality. Data were collected during the three phases of the ESTP (Table 24.1).

Semi-structured group interviews of approximately thirty minutes' duration were planned by the observer to capture participants' perceptions of the process and its utility following the completion of phase III. This was possible for eight of the ten reception service participants, all fourteen of those considering dissertation supervision and seventeen of the twenty-one involved in the provision of funding for social housing. Data were also collected approximately six months after the completion of the ESTP on its impact within each case study organization. This was obtained by telephone interview with the senior manager involved and triangulated with additional data collected from at least two of the participants in the ESTP.

These data were used to evaluate the process's ability to elucidate rich in-depth accounts and its utility for improvement agenda development. Initially the data collected were analysed and triangulated by ourselves independently, using the three phases of the ESTP as a framework. Where interpretation of these data varied, this was discussed further prior to agreeing a conclusion. By this process, problems of reliability associated with single-person interpretation were minimized (Miles and Huberman 1994).

Findings

Participant selection

Like any sample-based research, the utility of findings is dependent upon the sample from which data are collected. Within quantitative service quality studies, such as those using SERVQUAL, ensuring that the sample is representative and the results statistically significant enhances this. For qualitative studies, such as those using the ESTP, the utility of findings is dependent upon the characteristics of the sample of participants selected to generate the service templates, their subsequent commitment to the process and the richness of the data they provide. Time spent on careful selection of separate purposive samples of service users and deliverers, using clear service-specific criteria is therefore essential. In particular there is a need to ensure that the individuals selected are both critical to, and can between them account for and explain the extent and diversity (Patton 2002) of the service in question. Working with each of the three cases revealed that, to ensure the collection of useful data, sample size within each group would vary.

In examining the provision of funding for social housing for example, the sample of housing corporation managers needed to capture the discrete aspects of the service provision for which each was responsible. Six managers who interacted directly with local authorities and registered social landlords were therefore selected. As each manager was responsible for a different aspect of work and was at a different level in the hierarchy, individual meetings were held to generate separate service templates. In contrast each registered social landlord's development officer was undertaking a similar role and so a joint service template was developed. For the dissertation supervision case, discussion with the module leader emphasized a need to focus upon overall quality of dissertation supervision. Consequently, the purposive sample of service users consisted of eight students taking a level III dissertation who represented all degree combinations within that business school, while the six supervisors (service deliverers) encompassed the full breadth of supervisory and subject experience (Table 24.2).

Service quality measurement and data validation

Subsequent accounts of service quality and data validation emphasized the importance of the preparation stage (Table 24.1: phase II, stage 1). In all but the reception service case, between ten and fifteen minutes were devoted to explaining the nature and operation of ESTP in relation to a neutral example of a familiar service encounter, a supermarket checkout. Observer notes confirmed that this resulted in fewer questions of clarification and justification during the creation of the service templates for these cases. Despite this, observer notes highlight that, in all cases, participants often appeared sceptical at the start of the ESTP, needing to experience and understand the process as applied to their service situation before committing themselves.

In exploring a service's characteristics, and the 'ideal' and 'worst' descriptors, the facilitator sought clarity of meaning from the participants. This often resulted in discussion and revision of a single adjective to a short descriptive phrase, thought by the participants to capture their meaning. For example the 'ideal' descriptor for 'priorities' (Figure 24.1) is 'concise, clear and consistent'. Participants also tended initially to offer single adjectives, the 'ideal' being expressed as the opposite of the 'worst'. For example, the worst descriptor for 'priorities' (Figure 24.1) was originally 'inconsistent', participants commenting: ' "inconsistent" is just the opposite, it doesn't tell you any more . . how about "muddled"?' Observer notes indicate that partici-pants' confidence in generating their own descriptors grew as the process progressed, meanings often being clarified unprompted.

For all cases, participants understood and liked the visual representation of service quality in their service templates and the interactive process of plotting perceptions and expectations against their identified characteristics (e.g. Figure 24.2). They also liked the flexibility within the process and the fact that it allowed multiple perspectives, a typical comment being 'it allowed us to say what we thought was important'. Observer notes highlighted that, within each group, participants used phase II to discuss, explain and justify their perceptions to each other. They appeared surprised but pleased that the process was sufficiently flexible to measure and record within-group differences, this being typified by one respondent who declared he was 'interested that others may mention something we've never considered'. Through this process all gained an understanding of their group's perceptions and expectations across their agreed characteristics.

The final stage of phase II allows each group to weight the characteristics, thereby highlight-ing those considered most important. All approached this by allocating 100 points, the most common approaches to allocating points being group discussion or calculating the mean of group members' individual points allocations. Observer notes and research diary comments highlighted the difficulty that participants experienced in agreeing and prioritizing important characteristics. However, the resulting discussions helped each group further validate their group understanding of service quality, minor changes being made where requested.

Characteristic	WT	Ideal	10	9	8	7	6	5	4	3	2	1	Worst
Process timing	40	fair/formal	e	p									restrictive
Documentation – policy document	30	clear, detailed		e	p								too long
Publication of results – content	30	full explanation/justification			ep								no explanation/justification
Bidding document		comprehensive, helpful to registered social landlords' case			e		p						complex
Publication of results – time scale		generous	e	p									limited

Key: expectations   e   over lap   p   perceptions

Figure 24.2 Extract from service template reflecting a housing corporation manager's view on the provision of funding to develop social housing

The time taken to generate each of the service templates varied considerably, those involving more participants taking longer. Generation of the seventeen service templates created to examine the provision of funding to develop social housing took from sixty minutes for a single housing corporation manager to 270 minutes for the registered social landlords' development managers' template (Figure 24.1). For some participants, particularly those in more senior roles, this created problems, where they had only allowed the two hours requested. Immediately after a meeting, each service template was wordprocessed. Participants were given a choice regarding the order characteristics were presented in, but always requested they were presented in weighted order, emphasizing those that they considered most important.

Improvement agenda development

In all three of the cases there were difficulties in finding a time when all those involved in generating the associated service templates were available, highlighting the need for careful preplanning of meetings to ensure participants can attend. Consequently meetings were held up to two months after these templates had been generated and, other than for dissertation supervision, did not include all participants. Although appearing to have little impact on the interpretation of the service templates, the time delay between phases II and III meant participants welcomed the opportunity to refamiliarize themselves with their service templates prior to discussion.

Following assurances of individual confidentiality, service templates were explored jointly. Comments made by participants suggest this enabled them to develop a shared understanding of the range of views. Discussion was introduced by short presentations from each group explaining their templates, focusing on their high-weighted characteristics. Each participant received copies of all service templates and sought clarification as necessary. Subsequently, for the reception service and dissertation supervision cases participants chose to discuss and explore the templates collectively. Within this they focused on the major differences and similarities of the high-weighted characteristics and the gaps between perceptions and expectations, rather than precise values suggested by the numbers on the ten-point scale (Saunders and Williams 2005). In the case of the provision of funding to develop social housing, participants' interrogation of the templates generated by other groups was structured into four discussion rounds due to the larger number of templates and the involvement of service deliverers and users from three organizations. For each of the first three rounds participant groups agreed which other group they wished to have a forty-five-minute discussion with over their respective templates. For the final round, participants requested that representatives from all three groups meet together to explore their templates. Observer notes commenting on the design of this session suggested that tripartite presentations and discussions would probably have been more useful.

Observer notes emphasize that, within all three cases, there were many commonalities among the views expressed by the parties to the services in question regarding the characteristics determining service quality. For example, in the provision of funding to develop social housing there was commonality between those characteristics ranked highly by housing corporation managers and the registered social landlord development managers. This reflected their concerns for timing of the bidding process. In a housing corporation manager's service template, this characteristic was referred to as 'process timing' (Figure 24.2), while in the registered social landlord development manager's template it was referred to as 'timetable/ bidding timing' (Figure 24.1). Discussion highlighted that housing corporation managers were concerned with ensuring equity in the processes of bidding for and allocation of funds. In contrast, the development managers' focus was upon ensuring that the bidding process took up as little time as possible, thereby maximizing the time available for developing housing schemes. This was captured in their template by their extremes of 'concise' and 'protracted' (Figure 24.1). The views regarding the mismatch between perceived performance and expectations for both this and other housing corporation managers and the registered social landlord development managers highlighted that improvement could be achieved in this area. One outcome of their joint exploration of the service templates was the challenging of housing corporation managers' assumptions about what the registered social landlord development managers perceived to be important. Even where terms with apparently similar meaning are used within individual templates, observer notes highlight that the exploration of these terms means service users and deliverers can be confronted with hitherto unrecognized differing perspectives of the service relationship. Conversely, as in the reception service case, joint exploration of respective templates can result in users and deliverers commenting that, despite differences in language, 'all groups had raised the same issues'.

Participants in the three cases confirmed that, although time-consuming, joint exploration of the service templates was worthwhile, providing an opportunity for dialogue leading to jointly agreed service quality improvement agendas. The descriptors of each characteristic provided an additional level of detail to inform this process. For example, in the process of funding social housing, the practicalities of delivering 'programme(s)' of housing schemes within the 'annual' timescale imposed considerable pressure on the development managers (Figure 24.1). Their preference for a longer planning horizon in this relationship was emphasized by the 'ideal' descriptor 'rolling, three-year' for this characteristic, their expectations at the positive end of the scale and the large gap between these and their perceptions. The narrow range of perceptions recorded for this characteristic indicated a high degree of consensus relative to their expectations. Joint exploration of this issue led to proposals of how the concerns could be addressed. Participants commented that discussion allowed them to explain those aspects of the service where expectations were not met in sufficient detail to enable the associated problems to be defined clearly and for them to suggest possible improvements. In the dissertation supervision case, students commented they had enjoyed working with supervisors to develop quality improvement proposals. They said they found the process 'engaging' and that, unlike more traditional methods of evaluation they had experienced, felt their 'contributions were really valued'. Furthermore, the process facilitated the participants taking ownership of the process and its outcomes. Observer comments made during all three cases highlighted how participants took ownership of the process and appeared to enjoy participating.

These meetings required careful facilitation to help to focus dialogue on both learning and possible improvements, as well as to allow sufficient time for meaningful discussion and reflection. The time required for each of the three meetings varied from a time-limited meeting of 120 minutes for dissertation supervision, 155 minutes for the reception service and 300 minutes for the funding process, again reflecting the complexity of the service being considered.

The ESTP's utility in enabling service quality improvement agendas to emerge can be considered in relation to the use made of the data generated. For each of the three cases, participant groups drew up jointly a list of outcomes and suggestions for taking the project forward. In the case of the provision of funding to develop social housing, the importance of a partnership approach to the parties from the three bodies involved in the provision of social housing in the UK was reinforced, as was the need to develop further the method by which funding could be provided over longer time periods (Williams et al. 1999). For the reception service, there was consensus over a perceived conflict arising from the requirements for the receptionists to provide face-to-face service while operating the organization's main switchboard. One resulting outcome was the relocation of the main switchboard away from the reception area (Williams and Saunders 2006). The receptionists commented that they wished to continue to be involved in further improvements. For dissertation supervision, consistency of the supervisory process and assessment criteria and the timing of the research methods workshops were the main issues arising from phase III of the ESTP (Saunders and Williams 2005). As a result, consistency of advice was the subject of a staff development session where lecturers reconsidered the nature of the dissertation and assessment criteria. In addition, the research methods and the workshops were rescheduled to reflect more closely the stage students should have reached in their dissertations.

Discussion

Using clearly defined purposive samples of parties involved in a service, the ESTP has been shown to enable the characteristics that those service users and deliverers who are critical to the service believe are important to the quality of that service to be established and defined separately. Perceptions and expectations of performance are measured and recorded in a visual format using participant-defined and described descriptors. The resulting service templates provide a context for enabling joint understanding, problem definition and the development of an agenda for action.

The final phase of the ESTP enables these service templates to be compared and discussed by participants in the process, as they re-examine those characteristics they believe are important to that service's quality in conjunction with the characteristics highlighted by the other parties. Participant-generated characteristics and descriptors afford a high level of service-specific detail as a context for this discussion. Visual representation in the form of service templates appears to assist participants' understanding of their own and other groups' views in this process.

Discussion throughout the process means each party tests and defends the values and norms on which those characteristics they believe to be important are based. Despite an apparent lack of commonality in the language used to define a service, there were often elements of common ground regarding those characteristics that were important. Where this was not so, the service templates emphasized that the users and deliverers measured the service's quality within differing sets of norms. The ESTP therefore enables participants selected because they are critical to service delivery and usage to reflect in-depth upon the norms underlying their own assessments of service quality and their appropriateness in relation to other service participants. By highlighting differences and similarities in the norms and values upon which such assessments are based, new understandings, specific to the service in question can be developed by participants. The discursive and participative nature of phase III of the ESTP is instrumental in promoting shared understanding and ownership in the context of the specific service.

The research reported in this chapter highlights the importance of the facilitator in managing the process, helping the derivation, exploration and subsequent dialogue between service users and deliverers about service templates and the agreement of agendas for action. Fundamental to the process when measuring service quality is the separate generation of discrete service templates for service users and deliverers (phase II). Through these the facilitator ensures that key dimensions from both service user and deliverer perspectives are surfaced separately, measured and recorded in service templates. However, prior to use of the ESTP, a clear understanding and commitment by users and deliverers to both the process and the time required of individuals has been shown to be essential. This understanding incorporates the process of participant selection where the need to ensure the collection of useful data requires careful purposive selection and may necessitate deviation from the sample size range suggested.

Conclusion

In conclusion, the ESTP appears able to reflect the reality of dyadic interchange between users and deliverers involved in any public service and offers an additional, qualitatively based tool to the range of existing quality assessment processes. The ESTP is an alternative approach to measuring perceptions and expectations of service quality in a systematic manner. Because predetermined scales are not used, it is likely to be applicable without modification to evaluating quality across a range of public service encounters and relationships. Although time-consuming, users and deliverers are able to question and evaluate the appropriateness of the characteristics they believe are important within a service and achieve consistency of understanding. This can be a basis for empowering the parties to a service and promoting collaboration between them. Integral to this process is the need for discussion, learning and problem definition, deriving an agenda for improvement and developing ownership of agreed solutions.

Within qualitative research such as the ESTP, reliability in terms of the extent to which the account of service quality could be replicated by another enquirer is dependent upon the extent to which the procedures through which the data have been generated and interpreted are followed and documented carefully (Silverman 2006). In particular the involvement of clearly defined purposive samples of service users and deliverers, recording of their perceptions and expectations as service templates and subsequent testing of assumptions as the templates are explored is critical to maintaining reliability.

The cases outlined suggest the ESTP offers an alternative to measuring service quality and can assist in improvement agenda development within the arena of public service operations. As such, it is one response to Brysland and Curry's (2001: 393) call for 'a ready tool for evaluating and prioritising changes in current service quality, for public sector managers'.

References

Babakus, E. and Boller, G. W. (1992) 'An empirical assessment of the SERVQUAL scale', *Journal of Business Research*, 24(3):253–68.

Black, S., Briggs, S. and Keogh, W. (2001) 'Service quality performance measurement in public/private sectors', *Managerial Auditing Journal*, 16(7):400–5.

Borins, S. (2000) 'New public management, North American style', in K. McLaughlin, S. P. Osborne and E. Ferlie (eds) (2002) *New Public Management: Current Trends and Future Prospects*, pp. 181–94.

Brysland, A. and Curry, A. (2001) 'Service improvements in public services using SERVQUAL', *Managing Service Quality*, 11(6):389–401.

Carman, J. M. (1990) 'Consumer perceptions of service quality: An assessment of the SERVQUAL dimensions', *Journal of Retailing*, 66(1):33–5.

—— (2000) 'Patient perceptions of service quality: Combining the dimensions', *Journal of Services Marketing*, 14(4):337–52.

Chi Cui, C., Lewis, B. R. and Park, W. (2003) 'Service quality measurement in the banking sector in South Korea', *International Journal of Bank Marketing*, 21(4):191–201.

Cronin, J. J. and Taylor, S. A. (1992) 'Measuring service quality: A re-examination and extension', *Journal of Marketing*, 56(3):56–68.

Department of Environment, Transport and the Regions (1998) *Modern Local Government; In Touch With The People*, London: Stationery Office.

Donnelly, M., Kerr, N. J., Rimmer, R. and Shiu, E. M. (2006) 'Assessing the quality of police services using SERVQUAL', *Policing: An International Journal of Police Strategies and Management*, 29(1):92–105.

Edvarsson, B. and Enquist, B. (2006) 'Quality improvement in governmental services: The role of change pressure exerted by the "Market" ', *TQM Magazine*, 18(1):7–21.

Entwistle, T. and Martin, S. (2005) 'From competition to collaboration in public service delivery: A new agenda for research', *Public Administration*, 83(1):233–42.

Farnham, D. and Horton, S. (1993) 'The new public service managerialism: An assessment', in D. Farnham and S. Horton (eds) *Managing the New Public Services*, Basingstoke: Macmillan, pp. 237–54.

Flynn, N. (1995) 'The future of public sector management. Are there some lessons from Europe?', *International Journal of Public Sector Management*, 8(4):50–67.

Foddy, W. (1994) *Constructing Questions for Interviews and Questionnaires*, Cambridge, UK: Cambridge University Press.

Killmann, R. H. (1986) *Beyond the Quick Fix: Managing Five Tracks to Organizational Success*, San Francisco, CA: Jossey-Bass.

Krueger, R. A. and Casey, M. A. (2000) *Focus Groups: A Practical Guide for Applied Research*, 3rd edn, Thousand Oaks, CA: Sage Publications.

HMSO (1999) Local Government Act, London: HMSO.

Martin, S. (2002) 'Best value', in K. McLaughlin, S. P. Osborne and E. Ferlie (eds) (2002) *New Public Management: Current Trends and Future Prospects*, London: Routledge, pp. 129–40.

Miles M. B. and Huberman A. M. (1994) *Qualtiative Data Analysis: An Expanded Sourcebook*, 2nd edn, Thousand Oaks, CA: Sage Publications.

Newman, J. (2002) 'The new public management, modernization and institutional change. Disruptions, disjunctures and dilemmas', in K. McLaughlin, S. P. Osborne and E. Ferlie (eds) *New Public Management: Current Trends and Future Prospects*, London: Routledge, pp. 77–91.

Organization for Economic Cooperation and Development (OECD) (1995) *Governance in Transition: Public Management Reforms in OECD Countries*, Paris: OECD.

Parasuraman, A. (1995) 'Measuring and monitoring service quality', in W. J. Glynn and J. G. Barnes (eds) *Understanding Services Management*, Chichester: Wiley, pp. 143–77.

—— Zeithaml, V. A. and Berry, L. L. (1985) 'A conceptual model of service quality and its implications for future research', *Journal of Marketing*, 49(3):41–50.

—— Zeithaml, V. A. and Berry, L. L. (1988) 'SERVQUAL: A multiple-item scale for measuring consumer perceptions of service quality', *Journal of Retailing*, 64(1):12–40.

Patton, M. J. (2002) *Qualitative Research and Evaluation Methods*, 3rd edn, Thousand Oaks, CA: Sage Publications.

Pitt, F. F., Watson, R. T. and Kavan, C. B. (1995) 'Service quality: A measure of information systems effectiveness', *MIS Quarterly*, 19(2):173–87.

Pollitt, C. (2002) 'The new public management in international perspectives. An analysis of impacts and effects', in K. McLaughlin, S. P. Osborne and E. Ferlie (eds) (2002) *New Public Management: Current Trends and Future Prospects*, pp. 274–92.

Robinson, S. (1999) 'Measuring service quality: Current thinking and future requirements', *Marketing Intelligence and Planning*, 17(1):21–32.

Rosen, D. E. and Suprenant, C. (1998) 'Evaluating relationships: Are satisfaction and quality enough?', *International Journal of Service Industry Management*, 9(2):103–25.

Saunders, M. N. K. and Williams, C. (2005) 'From evaluation towards an agenda for quality improvement: The development and application of the template process', *Active Learning in Higher Education*, 6(1):60–72.

Schein, E. H. (1999) *Process Consultation Revisited: Building the Helping Relationship*, Reading, MA: Addison-Wesley Longman.

Silverman, D. (2006) *Interpreting Qualitative Data*, 3rd edn, London: Sage Publications.

Svensson, G. (2001) 'The quality of bi-directional service quality in dyadic service encounters', *Journal of Services Marketing*, 15(5):357–78.

Vidler, E. and Clarke, J. (2005) 'Creating citizen-consumers: New Labour and the remaking of public services', *Public Policy and Administration*, 20(2):19–37.

401

Williams, C. S. and Saunders M. N. K. (2006) 'Developing the service template: From measurement to agendas for improvement', *Service Industries Journal*, 26(5):1–15.
—— Staughton, R. V. W. and Saunders, M. N. K. (1999) 'An exploration of the process of funding social housing: Understanding service quality in the new public sector', *International Journal of Public Sector Management*, 12(4):366–79.
Wisniewski, M. and Donnelly, M. (1996) 'Measuring service quality in the public sector: The potential for SERVQUAL', *Total Quality Management*, 7(4):357–65.
Yin, R. K. (2003) *Case Study Research: Design and Methods*, 3rd edn, Thousand Oaks, CA: Sage Publications.

25

Marketing communication of public policy intentions

Dave Gelders

Introduction

Public sector marketing can be seen as a form of nonprofit marketing. Though this issue has received some academic interest during the past two decades (see e.g. Mokwa and Permut 1981), recently, it has received additional attention; see the final and broader chapter on public sector marketing in the second edition of the handbook *Marketing Management for Nonprofit Organizations* (Sargeant 2005: 375–95) and the explicit reference to this topic in the scholarly journal *Journal of Nonprofit and Public Sector Marketing*. Public sector marketing has become one of the important facets of human society in addition to third sector and private sector marketing (Sargeant 2005).

Traditional public administration studies consider 'policy processes' as a series of stages: preparation, adoption and implementation (for an overview of studies, see e.g. Weimer and Vining 1999). Marketing communication may play a role in each stage. Examples include helping 'politicians to convey the desirability of particular options and/or portray the wider benefit that will accrue to society as a consequence of a particular option' or encouraging 'individuals to exercise their democratic rights to vote' (Sargeant 2005: 380); stimulating citizens to participate in societal debates (Kotler 1988: 367–71); and trying to influence knowledge, attitude and/or behaviour of people by public communication campaigns used as a policy instrument in the implementation stage (besides legal and economic political instruments; e.g. Etzel and James 1970; Bemelmans-Videc *et al.* 1998; 'social marketing/ communication' in Sargeant 2005: 181–210).

Several authors focused on the role of marketing research in public policy decision-making (see Wilkie *et al.* 2002; Hugstad, 1979; Dyer and Shimp 1977; Ritchie and LaBréque 1975; Wilkie and Gardner 1974). This chapter deals with the 'marketing of public policy' with specific attention on one element of the marketing mix: the promotion or (external) communication of one aspect of policies such as public policy intentions or policy ideas that are made public by politicians (such as ministers) but that are not yet adopted by higher authorities (such as parliament).

We first describe why such marketing communication has become so important and will then sketch the specific public sector context in which such communication takes place. We then describe the most important arguments both for and against marketing communication about policy intentions. Finally, we study how the government may increase customers' satisfaction when it communicates about public policy intentions.

Why so important?

Recent developments in citizenry, politics and media clearly indicate that marketing communication about policy intentions is a highly relevant and delicate issue which merits close consideration. Let us note some of the most important and relevant developments: dissolution of political attitudes and affiliations previously thought to be strong anchors (Blumler and Gurevitch 1995); the voting behaviour of the citizenry is less predictable and the citizenry is more demanding. Politicians and political parties are involved in permanent campaigning (Norris 2000) during which the techniques of spin-doctoring, opinion polls and professional media management are increasingly applied to routine everyday politics. It has become common practice to float trial balloons in order to know the acceptable and appreciated policy intentions by the public. Arguing that the policy-making process should be less secretive and more transparent to the public, today's politicians often freely discuss their policy intentions before the eyes of the camera ('open debating culture').

Linsky (1986) states that in the past three decades, media in the USA has become the most important and in many cases is the only source of information used to inform citizens. The media serves as a basic tool for the government to learn about public opinion and needs, which are two basic functions originally executed by political parties. According to Linsky, the media has become the forum for policy discussion both in and out of the government. Where the policy dimension was originally developed outside the media, it increasingly occurs within the public space of the media (Meyer 2002 referring to O. Jarren). More often, one finds politicians floating trial balloons before definitively introducing policy intentions. After the proposals pass a series of tests in the media, politicians may define which proposed policy will become popular. In this way, the media helps to determine which policy will be accepted by political actors in addition to communicating about the decisions of political actors *post factum*. By introducing policy measures or reforms as intentions and not yet as well-developed proposals, politicians may, if the media's reply is negative, easily change their intentions, reformulate them and present them in a different format without consulting the party each time to be assured of their support. This is a negotiation process between politicians and media in which the media claims to reflect the (voice of) public opinion (which may be negative in future elections). In reality, the media does not always present public opinion but constructs it, as is illustrated by Meyer (2002). Cook (1989) also describes how politicians try to get bills adopted by means of the media. Cook states that the so-called 'inside strategies' (contacting a few strategically well-placed people behind the scenes) have not worked for two decades in the US Congress. Cook refers to James Baker, head of the White House staff under President Reagan, when stating that a message should first be sold to the public before selling it to Congress. Consequently, so-called 'outside-strategies' should also be followed. Authorities other than the president use this mechanism such as grassroots organizations (Fraser 1979) and public bodies such as the American Post. Linsky (1986: 151–68) describes how the 'American Postmaster General Winton Blount and his associates in the government' conducted a sophisticated marketing campaign (by paid and unpaid publicity; see below) in order to receive broad press attention and support for a reform plan of the postal system, hoping that the coverage would boost the public pressure on Congress to adopt the bill.

Interpretative reporting is a second evolution relevant to explaining the importance of marketing communication of policy intentions. Interpretative reporting is nearly as old as journalism itself but has only recently become the dominant model of news coverage; reporters questioning politicians' actions and commonly attributing strategic intentions to them provide politicians with fewer chances to speak for themselves (Patterson 1996). Striving for a story, the media does not always give the complete picture or exact status of policy issues (i.e. is it about a policy intention or a policy decision?). Consciously or not, the media supplies biased information to citizens whose reactions to policy decisions and policy-makers are based on what the media chooses to communicate and the manner in which they communicate it. This can influence the probability of whether or not a policy measure will be adopted and implemented successfully (Cobb and Elder 1981).

Typically, 'media logic' is that the 'politics of time' has increasingly turned into 'politics of news time' (Patterson cited by Wolfsfeld 2001). Meyer (2002) stresses that the media's perspective currently dominates the political perspective by stating that the (overall) 'media presentism' gives political leaders less opportunity to determine their support and results in a permanent pressure to float trial balloons (see also above). Increasingly, politicians take the news cycle (news deadlines, etc.) into account when communicating policy proposals. They devote more and more attention to the drafting of the message and are advised not to talk too much about general topics but rather about specific issues (i.e. not 'pleading for a traffic-safe city' but 'pleading for more cycle tracks on all school routes'). These proposals should not be communicated in an analytical manner but by means of warm, human-interest stories illustrated by a specific action of the politician presenting his policy intention. Politicians and their media advisers organize media events around their policy proposals. For example, in Belgium, an acrophobic minister parachuted in order to draw attention to a new system encouraging banks to lend money to new, small entrepreneurs. By the minister daring to jump, she hoped to encourage new entrepreneurs to start businesses by taking advantage of the new guarantee regulation of the government.

In addition to important factors such as timing and supporting actions (i.e. the parachute jump), the medium in which the policy intention is communicated has also become increasingly important. In Belgium, a minister announced his intention to host the Olympic Games in 2016 in a popular newspaper about sports and politics.

Specific context

In 1985, the American Marketing Association (AMA) added the concept of 'ideas' to the list of products suitable for marketing (Scammell 1999). Like products and services, (policy) ideas may be marketed. But Sargeant (2005: 27) wrote that 'despite the obvious benefits that marketing can offer a nonprofit, there are a number of important differences between the application of marketing in a for-profit and a non-profit context'.

When applied to the marketing communication of policy intentions, Gelders *et al.* (2007, forthcoming) state that such communication is important, but that it is also delicate as a result of the more complicated, unstable environment of the public sector and its political influences. The statutory characteristics of governmental operations result in so-called semi-products that governments communicate about. The complexity of the process is visible when politicians discuss the characteristics of policy intentions up to the 'point of sale' (Scammell 1999: 727). Without comparing and contrasting the openness versus closeness of the public and private sectors too much, the deliberative process in the private sector is an internal matter: if published, the decision is publicly communicated at the end of the policy-making process. It is hard to imagine that a private company would publicly discuss its product until the product is ready for consumption as often occurs in the public sector, as Scammell argues.

An important difference between the public and private sectors is that public organizations not only strive for efficiency (e.g. efficient policy implementation) but also for democratic values (e.g. respecting the authority of parliament by not anticipating its policy adoption).

Public communication about policy intentions is not obvious due to the greater organizational rigidity in the public sector: the relatively strict timing and budgeting of public communication is hard to fit in with the often capricious political policy-making process.

Pros and cons

The importance of marketing communication of policy intentions has already been discussed. During that discussion, there were references to important evolutions in politics, media and citizenry, and that politicians increasingly try to meet the needs of the media. Is this a negative? It depends on how far a politician goes. Though such practices are often negatively evaluated by journalists and opposition parties ('it is only about image . . .'), there are positive aspects. Thanks to good timing and drafting of messages, media events (e.g. the parachute jump) about more complicated issues may be made public in a shorter and more comprehensible way, and specific target groups may be reached sparking an interest in the issue. Media events are often 'symbolic events' or 'pseudo events' with no substantial policy consequences and are seen as occasions for politicians to demonstrate that they care about an issue. Media events are not a problem as they may promote the legitimacy of the governmental operation. But it is important that the problems discussed are eventually tackled. Additionally, the difference between the media event and the policy intention should not be too great. If, for example, the target groups, in addition to the broader population, do not see the link between the parachute jump and the guarantee regulation of the government or consider this link to be unclear, weak or irrelevant, the minister may be blamed or punished.

Paid publicity (leaflets, newspaper advertisements, etc.) used by government or ministers is most controversial in the marketing communication of policy intentions. This kind of publicity has been brought into question in several countries. The specific executive position of a minister may cast a shadow over the exact aim of the message. Is it (personal, political) propaganda and therefore a misuse of public money? Is it supplying transparent information in a democratic state aimed at informing and involving citizens and societal organizations regarding the formation of a policy?

These questions were raised during the campaign regarding reform of the Post Office in the USA (Linsky 1986). Leaflets on Operation Rescue and paying for local government did the same in the UK (Scammell 1999) while trial balloons on social security brought communication about policy intentions under discussion in Germany (Jarren cited in Meyer 2002). Other pre-eminent examples include the dissemination of leaflets on the introduction of toll-roads by the Dutch government (Kranendonk 2003) and the dissemination of leaflets on drug policy in Belgium (Gelders 2005).

Pros

Counterbalancing misleading or incorrect information from opponents and the media: an important argument for communication about policy intentions (by paid publicity) from government is that other actors such as the opposition, pressure groups and the media communicate one-sidedly or incorrectly about the policy intentions of government (Committee on the Future of Government Communication 2001). If it wants to be heard, government needs to communicate via paid publicity. When its communication is restricted to the free press (press interviews, press conferences), it is too hard to apply counter-pressure to the misleading or incorrect communication from other actors.

More efficient

Another argument for communicating policy intentions is that it can help government to implement and maintain the adopted policy. As a result, public policy becomes more efficient. Many policies within the formulation process are not controversial. In such cases, government only needs to communicate about a 'reservation of acceptance'. As a result, citizens and organizations can prepare for a policy that will most likely be adopted. For instance, if the rate modifications for the subsidies to be used in January of the following year are only published 'after acceptance by the Senate during the last meeting in December' (translated), Tiemeijer and Rijnja (2001: 190), this is considered inefficient for the implementation of public policy.

It is also argued that communication about policy intentions reduces or avoids unintended consequences later on, such as surprises, misunderstandings, resistance, frustrations and speculation among citizens and organizations. The extent of support and resistance by the public as well as the importance of the counter-arguments of citizens become clarified, thus creating opportunities to fine-tune the policy or for strengthening the arguments for the (intended) policy.

More democratic

Seydel *et al.* (2002) state that openness and freedom of information have evolved during the past few decades. In the past, openness and freedom of information were crucial conditions for public information provisions in the service of democracy. This idea has now been expanded to include the openness and transparency of the policy-making process itself. Presently, organizations must succeed in the traditional sense as well as in the current sense of procedure: they must be accountable to the often complicated working and policy-making procedures providing the basis of their qualitative products or services (Bouckaert 1995). Today, there seems to be a consensus on the use of paid publicity (e.g. campaigns) if government aims to stimulate citizens into participating in societal debates and thus seeks to stimulate interaction in the policy-making processes.

The proponents of more proactive communication about policy intentions (communication initiated by the government itself) stress that voters must be continuously informed about the political points of view and whether they are controversial. Government would also gain a realistic understanding of the possible reactions by population segments through publicly communicating policy intentions. Some authors even state that one bypasses the intermediary bodies of deliberative democracy (the organizations, pressure groups and parties) that in the past mediated political issues and brokered consensus, thus moving towards a more direct democracy (Meyer 2002).

Defenders of public communication about policy intentions also state that this type of communication clarifies what is going on within the political world ('the organized difference in opinion'). Politics would become more exciting and less detached from everyday life and people resulting in a general public more interested in politics and policies.

Cons

State propaganda

Opponents consider it dangerous when government uses public finances to communicate policy intentions unless its communication is explicitly meant to stimulate participation in interactive policy-making processes (Volmer 2000). Government would become too powerful when compared with the opponents of governmental policy. In addition, such ministerial or governmental communication may easily focus towards the minister as an individual politician rather than the content of the intended policy.

Less efficient

Some believe that prematurely publishing policy intentions may disturb the formulation or development of policy and eventually its success, thus wasting time and money when the plan is not implemented. Moreover, the internal deliberative processes between politicians and civil servants would come under pressure and thus hamper civil servants' operations (Van Gisteren and Wassenaar 2003).

Less democratic

The final important argument against governmental communication about policy intentions deals with the democratic characteristics of the policy-making process. Parliament is no longer the first body to be informed of government's intention and government overanticipates parliamentary adoption.

There is the risk of confusing policy intentions with policy decisions on two accounts: politicians often communicate about their policy intentions via the media and/or because politicians, the media and so on communicate in an incomplete and inconsistent manner.

Satisfying the customer: bridging the gap between expectations and perceptions

Based on the definition of Zeithaml (1981), Gelders (2005) argues that the marketing communication process about policy intentions may be seen as a 'service' that is intangible, inseparable, heterogeneous and perishable. Citizens may also be seen as 'customers' as argued by Bouckaert and Thijs (2003: 8). Zeithaml *et al.* (1990) developed a conceptual model about qualitative service delivery (the gap analysis model). This model maps five gaps; the final or fifth gap is between the customers' expected and perceived service delivery (his/her satisfaction). This gap may be explained by the four possible preceding gaps. The four gaps will be briefly described followed by arguments about what they may mean for the marketing communication of policy intentions.

Gap 1: Expected service vs. management perceptions of customer expectations

This refers to the difference between the customers' expected service delivery and the management perceptions of customer expectations that management believes the customer expects. Translated to our specific issue: politicians, or broader policy-makers, do not always know what

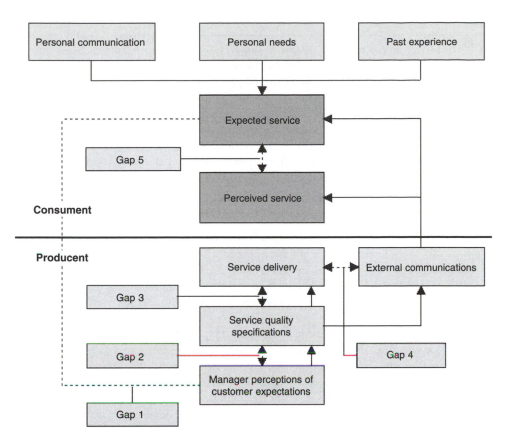

Figure 25.1 Gap analysis model

kind of information citizens would like regarding policy intentions (a down-to-earth or a more high-brow communication), in which format they prefer the information (policy letters of individual ministers, governmental agreements, trial balloons), how often citizens would like to be informed about these issues (every day, floating another trial balloon or not), and the manner in which the message is formulated (do citizens take offence at messages that do not communicate the status of the policy issue within the policy-making process?). Politicians will often be uncertain as to whether citizens would like to be confronted at all with preliminary policy communication. This first gap influences the final customer satisfaction in a significant way (Bouckaert and Vandeweyer 1999). The faults in the 'management perception' may be due to, for example, poor marketing research, improper bottom-up communication and too many management levels.

In order to gain better insight into which communication style, what information and how much information citizens wish to know about policy intentions, politicians may focus on several kinds of formal and informal market intelligence techniques, such as conversations with individual citizens, intermediary organizations, opinion polls, election results and image or reputation research. One should interpret these results carefully. For example, one should keep in mind that citizens do not easily change their attitude towards governmental bodies and policies (Van de Walle 2004).

Illustration

A TNS Media survey conducted among 1,084 Dutch-speaking people in September/
October 2004 in Belgium revealed that there were hardly any changes in party preferences
of citizens when compared with the Flemish regional elections as of 13 June 2004. However, the TNS Media survey was conducted after politically turbulent times; many open
conflicts and contradictory public declarations of policy intentions in the case of the night
flights at Brussels National Airport (Gelders and Facon 2004). 'Apparently, citizens do not
care so much about the day to day political wrestlings as the policymakers and the media',
explained a Belgian political journalist (*De Standaard*, 30 October 2004). According to him,
people are willing to 'see what will come' and have time to transform their opinion into a
political choice.

However, one finds that the gains that politicians make during elections, polls and reputation
studies are often seen as an indication of the extent to which politicians' communication styles
are appreciated. For example, the electoral win of the Flemish Christian-Democratic party
(slogan: 'Not words, but deeds') has been interpreted by several political analysts and politicians
as a sign that citizens did not like 'too much open debating culture' and that they want 'more
realism in politics'.

Studies about such topics as 'citizenship styles' may help to deduce information about
customers' expectations about communication of policy intentions, and consequently, they
may help to bridge the gap between the expected service delivery and management's perception of expectations. We can look to the large-scale survey conducted by Motivaction (2001)
among 8,010 Dutch people in 1997 to 2000. Based on this survey, Motivaction made a distinction between four types of citizenship styles: inactive citizens, dependent citizens, conformist
citizens and citizens critical of the social structure. Each kind of citizenship is characterized by
its own values and a preferred communication style (e.g. preference towards proactive vs.
reactive communication). It is useful to study the extent to which such styles relate to citizens'
expectations about the quality of communication of policy intentions.

Insight can also be generated by studies on the sources of citizens' dissatisfaction with and
distrust of government; based on an empirical research, Kampen *et al.* (2005) concluded that
a 'lack of transparency' (quantity and quality of information, etc.) is a major issue in citizens'
criticism of government.

Studies on the perceived pros and cons of the 'open debating culture' are useful. Using two
surveys conducted in 2004, we found that Flemish citizens are not as negative towards this issue
as politicians and journalists believe them to be.

Finally, one can also research the complaints and the questions of citizens about public
communication about policy intentions. But one should be cautious in interpreting the
data. Research shows that only 4 per cent of customers experiencing problems report their
complaints (Bouckaert and Vandeweyer 1999).

Gap 2: Management perceptions of customer expectations vs. service quality specifications

This deals with the differences between the management perception and service quality
specifications. Customers' wishes may not be correctly interpreted or translated into detailed
product specifications. Some wishes cannot be formulated into specific standards; this statement

is contested by Zeithaml *et al.* (1990) in that they consider a lack of involvement of the management in the quality of the service delivery as the cause for poor service quality specification.

Gelders (2005) analysed a series of quality criteria (i.e. factuality, completeness, timeliness) of communication that governments integrated in legal and deontological stipulations on public communication about policy intentions in several countries. These criteria cover acceptable principles but are insufficiently translated into details (Terrill 1994). Graber (2003) stresses that the assessment of quality of information is a highly subjective issue and it is difficult to determine objective evaluation standards measuring the quality of information in all variables: 'Consequently, officials find it difficult to determine whether available information is good enough to permit valid interferences and to serve as the basis for action.'

Gap 3: Service quality specification vs. service delivery

This refers to the difference between the quality specifications of service delivery and the service delivery itself: organizational members (in this case ministers) cannot or do not want to reach the assumed objectives or quality specifications. Ministers must not only know what customers expect (see Gap 1) and can translate this into standards (see Gap 2), but they also have to (want to) realize these standards. Scoring political points is often so important that even if governments stipulate strict conditions for communication about policy intentions, there will remain a gap between 'words and deeds'.

Gap 4: Customer service delivery vs. external communications

This deals with the difference between service delivery (communication about policy intentions) and the external communication about this service delivery in that the method of communication must communicate policy intentions. One can find this 'meta-communication' in deontological codes, interviews with ministers about their governing and communication style, and so on. For example, if a government states in a deontological code to strive for a cautious way of communicating policy intentions, this will influence citizens' expectations. The objectives that one formulates in such meta-communication should be realistic and the ministers should behave as such. A proper (meta-)communication policy is necessary as such communication steers the customers' expectations as well as their quality perception (Bouckaert and Vandeweyer 1999).

Illustration

The new Flemish government led by the Christian-Democratic Minister-President Yves Leterme could not easily drop the 'open debating culture' as the government had originally announced. The governmental agreement stressed that the essence of politics is making realistic choices and realizing them to obtain a strong, coherent team and a deontological code which must be respected. The new government affirmed an older code stipulating, for example, that each minister should hold back premature declarations when going public. Though this stipulation was not new, it held special meaning in light of the many statements by the Leterme Government to drop the 'open debating culture' and in light of practices illustrating that the open debating culture was 'still alive and kicking' (e.g. night flight debate; Gelders and Facon 2004).

411

Thus, there may be a gap between the way one intends to communicate (or wants to communicate) and the way one communicates in practice. The question to what extent the external communication policy about service delivery is more than a mere 'PR stunt' (Terrill 1994) may be brought forward.

Conclusion

Walsh (1994: 65) states that 'the way that policy is presented is seen as central to effective implementation' as Deacon and Goldin have previously stated. Public communication is much more than simply transferring information or persuading receivers. It is a tool that several actors use to create meaning in policy-making processes. One can speak of a transition from 'meaning of management' to 'management of meaning'.

Marketing communication on policy intentions is important as citizens and organizations can be informed about policy intentions and can be better involved in the policy-making process. However, this communication is delicate due to a fear of state propaganda and confusion among citizens and organizations between policy intentions versus real decisions. Confusion may be created due to the mere fact that government communicates something relating to as of yet unadopted policies and/or because government communicates in an incomplete and inconsistent manner.

Marketing communication on policy intentions is controversial: (a) several negative features make such communication objectionable, and (b) the question of publicly paid publicity (governmental leaflets, newspaper advertisements) in the policy preparation stage. In the following, there is an attempt to offer a balanced appreciation of these controversies.

Marketing communication on policy intentions: positive aspects

Such communication is not only positive for the image of a politician, party or government, but also for the policy a minister would like to realize. As such, image management is not objectionable. A positive image of a minister may also be good for his/her policy and vice versa. It is advisable to communicate policy intentions in an influencing (commercial/canvassing) manner as a way to stimulate citizens' participation in a societal debate. It may also open up debate with other politicians and citizens on possible new policies. Thanks to this communication, other politicians may be pushed to publish and argue their point of view or to go along with the ministerial intended policy for which the cooperation of other politicians (ministers, MPs) is necessary. Consequently, policy may be realized more efficiently. To the extent that policies strive for noble goals, there is something to be said for publicly communicating policy intentions. How far can a minister go in this matter? When does the activation end? When does putting pressure on colleagues start?

Some politicians, communication professionals and academics plead for discussing all policy ideas internally before going public, as was illustrated in Gelders' research. Others state: 'If you act in this way, the policy will not be enacted' (Gelders 2005). The question still remains regarding what happens when all the means (putting coalition partners openly under pressure) become admissible for reaching particular goals (realizing the policy). In that case, only the soft law of ministerial accountability plays a role. Although there is no real legal sanction, this soft law is not unimportant. If the voter disapproves of such a governmental communication style, he/she can blame government or the minister. A minister who continually communicates his policy intentions without taking into consideration the other parties risks retribution.

In some instances, governments do not want to signal their policy intentions in advance. For example, the US government was very secretive about the recent increase in taxes on US expatriates as part of the tax law approved in May 2006 because the proponents did not want lobbyists to have a chance to mobilize support against the proposal.

Influencing communication on policy intentions to accomplish noble goals

From a political science and communication science perspective, it can be argued that governmental communication about policy intentions should principally meet quality criteria such as a complete, factual, timely, consistent and comprehensible information provision. These criteria should also be applied to the communication occurring in the (free) press as stated by the politicians themselves (and thus not only in paid publicity). Political actions become less attractive in such a scenario. Ultimately, however, striving for quality criteria, as mentioned above, is good for the legitimacy of governmental operations.

The gap analysis model of Zeithaml *et al.* (1990) may be used as a rudimentary step-action plan to deal with the organizational quality policy (Bouckaert and Vandeweyer 1999). Though marketing communication of policy intentions often occurs in a politically strategic context, such a step plan is useful in practice (at least *ex post facto*) in order to know 'why events occurred as they occurred'.

The plan can be described by a means of five questions starting with the fifth and final gap – the gap between the customers' expected and perceived service delivery. If this first question is negatively answered, the other questions dealing with the four preceding gaps should be bypassed and possible corrective actions made. Questions that government can pose are:

1   Do citizens perceive the marketing communication of policy intentions according to what they expect? (See Gap 5.)
2   Do ministers assess citizens' expectations about such communication in a proper manner? (See Gap 1.)
3   Are the correct specific standards available to answer to the citizens' expectations about such communication? (See Gap 2.)
4   Does such communication fulfil the assumed standards? (See Gap 3.)
5   Does the external communication policy about the marketing communication of policy intentions occur in a proper manner? (See Gap 4.)

An important element in the research and practice of public administrations is the recent transition towards a market-driven mode of governance ('from government to governance'). As Haque (2001) extensively describes, this creates a serious challenge to the 'publicness' of a public organization. In particular, the current businesslike changes in goals, structures, functions, norms and users of public goods and services tend to diminish its publicness; see, for example, eroding public–private distinctions ('public–private partnerships'), shrinking socio-economic role, narrowing composition of service recipients, worsening condition of accountability and declining level of public trust (see also Roberts 2000). It is worth noting that public companies have to distribute commercially neutral products and are to be reserved in societal debates as they are expected to support the policy of their supervising government.

References

Bemelmans-Videc, M-L., Rist, R. and Vedung, E. (eds) (1998) *Carrots, Sticks and Sermons: Policy Instruments and their Evaluation*, New Brunswick, NJ: Transaction.

Blumler, J. and Gurevitch, M. (1995) *The Crisis of Public Communication*, London: Routledge.

Bouckaert, G. (1995) 'Remodeling quality and quantity in a management context', in A. Halachmi and G. Bouckaert (eds) *Public Productivity through Quality and Strategic Management*, Amsterdam: IOS Press, pp. 21–38.

Bouckaert, G. and Thijs, N. (2003) *Kwaliteit in de overheid*, Leuven: Instituut voor de Overheid.

—— and Vandeweyer, S. (1999) *Kwaliteit in de overheid*, Brugge: die Keure.

Cobb, R. and Elder, C. (1981) 'Communication and public policy', in D. Nimmo and K. Sanders (eds) *Handbook of Political Communication*, Beverly Hills, CA: Sage Publications, pp. 391–416.

Committee on the Future of Government Communication (2001) *In Dienst van de Democratie*, Den Haag: Sdu.

Cook, T. E. (1989) *Making Laws and Making News: Media Strategies in the US House of Representatives*, Washington, DC: Brookings Institution.

Dyer, R. and Shimp, T. (1977) 'Enhancing the role of marketing research in public policy decision-making', *Journal of Marketing*, 41(1):63–7.

Etzel, M. and James, D. (1970) 'Can government regulation replace marketing orientation?', *Journal of Retailing*, 46(4):14–23.

Fraser, E. (1979) 'Marketing public policy through grass roots action', *Public Relations Quarterly*, 24(2): 14–17.

Gelders, D. (2003) 'Publicly squabbling about policy ideas: The Belgian cannabis case', paper presented at Political Marketing Conference, London.

—— (2005) *Communicatie Over Nog Niet Aanvaard Beleid: Een Uitdaging Voor de Overheid?*, Leuven: Proefschrift Faculteit Sociale Wetenschappen, K.U. Leuven.

—— and Facon, P. (2004) 'Het Nachtvluchtendossier: Een Complexe Materie Voor Beleid En Communicatie', *Burger, bestuur & beleid: Tijdschrift voor bestuurskunde en bestuursrecht*, 1(4):317–64.

—— and Van de Walle, S. (2005) 'Marketing government reforms', *Journal of Nonprofit and Public Sector Marketing*, 14(1/2):151–68.

—— and Walrave, M. (2003) 'The Flemish customer contact centre for public information from a marketing and management perspective', *International Journal of Nonprofit and Voluntary Sector Marketing*, 8(2):166–80.

—— Bouckaert, G. and Van Ruler, B. (2007, forthcoming) 'Communication management in the public sector: Consequences for public communication about policy intentions', *Government Information Quarterly*.

Graber, D. (2003) *The Power of Communication. Managing Information in Public Organizations*, Washington, DC: CQ Press.

Haque, S. (2001) 'The diminishing publicness of public service under the current mode of governance', *Public Administration Review*, 61(1):65–81.

Hugstad, P. (1979) 'Barriers to the further utilization of advertising and marketing research in litigation and public policy formulation', *Current Issues and Research in Advertising*, 2(1): 65–71.

Kampen, J., Van de Walle, S., Maddens, B. and Bouckaert, G. (2005) 'Bronnen van Ontevredenheid en Wantrouwen in Vlaanderen: Een Open Vraag?', *Burger, Bestuur en Beleid: Tijdschrift voor Bestuurskunde en Bestuursrecht*, 2(1).

Kotler, P. (1988) *Marketing voor Non-Profit Organisaties*, Alphen aan den Rijn: Samsom Uitgeverij.

Kranendonk, S. (2003) *BOR: Bereikbaarheidsoffensief of Rekeningrijden? De Slag om het Bereikbaarheidsoffensief en het Rekeningrijden. De Invloed van de Geschreven Pers op Publieke Steun*, Scriptie VU Amsterdam, Amsterdam.

Lees-Marshment, J. (2001) *Political Marketing and British Political Parties: The Party's Just Begun*, Manchester: Manchester University Press.

Linsky, M. (1986) *Impact: How the Press Affects Federal Policymaking*, New York, NY: Norton & Company.

Meyer, T. (2002) *Media Democracy: How the Media Colonize Politics*, Cambridge: Polity Press.

Mokwa, M. and Permut, S. (1981) *Government Marketing: Theory and Practice*, Westport: Praeger.

Motivaction (2001) *Burgerschapsstijlen en Overheidscommunicatie*. Bijlage bij rapport In dienst van de democratie: www.minaz.nl/wallage/content/bijlagen/bijlage05_2.doc.

Norris, P. (2000) *A Virtuous Circle. Political Communications in Postindustrial Societies*, Cambridge: Cambridge University Press.

Patterson, T. (1996) 'Bad news, bad governance', *Annals of the American Academy of Political and Social Science*, 54(6): 97–108.

Ritchie, J. and LaBréque, R. (1975) 'Marketing research and public policy: A functional perspective', *Journal of Marketing*, 39(3):12–19.

Roberts, A. (2000) 'Less government, more secrecy: Reinvention and the weakening of freedom of information law', *Public Administration Review*, 60(4):308–72.

Sargeant, A. (2005) *Marketing Management for Nonprofit Organizations*, 2nd edn, Oxford: Oxford University Press.

Scammell, M. (1999) 'Political marketing: lessons for political science', *Political Studies*, 43(4):718–39.

Seydel, E., Van Ruler, B. and Scholten, O. (2002) 'Redactioneel: Overheidscommunicatie: de burger als medesubject en handelende partij', *Tijdschrift voor Communicatiewetenschap*, 30(4):274–8.

Stein, J. (1989) 'Cheap talk and the Fed: A theory of imprecise policy announcements', *American Economic Review*, 79(1):32–42.

Terrill, G. (1994) 'Guidelines for government media and information activity: Some considerations', *Australian Journal of Public Administration*, 53(1):54–62.

Tiemeijer, W. and Rijnja, G. (2001) 'De onhoudbare rem op communicatie over niet-aanvaard beleid', in B. Dewez, P. van Montfort, M. van Rooij and E. Voogt (eds) *Overheidscommunicatie: de nieuwe wereld achter Postbus 51*. Amsterdam: Boom, pp. 188–203 .

Van de Walle, S. (2004) *Perceptions of Administrative Performance: The Key to Trust in Government?*, Proefschrift Sociale Wetenschappen, Leuven: K.U. Leuven.

Van Gisteren, R. and Wassenaar, I. (2003) 'Geschiedenis van de overheidscommunicatie', in L. Jumelet and I. Wassenaar (eds) *Overheidscommunicatie*. Utrecht: ThiemeMeulenhoff, pp. 16–33.

Volmer, W. (2000) 'Central government communication', in J. Katus and W. Volmer (eds) *Government Communication in the Netherlands: Backgrounds, Principles and Functions*, The Hague: Sdu.

Walsh, K. (1994) 'Marketing and public sector management', *European Journal of Marketing*, 28(3):63–71.

Weimer, D. and Vining, A. (1999) *Policy Analysis: Concepts and Practice*, Englewood Cliffs, NJ: Prentice Hall.

Wilkie, W. and Gardner, D. (1974) 'The role of marketing research in public policy decision making', *Journal of Marketing*, 38(1):38–47.

—— Desrochers, D. and Gundlach, G. (2002) 'Marketing research and public policy: The case of slotting fees', *Journal of Public Policy and Marketing*, 21(2):275–88.

Wolfsfeld, G. (2001) 'Political waves and democratic discourse: Terrorism waves during the Oslo peace process', in W. Bennett and R. Entman (eds) *Mediated Politics. Communication in the Future of Democracy*, Cambridge, UK: Cambridge University Press, pp. 226–51.

Zeithaml, V. (1981) 'How consumer evaluation processes differ between goods and services', AMA Conference Proceedings.

—— Parasuraman, A. and Berry, L. (1990) *Delivering Quality Service – Balancing Customer Perceptions and Expectations*, New York, NY: Free Press.

415

Index

Note: *italic* page numbers denote references to figures/tables.

122; higher education institutions 262–3; market orientation impact on 16, 19–21; measurement of 19–20, 21, 22, 24, 78, 104; political parties 309; portfolio approach 76–7, 78, 80, 83–4, 85, *87*, 88, *90*; public sector 389, 399; relationship marketing 30; religious organizations 104; *see also* service quality

performing-arts organizations 227–40, 244–50; cultural economics 229–30; future research 238; government subsidies 230–3; managerial implications 237–8; marketing 233–7; *see also* arts

Perloff, R. M. 300

Perreault, W. D. 366

personal selling 101, 280

personality 119, *121*, 127

Peru 325

Petkus, E. Jr. 243

Petrie, R. 119–20, *120*

Petruska, R. *125*

Pharoah, C. 134, 186

philanthropy 1, 189; foundations 185, 187; middle class 185; motives for 131; new physics of 167–8; wealthy individuals 165–81; *see also* corporate philanthropy; e-Philanthropy

philia 175–6

physical evidence 102–3

Piercy, N. 257

Piferi, R. L. *129*

Piliavin, J. A. 117, *118*

Pinho, J. C. 19

pity 117, *118*, 130

place 102, 287

planned giving 4, 134–5, 203

Planned Parenthood 72

planning: foundations 187–8; higher education institutions 284, 286, 287–8; performing-arts organizations 228–9, 237; social marketing 335

pledge drives 100

political marketing 6, 299–315, 339; branding 302–4, 310–11; challenges facing marketers 300–1; comprehensive 316–29; consumer needs 301–2, 303, 304, 306, 311, 312; definitions of 310–11; delivery *319, 321, 326*; ethical concerns 326; global 323–5; implementation *319, 321*, 326–7; market orientation 318–22; political 'market' 301, 312; political 'product' 304–10, 311, 312, 317–18, *319*, 320, *321, 322*; *see also* public policy

political marketing management 310, 311, *311*

politicians: marketing communication of policy intentions 403, 404–5, 406, 408, 409, 412; political marketing 301, 309

Pollitt, C. 390

Polonsky, M. 157, 261

Porter, M. E. 311

portfolio analysis 75–91; building a portfolio model 79; individual input 86–8; inputs 80–1; interpretation of results 81–6; mission contribution 78, 81–2; performance (quality) contribution 78, 83–4; programme 77–8; resource contribution 78–9, 84–5; three-dimensional model 76–7, *76, 87*

positioning 4, 284

Posnett, J. 126, *128*

Post, J. E. *213*

PR *see* proportional representation

Prabhu, G. N. 210, *213*

Prentice, R. 241, 243

press 67, 113, 201; *see also* media

prestige 131

price: higher education institutions 282, 286–7, 290; religious organizations 101

Prince, R. A. 153

print materials 201

privatization 192, 193, 285

process 103

product: arts organizations 242; higher education institutions 282; lifecycle 366; political 304–10, 311, 312, 317–18, *319*, 320, *321, 322*; religious organizations 101; social marketing 335

professionalism 122, *123*

profit 12, 30, 149, 152, 263

project funding 187

promotion 101–2, 201, 403

propaganda 408

proportional representation (PR) 320, 325

prosocial behaviour 127

prospect research 204–5, 207

PTL Club 94–6

public benefit 192

public good theory 129

public opinion: AIDS coverage 349; marketing communication of policy intentions 404, 409; political marketing 318, *319*, 324, 326, 327

public participation 309, 310

public policy 125, 157–8; context 405–6; foundations 189–90; marketing communication of policy intentions 403–15; social marketing 341

public relations 4; higher education institutions 281, 282, 283; performing-arts organizations 234–5, 237; religious organizations 101

public sector: marketing communication of policy intentions 403–15; service quality 389–402; social entrepreneurship 219

publicity 406, 407, 412